The World War I Reader

The World War I Reader

EDITED BY

Michael S. Neiberg

New York University Press

NEW YORK AND LONDON

New York University Press
New York and London
www.nyupress.org

Library of Congress Cataloging-in-Publication Data
The World War I reader / edited by Michael S. Neiberg.
p. cm.
Includes bibliographical references and index.
ISBN-13: 978-0-8147-5832-8 (cloth : alk. paper)
ISBN-10: 0-8147-5832-0 (cloth : alk. paper)
ISBN-13: 978-0-8147-5833-5 (pbk.   )
ISBN-10: 0-8147-5833-9 (pbk.   )
1. World War, 1914–1918. 2. World War, 1914-1918—Sources. I. Neiberg, Michael S.
II. Title: World War One reader. III. Title: World War 1 reader.
D509.W85   2006
940.3—dc22   2006020767

New York University Press books

Manufactured in the United States of America
c 10 9 8 7 6 5 4 3 2 1
p 10 9 8 7 6 5 4 3 2 1

Contents

Acknowledgments

My thanks to Deborah Gershenowitz for her support of this project and to William Astore for providing a careful and intelligent reading of an early draft. I also thank the four anonymous reviewers for their helpful suggestions. Without the help of Shelia Smith and my wife, Barbara, this book would never have been written. Thanks!

As I was finishing this book, Hurricane Katrina struck Louisiana and Southern Mississippi. We left our home in Mississippi and showed up on the doorstep of our friends Paul, Bonnie, Bailey, and Bridget Bauman. They took in our brood of three adults, two children, and four cats until it was safe for us to return to our own home. For opening their home to us and for being such gracious hosts, I dedicate this book to them, with thanks and with love.

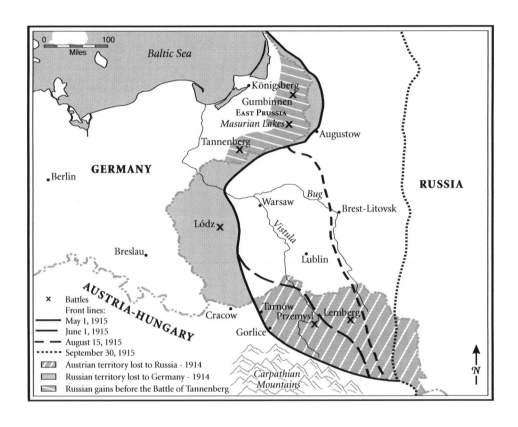

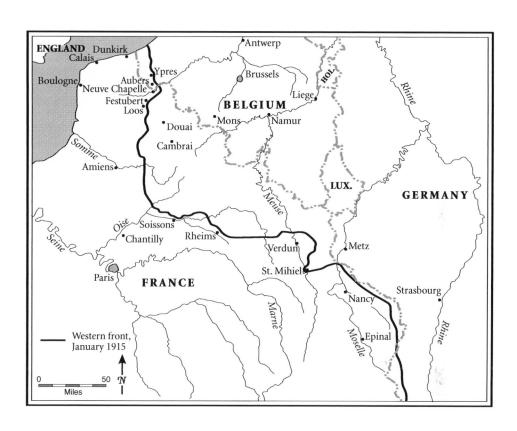

ENGLAND Dunkirk
Calais
Boulogne
Antwerp
Ypres
Brussels HOL.
Aubers
Neuve Chapelle
Festubert Liege
Loos BELGIUM
Douai Mons Namur
Cambrai
Amiens Rhine

LUX.
Oise Meuse GERMANY
Soissons
Chantilly Rheims
Seine Verdun Metz
St. Mihiel
Paris FRANCE Strasbourg
Nancy
Marne
Moselle Epinal Rhine

Western front,
January 1915

0   50
Miles   N

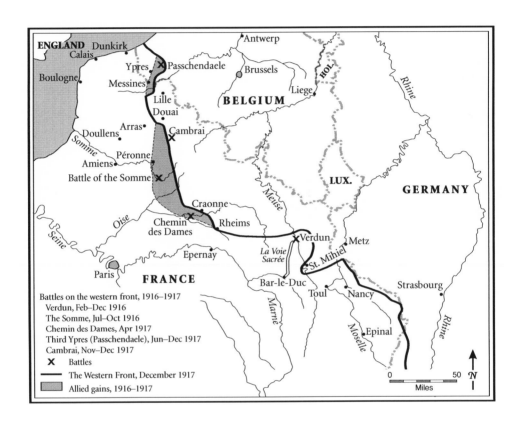

Battles on the western front, 1916–1917
Verdun, Feb–Dec 1916
The Somme, Jul–Oct 1916
Chemin des Dames, Apr 1917
Third Ypres (Passchendaele), Jun–Dec 1917
Cambrai, Nov–Dec 1917
X   Battles
—   The Western Front, December 1917
▨   Allied gains, 1916–1917

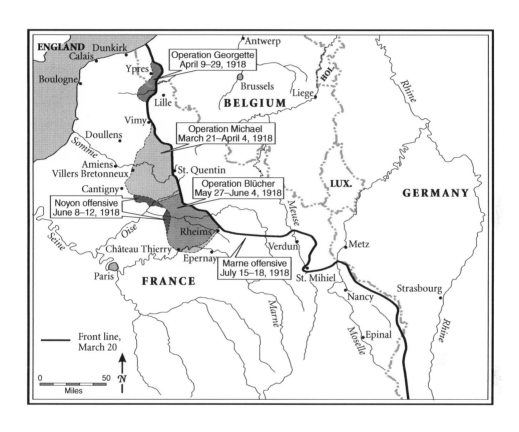

ENGLAND Dunkirk
Calais
Boulogne
Ypres

Operation Georgette
April 9–29, 1918

Antwerp

Brussels Liege

BELGIUM

Lille

Vimy

Doullens

Somme

Amiens
Villers Bretonneux
Cantigny

Oise

Noyon offensive
June 8–12, 1918

St. Quentin

Operation Michael
March 21–April 4, 1918

Operation Blücher
May 27–June 4, 1918

HOL.

LUX.

GERMANY

Rhine

Meuse

Rheims

Château Thierry

Epernay

Seine

Paris

FRANCE

Verdun

Marne offensive
July 15–18, 1918

St. Mihiel

Metz

Nancy

Strasbourg

Marne

Moselle

Epinal

Rhine

——— Front line,
March 20

0   50
Miles

N

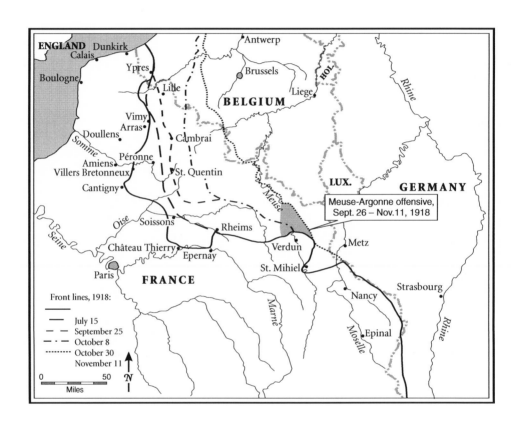

ENGLAND Dunkirk Antwerp
Calais
Boulogne Ypres Brussels
Lille Liege
BELGIUM HOL.
Vimy
Arras
Doullens Cambrai Rhine
Péronne
Amiens St. Quentin LUX. GERMANY
Villers Bretonneux
Cantigny Meuse-Argonne offensive,
Sept. 26 – Nov.11, 1918
Oise Soissons Metz
Château Thierry Rheims
Epernay Verdun
Paris St. Mihiel
FRANCE Nancy Strasbourg

Front lines, 1918:
——— July 15
– – – September 25
–·–·– October 8
········· October 30
November 11

0   50
Miles

N

Timeline of Major Events

1914

June 28	Assassination of Archduke Franz Ferdinand
July 23	Delivery of the Austrian Ultimatum to Serbia
August 4	German Invasion of Belgium
August 26 to 30	Battle of Tannenberg
September 4 to 10	First Battle of the Marne
September 17 to October 18	The Race to the Sea and Start of Trench Warfare

1915

February 19 to December 20	Gallipoli Campaign
May 7	German Sinking of the *Lusitania*
May 23	Italian Entry into the War
July 9	British Conquest of German Southwest Africa
October 3 to 5	Landing of Allied Troops at Salonika

1916

February 21 to December 15	Battle of Verdun
April 23	Start of the Easter Rising in Dublin
April 29	Surrender of British Garrison at Kut
June 6	Start of Arab Revolt
July 1 to November 18	Battle of the Somme
August 27	Romanian Entry into the War
November 28	First German Air Raid on London

1917

February 1	German Resumption of Submarine Warfare
March 11	British Capture of Baghdad

March 15	Abdication of Tsar Nicholas II
April 6	United States Entry into the War
April 16	Start of the Nivelle Offensive
July 31 to November 10	Third Battle of Ypres (Passchendaele)
November 16	Bolshevik Government Formed in Russia
December 9	British Capture of Jerusalem

1918

January 8	Announcement of Wilson's Fourteen Points
March 3	Signing of Treaty of Brest-Litovsk
March 21	Start of German Spring Offensives
October 3	Hindenburg Line Breached
October 20	Mutiny of German Sailors at Kiel
October 30	Surrender of Ottoman Empire and Austria-Hungary
November 11	Armistice Signed with Germany

1919

| January 12 | Opening of the Paris Peace Conference |
| June 28 | Signing of the Treaty of Versailles |

Brief Biographies of Important Figures Mentioned in the Text

Bethmann Hollweg, Theobald von (1856–1921). Chancellor of Germany from 1909 to 1917.

Bismarck, Prince Otto von (1815–1898). Prussian prime minister and German chancellor from 1862 to 1890. Played a large role in the unification of Germany.

Casement, Roger (1864–1916). British anti-imperialist who was involved in a plot to smuggle German weapons into Ireland. The British uncovered the plot and executed Casement.

Clemenceau, Georges (1841–1929). French war minister and prime minister from 1917 to 1919.

Enver Pasha (1881–1922). Ottoman military commander and minister of war.

Feisal, ibn Hussein, Prince (1885–1933). Son of ibn Ali Hussein (see below) and commander of Arab forces during the Arab revolt.

Foch, Ferdinand (1851–1929). French marshal named commander of all allied forces in 1918.

Franz Ferdinand, Austro-Hungarian Archduke (1863–1914). Heir to the throne of the Austro-Hungarian Empire and the man whose assassination sparked the July Crisis that led to the war.

Frederick II (1712–1786). King of Prussia. Both he and Frederick William used military power to increase the strength of Prussia in European affairs.

Frederick William (1620–1688). King of Prussia.

French, Sir John (1852–1925). Commander of the British Expeditionary Force, 1914–1915.

Groener, Wilhelm (1867–1939). Named German commander-in-chief in the last weeks of the war.

Haig, Sir Douglas (1861–1928). British soldier named to replace John French as commander of the British Expeditionary Force in 1915.

Hindenburg, Paul von (1847–1937). Commander of German forces from 1916 to 1918.

House, Edward (1858–1938). Confidante of President Wilson and Wilson's personal representative in Europe.

Hussein, Ibn Ali ibn Mohammed (1856?–1931). Sherif of Mecca and king of the Hejaz.

Jaurès, Jean (1859–1914). French socialist politician and advocate of a national militia instead of a professional army. He was assassinated in Paris just days before the war began.

Joffre, Joseph (1852–1931). French marshal and chief architect of France's 1914 war strategy. He commanded French forces until 1916.

Kemal, Mustapha (1881–1938). Ottoman military commander and future president of Turkey.

Kitchener, Lord Horatio (1850–1916). Architect of the British volunteer army system known either as the "Kitchener Armies" or the "New Armies."

Lloyd George, David (1863–1945). British prime minister from 1917 to 1922.

Ludendorff, Erich (1856–1937). German general and architect of the Spring Offensives of 1918.

Luxembourg, Rosa (1871–1919). German communist and leader of the Spartacist revolt.

McMahon, Henry (1862–1919). British high commissioner for Egypt, 1914–1916.

Maercker, Georg von (1865–1924). German general and founder of the *Freikorps*.

Mahan, Alfred Thayer (1840–1914). American naval theorist who argued that large navies were necessary for the protection of trade.

Millerand, Alexandre (1859–1943). French war minister from 1912 to 1913 and 1914 to 1915.

Moltke, Helmuth von (1848–1916). German general and chief architect of Germany's 1914 war strategy. He was removed from office after the failure of that strategy in 1914.

Monash, John (1865–1931). Innovative general named commander of the Australian Corps in 1918.

Nicholas II, Tsar of all the Russias (1868–1918). Nominal commander of Russian forces, 1915–1917. Abdicated in 1917 and was murdered by the Bolsheviks.

Nikolai Nikolaievich, Grand Duke (1856–1929). Uncle to Tsar Nicholas II and commander-in-chief of Russian forces in 1914 and 1915.

Nivelle, Robert (1856–1924). French general and commander of the disastrous Nivelle Offensive of 1917.

Noske, Gustav (1868–1946). German politician who encouraged the formation of *Freikorps* units.

Paléologue, Maurice (1859–1944). French politician and ambassador to Russia.

Pershing, John (1860–1948). Commander of the American Expeditionary Forces.

Pétain, Henri-Philippe (1856–1951). Commander of French forces in 1917 and 1918.

Poincaré, Raymond (1860–1934). President of the French Republic during the war.

Pourtalès, Count Friedrich von (1853–1928). German ambassador in Russia in 1914.

Rennenkampf, Pavel (1854–1918). Russian general responsible for some of Russia's worst defeats in 1914.

Schlieffen, Count Alfred von (1833–1913). Predecessor to Moltke as chief of the German general staff and originator of the key concepts of the German war plan of 1914, often called "the Schlieffen Plan."

Wilhelm II, German Emperor, or Kaiser (1859–1941). Nominal commander in chief of German forces. Abdicated in 1918.

Wilson, Woodrow (1856–1924), President of the United States and author of the Fourteen Points.

Introduction

Four years of total war turned large parts of the European continent into a series of muddy graves. It also altered the lives of Europeans in ways no one could have predicted. The war's ability to transform a failed Austrian art student, Adolf Hitler, into a German national hero is only one among many examples of how the war changed the course of lives and entire societies. Indeed, the manner in which Europe slid from the horrors of one world war into another further adds to the continued interest in the experience of 1914 to 1918. The sense of innocence lost remains attached to the outbreak of the First World War, but the dominant sense of the outbreak of the Second World War is much closer to resignation than innocence. As Canadian poet Milton Acorn noted in 1939, "This is where we came in; this has happened before / Only the last time there was cheering."

Even today parts of the World War I battlefields continue to kill, almost as if the spirits created on those fields had intentionally left behind reminders to future generations of the ways in which they had once killed one another.[1] Unexploded ordnance remains a danger to farmers living near former depots and battlegrounds. France and Belgium maintain weapons disposal units to assist locals who uncover rusted caches of unexploded munitions. Even well-maintained battlefield sites like Verdun and the Somme contain signs warning visitors to stay off certain paths that remain unsafe almost nine decades later. There are still places where plant life has not returned to normal. In at least one case, a large underground mine that failed to detonate in 1917 still sits somewhere under the soil of Belgium.

But these are silent and largely unobservable reminders of the war. The numerous cemeteries along the western front provide a vivid and painfully evocative reminder of the war's cost in human lives.[2] Driving through Belgium and eastern France, one comes across cemeteries dotting the now peaceful countryside. One can also find markers in every community in France commemorating the dead. Even towns too small to have their own post office often have markers with twenty or more names. Several major battle sites include much larger memorials to the dead and the missing. The high number of the latter testifies to the power of modern weaponry, most notably heavy artillery, to obliterate the human body.

Given these enormous sacrifices, it is hard to imagine even the victors going to war in 1914 if they had known the consequences. Britain and France emerged from the war victorious, but badly shaken, deeply in debt, and unable fully to deal with the social consequences of "victory." Germany, Austria-Hungary, and the Ottoman Empire, of course, dealt with those same traumas on top of the ignominy of losing and the need to develop political structures to replace those discredited during the war. More than eight million Europeans died in the war and millions more were permanently disabled. The number of orphans the war created remains a matter of conjecture. The war brought an end to the dynasties that had ruled the Habsburg, German, Russian, and Ottoman Empires; gave rise to Bolshevism and fascism; and ushered in a new relationship between the European powers and their colonies.

The war also had dramatic impacts outside of Europe. It helped to vault two powers, the United States and Japan, to unprecedented heights in global affairs. It struck China at a time of great domestic change, leading Chinese statesmen to try to use the war to unite the country and to interact with the Great Powers on equal terms for the first time.[3] Canada, India, and Australia all emerged from the war with a greater sense of independence from the British Empire. European colonialism itself underwent tremendous changes; British and French attempts to use the war to expand their colonial holdings under the veneer of the mandate system ultimately created more colonial problems than it solved. In Ireland, a rebellion against the British led to years of Anglo-Irish strife that eventually yielded the division of the island.

Although most of the major fighting occurred in Europe, contemporaries easily came to understand the war as the World War. Africa and southwest Asia saw sustained combat; Indochina, Senegal, China, and many other regions sent soldiers and laborers by the thousands to the fighting fronts. India raised the largest volunteer army in history to fight for the British and to prove to Britons that Home Rule for India would not compromise the integrity of the British Empire. The modern histories of both Asia and Africa (at least the colonized portions thereof) can be dated to the war. As we will see near the end of this volume, the transfer of Ottoman colonies to France and Great Britain ended one important period in the history of the Middle East and inaugurated another.[4]

American President Woodrow Wilson temporarily rallied his people with a call to fight a "war to end all wars." American soldiers, he said, would not fight for empire or for global power, but would fight to right a European political system corrupted by monarchy, imperialism, and excessive militarism. Once democracy and freedom had replaced tyranny, Europe would once again become a progressive and peaceful place, and Americans would never again have to go overseas to fight someone else's war. His call served to bring the United States together for two years, but debate over the wisdom of American entry meant that the war did not have a clear, single meaning for Americans. This ambivalence informed American foreign policy in the 1920s and 1930s, and even today Americans are hard-pressed to explain exactly why the nation fought.

Inside Europe, the war changed gender relations, created generational conflicts, and dramatically sped up the pace of social change.[5] The power of the state to intrude on peoples' lives reached new heights. The redirection of economies spurred a new round of urbanization and industrialization while bringing even remote rural areas into national systems. Perhaps most importantly, the war left Europe mourning the loss of so many young men for reasons that seemed hard to explain. Europe in 1919 was far from the "land fit for heroes" that British Prime Minister David Lloyd George had promised. To the contrary, several thoughtful Europeans understood quite clearly that neither the war nor the many ensuing peace agreements had established the conditions needed for a just and lasting peace.

As important as the war is to European, American, and world history, teaching it can be a difficult endeavor. In contrast to the Second World War, the First lacks a clear master narrative of good versus evil. The even greater destruction of the Second World War contributes to an understandable yet misleading image of the First as a senseless waste, the ultimate expression of a wrong war fought for the wrong reasons. Because the war produced relatively few heroes or even few villains, it also lacks a clear and easy identification with well-known people. As a result, the war becomes reduced to simplistic and familiar themes, especially when the teacher is short on time. These well-worn themes include the stupidity of generals, the innocence of soldiers, and the overall waste of the war. Like all simplifications, these tropes are based in an element of reality, but they disguise a tremendous level of complexity.

Instead of looking for consensus on the war, this book seeks to create a fuller understanding of the war by offering readers a range of contemporary and scholarly documents. By presenting both primary and secondary sources to readers, it strives to capture the experiences of the men and women who lived through the war, and to juxtapose these readings with recent work by academics. I do not capture the entirety of the war in this book, as no volume of this size can possibly reflect the widely divergent experiences of people and societies during wartime. Nor can this book track all of the debates and controversies in historical interpretations. Instead, I sought selections that provided particularly keen insight into critical facets of the war. Thus this book should not be read as a general history of the war, but as a sampling of how some people experienced it. In this way we can begin to see the First World War as the complex and critically important event that it was.

To get the most out of this book, the reader should challenge it. The primary sources, by definition, come from people who witnessed the events of the war themselves. As such, their selections bring with them questions of interpretation and bias. Readers should ask how those biases affected the ways that the authors understood their experiences. How did they come to understand the ways that the war tore their lives apart? How did they respond to those changes? The secondary readings offer a similar opportunity to examine how individuals and societies responded to these years of crisis. Readers should ask themselves about the evidence they see in the analyses of historians. Do their conclusions match the primary evidence? Do their arguments ultimately convince you based on what you have read here and elsewhere? What parts of the war do you better understand after reading these selections? Above all, I hope the reader will use these selections not as the final word, but merely as an introduction to the First World War.

Part One: Causes

Europe had no single or compelling reason to go to war in 1914. The crisis that broke out that summer need not have precipitated one year, let alone four years, of war. The assassination of Austro-Hungarian Archduke Franz Ferdinand did not directly impact the fundamental interests of any of the so-called "Great Powers," except Austria-Hungary itself; even the waning Dual Monarchy had many opportunities to push its case well short of war without any irretrievable loss of honor or international status. Across the continent, the assassination of the archduke produced no immediate fear or anxiety; instead, Europeans recalled the summer of 1914 as a particularly idyllic period, characterized by fine weather and a dependable economy. Many of these recollections, of course, came later, when the halcyon days of 1914 stood in especially dramatic contrast to the hell of the next four summers of war and many more summers of hardship and privation.

Europe in 1914 had its normal share of local hotspots, but none of these concerns threatened to provoke a general war. The most electric of these controversies, the question of Irish Home Rule, bore few wider European implications. Liberal and Labour politicians in Britain had agreed on the broad principles of a plan to give a Dublin Parliament control of internal affairs inside Ireland (including Ulster), while leaving foreign policy and military matters under the control of the London Parliament. The plan enjoyed wide support from those who viewed the compromise as the best way of easing sectarian tensions as well as from those who saw it as a way to bide time until a more amenable solution could be worked out. Conservative politicians and senior British military officials (including many officers who went on to important careers in World War I) disagreed; some had even threatened mutiny if the government ordered them to enforce Home Rule on rebellious Protestants. Although the debate over Home Rule remained unresolved at the outbreak of the war, it was clearly a British crisis with little potential to upset the continent more generally. The willingness of Irish Catholics and Protestants to volunteer for the British cause (although in separate divisions that were not placed together in the same corps) came as a great relief to British officials.

Neither were colonial disagreements sufficient to bring Europe to war. In fact, relations between European colonies were generally good, dependent as whites from neighboring colonies were upon each other for trade and the perceived need for mutual protection from native risings. If they needed any reminder of the need for the latter, they only needed to recall the violent 1901 Boxer Rebellion against European influence in China. By that time, Europeans had already agreed to settle their colonial disputes by negotiation, as witnessed by the serious diplomatic crisis between the British and French in the Sudan at Fashoda in 1898. That case also demonstrates that governments had the capability to resist going to war even when large sectors of their publics demanded it. Fashoda, moreover, was an exception to a more general diplomatic understanding that called for the Great Powers to respect the borders drawn in 1884 and 1885 at the Berlin Conference on Africa. Not all Europeans were entirely pleased with their share of the colonial pie, but most had long given up the idea of going to war for the sake of enlarging their slice.

Nor did tensions between rivals France and Germany destabilize the continent sufficiently to cause a war. French nationalists railed about the "lost territories" of Alsace and Lorraine (taken by Germany from France in 1871), but it had become harder and harder to motivate young people to feel patriotic grievances over lands that had never been French in their lifetimes. The flight of most Frenchmen from Alsace and

Lorraine in the ensuing years meant that the provinces had fewer cultural links to France as time passed. A French government decision to lengthen the period of conscription to three years had barely passed in 1913, indicating to many Europeans a general desire on the part of the French to avoid war. For their part, Germans, while unwilling to hand Alsace-Lorraine back to France, had no interest in seizing more French territory.

Socialists in both countries, led by Frenchman Jean Jaurès, spoke of the unity of the two countries' working classes against war. They hoped that class solidarity might make war between the two states impossible. Socialists threatened strikes that would disrupt mobilization, stop trains from moving soldiers to the front, and halt weapons production. The dreams of socialist leaders quickly faded when they lost Jaurès, their most charismatic spokesman, to a bullet fired by an ultranationalist assassin in a Parisian café just days after the assassination of the archduke. As the continental crisis built, moreover, it became obvious that the presumptive unity of the left was far too weak to stop the drift toward war. Hundreds of thousands of workers in all countries stood with their nation in 1914 instead of their class, causing disgruntled socialists like the Italian journalist Benito Mussolini to learn that nation, not class, held the deepest appeal to the hearts of Europeans. This notion helped him embrace the ideology of fascism, which he more fully exploited in the decades following the war.

In 1914 only two areas posed any threat to the general peace in Europe. The first involved the so-called "sick man of Europe," the dying Ottoman Empire. By all appearances, it was on life support, having failed to stop an Italian invasion of Libya in 1911 and having been humiliated in two small wars (1911–1912) by an alliance of minor Balkan powers. A new and vigorous generation of "Young Turks" reinvigorated Ottoman politics, but they provided more energy than solutions. Reasonable Europeans concluded that the Young Turks would be able to do little to stop the empire's slide into diplomatic irrelevance. This situation brought with it potentially enormous consequences. A weakened Ottoman Empire might leave the Straits of Constantinople dangerously exposed to a Russian power play for a warm-water port. Still, few statesmen among the Great Powers wanted to see the Ottoman Empire disintegrate and fewer still were willing to go to war either to prop it up or to destroy it.

The other remaining area of tension, the Balkans, had been a region of concern to European statesmen for decades. The region's rising nationalist tensions and dizzying ethnic diversity confounded all attempts to find lasting solutions to the seemingly endless conflicts between rival ethnic and religious groups. European diplomats understood that ethnic, economic, and political connections between Balkan groups and several of the Great Powers meant that a conflict in this region could easily expand.

Nevertheless, German Chancellor Otto von Bismarck's prophetic comment that "some damn fool thing in the Balkans" would start the next war was already several decades old by 1914. All of the Great Powers had financial and political interests in the region, with Austria-Hungary, Russia, and the Ottomans being the most heavily involved. Still, as in Asia and Africa, the region had thus far managed to avoid becoming an international chess board. Even the two regional wars there in 1912 and 1913 had failed to drag the Great Powers into the maelstrom of Balkan rivalries. Hungarians in the Dual Monarchy largely opposed any further expansion into the Balkans, slowing if not stopping Austrian grandstanding in the region. Talk of Pan-Slavism notwith-standing, many astute Russians had concluded that deep involvement in the region promised more trouble than an extension of Russian influence there could possibly be worth.

Thus, at first glance the assassination in Sarajevo seemed like just another in a long line of Balkan intrigues. Few Europeans expected it to lead to a large war, although another Balkan war seemed a distinct possibility. Even as the crisis grew in magnitude, most Europeans expected diplomacy and cooler heads to prevail, as they had so often in the recent past. British Foreign Secretary Sir Edward Grey had started planning for an international conference to seek compromises and arrive at a peaceful resolution to the situation. War for the sake of an unpopular Austrian archduke seemed far from the minds of most Europeans as they headed off to their summer vacations.

By the summer of 1914, moreover, many Europeans had concluded that large wars in the early twentieth century had become impossible. Polish banker Ivan Bloch's turn-of-the-century analysis of economic and military factors concluded that future wars would have to be brief. The tremendous expense of modern war, Bloch concluded, would render it too costly for even the wealthy states of Europe to engage in for long periods of time. Governments, therefore, would be unable or unwilling to commit the mass resources that modern weapons and soldiers required. Bloch, of course, was entirely right about the enormous costs of war, but equally wrong about the ability and willingness of states to assume those costs if they believed that they had no choice but to do so.[6]

The first selection in this collection, from Norman Angell's *The Great Illusion* (first published in 1910) followed a similar line of thinking. His book argued that states would not go to war because it was an essentially unprofitable endeavor. States and peoples would also seek to avoid war, Angell argued, because war was fundamentally out of step with civilized society. In the introduction to the 1933 edition of his book, written in the wake of one war and with the beginnings of the next already forming on the horizon, Angell explained his logic:

> The demonstration that war, however victorious, spells ruin, has results alike disastrous and incalculable (especially to capitalists, who are supposed to carry an especial load of guilt for war), produces a political and social chaos whose end no man can see—all this is too plain, too inescapable, not to make the desire to avoid it a genuine one. The explanation [for why wars happen] is that popular thought does not grasp the relation between policies which seem on the surface legitimate or advantageous, and their final effect as a cause of war and chaos. The problem is not merely to show that "war does not pay" (is not, that is to say, either advantageous to our country, a satisfaction to our pride in it, or necessary to the assertion of its rights), but to show why the policies which we pursue and which we believe do pay, must lead to war; to find why we pursue those policies and to create the will to reverse them.[7]

Angell therefore asserted that for Europe to be at peace, Europeans had simply to realize that war, even if successful, always brought more harm than did peace. In the years before World War I, pacifists and socialists found much to admire in this line of thinking, as it depicted civilized man as essentially rational and the future of Europe as a progressive journey toward greater peace and prosperity.

Angell's Europe contrasts rather starkly to the Europe of his contemporary, German officer Friedrich von Bernhardi. Like many Europeans of his generation, Bernhardi saw the continent as a place of inevitable competition. Whether influenced by the popular ideas of Social Darwinism, which emphasized a struggle for survival between races, or *Realpolitik*, which emphasized competition for power and resources between states, Bernhardi believed that war was both inevitable and a challenge to be accepted as a test of a race or state's fitness. Following this logic, he argued that a preemptive war was not only defensible, but that in some situations it made perfect sense. Bernhardi did not recommend that states invent reasons for war, but neither did he believe, as Angell did, that peace was always preferable to war.

Bernhardi's views took on a particular significance in Germany, where members of the German social, political, and military elite (to a greater degree than elsewhere on the continent the three groups overlapped) came to see their state as being the victim of an international conspiracy. This view of Germany came to be "a self-fulfilling vision" with a special venom directed at England, its presumably lucrative overseas empire, and its powerful fleet. The German elite "saw their country as being in a state of *Einkeisung* (encirclement), surrounded by enemies, hemmed in and oppressed. That attitude often provoked aggressive, even bellicose, responses that encouraged rivals to become enemies."[8] This self-fulfilling prophecy of national and racial insecurity, combined with the view of war espoused by Bernhardi and others, inclined many Austrians and Germans to use the July Crisis of 1914 as an opportunity to shoot first and rationalize the answers to the questions later.

Germany thus gave its Austro-Hungarian ally a "blank check" of support for the latter's reckless July policies. The Austro-Hungarian elite had already concluded that the assassinations of the archduke and his wife gave them a justification to fight a preventative war against Serbia in order to redress a balance of power that they saw tipping slowly but surely against them. The Austro-Hungarian ruling elite desperately needed German support in order to deter the Russians from providing material support to the Serbs because their own war plan called for deploying the bulk of their forces south, toward Belgrade. Germany agreed to the Austrian request because the German elite had concluded that their chances to win a war were more in their favor in 1914 than they would be in 1917 or 1920. None of the key decision makers fully understood the machines they were setting in motion nor did they understand that once the war began they would quickly lose control over the war machines themselves. Even as Germany lent its unqualified support to Austria-Hungary, it was preparing to send seven-eighths of its own army west against France. As a result, neither Germany nor Austria-Hungary was in any position to guard against the Russians, an astonishing oversight that says much about the ways that the two states failed to coordinate their strategies. This problem intensified as the war became too large for any man, staff, or state to control.

World War I occurred at a time when the ostentatious trappings of monarchy hid the inherent weaknesses of the Hohenzollern, Habsburg, and Romanov regimes. The ensuing four years of conflict quickly revealed the inability of monarchal systems to

deal with the pressures of total war. The almost surreal exchange of telegrams between cousins "Willy" (Kaiser Wilhelm II) and "Nicky" (Tsar Nicholas II) shows this
problem quite clearly. By the time declarations of war were being drafted for their signatures, the monarchs had already lost control of the international and domestic situations. Although both men tried desperately to prove to their subjects and to themselves that they still mattered, the war soon showed them to be incompetent even as
figureheads.

The scholarly debate on the origins of the war is at the same time voluminous and
incomplete. Explaining exactly why Europeans went to war remains a point of more
confusion than controversy, in large part because from our perspective no possible
war aims seem commensurate with the costs necessary to obtain them.[9] This volume
cannot possibly review all of the theories and schools of thought. Instead, it presents
excerpts from two works on the subject. They are not the final word on the subject,
but they give two examples of the way that historians have framed and treated the
subject.

Although most treatments of the First World War privilege the western front, the
war's immediate causes lay in eastern Europe. This excerpt from Dennis Showalter's
classic study of the battle of Tannenberg takes a long-term view of the causes of the
battle and the war of which it was a part. The strength of his analysis lies in his discussion of the ambivalent and flexible attitudes that Germans and Russians had of
one another. Without the tension in the Russo-German relationship, the crisis caused
by the assassination of Archduke Franz Ferdinand might well have remained localized. It is therefore critical to understand this relationship if we are to understand how
the Balkan crisis developed into a continental, and global, war.

Part of Germany's concern with Russia, of course, was based in Russia's close relationship with France. As Douglas Porch shows, until 1911, relations between France
and Germany had been relatively calm, if not friendly. After repeated German attempts to win influence in Morocco, however, both the British and the French saw the
growth of German power as antithetical to their own interests. The rising power of
the French Right after 1911 symbolized a fundamental change in French ideas. Few
Frenchmen supported an offensive war, but most recognized the need to prepare for a
possible war with their neighbors and rivals to the east. Nevertheless, even when war
became inevitable in August 1914, French politicians ordered the army to move away
from the Belgian and German frontiers in order that the German Army be clearly
seen as the aggressor.

The growth of the French Army and its position inside French politics and society
confirmed in German military minds the wisdom of their grand strategy. That strategy took as a given that any general war in Europe would require the German Army to
fight the French. Thus German war planning called for a rapid strike into France and
Belgium regardless of whether or not the diplomatic crisis leading the nation to war
involved France at all. The views of men like Bernhardi reinforced the sense of urgency and, consequently, sped up decision making. Even before the declarations of
war had the Kaiser's signature, German units were in neutral Belgium racing for the
key fortress complex around Liège. Such an approach to war "effectively precluded
any last-minute options for peace,"[10] but fit neatly into German views that war was

best fought when conditions favored victory, not as a last resort when all other options had been ruled out.

Part Two: Soldiers

No two veterans experienced the war in the same way. Some enjoyed relatively "good" wars in calm sectors of the front or in staff jobs behind the lines. Others endured titanic battles like those at Tannenberg, Verdun, the Somme, and the three costly engagements at Ypres. World War I soldiers and sailors fought in the air, under the sea, and in places as diverse as Belgium, Southwest Africa, Mesopotamia, and Poland. Similarly, no two soldiers remembered their place in the war in quite the same way. For some, the war had been the single defining experience of their lives. They wrote about the war, talked about the war, and did all they could to keep alive their roles in the war. For others, the war had been a horrifying and disgusting experience that led them into isolation and withdrawal.

For still others, the war had contained elements of farce. Jaroslav Hašek, who lived and wrote in Prague in the 1920s at the same time as Franz Kafka, served in an Austro-Hungarian army in which he did not believe for an emperor to whom he felt no loyalty. Taken prisoner during the war by the Russians and sent to a POW camp in Siberia, he had time to put together the ideas that come out in the bitingly satirical vignettes that became his masterful work, *The Good Soldier Schweik*. With its tales of atheistic chaplains and absurd army regulations, it anticipates Joseph Heller's unparalleled masterpiece from the Second World War, *Catch-22*.

Perhaps more importantly, the book gives us insight into the mindset of many of the men who went to war. Hašek's anti-hero was neither caught up in the throes of patriotic enthusiasm nor did he volunteer out of any great hatred for presumptive enemies. Instead, like millions of others, he went to war unaware of the larger issues involved in bringing the continent to war. He even has his title character, a Czech, suggest fighting on the side of the French against Germany in order to obtain independence for Czechoslovakia from the Austro-Hungarian Empire! Schweik was nevertheless caught up in the storm of mobilization and returned to uniform from his reserve status to fight a war he did not understand for a cause he suspected was not worth the sacrifice.

Not all soldiers, of course, were Schweiks. Many men willingly placed their lives on the line for causes in which they deeply believed. Defense of homeland, religion, and communal values figure prominently among the reasons given by men for going to war. So do less lofty matters such as the fear of being ostracized for not doing one's part, a boredom with the drudgery of civilian life, and a desire to join in a grand adventure. As the war continued, men came to have fewer choices as social and political pressures compelled them into military service. Open resistance to conscription was rare, although fears of its being extended to Ireland played a role in inspiring the Easter Rising of 1916.

Frederic Manning's brilliant work, *Her Privates We*, has justifiably become one of the best-regarded works on this or any other war. Manning, an Anglo-Australian who fought during 1916's bloody battle of the Somme, captured in the men's own slang the internal dynamic of a British unit. Manning brought out the comradeship among men from different backgrounds, their uncertainty as to the meaning of their own sacrifice, their ambivalence toward the blissfully ignorant civilians on the home front, and, above all, their hatred of the war. *Her Privates We* provides more insight into the thoughts and feelings of "ordinary soldiers" from World War I than any other book yet written.

The battle of the Somme carries a special poignancy in Britain. The first day of the battle, 1 July 1916, remains the bloodiest single day in the history of the British Army. Soldiers from Canada, South Africa, Ireland, Australia, and New Zealand lent their strength to a battle that the British high command never fully controlled. Even today considerable debate remains on what exactly the British Expeditionary Force's senior leadership hoped or expected to achieve.[11] Whatever the expectations, the battle continued into the fall amidst deteriorating weather and unrealizable objectives. At the end of the battle in November many British week-one objectives still sat in German hands. The British suffered more than 420,000 casualties, and the French 195,000 casualties; while the Germans' figures are harder to calculate, they may have risen as high as 600,000 casualties.

The perception of futility in the face of unprecedented effort only partially explains the British (and to a lesser extent German) fascination with the Somme. The British battalions that fought there were disproportionately amateur soldiers because Britain alone among the Great Powers had not employed conscription in the years before the war. New recruits to the British Army in 1914 and 1915 came through the "Pals" system, which allowed men to join up with their friends for the duration of the war. As a recruiting tool, it worked brilliantly, but it also meant that men who had enlisted together often died together. Because men tended to enlist with others from their hometowns and neighborhoods, the Somme battles left many localities without an entire generation of young men.

The power of Manning's book thus comes in part from its ability to bring the Pals battalions to life. As citizen-soldiers they had a more pronounced suspicion of officers and regular army soldiers than did their French and German counterparts. In another part of the book, Manning described the army thus: "Officers were scarce, but they might be scarcer by one or two, without much harm being done."[12] The comment is classically British and classically a part of the mentality of the Pals. By 1918, these men had themselves become grizzled veterans, inclined to see new draftees and arriving Americans as hopelessly amateurish.

The world of Britain's citizen-army is also the subject of Gary Sheffield's innovative study of officer-man relations. Because of the absence of prewar conscription, the British Army faced a particularly difficult problem in finding officers. Moreover, the high casualties suffered by the British in 1914 and 1915 left few experienced officers to train the new recruits. As a result, young Britons had to learn their jobs as they went. A cottage industry quickly developed that produced pamphlets written by old army veterans to help men learn their new trade.

The sharp divisions inside the British Army between officers and the "other ranks" further complicated the problem. Officers had to learn how to manage their new charges with fairness and dignity. In many cases, this task required them to ignore or modify the training they had received. Sheffield analyzes how military rank, social class, and politics interacted in the crucible of war. This excerpt also gives us insight into the understudied lives of the junior officers responsible for maintaining military effectiveness in their units under the most trying of circumstances. As these men quickly discovered, war is a terrible endeavor to try to learn on the job.

Like the British Pals battalions, men in Germany also volunteered in large numbers for military service. The question of exactly why they did so remains a point of scholarly contention. So, too, has been the rather unusual debate over how enthusiastically they did so. The question remains vividly alive in part because of the implications it carries for the larger issues of the war. Enthusiastic men have served either as examples of innocent lambs being led to slaughter by incompetent politicians and generals or as evidence of a popular groundswell in support of war that politicians could not resist. Jeffrey Verhey's book is an example of recent scholarship that tends to argue against the supposed depth of volunteer enthusiasm. Europeans, he argues, were not as anxious to become soldiers as surviving photographs, video reels, and contemporary news reports might suggest. Rather, he contends, the myths of war enthusiasm and national unity of purpose became more and more crucial as a means to pressure other men to follow in the footsteps of the presumably more patriotic men of 1914.

Perhaps no aspect of the war has elicited as much controversy as the competence (or lack thereof) of the war's senior commanders. Indeed, books on the subject carry titles such as *The Donkeys* and *British Butchers and Bunglers of World War One*. Even a complimentary biography of one of Britain's most successful divisional commanders carries the damning-with-faint-praise title *Far from a Donkey*.[13] Several individual biographies and campaign studies also offer scathing indictments of senior commanders wrapped up in petty rivalries, unaware of the realities of combat, and stubbornly holding to tactics and strategies that manifestly had no chance to succeed.[14]

More recent scholarship has emphasized the tremendous problems senior commanders faced. None of them had anticipated a war of the scale and scope of World War I. Few of them had commanded large units and fewer still had experience with the problems of trench warfare. The large sizes of World War I battlefields greatly complicated communications, leaving many commanders with enormous amounts of often contradictory information to interpret. The dominance of defensive technologies and the limitations of pursuit further hamstrung commanders who knew they had to attack to win. Even the most thoughtful among them could not find the formula that would allow them to succeed without incurring huge losses. As French General Charles Mangin rather disdainfully noted, "Whatever you do, you lose a lot of men." His statement has been read alternatively as a statement of his indifference to the lives of his men and as an expression of the frustrations faced by senior commanders. The former reading fits into the dominant images of the war more neatly, but the latter is much more likely.

Few generals wanted a war of immobility and attrition. German General Erich von Falkenhayn's plan to "bleed the French white" through carefully managed static warfare at Verdun stands out as an exception.[15] Almost all generals sought to win battles, and by extension the war, by restoring mobility to the battlefield; even as late as 1918 many battle plans included a cavalry charge and an advance into open country. Mobility became such an important goal in and of itself that larger strategic aims often got lost. German General Erich Ludendorff famously stated that the goals for his 1918 offensive were to "punch a hole. As to the rest, we shall see." That so few generals found ways to bring mobility back to the battlefield as a means of winning the war does not necessarily make them butchers, though bunglers several of them surely were.

Mangin, who was even nicknamed "the Butcher," is among those generals most often derided by historians, but not all senior commanders share his fate. Russia's Alexei Brusilov, Britain's Herbert Plumer, Australia's John Monash, and France's Ferdinand Foch all have reputations for excellence, at least in certain of the war's operations and campaigns. Brusilov's finest moment came in the summer of 1916 when he conducted a campaign that temporarily changed the fortunes of the faltering Russian Army. Brusilov, an aristocratic cavalryman by background, quickly lost faith in both the cavalry as an arm of warfare and the tsar as a leader for Russia. His memoirs, excerpted for this section, give us a window into his mind as well as a view of war on the important but often neglected eastern front.

Historian David Trask analyzes how the allied war efforts came together and how the United States fit into the alliance. By 1918 the relations between the allied powers remained characterized by a considerable deal of suspicion, but the senior generals and politicians had at long last realized the need for greater coordination of effort. Germany's mass offensives of that spring forced two changes in the nature of the alliance. First, the allies finally agreed to place one man in charge of all operations on the western front. General Ferdinand Foch had seen his star decline in 1915 and 1916 when his offensive-minded war plans produced huge casualties for little gain. In 1918, however, he proved to be remarkably adept at a job that had few precedents to guide it. Through personal persuasion, a deft handling of reserves, and an uncanny ability to read German intentions, Foch guided the defense of the western front and the allied counterpunches that led to victory in November.[16]

The second factor involved an increased role for the Americans. By the time the crisis of 1918 struck in March, the Americans had been in the war for almost a year, but had yet to translate their potential into fighting power. The Americans were still training soldiers, scrambling to find weapons for them, and developing their strategic and tactical concepts, many of which proved ill-suited to the challenges of war. To demonstrate their discomfort with the allies, the United States insisted on being called an "associated power" of the alliance and refused in principle to place American soldiers under European commanders, although in practice American officers proved to be more flexible than their policy allowed.

The selection from Trask in this section describes the situation in the allied high command after the crisis created by the German offensives from March to July had passed. Instead of merely defending French and Belgian territory, allied commanders were searching for ways to win the war in 1918. Failure to do so might give the Germans the chance to use the winter of 1918–1919 to regroup and refit. A prolonged war might also strain home fronts and the morale of the weary men under arms. A large American attack into the heavily defended Meuse–Argonne sector formed an important part of Foch's overall strategy for the final months of 1918. This selection thus allows for a discussion both of the ways that senior commanders from different nations worked together to determine operations and how the Americans handled their largest campaign of the war.

Part Three: Armageddon

The futility of combat in the First World War stands out as perhaps its single most defining characteristic. The dominance of defensive weapons and the strength of trench systems made classic breakthroughs and strategic envelopments rare. As science and technology, too, became mobilized for war, scientific solutions to military problems added misery to the lives of soldiers without materially affecting the course of the war. In 1915 the Germans added poison gas to the battlefield and in the following year they added the flamethrower. The British introduced tanks, an electrically powered device for firing gas shells, and more effective hand grenades. All armies built heavier and more powerful artillery pieces to destroy the defensive works soldiers built for self-protection, as well as lighter machine guns to provide them with mobile firepower as they advanced.

Despite the power of these weapons, a focus on technology can obscure the equally important developments soldiers made in what is known as, for lack of a better phrase, the art of warfare. Artillerists learned to use their guns in complex ways to protect the advance of their own infantry. At the same time other gunners were using sophisticated techniques to find hidden enemy guns and destroy them. Pilots learned to strafe and bomb targets on the ground, and specialized mining units developed ways to tunnel under enemy lines and detonate huge piles of explosives. The remnants of these craters are still visible on the western front. One such explosion in Belgium in 1917 was heard as far away as London.

The rapidly changing battlefield, of course, placed increasing strain on junior and senior officers to adapt to new ways of killing. The end result for soldiers was a battlefield vastly different from what they could possibly have imagined. Conditions at the front lines were abysmal even when no active battle was being fought. Besides the enemy, men had to contend with rats, lice, disease, a lack of proper food, and inconsistent medical care. Heroism lost its value and function in such an environment. To many men, the war had become a contest of machines in which their own survival had become a mere matter of chance.

The western and eastern fronts, although parts of the same war, often had little in common. The eastern front was simply too large for the creation of the types of solid defensive lines that so characterized the western front. Because of this difference in what armies call the force-to-space ratio, the eastern front occasionally experienced tremendous territorial shifts. During the 1915 Gorlice–Tarnow offensive, for example, the Germans advanced the line ninety-five miles in just two weeks. This mobility allowed for the use of cavalry and traditional operations such as pursuit and envelopment. It also meant that the war had a more direct impact on Polish civilians unfortunate enough to be in the path of advancing and retreating armies. With its relative lack of modern technology and higher incidence of disease, the war in the east often bore more resemblance to war in the nineteenth century than the twentieth.

On the western front, the war most directly impacted civilians in the occupied zone of Belgium and northeastern France. In 1914 the advancing German Army decided on a policy of ruthlessness toward Belgium in particular. In part this policy derived from the tight timetables the Germans had set for themselves (they had hoped to be in Paris within six weeks), but it also derived from an intense German dislike for irregular troops. The destruction of the Belgian university town of Louvain in response to alleged partisan activity particularly shocked people in the allied nations and stayed in their memories well after the war. The Treaty of Versailles even specified that "Germany undertakes to furnish to the University of Louvain, within three months . . . manuscripts, incunabula, printed books, maps and objects of collection corresponding in number and value to those destroyed in the burning by Germany of the Library of Louvain."

The first reading in this section provides eyewitness accounts of that notorious incident. The sacking of Louvain became a *cause célèbre* in allied and neutral nations and in allied eyes provided evidence of German bestiality. With astonishing speed the Germans had ceased to be seen as a nation of honorable, property-respecting soldiers. Instead they had become vicious beasts capable of real atrocities as well as those that allied propagandists and journalists embellished. Real and imagined atrocities became intermingled in the chaotic first months of the war. Although no one doubts that German soldiers committed atrocities in Belgium, the exact extent of those atrocities and their larger meaning for the war remain controversial today.[17]

Images of "Hun" brutality did much to help British recruitment in 1914. By 1916 those volunteers were at last ready for their first large test on the Somme. One of Britain's first accredited war correspondents, Philip Gibbs, captured the fateful July day that saw the opening of that battle. Gibbs needs to be read rather carefully, aware as he was that he might be censored and that he needed to sell newspapers back home. His optimism that the battle would produce victory in the end eventually faded, but in early July he, like thousands of British soldiers, believed in victory as a matter of faith. His early dispatches from the Somme also stand as evidence of the immense confusion that accompanied the early hours and days of a major campaign. In the case of the Somme, uncertainty about what was actually happening at the front, combined with the commanders' confidence in their eventual triumph, compelled them to lead wave after wave of men into the killing zone. The optimism of this excerpt can be read in contrast to Gibbs's *Now It Can Be Told*, a book he wrote after the war, when he could step back and see the war as a whole and when he no longer needed to fear the censor's pen.[18]

Historians Leonard Smith and Tony Ashworth provide two answers to the question of how men endured and responded to the seemingly unending horrors of the war. These historians' work fits into a generation of innovative scholarship that looked at the men of World War I as much more than anonymous victims in a vicious world that they could not control. Instead, Smith and Ashworth understand the soldiers of the war as responding to their environment in ways designed to fit into their own sense of morality and to enhance their chances of survival. In many ways, these actions either ignored or worked directly against the orders of their superiors. Men developed their own sense of battlefield ethics and their own notions of what was right and wrong within an environment seemingly bereft of traditional morality. The futility of the war bred contempt for fighting in ways that the men saw as unimaginative and needlessly bloody.

Smith's study analyzes French soldiers who took part in a mass mutiny following the disastrous Chemin des Dames offensive in April 1917. Senior French officers tended to look upon the mutineers as cowards, pacifists, or communists. Smith argues that the men were willing to fight for France, but they were not willing to throw away their lives for no obvious strategic purpose. Their mutiny was thus a way to express their unwillingness to be fed into senseless slaughter. It was not, however, an expression of cowardice or an unwillingness to put their lives on the line to defend France. Despite their refusal to advance, the vast majority of French soldiers stayed in their trenches and stood ready to defend France if the Germans attacked. Indeed, their mutiny was so carefully conducted that the Germans just a few miles away did not learn of it until it was far too late for them to take advantage of it.

As Tony Ashworth shows in his book *Trench Warfare, 1914–1918: The Live and Let Live System*, soldiers found other ways to deal with the dangers of the western front. In quiet sectors of the front men developed their own unwritten codes to take some of the senseless cost out of the war. By intentionally firing their daily allotment of shells inaccurately, men could signal to their enemies in the opposite trench their desire to keep the sector "quiet." If the enemy responded in kind, then an informal "live and let system" could develop, leaving some areas calm enough for men to grow vegetables in the trenches to supplement their bland diets and even keep cows in No Man's Land to provide fresh milk. In other sectors of the front men agreed not to shoot at ration parties or stretcher bearers. Of course, not all sectors saw such a system develop. Still, Ashworth shows us a side of the war that provides a dramatic contrast to the world of the large campaigns and battles. The live-and-let-live system stands as a warning to students of the war not to oversimplify their perceptions of combat in World War I.

Part Four: Home Fronts

Many soldiers returning home on leave found that those on the home front had little understanding of what the war was really like. Bombarded with propaganda (what the French called *bourrage de crâne* or "skull stuffing") and censored news stories, civilians often unquestioningly adopted the official version of events. Soldiers found it impossible to talk seriously with their relatives or friends about the war or their own experiences. Many men found it easier to tell civilians what they wanted to hear rather than try to explain in polite company how hellish their lives in the trenches really were. Attempting to find the words to tell a comrade's parents how their son had really died also proved too difficult for many soldiers.

Vera Brittain might have led an ordinary (if relatively privileged) English life had the war not changed her fate. The daughter of a prosperous businessman, Brittain was a bright student with a promising future that included an appointment at the University of Oxford. The war, however, took her away from that comfortable life and brought her repeated tragedy. During the course of the war, she lost her brother Edward, her fiancé, Roland, her brother's best friend, Geoffrey, and her fiancé's close friend Victor. All died of wounds suffered in battle before their twenty-third birthdays. All four of the young men had been a part of her circle of friends before the war, and Brittain maintained a remarkable correspondence with them during the course of the war.

Brittain learned about the war from this correspondence and through her own service as a volunteer nurse in the later years of the war. To follow her life is to see the depths of sadness and loss that the war could bring. She was in Brighton's Grand Hotel waiting for Roland to begin his leave when instead she received a telegram informing her of his death just two days before Christmas 1915. In 1917 Geoffrey and Victor died within a week of one another. Brittain responded to these losses by working even harder as a nurse and volunteering to serve in a clearing hospital in France until the illnesses of her parents forced her to return home. After the war, she turned to writing and dedicated herself to the cause of international pacifism.

Unlike Brittain, Princess Evelyn Stapleton-Bretherton Blücher had already led a far-from-ordinary life by the time the war began. Born into an aristocratic English family, she later married a German prince. When the July Crisis of 1914 began she and her husband were living in England, but they decided to move to Berlin as international tensions rose. In Germany she kept a diary that showed the increasing desperation on the German home front ironically caused in large part by the blockade enforced by her own nation's Royal Navy. Her position of privilege protected her from suffering the worst of these privations, but even her material conditions declined as time wore on. While Princess Blücher's situation was far from representative of the condition of ordinary Germans, her diary nevertheless shows the dramatic social changes wrought by four years of war.

Belinda Davis's research on food policies in Germany during the war shows us the life of the less fortunate. This chapter, "Home Fires Burning," details the loss of confidence ordinary Germans experienced in their own state. The German elite had delayed making economic and social changes needed for a long war and could not find an effective solution to the British blockade. Consequently, ordinary Germans turned to the black market or sought to exploit the systems put in place by local and state officials. The extent to which the food shortage impacted German war efficiency remains a point of debate, but, as Davis shows, there is little doubt that the government's inability to provide for the basic needs of its subjects contributed to its ultimate downfall.

The connection between military policy and the lives of men and women on the home front also appears in the work of Jennifer D. Keene. In this excerpt, she analyzes American conceptions of race and how they shaped military personnel policies. Her work also reflects a new generation of scholarship on the history of warfare by providing a critical link between the home and fighting fronts. Conceptions of race and the nature of American war fighting in 1917 and 1918 both shaped American policy on the home front and reflected the dominance of racial attitudes that ultimately made the war harder to prosecute.

As all of these selections show, it is important not to draw too sharp a line between home fronts and fighting fronts. Historians have much more work to do to bring these aspects of war together and explain how they impacted one another. The selections provided here show some of the ways that the two fronts can be seen as a unified whole.

Part Five: The End of the War

Nineteen seventeen had been a horrible year for the allies. British and French failures at Passchendaele and the Chemin des Dames had gravely weakened allied forces for little appreciable gain. The large, but inefficient Russian Army had left the war after a new Bolshevik government reluctantly agreed to sign the brutally one-sided Treaty of Brest-Litovsk. The Germans had already begun to amass grain and oil from eastern Europe to compensate for the British blockade and to prepare for one last offensive on the western front. The success or failure of that offensive would likely determine who would win the war and who would lose it.

In January 1918 the signs pointing to that offensive were mounting. The American army, on which the French and British had placed so much hope, had yet to make its presence fully felt on the western front. On January 8, President Woodrow Wilson issued his Fourteen Points, a statement of war aims upon which he hoped to base the postwar peace treaties. His view of the postwar world, however, differed greatly from those of America's allies. The British disliked the anticolonial tone of the Fourteen Points as well as the president's insistence on free trade and freedom of the seas. The French were no happier, with Prime Minister Georges Clemenceau allegedly remarking that Wilson had presented mankind with fourteen points, when God Himself had been content with just ten.

Wilson's words had, however, inspired Europeans to hope for a better world once the guns had ceased firing. Ironically, the Germans also reached out to the Fourteen Points, hoping that they might serve as a shield against the vengeance of the British and the French. Upon his arrival in Europe in 1919, Wilson received a rapturous greeting from crowds in England and France, but even by then it had become obvious that the Fourteen Points could not become the basis for negotiation.

American, British, and French differences with regard to their visions of the postwar world were reflected as well in the three nations' strategic and operational visions. A letter from the supreme allied commander, French Marshal Ferdinand Foch, reveals the state of mind of two senior military leaders in the last month of the war. Foch hoped to argue against the beliefs of British commander Sir Douglas Haig that the Germans still had the capacity to fight on. Haig recalled the German construction in 1917 of a series of fortifications known to the allies as the Hindenburg Line. As they retired to these positions, the German units enacted a policy of "scorched earth," leaving no resources intact. Haig feared that a repeat of this performance might impede any allied attempt to win the war in 1918. He therefore favored an armistice, if it could be concluded in such a way as to hamper future German efforts.

Pershing, in a letter written two weeks later, argued for fighting on. In command of the only army on the western front that grew stronger each day, Pershing advocated carrying the war into Germany if necessary in order to obtain an unconditional surrender. A 1919 offensive, he knew, would be led by mass armies built around fresh American soldiers and large supplies of heavy artillery pieces, airplanes, and tanks. Pershing therefore was willing to risk not winning the war in 1918 because he knew that a 1919 campaign would greatly favor the allies. With our hindsight knowledge of right-wing German activities in the postwar years, Pershing's observation that an early armistice might force the allies to forfeit "the chance actually to secure world peace on terms that would insure its permanence" seems more prophetic than it seemed to most of his European contemporaries.

In the end, Foch came closer to Haig's point of view than Pershing's. Foch argued that the point of military activity was to obtain from one's enemy conditions to end a war on victorious terms. Any blood shed after those conditions could be met, Foch believed, would be on his hands and his conscience forever. He therefore agreed to a German offer (broadcast over open airwaves and detected by the Eiffel Tower radio antenna) to discuss peace terms. In a forest clearing Foch had his chief of staff read his terms aloud. The German delegates expressed shock at how harsh those terms were, but they knew that the desperate conditions inside Germany gave them no choice but to agree and thereby end the war.

Even as the war was ending, German ultranationalists had begun to pass the blame for defeat away from the army and toward domestic enemies. They argued that German forces had been able to keep the allies out of Germany and that therefore the German Army must have still retained significant fighting power. The "stab in the back" theory thus blamed the failures of domestic governance to give the army the tools it needed to conclude a more favorable armistice. Whether Pershing's proposed way of ending the war would have discredited such arguments (and thereby have removed a major tenet of Nazism) remains pure speculation, but to people in a war-torn continent in 1918, Foch's decision seemed the right one because it ended the killing.

Wilhelm Deist's 1996 article on the condition of the German Army in 1918 shows beyond a doubt its debilitated condition. Deist chronicles the misinformed optimism and refusal to admit defeat that had become rampant among the German Army's senior leadership. He also shows the rapid loss of faith in that leadership in the war's final months among the German rank and file. His study should serve as a serious caution against the amateurish view of the German Army as consistently more devoted, more competent, and better led than its opponents. This view, which should have faded away long ago, remains a part of even scholarly and quasischolarly studies of the war's final months.[19] Deist's corrective allows us to see the Germans for what they were in 1918, a tired force with outdated weapons being asked to make monumental sacrifices for ultimately futile purposes by a deluded, if not deranged, senior command structure bereft of ideas.

The final essay in this section details the relationship between two armies that were improving as the war ended. The Australians had taken lessons learned from their monumental sacrifices at places like Gallipoli and the Somme to become a premier fighting force. The Australians and New Zealanders, under the command of General John Monash, took the lead in several critical operations in the war's final months, including the breaking of the Hindenburg Line. The Americans, for their part, had shown that their value far exceeded sheer numbers. They had learned how to fight and continued to improve with each campaign. Their mere presence in such large numbers and with such inspiring élan helped to rejuvenate tired French and British soldiers.

The contrast between the Australians and Americans on the one hand and the Germans on the other made the outcome of the war a *fait accompli*. The British and French, despite all of their losses over the four years, also retained significant striking power. Myths and attempts by German nationalists to shift blame for defeat do not hide the fact that the German Army was decisively beaten in 1918 by a combination of larger, more efficient, and better equipped armies.

Part Six: Peace

Trying to piece back together a world so badly torn apart by four years of global upheaval should have intimidated the statesmen of Europe. No precedent existed to guide them; their reliance on the 1815 peace settlement following the Napoleonic Wars proved to be misguided at best. They had not only to create a new Europe, but they also had to reconcile the many contradictory promises they had made to people around the world. From 1919 to 1925 the Great Powers held twenty major conferences in seven countries in a vain attempt to create the conditions for a lasting peace. Nine major treaties came out of these conferences, but none of them lasted more than a single generation. The Treaty of Sèvres, designed to create peace between the allies and the Ottoman Empire, lasted less than three years.[20] Whether or not the failure of this process created the conditions that made the Second World War inevitable has become a favorite point of classroom discussions. Of course, it is impossible to answer that question with any certainty despite the manifest failures of the Big Four.[21]

The first few pages of British diplomat Harold Nicolson's memoirs show that the diplomats in charge of the peace process understood the challenges in front of them, but that few of them thought the obstacles insurmountable. In this perception, they did not differ as greatly as they believed from the generals whom many of them despised. Just as the generals believed that no defensive position was too powerful to resist a well-crafted and properly supported plan, the diplomats believed that no international controversy existed that they could not solve by compromise, persuasive appeals to their fellow diplomats, or a redrawing of a border. Any unresolved issues or unforeseen problems could be handled through a Great Power–dominated League of Nations. The answers all appeared, if perhaps not simple, at least straightforward. It did not take long, however, for Nicolson and others to realize that they had quite seriously understated the intractability of the problems in front of them.

The second Nicolson excerpt comes from his diary entry on the day of the signing of the most important treaty, the Treaty of Versailles with Germany. Rather than being an occasion for tremendous celebration, Nicolson records that he went to bed "sick of life." Like many others, including David Lloyd George and Ferdinand Foch, Nicolson recognized fundamental flaws in the treaty (although the three men recognized different fundamental flaws). Nicolson had worked from January to June 1919 on the most important task of his generation, the completion of a lasting European peace, only to realize that his country's success had been "beastly," in large part because of its apparent impermanence.

Blaming the incompetence or the vengeance of diplomats and heads of state at the Paris Peace Conference for the failures of the peace process provides only part of the answer. The impossibility of creating a lasting peace had origins in the promises and hopes raised during the war itself. Wilson's Fourteen Points seemed to hold out hope to anyone and everyone who read them, even the Germans. The bright future that Wilson inspired formed a large part of the president's magnetic mystique, but the inevitable failure of the peace conference to meet even a fraction of those hopes led to a disillusion as powerful as the hope had once been.

The former Ottoman Empire reveals these contradictions and dashed expectations. In 1919 the problem of the Middle East (a phrase that first entered popular usage during the war) did not loom especially large to the diplomats gathered in Paris. The Ottoman Empire's former colonies would need a new status, but next to the monumental challenge of creating peace with Germany, the problems of the Middle East struck many as a secondary or tertiary issue. Nicolson makes scant mention of Turkey in his memoirs except to underscore the general British feeling that the Turks had behaved barbarically during the war (notably, he was referring to their treatment of British prisoners of war, not their mass murder of Armenian civilians) and, consequently, that they should expect little sympathy from the victorious powers.

Despite the general lack of concern given to the Middle East, the disarray that World War I created in that tortured part of world remains one of the war's most murderous legacies. The documents here show British diplomats making contradictory promises to Jews and Arabs. The Balfour Declaration effectively committed Britain to making Palestine a Jewish homeland after the war, but Arabs read the correspondence between Sherif Hussein Ibn Ali and Sir Henry McMahon as placing Palestine inside an Arab state. The British made both promises in secret in the hopes of gaining Jewish and Arab support against the Ottoman Empire. They also intentionally left the language and the borders vague, hoping to use the ambiguity either to create room for compromise or to delay any action they might be called upon to take.

Most perniciously, many members of the British government had little intention of meeting either obligation in the near future. Instead, they saw a chance to use the war's outcome to enlarge the British Empire in a strategically important area. In 1916 Sir Mark Sykes and French diplomat François Picot had, with Russian approval, concluded an agreement to place the former Ottoman colonies under British and French suzerainty. T. E. Lawrence, who had fought with the Arabs, exploded with anger when he heard of the deal and many British politicians were at least aware of the consequences created by the contradictions in British policy. Sykes and others had concluded, however, that Zionism, Arab nationalism, and British imperial interests could somehow be reconciled. This misjudgment, along with the arbitrary borders the diplomats drew, set the stage for the tumultuous and violent modern history of the

Middle East. Nicolson, Sykes, McMahon, Picot, and others became impresarios (many of them unwittingly) in a drama that continues to confront the British as well as the Americans.

The first real test of the postwar treaties occurred in Turkey. The unpopularity of the Treaty of Sèvres led to a rebellion headed by Turkey's greatest war hero, Mustapha Kemal. As David Fromkin shows, Kemal's patriotic movement soon led to the abdication of the sultan, a war between Greece and Kemal's Turkey, and a new treaty that shattered Sèvres and established the modern nation state of Turkey. Ironically, the state that Nicolson and others had derided as barbaric soon set out to reform and modernize itself along western lines. Kemal, who became president of Turkey under the name Atatürk (Father of the Turks), created a new state that looked to establish peaceful relations with the European powers while staying out of their wars in the future.

This volume ends with a discussion of the war's immediate impacts in Germany. News of the peace terms had sent right-wing Germans into the streets in protest. Crowds burned French battle flags from 1870 rather than see them returned to France as the Treaty of Versailles had demanded. Right-wing paramilitaries known as the *Freikorps* took advantage of the German government's weakness to conduct its own war of vengeance against socialists, Jews, and other presumptive enemies of the Reich. The government notably failed to clamp down on the paramilitaries; some army commanders even supported the demobilized soldiers who constituted the *Freikorps* by illegally arranging for weapons to be given or sold to them. Although the *Freikorps* violence eventually died down, the anger and bitterness of its members did not. The government's unwillingness to punish them for their crimes, moreover, indicated an acquiescence to their criminality. Many *Freikorps* members began drifting to groups like the Nazi Party's paramilitary *Sturmabteilungen* (SA), founded by Hitler in 1920 with the aim of violently overthrowing the Weimar Republic. The kaiser and many of his royal cousins had indeed departed, but exactly who might step up to replace them remained an unresolved question.

NOTES

1. See Donovan Webster, *Aftermath: The Remnants of War* (New York: Pantheon Books, 1996), chapter one.

2. These battlefields and cemeteries remain important to national identity, even far from Europe. See, for example, Ian McGibbon, *New Zealand Battlefields and Memorials of the Western Front* (Oxford: Oxford University Press, 2001).

3. See Xu Guoqi, *China and the Great War* (Cambridge: Cambridge University Press, 2005).

4. See David Fromkin, *A Peace to End All Peace: The Fall of the Ottoman Empire and the Creation of the Modern Middle East* (New York: Henry Holt, 1989) and Efraim Karsh and Inari Karsh, *Empires of Sand: The Struggle for Mastery in the Middle East, 1789–1923* (Cambridge: Harvard University Press, 1999).

5. See, among other works, Nicoletta Gullace, *"The Blood of Our Sons": Men, Women, and the Renegotiation of British Citizenship during the Great War* (London: Palgrave, 2004).

6. I. S. Bloch, *Is War Now Impossible?* (London: Richards, 1899).

7. Norman Angell, *The Great Illusion 1933* (New York: G. P. Putnam's Sons, 1933), p. 5.

8. William J. Astore and Dennis Showalter, *Hindenburg: Icon of German Militarism* (Dulles, Va.: Potomac Books, 2005), p. 12.

9. See, for example, Barbara Tuchman, *The Guns of August* (New York: Dell, 1963); James Joll, *The Origins of the First World War* (London: Longman, 1984; 2nd edition, 1992); Holger Herwig and Richard F. Hamilton, eds., *Decisions for War, 1914–1917* (Cambridge: Cambridge University Press, 2004); Annika Mombauer, *The Origins of the First World War: Controversies and Consensus* (London: Longman, 2002); and Hew Strachan, *The Outbreak of the First World War* (Oxford: Oxford University Press, 2004).

10. Annika Mombauer, *Helmuth von Moltke and the Origins of the First World War* (Cambridge: Cambridge University Press, 2001), p. 97.

11. Three recent books present differing accounts of the campaign. Gary Sheffield, *The Somme* (London: Cassell, 2003) provides a solid general introduction. For more detail, see Trevor Wilson and Robin Prior, *The Somme* (New Haven: Yale University Press, 2005). For an examination of some of the scholarly debates as well as a view of the French side see William J. Philpott, *The Somme* (London: Longman, 2006).

12. Frederic Manning, *Her Privates We* (London: Hogarth, 1986), p. 56.

13. Alan Clark, *The Donkeys* (London: Hutchinson, 1961); John Laffin, *British Butchers and Bunglers of World War One* (London: Alan Sutton, 1997); John Baynes, *Far from a Donkey: The Life of Sir Ivor Maxse* (Dulles, Va.: Brassey's, 1995). Clark's title comes from a well-known comment about the British as "an army of lions led by donkeys." The comment has been attributed to several people, including Napoleon.

14. See as examples Robin Prior and Trevor Wilson, *Passchendaele: The Untold Story* (New Haven: Yale University Press, 1996); Denis Winter, *Haig's Command: A Reassessment* (London: Viking, 1991); and Paul Fussell, *The Great War and Modern Memory* (Oxford: Oxford University Press, 1975).

15. Even with Falkenhayn there is considerable speculation. The claims that Verdun was to be a battle of attrition come from documents written after the war and from a 1915 memorandum by Falkenhayn. No copy of that memorandum survives, leading some scholars to contend that Falkenhayn used attrition as a postwar justification for the slaughterhouse that Verdun became.

16. See Michael S. Neiberg, *Foch: Supreme Allied Commander in the Great War* (Dulles, Va.: Brassey's, 2003).

17. See John Horne and Alan Kramer, *German Atrocities, 1914: A History of Denial* (New Haven: Yale University Press, 2001) and Larry Zuckerman, *The Rape of Belgium: The Untold Story of World War I* (New York: New York University Press, 2004).

18. Philip Gibbs, *Now It Can Be Told* (New York: Harpers, 1920).

19. For one example, see John Mosier, *The Myth of the Great War* (New York: HarperCollins, 2001).

20. A brief introduction can be found in Erik Goldstein, *The First World War Peace Settlements, 1919–1925* (London: Longman, 2002).

21. The term refers to Georges Clemenceau, David Lloyd George, Italian Prime Minister Vittorio Orlando, and Woodrow Wilson.

One

Causes

The Great Illusion, 1910

Sir Norman Angell

I think it will be admitted that there is not much chance of misunderstanding the general idea embodied in the passage quoted at the end of the last chapter. Mr. Harrison is especially definite. At the risk of "damnable iteration," I would again recall the fact that he is merely expressing one of the universally accepted axioms of European politics, namely, that a nation's whole economic security, its financial and industrial stability, its commercial opportunity, its prosperity and well-being, in short depend upon its being able to defend itself against the aggression of other nations, who will, if they are able, be tempted to commit such aggression because in so doing they will increase *their* power, and thus prosperity and well-being, at the cost of the weaker and vanquished.

I have quoted largely journalists, politicians, publicists of all kinds, because I desired to indicate not merely scholarly opinion, but the common public opinion really operative in politics, though in fact the scholars, the experts on international affairs, are at one with popular opinion in accepting the assumption which underlies these expressions, the assumption that military force if great enough can be used to transfer wealth, trade, property, from the vanquished to the victor, and that this latent power so to do explains the need of each to arm.

It is the object of these pages to show that this all but universal idea is a gross and desperately dangerous misconception, partaking at times of the nature of an optical illusion, at times of the nature of a superstition—a misconception not only gross and universal, but so profoundly mischievous as to misdirect an immense part of the energies of mankind, to misdirect them to such degree that, unless we liberate ourselves from it, civilization itself will be threatened.

As one of the most extraordinary features of this whole question is that the complete demonstration of the fallacy involved, the exposure of the illusion which gives it birth, is neither intricate nor doubtful. The demonstration does not repose upon any elaborately constructed theorem, but upon the simplest statement of the plainest facts in the economic life of Europe as we see it going on around us. Their nature may be indicated in a few simple propositions stated thus:

1. An extent of devastation, even approximating to that which Mr. Harrison foreshadows, as the result of the conquest of Great Britain, could only be inflicted by an invader as a means of punishment costly to himself, or as the result of an unselfish and expensive desire to inflict misery for the mere joy of inflicting it. Since trade de-

pends upon the existence of natural wealth and a population capable of working it, an invader cannot "utterly destroy it" except by destroying the population, which is not practicable. If he could destroy the population, he would thereby destroy his own market, actual or potential, which would be commercially suicidal. In this self-seeking world, it is not reasonable to assume the existence of an inverted altruism of this kind.

2. If an invasion by Germany did involve, as Mr. Harrison and those who think with him say it would, the "total collapse of the empire, our trade, and the means of feeding forty millions in these islands . . . the disturbance of capital and destruction of credit," German capital would, because of the internationalization and interdependence of modern finance, and so of trade and industry, also disappear in large part, German credit would also collapse; and the only means of restoring it would be for Germany to put an end to the chaos in Great Britain by putting an end to the condition which had produced it. Moreover, because also of this interdependence of our finance, the confiscation by an invader of private property, whether stocks, shares, ships, mines, or anything more valuable than jewelry or furniture—anything, in short, which is bound up with the economic life of the people—would so react upon the finance of the invader's country as to make the damage to him resulting from the confiscation exceed in value the property confiscated. So that Germany's success in conquest would be a demonstration of the economic futility of conquest.

3.For allied reasons, the exaction of tribute from a conquered people in our day has become an economic impossibility; the exaction of a large indemnity so difficult and so costly directly and indirectly as to be an extremely disadvantageous financial operation.

4. For reasons of a like nature to the foregoing, it is a physical and economic impossibility to capture the external or carrying trade of another nation by military conquest. Large navies are impotent to create trade for the nations owning them, and can in practice do nothing to "confine the commercial rivalry" of other nations. Nor can a conqueror destroy the competition of a conquered nation by annexation; his competitors would still compete with him—i.e., if Germany conquered Holland, German merchants would still have to meet the competition of the Dutch, and on keener terms than originally, because the Dutch manufacturers and merchants would then be within the German customs lines; the notion that the trade competition of rivals can be disposed of by conquering those rivals being one of the illustrations of the curious optical illusion which lies behind the misconception dominating this subject.

5. The wealth, prosperity, and well-being of a nation depend in no way upon its military power; otherwise we should find the commercial prosperity, and the economic well-being of the smaller nations, which exercise no such power, manifestly below that of the great nations which control Europe, whereas this is not the case. The populations of States like Switzerland, Holland, Belgium, Denmark, Sweden are in every way as prosperous as the citizens of States like Germany, Russia, Austria, and France. The wealth *per capita* of the small nations is in many cases in excess of that of the great nations. Not only the question of the security of small States, which, it might be urged, is due to treaties of neutrality, is here involved, but the question of whether military power can be turned in a positive sense to economic advantage.

6. No other nation could gain material advantage by the conquest of the British Colonies, and Great Britain could not suffer material damage by their "loss," however much such "loss" would be regretted on sentimental grounds, and as rendering less easy a certain useful social cooperation between kindred peoples. The use of the word "loss" is misleading. Great Britain does not "own" her Colonies. They are, in fact, independent nations in alliance with the Mother Country, to whom they are no source of tribute or economic profit (except as foreign nations are a source of profit), their economic relations being settled, not by the Mother Country, but by the Colonies. Economically, Great Britain would gain by their formal separation, since she would be relieved of the cost of their defense. Their "loss," involving no fundamental change in economic fact (beyond saving the Mother Country the cost of their defense), could not involve the ruin of the Empire and the starvation of the Mother Country, as those who commonly treat of such a contingency usually aver. As Great Britain is not able to exact tribute or economic advantage, it is inconceivable that any other country, necessarily less experienced in colonial management, would be able to succeed where Great Brain had failed, especially in view of the past history of the Spanish, Portuguese, French and British Colonial Empires. This history also demonstrates that the position of Crown Colonies, in the respect which we are considering, is not sensibly different from that of the self-governing ones (i.e., their fiscal policies tend to become their own affair, not the Mother Country's). It is not to be presumed, therefore, that any European nation, *realizing the facts*, would attempt the desperately expensive business of the conquest of Great Britain for the purpose of making an experiment which all colonial history shows to be doomed to failure.

The propositions just outlined—which traverse sufficiently the ground covered by those expressions, British and German, of the current view quoted in the last chapter—are little more than a mere statement of self-evident fact in Europe today. Yet the mere statement of self-evident fact constitutes, I suggest, a complete refutation of the views I have quoted, which are the commonly accepted "axioms" of international politics. For the purpose of parallel, I have divided my propositions into six clauses, but such division is quite arbitrary, and the whole could be gathered into a single clause as follows:

As the only feasible policy in our day for a conqueror to pursue is to leave the wealth of a territory in the possession of its occupants, it is a fallacy, an illusion, to regard a nation as increasing its wealth when it increases its territory. When a province or state is annexed, the population, who are the owners of the wealth, are also annexed. There is a change of political administration which may be bad (or good), but there is not a transfer of property from one group of owners to another. The facts of modern history abundantly demonstrate this. When Germany annexed Schleswig-Holstein and Alsace-Lorraine, no ordinary German citizen was enriched by goods or property taken from the conquered territory. Nor in these cases where there is no formal annexation, can the conqueror take the wealth of a conquered territory, for reasons connected with the very nature of wealth in the modern world. The structure of modern banking and finance have set up a vital, and, by reason of the telegraph, an immediately felt interdependence. Mutual indebtedness and world-wide investment have made the financial and industrial security of the victor dependent upon financial and industrial security in all considerable civilized centers. For these reasons wide-spread confiscation, or destruction of industry and trade in a conquered territory, would react disastrously upon the commerce and finance of the conqueror. The conqueror is, by this fact, reduced to military impotence as far as economic ends are concerned. Military power can do nothing commensurate with its cost and risk for the trade and well-being of the particular rulers exercising it. It cannot be used as an instrument for seizing or keeping trade. The idea that armies and navies can be used to transfer the trade of rivals from weak to powerful states is an illusion. Although Great Britain "owns" Canada, has completely "conquered" Canada, the British merchant is driven from the Canadian markets by the merchant of (say) the United States or Switzerland. The great nations neither destroy nor transfer to themselves the trade of small nations, because they cannot. Military power does not determine the relative economic position of peoples. The Dutch citizen, whose Government possesses no considerable military power, is just as well off as the German citizen, whose government possesses an army of two million men, and a great deal better off than the Russian, whose government possesses an army of something like four million. A fairly good index of economic stability, whether of a business organization or a nation, is the rate at which it is able to borrow money: risk and insecurity are very quickly reflected by a rise in the interest it must pay. Thus, as a rough-and-ready though incomplete indication of the relative wealth and security of the respective States, we find that the Three per Cents. of comparatively powerless Holland are quoted at 77 1/2, and the Three per Cents. of powerful Germany at 75; the Three and a Half per Cents. of the Russian Empire, with its hundred and twenty million souls and its four million army, are quoted at 78, while the Three and a Half per Cents. of Norway, which has not an army at all (or any that need be considered in this discussion), are quoted at 88. We thus get the paradox that, the more a nation's wealth is militarily protected, the less secure does it become.

The late Lord Salisbury, speaking to a delegation of businessmen, made this notable observation: The conduct of men of affairs, acting individually in their business capacity, differs radically in its principles and application from the conduct of the same men who they act collectively in political affairs.

The fact may explain the contradiction between the daily practice of the business world and the prevailing political philosophy, which security of property and high prosperity in the smaller States involves. We are told by the political experts that great navies and great armies are necessary in order to protect our wealth against the aggression of powerful neighbors, whose cupidity and voracity can be controlled by force alone; that as treaties avail nothing, and that in international politics might makes right, armaments are imposed by the necessity of commercial security; that our navy is an "insurance," and that a country without military power, with which their diplomats can "bargain" in the Councils of Europe, is at a hopeless disadvantage economically. Yet, when the investor studying the question in its purely material, its financial aspect, has to decide between the great States, with all their imposing paraphernalia of colossal armies and fabulously costly navies, and the little States, possessing relatively no military power whatever, he plumps solidly, and with what is in the circumstance a very great difference, in favor of the small and helpless. For a difference of twenty points, which we find as between Norwegian and Russian, and fourteen as between Belgian and German securities, is the difference between a safe and a speculative one.

Is it a sort of altruism or quixotism which thus impels the capitalists of Europe to conclude that the public funds and investments of powerless Holland and Sweden (any day at the mercy of their big neighbors) are 10 to 20 per cent. safer than those of the greatest Power of Continental Europe? The question is, of course, absurd. The only consideration of the financier is profit and security, and he has decided, thinking and acting as a financier, a practical economist, that the funds of the undefended nation are more secure than the funds of those defended by colossal armaments. Why does he reject the implications of this decision when he comes to settle matters of international politics?

If Mr. Harrison were right; if, as he implies, our commerce, our very industrial existence, would disappear did we allow neighbors who envied us that commerce to become our superiors in armament, and to exercise political weight in the world, how does he explain the fact that the great Powers of the Continent are flanked by little nations far weaker than themselves having nearly always a commercial development equal to, and in some cases greater than, their own? If the common doctrine be true, the financiers would not invest a pound or a dollar in the territories of the undefended nations. Yet, far from that being the case, they consider that a Swiss or a Dutch investment is more secure than a German one; that industrial undertakings in a country like Switzerland are preferable in point of security to enterprises backed by three millions of the most perfectly trained soldiers in the world. The beliefs of European financiers, as reflected in their acts, are in flat contradiction with the beliefs of European politicians as reflected in *their* acts. If a country's trade were really at the mercy of the first successful invader; if armies and navies were really necessary for the protection and promotion of trade, the small countries would be in a hopelessly inferior position, and could only exist on the sufferance of what we are told are unscrupulous aggressors. And yet Norway has, relatively to population, a greater carrying trade than Great Britain, and Dutch, Swiss, and Belgian merchants compete in all the markets of the world successfully with those of Germany and France.

The prosperity of the small states is thus a fact which proves a good deal more than that wealth can be secure without armaments. Exponents of the orthodox statecraft—notably such authorities as Admiral Mahan—plead that armaments are a necessary part of the economic struggle of nations, that without such power a nation is at a hopeless economic disadvantage.

The relative economic situation of the small States gives the lie to it all. This profound political philosophy is seen to be just learned nonsense when we realize that all the might of Russia or Germany cannot secure for the individual citizen better general economic conditions than those prevalent in the little States. The citizens of Switzerland, Belgium, or Holland, countries without "control," or navy, or bases, or "weight in the councils of Europe," or the "prestige of a great Power," are just as well off as Germans, and a great deal better off than Austrians or Russians.

Even if it could be argued that the security of the small States is due to the various treaties guaranteeing their neutrality, it cannot be argued that those treaties give them the military and naval power, the "weight in the councils of the nations," which Admiral Mahan and the other exponents of the orthodox statecraft assure us are such necessary factors in national prosperity.

I want, however, with all possible emphasis, to indicate the limits of the argument that I am trying to enforce. That argument is not that the facts just cited show armaments or the absence of them to be the sole or even the determining factor in national wealth or poverty. Nor indeed that there are no advantages in large national areas. Plainly there are (e.g. the absence of tariffs and fiscal barriers). But the facts cited do show that the security of wealth is due to other things than armaments; that the absence of political and military power is, on the one hand, no obstacle to prosperity any more than the possession of such power is a guarantee of prosperity; that the mere size of administrative area has no relation to the wealth of those inhabiting it, any more than it would be true to say that a man living in London is richer than a man living in Liverpool because the former city is larger and has a bigger budget.

A very common reply to the arguments just adduced is that the security of the small states nevertheless depends upon armaments—the armaments of the states which guarantee their neutrality. But, if treaty guarantees suffice for the protection of small states, why not of great? When that is suggested, however, the militarist is apt to turn round and declare that treaties are utterly valueless as a means of national security. Thus Major Stewart Murray:

> The European waste-paper basket is the place to which all treaties eventually find their way, and a thing which can any day be placed in a waste-paper basket is a poor thing on which to hang our national safety. Yet there are plenty of people in this country who quote treaties to us as if we could depend on their never being torn up. Very plausible and very dangerous people they are—idealists too good and innocent for a hard, cruel world, where force is the chief law. Yet there are some such innocent people in Parliament, even at present. It is to be hoped that we shall see none of them there in future.

But again, if the security of a nation's wealth can only be assured by force, and treaty rights are mere waste paper, how can we explain the evident security of the wealth of States possessing relatively no force? By the mutual jealousies of those guaranteeing their neutrality? Then that mutual jealousy could equally well guarantee the security of any one of the larger States against the rest.

The right understanding of this phenomenon involves, however, a certain distinction, the distinction between economic and political security. The political security of the small States is *not* assured; no man would take heavy odds on Holland being able to maintain complete political independence if Germany cared seriously to threaten it. But Holland's economic security is assured. Every financier in Europe knows that, if Germany conquered Holland or Belgium tomorrow, she would have to leave their wealth untouched; there could be no confiscation. And that is why the stocks of the lesser States, not in reality threatened by confiscation, yet relieved in part at least of the charge of armaments, stand fifteen to twenty points higher than those of the military States. Belgium, politically, might disappear tomorrow; her wealth would remain practically unchanged.

If this truth—that the wealth of an unprotected country is safe, that it cannot be seized—is recognized (as it is) by investors and financiers, the experts most concerned, whence comes the political danger, the danger of aggression? It is due surely to the fact that the truth recognized by investors, financiers, businessmen when dealing with facts belonging to their familiar world, has not been carried over into the realm of political ideas. The average businessman does not see the contradiction between his daily conduct as a businessman and the policy which he encourages his government to adopt. He sees no need of reconciling the fact that he will invest heavily in property that has no military or naval protection and his applause of Mr. Harrison, when the latter declares that, but for the British navy, the foreigner would run off with every penny that we possess, or words to that effect.

The actual policy pursued by financiers and investors implies that they do not believe that wealth, property can be "taken" by preponderant power. Yet preponderant power is pursued everywhere as the means of national enrichment. Power as an end is set up in European politics as desirable beyond all others. Here, for instance, are the Pan-Germanists of Germany. This party has set before itself the object of grouping into one great Power all the peoples of the Germanic race or language in Europe. Were this aim achieved, Germany would become the dominating Power of the Continent, and might become the dominating Power of the world. And, according to the commonly accepted doctrine of national advantage, such an achievement would, from the point of view of Germany, be worth any sacrifice that Germans could make. It would be an achievement so great, so desirable, that German citizens should not hesitate for an instant to give everything, life itself, in its accomplishment. Very good. Let us assume that, at the cost of great sacrifice, the greatest sacrifice which it is possible to imagine a modern civilized nation making, this has been accomplished, and that Belgium and Holland and Germany, Switzerland and Austria, have all become part of the great German hegemony: *is there one ordinary German citizen who would be able to say that his well-being had been increased by such a change?* Germany would then "own" Holland. *But would a single German citizen be the richer for the ownership?* The Hollander, from having been the citizen of a small and insignificant State, would become the citizen of a very great one. *Would the individual Hollander be any the richer or any the better?* We know that, as a matter of fact, neither the German nor the Hollander would be one whit the better; and we know also that, in all probability, both would be a great deal the worse. We may, indeed, say that the Hollander would be certainly the worse, in that he would have exchanged the relatively light taxation and light military service of Holland for the much heavier taxation and the much longer military service of the "great" German empire.

To the thesis here developed, the thesis that, while military conquest in the modern world involves a change of political administration which may be good, bad, or indifferent, it does not and cannot involve a transfer of property from one group of owners to another, the commonest objection is that I have overlooked the collection of taxes by the conqueror. While it may be true, say these critics, that a modern conqueror must respect titles to property since the insolvencies and insecurities produced by their destruction might well (almost inevitably would) affect securities, instruments of credits, loans, or what nots, held by persons of the victor state; produce, in other words, insolvencies, which would have dangerous repercussions—while all that may be true, it is said, I have overlooked the fact that the conqueror collects the taxes. It may be true that the Alsatians retained their farms and houses when the Germans took over the Province, they paid their taxes to Germany instead of France. Thus a writer in the *Daily Mail* argues: "If Alsace-Lorraine had remained French it would have yielded at the present rate of French taxation a revenue of eight millions a year to the State. That Revenue is lost to France and placed at the disposal of Germany," and on the basis of this the *Daily Mail* financier works out the "cash value" of the asset which France has lost and Germany gained.

Not once or twice since this book first appeared has that particular criticism been made. On hundreds of occasions have educated people written to me to point out this "oversight." I really had not thought this matter out sufficiently: obviously a nation was enriched by an addition to the receipts of its treasury. And never, in these criticism, is there any awareness that it constitutes a sort of Irish bull.

That this is perhaps the commonest of all the objections made to the argument of this chapter I regard as an extremely significant comment on the character of current political thinking. For this objection so commonly made is the outcome of pure confusion of thought, an illustration of what some writer has called "the unilateral illusion," the kind of illusion which leads us to think of a sale without realizing that it is also a purchase; that an export must also be an import; a failure to be clear as to the meaning of the terms we use, a mixing of the symbols with the things for which it stands. "Germany," says the *Daily Mail* critic, is now richer by eight millions a year which, but for the conquest, would have gone to "France." But who or what is "Germany" after the annexation? "Germany" now includes the people of Alsace-Lorraine, who not only pay the taxes but receive them—receive them, that is, as much as any other German. They belong to the new entity which "owns" the asset. The number of recipients have been increased in exact proportion to the number of the contributors.

To this particular critic I replied as follows:

Conquest multiplies by x it is true, but we overlook the fact that it also has to divide by x, and that the result is consequently, so far as the individual is concerned, exactly what it was before. My critic remembered the multiplication all right, but he forgot the division. The matricular contribution of Alsace-Lorraine to the Imperial treasury (which incidentally is neither three millions nor eight, but just about one) is fixed on exactly the same scale as that of the other States of the Empire. Prussia, the conqueror, pays *per capita* just as much as and no less than Alsace, the conquered, who, if she were not paying this million to Germany, would be paying it—or, according to my critic, a much larger sum—to France; and, if Germany did not "own" Alsace-Lorraine, she would be relieved of charges that amount not to one but several millions. The change of "ownership" does not therefore of itself change the money position (which is what we are now discussing) of either owner or owned.

If a great country benefits every time it annexes a province, and her people are the richer for the widened territory, the small nations ought to be immeasurably poorer than the great, instead of which, by every test which you like to apply—public credit, amounts in savings banks, standard of living, social progress, general well-being—citizens of small States are, other things being equal, as well off as, or better off than, the citizens of great States.

If the Germans are enriched by eight millions a year through the conquest of a province like Alsace-Lorraine, how much should the English people draw from their "possessions"? On the basis of population, somewhere in the region of a thousand million; on the basis of area, still more—enough not only to pay all our taxes, wipe out our National Debt, support the army and navy, but give every family in the land a fat income into the bargain. There is evidently something wrong.

In every civilized State, revenues which are drawn from a territory are expended on that territory, and there is no process known to modern government by which wealth may first be drawn from a territory into the treasury and then be redistributed with a profit to the individuals who have contributed it or to others. It would be just as reasonable to say that the citizens of London are richer than the citizens of Birmingham because London has a richer treasury; or that Londoners would become richer if the London County Council were to annex the county of Hertford, as to say that people's wealth varies according to the size of the administrative area which they inhabit. The whole thing is, as I have called it, an optical illusion, due to the hypnotism of an obsolete terminology. Just as poverty may be greater in the large city than in the small one, and taxation heavier, so the citizens of a great State may be poorer than the citizens of a small one, as they very often are.

But there is another phase of this confusion, characterized by a strange contradiction. In the militarist view, we must fight others for trade—fight them in a literal military sense, since the need of protecting our trade is invoked as the justification of a great navy. Their trade must be checked, restrained, their goods kept from our shores. Also, we add to our wealth when we conquer their territory. But, if we conquer their territory, we don't keep out their trade: the barriers against their goods are wiped away. The goods enter freely without let or hindrance. Conquest has not destroyed competition, it has wiped away all restraints upon it. We hear a good deal from Americans of the competition of Canadian trade, the need for barriers to keep out goods made in the factories of Ontario and Quebec. America is damaged by the free entry of those goods from those factories. So be it. But Americans of the nationalist and militarist type of mind talk of the ultimate conquest of Canada "and all its riches added to our nation's heritage." But it would mean that those same goods, made by the same hands in the same factories owned by the same people, would now compete freely with the goods of the conquerors. No American would dream of complaining any more than the people of Pennsylvania complain about the competition of Massachusetts (or those of Lancashire about the competition of Yorkshire). It would seem that it is the political status of the trader or manufacturer, not any economic fact, which determines whether he is a competitor or not. But then we do, indeed, labor under a delusion: the economic fight, the "inevitable biological struggle," has given place to a quarrel about flags. The "grim struggle for bread" ceases the moment that the rival comes under our flag. Is it not time we made up our minds what we are preparing to fight about: economic needs or national insignia?

We have never perhaps asked ourselves what it is we are really fighting about; as we certainly do not, for the most part, examine the nature of that wealth which we declare to be the object of the contest. Let us examine it.

NOTE

From *The Great Illusion* by Norman Angell (New York: Putman, [1910] and 1933), pp. 86–102.

Germany and the Next War

General Friedrich von Bernhardi

Prince Bismarck repeatedly declared before the German Reichstag that no one should ever take upon himself the immense responsibility of intentionally bringing about a war. It could not, he said, be foreseen what unexpected events might occur, which altered the whole situation, and made a war, with its attendant dangers and horrors, superfluous. In his "Thoughts and Reminiscences" he expresses himself to this effect: "Even victorious wars can only be justified when they are forced upon a nation, and we cannot see the cards held by providence so closely as to anticipate the historical development by personal calculation."

We need not discuss whether Prince Bismarck wished this dictum to be regarded as a universally applicable principle, or whether he uttered it as a supplementary explanation of the peace policy which he carried out for so long. It is difficult to gauge its true import. The notion of forcing a war upon a nation bears various interpretations. We must not think merely of external foes who compel us to fight. A war may seem to be forced upon a statesman by the state of home affairs, or by the pressure of the whole political situation.

Prince Bismarck did not, however, always act according to the strict letter of that speech; it is his special claim to greatness that at the decisive moment he did not lack the boldness to begin a war on his own initiative. The thought which he expresses in his later utterances cannot, in my opinion, be shown to be a universally applicable principle of political conduct. If we wish to regard it as such, we shall not only run counter to the ideas of our greatest German Prince, but we exclude from politics that independence of action which is the true motive force.

The greatness of true statesmanship consists in a knowledge of the natural trend of affairs, and in a just appreciation of the value of the controlling forces, which it uses and guides in its own interest. It does not shrink from the conflicts, which under the given conditions are unavoidable, but decides them resolutely by war when a favourable position affords prospect of a successful issue. In this way statecraft becomes a tool of Providence, which employs the human will to attain its ends. "Men make history," as Bismarck's actions clearly show.

No doubt the most strained political situation may unexpectedly admit of a peaceful solution. The death of some one man, the setting of some great ambition, the removal of some master-will, may be enough to change it fundamentally. But the great disputes in the life of a nation cannot be settled so simply. The man who wished to bring the question to a decisive issue may disappear, and the political crisis pass for the moment; the disputed points still exist, and lead once more to quarrels, and finally to war, if they are due to really great and irreconcilable interests. With the death of King Edward VII of England the policy of isolation, which he introduced with much adroit statesmanship against Germany, has broken down. The antagonism of Germany and England, based on the conflict of the interests and claims of the two nations, still persists, although the diplomacy which smoothes down, not always profitably, all causes of difference has succeeded in slackening the tension for the moment, not without sacrifices on the side of Germany.

It is clearly an untenable proposition that political action should depend on indefinite possibilities. A completely vague factor would be thus arbitrarily introduced into politics, which have already many unknown quantities to reckon with; they would thus be made more or less dependent on chance.

It may be, then, assumed as obvious that the great practical politician Bismarck did not wish that his words on the political application of war should be interpreted in the sense which has nowadays so frequently been attributed to them, in order to lend the authority of the great man to a weak cause. Only those conditions which can be ascertained and estimated should determine political action.

For the moral justification of the political decision we must not look to its possible consequences, but to its aim and its motives, to the conditions assumed by the agent, and to the trustworthiness, honour, and sincerity of the considerations which led to action. Its practical value is determined by an accurate grasp of the whole situation, by a correct estimate of the resources of the two parties, by a clear anticipation of the probable results—in short, by statesmanlike insight and promptness of decision.

If the statesman acts in this spirit, he will have an acknowledged right, under certain circumstances, to begin a war, regarded as necessary, at the most favourable moment, and to secure for his country the proud privilege of such initiative. If a war, on which a Minister cannot willingly decide, is bound to be fought later under possibly far more unfavourable conditions, a heavy responsibility for the greater sacrifices that must then be made will rest on those whose strength and courage for decisive political action failed at the favourable moment. In the face of such considerations a theory by which a war ought never to be brought about falls to the ground. And yet this theory has in our day found many supporters, especially in Germany.

Even statesmen who consider that the complete abolition of war is impossible, and do not believe that the *ultima ratio* can be banished from the life of nations, hold the opinion that its advent should be postponed so long as possible.

Those who favour this view take up approximately the same attitude as the supporters of the Peace idea, so far as regarding war exclusively as a curse, and ignoring or underestimating its creative and civilizing importance. According to this view, a war recognized as inevitable must be postponed so long as possible, and no statesman is entitled to use exceptionally favourable conditions in order to realize necessary and justifiable aspirations by force of arms.

Such theories only too easily disseminate the false and ruinous notion that the maintenance of peace is the ultimate object, or at least the chief duty, of any policy.

To such views, the offspring of a false humanity, the clear and definite answer must be made that, under certain circumstances, it is not only the right, but the moral and political duty of the statesman to bring about a war.

Wherever we open the pages of history we find proofs of the fact that wars, begun at the right moment with manly resolution, have effected the happiest results, both politically and socially. A feeble policy has always worked harm, since the statesman lacked the requisite firmness to take the risk of a necessary war, since he tried by diplomatic tact to adjust the differences of irreconcilable foes, and deceived himself as to the gravity of the situation and the real importance of the matter. Our own recent history in its vicissitudes supplies us with the most striking examples of this.

The Great Elector laid the foundations of Prussia's power by successful and deliberately incurred wars. Frederick the Great followed in the steps of his glorious ancestor. "He noticed how his state occupied an untenable middle position between the petty states and the great Powers, and showed his determination to give a definite character to this anomalous existence; it had become essential to enlarge the territory of the State and *corriger la figure de la Prusse* if Prussia wished to be independent and to bear with honour the great name of 'Kingdom.'" The King made allowance for this political necessity, and took the bold determination of challenging Austria to fight. None of the wars which he fought had been forced upon him; none of them did he postpone as long as possible. He had always determined to be the aggressor, to anticipate his opponents, and to secure for himself favourable prospects of success. We all know what he achieved. The whole history of the growth of the European nations and of mankind generally would have been changed had the King lacked that heroic power of decision which he showed.

We see a quite different development under the reign of Frederick William III, beginning with the year of weakness 1805, of which our nation cannot be too often reminded.

It was manifest that war with Napoleon could not permanently be avoided. Nevertheless, in spite of the French breach of neutrality, the Prussian Government could not make up its mind to hurry to the help of the allied Russians and Austrians, but tried to maintain peace, though at a great moral cost. According to all human calculation, the participation of Prussia in the war of 1805 would have given the Allies a decisive superiority. The adherence to neutrality led to the crash of 1806, and would have meant the final overthrow of Prussia as a State had not the moral qualities still existed there which Frederick the Great had ingrained on her by his wars. At the darkest moment of defeat they shone most brightly. In spite of the political downfall, the effects of Frederick's victories kept that spirit alive with which he had inspired his State and his people. This is clearly seen in the quite different attitude of the Prussian people and the other Germans under the degrading yoke of the Napoleonic tyranny. The power which had been acquired by the Prussians through long and glorious wars showed itself more valuable than all the material blessing which peace created; it was not to be broken down by the defeat of 1806, and rendered possible the heroic revival of 1813.

The German wars of Unification also belong to the category of wars which, in spite of a thousand sacrifices, bring forth a rich harvest. The instability and political weakness which the Prussian government showed in 1848, culminating in the disgrace of Olmütz in 1850, had deeply shaken the political and national importance of Prussia. On the other hand, the calm conscious strength with which she faced once more her duties as a nation, when King William I and Bismarck were at the helm, was soon abundantly manifest. Bismarck, by bringing about our wars of Unification in order to improve radically an untenable position and secure to our people health conditions of life, fulfilled the long-felt wish of the German people, and raised Germany to the undisputed rank of a first-class European Power. The military successes and the political position won by the sword laid the foundation for an unparalleled material prosperity. It is difficult to imagine how pitiable the progress of the German people would have been had not these wars been brought about by a deliberate policy.

The most recent history tells the same story. If we judge the Japanese standpoint with an unbiassed mind we shall find the resolution to fight Russia was not only heroic, but politically wise and morally justifiable. It was immensely daring to challenge the Russian giant, but the purely military conditions were favourable, and the Japanese nation, which had rapidly risen to a high stage of civilization, needed an extended sphere of influence to complete her development, and to open new channels for her superabundant activities. Japan, from her own point of view, was entitled to claim to be the predominant civilized power in Eastern Asia, and to repudiate the rivalry of Russia. The Japanese statesmen were justified by the result. The victorious campaign created wider conditions of life for the Japanese people and State, and at one blow raised it to be a determining co-factor in international politics, and gave it a political importance which must undeniably lead to great material advancement. If this war had been avoided from weakness or philanthropic illusions, it is reasonable to assume that matters would have taken a very different turn. The growing power of Russia in the Amur district and in Korea would have repelled or at least hindered the Japanese rival from rising to such a height of power as was attained through this war, glorious alike for military prowess and political foresight.

The appropriate and conscious employment of war as a political means has always led to happy results. Even an unsuccessfully waged war may sometimes be more beneficial to a people than the surrender of vital interests without a blow. We find an example of this in the recent heroic struggle of the small Boer States against the British Empire.[1] In this struggle they were inevitably defeated. It was easy to foresee that an armed peasantry could not permanently resist the combined forces of England and her colonies, and that the peasant armies generally could not bear heavy losses. But yet—if all indications are not misleading—the blood shed by the Boer people will yield a free and prosperous future. In spite of much weakness, the resistance was heroic; men like President Stein, Botha and De Wett, with their gallant followers, performed many great military feats. The whole nation combined and rose unanimously to the fight for the freedom of which Byron sings:

> "For freedom's battle once begun,
> Bequeathed from bleeding sire to sin,
> Though baffled oft, is ever won."

Inestimable moral gains, which can never be lost in any later developments, have been won by this struggle. The Boers have maintained their place as a nation; in a certain sense they have shown themselves superior to the English. It was only after many glorious victories that they yielded to a crushingly superior force. They accumulated a store of fame and national consciousness which makes them, though conquered, a power to be reckoned with. The result of this development is that the Boers are now the foremost people in South Africa, and that England preferred to grant them self-government than to be faced by their continual hostility. This laid the foundation for the United Free States of South Africa. President Kruger, who decided on this most justifiable, war, and not Cecil Rhodes, will, in spite of the tragic ending to the war itself, be known in all ages as the great far-sighted statesman of South Africa, who, despite the unfavourable material conditions, knew how to value the inestimable moral qualities according to their real importance.

The lessons of history thus confirm the view that wars which have been deliberately provoked by far-seeing statesmen have had the happiest results. War, nevertheless, must always be a violent form of political agent, which not only contains in itself the danger of defeat, but in every case calls for great sacrifices, and entails incalculable misery. He who determines upon war accepts a great responsibility.

It is therefore obvious that no one can come to such a decision except from the most weighty reasons, more especially under the existing conditions which have created national armies. Absolute clearness of vision is needed to decide how and when such a resolution can be taken, and what political aims justify the use of armed force.

This question therefore needs careful consideration, and a satisfactory answer can only be derived from an examination of the essential duty of the State.

If this duty consists in giving scope to the highest intellectual and moral development of the citizens, and in co-operating in the moral education of the human race, then the State's own acts must necessarily conform to the moral laws. But the acts of the State cannot be judged by the standard of individual morality. If the State wished to conform to this standard it would often find itself at variance with its own particular duties. The morality of the State must be developed out of its own peculiar essence, just as individual morality is rooted in the personality of the man and his duties toward society. The morality of the State must be judged by the nature and *raison d'être* of the State, and not of the individual citizen. But the end-all and be-all of a State is power, and "he who is not man enough to look this truth in the face should not meddle in politics."

Machiavelli was the first to declare that the keynote of every policy was the advancement of power. This term, however, has acquired, since the German Reformation, a meaning other than that of the shrewd Florentine. To him power was desirable in itself; for us "the State is not physical power as an end in itself, it is power to protect and promote the higher interests"; "power must justify itself by being applied for the greatest good of mankind."

The criterion of the personal morality of the individual "rests in the last resort on the question whether he has recognized and developed his own nature to the highest attainable degree of perfection." If the same standard is applied to the State, then "its highest moral duty is to increase its power. The individual must sacrifice himself for the higher community of which he is a member; but the State is itself the highest conception in the wider community of man, and therefore the duty of self-annihilation does not enter into the case. The Christian duty of sacrifice for something higher does not exist for the State, for there is nothing higher than it in the world's history; consequently it cannot sacrifice itself to something higher. When a State sees its downfall staring it in the face, we applaud if it succumbs sword in hand. A sacrifice made to an alien nation not only is immoral, but contradicts the idea of self-preservation, which is the highest ideal of a State."

I have thought it impossible to explain the foundations of political morality better than in the words of our great national historian. But we can reach the same conclusions by another road. The individual is responsible, only for himself. If, either from weakness or from moral reasons he neglects his own advantage, he only injures himself, the consequences of his actions recoil only on him. The situation is quite different in the case of a State. It represents the ramifying and often conflicting interests of a community. Should it from any reason neglect the interests, it not only to some extent prejudices itself as a legal personality, but it injures also the body of private interests which it represents. This incalculably far-reaching detriment affects not merely one individual responsible merely to himself, but a mass of individuals and the community. Accordingly it is a moral duty of the State to remain loyal to its own peculiar function as guardian and promoter of all higher interests. This duty it cannot fulfill unless it possesses the needful power.

The increase of this power is thus from this standpoint also the first and foremost duty of the State. This aspect of the question supplies a fair standard by which the morality of the actions of the State can be estimated. The crucial question is, How far has the State performed this duty, and thus served the interests of the community? And this not merely in the material sense, but in the higher meaning that material interests are justifiable only so far as they promote the power of the State, and thus indirectly its higher aims.

It is obvious, in view of the complexity of social conditions, that numerous private interests must be sacrificed to the interest of the community, and, from the limitations of human discernment, it is only natural that the view taken of interests of the community may be erroneous. Nevertheless the advancement of the power of the State must be first and foremost the object that guides the statesman's policy. "Among all political sins, the sin of feebleness is the most contemptible; it is the political sin against the Holy Ghost." This argument of political morality is open to the objection that it leads logically to the Jesuitic principle, that the end justifies the means; that, according to it, to increase the power of the State all measures are permissible.

A most difficult problem is raised by the question how far, for political objects moral in themselves, means may be employed which must be regarded as reprehensible in the life of the individual. So far as I know, no satisfactory solution has yet been obtained, and I do not feel bound to attempt one at this point. War, with which I am dealing at present, is no reprehensible means in itself, but it may become so if it pursues unmoral or frivolous aims, which bear no comparison with the seriousness of warlike measures. I must deviate here a little from my main theme, and discuss shortly some points which touch the question of political morality.

The gulf between political and individual morality is not so wide as is generally assumed. The power of the State does not rest exclusively on the factors that make up material power—territory, population, wealth, and a large army and navy: it rests to a high degree on moral elements, which are reciprocally related to the material. The energy with which a State promotes its own interests and represents the rights of its citizens in foreign States, the determination which it displays to support them on occasion by force of arms, constitute a real factor of strength, as compared with all such countries as cannot bring themselves to let things come to a crisis in a like case. Similarly a reliable and honourable policy forms an element of strength in dealings with allies as well as with foes. A statesman is thus under no obligation to deceive deliberately. He can from the political standpoint avoid all negotiations which compromise his personal integrity, and he will thereby serve the reputation and power of his State no less than when he holds aloof from political menaces, to which no acts correspond, and renounces all political formulas and phrases.

In antiquity the murder of a tyrant was thought a moral action, and the Jesuits have tried to justify regicide. At the present day political murder is universally condemned from the standpoint of political morality. The same holds good of preconcerted political deception. A state which employed deceitful methods would soon sink into disrepute. The man who pursues moral ends with unmoral means is involved in a contradiction of motives, and nullifies the object at which he aims, since he denies it by his actions. It is not, of course, necessary that a man communicate all his intentions and ultimate objects to an opponent; the latter can be left to form his own opinion on this point. But it is not necessary to lie deliberately or to practise crafty deceptions. A fine frankness has everywhere been the characteristic of great statesmen. Subterfuges and duplicity mark the petty spirit of diplomacy.

Finally, the relations between two States must often be termed a latent war, which is provisionally being waged in peaceful rivalry. Such a position justifies the employment of hostile methods, cunning, and deception, just as war itself does, since in such a case both parties are determined to employ them. I believe after all that a conflict between personal and political morality may be avoided by wise and prudent diplomacy, if there is no concealment of the desired end, and it is recognized that the means employed must correspond to the ultimately moral nature of that end.

Recognized rights are, of course, often violated by political action. But these, as we have already shown, are never absolute rights; they are of human origin, and therefore imperfect and variable. There are conditions under which they do not correspond to the actual truth of things; in this case the *summum just summa injuria* holds good, and the infringement of the right appears morally justified. York's decision to conclude the convention of Tauroggen was indisputably a violation of right, but it was a moral act, for the Franco-Prussian alliance was made under compulsion, and was antagonistic to all the vital interests of the Prussian State; it was essentially untrue and immoral. Now it is always justifiable to terminate an immoral situation.

As regards the employment of war as a political means, our argument shows that it becomes the duty of a State to make use of the *ultima ratio* not only when it is attacked, but when by the policy of other States the power of the particular State is threatened, and peaceful methods are insufficient to secure its integrity. This power, as we saw, rests on a material basis, but finds expression in ethical values. War therefore seems imperative when, although the material basis of power is not threatened, the moral influence of the State (and this is the ultimate point at issue) seems to be prejudiced. Thus apparently trifling causes may under certain circumstances constitute a full justifiable *casus belli* if the honour of the State, and consequently its moral prestige, are endangered. This prestige is an essential part of its power. An antagonist must never be allowed to believe that there is any lack of determination to asset this prestige, even if the sword must be drawn to do so.

In deciding for war or peace, the next important consideration is whether the question under discussion is sufficiently vital for the power of the State to justify the determination to fight; whether the inevitable dangers and miseries of a war do not threaten to inflict greater injury on the interests of the State than the disadvantages which, according to human calculation, must result if war is not declared. A further point to be considered is whether the general position of affairs affords some reasonable prospect of military success. With these considerations of expediency certain other weighty aspects of the question must also be faced.

It must always be kept in mind that a State is not justified in looking only to the present, and merely consulting the immediate advantage of the existing generation. Such policy would be opposed to all that constitutes the essential nature of the State. Its conduct must be guided by the moral duties incumbent on it, which, as one step is gained, point to the next higher, and prepare the present for the future. "The true greatness of the State is that it links the past with the present and the future; consequently the individual has not right to regard the State as a means for attaining his own ambition in life."

The law of development thus becomes a leading factor in politics, and in the decision for war this consideration must weigh more heavily than the sacrifices necessarily to be borne in the present. "I cannot conceive," Zelter once wrote to Goethe, "how any right deed can be performed without sacrifice; all worthless actions must lead to the very opposite of what is desirable."

A second point of view which must not be neglected is precisely that which Zelter rightly emphasizes. A great end cannot be attained except by staking large intellectual and material resources, and no certainty of success can ever be anticipated. Every undertaking implies a greater or less venture. The daily intercourse of civic life teaches us this lesson; and it cannot be otherwise in politics where account must be taken of most powerful antagonists whose strength can only be vaguely estimated. In questions of comparatively trifling importance much may be done by agreements and compromises, and mutual concessions may produce a satisfactory status. The solution of such problems is the sphere of diplomatic activity. The state of things is quite different when vital questions are at issue, or when the opponent demands concession, but will guarantee none, and is clearly bent on humiliating the other party. Then is the time for diplomatists to be silent and for great statesmen to act. Men must be resolved to stake everything, and cannot shun the solemn decision of war. In such questions any reluctance to face the opponent, every abandonment of important interests, and every attempt at a temporizing settlement, means not only a momentary loss of political prestige, and frequently of real power, which may possibly be made good in another place, but a permanent injury to the interests of the State, the full gravity of which is only felt by future generations.

Not that a rupture of pacific relations must always result in such a case. The mere threat of war and the clearly proclaimed intention to wage it, if necessary, will often cause the opponent to give way. This intention must, however, be made perfectly plain, for "negotiations without arms are like music-books with instruments," as Frederick the Great said. It is ultimately the actual strength of a nation to which the opponent's purpose yields. When, therefore, the threat of war is insufficient to call attention to its own claims the concert must begin; the obligation is unconditional, and the *right* to fight becomes the *duty* to make war, incumbent on the nation and statesman alike.

Finally, there is a third point to be considered. Cases may occur where war must be made simply as a point of honour, although there is no prospect of success. The responsibility of this has also to be borne. So at least Frederick the Great thought. His brother Henry, after the battle of Kolin, had advised him to throw himself at the feet of the Marquise de Pompadour in order to purchase a peace with France. Again, after the battle of Kunersdorf his position seemed quite hopeless, but the king absolutely refused to abandon the struggle. He knew better what suited the honour and the moral value of his country, and preferred to die sword in hand than to conclude a degrading peace. President Roosevelt, in his message to the Congress of the United States of America on December 4, 1906, gave expression to a similar thought. "It must ever be kept in mind," so the manly and inspiriting words ran, "that war is not merely justifiable, but imperative, upon honourable men and upon an honourable nation when peace is only to be obtained by the sacrifice of conscientious conviction or of national welfare. A just war is in the long-run far better for a nation's soul than the most prosperous peace obtained by an acquiescence in wrong or injustice. . . . It must be remembered that even to be defeated in war may be better than not to have fought at all."

To sum up these various views, we may say that expediency in the higher sense must be conclusive in deciding whether to undertake a war in itself morally justifiable. Such decision is rendered more easy by the consideration that the prospects of success are always the greatest when the moment for declaring war can be settled to suit the political and military situation.

It must further be remembered that every success in foreign policy, especially if obtained by a demonstration of military strength, not only heightens the power of the State in foreign affairs, but adds to the reputation of the Government at home, and thus enables it better to fulfil its moral aims and civilizing duties.

No one will thus dispute the assumption that, under certain circumstances, it is the moral and political duty of the State to employ war as a political means. So long as all human progress and all natural development are based on the law of conflict, it is necessary to engage in such conflict under the most favourable conditions possible.

When a State is confronted by the material impossibility of supporting any longer the warlike preparations which the power of its enemies has forced upon it, when it is clear that the rival States must gradually acquire from natural reasons a lead that cannot be won back, when there are indications of an offensive alliance of stronger enemies who only await the favourable moment to strike—the moral duty of the State towards its citizens is to begin the struggle while the prospects of success and the political circumstances are still tolerably favourable. When, on the other hand, the hostile States are weakened or hampered by affairs at home and abroad, but its own warlike strength shows elements of superiority, it is imperative to use the favourable circumstances to promote its own political aims. The danger of a war may be faced the more readily if there is good prospect that great results may be obtained with comparatively small sacrifices.

These obligations can only be met by a vigorous, resolute, active policy, which follows definite ideas, and understands how to arouse and concentrate all the living forces of the state, conscious of the truth of Schiller's lines:

> "The chance that once thou hast refused
> Will never through the centuries recur."

The verdict of history will condemn the statesman who was unable to take the responsibility of a bold decision, and sacrificed the hopes of the future to the present need of peace.

It is obvious that under these circumstances it is extremely difficult to answer the question whether in any special case conditions exist which justify the determination to make war. The difficulty is all the greater because the historical significance of the act must be considered, and the immediate result is not the final criterion of its justification.

War is not always the final judgment of Heaven. There are successes which are transitory while the national life is reckoned by centuries. The ultimate verdict can only be obtained by the survey of long epochs.

The man whose high and responsible lot is to steer the fortunes of a great State must be able to disregard the verdict of his contemporaries; but he must be all the clearer as to the motives of his own policy, and keep before his eyes, with the full weight of the categorical imperative, the teaching of Kant: "Act so that the maxim of thy will can at the same time hold good as a principle of universal legislation."

He must have a clear conception of the nature and purpose of the State, and grasp this from the highest moral standpoint. He can in no other way settle the rules of his policy and recognize clearly the laws of political morality.

He must also form a clear conception of the special duties to be fulfilled by the nation, the guidance of whose fortunes rests in his hands. He must clearly and definitely formulate these duties as the fixed goal of statesmanship. When he is absolutely clear upon this point he can judge in each particular case what corresponds to the true interests of the State; then only can he act systematically in the definite prospect of smoothing the path of politics, and securing favourable conditions for the inevitable conflicts; then only, when the hour for combat strikes and the decision to fight faces him, can he rise with a free spirit and a calm breast to that standpoint which Luther once described in blunt, bold language: "It is very true that men write and say often what a curse war is. But they ought to consider how much greater is that curse which is averted by war. Briefly, in the business of war men must not regard the massacres, the burnings, the battles, and the marches, etc.—that is what the petty and simple do who only look with the eyes of children at the surgeon, how he cuts off the hand or saws off the leg, but do not see or notice that he does it in order to save the whole body. Thus we must look at the business of war or the sword with the eyes of men, asking, Why these murders and horrors? It will be shown that it is a business, divine in itself, and as needful and necessary to the world as eating or drinking, or any other work."

Thus in order to decide what paths German policy must take in order to further the interests of the German people, and what possibilities of war are involved, we must first try to estimate the problems of State and of civilization which are to be solved, and discover what political purposes correspond to these problems.

NOTES

From General Friedrich von Bernhardi, *The Next War* (London: Edward Arnold, 1914), pp. 38–55.

1. During the Boer War (1899–1902) the British deployed 500,000 soldiers to subdue the Boers, Dutch settlers in modern-day South Africa.

The "Willy-Nicky" Telegrams

Kaiser Wilhelm II of Germany and Tsar Nicholas II of Russia

Telegram One: Tsar to Kaiser, July 29, 1914

In this serious moment, I appeal to you to help me. An ignoble war has been declared to a weak country. The indignation in Russia shared fully by me is enormous. I foresee that very soon I shall be overwhelmed by the pressure forced upon me and be forced to take extreme measures which will lead to war. To try and avoid such a calamity as a European war I beg you in the name of our old friendship to do what you can to stop your allies from going too far.

Nicky

Telegram Two: Kaiser to Tsar, July 29, 1914[1]

It is with the gravest concern that I hear of the impression which the action of Austria against Serbia is creating in your country. The unscrupulous agitation that has been going on in Serbia for years has resulted in an outrageous crime, to which Archduke Franz Ferdinand fell a victim. The spirit that led Serbians to murder their own king and his wife still dominates the country. You will doubtless agree with me that we both, you and me, have a common interest as well as all Sovereigns to insist that all the persons morally responsible for the dastardly murder should receive their deserved punishment. In this case politics plays no part at all.

On the other hand, I fully understand how difficult it is for you and your Government to face the drift of your public opinion. Therefore, with regard to the hearty and tender friendship which binds us both from long ago with firm ties, I am exerting my utmost influence to induce the Austrians to deal straightly to arrive to a satisfactory understanding with you. I confidently hope that you will help me in my efforts to smooth over difficulties that may still arise.

Your very sincere and devoted friend and cousin,

Willy

Telegram Three: Kaiser to Tsar, July 29, 1914

I received your telegram and share your wish that peace should be maintained. But as I told you in my first telegram, I cannot consider Austria's action against Serbia an "ignoble" war.

Austria knows by experience that Serbian promises on paper are wholly unreliable. I under-stand its action must be judged as trending to get full guarantee that the Serbian promises shall become real facts. My reasoning is borne out by the statement of the Austrian cabinet that Austria does not want to make any territorial conquests at the expense of Serbia. I therefore suggest that it would be quite possible for Russia to remain a spectator of the Austro-Serbian conflict without involving Europe in the most horrible war she ever witnessed. I think a direct understanding between your Government and Vienna possible and desirable, and as I already telegraphed to you, my Government is continuing its exercises to promote it. Of course military measures on the part of Russia would be looked upon by Austria as a calamity we both wish to avoid and jeopardize my position as mediator which I readily accepted on your appeal to my friendship and my help.

Willy

Telegram Four: Tsar to Kaiser, July 29, 1914

Thanks for your conciliatory and friendly telegram. Whereas official message presented today by your ambassador to my minister was conveyed in a very different tone. Beg you to explain this divergence! It would be right to give over the Austro-Serbian problem to the Hague conference. Trust in your wisdom and friendship.

Your loving Nicky

Telegram Five: Tsar to Kaiser, July 30, 1914

Thank you heartily for your quick answer. Am sending [Russian statesman] Tatischev this evening with instructions. The military measures which have now come into force were decided five days ago for reasons of defense on account of Austria's preparations. I hope from all my heart that these measures won't in any way interfere with your part as mediator which I greatly value. We need your strong pressure on Austria to come to an understanding with us.

Nicky

Telegram Six: Kaiser to Tsar, July 30, 1914[2]

Best thanks for telegram. It is quite out of the question that my ambassador's language could have been in contradiction with the tenor of my telegram. Count Pourtalès was instructed to draw the attention of your government to the danger and grave consequences involved by a mobilization; I said the same in my telegram to you. Austria has only mobilized against Serbia and only a part of her army. If, as it is now the case, according to the communication by you and your Government, Russia mobilizes against Austria, my role as mediator you kindly entrusted me with, and which I accepted at your express prayer, will be endangered if not ruined. The whole weight of the decision lies solely on your shoulders now, who have to bear the responsibility for Peace or War.

Willy

Telegram Seven: Kaiser to Tsar, July 31, 1914

On your appeal to my friendship and your call for assistance [I] began to mediate between your and the Austro-Hungarian Government. While this action was proceeding your troops were mobilized against Austro-Hungary, my ally. Thereby, as I have already pointed out to you, my mediation has been made almost illusory.

I have nevertheless continued my action. I now receive authentic news of serious preparations for war on my Eastern frontier. Responsibility for the safety of my empire forces preventive measures of defense upon me. In my endeavors to maintain the peace of the world I have gone to the utmost limit possible. The responsibility for the disaster which is now threatening the whole civilized world will not be laid at my door. In this moment it still lies in your power to avert it. Nobody is threatening the honor or power of Russia who can well afford to await the result of my mediation. My friendship for you and your empire, transmitted to me by my grandfather on his deathbed has always been sacred to me and I have honestly often backed up Russia when she was in serious trouble especially in her last war.

The peace of Europe may still be maintained by you, if Russia will agree to stop the military measures which must threaten Germany and Austro-Hungary.

Willy

Telegram Eight: Tsar to Kaiser, July 31, 1914[3]

I thank you heartily for your mediation which begins to give one hope that all may yet end peacefully. It is technically impossible to stop our military preparations which were obligatory owing to Austria's mobilization. We are far from wishing war. As long as the negotiations with Austria on Serbia's account are taking place my troops shall not make any provocative action. I give you my solemn word for this. I put all my trust in God's mercy and hope in your successful mediation in Vienna for the welfare of our countries and for the peace of Europe.

Your affectionate

Nicky

Telegram Nine: Tsar to Kaiser, August 1, 1914

I received your telegram. Understand you are obliged to mobilize but wish to have the same guarantee from you as I gave you, that these measures do not mean war and that we shall continue negotiating for the benefit of our countries and universal peace. Our long proved friendship must succeed, with God's help, in avoiding bloodshed. Anxiously, full of confidence await your answer.

Nicky

Telegram Ten: Kaiser to Tsar, August 1, 1914

Thanks for your telegram. I yesterday pointed out to your government the way by which alone war may be avoided. Although I requested an answer for noon today, no telegram from my ambassador conveying an answer from your Government has reached me as yet. I therefore have been obliged to mobilize my army.

Immediate affirmative clear and unmistakable answer from your government is the only way to avoid endless misery. Until I have received this answer alas, I am unable to discuss the subject of your telegram. As a matter of fact I must request you to immediately order your troops on no account to commit the slightest act of trespassing over our frontiers.

Willy

NOTES

The "Willy-Nicky" Telegrams were exchanged between Kaiser Wilhelm II (1859–1941) of Germany and Tsar Nicholas II (1868–1918) of Russia from July 29, 1914, to August 1, 1914.

1. Wilhelm II had not yet seen telegram one when he composed telegram two.
2. Telegrams five and six were sent at almost the same time.
3. Nicholas II had not yet seen telegram seven when he composed telegram eight.

The Circus Rider of Europe

Dennis Showalter

The relationship between Imperial Germany and tsarist Russia before 1914 was a complex mixture of attraction and repulsion. Anarchist Michael Bakunin's statement that nothing united Slavs like their hatred of Germans can be balanced by the German impact on Russia's Westernization. France might provide inspiration, but it was a long road from Paris to St. Petersburg. German professors filled most of the posts at the University of Moscow and the Academy of Sciences. German pietism shaped Russian religious thought. German concepts of natural law and philosophy prepared Russian ground not for individualism and empiricism, but for *Aufklärung* (Enlightenment), with its sensibility, its religiosity, its collectivism.

The assimilation of this quasi-German heritage was at best incomplete. Nevertheless in the aftermath of the Napoleonic Wars a bilingual, bicultural elite developed, an elite consciously seeking to fuse the best of Russian and German. An emerging Russian intelligentsia, initially self-absorbed and isolated, turned eagerly to Germany for cultural and intellectual models. The philosophy of Hegel and the literature of the Romantics were uncritically imitated east of the Vistula. Students were regularly sent to Germany for advanced education even in the darkest days of Nicholas I. Under Nicholas, too, a system of secondary schools on the German model was established for the entire empire. German scholars and artists basked in the admiration of their Russian counterparts. In turn they praised the spiritual depths of the Slavic soul and the unlimited promise of the Russian people.

The relationship was by no means one-sided. Restoration and *Vormärz* Prussia (1815–1848) accepted the Russia of Alexander and Nicholas as a bulwark against Austrian dominance, French revanchism, and popular revolution. Militarily too the traditional positions of Prussia and Russia reversed themselves during the Napoleonic Era. Prussia's martial arrogance was humbled at Jena and Auerstädt. After 1813 the war-hardened Russian army, with its long-service peasant conscripts, compared all too favorably in all too many respects with the improvised Prussian forces. The shortcomings of the postwar Prussian army seemed even more glaring when compared with the situation in Russia. Officers facing limited budgets periodically turned longing eyes to Russia, where the soldier-tsar Nicholas I appeared to stint his military establishment of nothing, where elaborate maneuvers were staged regardless of cost, where developments in weapons, organization, and tactics could be tested on an army-corps scale.

The Prussian foreign office recognized that Russia's diplomatic position in Europe, particularly after 1849, was less solid than it seemed. It also recognized Prussia's geographic, economic, and military weaknesses vis-à-vis both Western and Eastern Europe. Commitment to Russia meant the corresponding risk of becoming the tsar's battering ram against liberalism in general and France in particular. Prussia's "active neutrality" during the Crimean crisis of 1853–55 was deliberately designed to sustain good relations with Russia at the lowest possible price. The policy's initial success is indicated by Russian foreign minister K. R. Nesselrode's belief that the Prussian connection must become the cornerstone of Russia's relations with France in the aftermath of the Crimean War. Ultimately, however, Russia remained more concerned until 1866 with mending French fences than with supporting the aims of a Prussia whose good will was often taken for granted and whose capacities to implement an independent foreign policy seemed derisory.

The Seven Weeks' War of 1866 came as a corresponding surprise. Austria's unexpected collapse confronted Russia with a *fait accompli*. Should she intervene, it would be not to preserve a structure but to restore one—with proportionately increased risks. Four years later, on October 31, 1870, Russia collected a price for her abstention by unilaterally repudiating those clauses of the Crimean settlement that provided for neutralization of the Black Sea.

Bismarck was long in forgetting the minicrisis this generated. With Germany's armies too deeply stuck in the French tar baby to give him much freedom of action, the furious protests of Austria and Britain against Russia's action bade fair to escalate into a European war. It took all of the chancellor's skill to get the involved powers to a conference table, where Russia's action was eventually legitimated—at significant cost to Bismarck's nerves and with significant impact on his subsequent policies.

The new German empire inherited other liabilities in relation to its tsarist neighbor. A rising generation of Russian intellectuals blamed fifty years of playing safe, of hiding behind piles of paper, on Teutonic influences that stifled Slavic warmth and spontaneity. Pedantry and pettifogging were common hallmarks of the German in Russian literature. Among the least sympathetic minor characters of *War and Peace* is Captain Berg, who knows the army regulations better than the Lord's Prayer, yet sees nothing beyond them. Goncharov's *Oblomov* depends essentially for its comic effect on the contrast between Oblomov, the lazy, slovenly, ultimately lovable Russian and the dignified, efficient, ultimately sterile German Stoltz.

Literary Germanophobia was reinforced by economic changes. In a Russia historically lacking a middle class, opportunities for emigrants and migrants of all ethnic backgrounds had been extensive. The upper levels of the economy and the higher ranks of the bureaucracy were by no means dominated numerically by men of German ancestry. Germans, however, particularly from Baltic lands, constituted a highly visible element, one perceived as having a strong group identity. The Russian author who dubbed the Baltic Germans "the Mamelukes of the Empire" did not intend to pay them a compliment.

Russian nationalism in mid-century was also acquiring a sharp edge. A growing band of zealots, soldiers and bureaucrats, journalists and academicians, was developing a reasonably coherent set of visions conveniently grouped under the concept of

Panslavism. These Panslavs increasingly agreed on Russia's natural fitness for leadership of the Slavic communities. Works like Yuri Samarin's *Borderlands of Russia*, published in 1868, went farther and demanded the Russification of frontier minorities: Balts, Jews, and especially Germans.

Germany provided a focus for other anxieties as well. Even the limited constitutionalism of Bismarck's Reich seemed revolution incarnate to conservatives east of the Vistula. Russian liberals, on the other hand, saw a Germany abandoning her traditional role of mentor and model, falling prey instead to a militarism that threatened every form of human progress.

The impact of these attitudes was enhanced by a growing perception in the foreign office of a relative decline in Russian power and status. Paul Schroeder has argued that within nineteenth-century Europe's diplomatic structure Russia was restrained less by any internal moderate impulses than by the behavior of her friends and allies. Hostile coalitions, on the other hand, merely encouraged Russia to strike back by applying pressure in one of the many areas vulnerable to her. The point is reasonable as far as it goes. No successful statesman can afford to forget the fable of the wager between the north wind and the sun on who could first convince a man to remove his coat. But as George Lichtheim observes, Russians, never converted to Protestantism or liberalism, find it difficult to divorce politics from either ethics or metaphysics. The geopolitics of Peter the Great and the metapolitics of Alexander I had left a heritage—a sense of mission, of destiny, of purpose that generated in Russian statesmen a determination at least as great as Bismarck's to conduct Europe's orchestra, if not necessarily to drown out the other players.

Any theoretical propositions on how best to contain Russia had therefore to be balanced by consideration of the diplomatic and political prices she set on her friendship. Russia might hypothetically have responded positively to a systematic German policy that was conciliatory, self-effacing, and deferential. Such behavior corresponded neither to political and economic realities nor to the personality of Otto von Bismarck. The "white revolutionary" may have regarded Germany as a sated power whose interests were best served by maintaining the status quo. He saw that process, however, as dynamic rather than static, achieved only by constant, positive action initiated from Berlin.

In particular, Bismarck's policy of "balanced tension" reflected his increasing concern with Russia's dynamism, the pattern of Russian challenges to the European structure that he saw developing in the aftermath of the Peace of Frankfurt.[1] Even the limited Three Emperor's League of 1873 with Germany and Austria-Hungary, an agreement for mutual consultation rather than a formal treaty, was described as a threat to Russia's security and a brake on Russia's mission by diplomats who made no secret of their conviction that Germany was not being properly appreciative of Russia's moderation. From St. Petersburg's perspective, the Congress of Berlin in 1878 was ultimate proof of German perfidy. Bismarck's self-appointed role of "honest broker" seemed a mere mask for his real intention: the isolation and humiliation of Russia. A massive outburst of hostility in the press was accompanied by significant increases in the military establishment. The latter process survived the immediate crisis. It also confirmed and focused a broad structure of anti-Russian suspicions and hostilities in Germany.

German Russophobia existed on two levels. Throughout the nineteenth century the Left was hostile to its neighbor's form of government. After 1815, liberals and democrats saw Russia as a principal bulwark of reaction. Herder's nationalist disciples sympathized with the Poles rather than their Russian conquerors. Romantic poets and essayists described the coming conflict of West and East. In the Prussian Landtag and the German Reichstag alike, Russia was a familiar symbol of benighted oppression. *Zentrum* deputies expressing solidarity with Catholic Poles, Progressives, and National Liberals disgusted by increasingly overt anti-Semitism, contributed their voices to a negative chorus that maintained strong intellectual links to the Russian opposition.

German socialism's stand on Russia was strongly influenced by the views of its founders. Karl Marx's implacable hostility to tsarist despotism was matched by his attacks on a Russian character allegedly molded by centuries of subservience to oriental tyranny. Friedrich Engels, while usually exempting the Russian people from his general characterizations of Slavs as dogs, gypsies, bandits, and brigands, was even more critical than Marx of the aggressive behavior of a Russian government he described as dominated by alien adventurers.

To theorists like Karl Kautsky or Eduard Bernstein, the Russian Marxists were intellectual country cousins, approaching the master's doctrine with the sophistication of a locomotive, unable to grasp its subtleties, yet correspondingly concerned with provincial hair-splitting. To practical politicians, the Wilhelm Liebknechts and the August Bebels, their Russian comrades were poor relations, eating the bread of charity in exile or sustaining a hole-and-corner existence one step ahead of the *Okhrana*. Russia's masses of unlettered peasants, her small number of brutalized factory workers, were at best the remotest kind of raw material for socialism, particularly when compared to the increasingly literate, increasingly politically conscious proletariat of a Germany whose urbanization and industrialization seemed to be fulfilling the essence of Marx's predictions.

Where the tsarist political order was concerned, patronization gave way to implacable hostility. Social Democrats lost no opportunity in or out of the Reichstag to attack the tsarist system's legitimacy—an approach culminating in 1905, when the news of Bloody Sunday vitalized activists throughout Germany.[2] With *Vorwärts*[3] running a front-page box score of events, with local party groups collecting and dispatching funds for the revolution, Russian conservatives might well be pardoned for entertaining however briefly the suspicion that, for all the intimacy of the Willy-Nicky letters,[4] Germany's true feelings were best expressed by its political opposition.

Russia also faced increasing thunder from the German Right. As early as 1853 Paul de Lagarde advocated colonization of the East, with Germans as an aristocracy of talent among brutish or degenerate Slavs. Under the empire an expanding historical profession generated learned articles and journals devoted to Germany's eastward expansion. Gymnasium textbooks and university lecturers hammered home the point to generations of students. The Second Reich's best-known and most visible scholar of Russian history was Professor Theodor Schiemann. A Baltic German who emigrated at the relatively mature age of forty, he insisted on the inferiority of Slavic Russian culture, presenting the Russians as primitive, indifferent to beauty, lacking a sense of law. He described the need to destroy as part of the Russian nature, and argued that only force held the empire together.

In 1892, Schiemann edited *De moribus Ruthenorum*, a collection of diary entries made at mid-century by Victor Hehn, a Baltic German scientist. Its 250 misanthropic pages amount to one long indictment of a people with neither pride nor conscience, destroying itself through vodka and syphilis. The Slavic national animal, according to Hehn, was the louse. A cultivated Russian was a contradiction in terms. Their intelligentsia used Western ideas to destroy rather than construct. The lesser types were able to do nothing, whether make a watch, bake a cake, or drive a locomotive, without German models. Among prostitutes it was a known fact that the most famous were Baltic Germans; Russian ladies of the evening lacked the endurance, the inner nobility, to sustain such an unconventional life. Russian men could not even use modern plumbing correctly—a point made clear to anyone unfortunate enough to have recourse to public toilets in the tsar's empire.

The impact of such ideas was exacerbated by the ambiguous nature of nationalism in the new German Empire. Its roots at best were shallow, its symbols meager—a flag without a history, a monarchy without a heritage, an army without a common identity. The chauvinism that so offended Germany's neighbors in good part reflected deliberate government efforts to legitimate itself by creating a national self-consciousness. At the same time, exponential improvements in transportation and communication were shrinking the map of Europe. Space and spatial relationships grew correspondingly important. Time itself seemed to grow more compact. In this context the new Reich seemed for all its surface strength to be "a mollusk without a shell," vulnerable physically and psychically from all directions.

From this perspective it was a short step to visions of stabilization by expansion. Certain liberals, Friedrich Naumann, Lujo Brentano, and Gustav Schmoller, saw a partial solution to Germany's social problems in terms of a *Mitteleuropa*. Dominated culturally, politically, and economically by Germans, this entity would also secure the traditional heartland of the West against the threat posed by the emerging world empires: America, Britain, and above all Russia. The concept was, in the minds of its creators, a defensive reaction. Its advocates staunchly denied any interest in an *Ostimperium* (eastern empire) of Slavic helots under German rule. In this they stood in sharp contrast to those nationalists whose praise for the Germanizing of Slavic territory in the Middle Ages increasingly combined with fear of Panslavic expansionism to generate advocacy of a *Drang nach Osten*—the eastward expansion of German power.

Benign considerations of this process described Russia's quick defeat and permanent withdrawal into the wastes of Asia, then hurried on to discuss how the Danube and Vistula basins would become Edens under German hands. Other writers dwelt more lovingly on the prospect of Russian troops fleeing before German bayonets, of villages razed and peasants deported to make room for the younger, fitter race. Yet it seems worth noting that even the most extreme ideologues of the Pan-German League focused before 1914 on "internal colonization"—the resettlement of German peasants on German soil misused by Poles or Junkers. Their visions of conquest and resettlement were presented as reactions: consequences of Russia's unfortunate policies of aggression.

Even a fire-eater like Heinrich Class denied as late as 1912 any real grounds for war between Russia and Germany. Should the tsar be foolish enough to start trouble, Germany would fight. But her war aims would involve no more than territorial adjustments to create a more defensible frontier and some room for colonization. Class conceded that the latter process would involve displacing the present inhabitants. But at least before 1914, he expressed himself in such a circumlocutory passive construction that the point is almost lost—"woher die Evakuierung sich nicht umgehen lassen wird" ("where the evacuation would not let itself to be avoided").

The increasing anxiety Germans of all ranks and classes felt toward Russia and her ultimate intentions was reinforced during the 1890s from a previously unlikely source. In 1879, Bismarck's growing hostility to domestic supporters of free trade had resulted in a new and comprehensive structure of tariffs including a schedule of duties on imported Russian grain.

Retaliation was swift and enduring. In the eleven years after Bismarck's initiative, Russia's import duties on manufactured goods, already high, were increased four times. The direct economic impact of this escalation on German industry must not be exaggerated. As Walther Kirchner argues, we should expect to find industrialists complaining of high customs duties whenever they deal with their governments. Practical men proceeded to find ways around the barriers—improving production or marketing techniques, securing Russian patents, seeking purchase contracts from state agencies. These, however, were second-best solutions in a German business community regarding Russia as a virtually inexhaustible reservoir of potential customers, private and official, all the more attractive for being difficult of access. By the time Leo von Caprivi succeeded Bismarck as chancellor, the chorus of grievances encouraged the negotiation of a new set of commercial agreements with Russia—agreements the German chamber of commerce described as incorporating "unprecedented" reductions in tariffs on manufactured goods in return for significantly lower taxes on grain. A wave of protest from the agricultural East, including many letters from peasants and small farmers, was not enough to keep the Reichstag from approving the treaty on March 10, 1894.

This change in government policy contributed significantly to increase Russophobia on the agrarian right. Where businessmen saw markets, farmers saw competitors: a golden tide of cheap foodstuffs that would bankrupt estate owners and peasants alike. The anxieties generated by the Treaty of 1894 were further exacerbated as Russia embarked on a major program of railway construction. Its principal sponsor, Sergei Witte, made no secret of the fact that one of the main purposes of the improved transportation network was to enhance the marketability of Russian grain by reducing its delivery costs. The landowners of Germany's eastern provinces historically tended to identify with Russia's social and political order. But as more and more acres in previously isolated regions began contributing to the export pool, even the least imaginative of Junkers found no difficulty in seeing an economic threat from the East that could not be indefinitely conjured away by manipulating votes in the Reichstag.

The old order was changing. Nevertheless the impact of popular antagonisms must not be overstated. The proverbial lieutenant and ten men could not really have closed the Reichstag, but parliament's role in German foreign policy involved far more pointing with pride and viewing with alarm than systematic participation in decision making. Russia's foreign affairs were even more firmly in the hands of an elite—an elite not necessarily susceptible to journalistic attacks on German intentions and literary suspicions of German good will.

This was demonstrated in the aftermath of the Congress of Berlin. Tsar Alexander III, who succeeded his assassinated father in 1881, viscerally distrusted the bumptious industrial empire on his western border, a distrust in no way diminished by his love match with a Danish princess brought up on memories of 1864.[5] But his choice as foreign minister was N. A. Giers, who argued that Russia had too many internal problems to sustain overt antagonism with any of her neighbors. Bismarck for his part wished as far as possible to reknit the Russian connection. His Dual Alliance of 1879 was intended more to strengthen Germany's position vis-à-vis Russia than to underwrite either Austria's place among the great powers or any ambitions she might entertain in the Balkans.

The Second Three Emperors' League of 1881, renewed in 1884, marked on one level a triumph of common sense. The league linked the eastern powers in an agreement to remain "benevolently neutral" should any of them go to war with a fourth power. It secured Russia's European flank. It precluded the possibility of a Franco-Russian alliance and of Russo-Austrian rapprochement at Germany's expense. The league, however, also encouraged the bureaucratization of tension. Its very existence combined with Germany's insistence on playing a mediator's role to make Russia and Austria-Hungary aware on an ongoing basis of the problems in their relationship, and their fundamental insolubility within existing parameters.

For Bismarck this temporary stability was enough. He was confident of his ability to solve the tactical problems of diplomacy as they arose—a confidence exacerbated by his often-expressed contempt for the skills of his Russian and Austrian counterparts. But if Metternich had been the coachman of Europe, Bismarck was fast becoming its circus rider, standing with one foot on each of two galloping horses, hoping somehow to keep them moving in the same direction at the same pace. And the focus of tension between them, the Balkan Peninsula, was far too tempting a hunting ground for diplomats with delusions of genius, soldiers with illusions of glory, and businessmen with hopes of profit.

In periodically advocating a division of the peninsula into spheres of influence, Bismarck was by no means naïve enough to assume that either Russia or Austria would be permanently satisfied with a half share. But such a division would buy time, and as Bismarck grew older even short periods of time became ever more important to him. The chancellor had no desire to see Russia expand her influence anywhere in Europe. Such aggrandizement would mean both a direct threat to Germany and Austria and a significant disturbance of the territorial status quo Bismarck was committed to preserving. At the same time he had no will even to risk war with the tsar's empire. Apart from the golden opportunities this would offer France, Russia's very size mitigated against anything like the kind of total victory won against France in 1871—a victory which itself seemed increasingly anomalous.

From the inception of the German Empire, its military plans for the East were formulated in the context of a worst-case contingency: a two-front war against France and Russia. In such circumstances, Chief of Staff Helmuth von Moltke strongly favored seeking an operational decision in the East. While Russia was not likely to be overthrown in a brief campaign, the chances of knocking her out of a general war in a relatively short time were good—if the war was conceived as one of limited aims. A battle of annihilation was not a reasonable possibility. However, a series of theater-level victories might well disorganize her war effort to the point where the government would be amenable to negotiations if Germany offered reasonable terms.

The alternatives were hardly promising. In 1885 a general staff exercise projected a two-front war against France and Russia, with Austria initially remaining neutral and the bulk of Germany's army concentrated in the West. Four active corps, supported by a mixed bag of reserve and garrison troops, were left to hold the Eastern theater against twenty Russian divisions—a reasonable evaluation of Russia's capacities in the context of the problem. The best the Germans could manage was a fighting retreat across the Vistula. Four corps, Moltke sourly observed, could not hold East Prussia or protect Berlin against ten Russian corps no matter how cleverly they were maneuvered.

On the other hand, the long, open frontier between Germany and Russia offered correspondingly wide scope for offensive operations. The East Prussian salient might be threatened with immediate strangulation by a Russian blow at its base, but it provided an excellent sally-port against a Russian concentration in Poland. Moltke believed the best way for the Dual Alliance to defend the Eastern frontier was to attack, with Germans from the north and Austrians from the south meeting somewhere on enemy soil. This conviction, tested successfully in a staff exercise of 1886, was strong enough to lead the chief of staff increasingly to consider the possibility of a preventive war—a first strike, in cooperation with Austria, against the Russian garrisons in Poland and Galicia.

But what could Germany hope to gain from such a conflict? Intellectuals might dream of population shifts on a scale unseen since Genghis Khan. Bismarck was a practical statesman. The annexation of Alsace-Lorraine could be justified on the grounds of generating national identity while securing natural resources defended by Metz and the line of the Vosges. No such geographic barriers existed in the East. As for an economic equivalent to the iron mines of Lorraine, German agriculture was already alarmed at the prospects of competition from Russian grain. Territorial gains in the East would only mean an increase in the number of Poles, Balts, and Russians under German rule. Bismarck's distaste for the Poles of Posen and Silesia was already too marked for him to welcome that possibility.

Bismarck was, in short, not enthusiastic about challenging Russia for any reason, much less for the sake of Austria-Hungary's *beaux yeux*. He was unsympathetic alike to Cisleithanian businessmen's dreams of Balkan markets and to the Hungarian parliament's Russophobic rhodomontade. He spent much effort after 1878 warning Austria that Germany would not support her directly in the Balkans, particularly when it came to defending economic interests. The exact degree of Bismarck's acceptance of specific Russian claims and positions in the Near East remains debatable. In general, however, he seems to have regarded Russia's territorial ambitions as part of that stream of time human beings could neither create nor, ultimately, direct. His frequent references to Russia as an elemental force, no more to be changed than bad weather, strengthen images of inevitability subject, perhaps, to judicious guidance, but beyond anyone's power to terminate or modify.

This perception was reinforced as Russia's suspicion of Bismarck's good will reached new peaks during the Bulgarian crisis of 1885. Russia's position in the state it had helped establish only seven years earlier virtually collapsed from Russian heavy-handedness. Nevertheless Bismarck emerged as the villain, the wire-puller and manipulator. He was presented in St. Petersburg as simultaneously obstructing Russia's legitimate Balkan claims and encouraging her further involvement in the swamp of Bulgarian politics.

In this context golden bullets began acquiring new importance. Since the 1850s, Russia's domestic problems had been increasingly coalescing into what modern economic theory describes as a crisis of development. Costly foreign wars and territorial expansion in central Asia, combined with expensive programs of railroad building and industrialization, put unheard-of strains on the imperial treasury. The actual and potential supplies of private capital in Russia were limited. A political system neither strong enough nor autocratic enough to practice the forced bootstrapping common in the twentieth century turned logically to external sources.

German bankers and investors had been funding Russian economic enterprises for decades. Bismarck's own banker, Gerson Bleichröder, was deeply involved in the marketing of Russian securities, selling some of the paper to Bismarck himself.

The recipients of this German largesse were anything but suitably grateful. Nationalists argued that the interest rates were too high and the terms too short: Imperial Russia was being treated like a deadbeat gambler. Financiers were concerned with the growing complexity of a public debt contracted without any systematic planning. Panslavs took alarm at the threats posed by German involvement in Russia's economic life. Businessmen demanded higher tariffs, protecting their infant industries from German competition.

By the mid-1880s the German foreign office was also questioning the success of Bismarck's embryonic economic diplomacy. Germany seemed to have benefited little from official and private efforts to sustain Russia's development. The Cobdenite argument that, properly understood, a state's economic and diplomatic interests must coincide had never been widely accepted even in German liberal circles, much less among the group of young diplomatic Turks whose spokesman was Friedrich von Holstein.

Holstein's critics then and now have considered him a man of limited vision, blinded to the value of Germany's Russian connection by his hostility towards Bismarck, his sympathy for the ramshackle Habsburg Empire, and his identification with the saber-rattling militants urging a war of conquest in the East. Holstein was, however, by no means a blind Russophobe. Since joining the foreign office in 1876 he had observed and participated in Bismarck's increasingly desperate efforts to integrate Russia into a stable European network. The process had convinced him that the chancellor was making a fundamental error. Not France, but Russia, Holstein reasoned, was the greatest ultimate threat to Germany's security. France might be the clearer and more present danger, but a good big man can be expected to whip a good little man. Should France try conclusions with the German Empire, what happened in 1870–71 would happen again.

Russia, on the other hand, combined tremendous economic and military potential with the power of an idea. Her Alsace-Lorraine was the entire Balkan peninsula, if not Central Europe itself. In Holstein's view Russia's geopolitical ambitions threatened—or promised—not merely to bring all southeastern Europe under her sway, but to generate what later diplomatic generations would describe as Austria's Finlandization, if not her complete disappearance. In the aftermath of the Bulgarian crisis, Holstein worked in tandem with the chancellor to foster an anti-Russian coalition of the great powers. The Mediterranean Agreements of 1887, linking Britain, Italy, and Austria in defense of a regional status quo, gratified him at least as much as they did Bismarck. But the fundamental dichotomy between the foreign policy positions of the two men remained. Bismarck wanted to keep Germany in the middle, holding the balance between Russia on one hand, Austria and the other Mediterranean powers on the other. For Holstein and the increasing number of his supporters, the new treaties merely cleared the ground for a confrontation that would show Russia her place at the international table once more—a place she had to date been unwilling to accept by peaceful persuasion.

In a Russia already suspicious of German good will and German intentions, Panslavs and nationalists put increasing, and ultimately successful, pressure on Alexander to abandon the Three Emperor's League. An increasing number of voices suggested the virtues of a French connection. Bismarck responded by negotiating the Reinsurance Treaty of June, 1887. Its key was a mutual guarantee of neutrality except in case of a German attack on France or a Russian attack on Austria. But the belligerence and antagonism shown by the Russian press and the Russian foreign office during the negotiations boded ill for a long-term German-Russian entente. Should Germany's Western front explode, was any piece of paper strong enough to bind Russia to its terms?

Economic tension exacerbated diplomatic suspicions. Before the Reinsurance Treaty was negotiated, Bismarck was under pressure from both market agriculture and heavy industry to respond to a recent round of Russian tariff increases. In May, 1887, the tsar's government introduced new restrictions on foreign ownership of property in Russia, generating corresponding anxiety among actual and prospective German investors. Russian securities began to diminish in attractiveness and drop in value on the Berlin bourse. The German press, partly with Bismarck's encouragement, began to raise alarms. The Reichstag debated the wisdom, political and economic, of continuing to accept Russian commercial paper. On November 10, Bismarck issued the *Lombardverbot*.

The order's scope should not be exaggerated. It simply forbade the German state bank to accept Russian securities as collateral. Russia did begin transferring securities out of Germany after November 10. Some went to France, some back home for purchase by private banks, some to other European capitals. This, however, was not a politically motivated reaction to a diplomatic initiative. Russia's government still had no real cabinet structure. Ministries worked in separate compartments, often virtually unaware of each other's problems. Attempting to influence Russian foreign policy directly by financial pressure correspondingly resembled attracting the attention of a dinosaur by giving the beast a hotfoot. By the time the message reached its intended goal, any response was likely to be irrelevant to the current situation.

Austria for her part had reacted to the nonrenewal of the Three Emperor's League with a burst of anxiety. Russian troop concentrations in Poland and the Ukraine generated Habsburg demands for clarification of the Dual Alliance of 1879. Specifically, the Austrian generals pressed their German counterparts to accept clear Russian preparations for war as a *casus belli*. Their concerns found support in Germany. Moltke's deputy and designated successor, Quartermaster-General Alfred von Waldersee, shared with Holstein an ultimately pessimistic view of the prospects for retaining Russia's good will. By November, he and his aged superior were agreed on the military advantages of a preventive war, to be launched during the winter of 1887.

Bismarck rejected this concept out of hand. He insisted that provoking a war was directly contradictory to German policy. More to the point, he was unwilling to surrender the making of that policy to military considerations. Nor was he standing alone. Bernhard von Bülow, the future chancellor, at the time secretary in the German embassy to Russia, spoke during the winter for common sense. Should war be fought, Bülow declared, it must be a war to the finish, a war which would cripple Russia for at least a quarter-century. He described the Russians as more fanatical, more capable of sacrifice, and more patriotic than the French. For victory to be permanent, for Russia to be incapable of taking revenge, her black-earth provinces must be devastated, her coastal towns bombarded, her commerce and industry crippled. She must be driven from the Black and Baltic Seas. Ultimately, she must be deprived of her Western provinces. To do that would require a sequence of victories carrying German troops to the Volga—an eerie prefiguring of events in 1942. Given the obvious difficulties of winning such victories, Germany was far better advised to get along with her Eastern neighbor.

And there lay the rub. It took two to agree, but only one to quarrel. Bülow went on to castigate the weakness and stupidity of Russian government circles, the systematic poisoning of public and political opinions against Germany. Should Germany ever stand alone, Russia would immediately join with the French against her. Any promises to the contrary would be swept away by the tides of Panslavism and Germanophobia. The real guarantees of peace were armed force and alliances, particularly the alliance with Austria. Germany could expect favorable results only from a policy of mistrust expressed in the most determined terms.

Like other war scares before and since, that of 1887 blew over almost as rapidly as it emerged. But Bülow's letter reflected a changing attitude in German politics. Even those refusing to follow Holstein in regarding the tsar's empire as an implacable foe were beginning to concede a level of inevitability in Russo-German tensions that was foreign to Bismarck's argument that only interests, not friends or enemies, were eternal.

Military considerations sharpened the anxiety, especially for Waldersee, who finally succeeded Moltke in 1888. The new chief of staff's image as a Russophobic political general should not obscure the reasonable questions of strategy and operations that influenced his views on broader issues. The East, Waldersee had declared in 1884, was a far more dangerous theater for Germany than the West. Not only was the road to Berlin virtually without natural obstacles, but every yard of ground abandoned meant the loss of historic Prussian territory to an all-destroying enemy.

The existing war plans developed by Moltke depended on Russian cooperation: specifically, Russian readiness to deploy substantial forces in the Polish salient, exposed to an Austro-German pincer. Since the 1880s, in an effort to counterbalance Germany's advantage of rapid mobilization, almost half the Russian army had been concentrated in the empire's Western military districts. A British war office report circulated in January, 1893, highlighted the fact that in the previous decade the garrisons of those military districts not on the European land frontier had remained almost the same size. In Kiev, Vilna, and Warsaw, on the other hand, the garrisons had been augmented by 124 battalions, 148 squadrons, and 61 field batteries.

These formidable forces were not projected to remain obligingly in place. The Russians had become sufficiently aware of German intentions to have altered their own. Rather than holding forward positions, their main armies now expected to retreat eastward, drawing their enemies after them. Waldersee's initial response was a strategy of hot pursuit, with one German army attacking south into Russian Poland towards the Narew River, and another, smaller force advancing east across the Nieman River, on towards Kovno and Vilna. The new plan was risky at best, involving as it did movement in diverging directions against superior forces. It left almost no margin for human error or acts of God. In particular, Waldersee fretted about the possible impact of weather conditions on his projected offensive. Mud would slow the German infantry. It would immobilize the artillery whose firepower was regarded as an indispensable counterweight to Russian numerical superiority. By the end of his term in office Waldersee was even suggesting that should war begin during the wet season, Germany might be better advised to reduce its forces in the East in favor of the West until the weather changed. The rain clouds on the chief of staff's horizon foreshadowed a basic change in Germany's plans for the contingency of a two-front war.

Meanwhile, Russian relations with France steadily improved in the financial and military spheres. French bankers, eager to take Germany's place exploiting the Russian market, negotiated in the summer and fall of 1888 a major conversion loan giving Russian credit a much-needed boost. The respective general staffs were also beginning a series of systematic exchanges. Widely publicized improvements in French organization, armament, and training during the 1880s did not go unnoticed in a Russia increasingly dubious of Germany's probable attitudes in any European conflict. French generals for their part were all too aware of the enduring weaknesses of even their revamped military system. A Russian connection seemed to promise a quick fix, as opposed to dreary efforts to overhaul the army in the face of successive governments unable to pursue any policy over a long term.

Bismarck's resignation on March 18, 1890, marked a watershed in German-Russian relations. The Reinsurance Treaty expired in June. Kaiser William II, logically enough, turned over the negotiations for its renewal to his new chancellor. Leo von Caprivi had no experience in foreign affairs. He had never even seen the texts of the treaty—hardly the best preparation for dealing with Holstein and his allies in the foreign office, who immediately sought to change the kaiser's mind. They described the Reinsurance Treaty as conflicting with Germany's other agreements, above all the Austrian alliance. Bismarck, the critics asserted, had been able to keep his complicated diplomacy alive because he was Bismarck. His reputation was such that even his follies were taken for wisdom. No successor could expect to have anything like the same status—or if it came to that, the same mind-set, with his enthusiasm for keeping a half-dozen balls in the air simultaneously. Clear-cut, unmistakable policies were preferable for a new administration under a young ruler.

Caprivi knew his own limitations. He was reluctant to assume Bismarck's mantle and risk keeping apparently conflicting commitments to five powers at once—particularly in the context of the domestic conflicts that had been the immediate cause of Bismarck's downfall and now demanded prompt attention. Responding to the overwhelming advice of his counselors, William informed Giers that the recent changes in the government impelled Germany to avoid far-reaching commitments, at least temporarily. The Reinsurance Treaty would therefore not be renewed, but Russia could remain assured of Germany's friendship and good offices.

Giers, shocked and upset, did everything in his power to change William's mind. His desperation was enhanced by his isolation. Russia's current chief of staff argued that the Congress of Berlin should have been lesson enough that Russia's most dangerous enemy was not the one who fought her directly, but the one who awaited her weakening to dictate terms of peace.

A government's policy is not always best evaluated by the opinion of its generals. But in March, 1892, Tsar Alexander suggested to a shocked Giers that a major order of Russia's business in any future war would be to correct the error of German unification by breaking up the Reich into a number of small, weak states. Such attitudes, expressed not in journalistic or academic circles, but at the highest policy-making level, suggest that Germany was not exactly abandoning a willing partner—unless "willing" be interpreted as an equal desire to embrace or to annihilate the object of one's affections.

Nonrenewal of the Reinsurance Treaty was not an overt step towards considering alliances in terms of their value in preparing for war, as opposed to sustaining peace. Holstein warned consistently against fatally alienating Russia at the wrong time by challenging her too sharply in a specific situation. Better by far to contain her through a structure functioning without Germany's direct intervention. Rejection of the Reinsurance Treaty had been a necessary taste of the stick. Now, Holstein argued, it was time for carrots—trade agreements, political concessions, perhaps even a new treaty. But all must take place within the status quo.

Russia was in no position to issue direct challenges to any of the great powers. Her sponsorship of the Hague disarmament conference of 1899 reflected more a general consensus of the state's military backwardness than an altruistic concern for international order. Russian military appropriations had the highest growth rate of any European power during the 1890s. After 1892 Russia consistently outspent France; after 1894 Germany too fell behind the tsar's empire. But though Russia did move increasingly toward self-sufficiency in terms of arms production, on the whole the amount of security purchased did not match the actual outlay of rubles. This reflected less internal inefficiency and corruption than the sheer size of the Russian military establishment—almost a million men during the 1890s, as opposed to the half-million or so kept with the colors by France and Germany. Russia's extensive frontiers, the lengthy period of active service considered necessary to train peasant conscripts for modern war, and the slow mobilization imposed by an underdeveloped transportation network combined to generate a conviction that Russia needed the largest peacetime army she could possibly support. This in turn meant more money spent on maintaining the structure than improving it.

It was scarcely surprising in this context that Russian relations with Germany remained if not consistently warm, at least generally harmonious. French capital might dominate the official money market, but German investment in railroads and industrial enterprises steadily increased. German consumer goods made headway everywhere in Russian markets. Periodic vitriolic outbursts from Moscow or St. Petersburg over the inequities of the economic relationship were by this time familiar enough to be overridden. Where it counted the governments were well able to cooperate.

Nor was Holstein's conviction that Imperial Russia and Republican France could sustain anything but the most fragile relationship directly disproved by the course of events. The first official French references to an "alliance" with Russia were made only in 1895. Not until 1897 would a Russian tsar acknowledge the treaty in public—and then it was Nicholas II, who in 1894 succeeded a father never proud of his French connection.

The new Russo-German relationship represented a significant departure from the direct influence Bismarck consistently sought to exercise. But restraints can be no less binding for being relatively loose. The possibilities of integrating Russia into a flexible network of diplomatic relationships seemed enhanced as France's moderate attitude suggested the survival, or perhaps the rebirth, of that Concert of Europe Bismarck had done so much to demolish. Holstein and his colleagues in the foreign office were by no means hostile to the concept. A Europe subdivided into rigid alliance systems offered too little scope for the exercise of the diplomatic talents on which they prided themselves. Inflexibility bade fair to neutralize the economic and military strength, the geographic position, and not least the mixed form of government that, in the minds of Germany's leaders, gave her such advantages as mediator and pivot point of an open international order. As early as 1895 Holstein asserted that "the Russians will need us before we will need them." Germany could safely afford to wait for her Eastern neighbor while preserving as far as possible a free hand towards the rest of the world.

An important aspect of this freedom was the search for a British connection. Holstein's vision of such a relationship involved accord rather than alliance: specific action in common for common specific ends. Yet even this modest goal remained out of reach. Paul Kennedy has demonstrated that above all Germany's rapid economic growth created a fundamental antagonism between the two powers that would have been difficult to overcome given the most conciliatory diplomatic behavior on both sides. Gregor Schollgen speaks of "ignorance," of a young and inexperienced nation pursuing a tragic course in its relations with the older power, ultimately failing to recognize that its goals of *Weltpolitik* could best be achieved as Britain's junior partner. Peter Winzen is more critical. He accuses Bülow, who became secretary of state for foreign affairs in 1897, of consistent bad faith, of sabotaging Anglo-German relations for the sake of a grand design that would ally Russia to Germany in the course of an Anglo-Russian war Bülow regarded as inevitable.

These approaches overlook the basic fact that Britain and Germany had no common enemy, no common concrete danger strong enough to bring them together. The enduring continental alliances, Austria and Germany, France and Russia, were essentially insurance policies against objective threats, geographic possibilities that remained constant whatever treaty relationships might exist. Britain and Germany had no equivalent situation. Without one their relationship was likely to remain at best alignment without alliance, connection without commitment.

Holstein was correct in reasoning that Britain's interests, like Germany's, were best served by sustaining the existing order. Where he failed was in overestimating the strength of the British Empire. Britain was not merely sated, but saturated. Appeasement seemed by far the wisest course. This approach is historically congenial to imperial powers in decline. It reflected as well the position of the bourgeois-conservative elites that dominated Britain, and demanded global grandeur with limited liability.

Toward whom should that appeasement be directed? Keith Wilson exaggerates when he speaks of Germany as "invented" to suit the role Britain needed to play in order to sustain its policies. Yet the weakness of the concrete points of friction, even the naval issue, between Britain and Germany does suggest that Britain's commitment against Germany was a secondary, rather than a primary, fact of twentieth-century international relations. It was a by-product of the French and Russian ententes Britain needed to sustain her position as a world power. As such, it lay farther outside of German control than successive German governments were willing to concede.

In view of the continued failure of its British policies, German encouragement during the 1890s of Russia's expansion in central Asia and towards the Pacific appeared almost brilliant in the first years of the new century. Russian advances in Korea and Manchuria generated resistance from Japan and increasing opposition from Britain, Japan's ally since 1902.

Bülow, promoted from the foreign office to the chancellorship in 1900, was enthusiastic over a situation he regarded as an inviting opportunity for creative diplomacy. Bülow viewed international relations in a traditional context of alliances, balances of power, and national security. His concept of *Weltpolitik* was anything but a coherent program of economic or political imperialism. Depending on perspective, it can be described negatively, as the constant search for cheap successes at low risk or, positively, as the flexible exploration of a spectrum of options to solve long-standing problems of international relations. To date the Franco-Russian alliance had been essentially a free ride for both partners. What might happen if a price tag suddenly appeared on the relationship? In Bülow's opinion a German initiative, properly couched and timed, could mean re-establishing close relations with Russia at bargain-basement terms. The Russians seemed in no position to be selective. A Russo-German alliance might in turn draw France into its orbit—particularly in view of that country's recent initiatives in Morocco. Germany's interests there were significant, but not vital. They could be negotiated, even bartered. The Franco-Prussian War had been history for over three decades; times seemed propitious for dramatic changes in great-power relationships.

Bülow's underlying attitude towards Russia had changed little since 1887. She was not a shambling giant with feet of clay—that status Bülow reserved for Austria—but a power whose attitudes and behavior held the keys to Europe's stability. His policy depended heavily on Russian support to bring France to terms. But far from acting as the sophisticated mediator of interests and attitudes, the Russian government behaved more like a *Luftmensch* (overseer) from the empire's own *shtetls*. Themselves with nothing to trade, the Russian delegates to the First Moroccan Conference devoted all their energies to persuading Germany into concessions. The foreign ministry officially stated that Russia would stand by France should war over Morocco arise. With the French government firmly refusing to negotiate directly with Germany, with even Austria-Hungary pressing Germany to back down, Bülow faced a choice: fight or quit. Germany chose to quit, accepting one of the twentieth century's most complete diplomatic defeats rather than risk a war that suddenly very few Germans seemed to want, no matter how belligerent their previous rhetoric might have been. And in April, 1906, Russia collected its payment—a new French loan on unusually favorable terms.

German restraint in 1905 is frequently described as at best a temporary reflection of current shortcomings in armament and equipment, an anomaly in a political-military strategy essentially offensive in nature. The strategy is in turn most often presented as reflecting both extensive geopolitical aims and an institutional bias in favor of the offensive, which was considered to express most fully the values at the heart of the German military system: courage, decisiveness, initiative, and similar caste-influenced attitudes. Germany's sudden backdown did owe much to the fact that her policy during the crisis had been no more than a set of diplomatic initiatives. Coordination and consultation between the foreign office and the general staff was minimal. Yet for all of his rhetoric about the desirability of war with France in the context of current Russian weakness, even Chief of Staff Alfred von Schlieffen seemed reluctant to push his arguments to the limit in 1905.

This caution was not specific to the situation. Germany's mainstream military theorists had moved a long way from Waldersee's ebullient advocacy of preventive war. Since the turn of the century they had become increasingly dubious about their country's prospects. For all of Tirpitz's elaborate building programs, naval planning against likely combinations of enemies more and more assumed the nature of the Mad Hatter's tea party in *Alice in Wonderland*. The army's consideration of invading Denmark and Holland, and Schlieffen's eventual decision to attack Belgium, reflected a sense of weakness rather than strength, a view that these small states would become sally-ports for future enemies, and a corresponding search for compensating advantages however ephemeral and costly these might be in the long run. As late as November, 1909, the general staff asked the navy to evaluate which Dutch harbors would be suitable for a major British landing.

This pessimism reflected Germany's increasingly unfavorable diplomatic situation. It responded to the domestic strains engendered by increased military preparation: the social consequences of enlarging the army and the financial burdens of expanding the navy. At the cutting edge, however, it was a function of professional anxiety at two

levels. Schlieffen's growing commitment to an all-out offensive against France represented at least as much a turn away from the East as a focus on the West. In a quarter-
century's alliance between Germany and Austria, the Habsburg army had developed
an image and a self-image as a military Avis—not exactly a poor relation, but an attendant lord, suited to start a process and swell a scene or two but able to do nothing
the Germans could not do better. In Schlieffen's opinion the Austrian army could not
even protect its own state from a determined Russian offensive.

His judgment is open to question. Unit for unit, in equipment, efficiency, and command, there was arguably little to choose between Habsburg and Romanov. Psychic
reality, however, was more important than hindsight. In his early years as chief of staff
Schlieffen believed that if the main German strength were not deployed in the East
Austria might collapse completely. Much to Waldersee's chagrin, he therefore replaced
Moltke's pincer movement with a side-by-side German-Austrian offensive from Silesia and Galicia into southern Poland.

This new concept left East Prussia completely exposed to a Russian attack. It meant
deploying almost a million men in an area where road and railway networks were
poor on both sides of the frontier. Its only advantage was the possibility of providing
direct German support for an inefficient ally. And Schlieffen increasingly doubted
whether the advantages of this operation justified its risks. A large part of the active
Russian army was stationed on the Western frontier. To expedite the deployment of
the remainder, railroads were being built in European Russia with all possible speed.
Russian strategic concepts had correspondingly altered. Revised war plans now incorporated one offensive from the Niemen against the German left, and another against
the Austrian right flank in southern Galicia. Each ally would therefore have to secure
its own respective flank before any combined operations would be possible. This in
turn encouraged a tendency to establish two separate secondary theaters of war,
whose geographically diverging objectives were likely to absorb critical numbers of
the available troops.

The possibility of winning even the kind of limited victory Moltke originally projected was substantially reduced. And if the allies could cope with the new strategic
situation, what would they have gained? Moltke's original hypothesis that victory
would encourage negotiation in the East depended on at least a stable front in the
West. Schlieffen's ultimate dream may have been a repetition of the victory of Cannae
on a European scale. But that dream was the fruit of his nightmare: a series of meaningless victories in the East, drawing German armies even deeper into Russia while a
rejuvenated France drove at the Vosges and the Rhine.

For all its positive qualities, however, the French army was to Germany what the
German navy was to Great Britain—a challenge that no one doubted could be
matched. This by no means made the French a foe to be despised. But since 1870 the
French military had essentially formed itself according to patterns set in Germany.
Despite specific advantages in some areas, it continued to sustain the image of a
blurred copy of its original. Even without the advantage of a larger population, German military planners were convinced that France could be beaten both by sheer numerical superiority and man for man, corps for corps. The growing faith among Europe's military planners in the tactical and operational superiority of the offensive

only strengthened the conviction that an all-out attack on France would remove not only an immediately dangerous enemy, but the one most vulnerable to a Germany herself in no position to sustain a long, drawn-out war.

Schlieffen's concern for the Eastern theater also provided him with the beginnings of a solution to his greatest practical anxiety: the fundamental imbalance in manpower between Germany on one hand and France and Russia on the other. Even by training every fit man, Germany could not hope to match her enemies numerically. In an age when all armies were trained, armed, and equipped essentially alike, the prospects for securing more than a marginal advantage in quality seemed severely limited. These problems posed a corresponding challenge to professional skill. The window of vulnerability must become a door of opportunity. The general staff exercises of the 1890s indicated the possibilities even under modern conditions of a small force defeating a larger one by concentrating against an enemy's flank, then driving against its lines of retreat. Far from ignoring or denigrating the power of modern weapons, Schlieffen proposed to take advantage of them by reducing the strength of covering and screening forces to what seemed an unacceptable minimum to more conservative colleagues. Instead of playing to its enemies' strengths by a series of frontal encounter battles, the German army must seek to change the rules, to impose a plan so comprehensive, so cohesive, that the enemy would be able to do nothing except react.

Orthodox general staff wisdom held that Germany's long and exposed Eastern frontier could only be defended by a strategic offensive, by thrusts into Russian territory. This opinion was unchallenged by Bismarck and shared by his successors, Caprivi and Hohenloe. Schlieffen for his part was willing to test the hypothesis that the East and in particular its most vulnerable area, the province of East Prussia, could be held even against heavy odds by relatively weak forces. East Prussia's complex network of lakes, swamps, and woods offered excellent possibilities to well-trained, boldly commanded defenders. The geography of the area and the disposition of the Russian railroad network encouraged dividing invading Russian forces into two halves, one advancing westward from the Niemen, the other northwest from the Narew. And this in turn offered excellent prospects for operational ripostes that would overwhelm the invaders in detail.

The general staff exercise of 1891 featured a simultaneous Russian invasion of Posen and East Prussia, with Schlieffen's summary highlighting the probable moral impact if even one invading column was destroyed. The problem for 1898 saw the East Prussian garrison threatened on three sides, with Schlieffen insisting the optimal response was to engage the nearest enemy force as quickly as possible, decisively defeat it, then turn against the other two adversaries. In 1899 the Germans again countered numerical inferiority by crushing one of the Russian flanks, then moving against their lines of communication.

By the turn of the century it had become a textbook solution: throw the entire German strength at whichever enemy first came within range, then concentrate against the other. Time and again the concept succeeded in war games. On one memorable occasion a general staff lieutenant-colonel charged with leading one of the "Russian" armies found himself so completely surrounded that the rules demanded a surrender.

The officer insisted that no force he led would ever lay down its arms. Schlieffen, who was not without a sense of humor, amended the final report to read that the "Russian" commander, recognizing his hopeless situation, sought and found death in the front line!

Such an outcome was, however, considered an optimal result. Schlieffen had a healthy respect for the size of the Russian army, and a high regard for the uncertainties of battle. After 1901 the mobilization plan reduced Germany's Eastern force to an average of three corps, four reserve divisions, and two to four cavalry divisions. Schlieffen did not expect miracles from such a weak instrument. He recognized the possibility that a well-coordinated Russian advance, or a German defeat in the opening rounds, might require drawing troops from the West. But he also warned that once the reinforcements were on the scene, nothing would prevent the Russians from withdrawing until French pressure constrained the Germans to send troops westward, then resuming the advance. This sort of counterpunching, Schlieffen roundly declared, would lead in the long run to the complete annihilation of the German army. Instead, Ostheer should expect to fight with what it had, do as much damage as possible, and wait for the decisive victory over France. If necessary, Schlieffen was prepared to return to the concept of the 1880s, abandoning most of East Prussia and making a stand on the Vistula River. By 1903 the railway section of the general staff felt able to guarantee the transportation of eleven corps eastward as soon as France should be overthrown. And this would be only the vanguard of a German army strong enough not merely to drive Russian invaders out of East Prussia, but to pin them there and destroy them.

Schlieffen's strategic conceptions incorporated his reflections on the changing nature of war. Often derided for their shortsightedness in failing to predict a war of attrition, Europe's generals were if anything even less correct in evaluating the pace of destruction in modern war. Far from being technological illiterates, soldiers were well aware of what modern weapons, the rapid-firing field gun, the machine gun, and the magazine rifle, could do in theory. What they were expecting was not a gentlemen's war, not a repetition of 1866 or 1870, but an Armageddon in quick time, with events proceeding at the outer limits of comprehension and control. I. S. Bloch's *La guerre future* was not only discounted because of its pessimistic predictions of indecisive mass war. More and more experts agreed that the rates of loss under modern conditions made a war of attrition on the Bloch model impossible.

Military planners prior to 1914 are often described as underestimating the resilience of their war machines and the societies sustaining them. What they actually did was to overestimate the rates at which men would be killed and machines destroyed. They saw vulnerabilities more clearly than durabilities—and it was the latter that gave Europe time to adjust to the initial casualty rates of 1914–15. Given the nature of prewar anticipations, it by no means indicated lack of faith in one's people to assume that countries facing such a catastrophe were likely to collapse from psychic shock and physical stress. Schlieffen was hardly isolated in his growing belief that the armed forces available to modern nations could be maintained for any length of time only at the expense of the economic, social, and political institutions they were supposed to sustain. And in this context Russia, combining tremendous reserves of human and material resources with a relatively primitive social structure, emerged as the most likely survivor of a protracted war.

The essence of strategy is the calculating of relationships among ends, means, and will. Let the process of calculation obscure the values of the relationships, and the result is not bad strategy but no strategy. Neither the German Empire's power nor the German Empire's finesse was sufficient to establish her as the focal point of European diplomacy during the Bülow years. Instead, Germany remained one power of several—at the very time when increasing concern for her military position generated a corresponding policy of *Flucht nach vorne* (flight forward). The German army in the years before 1914 became increasingly concerned with processes, methods, and techniques. Arguably, Schlieffen's essential flaw as a strategist was his acceptance of Germany's international position as defined by civilian political authority. He responded with a desperation move: a staff college *tour de force*, but a military myth requiring everything to go impossibly right to have a real chance of succeeding.

"Everything" included political and diplomatic factors, which between 1905 and 1914 became increasingly subordinated to this gambler's gambit. The Schlieffen Plan, however, had one supreme psychological virtue. It offered hope through diligence. If everyone did his bit and played his part, the empire might have a chance. The plan's rapid evolution into dogma owed much to the increasingly narrow perspective of German military thinking. But that development in turn represented in large part a response to a paradox. The imperial army was given—and accepted—the task of planning for a war which its own calculations suggested might well be so destructive as to be unpredictable, uncontrollable, and ultimately unwinnable. In this context, a withdrawal into procedures, a concentration on mobilization schedules and corps-level tactics, was natural if not exactly inevitable. The Schlieffen Plan was a sophisticated security blanket. Had it not existed its equivalent would almost certainly have been designed.

The climate of anxiety in Germany was reinforced by a new set of public shouting matches with Russia. In the agonizing reappraisals that followed the Peace of Portsmouth, Germany bore the brunt of the blame in St. Petersburg for encouraging Russia's disastrous Far Eastern policies. Even Witte criticized Berlin for "forcing" Russia to pursue her arms in Manchuria rather than closer to home. Holstein was not being blindly Russophobic when he acidly described "Russia of the Russians, where the 'inevitable' war with Germany is discussed in every *Zemstvo* . . . even if a treaty actually existed between Russia and Germany, the popular prejudices of the Russian people would today probably override it."

Russia's increasing and unexpected postwar rapprochement with Britain generated corresponding despondency in the German foreign office. Both powers had significant reasons for settling their imperial rivalries. Britain was unwilling to maintain the land forces necessary to project her power into the Middle East and central Asia in the face of Russian opposition. Russia for her part needed above all a period of stability in international affairs. These positive factors drew Britain and Russia together independently of anything Germany was able to do. With France as an enthusiastic go-between, the Anglo-Russian entente of 1907 quickly emerged as something more than just another paper agreement.

Both powers were concerned to reassure Germany that their improved relationship was not aimed at her. In his annual reports for 1906 and 1907 Ambassador Sir Arthur Nicolson was impressed by the "intimate and cordial" relations between Russia and Germany's courts and governments—relations he ascribed both to the unusual skill with which Germany managed her Russian affairs, and by the absence of direct points of friction between the empires. In the European field, he declared, "there is a desire on the part of the Russian Government to live on the best possible terms with Germany." Nevertheless, no interpretation of the entente as a "warning," a structure aimed at containing a provocative and insatiable German diplomacy, can deny the objective reality of encirclement. Even Fritz Fischer concedes that Germany after 1907 "lived permanently under the threat of a war on two fronts." The continued failure to negotiate a naval limitation treaty with Britain set the seal of Germany's isolation. The Bosnian crisis of 1908 demonstrated its consequences.

Notes

From Dennis Showalter, *Tannenberg: Clash of Empires*, chapter 1: The Circus Rider of Europe (Dulles, Va.: Brasseys, 2004), pp. 13–35. Reprinted with permission of Potomac Books, Inc., formerly Brassey's, Inc.

1. The peace treaty that ended the Franco-Prussian War of 1870–1871.
2. The shooting of protestors at the tsar's Winter Palace in St. Petersburg in 1905.
3. Germany's socialist party newspaper.
4. See reading 1.3.
5. In 1864 Prussia soundly defeated Denmark and seized the provinces of Schlesswig and Holstein.

The Army and the Nationalist Revival

Douglas Porch

In the history of the French army before the Great War, 1911 marked a turning point. The Moroccan crisis of that year introduced a new note of urgency into military debates. Beneath the threat of war, politicians like Poincaré, Messimy and Millerand set out to rehabilitate a war machine which had grown rusty from over a decade of neglect and restore the army as the focal point of French patriotism and national pride.

The Nationalist Revival, as the period between the Agadir crisis of 1911 and the outbreak of war has come to be called, was the product of a serious deterioration in Franco-German relations which began with the first Moroccan crisis of 1905.[1] While no threat of war existed, Frenchmen could indulge a witch-hunt against soldiers, priests and other enemies of the republic. When Germany suddenly appeared as a serious threat to peace, public complacency was shaken. By 1911, when Germany again challenged France over Morocco, French public opinion had hardened—in 1905, few wanted to fight. By 1911, a significant number of people were prepared for a showdown with the Kaiser. This change of attitude had first become apparent at the top. In 1905, the high command had informed the government that the French army had no chance of winning a war with Germany. Two years later, the chief of the general staff, General Hagron, resigned, giving as his reason France's abysmal state of military preparedness which the government seemed in no haste to repair. However, from the 1908 affair of the Casablanca deserters which again strained relations between the two countries, the attitude of leading Radicals toward the army began to mellow: Clemenceau named Foch to command the *Ecole de guerre*, despite his Catholic background, while reports of the annual military budget began to suggest improving the conditions of service for professional soldiers as a means of reviving sagging army morale. With the second Moroccan crisis of 1911, the restoration of military strength had become a first priority among Radical politicians. While one must not exaggerate the scope of the Nationalist Revival which especially influenced the young, the intelligent and the Parisian, by 1911 nationalism had become a significant factor in French politics responsible for the election of Poincaré as president in 1913 and for the passage in that year of the three-year service law.[2]

For the reformist historians of the inter-war years, whose views have never been fundamentally challenged, the Nationalist Revival issued in a catastrophic period of reaction which bolstered the prestige of professional soldiers and, in the words of left-wing historian Georges Michon, 'returned the army to its pre-Dreyfus affair state.'[3]

Monteilhet, who sees the history of French military institutions from 1875 to 1914 as 'basically the struggle for survival by the professional army . . . against the nation-in-arms,' believed that these three years saw a fundamental shift in the balance of power in favour of the former. The history of the army in the Third Republic[4] is seen as one of a conflict between two systems. The Nationalist Revival announced a reversal of policy which, by pandering to the professional interests of the army, led inexorably to three-year service, the offensive *à outrance*, 'the disdain of heavy artillery, machine guns, field fortifications as well as the worth of reserves.' In short, the politicians of the Nationalist Revival had relinquished the political control over the army conquered so painfully during the Dreyfus affair, and thus condemned Frenchmen in uniform to suffer all of the idiocies, blind prejudices, lack of foresight and slaughter of the war's opening months.

How true a picture is this of military policy in the three years before the war? The politicians in power after 1911, and particularly Alexandre Millerand, war minister for most of 1912, certainly set out to modify many of the policies inaugurated under the André ministry.[5] Conscious that war loomed large, they set themselves the task of restoring the tumbled-down authority of military leaders and rekindling enthusiasm for French defence in a population grown apathetic during decades of peace, while bolstering the badly shaken morale of officers and NCOs. The question of how far they succeeded in restoring patriotism as a fashionable sentiment in the nation at large is answered by other authors. But what of the effect of the Nationalist Revival on the authority of the high command and the morale of the forces?

The reforms of the high command pushed through by Galliffet and André had strengthened the position of the war minister and reduced that of the generals. The chief of the general staff, chosen from among rather junior major generals, was from this period simply a senior ministry functionary without power to command service directors. The vice-president of the *conseil supérieur de la guerre* (Supreme War Council, or CSG), who was to command the armies in the field, had no organized staff in peacetime. Nor were the designated corps commanders allowed to organize and train their staffs or to inspect the troops who would make up their wartime commands. This was a system which sprang from the fear of a *coup d'état* rather than one designed to ensure military efficiency.

The obvious weaknesses of this arrangement were exposed in 1911 when the war minister, General Goiran, was questioned in the Senate on the role of the generalissimo. 'There is no generalissimo, there is only a vice-president of the *conseil supérieur de la guerre*,' Goiran replied. On the outbreak of war, the vice-president would take command of the principal north-east army group while the chief of the general staff would remain with the war minister in Paris. 'The government must control the overall wartime operations. The war minister is its executor. There are army group commanders, each of whom has a mission.' Senators, deputies and public opinion, shaken by the Moroccan crisis and aware that the French army might not be capable of repelling an invasion, failed to find this answer satisfactory. Goiran's reply brought down the Monis government.

The major task of re-structuring the high command fell to Adolphe Messimy, who replaced Goiran on 27 July 1911, and his successor of 15 January 1912, Alexandre

Millerand. Both men sought to make the chief of the general staff the undisputed military chief, answerable to the government through the war minister, and to bolster the power of the *CSG* as a central organ of policy making, direction and standardization in the forces. André, in his 1903 reform of the high command, had failed to define the relationship between the vice-president of the *CSG* and the chief of the general staff, and resulting constant friction between them sabotaged war planning. The 1911 decree abolishing the vice-presidency noted the defects of the old system: 'The presence of a vice-president isolated and without constant contact with the chief of the army general staff has resulted in an unfortunate overlapping of duties. The chief of the army general staff, who must prepare for war, works independently and without direct contact with the general officer destined to command the principal army group.'

In 1911, Messimy overcame republican fears of strong army leadership and appointed Joffre chief of the general staff. The following year, War Minister Millerand abolished the post of chief of the army general staff to end the bickering between Dubail and Castelnau over their relative functions, leaving Joffre in undisputed command. But how extensive were Joffre's powers? Very extensive indeed, according to Professor David Ralston who argues that Joffre was now even more powerful than his German counterpart: 'The military situation created for Joffre by the 1911 decree in the democratic and republican state of France was actually stronger than that of his counterpart in aristocratic, militaristic Germany, the younger Moltke,' Ralston writes. 'Joffre had virtually unlimited power with regard to the army,' but even more: 'These . . . steps . . . gave to the army almost complete autonomy within the state."

The power of the chief of the general staff over the army and the degree of autonomy which the 1911 decree gave the army within the republic, however, was more than a simple question of legal phrasing. These depended ultimately on the personality of the new chief and on the habits and traditions of the forces. Had Messimy's first choice, General Galliéni, not declined the post, the history of the army might possibly have been different. A colonial man who possessed a lively and imaginative mind, Galliéni was well known for his intolerance of the bureaucratic and timorous ways of the metropolitan army. Whether he possessed the ruthlessness to sweep out the Augean Stables which the war ministry had become and to establish the chief of the army as a real power in the republic will never be known, for he reminded Messimy that he was too near retirement to take up a task which would require some years to complete. 'I see two men," Galliéni told Messimy, 'Pau and Joffre.'

General Pau was the army's candidate. An austere Catholic whose loyal and frank character had won the respect of his fellow officers, he was an excellent administrator. However, his interview with Messimy did not go well. Pau told him that, were he appointed chief of the general staff, he would insist upon taking over the prerogative reserved for the war minister of selecting generals. This was clearly not the man in whom to confide the delicate and sensitive task of leading the army.

The mantle of army leadership fell therefore by default on Joffre. Joffre seems to have been somewhat surprised by Messimy's offer, and well he might have been, for there was little in his background or career which had singled him out for the post of commander-in-chief. A graduate of the *Ecole polytechnique* with a mediocre school record, he owed his rapid promotion to the expansion of the army after 1871 and his colonial service. He was a competent technician, but he frankly acknowledged that he knew nothing of staff work. And this was the man whom Messimy chose as chief of the general staff!

Joffre's ability to impose a coherent tactical doctrine and armaments policy, his 'virtually unlimited power with regard to the army,' will be discussed elsewhere. But what of the charge that the Messimy-Millerand reform 'gave to the army almost complete autonomy within the state'? Even a superficial acquaintance with Joffre's character reveals that he was hardly an empire builder. The traits which had made him a successful and popular soldier—forthrightness, honesty, consideration for subordinates—were positive liabilities in the new world which he now entered, a jungle of parliamentary manoeuvre and clever debate. He could be ruthless, as his axing of commanders found wanting in 1914 demonstrates. But this soft-spoken, unimaginative and somewhat feckless man was utterly devoid of the ambition and deviousness required to carve out a position of power within the state. Instead, that power was thrust upon him in the crucible of war in 1914.

Nor was it the intention of the leaders of the Nationalist Revival that the army should ever escape their political control. Pau was rejected, Messimy states quite categorically, because the war minister had no intention of relinquishing control over officer promotion. Millerand's critics argue that he deferred too much to the advice of his service chiefs and allowed the conservative officer corps to regain control of military policy. Millerand believed that the role of the war minister was to act as the army's political chief, its defender against attack and arbiter in controversial issues. He had no knowledge of strategy and tactics, nor was he competent to deal with questions of materiel. But then few politicians were. The decrees reorganizing the high command simply recognized that the war minister could not be the administrative, technical *and* the political head of the army.

At least, not in the Third Republic, where the war ministry was plagued by instability and inexperience. Appointments often fell to generals and specialists, 27 per cent of whom served only one term of office then quit government altogether. Twelve per cent of foreign ministers and only ten per cent of those who served in the finance and interior ministries had such a brief passage in power. The Dreyfus affair had done nothing to increase the desire among senior army officers to swap a stable command for the rough and tumble of parliamentary debate. Consequently, as before 1899, rather junior divisional commanders were most often named, as was the case with André, Picquart and Goiran. Messimy was scathing in his criticism of the phlegmatic General Brun, war minister in 1910, a view shared by Emile Mayer: 'The man was a real sceptic (sic),' he wrote. 'He did not believe that war would break out, so he did as little as possible to prepare for it.' Civilians named to the rue Saint-Dominique (the location of the War Ministry) were usually selected from among second rank politicians like Messimy, Lebrun and Noulens. Bertreaux, a man who had fixed his ambitions on the presidency until a tragic accident cut short his career in 1910, paid little attention to the needs of the army during his two terms as war minister. The main concerns of Etienne, who served six terms as war minister, were colonial, not military: 'No man more ignorant of military affairs has ever occupied the rue Saint-Dominique,' Montheilhet said of him. Millerand was the only class politician to sit in the war ministry after Freycinet's resignation.

Politicians in the rue Saint-Dominique often placed the direction of the army low on their list of priorities. Parliamentary sessions, committee meetings, dealing with favour seekers, party or constituency business left ministers little time for the nuts and bolts of ministry business. When in 1905 Jonnart, the governor general of Algeria, attempted to see War Minister Berteaux, he was told that the minister was busy on a speech for a dedication at Mauberge: 'and his private secretary told me how difficult it is to speak in a town where the municipal council is divided in two, where the deputy is a socialist and the councilors are centre-left,' Jonnart wrote to Lyautey.

> I profoundly shocked him when I timidly suggested that perhaps (I said perhaps!) the Minister should not have accepted to speak at the Mauberge dedication. I am told that between now and 15 October, this extraordinary man must attend *nine* dedications. He obviously has the primary quality of a military leader: endurance. But for me he is invisible when it is a simple question of service matters.

The absence of firm ministerial direction told in the rickety organization of the war ministry and the high command. The ministry's 14 services and 'directions' worked independently, while the high command counted 11 technical committees and 100 temporary ones, often with identical functions and little inclination to leave the stage. Between them the ministry and the high command employed nearly one-third of France's 330 generals in 1909 in purely administrative jobs. 'It is materially impossible for even a talented and diligent minister to coordinate and direct so many different sections,' Gervais, a member of the parliamentary army committee, wrote in *France Militaire* on 15 February 1914. 'With only the minister to coordinate them, they work independently.'

The reorganization of the high command ended the fiction that the war minister could act as a substitute for a chief of the general staff. What it did not do was to make Joffre more independent than Moltke. The difference in the positions of the two men remained fundamental: Joffre was the soldier of a republic answerable to parliament through the war minister, while von Moltke commanded in a garrison state where military considerations increasingly gained the high ground in important policy decisions, owing explanation only to the Kaiser. Millerand and his immediate successors believed it their duty to protect the commander-in-chief from undue political interference, but civilian legal restraints remained and only awaited a Clemenceau to tighten them in the dark days of 1917. In contrast, the German commanders went from strength to strength and ended by ruling their country behind the thinnest trappings of civilian power. While Joffre no doubt had a powerful say in the nominations for top army positions, he found his ability to influence many aspects of military policy, especially concerning armaments, severely limited. Although on paper, the new generalissimo might have extensive powers, in practice war ministers often took decisions without consulting him, while entrenched service directors refused to recognize his authority to dictate an overall scheme of army needs. And, of course, Joffre *always* deferred to the government in questions of strategic planning and the declaration of war, insisting upon a clear directive before he undertook the invasion of Belgium. Schlieffen and his successors hardly worried about such diplomatic niceties, giving assurances to Austrian Chief of Staff Conrad of German support in any war with Serbia, openly pressing for war with France, demanding the invasion of Belgium as a military necessity and slamming the door in the face of the last bids for peace in 1914. In Germany, the influence of soldiers in policy decisions was immense; in France, the republic left them in no doubt about who was in charge. The republic did not forfeit control of its soldiers in 1912, as Ralston and others have argued. Joffre's relative independence from government control dated from his (September, 1914) victory on the Marne, which transformed him overnight into a national hero.

In 1912 Millerand stated categorically that, in a war, the government directed the overall strategy while the soldiers conducted operations designed to achieve the goals of that plan: 'In short, one can say that the government *directs the war*, leaving the *conduct of operations* to the supreme command.' This hardly spells a doctrine of independence from civilian control. On the contrary, the Nationalist Revival strengthened government control over the conduct of military policy: the *comité supérieur de la défense nationale* was re-constituted in July 1911 to include the ministers most concerned with defence and mobilization as well as top generals, admirals and civil servants with the goal of unifying and rationalizing defence policy. Millerand also divided the great general staff and ministry bureaux into a mobile section to leave with the generalissimo on the outbreak of war and a sedentary group to remain in Paris with the war minister:

> The sedentary section which will remain with the Minister is aware of all the questions of organization, mobilization, concentration and preparation and is able to furnish all the useful information as well as, of course, the deputy chiefs of the general staff . . . (two of which) aware of all of the questions considered at the general staff remain in Paris next to the Minister.

Millerand failed to realize, however, that the conduct of operations themselves was bound to have political consequences. His refusal to check the bloody futility of Joffre's 'nibbling' strategy in the war's first two years gradually built up resentment which tumbled the commander-in-chief and brought Père-la-Victoire (Georges Clemenceau) to power on the crest of a growing belief that 'war is too important to be left to the generals.'

A revitalized and strengthened *conseil supérieur de la guerre* set out to coordinate vital military reforms. 'The great merit of the 28 July 1911 decree,' Millerand told the Chamber on 22 March 1912, '. . . is precisely to have united, tied together, these two indispensable organs of war preparation which for twenty years were isolated: the *conseil supérieur de la guerre* and the general staff.' Virtually moribund since its creation in 1872, the *conseil supérieur de la guerre* was revived by Freycinet in 1888, to 'coordinate and centralize the work undertaken to strengthen the army and national defence.' The task proved a difficult one. 'They do not train the high command seriously,' Messimy wrote in 1907. Among its twelve members were the designated army commanders, although neither the armies nor the army staffs existed in peace time. On 27 February 1901, André abolished their right to inspect the corps which could make up their wartime commands in the conviction that local commanders could best judge their own troops, so eliminating an important element of central control and standardization. Army commanders were named only provisionally and army organization was limited to an annual meeting between the designated army leader and his staff chief for a map exercise. Messimy's 28 July 1911 decree reinstated inspections by members of the *conseil supérieur de la guerre*, strengthening their powers over the troops who would make up their wartime command, bolstering the authority of the future army commanders, so vital in an army which admitted no rank above that of major general. The nuclei of the army staffs were also created. When the Left complained that these reforms blessed the army with too much potentially dangerous independence, Millerand replied that army discipline and loyalty were beyond question and that military efficiency, not politics, should dictate military reform. He brushed aside charges that he had reinstalled a covey of pro-clerical generals in the rue Saint-Dominique and told the *Radical* on 21 September 1912:

> General Castlenau has never been involved in any placement of personnel: his sole mission is the preparation of the army for its great tasks, and it is impossible not to recognize the great technical abilities which he exercises in carrying out his task. General Joffre is responsible for controlling nominations and General Legrand, chief of the general staff on an equal footing with General Castelnau, prepares with the generalissimo all of the promotion lists and personnel movement. Now, General Legrand is not, I imagine, suspect by the republicans; nor General Joffre.

Political leaders looking over their shoulders at the time of the Agadir crisis feared that a decade's obsession with political loyalty had compromised the quality of the high command. As influence had replaced ability in the promotion stakes under the André ministry, the quality of leadership had declined. Candidates for high office had to please in high places, whether this meant putting on a republican face or simply avoiding causing their patrons embarrassment. Joffre had been named generalissimo not because he was the best candidate but because he was a 'Republican' officer. Senior army positions were soon occupied by officers who had staked out careers in the ministry or in the corridors of parliament.

The sorry state of French military leadership was a matter of open discussion. Already in 1904 Lyautey had noticed that Radical attacks upon the army had undermined the confidence of commanders. The conservative *Porte-Voix* noted on 11 February 1912:

> When you compare the generals of 15 or 20 years ago to those of today, you are struck by the inferiority of the latter . . . line officers are frequently amazed by the feebleness of their appointed leaders. Ill-at-ease in the field, they are utterly incompetent and at sea in regimental service. . . . In short . . . the products of the presidential and ministerial antechambers do not exactly shine.

An inspection report by General Dubail in November 1913, just months before the outbreak of war, said that top officers were 'timid and indecisive. . . . Nowhere do they act with resolution. We must develop character, a taste for risk and responsibility.'

French generals, with an average age of 61 in 1903 against 54 in Germany, were often too old or too ill to campaign. But officers refused to denounce them and they stayed on . . . and on. On 1 November 1910, the *Porte-Voix* estimated that at least 30 generals, 20 colonels, 25 lieutenant colonels, 80 majors and 100 captains were physically unfit to campaign. But a stern letter from War Minister Brun before the 1910 manoeuvres had resulted in the retirement of only two colonels, two lieutenant colonels, sixteen majors and six captains. Messimy complained on 27 July 1911 that 'ministerial orders have for too long remained a dead letter,' and ordered into retirement any officer unable to ride a horse. He met with no more success than did Brun. Emile Mayer reckoned that had this measure been strictly applied, the corpulent Joffre, whose efforts to mount a horse provided an early morning pick-up for his neighbours, would have been among the first to collect his pension. The *Cri de Paris* published a cartoon of a general ordering a captain to list officers unable to campaign: 'Of course, general,' the captain replied. 'Shall I place you on the list?'

Manoeuvres provided sad testimony to the declining quality of French leadership. After viewing those of 1905, Gervais, a member of the Parliamentary army committee, wrote: 'Our leaders were obviously poorly trained . . . in practice, many generals, caught unprepared, lacked composure, judgement and common sense. . . . I have no wish to enumerate all the mistakes I have seen . . . some of them worse than absurd.'

One of the two generals chosen to lead a manoeuvre army each year between 1909 and 1914 had reached the retirement age. Autumn manoeuvres, a dry run for war, were thus transformed into an elaborate retirement ceremony. In 1912 manoeuvres climaxed on the third day, when army commander General Galliéni captured his opposite number, General Marion, his entire staff, one of his corps commanders and his staff, the corps artillery and four aeroplanes. In 1913, both commanders retired soon after manoeuvres finished. Jaurès complained in 1910:

> The grand manoeuvres are nothing but a parade where military leaders hope to be noticed, not through good planning and organization, but by the press and politicians. The point is not who best directs his forces to achieve precise goals, but who will have the most influential newspaper editor in his car. . . . The best part of their strategy goes into press campaigns against their rivals, while battalions, regiment and brigades move in a void, without firm direction or goal.

In 1911, Messimy found the top positions at the rue Saint-Dominique in poor hands: 'There now was no-one at the top of this hierarchy. Deprived of real leaders, general staff officers had divided into factions, primarily according to doctrine. Little "sects" had been established.' The generalissimo designate in wartime, General Michel, a product of the ministries and favoured aide-de-camp assignments, was 'terrified of responsibility.' The chief of the army general staff, Laffon de Ladébat, was 'a perfect bureaucrat.'

Messimy and Millerand sought to recast the high command, but found their ability to dismiss incompetent generals limited. Joffre pointed out that once a general was named, it was virtually impossible to sack him: 'When it is a question of eliminating a general for professional incompetence, the war minister is almost entirely disarmed in the present state of our legislation,' he wrote to the war minister in October 1911. Consequently, Messimy was forced to fall back upon the inadequate expedient of premature retirement for the grey and the unfit.

Although, before the wholesale purges of August–September 1914, Messimy, Millerand and Joffre could do little to eliminate incompetent leaders, they sought to bolster the military competence of the army's next generation of generals. On 9 January 1912, Messimy told members of the *conseil supérieur de la guerre* that he expected a frank appreciation of officers whom they were to inspect: 'In spite of the observations and the repeated orders of the minister, the reports on officers still do not give an exact idea of their true worth,' he wrote.

> Usually written in terms marked by a vague and unenlightening kindness, generally silent on the defects of the officers and on their physical and intellectual shortcomings, sometimes manifestly exaggerating their qualities, they do not supply the minister with sufficient information which permits him to single out meritorious officers from those whose career has gone far enough or even should be eliminated. This situation is particularly serious where the promotion of colonels and generals is concerned.

Millerand set out to correct the abuses in the promotion system introduced by the Radicals, which he believed had pushed the wrong men to the top: 'The goal is to assure the recruitment of generals who are competent,' he noted after a conversation with General Pau. 'It is a question of 500 officers. Ten years ago, we could have found competent men by the hundreds. For promotion, the only rule must be absolute order of merit; all questions of age, seniority, campaigns are abstract.'

On 25 January 1912, Millerand abolished prefectorial notes on the political opinions of officers, to limit the influence of politics in promotion calculations. He then withdrew, except in exceptional circumstances, an officer's right, accorded in 1905, to see the efficiency report on him drawn up by his superior. In this way, he hoped that banal reports would give way to a more candid appreciation of an officer's qualities. He re-established promotion committees at various points in the hierarchy, capped in each army and service by a council containing generals from outside the Paris garrison to break the hold of the capital and ministry on officers promotion. He vowed to stick closely to their recommendations. An 11 January 1913 circular encouraged corps commanders to discuss their promotion recommendations with their subordinate commanders rather than simply gather them together to read them out.

Promotion chances were also affected by garrison assignments. Officers in and near Paris enjoyed a higher promotion rate, while the crack sixth corps on the German frontier ironically had the lowest rate. 'The Paris garrison and the large cities are reserved for those protected by the powers of the day,' the *Porte-Voix* complained on 11 March 1912. Millerand ordered a more frequent turnover of Paris personnel, but like the orders of so many of his predecessors these too fell on deaf ears at the war ministry. Charles Humbert complained in the *France Militaire* on 1 February 1912 that the worst graduates of the officer schools were packed off to eastern garrisons, while generals regarded an eastern command as a punishment, a statement which was only partially true. Millerand also promised to favour eastern garrisons for promotion and decorations. However, this did little to loosen the iron grip staff officers held upon promotion. In 1910, 9.6 per cent of brevet staff captains serving infantry regiments were promoted to major, against 1.3 per cent of non-brevet captains. The figures were 9.3 per cent against 1.5 per cent in 1911 and 11.75 per cent against 1.2 per cent in 1912. The surest tickets to promotion were those of an aide-de-camp of a ministerial assignment. Of 130 infantry captains promoted to major in 1906, 23 were aides-de-camp. In the same year, eighteen per cent of all infantry captains who were aides-de-camp were promoted while barely two per cent of infantry captains otherwise employed moved up. In 1910, 34.5 per cent of the captains serving in the infantry department of the war ministry received discretional promotions to major; in 1911, the figure shot up to 62.5 per cent. These figures went down slightly under Millerand, but favoured positions in the ministry, military schools and other special assignments were well rewarded.

The men who felt the warm breath of war in 1911 feared that they might be forced to fight it with an army whose morale had bottomed out. Millerand capitalized on the mood of public resentment over German bullying at Agadir in July 1911 and over the November signing of the Franco-German agreement on Morocco, the Congo and the Cameroons to encourage a martial spirit in the nation with weekly military parades in garrison towns. A 2 March 1912 military retreat in Paris drew an estimated 10,000 spectators. Those in Nancy, Lyon and other towns were equally spectacular, only occasionally marred by anti-militarist counter-demonstrations. 'Do not think that the restored tattoo is mere child's play, it is the sign of a revival,' the *Echo de Paris* wrote. From June 1912, drums and bugles, abolished by Picquart in 1906, once more punctuated daily regimental routine 'in order to give barrack life a gaiety and an animation desirable from all points of view.'

But the politicians of the Nationalist Revival realized that it would take far more than noise to raise the morale of the armed forces. Historians have noted that army morale hit its nadir during Clemenceau's first ministry, but they have not pointed out that it continued to bump along rock bottom until August 1914 and that one of the major results was the first tentative steps towards unionization of professional soldiers.

A fierce battle to unionize teachers and civil servants had been fought during Clemenceau's first ministry, and soldiers could hardly be blamed if they began to move toward the sound of guns, especially after the *Vincennoise* had pressed so effectively for a new deal for administration officers. 'The administration officers have obtained . . . some very substantial advantages in the last few years, and no one can blame them: they have triumphed because of the cohesion of their assault upon governmental favours,' the *France Militaire* wrote on 11 October 1905. 'Encouraged by their success . . . now perhaps they are going too far, or too fast, in their claims.' In 1904, André stifled an attempt to form a 'union of officers promoted from the ranks,' while in 1907, Picquart forbade the '*Union des sociétés des officiers*,' an umbrella organization grouping the military school mutualist societies, fearing that it might actively fight for military reforms. In 1909, the war ministry founded a '*Société nationale de secours mutuels*' probably hoping to undercut the *Saint-Cyrienne, Versaillaise* and other mutualist officer societies which were beginning to act as vehicles for officer discontent.

By 1909, officer grumblings began to take on more serious manifestations. Not surprisingly, the first shock waves came from the colonial army where the traditional complaints against Radical military policies combined with slow promotion to produce a crisis in a force where career expectations were high. Discontent was directed both at politicians and at generals, who, it was felt, had done little to protect the interests of their subordinates. In the atmosphere of the post–Dreyfus affair army, only conscripts, not professionals, were worthy of the attentions of generals. Promotion, they claimed, went almost exclusively to staff officers, aides-de-camp, and the well-connected: 'One can say that favouritism counts for five tenths, nepotism four tenths and merit one tenth.' An attempt by colonial officers at Toulon to set up 'study centres' in each colonial regiment to send delegates to a Paris conference crumbled when General Archinard persuaded officers that they must look to their military superiors to protect their interests. However, Toulon police reported that officer discontent again raised its head in 1911 with the Raiberti bill to fuse the colonial and metropolitan armies. Attempts to direct discontent in colonial regiments never got off the ground, but they did cause the government some concern: 'Since (1909), many southern garrisons, particularly Toulon and Perpignan, have been the scene of the same sort of agitation,' the war minister wrote to the prime minister in 1911. 'In any case, this agitation was never so serious that the military authorities had to intervene. . . . It is also true that the turnover of personnel in colonial regiments makes the creation of permanent associations more difficult.'

The organization of metropolitan officers presented a more serious threat: 'It is hardly surprising that the soldiers, who feel abandoned, who are not organized . . . feel tempted to give themselves the same power as other servants of the nation,' wrote Paul Boncour, deputy for the Loire-et-Cher, in 1909. Demands to organize officers reached a peak in 1911–12. In February 1911, a group of officers promoted through the ranks claimed that unionization was the only way to force the gates of the army's senior grades: "We demand not to be systematically sacrificed and shoved aside in the promotion lists,' read their manifesto. 'There is but one way, dear comrades, to be heard, and this consists, without prejudicing our professional duties, that is remaining respectful and disciplined, in having but one unified leadership, one unified tactic. . . . Dispersed, we are ineffective, without cohesion, consequently powerless. Think what authority a group like ours could have." Messimy broke up the *Union central* in 1911 by scattering its organizers to the four winds while an attempt by the editor of the socialist *Petit-Var* at Toulon to form a naval officers' union was crushed by police who surrounded the café where officers had been invited to an 'apéritif de solidarité.' In March 1911, Radical General Pédoya attacked retired right-wing Major Driant's *ligue militaire*, which claimed a membership of 635 officers and 63 generals, focusing parliamentary attention on the growing dissatisfaction in the officer corps.

The 14 March debate woke up many to the new mood of militancy in the forces: 'Despite the government, one can fear that soon there will be powerful associations in the forces with which one must negotiate,' *Le Temps* wrote on 20 March 1911. Although officer associations like the *ligue militaire* generally grouped retired officers to place them beyond the reach of the government:

> their influence can be exerted over young serving officers. But what is disturbing in the army ... is that the attitudes of officers have changed entirely over the past few years. It is not the attitudes of generals or of men serving in high military positions which have been modified, but those of subalterns, lieutenants and captains. Whether they come from Saint-Cyr or through the ranks, they are unanimous in declaring that the hour for associations and groups has arrived for them. What is the origin of this change? From several causes, first of which is incontestably that the prestige of the uniform is much diminished in France. Have we not also for the last few years debased too much the merit and the mission of officers? ... If the prestige of the officer has disappeared little by little in the nation, it is even more evident that his authority in the barracks has become more and more precarious.

It was this new mood of militancy in the armed forces, the feeling among professional soldiers that they had for too long been treated unfairly by the government and by their own leaders, which worried many politicians. The Leroy committee formed to investigate the growth of NCO 'friendly societies' in Paris and other garrisons in 1911 concluded in October 1912 that the forces had only narrowly escaped unionization. Ajam, deputy for Sarthe and a member of the parliamentary army committee, also reckoned that unless the government took steps to rectify fundamental professional grievances, unionization for the forces was certain.

As if to underline this point, newspapers specializing in military affairs buried their substantial political differences to co-ordinate a campaign for political rights for officers. A poll carried out by the left-wing *Armée et Démocratie* in 1911 revealed that the overwhelming mass of officers called for the same political rights as other citizens: 8,589 officers wanted to be given the vote, against only 211 who did not. 6,541 called for officers to be allowed to run for office against 2,728 who thought it a bad idea. 'Professional soldiers have no way to defend their material and moral interests,' the newspaper wrote. 'They constitute a group of untouchables in the nation.' Captain d'Arbeaux pointed out the inconsistency of calling upon officers to lead the moral regeneration of the country and then refusing the basic political rights, an attitude which made the question asked in 1910 of prospective Saint-Cyr cadets 'describe the different voting methods in France since 1789,' something of a joke. Jaurès, too, complained in the *Armée nouvelle* published in 1910 that the refusal to give professional soldiers the right to vote had entrenched a 'spirit of clan, routine and intrigue' in the forces.

Radicals hotly opposed political rights for officers: 'If by some misfortune they acquire any political influence ... the era of pronunciamientos will be open,' Ajam told parliament. However, pressure continued to mount, even from the Left, to give all soldiers the right to vote: 'The exercise of civic rights abolished by the accomplishment of the first of civic rights, that of defending the city of the Fatherland!' cried Guesde.

'What a contradiction not to say aberration.' The *France Militaire* claimed that deputies would only wake up to the needs of the army and soldiers recover their confidence once the officers conquered the votes.

Unions never really threatened to take root in the officer corps: a strong middle-class aversion to unions, respect for the traditional military hierarchy and, above all, government repression combined to weigh against the campaign for unionization. On 4 September 1912, Millerand simply forbade soldiers to join Driant's *ligue militaire*. But professional grievances continued, a smouldering revolt which could only be quenched by reforms to prove to officers that the army was back in favour with the power elite.

The unionization debate was important, not because unions threatened to sweep the officer corps but because they forced the government toward reforms destined to raise the prestige and the morale of professional soldiers, to demonstrate to officers that the government and the military chiefs, not union organizers, were their real patrons. Millerand's 24 July 1912 decree abolishing many of the advantages won by administration officers was designed to deflate the influence of the *Vincennoise*, demonstrating to combat officers that organized pressure group activities no longer influenced government military policy. 'I decided to use all my powers to finish with a practice which threatened to destroy the army,' he said of this decree. His 2 January 1913 order forbidding officers to contribute to any fund destined to further professional military interests tried to dry up money paid by administration officers to support pressure group activities.

'The Millerand reforms soon appeared to be sops to the General Staff who were seeking revenge for the Dreyfus affair and the republican military reforms carried out since 1899,' wrote George Michon. But Millerand's substantial programme of military reform was not a gift from conservative politicians to professional soldiers, an attempt to tip the scales against the 'nation-in-arms,' but was forced upon them by the realization that unless steps were taken to rectify basic professional grievances, the government might face a trauma of unionization in the forces which would make those of teachers and postal workers look trivial in comparison.

Millerand's reforms set out to remedy many of the basic grievances which fed the army's morale crisis and to hoist army prestige back onto the pedestal from which it had been tipped in 1899. The uniform provided a visible symbol of this determination. He reinstated the infantry epaulette abolished by Messimy and strictly curtailed the wearing of civilian dress, especially for NCOs and soldiers: 'Civilian dress can expose NCOs to unfortunate temptations and push them to expenses which they cannot afford,' he wrote. 'These temptations are especially troublesome for young NCOs.'

This coupling of the uniform with military prestige had unfortunate consequences, for it undercut attempts to introduce a camouflaged battledress adopted by most other European armies before 1914. The question had been under study since 1899, and in 1911 three regiments were kitted out with a less target-worthy green for the autumn manoeuvres. The Right, however, denounced any attempt to put the traditional red trousers in storage as a deliberate coup against military panache. The *Echo de Paris* typically believed the dull colours to be the fruits of a Masonic plot: 'The camouflaged uniform . . . seems calculated to diminish (the army's) already compromised prestige,' it complained on 2 October 1911. 'Thus the goals of the masonic covens are achieved.' The green uniform was discarded in December 1911 after Clémentel, the budget reporter, complained that the camouflaged uniform 'went against both French taste and against the needs of the army. . . . The red trousers have something national about them.' War Minister Etienne was more categorical: 'Abolish red trousers?' he asked the parliamentary army committee in 1913. 'No! Red trousers, c'est la France!' Credits for camouflaged uniforms were voted only 15 days before the outbreak of war.

Millerand turned his attention to rebuilding officer corps solidarity badly shaken since 1899. In July 1912 he re-established the obligatory mess for bachelor lieutenants, abolished by André in 1903 after a poll of corps commanders found only one who opposed it. He also attempted to tighten army discipline. Radicals had set their sights on a root and branch reform of the court martial since the Dreyfus affair. In November 1912, Millerand intervened in the Senate to modify reforms proposed by the Chamber to send many military cases to civil tribunals and considerably soften the penalties. 'Even Switzerland has court martials,' he told senators. Court martials were reprieved by the German attack of 1914. Millerand also upset a 1905 law which had dumped many men convicted of civilian crimes straight into the regiments rather than into the disciplinary *bataillons d'Afrique*, leading many to associate the increasing indiscipline in the forces with the influx of men with prison records. Discipline companies attached to each regiment to take men who bent unwillingly to military life were reorganized in areas away from the civilian population and more suitable for training. Corporals, sergeants and lieutenants had the right to punish soldiers, removed in May 1910, restored on the condition that each punishment was confirmed by the company commander after hearing the soldier: 'The right to punish is a corollary . . . which must be considered one of the prerogatives inseparable from authority,' read the 13 May 1912 decree. However, officers were required to keep some of their number on duty in the barracks at all times.

The abusive application of the other Radical reforms was also brought to heel. Co-operatives set up by André both to keep soldiers off the streets and to teach them the value of common enterprise had, Millerand complained, 'exceeded little by little the precise and limited goals established by . . . my predecessors.' Once officers realized the enormous profits to be made, co-operatives spread like wildfire and with them incidents of drunkenness and, to a lesser degree, graft. Charles Humbert complained that the co-operatives, originally meant to be morally uplifting, had degenerated into low cabarets 'where the soldiers stroll from one to another in a sort of Grand Duke's round with the corporals leading the dance. The cases of drunkenness are numerous and . . . alcoholism replaces the games of cards, backgammon and billiards which we thought we were encouraging.' Humbert also complained that they creamed off men, especially NCOs, who would be more usefully employed in training. Millerand limited each regiment to one co-operative, forbade the sale of alcoholic drinks formerly permitted mainly to boost the receipts of depressed south-western wine growers and ordered profits to be paid into regimental funds or beneficial activities rather than into soldiers' pockets. He also gave the right to permit leave, especially for agricultural work, back to regimental commanders. A 23 August 1910 circular had required prefects to determine which soldiers would be permitted home for the harvests. On 28 June 1912, several deputies claimed that this system had led to abuse, with the best-connected rather than the most needy allowed home.

Millerand was forced to resign on 12 January 1913 after the reintegration into the territorial army railway troops of Lieutenant Colonel du Paty de Clam, a prominent anti-Dreyfusard retired from the army in 1906, provoked a political storm among deputies who claimed that Millerand was handing the army to the forces of reaction. In his defence, Millerand pointed out that he was simply honouring a promise made by his two immediate predecessors to admit du Paty de Clam into the territorials if he dropped a standing complaint against the war ministry. Millerand stuck on a 'question of honour' and so forfeited his portfolio. Paléologue blamed Poincaré's 'inexcusable weakness' for Millerand's departure; 'The effect abroad of Millerand's brusque resignation is deplorable,' he told Briand. 'They will be dancing in Berlin.'

Historians have claimed that the passage of Messimy and Millerand through the rue Saint-Dominique had a 'tonic effect' upon army morale. Certainly, the *Porte-Voix* noticed a revival of morale in the army in 1912, stimulated by fears of war in the population and by a renewed interest in military reform in government circles. But while ministry officers and generals close to power perhaps appreciated a new determination to bolster national defence, it is unlikely that this filtered through to provincial garrisons. Eugen Weber noted that the Nationalist Revival was a Parisian phenomenon which only occasionally touched the provinces. Military newspapers, even the pro-government *France Militaire*, continued to point out that military life had retained all its servitudes but little of its grandeur. While Messimy's reform of the high command did something to prepare the army to counter the Schlieffen plan,[6] officers could not be expected to take to their bosom a man who had pitched his political appeal on the defiance of his military superiors: 'Jealous of their stars, this ex-captain of chasseurs à pied treated our generals as underlings without importance,' the *Porte-Voix* complained after the fall of Messimy's ministry. He was remembered not for his reorganization of the high command but for his request for prefectorial reports on the political opinions of officers and even the religious habits of their wives: '(The officer) is fed up with knowing that his career, already difficult enough, is at the mercy of information taken from unknown sources,' the *Porte-Voix* wrote on 12 January 1912. Emile Mayer thought Messimy: 'a light-weight politician, inconsistent, who believed that his time spent in the army and the two years at the Ecole de guerre should be taken seriously and who took himself for a real soldier.' According to his son Jacques, Alexandre Millerand believed Messimy to be 'un agité, un peu fou' (an excitable man, a bit crazy), an opinion given substance by Messimy's repeated letters to Joffre during 1914, demanding that officers found wanting be dragged before a firing squad. Historians have claimed that Millerand courted army popularity by acting as the agent for the desires of the high command. However, Joffre argued that Millerand did not consult his generals enough: one of his first acts in January 1912 was to slash a promised 240 million francs in extra credits, earmarked for vital improvements in artillery and training camps painfully squeezed out of Messimy, to 50 million after a single tête-à-tête with Finance Minister Krantz.

Nor were many of Millerand's reforms popular in the forces, however well intentioned or useful they might have been. The obligation to remain in barracks at night, the restrictions placed upon the wearing of civilian clothes, garrison rotations which hit the pockets of married officers and NCOs, the abolition of the right to see personal files and charges of promotional favouritism which were thought especially bad under Messimy, caused the *Porte-Voix* to lump Millerand with the worst war ministers: 'Millerand's work can be summed up in a few lines,' it wrote on 20 January 1913. 'He looked to terrorize officers by every means. Did he succeed? Yes!'

Raoul Girardet believed that the army recovered quickly from a 'brief' crisis at the beginning of the century. Rather, the Dreyfus affair can be seen as the beginning of a long crisis of morale which continues even today, a period only briefly punctuated by the Great War. After a very short victory celebration in 1918, the army again fell from fashion, attacked from the Left, held in low esteem by the middle class and stumbling from defeat to defeat.

'Millerand, at the ministry of war, was doing his best to save the confidence of the people in its army and of the army in itself,' wrote Weber. But the confidence of many professional soldiers in the government remained low. The three-year-law riots of 1913 demonstrated that officers had yet to shake out the wrinkles of the morale crisis and that their authority over their troops wobbled even in the patriotic eastern garrisons. Coming on the heels of a year of intense agitation surrounding the Aernoult affair, which saw over 100,000 people attend the dead soldier's funeral, the three-year-law riots revealed an army whose nerves were still frayed. On 29 March 1913, meetings were held through France to protest against the government's proposed additional service year. When the cabinet announced in May that conscripts would be retained in the forces beyond their statutory two years' service, several garrisons erupted with discontent. In Toul, 200 soldiers shouted "Hou! Hou! Les trois ans!' and dispersed only after 25 were arrested. Soldiers at Belfort and Nancy sang the *Internationale*. Both Rodez and Mâcon witnessed demonstrations by up to 300 soldiers. Twenty garrisons reported serious trouble while many others recorded a 'restlessness' which threatened to break into open revolt.

Noting the presence in many infected eastern garrisons of large contingents of Parisians, officials suspected that anti-militarists had carefully prepared the ground for these revolts. 'We are not faced with a military mutiny, but with a political movement,' General Pau, sent to investigate the disorders, reported. Pichon told Paléologue that the *CGT* (the *conseil générale du travail*, a large conglomeration of trade unions) had stirred the conscripts' revolt while the police reckoned that 'the incidents at Toul and Belfort, which will probably occur in other garrisons, are nothing but the logical outcome of propaganda.' Many Paris newspapers also bought and sold an anti-militarist conspiracy.

On 25 May, the minister of the interior asked prefects to forward the names of known anti-militarists serving in the troubled regiments and lists of *Bourses du travail* or *Unions des syndicats* in garrison towns. One Paris regiment claimed to have 17 syndicalists in its ranks. Otherwise only one of 28 regiments which had experienced trouble listed as many as two known anti-militarists; four regiments had one each. Of 20 garrison towns reporting trouble, only five had a *Bourse du travail* and six a *Union des syndicats*. Toul and Rodez, where the worst disorders had been reported, listed no militant anti-militarists either in the regiments or in the civilian population. The trial of five soldiers accused of leading the demonstrations at Toul revealed that they had no anti-militarists nor trade union connections but were exemplary soldiers. The riots appear to have been a spontaneous eruption of discontent against the announcement of extended service.

Officials, however, remained on their guard, convinced that anti-militarists stood behind the troubles. Paris police raided anti-militarist haunts on 6 June, and when the Left announced plans for large 1 October demonstrations to coincide with the normal departure date of the class of 1910, the war minister, acting on rumours that a large demonstration was being prepared in the 162nd infantry at Verdun, ordered an enquiry in to the morale of the eastern garrisons. Police reported that army morale was good, but urged the government to set a definite liberation date for the 1910 class. Poincaré predicted mass desertions on the day the conscript class should be liberated. On 2 October, the day after the class should have been sent home, the prefect of the Haute-Sâone reported that no *CGT* agents had turned up to incite soldiers and that garrisons had remained calm.

Historians have tended to skip over the 1913 riots, ignoring them as slight ripples in the mounting tide of the Nationalist Revival. But while the riots were undoubtedly isolated events springing from a very understandable disinclination on the part of many conscripts to remain under the colours indefinitely, many at the time saw the riots as cast-iron proof of the progress of anti-militarism in the French ranks and of the basic lack of patriotism in the country: 'Incidents of collective insubordination are multiplying to a terrifying degree,' one German newspaper reported to its readers. 'This wave of anti-militarism demonstrates how much patriotic sentiment has declined in France. The Kaiser was delighted that a measure so obviously calculated to show French resolve in the face of German military expressionism had backfired; 'How can you ally with the French?' he asked the Czar, on a visit to Berlin in May 1913. 'Don't you see that the Frenchman is no longer capable of becoming a soldier?' Poincaré was thrown into a depression so black that he even threatened to ask his arch-enemy Clemenceau, 'as patriotic as the Jacobins of 1793,' to form a government if Barthou were overthrown on the three-year-law.

The riots also revealed an officer corps whose faith in itself and in its leaders had not been strengthened by the Nationalist Revival. For many, 1913 was simply 1907 six years on: 'I was saddened and struck during the recent mutinies less by the anger of the soldiers than by the reserve of the officers,' wrote Edmond de Mesnil. 'They seemed to me to lack initiative and decisiveness. . . . I believe that their failure to act and their resignation revealed a fear of responsibilities which betrays a crisis of morale.'

Typically, the government blamed the officers for failing to snuff out the mutiny rather than their own ill-advised decision to retain the 1910 conscript class indefinitely. War Minister Etienne demanded a list of officers 'remote' from their men and tightened surveillance in barracks: more officers were kept on duty at night, leave was suspended and restrictions placed upon the wearing of civilian clothes. Several regiments were transferred to Algeria and Corsica and a double dose of training was ordered for others. 'In some places, the life of officers and NCOs has become hell,' the *Porte-Voix* complained on 1 July.

In the final analysis, the Nationalist Revival, far from restoring the army's confidence, appeared only to emphasize how far army morale had slipped: military unions, continued resignations of well-qualified officers, especially polytechnicians, low pay, slow promotion, a shortfall in NCO recruitment and the widely held belief that many regiments were rotten with anti-militarism as shown by the 1913 riots all demonstrated that morale had not crawled from the abyss into which it had fallen after 1900. Had politicians really looked to conquer military affection, they should have rewritten Clemenceau's deeply resented precedence decree of 1907. But even Millerand did not alter that. Professional soldiers might be forgiven for failing to distinguish the Messimys and Millerands, who for years carried the torch of anti-militarism, from those who now claimed to be stoking the flames of French patriotism.

Nor did the Nationalist Revival restore the authority of the high command. It is simply ludicrous to suggest, as does Ralston, that Joffre was more powerful than Moltke. The government may have become reconciled in the face of the growing German threat to name a chief of the general staff. But Joffre's authority was hedged by so many safeguards—not the least of which was his personality and lack of experience—that the army continued to function, or not to function, largely as before. War ministers and ministry officials often simply ignored him. For his part Joffre considered himself simply as 'a direction equal to other directions,' who could request and supplicate, but whose ability to command was circumscribed.

Notes

From Douglas Porch, *The March to the Marne: The French Army, 1871–1914*, chapter 9: The Army and the Nationalist Revival (Cambridge: Cambridge University Press, 1981), pp. 169–90. Reprinted with the permission of Cambridge University Press.

1. In 1905 and 1911 two diplomatic crises over Morocco increased tensions between Germany and France. In both cases, the Germans sought to use Moroccan ports as German naval bases. The French, who had declared a protectorate over Morocco, reacted sharply. In both cases, British support for France helped to undermine German plans.

2. With Franco-German tensions rising the French narrowly and controversially passed a law extending the term of mandatory military service from two to three years.

3. The Dreyfus affair of the 1890s pitted conservative supporters of the army against Republican defenders of Jewish Captain Alfred Dreyfus, who had been wrongly accused and convicted of treason.

4. The Third Republic refers to the political system that governed France from 1877 until 1940.

5. Under Minister of War General Louis André, the French government sought unsuccessfully to remove all influences of Catholicism from the senior ranks of the French officer corps.

6. The German war plan that called for Germany to concentrate seven of its eight field armies against France no matter what the cause of the war.

Two

Soldiers

The Good Soldier Schweik

Jaroslav Hašek

"So they've killed Ferdinand," said the charwoman to Mr. Schweik who, having left the army many years before, when a military medical board had declared him to be chronically feeble-minded, earned a livelihood by the sale of dogs—repulsive mongrel monstrosities for whom he forged pedigrees. Apart from this occupation, he was afflicted with rheumatism, and was just rubbing his knees.

"Which Ferdinand, Mrs. Müller?" asked Schweik, continuing to massage his knees. "I know two Ferdinands. One of them does jobs for Prusa the chemist, and one day he drank a bottle of hair oil by mistake; and then there's Ferdinand Kokoska who goes around collecting manure. They wouldn't be any great loss, either of 'em."

"No, it's the Archduke Ferdinand, the one from Konopiste, you know, Mr. Schweik, the fat, pious one."

"Good Lord!" exclaimed Schweik. "That's a fine thing. And where did this happen?"

"They shot him at Sarajevo with a revolver, you know. He was riding there with his Archduchess in a motor car."

"Just fancy that now, Mrs. Müller, in a motor car. Ah, a gentleman like him can afford it and he never thinks how a ride in a motor car like that can end up badly. And at Sarajevo in the bargain, that's in Bosnia, Mrs. Müller. I expect the Turks did it. I reckon we never ought to have taken Bosnia and Herzegovina away from them. And there you are, Mrs. Müller. Now the Archduke's in a better land. Did he suffer long?"

"The Archduke was done for on the spot. You know, people didn't ought to mess about with revolvers. They're dangerous things, that they are. Not long ago there was another gentleman down our way larking about with a revolver and he shot a whole family as well as the house porter, who went to see who was shooting on the third floor."

"There's some revolvers, Mrs. Müller, that won't go off, even if you tried till you was dotty. There's lots like that. But they're sure to have bought something better than that for the Archduke, and I wouldn't mind betting, Mrs. Müller, that the man who did it put on his best clothes for the job. You know, it wants a bit of doing to shoot an archduke; it's not like when a poacher shoots a gamekeeper. You have to find out how to get at him; you can't reach an important man like that if you're dressed just anyhow. You have to wear a top hat or else the police'd run you in before you knew where you were."

"I hear there was a whole lot of 'em, Mr. Schweik."

"Why, of course, there was, Mrs. Müller," said Schweik, now concluding the massage of his knees. "If you wanted to kill an archduke or the Emperor, for instance, you'd naturally talk it over with somebody. Two heads are better than one. One gives one bit of advice, another gives another, and so the good work prospers, as the hymn says. The chief thing is to keep on the watch till the gentleman you're after rides past. . . . but there's plenty more of them waiting their turn for it. You mark my words, Mrs. Müller, they'll get the Czar and Czarina yet, and maybe, though let's hope not, the Emperor himself, now that they've started with his uncle. The old chap's got a lot of enemies. More than Ferdinand had. A little while ago a gentleman in the saloon bar was saying that there'd come a time when all the emperors would get done in one after another, and that not all their bigwigs suchlike would save them. Then he couldn't pay for his drinks and the landlord had to have him run in, and he gave him a smack in the jaw and two to the policeman. After that they had to strap him down in the police ambulance, just to bring him to his senses. Yes, Mrs. Müller, there's queer goings on nowadays; that there is. That's another loss to Austria. When I was in the army there was a private who shot a captain. He loaded his rifle and went into the orderly room. They told him to clear out, but he kept on saying that he must speak to the captain. Well, the captain came along and gave him a dose of c.b. Then he took his rifle and scored a fair bull's-eye. The bullet went right through the captain and when it came out the other side, it did some damage in the orderly room in the bargain. It smashed a bottle of ink and the ink got spilled all over some regimental records."

"And what happened to the private?" asked Mrs. Müller after a while, when Schweik was getting dressed.

"He hanged himself with a pair of braces," said Schweik, brushing his bowler hat. "And the braces wasn't even his. He borrowed them from a jailer, making out that his trousers were coming down. You can't blame him for not waiting till they shot him. You know, Mrs. Müller, it's enough to turn anyone's head, being in a fix like that. The jailer lost his rank and got six months as well. But he didn't serve his time. He ran away to Switzerland and now he does a bit of preaching for some church or other. There ain't many honest people about nowadays, Mrs. Müller. I expect that the Archduke was taken in by the man who shot him. He saw a chap standing there and thought: Now there's a decent fellow, cheering me and all. And then the chap did him in. Did he give him one or several?"

"The newspaper says, Mr. Schweik, that the Archduke was riddled with bullets. He emptied the whole lot into him."

"That was mighty quick work, Mrs. Müller, mighty quick. I'd buy a Browning for a job like that. It looks like a toy, but in a couple of minutes you could shoot twenty archdukes with it, thin or fat. Although between ourselves, Mrs. Müller, it's easier to hit a fat archduke than a thin one. You may remember the time they shot their king in Portugal. He was a fat fellow. Of course, you don't expect a king to be thin. Well, now I'm going to call around at The Flagon and if anybody comes for that little terrier I took the advance for, you can tell 'em I've got him at my dog farm in the country. I just cropped his ears and now he mustn't be taken away till his ears heal up or else he'd catch cold in them. Give the key to the house porter."

There was only one customer at The Flagon. This was Bretschneider, a plain-clothes policeman who was on secret service work. Palivec, the landlord, was washing glasses and Bretschneider vainly endeavored to engage him in a serious conversation.

"We're having a fine summer," was Bretschneider's overture to a serious conversation.

"All damn rotten," replied Palivec, putting the glasses away into a cupboard.

"That's a fine thing they've done for us at Sarajevo," Bretschneider observed, with his hopes rather dashed.

"What Sarajevo's that?" inquired Palivec. "D'you mean the wineshop at Nusle? They have a rumpus there every day. Well, you know what sort of place Nusle is."

"No, I mean Sarajevo in Bosnia. They shot the Archduke Ferdinand there. What do you think of that?"

"I never shove my nose into that sort of thing. I'm hanged if I do," primly replied Mr. Palivec, lighting his pipe. "Nowadays, it's as much as your life's worth to get mixed up in them. I've got my business to see to. When a customer comes in and orders beer, why, I just serve him his drink. But Sarajevo or politics or a dead archduke, that's not for the likes of us, unless we want to end up doing time."

Bretschneider said no more, but stared disappointedly around the empty bar.

"You used to have a picture of the Emperor hanging here," he began again presently, "just at the place where you've got a mirror now."

"Yes, that's right," replied Mr. Palivec. "It used to hang there and the flies left their trade-mark on it, so I put it away into the lumber room. You see, somebody might pass a remark about it and then there might be trouble. What use is it to me?"

"Sarajevo must be a rotten sort of place, eh, Mr. Palivec?"

Mr. Palivec was extremely cautious in answering this deceptively straightforward question. "At this time of the year it's damned hot in Bosnia and Herzegovina. When I was in the army there, we always had to put ice on our company officer's head."

"What regiment did you serve in, Mr. Palivec?"

"I can't remember a little detail like that. I never cared a damn about the whole business, and I wasn't inquisitive about it," replied Mr. Palivec. "It doesn't do to be so inquisitive."

Bretschneider stopped talking once and for all, and his woe-begone expression brightened up only on the arrival of Schweik, who came in and ordered black beer with the remark: "At Vienna they're in mourning today."

Bretschneider's eyes began to gleam with hope. He said curtly: "There are ten black flags at Konopiste."

"There ought to be twelve," said Schweik, when he had taken a gulp.

"What makes you think it's twelve?" asked Bretschneider.

"To make it a round number, a dozen. That's easier to reckon out and things always come cheaper by the dozen," replied Schweik.

This was followed by a long silence, which Schweik himself interrupted with a sigh. "Well, he's in a better land now, God rest his soul. He didn't live to be Emperor. When I was in the army, there was a general who fell off his horse and got killed as quiet as could be. They wanted to help him back onto his horse and when they went to lift him up, they saw he was stone dead. And he was just going to be promoted to field marshal. It happened during an army inspection. No good ever comes of those inspections. There was an inspection of some sort or other at Sarajevo, too. I remember once at an inspection like that there was twenty buttons missing from my tunic and I got two weeks solitary confinement for it, and I spent two days of it tied up hand and foot. But there's got to be discipline in the army, or else nobody'd care a rap what he did. Our company commander, he always used to say to us, 'There's got to be discipline, you thickheaded louts, or else you'd be crawling about like monkeys on trees, but the army'll make men of you, you thickheaded boobies.' And isn't it true? Just imagine a park and a soldier without discipline on every tree. That's what I was always most afraid of."

"That business at Sarajevo," Bretschneider resumed, "was done by the Serbs."

"You're wrong there," replied Schweik, "it was done by the Turks, because of Bosnia and Herzegovina."

And Schweik expounded his views of Austrian international policy in the Balkans. The Turks were the losers in 1912 against Serbia, Bulgaria, and Greece. They had wanted Austria to help them and when this was not done, they had shot Ferdinand.

"Do you like the Turks," said Schweik, turning to Palivec. "Do you like that heathen pack of dogs? You don't, do you?"

"One customer's the same as another customer," said Palivec, "even if he's a Turk. People like us who've got their business to look after can't be bothered with politics. Pay for your drink and sit down and say what you like. That's my principle. It's all the same to me whether our Ferdinand was done in by a Serb or a Turk, a Catholic or a Moslem, an anarchist or a young Czech liberal."

"That's all well and good, Mr. Palivec," remarked Bretschneider, who had regained hope that one or other of these two could be caught out, "but you'll admit that it's a great loss to Austria."

Schweik replied for the landlord. "Yes, there's no denying it. A fearful loss. You can't replace Ferdinand by any sort of tomfool. Still, he ought to have been a bit fatter."

"What do you mean?" asked Bretschneider, growing alert.

"What do I mean?" replied Schweik composedly. "Why, only just this: If he'd been fatter, he'd certainly have had a stroke earlier, when he chased the old women away at Konopiste, when they were gathering firewood and mushrooms on his preserves there, and then he wouldn't have died such a shocking death. When you come to think of it, for him, the Emperor's uncle,[1] to get shot like that, oh, it's shocking, that it is, and the newspapers are full of it. But what I say is, I wouldn't like to be the Archduke's widow.[2] What's she going to do now? Marry some other archduke? What good would come of that? She'd take another trip to Sarajevo with him and be left a widow for the second time. A good many years ago there was a gamekeeper at Zlim. He was called Pindour. A rum name, eh? Well, he was shot by poachers and left a widow with two children. A year later she married another gamekeeper from Mydlovary. And they shot him, too. Then she got married a third time and said: 'All good things go by threes. If this turns out badly, I don't know what I shall do.' Blessed if they didn't shoot him, too, and by that time she'd had six children with all those gamekeepers. So she went to the Lord of the Manor himself at Hluboka and complained of the trouble she'd had with the gamekeepers. Then she was advised to try Jares, a pond keeper.

Well, you wouldn't believe it, but he got drowned while he was fishing and she'd had two children with him. Then she married a pig gelder from Vodnany and one night he hit her with an axe and gave himself up to the police. When they hanged him in Pisek, he said he had no regrets and on top of that he passed some very nasty remarks about the Emperor."

"Do you happen to know what he said?" inquired Bretschneider in a hopeful voice.

"I can't tell you that, because nobody had the nerve to repeat it. But they say it was something pretty awful, and that one of the justices, who was in court at the time, went mad when he heard it, and they're still keeping him in solitary confinement so as it shouldn't get known. It wasn't just the ordinary sort of nasty remark like people make when they're drunk."

"What sort of nasty remarks about the Emperor do people make when they're drunk?" asked Bretschneider.

"Come, come, gentlemen, talk about something else," said the landlord, "that's the sort of thing I don't like. One word leads to another and then it gets you into trouble."

"What sort of nasty remarks about the Emperor do people make when they're drunk?" repeated Bretschneider.

"All sorts. Just you have too much to drink and get them to play the Austrian hymn and you'll see what you'll start saying. You'll think of such a lot of things about the Emperor that if only half of them were true, it'd be enough to disgrace him for the rest of his life. Not that the old gentleman deserves it. Why, look at it this way. He lost his son Rudolf at a tender age when he was in the prime of life. His wife was stabbed with a file; then Johann Orth got lost and his brother, the Emperor of Mexico, was shot in a fortress up against a wall. Now, in his old age, they've shot his uncle. Things like that get on a man's nerves. And then some drunken chap takes it into his head to call him names. If war was to break out today, I'd go of my own accord and serve the Emperor to my last breath."

Schweik took a deep gulp and continued, "Do you think the emperor's going to put up with that sort of thing? Little do you know him. You mark my words, there's got to be war with the Turks. Kill my uncle, would you? Then take this smack in the jaw for a start. Oh, there's bound to be war. Serbia and Russia'll help us. There won't half be a bust-up."

At this prophetic moment Schweik was really good to look upon. His artless countenance, smiling like the full moon, beamed with enthusiasm. The whole thing was so utterly clear to him.

"Maybe," he continued his delineation of the future of Austria, "if we have war with the Turks, the Germans'll attack us, because the Germans and the Turks stand by each other. They're a low lot, the scum of the earth. Still, we can join France, because they've had a grudge against Germany ever since '71.[3] And then there'll be lively doings. There's going to be war. I can't tell you more than that."

Bretschneider stood up and said solemnly, "You needn't say any more. Follow me into the passage and there I'll say something to you."

Schweik followed the plain-clothes policeman into the passage where a slight surprise awaited him when his fellow toper showed him his badge and announced that he was now arresting him and would at once convey him to the police headquarters.

Schweik endeavored to explain that there must be some mistake; that he was entirely innocent; that he hadn't uttered a single word capable of offending anyone.

But Bretschneider told him that he had actually committed several penal offences, among them being high treason.

Then they returned to the saloon bar and Schweik said to Mr. Palivec, "I've had five beers and a couple of sausages with a roll. Now let me have a cherry brandy and I must be off, as I'm arrested."

Bretschneider showed Mr. Palivec his badge, looked at Mr. Palivec for a moment, and then asked, "Are you married?"

"Yes."

"And can your wife carry on the business during your absence?"

"Yes."

"That's all right, then, Mr. Palivec," said Bretschneider breezily. "Tell your wife to step this way. Hand the business over to her, and we'll come for you in the evening."

"Don't you worry about that," Schweik comforted him. "I'm being run in only for high treason."

"But what about me?" lamented Mr. Palivec. "I've been so careful what I said."

Bretschneider smiled and said triumphantly, "I've got you for saying that the flies left their trade-mark on the Emperor. You'll have all that stuff knocked out of your head."

And Schweik left The Flagon in the company of the plain-clothes policeman. When they reached the street Schweik, fixing his good-humored smile upon Bretschneider's countenance, inquired, "Shall I get off the pavement?"

"How d'you mean?"

"Why, I thought now I'm arrested I mustn't walk on the pavement."

When they were passing through the entrance to the police headquarters, Schweik said, "Well, that passed off very nicely. Do you often go to The Flagon?"

And while they were leading Schweik into the reception bureau, Mr. Palivec at The Flagon was handing over the business to his weeping wife, whom he was comforting in his own special manner. "Now stop crying and don't make all that row. What can they do to me on account of the Emperor's portrait where the flies left their trade-mark?"

And thus Schweik, the good soldier, intervened in the World War in that pleasant, amiable manner which was so peculiarly his. It will be of interest to historians to know that he saw far into the future. If the situation subsequently developed otherwise than he expounded it at The Flagon, we must take into account the fact that he lacked a preliminary diplomatic training.

NOTES

From Jaroslav Hašek, *The Good Soldier Schweik* (New York: Crowell, 1974), pp. 21–29.

1. The archduke was, in fact, the emperor's nephew.
2. Archduchess Sophie was sitting next to her husband and died at the same assassin's hand.
3. In 1871 the Germans seized the French provinces of Alsace and Lorraine.

Her Privates We

Frederic Manning

Bourne roused himself, and, after a few minutes of dubious consciousness, sat up and looked round him, at his sleeping companions, and then at the rifles stacked round the test-pole, and the ring of boots surrounding the rifle-butts. His right hand finding the opening in his shirt front, he scratched pleasurably at his chest. He was dirty, and he was lousy; but at least, and he thanked God for it, he was not scabby. Half a dozen men from Headquarter Company, including Shem as a matter of course, had been sent off yesterday to a casualty clearing station near Acheux, suffering or rejoicing, according to their diverse temperaments, with the itch. The day after their arrival at Mailly-Maillet, the medical officer had held what the men described irreverently as a prick-inspection. He was looking for definite symptoms of something he expected to find, and because his inquest had been narrowed down to a single question, it may have seemed a little cursory. The men stood in a line, their trousers and underpants having been dropped round their ankles, and as the doctor passed them, in the words of the regimental sergeant-major, they 'lifted the curtain,' that is to say the flap of the shirt, so as to expose their bellies.

Scratching his chest, Bourne considered the boots: if a sword were the symbol of battle, boots were certainly symbols of war; and because by his bedside at home there had always been a copy of the Authorised Version, he remembered now the verse about the warrior's boots that stamped in the tumult, and the mantle drenched with blood being all but for burning, and fuel for the fire. He lit a cigarette. It was, anyway, the method by which he intended to dispose of his own damned kit, if he should survive his present obligations; but the chance of survival seeming to his cooler judgment somewhat thin, he ceased spontaneously to be interested in it. His mind did not dismiss, it ignored, the imminent possibility of its own destruction. He looked again with a little more sympathy on his prone companions, wondering that sleep should make their faces seem so enigmatic and remote; and still scratching and rubbing his chest, he returned to his contemplation of the boots. Then, when he had smoked his cigarette down to his fingers, he rubbed out the glowing end in the earth, slipped out of the blanket, and reached for his trousers. He moved as quickly as a cat in dressing, and now, taking his mess-tin, he opened the flap of the tent, and went out into the cool morning freshness. He could see between the sparse trees to the cookers, drawn up a little off the road. The wood in which they were encamped was just behind Mailly-Maillet, in an angle formed by two roads, one rising over the slope to Mailly-

Maillet, and the other skirting the foot of the hill towards Hedauville. It was on a rather steep reverse slope, which gave some protection from shell-fire and there were a few shelter-trenches, which had been hastily and rather inefficiently dug, as a further protection. It was well screened from observation. The trees were little more than sapling, young beech, birch, and larch, with a few firs, poorly grown, but so far un-shattered. Bourne strolled carelessly down to the cookers.

"Good morning, Corporal; any tea going?"

Williams stretched out his hand for the mess-tin, filled it to the brim, and then, after handing it back to Bourne, went on with his work, without a word. Bourne stayed there, sipping the scalding brew.

"Go up the line, last night?" Williams inquired at last.

"Carrying-party," answered Bourne, who found his Dixie so hot he could scarcely hold it, so he was protecting his hands with a dirty handkerchief. "I was out of luck. I was at the end, and when they had loaded me up with the last box of ammunition, they found there was a buckshee box of Verey lights to go, too. The officer said he thought I might carry those as well; and being a young man of rather tedious wit, he added that they were very light. I suppose I am damned clumsy, but one of those bloody boxes is enough for me, and I decided to dump one at the first opportunity. Then Mr Sothern came back along the top of the communication trench, and, finding me weary and heavily laden, said all sorts of indiscreet things about everybody concerned. 'Dump them, you bloody fool, dump them!' he shouted. I rather deprecated any extreme measures. 'Give me that bloody box,' he insisted. As he seemed really angry about it, I handed him up the box of ammunition, as it was the heavier of the two. He streaked off into the darkness to get back to the head of the party, with his stick in one hand, and a box of ammo in the other. I like these conscientious young officers, Corporal."

"'e's a nice chap, Mr Sothern," observed Williams, with a face of immovable melancholy.

"Quite," Bourne agreed. "However, there's a big dug-out in Legend Trench, and between that and the corner of Flag Alley I saw a box of ammunition that had been dumped. It was lying by the duck-boards. It may have been the one I gave Mr Sothern: 'lost owing to the exigencies of active service.' That's what the court of inquiry said about Patsy Pope's false teeth."

Williams went on with his work.

"It won't be long before you lads are for it again," he said in his quiet way.

"No," said Bourne, reluctantly, for there was a note of furtive sympathy in Williams' voice which embarrassed him.

"The whole place is simply lousy with guns," continued the cook.

"Why the hell can't you talk of something else?" exclaimed Bourne, impatiently. "Jerry chased us all the way home last night. Mr Sothern, who knows no more about the bloody map than I do, tried a short cut, and wandered off in the direction of Colincamps, until we fetched up in front of one of our field batteries, and were challenged. Then an officer came up and remonstrated with him. After that, when we got on the road again and Fritz started sending a few across, you should have seen us! Leaning over like a field of corn in the wind."

"A lot o' them are new to it, yet," said Williams, tolerantly. "You might take a drop o' tea up to the corporal, will you? 'e's a nice chap, Corporal 'amley. I gave 'im some o' your toffees last night, an' we was talking about you. I'll fill it, in case you feel like some more."

Bourne took it, thanking him, and lounged off. There was now a little more movement in the camp, and when he got back to his own tent he found all the occupants awake, enjoying a moment of indecision before they elected to dress. He poured some tea into Corporal Hamley's tin, and then gave some to Martlow, and there was about a third left.

"Who wants tea?" he said.

"I do," said Weeper Smart, and in his blue shirt with cuffs unbuttoned and white legs sprawled out behind him, he lunged awkwardly across the tent, holding out his Dixie with one hand. Smart was an extraordinary individual, with the clumsy agility of one of the greater apes; though the carriage of his head rather suggested the vulture, for the neck projected from wide, sloping shoulders, rounded to a stoop; the narrow forehead, above arched eyebrows, and the chin, under loose pendulous lips, both receded abruptly, and the large, fleshy beak, jutting forward between protruding blue eyes, seemed to weigh down the whole face. His skin was an unhealthy white, except at the top of the nose and about the nostrils, where it had a shiny redness, as though he suffered from an incurable cold: it was rather pimply. An almost complete beardlessness made the lack of pigmentation more marked, and even the fine, sandy hair of his head grew thinly. It would have been the face of an imbecile, but for the expression of unmitigated misery in it, or it would have been a tragic face if it had possessed any element of nobility; but it was merely abject, a mask of passive suffering, at once pitiful and repulsive. It was inevitable that men, living day by day with such a spectacle of woe, should learn in self-defence to deride it; and it was this sheer necessity which had impelled some cruel wit of the camp to fling at him the name of Weeper, and make that forlorn and cadaverous figure the butt of an endless jest. He gulped his tea, and his watery eyes turned towards Bourne with a cunning malevolence.

"What I say is, that if any o' us'ns tried scrounging around the cookers we'd be for it."

Bourne looked at him with a slightly contemptuous tolerance, gathered his shaving-tackle together, flung his dirty towel over his shoulder, and set off again in the direction of the cookers to scrounge for some hot water. He could do without the necessaries of life more easily than without some small comforts.

Breakfast over, they cleaned up and aired the tent, and almost immediately were told to fall in on parade with Headquarter Company. Captain Thompson, watching them fall in from the officers tents, knocked his pipe out against his stick, shoved it in his tunic pocket, and came up the hill, carrying his head at a rather thoughtful angle. He had a rather short, stocky figure, and a round bullet head; his face was always imperturbable, and his eyes quiet but observant. Sergeant-Major Corbett called the company to attention and Captain Thompson acknowledged the salute, and told the men to stand easy. Then he began to talk to them in a quiet unconventional way, as one whose authority was so unquestioned that the friendliness of his manner was not likely to be misunderstood. They had had a good rest, he said (as though he were talking to the same men who had fought their way, slowly and foot by foot, into Guillemont!), and now there was work in front of them: difficult and dangerous work: the business of killing as many superfluous Germans as possible. He would read out to them passages from the letter of instructions regarding the attack, which as fresh and reconditioned troops they would be called on soon to make. He read; and as he read his voice became rather monotonous, it lost the character of the man and seemed to come to them from a remote distance. The plan was handled in too abstract a way for the men to follow it; and their attention, in spite of the gravity with which they listened, was inclined to wander; or perhaps they refused to think of it except from the point of view of their own concrete and individual experience. Above his monotonous voice one could hear, now and again, a little wind stray down through the drying leaves of the trees. A leaf or two might flutter down, and scratch against the bark of trunk or boughs with a crackling papery rustle. Here and there he would stress a sentence ever so slightly, as though its significance would not be wasted on their minds, and their eyes would quicken, and lift towards him with a curious, almost an animal expression of patient wonder. It was strange to notice how a slight movement, even a break in the rhythm of their breathing, showed their feelings at certain passages.

". . . men are strictly forbidden to stop for the purpose of assisting wounded . . ."

The slight stiffening of the muscles may have been imperceptible, for the monotonous inflexion did not vary as the reader delivered a passage, in which it was stated, that the Staff considered they had made all the arrangements necessary to effect this humanitarian, but somewhat irrelevant, object.

". . . you may be interested to know," and this was slightly stressed, as though to overbear a doubt, "that it is estimated we shall have one big gun—I suppose that means hows, and heavies—for every hundred square yards of ground we are attacking."

An attack delivered on a front of twenty miles, if completely successful, would mean penetrating to a depth of from six to seven miles, and the men seemed to be impressed by the weight of metal with which it was intended to support them. Then the officer came to the concluding paragraph of the instructional letter.

"It is not expected that the enemy will offer any very serious resistance at this point . . ."

There came a whisper scarcely louder than a sigh.

"What fuckin' 'opes we've got!"

The still small voice was that of Weeper Smart, clearly audible to the rest of the section, and its effect was immediate. The nervous tension, which had gripped every man, was suddenly snapped, and the swift relief brought with it an almost hysterical desire to laugh, which it was difficult to suppress. Whether Captain Thompson also heard the voice of the Weeper, and what construction he may have placed on the sudden access of emotion in the ranks, it was impossible to say. Abruptly, he called them to attention, and after a few seconds, during which he stared at them impersonally, but with great severity, the men were dismissed. As they moved off, Captain Thompson called Corporal Hamley to him.

"Where will some of us poor buggers be come next Thursday?" demanded Weeper of the crowded tent, as he collapsed into his place; and looking at that caricature of grief, their laughter, high-pitched and sardonic, which had been stifled on parade, found vent.

"Laugh, you silly fuckers!" he cried in vehement rage. "Yes, you laugh now! You'll be laughing the other side o' your bloody mouths when you 'ear all Krupp's fuckin' iron-foundry comin' over! Laugh! One big gun to every bloody 'undred yards, an' don't expect any serious resistance from the enemy! Take us for a lot o' bloody kids, they do! 'aven't we been up the line and . . ."

"You shut your blasted mouth, see!" said the exasperated Corporal Hamley, stooping as he entered the tent, the lift of his head, with chin thrust forward as he stooped, giving him a more desperately aggressive appearance. "An' you let me 'ear you talkin' on parade again with an officer present and you'll be on the bloody mat, quick. See? You miserable bugger, you! A bloody cunt like you's sufficient to demoralize a whole fuckin' Army Corps. Got it? Get those buzzers out, and do some bloody work, for a change."

Exhausted by this unaccustomed eloquence, Corporal Hamley, white-lipped, glared round the tent, on innocent and guilty alike. Weeper gave him one glance of deprecatory grief, and relapsed into a prudent silence. The rest of the squad, all learners, settled themselves with a more deliberate obedience: there was no sense in encouraging Corporal Hamley to throw his weight about, just because he had wind up. They took up their pencils and paper, and looked at him a little coolly. Weeper was one of themselves. With the corporal sending on the buzzer, the class laboriously spelt out his messages. Then he tried two men with two instruments, one sending, and the other answering and repeating, while the rest of the squad recorded.

"You've been at this game before," he said to Weeper.

"I, Corporal?" said Weeper, with an innocence one could see was affected; "I've never touched one o' these things before."

"No?" said the corporal. "Ever worked in a telegraph office? You needn't try to come that game on me. I can tell by your touch."

He was not in a humour to be satisfied, and the men, thinking of the show they were in for, did not work well. A sullen humour spread among them. Bourne was the least satisfactory of all.

"You're just swinging' the lead," said Corporal Hamley. "Those of you who can't use a buzzer will be sent out as linesmen, or to help carry the bloody flapper."

Things went from bad to worse among them. There was a light drizzle of rain outside, and this gradually increased to a steady downpour. Their sullen humour deepened into resentment, fretting hopelessly in their minds; and the corporal's disapproval was expressed now and again with savage brevity. Then the stolid but perfectly cheerful face of Corporal Woods appeared between the flaps of the tent.

"Kin I 'ave six men off you for a fatigue, Corporal?" he asked pleasantly.

"You can take the whole fuckin' issue," said Corporal Hamley, with enthusiasm, throwing the buzzer down on his blankets with the air of a man who has renounced all hope.

Shem returned, wet and smelling of iodine, at dinner time. All that day it rained, and they kept to the tents, but their exasperation wore off, and the spirit of pessimism which had filled them became quiet, reflective, even serene, but without ceasing to be pessimism. Mr Rhys paid them a visit, and said, that, taking into account the interruption of their training by other duties, their progress had been fairly satisfactory. He, too, picked out Weeper Smart as an expert telegraphist, and Martlow as the aptest pupil in the class; as for the other new men, it would be some time before they were qualified for their duties. At a quarter to three he told the corporal that they might pack up for the day. If the weather had cleared they would have gone out with flags; but they had been on the buzzer all the mornings, and in the monotony of repeating the same practice, hour after hour, men lose interest and learn nothing. From outside came the dense unbroken murmur of the rain, which sometimes dwindled to a whispering rustle, through which one could hear heavy drops falling at curiously regular intervals from the trees on to the tent, or a bough laden with wet would sag slowly downward, to spill all it held in a sudden shower, and then lift up for more. These lulls were only momentary, and then the rain would increase in volume again until it became a low roar in which all lesser sounds were drowned. There was little wind.

Mr Rhys told them they might smoke, and stayed to talk with them for a little while. They all liked him, in spite of the erratic and hasty temper which left them a little uncertain as to what to make of him. From time to time, without putting aside anything of his prestige and authority over them, he would try to get in touch with them, and learn what they were thinking. Only a very great man can talk on equal terms with those in the lower ranks of life. He was neither sufficiently imaginative, nor sufficiently flexible in character, to succeed. He would unpack a mind rich in a curious lumber of chivalrous commonplaces, and give an air of unreality to values which for him, and for them all in varying measure, had the strength, if not altogether the substance, of fact. They did not really pause to weigh the truth or falsity of his opinions, which were simply without meaning for them. They only reflected that gentlefolk lived in circumstances very different from their own, and could afford strange luxuries. Probably only one thing he said interested them; and that was a casual remark, to the effect that, if the bad weather continued, the attack might have to be abandoned. At that, the face of Weeper Smart became suddenly illumined by an ecstasy of hope.

When at last Mr Rhys left them, they relaxed into ease with a sigh. Major Shadwell and Captain Malet they could understand, because each was what every private soldier is, a man in arms against a world, a man fighting desperately for himself, and conscious that, in the last resort, he stood alone; for such self-reliance lies at the very heart of comradeship. In so far as Mr Rhys had something of the same character, they respected him; but when he spoke to them of patriotism, sacrifice, and duty, he merely clouded and confused their vision.

"Chaps," said Weeper, suddenly, "for Christ's sake let's pray for rain!"

"What good would that do?" said Pacey, reasonably. "If they don't send us over the top here, they'll send us over somewhere else. It 'as got to be, an' if it 'as got to be, the sooner it's over an' done wi' the better. If we die, we die, an' it won't trouble nobody, leastways not for long it won't; an' if we don't die now, we'd 'ave to die some other time."

"What d'you want to talk about dyin' for?" said Martlow, resentfully, "I'd rather kill some other fucker first. I want to have my fling before I die, I do."

"If you want to pray, you 'ad better pray for the war to stop," continued Pacey, "so as we can all go back to our own 'omes in peace. I'm a married man wi' two children, an' I don't say I'm any better'n the next man, but I've a bit o' religion in me still, an' I don't hold wi' sayin' such things in jest."

"Aye," said Madeley, bitterly; "an' what good will all your prayin' do you? If there were any truth to religion, would there be a war, would God let it go on?"

"Some on us blame God for our own faults," said Pacey, coolly, "an' it were men what made the war. It's no manner o' use us sittin' 'ere pityin' ourselves, an' blamin' God for our own fault. I've got nowt to say again' Mr Rhys. 'e talks about liberty, an' fightin' for your country, an' posterity, an' so on; but what I want to know is what all us'ns are fightin' for . . ."

"We're fightin' for all we've bloody got," said Madeley, bluntly.

"An' that's sweet fuck all," said Weeper Smart. "A tell thee, that all a want to do is to save me own bloody skin. An' the first thing a do, when a go into t'line, is to find out where t' bloody dressing stations are; an' if a can get a nice blighty,[1] chaps, when once me face is turned towards home, I'm laughing. You won't see me bloody arse for dust. A'm not proud. A tell thee straight. Them as thinks different can 'ave all the bloody war they want, and me own share of it, too."

"Well, what the 'ell did you come out for?" asked Madeley.

Weeper lifted up a large, spade-like hand with the solemnity of one making an affirmation.

"That's where th'ast got me beat, lad," he admitted. "When a saw all them as didn' know any better'n we did joinin' up, an' a went walkin' out wi' me girl on Sundays, as usual, a just felt ashamed. An' a put it away, an' a put it away, until in th' end it got me down. A knew what it'd be, but it got the better o' me, an' then, like a bloody fool, a went an' joined up too. A were ashamed to be seen walkin' in the streets, a were. But a tell thee, now, that if a were once out o' these togs an' in civvies again, a wouldn't mind all the shame in the world; no, not if I 'ad to slink through all the back streets, an' didn' dare put me nose in t'Old Vaults again. A've no pride left in me now, chaps, an' that's the plain truth a'm tellin'. Let them as made the war come an' fight it, that's what a say."

"That's what I say, too," said Glazier, a man of about Madeley's age, with an air of challenge. Short, stocky, and ruddy like Madeley, he was of coarser grain, with an air of brutality that the other lacked: the kind of man who, when he comes to grips, kills, and grunts with pleasure in killing. "Why should us'ns fight an' be killed for all them bloody slackers at 'ome? It ain't right. No matter what they say, it ain't right. We're doin' our duty, an' they ain't, an' they're coinin' money while we get ten bloody frong a week. They don't care a fuck about us. Once we're in the army, they've got us by the balls. Talk about discipline! They don't try disciplinin' any o' them fuckin' civvies, do they? We want to put some o' them bloody politicians in the front line, an' see 'em shelled to shit. That'd buck their ideas up."

"I'm not fightin' for a lot o' bloody civvies," said Madeley, reasonably. "I'm fightin' for myself an' me own folk. It's all bloody fine sayin' let them as made the war fight it. 'twere Germany made the war."

"A tell thee," said Weeper, positively, "there are thousands o' poor buggers, over there in the German lines, as don' know, no more'n we do ourselves, what it's all about."

"Then what do the silly fuckers come an' fight for?" asked Madeley, indignantly. "Why didn' they stay t' 'ome? Tha'lt be sayin' next that the Frenchies sent 'em an invite."

"What a say is, that it weren't none o' our business. We'd no call to mix ourselves up wi' other folks' quarrels," replied Weeper.

"Well, I don't hold wi' that," said Glazier, judicially, "I'm not fightin' for them bloody slackers an' conchies[2] at 'ome; but what I say is that the Fritzes 'ad to be stopped. If we 'adn't come in, an' they'd got the Frenchies beat, 'twould 'a' been our turn next."

"Too bloody true it would," said Madeley. "An' I'd rather come an' fight Fritz in France then 'ave 'im come over to Blighty an' start bashin' our 'ouses about, same as 'e's done 'ere."

"'e'd never 'ave come to England. The Navy'd 'ave seen to that," said Pacey.

"Don't you be too bloody sure about the Navy," said Corporal Hamley, entering into the discussion at last. "The Navy 'as got all it can bloody well do, as things are."

"Well, chaps," said Glazier, "maybe I'm right an' maybe I'm wrong, but that's neither here nor there; only I've sometimes thought it would be a bloody good things for us'ns, if the 'un did land a few troops in England. Show 'em what war's like. Madeley an' I struck it lucky an' went 'ome on leave together, an' you never seed anything like it. Windy! Like a lot o' bloody kids they was, an' talking no more sense; 'pon me word, you'd be surprised at some o' the questions they'd ask, an' you couldn't answer sensible. They'd never believe it, if you did. We jes' kep' our mouths shut, and told 'em the war was all right, and we'd got it won, but not yet. 'twas the only way to keep 'em quiet."

"The boozers in Wes'church was shut most of the day; but Madeley and I would go down to the Greyhound, at seven o'clock, an' it was always chock-a-block wi' chaps lappin' it up as fast as they could, before closin' time. There'd be some old sweats, and some men back from 'ospital into barracks, but not fit, an' a few new recruits; but most o' them were miners, the sort o' buggers who took our job to dodge gettin' into khaki. Bloody fine miners they was. Well, one Saturday night we was in there 'avin' a bit of a booze-up, but peaceable like, when one of them bloody miners came in an' asked us to 'ave a drink in a loud voice. Well, we was peaceable enough, an' I dare way we might 'ave 'ad a drink with 'im, but the swine put 'is fist into 'is trousers' pocket, and pulls out a fistful of Bradburys an' 'arf-crowns, an' plunks 'em down on the bar counter. 'There,' he says, 'there's me bloody wages for a week, an' I ain't done more'n eight hours' work for it, either. I don't care if the bloody war lasts for ever,' 'e says. I looks up an' sees Madeley lookin' white an' dangerous. 'Was you talkin' to me?' says Madeley. 'Aye,' 'e says. 'Well, take that, you fuckin' bastard!' says Madeley, an' sloshes 'im one in the clock. Some of 'is friends interfered first, and then some of our friends interfered, an' in five seconds there was 'ell's delight in the bloody bar, wi' the old bitch be'ind the counter goin' into 'ysterics, an' 'ollerin' for the police.

"Then Madeley got 'old of 'is man, who was blubberin' an' swearin' summat awful, an' near twisted 'is arm off. I were busy keepin' some o' the other buggers off 'im, but 'e didn't pay no attention to nobody else, 'e just lugged 'is man out the back door an' into the yard, wi' the old girl 'ollerin' blue murder; and Madeley lugs 'im into the urinal, an' gets 'im down an' rubs 'is face in it. I'd got out the back door too, be that time, as I seed some red-caps comin' into the bar; an' when 'e'd finished I saw Madeley stand up an' wipe 'is 'ands on the seat of 'is trousers. 'There, you bugger,' 'e says, 'now you go 'ome an' talk to yourself.'—''op it,' I says to 'im, 'there's the fuckin' picket outside'; an' we 'opped it over some palin's at the bottom o' the yard; one of 'em came away, an' I run a bloody great splinter into the palm o' me 'and. Then we just buggered off, by some back streets, to The Crown, an' 'ad a couple o' pints an' went 'ome peaceable."

"Look at ol' tear-gas!" Martlow cried. "Thought you didn't like fightin', Weeper?"

Weeper's whole face was alight with excitement.

"A like a scrap as well as any man, so long as it don't go too far," said Weeper. "a'd 'ave given a lot to see thee go for that miner, Madeley. It's them chaps what are always on the make, an' don't care 'ow they makes it, as causes 'arf the wars. Them's the bloody cowards."

"Is it all true, Madeley?" asked Corporal Hamley.

"It were summat like, but I misremember," said Madeley, modestly. "But it's all true what 'e says about folks at 'ome, most on 'em. They don't care a fuck what 'appens to us'ns, so long as they can keep a 'ole skin. Say they be ready to make any sacrifice; but we're the bloody sacrifice. You never seed such a windy lot; an' blood-thirsty ain't the word for it. They've all gone potty. You'd think your best friends wouldn't be satisfied till they'd seed your name on the roll of honour. I tol' one of 'em 'e knew a bloody sight more'n I did about the war. The only person as 'ad any sense was me mother. She on'y fussed about what I wanted to eat. She didn't want to know anything about the war, an' it were on'y me she were afraid for. She didn't min' about aught else. 'Please God, you'll be home soon,' she'd say. An' please God, I will."

"An' then they give you a bloody party," said Glazier. "Madeley an' I went to one. You should a seed some o' the pushers. Girls o' seventeen painted worse nor any Gerties I'd ever knowed. One of 'em came on an' sang a lot o' songs wi' dirty meanings to 'em. I remember one she sang wi' another girl, 'I want a Rag.' She did an' all, too. When this bloody war's over, you'll go back to England an' fin' nought there but a lot o' conchies and bloody prostitutes."

"There's good an' bad," said Pacey, mildly, "an' if there's more bad than good, I don't know but the good don't wear better. But there's nought sure in this world, no more."

"No, an' never 'as been," said Madeley, pessimistically.

"There's nought sure for us'ns, anyway," said Weeper, relapsing. "Didst 'ear what Cap'n Thompson read out this mornin', about stoppin' to 'elp any poor bugger what was wounded? The bloody brass-'at what wrote that letter 'as never been in any big show 'isself, that a dare swear. 'e's one o' them buggers as is never nearer to the real thing than G.H.Q."[3]

"You don't want to talk like that," said Corporal Hamley. "You've 'ad your orders."

"A don't mind tellin' thee, corporal," said Weeper, again lifting a large flat hand, as though by that gesture he stopped the mouths of all the world. "A don't mind tellin' thee, that if a see a chum o' mine down, an' a can do aught to 'elp 'im, all the brass-'ats in the British Army, an' there's a bloody sight too many o' 'em, aren't goin' to stop me. A'll do what's right, an' if a know aught about thee, tha'lt do as I do."

"You don't want to talk about it, anyway," said Corporal Hamley, quietly. "I'm not sayin' you're not right: I'd do what any other man'd do; but there's no need to make a song about it."

"What beats me," said Shem, sniggering, "is that the bloody fool who wrote that instructional letter, doesn't seem to know what any ordinary man would do in the circumstances. We all know that there must be losses, you can't expect to take a trench without some casualties; but they seem to go on from saying that losses are unavoidable, to thinking that they're necessary, and from that, to thinking that they don't matter."

"They don't know what we've got to go through, that's the truth of it," said Weeper. "They measure the distance, an' they count the men, an' the guns, an' think a battle's no' but a sum you can do wi' a pencil an' a bit o' paper."

"I heard Mr Pardew talking to Mr Rhys about a course he'd been on, and he told him a brass-hat had been lecturing them on the lessons of the Somme offensive, and gave them an estimate of the total German losses; and then an officer at the back of the room got up, and asked him if he could give them any information about British losses, and the brass-hat said: No, and looked at them as though they were a lot of criminals."

"It's a fact," said Glazier; "whether you're talkin' to a civvy or whether you're talkin' to a brass-'at, an' some o' the officers aren't no better, if you tell the truth, they think you're a bloody coward. They've not got our experience, an' they don't face it as us'ns do."

"Give them a chance," said Bourne, reasonably; he hadn't spoken before, he usually sat back and listened quietly to these debates.

"Let 'em take my fuckin' chance!" shouted Weeper, vindictively.

"There's a good deal in what you say," said Bourne, who was a little embarrassed by the way they all looked at him suddenly. "I think there's a good deal of truth in it; but after all, what is a brass-hat's job? He's not thinking of you or of me or of any individual man, or of any particular battalion or division. Men, to him, are only part of the materiel he has got to work with; and if he felt as you or I feel, he couldn't carry on with his job. It's not fair to think he's inhuman. He's got to draw up a plan, from rather scrappy information, and it is issued in the form of an order; but he knows very well something may happen at any moment to throw everything out of gear. The original plan is no more than a kind of map; you can't see the country by looking at a map, and you can't see the fighting by looking at a plan of attack. Once we go over the top it's the colonel's and the company commander's job. Once we meet a Hun it's our job . . ."

"Yes, an' our job's a bloody sight worse'n theirs," said Weeper.

"It's not worse than the colonel's, or the company commander's," said Bourne. "Anyway, they come over with us. They've got to lead us, or drive us. They may have to order us to do something, knowing damned well that they're spending us. I don't envy them. I think that bit in the letter, about not stopping to help the wounded, it's silly. It's up to us, that is; but it's up to us not to make another man's agony our excuse. What's bloody silly in the letter is the last bit, where they say they don't anticipate any serious resistance from the enemy. That is the Staff's job, and they ought to know it better."

"We started talking about what we were fighting for," said Shem, laughing. "It was Mr Rhys started it."

"Yes, an' you've been talkin' all over the bloody shop ever since," said Corporal Hamley. "You all ought to be on the bloody Staff, you ought. 'oo are orderly-men? Shem and Martlow; well, tea's up."

Shem and Martlow looked at the straight rain, and then struggled into their greatcoats.

"All that a says is, if a man's dead it don't matter no more to 'im 'oo wins the bloody war," said Weeper. "We're 'ere, there's no getting' away from that, Corporal. 'ere we are, an' since we're 'ere, we're just fightin' for ourselves; we're just fightin' for ourselves, an' for each other."

Bourne stared as though he were fascinated by this uncouth figure with huge, ape-like arms, and melancholy, half-imbecile face. Here was a man who, if he lost his temper with them, could have cleared the tent in ten seconds; and he sat with them, patient under daily mockery, suffering even the schoolboy cheek of little Martlow indifferently, and nursing always the bitterness and misery of his own heart. Already dripping, Shem and Martlow dumped the dixie of tea in the opening of the tent, almost spilling it, as they slipped on the greasy mud, where many feet had made a slide by the doorway.

"I never knowed such a miserable lot o' buggers as you all are," said Corporal Hamley. "'and me over that pot o' pozzy."

"I'm not miserable, Corporal," said little Martlow. "We're not dead yet. On'y I'm not fightin' for any fuckin' Beljums, see. One o' them buggers wanted to charge me five frong for a loaf o' bread."

"Well, put a sock in it. We've 'ad enough bloody talk now."

They ate, more or less in silence, and then smoked, contentedly enough. The rain was slackening, and there was more light. After they had smoked for awhile, Glazier took his tunic and shirt off, and began to hunt for lice. One after another they all followed his example, stripping themselves of trousers, underpants and even socks, until the tent held nothing but naked men. They would take a candle, or a lighted match, and pass it along the seams of their trousers, hoping that the flame would destroy the eggs. A hurricane lamp hung by a nail on the tent-pole, and after it was lighted they still continued the scrupulous search, its light falling on white shoulders studiously rounded as they bent over the task. They were completely absorbed in it, when the air was ripped up with a wailing sigh, and there was a muffled explosion in the field behind them. They stopped, listening intently, and looking at each other. Another shell, whining precipitately, passed overhead to end with a louder explosion in some fields beyond the little wood, and well over the lower road. Then there was a silence. They sighed and moved.

"If Jerry starts shellin' proper," said the corporal, as they dressed themselves again, "you want to take shelter in them trenches."

"They're no' but rabbit-scrapes," said Weeper.

"Well, you get into 'em," said the corporal, "an' if they're not good enough for you, we can dig 'em deeper tomorrow."

Nothing more was said. They were bored a little, lounging there, and smoking again, but they took refuge with their own secret thoughts. Outside, the rain had stopped. They were all going up the line with a big carrying-party that night. At about six o'clock they heard from the road below a heavy lumbering and clanking, and they listened with ears cocked. Then they heard hurrying movements outside.

"What is it?"

"Tanks! Tanks!"

They rushed out of their tent, and joined, apparently with the whole camp, in a wild stampede through the trees to the road below. None of them as yet had seen a tank. It was only a caterpillar tractor, which had come up to move a big gun to or from its lair. Officers hurried out to see what was the matter, and then returned disgusted to their own tents. Sergeants and corporals cursed the men back to their own lines. As Bourne turned back with the others, he looked up to a clear patch of sky, and saw the sharp crescent of the moon, floating there like a boat. A bough threw a mesh of fine twigs over its silver, and at that loveliness he caught up his breath, almost in a sob.

Notes

From Frederic Manning, *Her Privates We* (London: Serpent's Tail, 1999), pp. 142–57. Reprinted with permission.

1. "Blighty" meant England. A blighty was therefore a wound serious enough to send a man back home, but not serious enough to cause permanent disability.

2. Conscientious objectors.

3. General Headquarters.

A Soldier's Notebook

Alexei Brusilov

On September 14, if I remember rightly, orders were received to the effect that General Radko-Dmitriev should at once proceed to take over the command of the Third Army, General Ruzski having been appointed Commander of the North-West Front, in place of General Jilinski, who had been relieved of his command in consequence of the heavy defeat sustained by the Second Army under General Samsonov in East Prussia, and the disorderly and costly retreat of the First Army under General Rennenkampf. I had to appoint a successor to Radko-Dmitriev in command of the VIII Corps. The senior Divisional Commander in my army was Lieut.-General Orlov, an officer with a curious reputation dating perhaps from the Chinese campaign, or more probably from the Russo-Japanese War. During the Chinese campaign he had attempted to break loose from his Chief and win himself some easy laurels; in the Japanese War he had been held responsible for Kuropatkin's reverses, and it was believed that he had been made the scapegoat after our loss of the battle of Liao-Yang. Just before the War he had been in charge of the 12th Division in the XII Army Corps under my own command. I had observed his work in the grand manœuvres, and it had been admirable. His division had been in every respect capably handled and well trained. In several of the early battles won by the Eighth Army the operations conducted by Orlov had been above criticism. For these various reasons, I requested that he might be posted as Commander of the VIII Army Corps, in spite of the fact that in peace-time his name had most consistently been struck out of the list of candidates for promotion to the command of an Army Corps. My suggestion was considered favourably , and Orlov was appointed to the post.

In conformity with the instructions of the Commander-in-Chief, all the armies of the South-West Front continued to move westward, my army keeping to the south of the Lemberg-Gorodok-Przemysl line. Since we formed the extreme left of our whole Western Front, my duty, in general terms, was as before, to screen our left against any attacks which might threaten, whether from the south or the west. My task became more and more complicated the further we advanced, for our lines of communication grew longer and it became increasingly difficult to safeguard our left and rear from enemy assaults. It seemed to me that for this purpose my army should have received periodical reinforcements, all the more because in the course of the battle of Gorodok I had been forced to call up the solitary infantry brigade which was guarding the rear of our left flank. At the conclusion of the battle my army, in the absence of reinforcements, had been so weakened by the losses it had suffered that I had not considered it possible to send this brigade back to the rear on the right bank of the Dnestr, and had left it attached to its division. I urgently begged the Front Commander to reinforce my army with one Army Corps, for on the right bank of the Dnestr, on a front of nearly 200 versts, our flank was protected by no more than three Caucasian Cossack divisions—an obviously inadequate safeguard. The result of my representations was that the 71st Infantry Division of the Second Line was detailed to replace the brigade which I had transferred from the river; which was enough for the moment. On principle, I did not think fit to ask for useless reinforcements, or to paint too lurid a picture of the situation, since on this flank the enemy's forces were inconsiderable, mostly Landsturm[1] and not enough to be a serious menace to our rear. On the right bank of the Dnestr we had a division of infantry and three Cossack divisions engaged on similar duty; at my suggestion all these four divisions were united under a single command and given the designation of the XXX Army Corps.

Having settled the question of our rear and satisfied myself that all was as it should be with the rear of my own army, I moved my Staff from Lemberg to Luben-Velki. My whole army was now on the right bank of the Vereshchitsa, and I was moving forward on the line Przemysl-Nizankovitse-Dobromil-Khyrov. I had sent the 10th and 12th Cavalry Divisions forward on the Dynov-Sanok line, on the River San and beyond it, so as to keep in touch with the enemy, and the 2nd Composite Cossack Division by way of Sambor and Staroie-Mesto in the Carpathians toward Mount Turka to try to seize and hold the summit of the great pass leading from the Hungarian valley. Leaving a considerable garrison at Przemysl,[2] the enemy forces had fallen back to the west on to the left bank of the San, where they had halted to restore their formation after the heavy defeats they had suffered. It seemed to me that we ought not to allow them to pull themselves together again but should follow close on their heels and complete their overthrow, merely leaving a strong force on the watch before Przemysl. The objection to this was that our lines of communication were lengthening unconscionably and were not in good order; the nexus of railways at Lemberg was in a state of chaos, and was so congested that we experienced great delay in obtaining supplies. I had no means of remedying this wretched state of affairs because this branch was in the province of the General-Quartermaster of the armies on the Front, directly under the Front Commander, and with him my protests and complaints counted for little. Still, I think that a little goodwill and management would have enabled us to put things right in our rear with greater rapidity and at the same time bring about the complete overthrow of an enemy already beaten, by not allowing him time to receive reinforcements or to rest and recuperate.

The investment of Przemysl was entrusted to the new Commander of the Third Army, Radko-Dmitriev, who when he was in command of the VIII Corps of my army, and earlier, in the Turco-Bulgarian War, had struck me as a strong-minded, quick-witted and capable officer. I did not doubt for a moment that at this juncture he would display these same military qualities and would attempt to take Przemysl without more ado, which would have freed our hands, established us firmly in Eastern Galicia, and given us an opportunity of pushing onward without meeting any resistance and without leaving behind us an enemy fortress and a besieged army. Indeed, after such a succession of defeats and heavy losses, the Austrian Army was so demoralized and Przemysl so little prepared to stand a siege (for its garrison, composed of beaten troops, was far from steady), that I was absolutely convinced that by the middle of October the place could have been taken by assault without any serious artillery preparation. But the days passed and no effort was made to take Przemysl. However, it was no business of mine, and I therefore did not think that I had any right to interfere with the plans of a colleague or to influence his decisions one way or the other.

Until the early part of October, we remained inactive on the line determined for us and enjoyed a complete rest. I had only one thing to worry me—viz., the inadequacy of my reinforcements, and in addition, the fact that the drafts which arrived were not properly trained as soldiers. At first I was inclined to attribute this to the fact that the reserve battalions had only just been formed and had not yet properly organized their work; but I was grievously mistaken. At no stage of the War did we receive properly trained reinforcements. As time went on, the reserve troops became worse and worse, not only in the matter of military training, but morally and politically. Not a single man could answer me when I asked them about the causes of the War, what we were fighting for and why. It is impossible not to fix the blame for the existence of this mental condition on the War Office which had established such a faulty system of training at the depots.

In the early days of October, the disorder on the railways, especially at the railhead at Lemberg, grew still worse. The lines there were so choked that it had become an absolute bottle-neck in which it was impossible to sort out the contents of the trains and send off what was required at the proper time. This matter was not part of my duties, but since my representations came to nothing, I took it upon myself to issue instructions at Lemberg so as to bring this important system of lines into something like order. The position of General Dobryshin, the railway specialist, was a delicate and trying one. He possessed no authority, but was striving his utmost to relieve the congestion at Lemberg and to restore normal working. The city was, as I have said, outside the area of my command, and the Railway Service was in no sense under my control, and I was interfering with someone else's business; but the welfare of my army was beginning to be affected by the disorganization of the railway system, and no one would listen to my protests. Accordingly, I took upon myself, not without some qualms, the responsibility of appointing General Dobryshin as Officer Commanding the railhead at Lemberg. I must admit that if previously no one had attended to my complaints, at least no one now hindered me from interfering in what was really not my affair.

At this same period the formation of the Eleventh Army was announced, whose task was that of besieging Przemysl; it was to be composed of a number of Second Line divisions and a brigade of militia. Its Commander was General Selivanov, an elderly man, whose military ability as displayed in the Japanese War had been less conspicuous than the strength of character he had shown at the time of the revolt at Vladivostok, during the revolutionary movement that shook the whole of Russia in 1905 and 1906. He was an unimaginative, rigid man, and, in my opinion, ill-fitted for the task entrusted to him.

North of the Third Army our affairs were progressing more and less successfully, the attention of the Front Commander and Staff of the South-West Front being concentrated on the Vistula. I was now entrusted with the command of a group consisting of the Third, Eleventh, and Eighth Armies, with instructions to stay where I was for the time being. I accordingly moved my Staff to Sadova Vishnia, which was a more convenient headquarters for my new duties. General Shcherbachev, commanding the IX Corps of the Third Army, had been appointed, pending the arrival of General Selivanov, to direct the siege of Przemysl. I had known him for many years, ever since my St. Petersburg days. He now reported to me that after seriously considering the situation of Przemysl, he thought that the fortress could at the moment be taken by storm and he would guarantee to do it. The proposal was an enticing one, even though our casualties were bound to be serious, for the fall of Przemysl would have released the newly constituted Eleventh Army and notably strengthened the front held by the Third and Eighth Armies. Besides, it was beyond all doubt that the enemy, in view of the general situation and the inactivity of our left, would very shortly resort to strong offensive measures in order to relieve a stronghold which was the most important fortress in the whole Austro-Hungarian Empire. If, however, the place fell, the reason for any such offensive would cease to exist, and we should be able without misgivings to develop and extend our own offensive, which might have a salutary effect on the long-drawn battle on the Vistula. These various considerations and my own personal opinions urged me to consent to the storming of Przemysl. After going into the whole matter thoroughly and drawing up a detailed report to the Front Commander, I asked his permission to carry out this operation and received a favourable reply. I felt that the real moment for the taking of Przemysl by sheer assault had passed, and that the task was far more serious and less promising of certain success than it would have been three weeks previously; still, the advantages outweighed the risks.

In drawing up a plan for the assault of the fortress there were certain points on which the views of General Shcherbachev and myself were at variance. In his opinion, we ought to attack the most important group of forts, those to the east, where the works were the strongest and most up-to-date, and especially Fort Syedlitski; the General considered that once these forts fell, Przemysl could no longer hold out. I agreed, but I thought that the capture by assault of the eastern forts, particularly Fort Syedlitski, was problematic, whereas to attack the western forts, which were not so well armed, gave great promise of success and would cut off the retreat of the garrison. The chief difficulty in the attack on the city arose from the fact that the westerly withdrawal of the Austrian Army had left it at the moment only three or four days' march from the fortress, and it had already succeeded in pulling itself together and filling up its ranks. Consequently it would soon be ready to resume the offensive so as to assist the garrison and save the city. This possibility had to be borne in mind, for it meant that the enemy force must be held back during our assault on the fortress, and for that purpose a fighting front had to be established to meet any such offensive. We decided to attack the eastern group of forts first, in order to divert the attention and reserves of the enemy to that side, and at the same time to surround Przemysl on all the other sides and to direct our assault on the north-west and south-west forts. The cavalry were ordered to redouble their vigilance and to be specially active in reconnaissance so as to warn us in due time of any assumption of the offensive by the enemy.

At this point the 2nd Composite Cossack Division, which I had despatched, as has been mentioned above, into the Carpathians in the direction of Mount Turka, had halted and were being hard pressed by a Hungarian division. General Pavlov asked for assistance to check the Hungarians by a counter-offensive, and I instructed General Tsurikov to detail a regiment of infantry from the XXIV Corps to reinforce this division.

General Radko-Dmitriev, commanding the Third Army, now asked for reinforcements because he doubted whether he would be strong enough without them to hold the left bank of the San to the north of Przemysl. I thought his fears were exaggerated, but the Front Commander instructed me to lend him my VII Army Corps and I did so. I detailed the XII Army Corps (General Lesh) to assist General Shcherbachev in the assault on Przemysl; so that now I had only two Army Corps to the south of this city, the VIII and the XXIV.

Apart from the Eleventh Army troops, the 19th Division of the XII Army Corps was to attack the forts of the Syedlitski group, the 12th Division was to seize the northwest forts (which were the weakest), and the 3rd Brigade of Sharpshooters the southwest. Two brigades of heavy artillery and two howitzer brigades were selected to prepare our attack on the Syedlitski forts. Our artillery preparation could not be of sufficient intensity or duration because of our lack of ammunition; however, our firing was good and it silenced that of the Austrians because, although our guns were smaller in number and in caliber, the quality of their fire was immeasurably superior. General Shcherbachev, who was in charge of the operations, was convinced of the success of our enterprise; and indeed, two of the Syedlitski forts were stormed by the 19th Infantry Division, the Crimean Regiment particularly distinguishing itself, and the entire attention of the besieged troops and the greater part of their reserves were, as we had hoped, drawn off to this area; the right moment had arrived for an attack on the north-west and south-west forts.

But just then the very thing we had been afraid of came to pass. The Austrians took the offensive in order to save Przemysl. They were only four marches away, and could soon join issue with us. The assault on the city had therefore to be broken off at once. Indeed, according to the information we received, the enemy forces moving against us were superior in numbers and were marching partly against the Third Army and partly against the Eighth, at a time when I had nothing but two Army Corps, which would be quite powerless to hold the enemy back. After examining the situation in consultation with General Shcherbachev, I came to the conclusion that the attack on Przemysl would require another five or six days and that we no longer had this amount of time in hand. We therefore had to give up this promising operation and withdraw the XII Corps from before the city and order the Eleventh Army to relinquish the siege and take up a position with its right resting on the left of the Third Army and its left on the right of the Eighth. By about October 10, therefore, my three Army Corps practically held the front between Popovishche and Staroie-Mesto.

General Radko-Dmitriev, in charge of the Third Army, under my command, now reported that he thought it hazardous to keep his ground on the left bank of the San with a river behind him on which he did not hold a sufficient number of crossing-places, and asked for authority to withdraw to the right bank. I am bound to say that this proposition did not appeal to me at all, for the simple reason that if the Third Army retired behind the river (which was now swollen by the autumn rains) it would be quite incapable of taking the offensive, although admittedly it would be free from enemy attacks. It might easily be imagined that the Austrians, having Przemysl in their hands, would leave only a small force to face the Third Army and would shift the bulk of their forces from north to south, in which case my army, small in number and with nothing to protect its front, would find overwhelming enemy forces descending on it and would be seriously jeopardized. It was, however, very difficult not to fall in with the plan of Radko-Dmitriev to retire behind the San, because, if he had by any chance suffered a severe reverse, his excuse would be that I had exposed him to it for selfish considerations of my own. As the question involved personal interests, military ethics forbade my putting up any strong opposition to his wishes. I hoped that the Front Commander would judge between us and would come to a decision which would serve the interests of both of us. Unfortunately my calculations proved incorrect: Radko-Dmitriev was instructed to retire, and my army was thus left to the hazard of Fortune. In this awkward position I had only one course possible, to ask for the return of the VII Corps from the Third Army, and further, for another infantry division so that I might attempt to put my forces on a par with those of the enemy.

However, I had succeeded in consolidating my front by the time the Austro-Hungarians arrived, and as was my custom I myself assumed the offensive on their approach, with a view to dealing them a swift blow so as to upset their plans. Once more I was successful. The roads to the south of Przemysl were few and the country hilly; and the fact that the Austrians were in deep formation, since they had no chance of deploying at the right moment, forced them to accept battle in circumstances not to their advantage, because they could only make use of their advanced troops. From intercepted telephone conversations and the reports and orders we captured it was clear that about the middle of October the Austrians considered their situation uncomfortable, if not desperate. Their High Command attempted to put heart into the troops by informing them that to the north of Przemysl the Russians had fallen back behind the San and that considerable reinforcements were on the way there.

Here, for the first time since the opening of the campaign, my army was forced to carry on for about a month a war of position, and that under most adverse conditions. Its right wing practically had its back to the enemy fortress. The Eleventh Army, being composed of Second Line divisions and a militia brigade, was rather shaky, and needed constant support. The enemy was persistently increasing his pressure on our front and continually strengthening his numbers. At the same time our left was beginning to feel the effect of the strong enemy thrust from the Carpathians, which looked like outflanking my XXIV Corps. Further, equally important enemy forces were moving from Skole and Bolekhov on Stryi and Mikolaiev—i.e., directly against Lemberg and in our rear. In spite of my earnest requests for reinforcements in view of the enemy's numerical superiority and the peculiar difficulty of my strategical position, the Front Commander contented himself with making arrangements for the evacuation of Lemberg. I was more or less jettisoned, as though the annihilation of my army, the appearance of the enemy in my rear, and the recapture of Lemberg were not of the same grave import for all our armies. Even to-day, looking back, I fail to understand such an inexplicable treatment of my army, a policy which might have had the most disastrous consequences not only for me, but for the whole-South-West Front; nor can I imagine the motives of General Ivanov and General Alexeiev, his Chief of Staff. I was told that on the Staff on the South-West Front people were saying, "Brusilov will wriggle out," or "Let him wriggle out!" This sort of thing is only gossip, but it is typical, and it is a mistake to trifle with public dissatisfaction by letting such rumours get about. The rank and file hearing these tales would for their part add, "Yes, of course, our General will wriggle out, but only at the cost of our blood and bones." All of which did nothing to keep up the stoutness of heart that is so needful in time of war.

To resume, I had to face a frontal attack by an enemy force of a strength twice my own. My left was being outflanked by troops moving from the Carpathians by way of Turka, while other hostile forces making for Lemberg via Stryi and Mikolaiev were coming straight down on my rear in numbers considerably superior to those who had to defend that line. On my actual front my position was a fairly strong one, but I was uneasy about the left of the Eleventh Army, which was being bombarded by the heavy artillery from the fortress of Przemysl and showed signs of breaking. When one of the Second Line divisions was attacked one night by an Austrian Army Corps, it abandoned its trenches, evacuating them altogether. Enquiries were made, but it was impossible to discover who was responsible; the brigadier reported that he had received definite orders from the Divisional Commander, but this the latter categorically denied. However that may be, the result of this business was that the enemy rushed great forces through the breach thus created. Fortunately, the Austrians, after penetrating our lines, lost their bearings in a forest, and were unable to turn their success to account quickly enough. I was at once informed by telegraph of the break in our line and despatched the 9th and 10th Cavalry Divisions, which I was holding in reserve, to the scene with orders to prevent the gap from spreading at any cost, and not to allow the Austrians to penetrate any further into our formations. At the same time I instructed the General commanding the XII Army Corps to attack the enemy vigorously in the forest they had occupied and retrieve the situation, and ordered the division which had quitted its trenches without orders to get back into them. This Second Line division was short of officers, and such few as there were hardly showed themselves up to their work; but the cavalry division came to their assistance, and of its own accord detailed a number of its officers who volunteered to take over the command of companies and battalions of the Second Line division and put it straight again. These new officers were greeted with enthusiasm by the men, who went to work with a will to redeem their error, and recaptured the trenches that they had abandoned. However, to strengthen this sector of the front, I had sent up the last of my reserves, which were stationed at Mostsisk at the disposal of the XII Army Corps. By such means, albeit with great difficulty, our front was restored and the Austrian II Army Corps, which had pierced it, was driven out. Hard as it was to stand firm under the heavy fire of the Przemysl batteries at the point where the two armies joined, our troops braved this ordeal as long as they remained in those positions.

The situation of the left of the army presented greater difficulties, for, well before this date, I had been obliged to lend General Tsurikov, commanding the XXIV Army Corps, all my available reserves to prevent this wing from being enveloped. General Tsurikov proposed to assemble as large a body as possible of his available forces on his extreme left, on the right bank of the Dnestr, and with it to assume the offensive and save his flank from being turned. To do this successfully meant that we must not only drive back the enemy and extend a screen of troops southwards to meet his forces coming from Turka, but must ourselves attempt to envelop the enemy right. I entirely approved of this scheme. I believed then, as I believe now, that the best method of defence is to assume the offensive if there is the slightest chance of doing so, and not to remain inactive (which is to court defeat), but to adopt vigorous measures and strike the enemy a telling blow on some vital spot. I hoped by so doing to safeguard my own position and at the same time secure my left wing, which had been surrounded.

We had yet to devise some means of parrying the enemy offensive against Lemberg via Mikolaiev. Fortunately for me, the Austrians, calculating on having to encounter merely the small and scattered bodies of troops that I had kept on the right bank of the Dnestr, and judging that it would be impossible for us to collect these at any one point, brought inadequate forces to bear on Stryi and Mikolaiev. Had they disposed their troops differently and despatched two or three Army Corps there, they would have been able to compel me to fall back a good distance to the east, which would have had disastrous and far-reaching consequences on the whole of the South-West Front. As things were, it was no use sending less than a division of infantry to Mikolaiev to repel the enemy forces which had appeared in my rear, for the few battalions of the 71st Division which had been rapidly assembled at Stryi had been driven out and were slowly withdrawing, fighting as they went, towards Mikolaiev. The Cossack Division had not carried out the duties assigned to it and had retired without my orders on Dragobych (Drohobycz). Its general, who was responsible for this, was in consequence relieved by me of his command.

I had now no reserves of any sort or kind, as I had been forced to use them all in the various engagements fought on my front, as I have already mentioned, and the numerical superiority of the enemy precluded me from withdrawing a single man from the fighting line. I therefore determined to move a division (the 58th) from the inactive sector of the Eleventh Army—i.e., the right bank of the San, north of Przemysl. The great difficulty of this step was to ensure the arrival of this division at Mikolaiev at the earliest possible moment, and in time to prevent the Austrians from Stryi from crossing to the left bank of the Dnestr.

In this connection it is only just to mention the services rendered by the 8th Railway Battalion; this battalion was not in any way under my control, but realizing the need for rapid transport, they put forth literally superhuman efforts and accomplished their task with amazing expedition. The infantry were moved by railway; the artillery by various means proceeded by the high road and likewise reached Mikolaiev in time; the convoys followed also by road. The officer commanding this division, General Alftan, with whom I had conferred in detail at Army Headquarters, carried out his mission brilliantly. Although his division was not yet completely reformed, seeing that time pressed, he took the offensive from Mikolaiev, rallied the retreating units of the 71st Division, and came heavily down upon the Austrians to the north of Stryi. After two days' fierce fighting the enemy were defeated and began to retire rapidly, abandoning Stryi, and falling back on Skole and Bolekhov. Thus, by about October 28, I had definitely secured my rear. At this juncture my left assumed the offensive and in a continuous series of engagements began to drive back the enemy, partly towards the east and partly towards the south in the direction of Turka. It was only for want of sufficient forces that I was unable to outflank the Austrian right.

By the middle of November, then, I had succeeded in holding my ground firmly, covering Lemberg to the south, and achieving my task of safeguarding the left of the entire Western Front of the Russian Army.

My position was not a cheerful one, however, and as a matter of fact it was one of great difficulty and discomfort. We had been fighting continuously for about a month against very powerful enemy forces, we had received no reinforcements, and, in spite of all my complaints, supplementary drafts reached me in quite insignificant numbers. Those that were sent me were, unhappily, ill-trained and by no means fit to be put into the line at a time when, owing to incessant casualties in killed, sick, and wounded, the ranks of my troops were thinned out; regiments dwindled away faster and faster and the exhaustion of the men was extreme.

At this critical moment there arrived at my Headquarters Prince Alexander Petrovich Oldenburgski, the Head of the entire Russian Medical Service. He felt keenly and sympathetically the distressing state of the Eighth Army and despatched a telegram on the subject direct to the Commander-in-Chief, the grand Duke Nikolai Nikolaievich. It was undoubtedly then and then only that the Stabka (Russian General Staff Headquarters) realized how we were placed. Obviously the Staff on the south-West Front had been either unable or unwilling to get an accurate idea of our position, thinking, no doubt, that my reports were exaggerated; I can find no other explanation. The Commander-in-Chief at once issued instructions for the dispatch of two infantry divisions to reinforce the Eighth Army. The first, the 12th Siberian Division of Sharpshooters, arrived very soon; the second was stopped on the way by the Staff and despatched to the Third Army.

I had intended to combine these two divisions when they arrived and to use them with the VIII Army Corps to break through the enemy's front in the direction of Khyrov; but, as I have said, the second division never reached me. I therefore attached the 12th Siberian Division to the XXIV Corps because I could not effect a break-through with one division only, and I preferred to strengthen my left for the purpose of outflanking rather than breaking the enemy's lines. The latter manœuvre, in the case in point, might perhaps bring me less decisive results than a break-through at Khyrov, but I hoped, by strengthening my left, to be able to drive back for good and all the enemy forces which were approaching from Turka over the crest of the mountain. However, the commander of the XXIV Corps was forced by the weakness of the 48th and 49th Infantry Division (which were now merely the ruins of their original regiments) to move the 12th Siberians Division, not in the direction of Turka, where our 65th Infantry brigade and 4th Brigade of Sharpshooters were operating, but as a reinforcement to the 48th and 49th divisions.

At this juncture the Third Army, by the orders of the Front Commander and in conformity with the general situation, began to recross to the left bank of the San. In so doing it drew off part of the enemy forces and at the same time lightened to some extent the task both of the Eighth Army and of the Eleventh Army. On the previous occasion when the Third Army had moved over the river from the left bank to the right, it had imprudently destroyed all the crossings; and now these had to be restored under the enemy's fire, involving us in losses which might easily have been avoided.

Some time early in November, our airmen reported that they had observed long convoy columns moving back westward from the enemy front, a clear sign that the Austrians considered this long-drawn battle as a defeat, and were preparing to retire. I at once issued orders to all my troops to prepare to make a brisk advance and fall upon the enemy. Sure enough, the latter had begun to withdraw during the night, and my army attacked their rearguard at dawn and fought its way onward despite the utter weariness of the troops, taking a number of prisoners, convoys and guns.

This battle of Przemysl, which had continued incessantly for a whole month, was the last one in which I can say that I had an army that had been properly taught and trained before the War. After hardly three months of war the greater part of our regular, professional officers and trained men had vanished, leaving only skeleton forces which had to be hastily filled with men wretchedly instructed who were sent to me from the depots; while the strength of the officers was kept up by promoting subalterns, who likewise were inadequately trained. From this period onwards the professional character of our forces disappeared, and the Army became more and more like a sort of badly trained militia. The question of N.C.O.'s became a particularly acute one; we had to institute training squads so as to provide, hastily and anyhow, N.C.O.'s who assuredly could not take the place of their well-trained predecessors. On this point also one is bound to blame the War Ministry for not foreseeing these difficulties in their preparations for war. I repeat, the new officers came to us absolutely unqualified and in insufficient numbers; the N.C.O.'s, of whom there were great numbers in the Reserve, had not been put specially through a fresh course of training as a valuable body of subordinate officers with a view to their ultimate use in that capacity. Many of them were put into the ranks as privates during mobilization, and at the beginning of the campaign we had far too many N.C.O.'s, while later on we had none at all. We who were in charge of operations were obliged to have instructional squads behind the line for each regiment. Last of all, the men sent to replace casualties generally knew nothing except how to march; none of them knew anything of open order, and many could not even load their rifles; as for their shooting, the less said about it the better.

In every regiment, then, we had to have the new drafts put through a course behind the lines before they could go into the ranks. But even so, our losses in the bigger battles were so enormous that very often we had to dump men into the line who had had absolutely no training whatever. Such people could not really be considered soldiers at all; they did not always show the necessary steadiness during the fighting, and they had no proper discipline. On top of this, the standard of training of the drafts sent up to us got worse and worse despite all the protests, complaints, and recriminations of those in command. True, very many of these officers, N.C.O.'s, and privates, trained at express speed, afterwards turned out skilful fighting-men and filled their respective posts with distinction; but what an amount of useless waste, disorder, and delay was caused as a result of these second-rate, unorganized drafts!

My army, driving the enemy before it, continued to advance rapidly towards the Dynov-Sanok line, situated behind the San, on which the enemy were hastily retiring. At this time of year the river presented no difficulty to our troops; we crossed it rapidly and unimpeded, and drove the Austrians back still further west. The enemy did not put up much resistance, continuing to withdraw towards positions previously prepared so as to cover the Carpathian passes and prevent us from descending into the Hungarian Plain. They thus occupied a flank position in relation to the Eighth Army. At this moment the Third Army, moving to the north of Przemysl without having to face any considerable enemy force, had arrived outside Krakov. To my amazement I now received orders from the Front Commander to occupy the Carpathian passes with part of my troops, and proceed in person with my main body with all haste towards Krakov to support and protect the left wing of the Third Army and facilitate the capture of that city. On the left of my army, as I have said, I had four Austrian Army Corps which would have been certain to attack me in the rear and cut off my communications. I therefore reported that I could not carry out the order until I had definitely defeated the enemy and driven him from the Carpathians.

Of the four Army Corps under me, one (the VII) had been left to safeguard my left and mask the siege of Przemysl. How then could I possibly leave a screen of troops opposite the four Austrian Army Corps when I had only three Corps at my disposal? If I had decided to leave two Army Corps, I could not have marched westward with only one, and in all probability the two Army Corps, strung out over a front 100 versts (65 miles) long, would have been pierced and my army defeated piecemeal. Having taken all this into consideration, I again reported that I was about to attack the enemy troops on my flank with all available forces, and that until I had defeated them I could not move further. I was answered that there was no time to lose; that the Third Army might find itself in a critical position, that I was to defeat the enemy as quickly as possible and then hurry westward without a pause to aid the Third Army I again stated that I could not carry out the order at the moment, that I would lose no time, and was about to attack immediately, but that I could not calculate exactly at what moment the enemy would be put out of action. At the same time I reported that my army, which had been fighting without respite all November in the Carpathians, was literally unclad. Their summer clothing was worn out; there were no boots; my men, up to their knees in snow and enduring the most severe frosts, had not yet received their winter kit. I added that I considered this as nothing less than a crime on the part of the Commissariat on this front, and demanded the immediate despatch of boots, *valenki*, and warm clothing. At the same time, without waiting for any measures that the Commissariat might take, I issued a personal order for warm clothing to be purchased beyond the lines and brought up to our troops at once.

I should add that the question of warm clothing was one that I had raised as far back as September; but I was informed that the troops on the North-West Front must be provided with warm clothing first because of the more trying climate. Nobody appeared to have realized that in the Carpathians the winter is much more severe and that troops in mountainous country have far greater need of winter kit. Anyhow, I thought that all the troops might well have been supplied with it in November, and their lack of it was due to criminal negligence on the part of the Commissariat. Very shortly after my report I received a fresh telegram from the Front Commander accusing me of being carried away by personal motives, of unnecessarily protracting my operations against the Austrian force which barred my way to the Hungarian Plain, and of putting forward apparently honourable objections in order to conceal my unwillingness to carry out his instructions. Such was the gist of this inexplicable telegram. I had to reply that I simply could not understand how I could loosen my hold on an enemy who was still perfectly capable of fighting and was more numerous than my forces, and leave him on my flanks and rear without abandoning my lines of communication; if I did so I should be clearing the way for him towards Przemysl and Lemberg, and should have to make a new base at Rjeshov, Landshut (Lantsut), and Yaroslav, which would have been equivalent to a defeat.

I ought to say here that right from the beginning of hostilities I had never been able to find out anything about our general plan of campaign. When I was assistant to the General Commanding the Warsaw Military Region, I was acquainted with the general plan then in being in the event of war with Germany and Austro-Hungary. It was strictly defensive and in my opinion ill-conceived from many points of view; but it was not put into execution because circumstances forced us into an offensive campaign for which we had made no preparations. What was this new plan? It was a dead secret to me, and obviously equally so to the General in Command of the Front. It is quite possible that no new plan was ever established at all, and that we followed the special policy determined by the needs of any given moment. However that may be, it seemed to me truly strange that we should think of advancing without looking to our rear, and that no attention whatever should be paid to my left flank. We were continuing to lengthen our lines of communication, we were stringing our troops out indefinitely along the front, and we had no adequate reserve, without which, as we had already found, we could not be safeguarded either against various unpleasant surprises or even against a disaster which might absolutely turn the tables on us in a campaign which had opened so auspiciously. The danger of a dissipation of our forces involved in the ever-growing length of our lines of communication was increased by the fact that we were constantly receiving insistent warnings as to the inadequate supply of munitions that was left to us, especially in the artillery, and the impossibility of finding a quick remedy for this terrible state of affairs.

At the end of November and the beginning of December, the Eighth Army, capturing one position after another, dealt the enemy a staggering blow and forced him to retire on a position south of the Carpathians, leaving the passes unguarded. The fighting was severe and bloody, and we had to use the least possible amount of ammunition in it and yet drive the enemy from ridge to ridge; it had cost our troops dear, and our losses had been serious. Every ridge had been fortified beforehand in the most solid manner with three or four lines of defence. The Magyars especially showed desperate ferocity in defending the passages to the Hungarian Plain, which, as a matter of fact, was not our present objective. The fighting had been particularly fierce at Mezo-Laborch, and the brunt of it had been borne by the VIII Corps, under General Orlov.

The position of this officer was a peculiar one. He was a man of intelligence, with a thorough knowledge of his profession, ingenious, and hard-working; yet his men hated him and did not trust him. From the very beginning of the campaign I had been always hearing complaints that he was an impossible leader and that the troops under him were thoroughly miserable. I attempted to find out for my own purposes what was at the bottom of this, and discovered that his officers disliked him because he was sparing of rewards, very rarely spoke to them, and, in their opinion, looked down on them. The men disliked him because he generally did not give them the usual greeting, never went round the cookhouses, did not sample the food, never thanked them for what they had done, and altogether appeared to ignore their existence. In actual fact he took a great interest in both officers and men, attempted by all the means in his power to achieve results with the least possible bloodshed, and was constantly offering me the most happy suggestions for the improvement of food and kit; but he scorned to let his men know it, or else did not understand how to tell them. I have known other Commanders who took no sort of trouble about anything and yet were loved by their men and called "Father." I warned General Orlov of this weakness, but my words had little effect; he did not know how to win the affection of those under him.

At this moment, the XXIV Corps was attacking further east from Liski towards Baligrod, Tsisna, and Rostovki. Naturally this Army Corps had been given instructions not to advance beyond the crest of the mountain. General Kornilov, however, again attracted attention in no very desirable fashion. Carried away by his fiery spirit and his eagerness to win distinction, he did not limit himself to the instructions of his Army Corps Commander, but without asking for permission, went on down from the mountains, and contrary to definite orders, reached Gumennoye. Here he found the 2nd Composite Cossack Division, which in its capacity as a body of cavalry had been instructed to carry out a raid into the Hungarian Plain, without taking artillery, to create a panic there, and then return speedily. Of his own motion, Kornilov took upon himself a similar duty, and received the punishment he deserved. A Hungarian division moving from Ungvar towards Turka wheeled on Stakchin and came upon the rear of his division, cutting off his line of retreat. He attempted to fight his way back through their lines, but failed and had to abandon a mountain battery which he had with him, his limbers, some of his lorries, and nearly two thousand prisoners, and return with the remnant of his division by mountain paths. I considered it necessary to bring him before a Court of Enquiry for persistently failing to carry out the orders of his Army Corps Commander; but General Tsurikov again begged me to spare Kornilov, speaking of him as a zealous paladin, and himself taking the responsibility, saying that, knowing Kornilov's character, he should have kept a tighter hold on him, and after all had actually done so, but that in this particular instance Kornilov had suddenly slipped through his hands. He implored me not to punish a man for what was sheer intrepidity, even if ill-advised, and promised that it should not occur again. The incident closed with a reprimand in Army Orders to both Tsurikov and Kornilov. Subsequently, when Kornilov was with the Third Army, he once again disobeyed Tsurikov's orders at the moment when their front was broken; this time he was completely surrounded and taken prisoner. When it was too late I regretted the misplaced leniency which had thus led to the utter ruin of this splendid division. Curiously enough, Kornilov never spared his troops, and in all the battles in which this division took part under him it suffered terrible losses, yet both officers and men loved him and trusted him. The fact is that he had magnificent personal courage and used it to push headlong forward.

The enemy was beaten, there was no doubt of that; but he was not destroyed and still remained capable of fight. I had therefore, with a heavy heart, to order my troops to come to a halt, leaving their task half done—i.e., without having reduced the enemy to impotence. In obedience to the orders of the Commander-in-Chief, I now left the XII Army Corps, consisting of three infantry divisions and a division of cavalry, to hold the passes, and despatched westwards the VIII Army Corps, followed by the XXIV, to assist the Third Army, which was now before Krakov and in a really critical situation. I nevertheless reported that I considered my rear to be insecure, and that as soon as I moved forward the enemy would renew the offensive behind me and would certainly overwhelm the XII Army Corps, which by its composition was unfitted to face a numerically much superior enemy force. I added that the Carpathians, especially their western regions, which were much lower than those further east, were not in themselves a serious obstacle, and that infantry with mountain batteries could go anywhere among them so easily that our holding the passes was no guarantee for our safety. But I was again notified that it was imperative that I should hurry to the relief of the Third Army, and I made my best haste. Thus the Eighth Army with four Army Corps on its flank was spread over between two hundred and fifty and three hundred versts from the Russian frontier. Our front line (and we had no reserves) was so thinly held that the enemy obviously could break it at any point where he might concentrate to strike a blow. To reinforce the Third Army I had only two Army Corps, which were much below strength. I could not understand a strategic situation of this kind: I regarded the position of our army as highly critical, and I was convinced that the Austro-Hungarians would be bound to take advantage of so favourable an opportunity. As will be seen later, these fears were justified all too quickly. Even to-day I cannot understand how, with our shortage of munitions, we could pursue this reckless westerly thrust, nor what possessed my Chief to let us advance so far from our base, and particularly to endanger our left and our rear.

NOTES

Alexei Brusilov, *A Soldier's Notebook* (Westport, Conn.: Greenwood, 1971), pp. 76–103.

1. German reserves.
2. A main Austro-Hungarian fortification, one of the most powerful in Europe. The Russians bypassed it and besieged the garrison, finally capturing it in March 1915, only to lose it again later in the year.

Officer-Man Relations
The Other Ranks' Perspective

G. D. Sheffield

> Officers fell into two categories. If they passed dirty
> rifles, handled a spade, or carried a bag of cement, they
> were 'aw reet.' If not, they were 'no bloody bon.'
> —Pte W.V. Tilsley, a 'Derby' infantryman of 55th Divsion

Other Ranks did not respect their officers merely because they held the King's commission. Rather, the soldier's respect had to be earned by the officer, who had to demonstrate a number of leadership qualities. Working-class rankers tended to judge officers by a simple set of criteria. The views of working-class soldiers in 2/5 Glosters[1] support Tilsley's comments:

> A bad officer, that is, a bully, is a—! A good officer, that is, a (sic) considerate, is 'a toff.'
> 'I'd follow him anywhere.' 'The men's friend'; or simply, put in significant tones, a 'gentleman'!

Other Ranks tended to judge officers almost entirely in terms of the deferential dialectic. Expressed more simply, the ranker's view of the officer was largely determined by the way the officer behaved towards him. Officers had to juggle two aspects of their duties. They had to be both militarily efficient and also protective of their men, and these two roles could sometimes conflict. Inevitably, a ranker's view of his officer could vary according to the circumstances. A ranker recalled that on one occasion hungry, cold men on a long march took a dim view of a normally popular officer, but that attitude changed to one of genuine gratitude when a surprise Christmas dinner was provided for the men.

Other factors were far less important in determining a soldier's perception of an officer. Strict disciplinarians were not necessarily unpopular, as they could also possess other qualities, such as leadership, of which the men approved. An officer's youth was not necessarily a barrier to winning his men's approval. In later life, Lt W. R. Bion (Tank Corps) wondered if anybody, 'outside of a public-school culture, believe[s] in the fitness of a boy of nineteen to officer troops in battle?' The answer was that the non-public school classes of 1914–18 accepted 19-year-old boys as military leaders provided the latter behaved in an officer-like manner. An incident in Bion's career suggests that a form of reverse paternalism could exist, in which rankers made concession to the youth of officers. When his tank broke down in action in 1917, Bion was calmed by the 38-year-old 'grandfather' of the crew who showed him photographs of his family. Pte Clarkson of 5/6 Royal Scots recalled that green young officers were inclined to try to teach old sweats their business, but nevertheless he admired their courage.

Pte A. Jobson (39th Division Field Ambulance) placed officers into three categories: 'Good, Bad and perfectly Bloody.' While this over-simplified the ambiguities inherent in the officer-man relationship, Jobson's view may mean that good officers fulfilled their paternal role, bad officers did not, while 'perfectly Bloody' officers were those who were deliberately unpleasant or oppressive towards the men. Broadly speaking, there were three major reasons why officers were disliked by Other Ranks: failures in paternalism; failures of leadership; and deliberate unpleasantness.

Possibly the most important factor in determining a soldier's attitude to his officer was the extent to which he cared for the well-being of his men. The diary of a ranker of 27th Division Ammunition Column shows a direct correlation between his low morale and poor conditions and food, for which he blamed his officers: 'Rotten lot of officers—they fare alright but they don't mind about us. . . . Fed up.'

Rankers also expected their officers to show leadership qualities in battle. Pte S.B. Abbot (86th MG Company) condemned one of his officers (nicknamed 'The Orphan') as a 'thruster,' prepared to endanger his men's lives by unnecessary displays of excess zeal in 'strafing' the enemy positions, while simultaneously appearing to be overconcerned for his own safety. Abbot implicitly compared The Orphan with another officer, referred to respectfully as Mr Street, who was 'a splendid man,' a paternalist who was mourned as 'our brave and kind officer' when he was killed in April 1917. The essence of leadership is diverting the cohesion of the group to the ends desired by the military hierarchy; but this example demonstrates that if officers are perceived to be too eager to take risks, and thus jeopardise their troops, at the very least they forfeit the respect of their men. This seems to have happened, temporarily at least, in 2/Royal Sussex after the battle of Aubers Ridge in May 1915. According to one sergeant, the men blamed the officers for adopting tactics which resulted in heavy casualties. Conversely, in the eyes of his men, an officer's courage could compensate for other failings. A group of rankers, discussing their officer, were heard to say 'Now that little one don't know much, but he's always about when it comes on to shell.'

In general, a middle-class Territorial ranker wrote, officers' 'outward and visible standard of courage' was higher than that of the Other Ranks. 'Windy' officers were usually regarded with some disgust. Both senior and junior non-commissioned ranks felt contempt for an officer of 1/13 Londons 'for showing his fear in front of the men he was supposed to be leading,' by ducking on hearing shells explode, the RSM[2] going so far as to shout at him to 'keep his head up.' An officer of 22/Royal Fusiliers was once found cowering at the bottom of a trench at the beginning of an attack; his platoon sergeant swore at him, and physically bundled him over the parapet. George Coppard (37th MG Company) mingled his disgust for an officer who refused to emerge from a dugout with pity for his physical and mental condition. Although one ex-ranker wrote of men covering up the 'deficiencies' of 'dud' officers, this attitude does not seem to have been typical. Many soldiers appeared to have shared Lord Moran's view that courage was very much a matter of character and willpower, that everyone felt fear, but only cowards gave way to it. Officers were expected by their men to set an example of courage. Cowards had, in the eyes of the Other Ranks, forfeited all right to commissioned status, and the privileges that went with it.

Rankers also expected their officers to behave in a fitting, gentlemanly manner when out of action. Genteel disgust at the loutish behaviour of some 'temporary gentleman' was shared by some rankers. An interesting insight into this is given by Pte Eric Linklater (4/5 Black Watch). One evening, Linklater was sitting in an estaminet with some sergeants when the peace was disturbed by a drunken, argumentative and visibly sexually aroused temporary officer chasing the hostess. The sergeants, working-class slum-dwellers in civilian life, were 'incensed by such behaviour in an officer of their regiment.' Officers did not have to make an exhibition of themselves to be condemned as ungentlemanly by their men. Passages in the diary of the officers' mess sergeant of a TF[3] unit, 1/5 Buffs, indicate that he respected the original officers of the battalion, who were gentlemanly and paternal, but he disliked their replacements who lacked these qualities. The sergeant was greatly aggrieved when his pay was reduced because the six surviving officers judged that he had less work to do: 'A gentleman's thanks,' he commented sarcastically, 'for what you have done for them.' This sergeant was reacting to his hierarchical superiors' failure to keep their side of the deferential bargain.

While failures of paternalism and leadership might be ascribed, by charitably-minded soldiers like Coppard, to the frailties of human nature, deliberate unpleasantness on the part of officers was deeply resented. Pte A.J. Abraham came across two officers who were regarded as petty tyrants. One, at a training unit, was nicknamed the 'Black Bastard.' He was 'a mean type and we hated his guts.' The other, Abraham's platoon officer in 8/Queen's, made a decision which long rankled with Abraham, when he refused to allow the men to wear greatcoats or groundsheets in heavy rain. This failure to improve the conditions of the men was just one of many reasons why Abraham had a low opinion of this officer. However, Abraham had a very different attitude towards others: 'Some of our officers were born leaders, men we instinctively trusted and respected.'

It is rare indeed to find a blanket condemnation of officers in soldiers' memoirs, diaries or letters. A furious denunciation of one officer is likely to be followed by a complimentary reference to another. Pte Frank Dunham of 1/7 Londons was scathing about one officer, nicknamed 'Nellie,' but wrote about Capt. K.O. Peppiatt in glowing terms. Peppiatt was 'a sport,' a 'fine soldier . . . , [who] was not afraid to take his share in any of the risky jobs.' In fact, it is uncommon to discover an officer who was actively hated by his men, as opposed to one who was criticised for neglecting his men or for thoughtlessness. One such was a Northamptonshire Yeomanry officer, known as 'the Bloody Bastard,' described by one ranker as 'the most detested and hated officer I ever met in two world wars.' The interesting point is not that this officer was despised, but that he suffered by comparison with the officer whom he had replaced, who had been popular with the men. Because most officers were paternal and lived up to their side of the unspoken deferential bargain, officers who did not conform to the general pattern of officer-man relations were regarded with especial distaste by rankers.

Favourable references to officers can often be found in the writings of Other Ranks, although not as frequently as complementary references to men occur in officers' letters and diaries. In part this was a reflection of the differing perceptions of the relationship. It was also a product of the generally healthy state of officer-man relations. Only if an officer was exceptionally good, or exceptionally bad, or if a particular officer suddenly came to mind, if he was killed or wounded for instance, was he likely to be mentioned in the letters or diaries of an Other Rank. To take one instance, the first fatal casualty mentioned by name in the diary of L/Cpl Joe Griffiths (1/King's Royal Rifle Corps) was 2/Lt Bentall, 'who was only 18 a real good sort & was liked & respected by his men.' His sense of loss prompted Griffiths to record his appreciation of this officer which otherwise would have been unknown.

Officers' privileges were resented by some, mostly middle-class, rankers. One was a private of the London Scottish who objected to the greater opportunities for leave available to officers. His complaints were echoed three years later by a conscript Pay Corps private. The artist Stanley Spencer, who served as a ranker with 7/Royal Berks, slipped an oblique comment into his painting *The Resurrection of the Soldiers*. In among scenes of dead soldiers rising from their graves and shaking hands with their mates is a glum-looking officer—identified by his brown boots—cleaning his own kit.

These criticisms were fairly exceptional. Pte Coppard had no doubt about the reason why most soldiers accepted the disparity in privileges without complaint: 'the Tommy accepted it as the natural order of things,' although they might joke about the differences, for example by referring to 'Old Orkney' whisky as "Officers Only." Provided that an officer behaved in a certain way, his privileges were not resented by the ordinary working-class soldier. If an officer behaved in an 'unofficerlike' way, by acting unfairly, neglecting his men or acting in a cowardly manner, in his men's eyes he forfeited his rights to his lifestyle.

This point is illustrated by an incident that occurred on a troop ship *en route* to the Dardanelles in August 1915. On two days officers were allowed ashore while the men were kept on board ship. Several revealing remarks about this appear in Pte G. Brown's diary. First, he commented that the officers 'didn't play the game with us.' Secondly, while admitting that to send a large number of men on shore leave presented difficulties, he argued 'the OCs should have been sports and tried some arrangement.' The use of public school sporting imagery reinforced the sense of unfairness experienced by these rankers. Whether in the trenches or on board a troopship, ordinary soldiers accepted that the officer might retire to a well-appointed dugout or cabin, but only after he had ensured that his men were fed and made as comfortable as possible. In this case the officers had neglected their paternal duty and officer-man relations suffered as a result; '[There was] Bad feeling about the business and officers were booed leaving.'

In 1916, an upper-class gentleman ranker wrote of a temporary officer who had joined a New Army[4] battalion at the beginning of the war, knowing as little about military life as the men he commanded. Gradually he trained as a soldier alongside his men. Little by little he learned the character of each individual soldier of his platoon. By his kindly and tactful handling of the men, he won their confidence, affection and love. The troops grew to feel that they belonged to him, and he belonged to them. His smile 'was something worth living for, and worth working for,' while 'his look of displeasure and disappointment was a thing that we would do anything to avoid.' In the trenches, the men worried for his safety, and they mourned him when he was killed. In the final paragraph, the 'Beloved Captain' appears alongside Christ in heaven.

The author, Donald Hankey, despite his upper-class origins, served in the ranks of 7/Rifle Brigade for a year in 1914–15. Later, as an officer in 1/Royal Warwicks, Hankey does seem to have been brave and paternal. His idealised portrait of 'The Beloved Captain,' which first appeared in the *Spectator*, reflects, in exaggerated form, the feelings of many rankers towards good officers. It would be ludicrous to claim that all rankers regarded all officers in this way, but some soldiers, working-class and middle-class alike, certainly had a very high opinion of some of their officers. Some younger soldiers hero-worshipped their officers, just as other youths idolised sportsmen or popular masters at school. More mature men respected officers for their courage and their demeanour. Ernest Shephard, a prewar Regular NCO of 1/Dorsets, described Capt. Algeo as 'a real example of the Regular 'Officer and Gentleman.' . . . Absolutely fearless and [whose] first and last thought [is] for the men.' A private of 1/15 Londons wrote that his company commander

held the devotion and respect of all who served him. . . . His officers and men were his family. He knew their foibles and most of their hopes and fears. They executed his orders explicitly and confidently.

Pte Giles Eyre (2/King's Royal Rifle Corps) also wrote of men defending the honour of their officer against a rival platoon: 'There ain't no one in the Batt. like Mr. Walker, and you can swank as much as yer likes. We know's 'im and wouldn't swap 'im for nuffink.'

Just as the Beloved Captain's platoon throve on his smile, it does seem that small acts of kindness and friendship on the part of officers had a disproportionate effect on rankers' morale. In a letter of July 1915 a lance-corporal of 7/Norfolks, who, interestingly, was of middle- rather than working-class background, and an artist in civilian life, mentioned that he had attended an early-morning Communion service. His former platoon commander, a fellow scoutmaster, 'came up and spoke to me afterwards, which was very decent of him.'

Rather more practically, in mid-1915 an officer of 2/Rifle Brigade told his men who had been selected for a working party that it was unfair for them to be called upon 'to do fatigues while we were at rest, and told the men not to work too hard.' There are two points of particular interest about this incident. First, it appears in the unpublished memoirs of J.W. Riddell, who was not a sensitive middle-class artist but a hard-bitten prewar Regular NCO. Second, the officer's advice was well-intentioned, but if the troops had taken it, they would have been condemned to a longer spell in the trenches. The fact that Riddell bothered to record the incident in his postwar memoirs, which were extremely critical of military authority, indicates that he appreciated the officer's kindness and concern for his men, and his desire to protect them against the unfair demands of the military system. It also illustrates the gulf in perceptions between the commissioned and non-commissioned ranks.

How common a figure was the "Beloved Captain'? A partial answer occurs in an interesting analysis of the officer-man relationship which appeared in 1938. Its author was an anonymous former ranker. This article drew attention to the ambiguities in the officer-man relationship. When he tried to recall his officers, he wrote, a trick of memory produced a composite figure:

> boyish and middle-aged, cool and reckless, grave and humourous, aloof and intimate; a martinet lapsing into an indulgent father; a thwarter becoming an aider and abetter; an enemy melting into a friend.

This ex-ranker's analysis of the attributes of the good officer, interestingly enough, had many points in common with the 'official' view of military leadership discussed in an earlier chapter. He regarded the officers' battlefield role as important: '[we] despised some for their deficiencies on parade, while admiring their imperturbability under fire.' However, other attributes of the 'good' officer were perhaps less likely to be approved by the powers-that-be: 'no officer was good who had not learned when to be deaf, dumb, and blind—and when not to be.' Most officers, the writer asserted, acquired these skills on active service. They also learned to question both Rudyard Kipling's opinions of the private's 'psychology and character,' which were, after all, some forty years out of date by the 1914–18 war, and also textbook views on 'the behaviour of men in the mass.' In the field, officers learned man-management, and their effectiveness in this sphere greatly influenced their men's opinion of them. The ideal officer, in the writer's view, would have been a man of all-around talent. However, a paternal officer who genuinely cared about the welfare of the troops under his command would be forgiven many sins of omission and commission by the ordinary soldier. One of the writer's officers was renowned for his ineptitude on the drill square 'yet this officer was the best in the battalion for the care of his men in the trenches.'

> 'Looking back,' this writer argued, 'with a better appreciation of their difficulties than we then had, at the officers under whom we served, we can have nothing but admiration for almost all of them—admiration with a tinge of affection.'

Officers who fell short of the ideal in some way, 'we can afford to forgive':

> We do not need to be reminded that if in civil affairs we could get as square a deal and as much consideration from our superiors as we got from officers when we were in the Army, the world would be a pleasanter place to live in that some of us are finding it.

Thus the writer was suggesting that most regimental officers were effective man-managers who possessed, in some measure, the attributes and attitudes of the 'Beloved Captain.' This view lacks the sentimentality of Hankey's idealised portrait, depicting instead officers as fallible human beings. However, like Hankey's article, it expresses the rankers' admiration of brave and paternal officers, and recognises the officer's role in making life bearable for the soldier. The impact of the officer on the morale of the private perhaps only became apparent in retrospect. Back in civilian life, former soldiers who were now unemployed, or who worked in dangerous or unrewarding jobs, had no paternal subalterns to look after their interests.

Traditionally, Regular officers believed that working-class soldiers preferred to be commanded by gentlemen rather than by officers of humble origin who had been promoted through the ranks. How, then, did ordinary soldiers regard the large numbers of officers of lower-class origin commissioned during the Great War?

The traditional view of ranker officers was slow to disappear. Pte John Tucker (1/13 Londons) recalled the lower ranks of this class corps disdaining a subaltern because he was a former bank clerk and spoke 'with a slight cockney accent.' Interestingly, Tucker, who recognised in retrospect that this snobbish prejudice was ludicrous, was himself a city clerk before the war. A.M. Burrage, a middle-class journalist turned embittered private soldier, wrote scathingly of some officers he encountered who

> judging by the[ir] manners and accents . . . were nearly all 'Smiffs,' late of Little Buggington Grammar school, who had been 'clurks' in civil life . . .

In 1917 Pte R. Cude (7/Buffs) commented that some newly-arrived officers were only commissioned because of the manpower shortage: 'Pon my word, if this is the best that England can do, it is time she packed [up].' However Cude, who seems to have been an artisan in civilian life, also described his platoon officer as 'a thorough Gentleman.' He made this comment in September 1915, before his unit had taken heavy casualties and replacements for the original public school subalterns arrived.

Some commentators attempted to rationalise the dislike of Other Ranks for lower-class officers. G.W. Grossmith's evidence supports the traditional view of ranker-officers. He believed that rankers preferred officers to be recognisable as such by their speech and behaviour, and once heard a ranker comment that his new platoon commander was 'only one of us.' Grossmith served in the rank of 7/Bedfords and was later commissioned into a Regular battalion, 2/Leicesters. Such views may have been typical of Regular units, for a Regular RSM of 1/HLI believed that humbly-born temporary officers, not being 'born and bred' to leadership, did not command the same loyalty given by the men to public school–educated officers.

Others offered more specific reasons for the common dislike of lower-class officers. A temporary officer of 1/6 Royal West Kent believed that tanker-officers were unpopular with the men because 'they knew their job' and were aware of the various tricks and dodges employed by the ranks; in other words, they were poachers turned gamekeepers, and as gamekeepers they were rather too effective for the men's liking. A working-class private of 23/Royal Fusiliers thought that former NCOs found it necessary to assert themselves with officious behaviour. Burrage held a similar view:

> Quite the worst type of officer was the promoted sergeant-major. . . . Whatever rank they achieved they were still warrant-officers in spirit. They could never be anything else.

An ex-Regular NCO who served as an officer in 2/Camerons seemed to fit this pattern. According to a fellow officer, writing in 1916, 'like most rankers, but not all, [he is] not too well liked by the men. He is apt to be fussy and bullying in matters of detail.' This opinion is of interest not least because the writer was himself a ranker-officer, although having served in the ranks of the London Rifle Brigade, a Territorial class corps, he clearly regarded himself as being in a very different category from a former Regular NCO.

It is not surprising that attitudes such as these should be so widespread, given the degree of class consciousness in British society and the assumptions underlying the deferential/paternal relationship. A study of the Leeds Rifles (1/7 and 2/7 West Yorks) concluded that the men of these Territorial units insisted on gentlemanly officers, and would not accept officers who were not gentlemen, although this may not have been an attitude which was typical of the Territorial Force in its entirety.

Other wartime soldiers thought differently. J. Gibbons, who served in the ranks of a London TF unit, believed that working-class replacements for public school officers were just as effective as their socially elite predecessors. M.L. Walkington, a grammar-school boy who served as a ranker in a TF class corps (16/Londons) before being commissioned, believed that competent but poorly educated NCOs who received commissions generally made valuable officers. The prospect of officer status gave 'great encouragement to young NCOs who developed ambition.' The usual practice was for newly commissioned officers to be posted to units other than the one in which they had served as rankers, but some cohesive 'family' Territorial and New Army units preferred to take back their 'old boys.' This practice can also be found in some Regular units throughout the war. CSM Sayers of 4/Middlesex was commissioned in the field in October 1914 and served with the battalion until his death in 1915, while Sgt Fenner (3/Rifle Bde) was commissioned in his battalion in 1917.

Commanders of units such as these presumably considered that the discipline and cohesion of their battalion or battery was strong enough to overcome any problems that might have resulted from allowing ranker officers back into their original unit, although often such men were posted to different companies. One such officer, G.H. Cole, commented that he had no problems adjusting to officer status because he 'grew up' as a ranker in his battalion, 1/20 Londons. Cole also saw the matter from the ranker's perspective. As a private, his company commander was a man who had been in his form at school. 'In public, of course,' Cole wrote, 'No-one would have known that we had ever met.' Although there was some prejudice against ranker-officers among Other Ranks, it is rare indeed to find criticism of a specific officer whom a ranker had known in his previous incarnation as an ordinary soldier.

Even outside 'family' units, soldiers meeting friends who were now commissioned officers seem to have observed the spirit, if not the letter, of discipline. Other Ranks sometimes talked informally with officer friends but rarely took advantage of this relationship. The British army could have followed the Australian practice and allowed more ranker-officers to return to their old units. Generally speaking, the self-discipline of Other Ranks was strong enough to ensure that military efficiency did not suffer from the commissioning of officers within a unit. It may even have enhanced it, rather as Walkington suggested, by encouraging rankers to strive for excellence, in the knowledge that they would not have to be posted away from their battalion on becoming an officer.

By the end of the war the officers of the British army were drawn from a wider social spectrum than ever before. It is possibly significant that Tucker's comments quoted above refer to 1915, a time when lower-class officers were somewhat rarer than was to be the case later in the war, for if mistrust of working-class and lower-middle-class officers had been as widespread as some have claimed, officer-man relations should have been poor throughout the army by 1918. Indeed, following this argument through to its logical conclusion, the British army should have disintegrated in 1917–18 because Other Ranks would have refused to follow the lower-class officers commissioned to in place of the 'gentlemanly' officers who had been killed. Of course, this did not happen: officer-man relations remained generally cordial throughout the war.

Ultimately, an officer's relations with his men were determined not by his social class, or by his previous service in the ranks, but by his competence, leadership skills, paternalism and courage. It is true that some former Regular NCOs did not find the transition to commissioned rank easy, and that some lower-class officers had some difficulty in establishing their credibility with their soldiers. However, it should not be forgotten that officer training was remarkably effective in educating ranker-officers in the ethos and methods of the Regular officer class, and that from early 1916 onwards most commissions had to be earned on the battlefield. A newly-commissioned officer had to give practical demonstrations of his paternalism and leadership qualities in the trenches and on the battlefield, and this compensated for any lack of social standing, whatever misgivings private soldiers might originally have had about the social origins of an officer. Confirmation of this theory comes from a surprising source. That scourge of the temporary gentleman, Pte A.M. Burrage, concluded that officers

> who came from shops and offices, with little education and less tradition, did their job somehow and did it well. I hated being jiggered about (we used a slightly different phrase) by people that I considered my inferiors . . . but I who was a private, and a bad one at that, freely own that it was the British subaltern who won the war.

There is a very useful phrase of Great War vintage: 'On parade, on parade; off parade, off parade,' meaning 'what was permissible on certain occasions might be a military crime on others.' This phrase aptly describes the relations of many officers with their men; 'regimental' on some occasions, informal on others. In the trenches, relations between officers and men were generally characterised by a greater degree of informality than was the case behind the lines. Officers and men quietly dispensed with much of the pomp and ceremony. In one extreme example, an 18th Division private reported (in a scandalised manner) that officers of a 32nd Division unit 'were known to the men by their Christian name.' More commonly, some officers used soldiers' nicknames. Such informality was not always appreciated by higher military authorities, the lack of 'regimental' soldiering in XI Corps in 1916 leading, in the view of Corps staff, to a dangerous slackening of discipline.

In the trenches, it would often be difficult for the casual observer to tell officers and men apart. A newly-commissioned ranker-officer was helped to play the part of a gentleman by his uniform, which was 'the khaki equivalent of hunting dress,' very different from the 'shabby garb of the artisan' worn by the private. However, in some units, officers carried rifles and packs and wore privates' uniforms, the rank badges on the sleeve replaced by unobtrusive pips on the shoulder. While this adoption of rankers' dress as a protection against snipers was not universally popular, some officers arguing that it was wrong that men could not easily recognise their officers, it aptly symbolised the decrease in formality in inter-rank relations that generally occurred in the line.

Coppard somewhat cynically referred to the decreased gap between officers and men in the trenches as 'a temporary attempt at chumminess.' In some units it might be the case that only in the trenches were junior officers, out of sight of their superiors, able to establish informal relations with their men. However, in other units officer-man relations achieved a degree of informality out of the trenches. A sergeant of 2/6 Lancashire Fusiliers recalled that in June 1917 D company was 'one great happy family. After parades discipline was relaxed and we were at liberty to spend most of our time in our own way.' There was a 'close bond' between officers and men, a 'very dear thing in the throes of war.'

Coppard also was not unsympathetic to officers. He commented on the weight of responsibility that they bore for their men's lives. One mistake could kill the men of their platoon: 'The nervousness, strain and irritability of his officers could be responsible for a lot of what Tommy had to put up with.' Similarly, the stress of waiting to go into battle caused one artillery officer to verbally abuse the officers' servants. Coppard also made an important point about the way in which one of the artificial barriers of rank was reduced on active service. He believed that he became less scared of officers as time went on, not because officers became 'any more friendly, but because we youngsters were growing up.' In action, officers could not hide behind their status and rank. They had to prove themselves as leaders, and inevitably some made mistakes and demonstrated that they were far from omnipotent. A private of 32nd Field Ambulance saw this process in operation on 7 August 1915, at Suvla Bay:

> You could see the spreading dismay as the ordinary Tommies recognised their own fear and hesitation in the eyes of these one-pip striplings [second lieutenants]. Men under fire . . . watch each other with nerves on edge. 'Blimey! Even the bloody officers are lost!
> . . .

Such comments suggest that Capt. T.M. Sibley was to some extent correct when he wrote in June 1916 that the gulf between officers and men was 'a very important part of the British Army system' and soldiers would lose their respect for some officers if they came to know them. This remark gives a salutary reminder of the difficulties of generalising about inter-rank relations in an organisation as big as the British army.

In the words of a subaltern of 2/King's Own Yorkshire Light Infantry, 'the horizon of the Infantryman in the Great War was small, but his philosophy was straightforward'; the war had to be fought, and if mail, food and cigarettes were available, the war was going well. One private was not untypical in regarding himself as belonging first to his platoon, then to his company, and then to his battalion. For the most part, higher formations meant little to the private, although some divisions such as 18th (Eastern), 51st (Highland) and 56th (London), did acquire a measure of divisional *esprit de corps*. Junior officers and rankers alike shared this narrowness of vision. In this tiny, insular world, it is not surprising that men turned in on each other for affection, or that minor acts of benevolence were greatly appreciated. Many officers regarded it as part of their duties to write letters of condolence to the families of soldiers who had been killed or wounded while serving under their command. While this could be interpreted as just another aspect of military paternalism, there are also many examples of NCOs and privates writing to the families of their officers. It was not uncommon for soldiers on leave to visit the families of their officers, or officers the families of soldiers. Indeed, one historian, citing the correspondence of a ranker with the widow of his officer, has suggested that 'mourning for the same man created a strong bond' between disparate individuals.

Apart from demonstrating the affection and comradeship felt by men for their officers, and vice versa, such letters also helped to relieve one of the principal factors that undermined the morale of fighting men: worry about their families. The soldiers could face death knowing that their loved ones would receive some comfort, however small. Letters of sympathy from ordinary rankers were perhaps especially comforting to officers' families, because they gave evidence of the effectiveness of their military leadership, of a duty performed unto death, of a sacrifice nobly given. In many cases, it took a real effort for ill-educated privates to write a formal letter of this sort. This obviously did not apply to Pte S. Brashier of 22/Royal Fusilliers, who wrote to the family of the late Capt. G.D.A. Black:

> To us he was life itself, and the confidence we placed in him was great. Really we used to say—'He knew no fear' and so though we greatly miss him we realize what sorrow and grief it (sic) has come to you, and so our thoughts go out to you in your great sorrow.

This letter was copied and circulated among Black's family. It obviously did provide some comfort, since it has been treasured in the family down to the present day.

Some point of mutual interest, such as common regional loyalties or language, helped to break down barriers between the ranks. Edmund Blunden actually found it easier to get on with his soldiers, fellow Sussexmen, than with some of his brother officers. Welsh-speaking officers and men of 15/Royal Welsh Fusiliers talked freely together; English was regarded as 'the language of the Army, Welsh the language of friendship and companionship' and the use of Welsh formed 'a bond of unity, that sense of being an enclave within a community.' Likewise, in Scots units, enthusiasm for bagpipes, 'which were played by Scottish gentlemen,' 'reinforced the bond' between rankers and officer.'

Some close relationships developed between officers and men when a soldier emerged from the khaki mass. NCOs would sometimes find themselves alone with officers, and mutual respect could blossom into greater intimacy. This happened in, of all units, the South Persia Rifles, where a middle-class officer (formerly a ranker in the 7/Royal Dublin Fusiliers) was thrown into the company of a British sergeant. Similarly, Anthony Eden (21/King's Royal Rifle Corps) wrote movingly of nights spent on watch in Plugstreet Wood, when he would hold long discussions with a platoon sergeant, Norman Carmichael, whom Eden counted as a friend. (See below for a further discussion of officer-NCO relations). The authors Stephen Graham and Wilfred Ewart served together in the Scots Guards, and struck up a friendship, even though the former was a private and the latter a captain. Ewart's fellow officers apparently disapproved of the relationship.

Soldier-servants and officers could become friendly within the bounds imposed by rank and class. A public school officer of 1/North Staffords summed up his relationship with Tidmarsh, his working-class 'old-soldier' batman, in these words:

> We were not exactly friends because of the differences of social class, but, accepting these differences, we were not separated by them. Each regarded the other as a personality to be respected.

Soldier-servants had a unique opportunity to get to know their officers, 'warts and all.' One prewar soldier-servant's duties commenced each morning at 6 a.m., when he had to take a glass of whisky to his officer's bedroom, followed by two boiled eggs and more whisky. Soldiers had good reason to be friendly to their officers. As a private of Worcestershire Yeomanry pointed out, being an officer's servant 'is much better than being in the troops' since he received many luxuries and was excused night guards. It is certainly true that many servants had a privileged position. These privileges might take the form of physical comfort—a company commander of 2/21 Londons shared a tent and pooled rations with his servant while on campaign in Palestine—but there were also more subtle benefits to being an officers' servant. This is indicated by the obvious delight of a mess cook who summoned other servants to watch the spectacle of a newly-arrived subaltern making a fool of himself. This incident, in which the officer had to be disentangled from coils of wire by the grinning cook, also indicates that soldier-servants were allowed a certain amount of license, an aspect of the relationship which is beautifully captured by some of the comic scenes in Sherriff's play *Journey's End*.

An unfriendly or surly servant, let alone an incompetent one, ran the risk of being returned to normal duty and forfeiting his privileged existence, so it was in his own interest to be pleasant. However, some genuine friendships developed between officers and servants. An officer of 11/Cheshires 'witnessed a most touching farewell' between the battalion commander and his old servant: 'they embraced and both shed tears.' Pte Harry Adams (6/Queens) developed a 'real attachment' to his officer, Mr Jefferies, and experienced 'great grief' when he heard of his death in 1918. Capt. V.F. Eberle (48th Division Royal Engineers) commented that 'the relationship between a good batman and his officer is often no mean criterion of the latter.'

Other rankers who emerged from the anonymity of the ranks also enjoyed more than usually intimate relations with officers. Pte Clarkson, a runner for a company commander in 5/6 Royal Scots, wrote that mutual respect was high and that he learned to trust his officer. In a common act of friendship, the officer would often give Clarkson extra rum on cold nights. Another soldier with a semi-independent existence was Sgt Jones, 'of Jones's water dump,' on Gallipoli, whom an officer compared to a friendly 'inn-keeper.' Officers and men alike would congregate in Jones's dugout to hear the latest rumours. All of these examples indicate the type of informal, friendly relations which could develop between officers and men when circumstances allowed individuals to get to know each other as men.

However, it is clear that for the most part, circumstances did not allow rankers and officers to develop this sort of relationship. The restraining hand of the NCO was one of the factors why inter-rank relations did not often grow from friendliness into real intimacy. This is well illustrated by a scene in an autobiographical novel by a ranker-officer, where a newly-arrived subaltern briefed his men and then asked them if they had any questions. This was clearly regarded as unusual, and to 'continue the feeling of part-intimacy with the officer' a private took advantage of the invitation and actually asked a question. On receiving a polite and informative answer the private was emboldened to ask another. However, the private was well aware of the disapproval of his sergeant, who suspected insolence, although none was intended. The moral of this episode was even if the private and the subaltern were prepared to establish an informal relationship, the NCO, who in many ways had the greater influence over the life of the private, was capable of being less broad-minded.

The relationship between the non-commissioned officer and the officer deserves special consideration. The NCO played a crucial role in the maintenance of discipline, and the administration and management of military units. During the Great War, as before and since, NCOs were the 'backbone' of the British army. They formed the crucial link between the officer and the ranker, passing orders down the chain of command and performing, as a contemporary commentator noted, the 'grave and all-important task of enforcing that prompt obedience to orders that is the life's blood of an army.' As noted above, the NCO, rather than the officer, was often the figure of authority who had the greatest impact on the life of the ordinary soldier, although it is fair to say officers and men came into contact more frequently on active service than in peacetime. NCOs varied greatly in status. They included the lance-corporal, 'one who has position, but no magnitude,' an appointment which was only one step up from a private and was often held in an acting and unpaid capacity. For our purposes it also included the senior non-commissioned rank in a unit, the regimental sergeant major (RSM). The RSM, technically a warrant officer (WO), was, in contrast to the unfortunate 'lance jack,' a powerful and often respected figure. The British NCOs of 1914–18 deserve a major study, but here we can reflect only on those aspects of their role that directly affected officer-man relations.

There were two basic species of NCO. First, there were the Regular NCOs encountered by all soldiers at training establishments throughout the war. Some of whom were the 'old soldier' types immortalised by C.E. Montague: men who preferred drinking to training, who were open to bribes, and who stole army property. Many were older men, reservists who were medically unfit for active service. Second, there were NCOs appointed from the ranks of wartime volunteers and conscripts. In the earlier part of the war, some difficulty was experienced with such NCOs, as attempts to enforce the separation from the rank and file deemed necessary by the army were not always successful in New Army and Territorial units.

NCOs had reached positions of responsibility because officers believed they were more intelligent than privates and had the ability to administer, and indeed accept, discipline although the degree of trust reposed in NCOs varied from unit to unit, depending on the personality of the commanding officer. A former farm labourer, serving as a junior NCO in a trench mortar battery, summed up the relationship between NCOs and men in these words:

> it dose (sic) not do for us [the NCOs] to sleep with them [the men] for we are like Masters on a farm and the men under us you see how the thing works.

Like civilian foremen, NCOs ensured smooth running of a unit, keeping a finger on the pulse of a complex organisation. Thus the word of an NCO was usually taken at face value, even if it conflicted with that of a private. Reinforcement of the NCO's authority was seen as being of greater importance than the strict administration of justice. NCOs were known to impose punishments which were illegal but nonetheless tacitly condoned by officers. Thus it was vital that NCOs could be trusted by their officers. Capt. Hamond, in a typically forthright sentence, wrote that an NCO who was a liar or who manufactured evidence 'must be destroyed at once.'

The NCOs' duties were not simply concerned with discipline. They had a vital role in training, both on active service and at home. One gunner commented that he did not come into contact with a single officer during his training in England, for NCOs carried out all the work. C.S. Lewis, an officer of 3/SLI, a Special Reserve unit based in England, wrote in October 1917 that all the training was carried out by NCOs; 'All you do is to lead your party onto parade, hand them over to their instructor, and then walk about doing nothing at all.' On active service, a whole host of other duties came the way of the NCO, including ensuring a fair division of food when in the line, and also responsibility for kit, arms and equipment. Less formal duties included protecting soldiers against higher authority, and inculcating regimental traditions. On the battlefield, NCOs had to lead men, to command platoons if the officers were killed or wounded and promote and sustain morale. It is not surprising that one ex-ranker wrote 'Platoon sergeants—what would the War have been without them? Why, they ran the thing! At least, that was the impression we received.'

The NCO's role therefore overlapped with that of the officer. Although the military hierarchy imposed 'distance' between the private and the NCO, it was not as great as that between privates and officers. Junior NCOs, for instance, often shared many of the living conditions of Other Ranks, and some NCOs operated on the principle of 'on parade, on parade; off parade, off parade' with their men. NCOs could also do things that an officer officially could not, such as physically lay hands upon the men. Most importantly of all, since NCOs were usually appointed from within the unit, they were in a position to gain more detailed knowledge of the men than even the most paternal and informal office could ever hope to obtain. In 1917, RQMS Young of 2/17 Londons reflected on his methods of command: 'By a word, I can hold them in check; when they get unruly, because I know them and their East End spirit.'

Given the wide range of types and functions of NCOs, it is difficult to generalize about the state of relations between the NCOs and privates. Driver R.L. Venables, for instance, served under two very different battery sergeant-majors. The BSM in his battery of 31st Division artillery was a foul-mouthed 'nasty piece of work' from the metropolis gutter,' while the BSM in his previous battalion, in 32nd Division, was 'first-class,' never using foul language on parade. Moreover, Venables believed that the discipline in the 32nd Division unit was superior. Broadly speaking, the relationship between privates and NCOs within the unit was more often than not characterized by respect.

It can be seen that many of the NCO's duties, responsibilities and experiences were paralleled by those of officers:

> . . . I am learning how to mix discipline and persuasion. . . . I have got to know the roughs in our platoon pretty well. . . . You never get to the stage of really trusting them, but you can establish working relationships with them by expedients which seem almost childish, silly jokes and a kind of assumed (for me) music-hall, pub-loafing heartiness. It's acting, of course, but I come to feel more and more that all leadership is in a way acting, conscious or unconscious.

This passage could easily have been written by a subaltern but it was in fact penned by a Wykehamist NCO of 6/Duke of Cornwallis Light Infantry. The experiences of Sgt. C.F. Jones of 2/15 Londons also have many points of comparison with those of officers. In his time he defended a new draft of boys, 'as a lioness its whelps' against what he perceived to be the unfair demands of a higher authority, in this case, the orderly sergeant. The good NCO, Jones believed, could play a vital role in 'getting the best out of his men' by seeing that rations were fairly distributed. Clearly, the good NCO, like the good officer, was a paternalist. According to an officer of 1/Royal Welsh Fusiliers, the acid test of 'good' and 'useless' NCOs was their behaviour during a 'working party in the rain.' The useless NCO would take shelter. The good NCO would help the men with their tasks.

In practice, NCOs could become the junior partners of regimental officers in running a platoon, company or battalion. Frederic Manning's fictional RSM concisely expressed the importance of the relationship between the officer and the NCO:

> [W]hen you're an officer you won't know your men. You'll be lucky if you know your NCOs, and you'll have to leave a lot of it to them. You'll have to keep them up to the mark; but you'll have to trust them, and let them know it.

The fact that in the latter part of the war many officers had served as NCOs undoubtedly aided the building of good working relationships. Sgt R.H. Tawney (22/Manchesters), writing of the moments just before going into action on the Somme in 1916, noted that his platoon officer 'had enough sense not to come fussing round'; sense gained, it is implied, as a result of his previous experience as an NCO.

Wyn Griffith, a company commander in 15/Royal Welsh Fusiliers, left a pen-portrait of his relationship with his company sergeant-major. Just as a company commander would often hold an informal 'board meeting' with his subaltern, Griffith and his CSM would relax together over a glass of whisky and a pipe in the company officers' mess and gossip about the men of the company. Griffith made two revealing remarks about this relationship. First, 'Our life thrust us close together; his [the CSM's] position was in its way as solitary as my own.' Both had responsibility for their men. Both needed to strike a delicate balance between being part of the company 'team' and being slightly aloof from it. Second, the gossip allowed Griffith to find out incidents in the life of the company 'unknown to the least unapproachable of company commanders, unguessed at in spite of the close contact of life in the trenches.' For example, 'Had I heard what Delivett said when a pip-squeak blew some mud in his mess tin . . . ?' In short, the CSM provided an important link between the private and the company commander. In this case, and many others, the NCO and officer worked together as a harmonious team. Similar relationships could exist between other grades of NCO and officer, but in all cases, they had to be founded upon mutual goodwill and carefully nurtured.

It is instructive to compare Griffith's relationship with his CSM with the comments of Sgt S.F. Hatton (Middlesex Yeomanry) concerning an officer who tried to

> court popularity by being over-friendly with the sergeants, and coming into the sergeants' mess to stand drinks. . . . In fact, you have to be just the right type of officer to ever receive an invitation into the sergeants' mess, to be able to drink with them, and preserve their loyalty and your own dignity. . . . [A] sergeant no more wants a young and inexperienced officer in the mess than a man really wants a woman in a public-house.

This passage neatly encapsulates the problem that faced officers who wished to demonstrate respect and friendship for their NCOs. Hatton's subaltern breached some of the important ground rules, recognised by officers and NCOs alike, as essential for the maintenance of discipline. To buy drinks for NCOs could be interpreted as an attempt to buy loyalty. In addition, the good officer understood that the NCOs were entitled to privacy in their mess, their home. No matter how friendly an officer might be, it was impossible for a subordinate to be completely relaxed in a superior's company. While an experienced officer would know enough not to abuse the privilege of admission to the sergeants' mess, to talk to the sergeants in an appropriate way and to make a tactful withdrawal, this inexperienced officer clearly outstayed his welcome on a number of occasions. The fact that the Middlesex Yeomanry contained a large number of middle-class men, and enjoyed very informal relations with their officers, makes Hatton's insistence on the rights of the NCO all the more striking.

More generally, it may be suggested that for the most part privates and NCOs did not want their officers to be too friendly, but rather preferred them to maintain a certain social distance, to avoid role-ambiguity. Even before a man left his unit to go for officer training, a subtle change came over his relations with his comrades, impending promotion 'already dividing him from them.' It is in fact very rare to come across an officer misguided enough to endanger his authority by becoming over-familiar with his soldiers. One suspects that service in the ranks and training at an OCB gave most subalterns a firm grasp of the correct way to treat their men.

Many officers relied heavily on their NCOs. This was especially true of young sub-alterns, fresh out from England, with no previous war experience. The steady, experi-enced NCO supporting the 'green' subaltern with a whispered word of advice is al-most a commonplace. In late 1915 one gunner officer wrote that subalterns fresh from (the training base of) Woolwich 'know very little about the interior economy of their batteries. They step into the machine and glide along with a first class B.S.M. and Q.M.S. behind them.' For the sake of discipline, it was important that the position of the NCO should not be undermined. In 1915, Sgt T. Boyce (1/10 Londons) was rudely treated by his CO in front of his men; this incident still rankled with Boyce fifty years later. In fact most senior officers were well aware of the importance of the NCO in the smooth running of a unit. If a subaltern was to undermine the position of an NCO, for instance by swearing at him or rebuking him in front of his men, a senior officer was likely to take the part of the NCO. Experienced NCOs were invaluable, while sub-alterns were all too easy to replace. The chastening experience of one young Territorial gunner officer underlines the relative importance of the newly arrived subaltern and the battle-hardened NCO. On one occasion in 1917, a working party was unloading wagons under shellfire. Lt P.J. Campbell called to Sgt Denmark to come over to him. Denmark flatly disobeyed, demanding, with a 'face of thunder,' 'Who's taking charge here, are you Sir, or am I?' Campbell was left feeling humiliated and crushed. Den-mark's appreciation of the situation was correct, as Campbell apparently recognised in retrospect; the NCO was carrying out a dangerous task that needed to be com-pleted as swiftly as possible without interruption. Campbell did not even contemplate making a disciplinary issue of Denmark's insubordination, fearing that even to con-fide in a fellow officer would only result in Campbell looking even more foolish. In-stead, Campbell worked to try to win his sergeant's respect.

A case could be made that the NCO corps was damaged by the wholesale commis-sioning of corporals and sergeants who showed leadership ability. One temporary officer believed that the commissioning of warrant officers was a mistake, because an RSM enjoyed much greater prestige than a mere subaltern. A number of Regular NCOs had poor opinions of their New Army and Territorial counterparts. One officer's belief that most NCOs were ineffective under shellfire and the exceptions 'ought to be officers,' while no doubt a broad generalisation, is indicative of the gen-eral belief that the place for those soldiers with leadership qualities was as officers, not as sergeants. Many NCOs were held in high regard by their officers, as men, as leaders and as partners in the administration and management of military units. After a bat-tle in 1917, Lt R.L. Mackay of 11/Argylls described Sgt McQuarrie as:

> one of the bravest and best gentlemen I have ever met. He has been utterly invaluable to me on this job. . . . I have more respect for this man than for any other dozen I have ever met.

The language used by Mackay is revealing. McQuarrie was a courageous 'gentleman,' perhaps not by birth, but certainly by behaviour, who had earned Mackay's respect. In short, he fulfilled most of the criteria demanded by Other Ranks of their officers. Mc-Quarrie had, one might say, 'leadership qualities.' Similarly, the picture that emerges from the diaries of CSM Ernest Shephard, a prewar Regular soldier of 1/Dorsets, is of a man who 'nursed' inexperienced officers, who acted as a rock of stability and continuity after the battalion had taken heavy casualties, and who admired, and had good relations with, various officers. One of the major factors in maintaining the cohesion of the British army through the long years of attrition was the presence of Regular, Territorial and New Army NCOs like Shephard, Denmark and McQuarrie.

During the war years, there was much talk among civilians about the positive effects of war service on social cohesion. In 1916 the Bishop of London spoke of a 'brotherhood' being 'forged of blood and iron' in the trenches, which should be maintained into peacetime, thus ending the class war between 'Hoxton' and 'Belgravia.' Subsequently historians have pointed to the growth of solidarity among front-line soldiers of all nations as a reaction to the politicians, capitalists and shirking or striking workers on the home front, and as argued above, generals and staff officers.

Is it, then possible to talk about the existence of *Grabenkameradeschaft*, a comradeship of the trenches, which united British front-line soldiers, regardless of rank, into a common fraternity? Many officers believed that it was. 'Through all their ordeals and sufferings' wrote one, 'they knew they had become a brotherhood of all ranks. . . .' The padre of 12/Highland Light Infantry argued, from personal experience, that men who had fought in battle had 'proved our manhood to ourselves and to one another,' the 'bond' of a shared experience of battle being

> finer and more intimate than could be forged by any other association . . . we shall for ever have in common a host of dearly-bought memories, sacred and incommunicable.

I have argued elsewhere that war experience did make an impact on 'officer-class' perceptions of the working classes, a phenomeneon which had considerable repercussions for postwar British society and politics. But how far, if at all, did Other Ranks regard themselves as sharing a common war experience with their officers, an experience which transcended rank?

At one level, men of whatever rank who had undergone the experience of battle shared an experience denied to everyone else. The working-class private who wrote to Edmund Blunden after the war to say that *Undertones of War* had put his war experience into words was also testifying that, even if the officer and the private had nothing else in common, they shared the experience of battle. Combat had the ability to dissolve the formal bounds of rank, at least temporarily. Capt. E.G.D. Living (2/19 Londons) wrote of returning from an action in Palestine. A ranker marched beside him

> and, officer and man, we opened our hearts to one another as everyone else in the stumbling fours in front of us was doing, and as only those can who have been through terrible experiences together.

Studies on other twentieth-century armies drawn from western industrialised societies suggest that the small cohesive group, offering mutual support and affection, is of vital importance in sustaining morale in war. A private's view that the 'set of mucking-in pals' was 'the true social unit of the army' of the 1914–18 war would tend to re-inforce this view. Some very deep relationships were forged between soldiers during the First World War, especially on active service. The commonly held view that, in war, life and human relationships were especially vivid was held by a very ordinary private of 2/4 Londons, Jack Mudd, who wrote to his wife of the importance of com-radeship in the trenches:

> Out here dear we're all pals what one hasn't got the other has we try to share each others troubles get each other out of danger you wouldn't believe the Humanity between men out here. . . . It's a lovely thing is friendship out here.

There is much evidence from the writings of Great War soldiers that comradeship was indeed of vital importance in maintaining morale. Conversely, men who were ex-cluded from primary groups usually had a miserable time, and this was an important factor in the disillusionment of specific individuals.

Primary groups could transcend social class, for although some middle-class rankers could be rather uncomfortable serving alongside working-class soldiers, other happily 'mucked-in' with their proletarian comrades. An artist serving in the ranks of 8/Rifle Bde noted that:

> I have gained a knowledge of the 'workers' point of view, opinions & workings of his mind, that would be invaluable if I were going to do anything in the political or socio-logical line!

In his diary, a middle-class conscript infantryman referred to "The splendid qualities of the men with whom one is associated.' Later he wrote:

> It is very educative to mix among these men, whose ideas and characters are as diverse—sometimes as grotesque—as the burrs or drawls of their speech. . . . They are all very nice to me. . . .

These quotations sit neatly alongside similar ones from socially privileged officers such as Alec Waugh (Machine Gun Corps), who wrote in the 1960s that

> for many young soldiers, certainly for me, there came a newly awakened social con-sciousness. . . . The young officer began to feel differently about the men he led in action.

J.R.R. Tolkien (11/Lancashire Fusiliers) described 'Sam Gamgee,' a character in his novel *The Lord of the Rings*, as a portrait 'of the English soldier, of the private and bat-men I knew in the 1914 war, and recognised as so far superior to myself.'

Could this process be taken a stage further? Could officers, as well as middle-class Other Ranks, form a comradeship group with working-class soldiers? Rank and disci-pline placed considerable barriers in the way of uninhibited friendship between lead-ers and led, but some individuals came close to breaking these down. R.C. Foot, a temporary gunner officer of 62nd Division claimed that:

Officers shared the same food and slept in the same ditches as their soldiers; about the only thing they [the Other Ranks] could not share was their responsibility, and the soldiers recognised this.

It is possible that Foot exaggerated the closeness of inter-rank relationships in his unit, but he certainly seems to have formed a bond of mutual friendship and trust with an NCO. Long after the war Foot was visited by the daughter of his old sergeant. This lady had a personal problem, and she had been told that she could refer to Foot in time of trouble, but as he wrote,

that incident, some twenty five years later than her father's service and friendship with me, rather took my breath away at the time.

Foot went on to argue that 'such friendship, based on mutual individual respect' and the comradeship engendered by a male society made it possible to endure the horrors of war.

A similar incident occurred in 1969, when W.M. Jenner, a former ranker, wrote to the family of Capt. Peter Blagrove, after seeing his old officer's obituary in a newspaper. Jenner wrote that 'To me he was a friend as well as a superior officer,' and said that all of the men of his trench mortar battery were proud of Blagrove, who was regarded as 'a real gentleman and a very brave man.' One of the things which endeared him to Jenner was that, when short of labour, Blagrove helped the men with hard physical work. In the eyes of his subordinates, Blagrove displayed the traits of a 'Beloved Captain,' being gentlemanly, courageous and paternal. Blagrove and Jenner last met in December 1918. For a ranker to treasure the memory of an officer for over fifty years is evidence that *Grabenkameradeschaft* existed in this particular case.

Perhaps Maurice Bowra, who served as a temporary gunner subaltern, captured the essence of many relationships between officers and soldiers when he wrote that his dealings with his men 'were more formal but in the end hardly less intimate' than his relations with his brother officers. The men looked after one another, and Bowra, with 'protective care' and 'In moments of danger or excitement or even of frustrating tedium they would relax their restraints and tell me about their families and their jobs in time of peace.

The fact that junior officers and rankers shared much the same dangers in battle was important. Charles Crutchley, who served in the ranks of 135th MG Company in Mesopotamia, captured the way in which shared danger could forge men into a community, if only temporarily, regardless of rank:

Thousands of rounds of empty ammunition cases were strewn around a deserted machine-gun emplacement. 'Nasty bit of good' said our officer. . . . 'I wonder how many they got with that little lot.'

The look on his face made me wonder if he were (sic) also thinking of our own 'nasty bit of goods.' . . . We squatted around: a mere handful of us, on a lonely ridge in the desert. . . . Dreamy said it was his twenty-first birthday, and my officer fished out a flask [of whisky] from his haversack.

'Pass it around, sergeant,' he said. . . . That drink, taken from the same flask, cemented our comradeship.

Clearly at least *some* officers were regarded by *some* men as comrades; even if rank and the disciplinary structure prevented the uninhibited friendship possible between two privates. Without a host of case studies of individual units and individual soldiers, it is impossible to assess how widespread was this sense of inter-rank comradeship. Nevertheless the resolutions passed by the 'Soldiers and Workers Council, Home Counties and Training Reserve Branch' held at Turnbridge Wells on 24 June 1917 offers an important clue. These resolutions were for the most part closely akin to trades union demands, calling for an increase in separation allowances, relaxation of the Defence of the Realm Act and so on. However, two of the resolutions read:

5. That the general treatment of soldiers be brought into line with the spirit of the Officers and men in daily contact. As things stand, the Army Council continually issues orders which have the effect of reducing the organisation to a cross between a reformatory and a lunatic asylum. Only the goodwill and tolerance of the Officers and men make life endurable. We be neither dogs, criminals, or children.
6. We ask for a more generous treatment of younger Officers who, out of a daily casualty list of over 4,000, suffer the heaviest proportionate burden.

This document gives a clear indication of the general state of officer-man relations, although it is fair to note that soldiers involved with this council were obviously atypical. Although far from revolutionary in its aims, the very existence of this body represented a direct challenge to the formal hierarchical and disciplinary structure of the army. Yet Resolution 5 demonstrates that the council members drew a sharp distinction between senior officers, who were seen as inflicting a humiliating disciplinary system on the men, and regimental officers who were 'in daily contact' with the men and who did their best to modify the system. Resolution 6 not only offers evidence of the sympathy that existed for junior officers among some other ranks, but can also be interpreted as recognition that a community of interest existed between soldiers and regimental officers, many of whom had risen from the ranks. It was in the interests of those striving for better conditions for the ranks to do the same for junior officers, because some of the rankers would eventually receive a commission. By 1917, it was no longer valid, if indeed it had ever been, to think of officers and men as belonging to two distinct, water-tight groups, possessing no knowledge of each other's conditions.

Only a minority of wartime soldiers joined ex-service organisations after the war, but the existence and longevity of an Old Comrades Association (OCA) can offer a broad hint as to the *esprit de corps* and state of officer-man relations of a unit. While not all cohesive units formed an OCA, and some units and formations such as 66th Division had associations for officers only, many OCAs seem to have been organisations in which former officers and Other Ranks could meet on approximately equal terms. In the interwar years, the OCA of 32nd Division Trench Mortar Battery met once a year for dinner. This OCA, wrote its Honourary Secretary, a former ranker, spells brotherhood first and last, and class distinction is taboo'd (sic). The old Tock-Emma [i.e. trench mortar soldier] is welcome for what he did 'out yonder,' and not necessarily for what he is today.

Many OCA members probably had little in common apart from a wish to share and rekindle memories of wartime service in a particular unit, to fulfil a deep psychological need. Former soldiers usually dwelt on the humour and comradeship, rather than the horrors, of war. Some OCAs, and other veterans' organisations, such as the British Legion and the Old Contemptibles Association, had a charitable function. In these bodies the paternal pattern of the war years was extended, with ex-officers and ex-soldiers working together to provide financial and other help for poorer members and their families. This was especially important since 'in the immediate post-war period "unemployed man" and "unemployed ex-serviceman" were close to synonymous.' Some OCAs continued in operation for many years. The 22/R. Fusiliers' OCA existed from 1919 to 1976, while the Machine Gun Corps OCA had a similar lifespan. Nostalgia for comradeship and paternalism, which contrasted starkly with many ex-soldiers' (and indeed ex-officers') experiences of the harshness of life in a land which was far from 'fit for heroes,'[5] was undoubtedly a factor in the popularity of OCAs.

Even in the absence of a formal unit OCA, former members of a unit could continue to demonstrate comradeship and respect in time of peace. When, in the 1920s, a former officer of the Accrington Pals died, his chief mourners included five members of the battalion, four of them rankers, the officer having 'no family.' Former officers and soldiers of many units, particularly locally raised battalions, also met to commemorate the dead, whether at memorial services in Britain or on 'pilgrimages' to the battlefields. Unit histories, especially those of disbanded service units, were another means of commemorating the dead and recapturing wartime *esprit de corps*. Those produced between 1918 and 1923 in particular, 'although not overtly consensual in tone' often portrayed officer-man relations in terms of a community of interest. Although contributions from Other Ranks were often included, most unit histories were written by officers.

All members of the Old Contemptibles Association were, somewhat artificially, referred to as 'chum,' regardless of rank. Regimental journals, particularly those produced by OCAs of service units, were full of obituaries, articles and reminiscences written by former soldiers of all ranks, which stressed, consciously or not, that a spirit of comradeship which encompassed all ranks had existed and continued to exist. In sum, the postwar activities of veterans of all ranks offer further evidence that rankers could, and did, regard officers as comrades.

Taking all this evidence into account, one is led to the conclusion that it is indeed valid to talk of a British 'war generation' who shared a common experience. In Janet Roebuck's words,

> Under battle conditions class lines came to be overshadowed by the shared experiences of combat and the mutuality of death. . . . The conditions of war made contact between upper-class officers and lower-class soldiers inevitable and gave them a set of common experiences which neither group shared with civilians of their own class.

There is much to be said for Marc Ferro's idea that a 'special 'ex-serviceman's' outlook grew up from bitterness and nostalgia' leading to postwar idealisation of the war years although, in the case of Britain, he underestimates the degree of continuity with wartime relationships. Clearly, it would be wrong to assume that all Other Ranks regarded all officers as comrades. It is likely that some of the more sweeping claims made by officers about the existence of a community of the trenches which united soldiers of all ranks contained a large element of wishful thinking; we return to the fact that Other Ranks tended to judge their officers on an individual basis, rather than giving their loyalty to officers as a group.

Some politicians attempted to capitalise on their war service in an attempt to win veterans' votes. One such was Sir George McCrae, a Liberal Member of Parliament who had raised and commanded 16/R. Scots. In a 1923 election address he claimed to be 'an ex-service man' who, having 'shared their dangers and hardships' would support the fight of former soldiers for fair treatment. It is instructive that men like McCrae and two future prime ministers, Clement Attlee (described as 'Major Attlee' between the wars, partly in an attempt to stress Labour's respectability) and Anthony Eden (who used a photograph of himself in uniform on the cover of his 1922 election address) were members of the three major established parties. No 'military party' emerged as a force in British politics. Mosley's British Union of Fascists, which promoted militaristic values and attempted to appeal to ex-servicemen, was electorally unsuccessful. Ex-servicemen's organisations had a minimal political impact. All this suggests that the British war generation was a rather different beast from its German counterpart.

But a British war generation did exist, in the form of individual relationships between officers and men, forged in the face of hardships and dangers shared, to a greater or lesser extent, by all ranks. Many of these relationships continued after the war through the medium of ex-servicemen's organisations. Memories of wartime relationships between officers and men were treasured long after the war, even if, like Capt. Blagrove and Gunner Jenner, they lost contact in 1918. Writing nearly fifty years after the event, ex-L/Cpl S.A. Boyd of 10/R. Fusiliers stated that 'My lasting impression of the Somme battle is the fine young officers who led us so well. They were extremely brave but so young, many under the age of 20.'

Just as the character, ethos and experience of no two military units was the same, war veterans reacted to peace in different ways. Cohesive 'family' units were probably more likely to establish and maintain OCAs than other units. Nevertheless, as the evidence of soldiers referring in affectionate terms to officers with whom they had lost contact long ago suggests, the British war generation should not be located solely in the reunion dinners and magazines of OCAs of disbanded Pals battalions. The British war generation was characterised by general, if unquantifiable friendly feeling between ranks and classes. Although unquantifiable, it was nonetheless real.

The failure of British veterans to create cohesive political organisations did not mean that their war generation was politically insignificant. In their study of French, German and British literature on the Great War, Bessell and Englander concluded that the war generation 'existed only for so long as it remained under fire,' and that on demobilisation 'it appears to have disintegrated into its constituent parts.' This interpre-

tation ignores the many ties of affection and comradeship that continued to bind former soldiers of all ranks in peacetime Britain. G.H. Roberts, a trade unionist MP and
Minister for Labour, noted after a tour of the Western Front in September 1918 that
not only were officer-man relations 'excellent,' but that officers wanted 'conditions at
home' to improve for their men after the war. Men had come to 'respect their officers'
while officers had come to

> know and appreciate the lives of their men at home. They have been taught to give every
> consideration to their comfort in the field, and many of them evidently regard it as their
> duty to do the same for them at home when the war is over.

This wartime comradeship and concern was not simply abandoned or forgotten at
the Armistice. As noted above, some veterans' organisations were an extension of
wartime paternalism by other means, and more importantly, in John Keegan's words,
many officers conceived

> an affection and concern for the disadvantaged which would eventually fuel that trans-
> formation of middle-class attitudes to the poor which has been the most important so-
> cial trend in twentieth century Britain.

Recently Gerard J. DeGroot has argued that a 'myth' about the Great War has
arisen which sees 'class antagonism as the product of 'ignorance, which the trench experience eradicated.' While he correctly argues that 'paternalism should not be confused with . . . equality,' he seriously underestimates the extent to which inter-rank
barriers came down on active service. Class antagonism was not eradicated by the
trench experience, but it was modified. The wartime officer-man relationship and its
impact on postwar class relations was rather more subtle than DeGroot's analysis indicates.

To try to assess something as nebulous as the social attitudes of such a large and diverse group as British veterans of the Great War over twenty or more years is a difficult task, to put it mildly; but by the 1940s the idea that a total war entitled the participating population to a 'decent existence' was firmly established. This stood alongside
the belief that after 1918 'the rank and file of the nation had been denied their entitle-
ment.' This of course is a prime example of Andreski's 'military participation ratio' in
action, and Keegan's 'process of discovery' undoubtedly played a part in this phenomenon.

The argument that the concept of the war generation as such should be left behind
in favour of analysis of 'those constituent parts which temporarily comprised it' has
much to commend it, but to abandon the idea of a war generation altogether is to risk
throwing out the baby with the revisionist bathwater. Although this subject is in need
of further examination, it is safe to state that many British officers and rankers believed themselves to be part of a war generation, united by comradeship and the
shared experience of combat.

Notes

From G. D. Sheffield, *Leadership in the Trenches: Officer-Man Relations, Morale, and Discipline in the British Army in the Era of the First World War*, chapter 7: Officer-Man Relations: The Other Ranks' Perspective (London: Macmillan Press, 2000), pp. 103–34. Reprinted with permission of Palgrave Macmillan Press.

1. The numerical designation indicates the battalion. The words indicate the regiment. Regiments were often associated with a particular region of Britain. Thus in this example, "2/5 Glosters" means the 2/5 battalion of the Gloster Regiment. A full list of British regiments from the First World War can be found at www.1914-1918.net.

2. Regimental Sergeant Major, the highest ranking enlisted man.

3. Territorial Forces.

4. The "New Army" refers to the volunteer, locally recruited units raised by the British in 1914 and 1915.

5. David Lloyd George's campaign slogan in 1918 was his promise to make Britain "a land fit for heroes."

"War Enthusiasm"
Volunteers, Departing Soldiers, and Victory Celebrations

Jeffrey Verhey

Although the carnivalesque crowds speak of a certain enthusiasm in the population it was an "enthusiasm" which required no sacrifices. It was an enthusiasm for enthusiasm's sake—for the pleasure of being rowdy, of letting off tension. Although an essential part of the "August experiences," such enthusiasm can scarcely be cited as evidence of "war" enthusiasm, and indeed, contemporaries seldom discussed it in this context. Rather, for evidence that Germany was united in "enthusiasm" myth-makers cited the enthusiastic crowds parading in the streets, the crowds applauding the departure of the troops, the mood of the soldiers departing to the front, the outpouring of charity, and the large numbers of volunteers. Of these the number of volunteers was, in the words of Matthias Erzberger, the "best judge of the enthusiasm of the people."

On 4 August newspapers reported that vast crowds of young men were gathering in front of the barracks, volunteering for the army, and that vast crowds of young women were volunteering for the Red Cross. On 11 August newspapers reported that over 1,300,000 men had already volunteered. On 16 August the *Norddeutsche Allgemeine Zeitung* repeated this information, making it official, and it (or a larger number) would be repeated throughout the war, and in most history books up till the present day.

Yet the press vastly exaggerated. About 185,000 men volunteered in August 1914. (In 1926, the War History Division of the Prussian Army did a study on manpower in the First World War. The author of this study—employing archival materials destroyed in the Second World War—wrote that up till 11 August 1914 the Prussian army reported that 260,672 had attempted to volunteer; of these 143,922 were accepted. If one adds up the figures for the other armies [32,000 for Bavaria, 8,619 for Wurttemberg, and probably around 10,000 for Saxony] one comes up with 185,000.)

Although the press vastly exaggerated, 185,000 is evidence of a broad enthusiasm among at least sections of German youth. In the war of 1870/1871, there were less than 10,000 volunteers in the whole North German Federation. The German army's manpower needs were met through the draft, meaning that most young men could not volunteer—they were already assigned to a division. Only those under seventeen or over fifty, those who had had an exemption, or whose reserve division had not yet been called up, could volunteer. Moreover, the draft meant that those who did wish to volunteer had difficulties finding an army division with an opening. As most divisions were not accepting any volunteers, young men gathered in long queues in front of the few divisions that were. Recognizing this difficulty, the government provided prospective volunteers with free train travel. As most youths visited many barracks before finding one with an opening, they were undoubtedly counted many times. Not surprisingly, many young men who grasped this opportunity had no intention of volunteering. Rather, as the War Ministry noted, they "have used this piece of paper to travel from one end of the country to the other."

According to bourgeois journalists, the volunteers came from all social classes, and were thus evidence of enthusiasm among the population as a whole:

> Over 2,000,000 volunteers have come forward from all social classes, from the rich to the poor. Without any class differences, wearing the same uniform, the rich and the poor are all united—welded together through discipline and through the courageous idea: we must, we will win.

Was this the case? Given the available evidence, it is almost impossible to answer this question adequately. However, an examination of the rolls of two divisions suggests that the social composition of the volunteers corresponded broadly to that which journalists described for the "enthusiastic" crowds. The "enthusiasm" was found in its greatest concentration among the educated elite, but no part of German society was immune from it. There were many students; there were also many young businessmen and professionals, as well as some tradesmen. The working class was under-represented but not fully absent.

Why did the young men volunteer? Many tradesmen, unemployed and facing a dismal economic future, may have decided to join the army as a means of getting through these difficult times. For many youths, however, especially educated youths, "enthusiasm" is a fair description of their motivations. But what is meant by "enthusiasm?" Some greeted the coming of the war as an opportunity for personal growth, a chance to develop their personality. As George Mosse has noted, in 1914 war still had the aura of fear and courage for young intellectuals; its violent nature was still believed to be the true touchstone of a man. War was a rite of passage, a "test of fire," a "male baptism."

Many youths were glad to have a goal, a meaning, and a purpose in their lives, even if it was only a vaguely defined desire for adventure, of not returning to school, or of just getting over a relationship. They were less "enthusiastic" than curious. The philosopher Karl Löwth explained his motivations in his memoir:

> the desire to be emancipated from the confined bourgeois space of the school and home, a difficult struggle with myself after my first love affair, the charm of a "dangerous life," for which Nietzsche had been enthusiastic, the desire to try out a new adventure . . . these and similar motives made me welcome the war as a chance for life and death.

Ernst Toller, for example, volunteered because:

> Yes, we are living in a rush of emotions. The words Germany, fatherland, war have a magical power, when we say them they do not disappear, they hang in the air, circle themselves, ignite themselves and us.

"War is like Christmas," a young lieutenant is supposed to have said in 1914, and even if he did not, many "enthusiastic" youths believed something similar.

Others volunteered out a sense of duty. The letters of the students collected and published by Phillip Witkop are replete with noble phrases, the model for which seems to be the Greek and Roman conceptions of honor and love for one's country which they had learned at school. Indeed, among the children of better-educated families, Bernd Ulrich has suggested, peer pressure was such that it was difficult not to volunteer. Over half of the 32,000 eligible university preparatory high-school (*Gymnasium*) students volunteered in 1914 (and, although I could find no figures there was most probably a similar percentage among the 64,000 university students). In some places, whole school classes signed up for the army.

Many youths, especially in the youth movement, were enthusiastic less for themselves than for Germany. They believed that war would move German society away from bourgeois "materialism" toward an aesthetic idealism, move people away from the world of outer appearances back to inner truths. In place of greed and egotism the war experience would validate humility, sacrifice, and courage. As Jakob Müller has noted, the members of the youth movement displayed—as shown in their magazines and letters—little chauvinism and, indeed, little actual "enthusiasm." Indeed, they had difficulty explaining their motivations to older, less-well-educated soldiers. As Hans-Gerd Rabe (a member of the *Wandervögel* from Osnabrück) wrote in his memoirs, many of them did not understand their motivations:

> what [our officer] never fully grasped was the fact of our volunteering. This was true not only for him but for many much higher up. . . . We broke through the fat peace of the quiet order of the bourgeois world, a world which was already troubling for the *Wandervögel*, above all through our free decision.

Many historians have taken such explanations at face value and seen in the enthusiasm the transformation of personalities, a change in identity, a liberation from Wilhelmine bourgeois culture. Yet it is telling that most contemporaries did not judge the enthusiasm as a rejection of Wilhelmine society and values but as an affirmation. The breadth of enthusiasm, the popularity of the romanticism of war, demonstrated the success of the Wilhelmine education system and government sponsored youth organizations. This sort of rejection of "bourgeois" culture, this emphasis on the "heroic" ideal, was at the heart of Wilhelmine bourgeois culture, a part of the internal contradictions of the German bourgeois identity.

The second piece of evidence cited for a Germany united in enthusiasm was the enthusiastic crowds accompanying the departing troops, As noted, the departure of the troops was at first a solemn affair. Only toward the middle of the month, after the first victories, did the departure become a festive event. Then, thousands of men, women, and children turned out to watch the regimental parade, to give the soldiers

Liebesgaben such as chocolate, food, flowers, and cigars. Yet even before this sort of cheering audience became institutionalized, from the very beginning of the war, in almost all German towns and cities a committee greeted the troops passing through. When the troops arrived the mayor, or some other notable, made a patriotic speech and then the young women of the Red Cross, especially popular with the troops, handed out *Liebesgaben* (literally: gifts of love) such as flowers, food, and cigars, often more than the soldiers could consume. It would all be repeated in the next town or city, often only a little way away.

A Social Democratic journalist wrote of the mood at the train stations in Cologne:

A long train stands ready to depart. Let's walk alongside it . . . the wagons are decorated with freshly cut foliage. Everything so pleasant and pretty as if the soldiers were returning home from a maneuver, as if they would soon be out of their soldier's clothing. Yet they are going to bloody battles which will extend their term of service by who knows how many months.

Friedrich Ebert, the Social Democratic politician and future President of Germany, wrote in his diary for the middle of August: "at the train stations the people stand thickly next to one another. They greet the train with hurrahs. From almost all houses towels are waved." As these were the first audience crowds which became enthusiastic crowds, the first example of an "enthusiastic" crowd in which all classes, generations, and gender participated, it is not surprising that many Germans considered the train trips as the highpoint of the August enthusiasm, the best evidence of a people united in "enthusiasm."

For their part, the soldiers covered the sides of their trains with slogans displaying a naïve innocence of the nature of the war they were about to fight, such as "breakfast in Paris, we will thresh them," or:

> We won't stop
> Till the French are fasting.
> > French, Russians, Serbian,
> > All must die.

> Czar, it is an ape-like shame
> What we must do to you and your band
> First, we will disinfect
> And then thoroughly cultivate.

> (Zar, es ist 'ne Affenschande,
> Daß wir dich und deine Bande
> Müssen erst desinfizieren
> Und dann gründlich kultivieren.)

> When it rains of Russian heads,
> And when French heads come down like snow

Then we will ask the Lord God
That the weather remain so.

(Wenn es Russenköpfe regent
Und Franzosenköpfe schneit;
Dann bitten wir den lieben Gott,
Daß das Wetter noch so bleibt!)

Postcards depicted the slogans which the soldiers had written. Caricatures in similar bad taste were published by the popular "humor" weeklies, *Kladderadatsch* and *Simplicissimus*.

This enthusiasm, too, had little to do with the real war. The troops enjoyed being waved at, being taken care of at the train stations, especially by the young women. As one *Berliner Morgenpost* journalist noted, "the taking care of the troops has taken on the character of a party ... young women dressed in their prettiest clothes," were "living out their instincts." Already on 6 August, according to the diary of one minister in a small town in western Germany, "the people are talking about the war as if it was just a maneuver, as if glorious victories were inevitable." As one soldier wrote in a letter home: "the mood of the troops is fresh and humorous. . . . No one believes that we can be defeated; the will to victory is in us all." The troops expected to be home by Christmas.

This romantic vision of war did not survive the first experience with the real war, the first sight of death. The superficiality of such "enthusiasm" was noted by a Bremen soldier who wrote in a letter home that on 26 August his train going to the front passed a train of wounded in Berlin: "after our train once again started moving you no longer heard any more songs, for each of us had become aware that we stood a chance of becoming wounded or dying on the battlefield." Not only was such enthusiasm naïve, if one looked under its surface one discovered what an American military psychologist has aptly termed "apprehensive enthusiasm." Such enthusiasm, wrote the psychologist, "relates to fear of death. . . . The enthusiasm is a reaction formation against these feelings."

The experience of the crowds applauding the troops departing on the trains was the first broader experience of unity. Yet this experience was ephemeral. Charity provided the first institutional framework for a German community transcending class boundaries. In 1914 there was a vast spontaneous outpouring of private charity. Throughout Germany local committees, generally led by the Red Cross, the local "National Women's Service," or the city government, collected enormous sums to help the needy. All women's organizations, including the Social Democratic women's organization, participated in the "National Women's Service," organized in the first days of the war by the leader of the "Association of German Women" (*Bund deutscher Frauen*), Gertrud Bäumer. Bäumer could thus with justice claim that "war charity work is one of the first examples in which the dissolving of the parties into a large *Volksgemeinschaft* became reality." Indeed, it was here—in local political organizations such as women's charities—where the SPD did its most effective work during the war.

Soldiers were the focus of the charity. Girls at school, female students at the university, or just groups of women knitted and sewed clothes to send to the soldiers. Marlene Dietrich, a university student in Berlin at the time, wrote in her memoirs:

> when school began after the summer vacation in 1914 we went to the large auditorium. . . . There we heard thunderous speeches; we could scarcely understand their significance. . . . We would, they said, instead of learning at school, learn to knit.

All of these efforts came together at Christmas 1914 when vast amounts of *Liebesgaben* were sent to the front. (The city government of Frankfurt/Main required fifty train wagons in order to transport its gifts.)

Such charity was not limited to soldiers but extended as well to those citizens negatively affected by the war, those unemployed, or those whose husbands were only earning a common soldier's wages. Charity organizations set up in August 1914 their first soup kitchens, created employment for unemployed women in sewing rooms, or set up centers to help citizens through the maze of government bureaucracy. And many organizations paid unemployment assistance. The Free Trade Unions, for example, spent over one-fourth of their savings in the first year of the war on unemployment assistance, assistance to the families of those drafted, and the like. Many industrialists patriotically proclaimed that they would continue to pay the salaries (or a portion thereof) of their employees who had been drafted.

Although these private efforts were considerable, the efforts of local governments were even greater. This outpouring of charity was evidence that the idea of community had taken hold among well-to-do Germans in August 1914. But it was a certain form of community. Charity remained mostly women's work. Indeed, for Gertrud Bäumer, the leader of the *Bund deutscher Frauenverein* (BdF), "charity work (*Heimatdienst*)" was the translation during the war of "women's movement." Bourgeois women embraced this opportunity, as Barbara Guttmann has noted, not only because it was almost their only opportunity to participate in the "Great Times," but also because through such work they could prove they were capable citizens. As the war continued the charity decreased. Already in 1915 firms ceased paying the salaries of workers who had become soldiers, and private citizens stopped making large contributions to charity. There were few trains filled with *Liebesgaben* in 1916 and 1917.

The idea of a people's community could not be sustained through philanthropy alone. Charity did not decrease the distance between the classes; traditional elites warned against charity which out of "false" warmth broke down social distinctions. In August 1914 the governmental *Norddeutsche Allgemeine Zeitung* asked wealthy women not to invite hungry children to their homes because they might see vast differences in living standards and no longer be able to be happy. They asked that such charity take place outside the home, in schools, or in other public buildings.

Finally, the charity could not hide the fact that in August there was a great deal of greed. Many well-to-do women informed their servants either that they would not be paid for the duration of the war or that their salaries would be drastically reduced. The Braunschweig Trade Association suggested that one should use the economic downturn to fire one's employees and rehire them at cheaper wages.

A wider experience of war enthusiasm came at the end of August, aptly character-ized by one contemporary as "the extra edition bringing the news of victory." In Hei-denheim (Brenz), when mobilization came, "at first everywhere there was great dis-may, as we were aware of how serious it was . . . enthusiasm first showed itself with the victories." The enthusiasm, in other words, was engendered by relief.

The first victory was celebrated on Friday, 7 August, when, from the steps of the Berlin palace, an officer proclaimed the German victory at Liège (a week too soon, it turned out). Twenty policemen on horses carried the news through Berlin. After hear-ing the news, cheering, singing crowds once again sauntered up and down Unter den Linden. Church bells rang throughout the city, and the children received a school hol-iday on Saturday. Again on 10 August crowds milling around in the streets of Berlin saw a car rush towards the palace. Out of the car a General Staff officer yelled "victory of the Germans in Alsace." Again a parade formed on Unter den Linden, led by some-one carrying a bust of the Kaiser covered with a green wreath. At exactly that mo-ment, a group of elite troops marched down Unter den Linden on their way to the train station. Not surprisingly, they were cheered enthusiastically, and given roses for their rifles and uniforms. In the words of the *Norddeutsche Allgemeine Zeitung* jour-nalist, "already the effect of the heroic, hard-won victories shows itself among our population. The faces, which in the beginning only too often showed the expression of anxious worry, have relaxed. One reads solid trust in all." These victories were cele-brated only in Berlin. Throughout Germany the first victory celebration came on 20 August 1914.

Beginning on 20 August and lasting for about the next three weeks, the victories came one after another. In Berlin, on Friday 21 August 1914, late-afternoon extra edi-tions proclaimed the victory of the Bavarian army on the French-German border. Church bells sounded throughout the city, and crowds celebrated on Unter den Lin-den. 22 August was a school holiday. Outside of Berlin, even in the smaller towns and the countryside, the victory was also celebrated with the ringing of church bells and the flying of flags from almost every house. In Hanover the mayor proclaimed "out with the flags. Do away with any small-minded, depressed feelings. Express your joy." Another victory celebration took place in Berlin on Saturday, 22 August, when the Germans moved into Brussels. Now flags flew on houses and apartments throughout Berlin. Sunday saw even more victory celebrations. A *Tägliche Rundschau* journalist wrote with relief that "the great times of heroes, which had almost become a legend, have returned. So, too, did our sons and brothers march off into the holy war." Victory was celebrated again on 24 August (after the fall of Namur), especially in Wurtten-berg, for troops from Wurttenberg had assisted in this victory.

On 2 September 1914, Germans commemorated the victory at Sedan in 1870 with parades they fully expected were, in the words of a *Tägliche Rundschau* journalist, "a trial-run for the victory parade." In Berlin, hundreds of thousands on Unter den Linden watched captured French war materiel pass by. Theodor Wolff wrote "all of Berlin is excited . . . it looks as if there were never as many people . . . in Berlin as now." In the next week, "a serious old General warned the Berlin house owners . . . not to rent their windows for the victory parade at too high a price." It was a rare contemporary who warned that the war had not yet been won, that the celebrations occurred too often, and that a depression was bound to follow if victory did not come quickly.

The enthusiasm even spread to Berlin's working-class districts. For the first time black, white, and red flags flew from working-class apartments, something right-wing newspapers commented on with glee. A minister from Moabit (a working-class suburb of Berlin) reported that:

> out of the windows flags are hanging . . . an amazing picture for those who know the conditions. Usually there is not a single flag on, for example, the Kaiser's birthday. . . . The Social Democratic worker is proud that he can show his patriotism.

Bourgeois journalists claimed to have heard patriotic songs in bars where Social Democrats were known to congregate. Some Social Democrats wore black, white, and red ribbons, and some working-class women knitted black, white, and red scarves for their men to wear. Especially Social Democratic youths were taken in by the "war enthusiasm." According to a minister from a working-class suburb of Berlin, "the youth is naturally enthusiastic. In my youth group, which previously was not known for being patriotic, one sings, standing, every Sunday evening "Heil dir im Siegerkranz." More significantly, the black, white, and red flags even flew in Berlin's working-class districts on monarchical holidays such as the Queen's birthday (22 October) and the Kaiser's birthday in January 1915.

These crowds had a profound impact upon contemporaries; almost all of the descriptions of them use terms like "enveloping, moving." It seemed that the whole population had become infected with "war enthusiasm." One journalist, describing the victory celebration in Bremen on 24 August 1914, wrote:

> we lack the words to describe these experiences. . . . We are standing in the middle of the greatest joys of our lives. Our victory wagon has departed and will no longer be able to be held back. . . . We, young and old, will be allowed to remember always the Sunday passed as a day of unforgettable wonderful experiences.

Yet limits to the enthusiasm remained. Only in Berlin did flags fly in working-class suburbs. In Düsseldorf government officials held a conference on 31 August in order to discuss ways to have the working class in the Ruhr fly the German flag. More importantly, the "enthusiastic" crowds were ephemeral. The "spirit of 1914," the carnivalesque, festive public expression of patriotism, lasted only about six weeks. After Sedan day (2 September 1914) a month passed before the next victory celebration on 10 October, when Antwerp fell. As the war continued the "war enthusiasm," too, passed. Already by 23 August, "the only recently so feverishly excited Berlin, which pulsated with violent changes of mood and hourly changing strong emotions, had become a quiet, serious city—had returned to its customary work." Toward the end of September, "the loud coming together of people in the streets—often caused by false reports of victories—has stopped. There are no more demonstrations in the cafés and bars." In 1915 and 1916, no crowds greeted the wounded heroes, no spectators put flowers in the guns of departing warriors.

Instead, different sorts of crowds would form. On 9 August the government published the first list of the dead, wounded, or missing. Such lists would be published approximately every three days for the next four years. In August the lists were published in the newspapers, and they were long—too long. In September the government decided to forbid their full publication. (Only partial lists—of the local dead, wounded, and missing—could be published, and only in the smaller cities or towns.) But the full lists were still posted on boards in front of the War Academy on the Dorotheenstrasse in Berlin. By the end of September, except for the celebrations of an occasional victory, the largest crowds in Berlin were composed of people searching for names on these long lists. And thus the War Academy, one of those "national" sites which the patriotic parades visited in the last week of July, slowly but surely became in the popular mind the symbol of the horror of war's reality, a place where one might find the name of a loved one or a friend.

In August 1914 Germans could read that they had all experienced the outbreak of war in the same way, that through the August experiences a "national" identity had come to replace the various local or class identities as the most important social identity. Yet, as the liberal sociologist Leopold von Wiese noted in late 1914, "people are different, and the great, serious, days—very moving through their very simplicity—were, so far as I could tell, experienced differently according to a person's disposition and experience."

There was a great deal of public "war enthusiasm." Even if not all of this is adequately described with the term "enthusiasm" the opportunity to go to war was a moment of great adventure such as few generations are given. Within the active, purposive, enthusiastic crowds, people experienced themselves as a community, capable of acting as a collective and coherent entity. For many, especially for academic intellectuals, this experience was the experience of a lifetime.

Yet there were generational, occupational, temporal, gender, and geographical differences in German public opinion in August 1914. "War enthusiasm" was mostly limited to large cities, where it was localized among the better classes, especially the educated youth. The enthusiasm may have helped bridge some differences among Germans—the enthusiasm was found both in Catholic and in Protestant areas, among north and south Germans, among Christians and Jews, among men and among women. But the feeling of unity, of community, was limited to a small section of the urban population.

"War enthusiasm" does not seem to have extended outside the city bourgeoisie. There was little public enthusiasm in the smaller towns, in the countryside, and in the working-class sections of the large cities. In villages and in farming towns the mood was more somber than exuberant. And there was little enthusiasm in the larger cities near the border. "Enthusiasm" was also not felt by families, who had to cope with fear and uncertainty. Men were more "enthusiastic" than women. Many women were genuinely worried and upset at the beginning of the war. All told, it seems safe to say that the majority of Germans in July and August 1914 did not feel "war enthusiasm." If a referendum had been held on 1 August on whether or not there should be a world war it would have been overwhelmingly rejected.

And yet it would be a mistake to search too closely for a sociology of German public opinion in August. People had mixed emotions, as a Berlin journalist noted on 2 August:

> neither the enthusiastic crowds tumbling down the street nor the signs of pure fear, produced by conceptualizations of undistilled nervous worrying, can be considered the single description for the mood of the Berlin population in these days. There has never been a better example of the concept of "mixed emotions."

The essence of the August experiences was not so much enthusiasm but excitement, a depth of emotion, an intensity of feeling. It was a time lived and perceived by the participants as a historical time. Germans felt pride, enthusiasm, panic, disgust, curiosity, exuberance, confidence, anger, bluff, fear, laughter, and desperation. All of these emotions may have been felt by the same person. At the very least they were found in the same place. In front of the barracks there were families—most often women and children—saying goodbye to their men, or, biting their nails, waiting to see one of them. They were often crying. Alongside them were groups of enthusiastic, boisterous young boys, trying to look older, trying to volunteer. Nearby were crowds of curious bystanders, who had come to watch a piece of history unfold, to be able to tell their grandchildren that they had seen this world theater.

Did identities change as a result of the August experiences? Certainly some individual identities changed. Some drifters, such as Adolf Hitler, found a purpose in life. Yet social identities did not change. Most Germans responded to the outbreak of war more or less as one would have expected. The Germans were united, not in their enthusiasm but in their purpose.

A historical curiosity, an innocent and naïve playing at heroism, a moment of profound tragedy, the end of a militaristic innocence, these are some of the possible narratives of the "August experiences" if the narrative had been based on the sum of individual experiences. Such a narrative was not written because a different narrative of these days, a social memory was being composed at the time. This social memory would come to shape people's individual memories of their own experiences. The rest of the story is the history of the memories of those warm days in July and August 1914.

NOTE

From Jeffrey Verhey, *The Spirit of 1914: Militarism, Myth, and Mobilization in Germany*, from chapter 3, "War Enthusiasm": Volunteers, Departing Soldiers, and Victory Celebrations (Cambridge: Cambridge University Press, 2000), pp. 97–114. Reprinted with the permission of Cambridge University Press.

Foch's General Counteroffensive, Part I
26 September to 23 October 1918

David Trask

After the Allied victories during the period 8 August–16 September 1918, Ludendorff's shaken armies fell back grudgingly to the Hindenburg line. These defenses protected their lateral communications. General headquarters moved from Avesnes to Spa. The number of German divisions declined from 207 late in May to 185 by the third week in September, and German infantry battalions were reduced from four to three companies. Twenty-two divisions had to be cannibalized, and the continuing arrival of new American divisions constantly increased Foch's superiority in rifle strength. Ludendorff observed telltale signs of declining German morale. "Shirking at the front became more prevalent, especially among men returning from home leave. Overstaying of leave increased, and the fighting-line was more thinly manned." The first quartermaster general could only plead for determined resistance to impending attacks. On 15 September, reacting to an Austrian bid for peace negotiations, he stated: "The German army . . . must prove to the enemy that we are not to be conquered. As we fight we must wait and see whether the enemy's intentions are honorable, in case he is ready to engage in peace negotiations this time, or whether he will again reject peace with us, or we are to purchase this peace on terms which will destroy the future of our people." Foch feared that Ludendorff might order a retreat to the line Antwerp–Brussels–Namur–the Meuse–the Chiers–Metz–Strasbourg, shortening his front and concentrating his remaining manpower. Unremitting pressure prevented any such movement.

Foch realized that he should now attack the Hindenburg line in front of the British troops on the line Cambrai–St. Quentin–La Fere–St. Gobain, but he recognized that he also must engage the enemy elsewhere. If he advanced only in Picardy, he "ran the risk of seeing all the enemy reserves massed to meet the onslaught of our armies, and, aided by a powerful system of fortification, in a position to frustrate our efforts." He must therefore launch a series of coordinated attacks that would immobilize the enemy forces elsewhere than in Picardy and "by their convergent directions, make them harmonize their efforts with those produced by our already successful enterprises. In short, extend the front of our offensive while keeping it always headed in the same general direction." The employment of the American army on the right and the Belgian army on the left would create this extension. Foch's grand conception entailed the destruction of the grand salient, sometimes called the Laon bulge, that the German army had driven into France and Belgium. Powerful attacks on the west and south faces of the salient would force a retreat at least to the line Antwerp–the Meuse.

On 3 September, following his discussions with General Pershing about the future operations of the American First Army, Foch issued the initial directive for his huge enterprise. The British army would attack eastward in the general direction of Cambrai–St. Quentin. The French armies in the center would drive the enemy beyond the Aisne and the Ailette. On the right, the Americans would strike northward between the Meuse and the Argonne in the general direction of Mezieres. They would coordinate their operations with those of the French Fourth Army on the left. The American First Army's attack would reach the line Dun-sur-Meuse–Grandpre–Challerange–Sommepy and then it would move on to the line Steny–LeChesne–Attigny, from which it would threaten Mezieres. The basic objective was to interdict the railway behind the Hindenburg line that ran from Lille in the north through Aulnoye, Avesnes, Hirson, Mezieres, Sedan, and Metz to Strasbourg. The British would drive to the Maubeuge–Aulnoye area and the Franco-American force to the Mezieres–Sedan area. These operations would deprive the Germans of an essential rail connection and force a broad retreat.

The plan for the general counteroffensive also included an inter-Allied attack in Flanders toward Ghent from the positions gained early in September. This movement was part of Foch's effort to keep Ludendorff occupied along the entire western front so that he could not reinforce the most threatened areas. A thrust north of the Lys River would clear the Belgian coast and threaten German communications north of the Ardennes region. On 11 September, Foch formed the Flanders Group of Armies to undertake this attack. King Albert of Belgium commanded this group with the help of the French General Jean Degoutte. It included the Belgian Army, the British Second Army (Plumer) the French Cavalry Corps, and the French VII and XXXIV Corps. Just to the south, the British Fifth Army (Birdwood) would move against Lille.

Foch soon fixed the schedule for the three coordinated thrusts that made up the general offensive:

September 26: Franco-American attack towards the Mezieres–Sedan area between the Meuse and Suippe rivers on a front of 44 miles, the American First Army (fifteen double-sized divisions) and the French Fourth Army (twenty-two divisions), the two forces joining at the west side of the Argonne forest.

September 27: British attack in the general direction of Cambrai between Peronne and Lens by the First Army (twelve divisions) and Third Army (fifteen divisions).

September 28: Belgian-French-British attack by the Flanders Group of Armies toward Ghent between the English Channel and the Lys River (British Second Army [ten divisions], Belgian Army [twelve divisions], French Sixth Army [six divisions]).

September 29: Franco-British attack toward Busigny between Peronne and La Fere by the British Fourth Army (seventeen divisions, including two American divisions) and the French Tenth Army (fourteen divisions).

Two hundred miles separated the Flanders Group of Armies in the north and the American First Army in the South. The numbers of troops engaged far exceeded the total of those who took part in the preliminary battles during August–September 1918. Britain's official history noted the distinctive feature of this plan. During previous Allied offensives the enemy had managed to reinforce threatened locations. "Now he was attacked everywhere at once, was forced to disperse his reserves, and although the Allied margin of superiority was not very great, he was, in the result, nowhere strong enough to hold his ground."

On 25 September, just preceding the opening of the offensive, and on 27 September, just afterward, Foch drew the attention of the national commanders-in-chief to certain essential considerations. He was concerned above all with engaging the enemy and maintaining unremitting pressure. His commanders were enjoined to exploit all ruptures of the line of resistance and to avoid any halts in exploitation. These injunctions applied particularly to the French Fourth Army and the American First Army. "Under the conditions now existing, the main thing is to develop before anything the shock power of the Allied armies." Foch hoped to prevent the enemy from organizing a defense. "If we do not give him time enough to pull himself together, we shall be confronted everywhere with nothing but disorganized units, mixed up together, or, in any event, improvisations hastily made." These instructions were designed to prevent the German army from effectively reconstituting defensible positions after the initial engagement.

The terrain features of the Meuse–Argonne sector posed exceptionally difficult obstacles for the American First Army. To its right ran the Meuse, an unfordable river, and on its right bank rose the heights of the Meuse. These hills overlooked a region to the west that included several ridges, of which the most imposing was the hill of Montfaucon, 342 meters high. To the north, the wooded heights of Romagne and Cunel provided excellent observation of the surrounding territory. On the First Army's left the Argonne forest allowed the German defenders to observe the territory to the east and provided cover for troops within it. A small stream, the Aire River, flowed northward parallel to the forest, emptying into the Aisne River at Grandpre. The region constituted a double defile with a hogback down the middle that passed through Montfaucon and the Romagne–Cunel heights. The attacker must move up the defiles on both sides on the hogback. Only two inadequate roads gave access to the battlefield. It is hard to imagine a more difficult position to attack.

The German defenders constructed four distinct sets of fortifications, taking advantage of east–west ridges. The southernmost of these, the first defensive position, followed the line Regneville–Bethincourt–Boureuilles–Vienne-le-Chateau. Five kilometers north of this position lay the Giselher Stellung. Six kilometers farther came the most formidable barrier, the Kriemhilde Stellung, running through the wooded heights of Cunel and Romagne. It was an eastward extension of the main Hindenburg fortifications running through the Aisne valley known as the Hunding–Brunhilde Stellung. The fourth line, the Freya Stellung, was much less developed. It bestrode the Barricourt heights, another strong wooded position. Various intermediate lines and switch positions further strengthened the defense. Throughout the region well-sited machine-gun nests, pill boxes, barbed wire entanglements, and artillery batteries added to the natural strength of the Meuse–Argonne defenses.

These fortifications were deemed so formidable that the German Group of Armies Gallwitz (nineteen divisions) allocated only the German Fifth Army of five divisions to their defense. The First Army staff calculated that German command could reinforce the area at the rate of four divisions on the first day, two on the second, and nine on the third. German reserves were concentrated around Metz, probably to guard against an attack eastward from the St. Mihiel salient. The defending divisions were generally of poor quality, including Saxon and Austrian organizations of dubious dedication. These units were seriously depleted, at a third of their normal complement. However, the German command was sufficiently competent and the region so favorable for defense that an attacking force could expect stubborn resistance.

Pershing had only ten days to concentrate his forces. He had to relocate three corps headquarters, fifteen divisions, and corps and army troops. Seven divisions came from the St. Mihiel area, three from the Vosges Mountains, three from the Soissons area, one from a training area in the Haute-Marne, and one from near Bar-le-Duc. This circumstance led to unfamiliar command relationships. For example, General Liggett's I Corps for the Meuse–Argonne attack included the 28th and 77th Divisions from the Vesle River sector near Soissons, the 92d Division from the Vosges Mountains, and the 35th Division from the vicinity of Nancy. None of these divisions had been under Liggett's command during the reduction of the St. Mihiel salient. Col. George C. Marshall, who coordinated the movement, made use of trains, motor transport, and marching columns, all moving at night to conceal the concentration from the enemy. Somehow about 200,000 French troops were moved out of the Meuse–Argonne sector and about 600,000 Americans into it. Despite continuous confusion and monumental traffic jams, the movement was completed by 26 September. Many French troops—the II Colonial Corps, the XVII Corps, and the 5th Cavalry Division, seven divisions in all—were assigned to the First Army. They were placed just to the east of the Meuse River with some American troops.

The gap of only ten days between the conclusion of the St. Mihiel attack and the beginning of the Meuse–Argonne offensive meant that Pershing must employ untested troops during the initial phases of the second operation. Experienced divisions were unavailable, notably the 1st, 2d, 26th, and 42d. Only four of the nine divisions designated for the attack on 26 September had seen action. Four of these lacked their organic artillery, entering the battle without an opportunity to familiarize themselves with the guns assigned to them. Some units had neither completed their training nor served in quiet sectors of the front. The only veteran outfit was the 33d Division.

General Pershing's objective was somewhat altered just before D-day. Mezieres had been designated as the American objective in early discussions, but by 16 September, the French Fourth Army, operating between the Argonne forest and the Suippe River, had inherited this task. Gen. Henri Gouraud's troops were to gain the line Rethel–Attigny on the Aisne "with subsequent direction toward Mezieres." The American First Army was to move first to the line Dun-sur-Meuse–Grandpre, linking with the French north of the Argonne forest. It would then advance to the line Steny–Le Chesne, aiming at Buzancy and Stonne. These operations would support the French task of clearing the line of the Aisne River preparatory to the French capture of Mezieres, which would interdict Ludendorff's lateral rail communications. However, the principal effort on the right wing of Foch's converging offensive must come from the First Army. Pershing apparently construed his objective as the section of the railroad between Carignan and Sedan southeast of Mezieres, although Foch did not specifically assign it to him. Characteristically, he insisted that "the sector assigned to the American Army was opposite the most sensitive part of the German front then being attacked."

The First Army's plan of attack, Field Order No. 20 issues on 20–21 September, aimed at a rapid, deep penetration of the German defenses, seeking to overrun them before the enemy could bring up reinforcements. Three corps on line were to advance in two days through the main battle line, the Giselher Stellung, and the Kriemhilde Stellung. This surge of about 10 miles would reach the line Dun-sur-Meuse–Grandpre. After completing this great effort, another bound of about 8 to 12 miles would put the First Army on the line Steny–Le Chesne. Then Pershing's forces to the east of the Meuse, largely French, would seize the heights of the Meuse, securing his right flank. Finally, the Americans would move on the Sedan–Carignan railroad.

The critical aspect of the plan was the initial assault on a front of twenty miles intended to penetrate the Kriemhilde Stellung in two days. The V Corps (91st, 79th, and 37th Divisions), commanded by Maj. Gen. George H. Cameron, was to capture Montfaucon Hill on the first day. The I Corps (77th, 28th, and 35th Divisions), commanded by Gen. Liggett, would advance on the left down the valley of the Aire River. Maj. Gen. Robert L. Bullard's III Corps (4th, 80th, and 33d Divisions) would move forward to the east of Montfaucon Hill. These drives would create deep salients on each side of the elevation, outflanking it and assuring its fall. Then the Americans would pierce the Kriemhilde Stellung. The advance of the I Corps east of the Argonne and that of the French Fourth Army west of the Argonne would outflank that formidable wooded barrier and force its defenders to withdraw. The artillery of I Corps would suppress enemy fire from the Argonne, and that of III Corps would neutralize enemy artillery firing from the heights of the Meuse. Some artillery support would also come from the troops on the line just ease of the Meuse, the French XVII Corps and the American IV Corps. Besides almost 2,800 guns, the Americans had at their disposal 182 small tanks, 142 of them manned by Americans under the command of Col. George S. Patton, Jr., and attached to the I Corps, and 821 airplanes, of which Americans manned 604.

Pershing's plan was extraordinarily demanding, but various considerations led him to adopt it. He counted heavily on surprise. Besides, he expected to enjoy an enormous preponderance of manpower during the first days of the battle. He would send nine double-strength divisions close to full complement against only five weak German divisions at no more than one-third strength. Of great importance was also his faith in his men, so often proclaimed during the controversies over the formation of an independent force. "It was thought reasonable to count on the vigor and the aggressive spirit of our troops to make up for their inexperience." The difficulty with this plan, as Allan Millett has observed, was the inability of the American artillery to reach the Kriemhilde Stellung. The inexperienced American staff could not yet move artillery forward quickly. It was hoped that aircraft and tanks could provide sufficient support to ensure success. At 2030 on 26 September, a tremendous barrage from 2,775 artillery pieces, most of them French, opened on the German front line between the Meuse and the Argonne, and at 0530 the three American corps began their advance behind a rolling barrage. To the left, the French Fourth Army also attacked, the two armies advancing on a front of 44 miles between the Meuse and the Suippe. The First Army had made strenuous efforts to gain surprise, and initially the attack went well; the first German line was quickly overrun. Soon after that, progress began to slow. The inexperienced 79th Divisions, given the task of seizing Montfaucon Hill, encountered strong resistance. German defenders made their principal stand on the second line of defense, the Giselher Stellung, which ran through the hill. Despite desperate efforts, the VI Corps did not capture Montfaucon until midday on 27 September. The 4th Division to the right in the V Corps had an opportunity to seize the hill but adhered to rigid boundary assignments and did not do so. By this time, the first German reinforcements were arriving. Instead of quickly bursting through the German third line of defense, the First Army did not pass beyond the Giselher Stellung.

General Bullard, commanding the III Corps next to the Meuse River, recalled the complications that developed during the first four days of the battle. "The resistance of the enemy was steadily stiffening. Wherever his machine guns were encountered— and they were encountered after the passage of the first line—the progress was exceedingly difficult. Indeed his first defence seemed to be almost wholly machine guns." After that a new challenge presented itself. "We began to catch a heavy artillery fire from the high ground on the right bank of the Meuse. It was becoming exceedingly annoying, the more so as we advanced." Only local gains were recorded after the initial attack. Pershing's growing anxiety was reflected in a directive transmitted to the corps commanders. He ordered them to locate their division and brigade commanders "as far up toward the front of the advance of their respective units as may be necessary to direct their movements with energy and rapidity in the attack. . . . All officers will push their units forward with all possible energy." He also authorized condign measures against leaders who did not respond effectively. Corps and division commanders received authority "to relieve on the spot any officer of whatever rank who fails to show in this emergency those qualities of leadership required to accomplish the task that confronts us."

Information from the three corps confirms Bullard's view. On 27 September, I Corps, next to the Argonne forest, reported: "We progressed against strong resistance." On the 28th, "infantry advancing . . . met with determined resistance. The line was practically unchanged." On the 29th, the enemy was reported as "harassing our forward troops with machine-gun and artillery fire, particularly from the east edge of the Foret d'Argonne." Bullard's III Corps reported that, on 2 September it "continued to encounter heavy M.G. [machine gun] fire from the left flank . . . also artillery fire from the northwest and heavy M.G. fire from the front. Early this morning [28 September] our line remained approximately the same as last night." On 28–29 September, "the infantry met considerably more resistance. Very heavy M.G. and artillery fire prevented further advance during the day." On 30 September, II Corps noted that an attack by the 4th Division had failed "because of heavy artillery fire. . . . No advance of our line. . . . Our line at present stabilizing." V Corps, attacking in the center, noted the capture of Montfaucon, reporting that "the enemy had but few troops engaged in the defense of Montfaucon. . . . they relied heavily upon machine-gun fire to check our forces. . . . The advance of our troops was hindered everywhere by machine-gun fire and intermittent shelling by the enemy." During the period 28–29 September, the reports remained the same: "Small machine gun groups, favorably located have proved a constant hindrance to the attackers. Artillery activity of the enemy is on the increase." On 30 September, this refrain was repeated: "The enemy is strongly resisting the advance of this corps. His line has been reinforced and volume of hostile artillery fire has increased. . . . The enemy is making stubborn resistance along entire front."

Pershing continued to exhort his troops to advance, but he was eventually forced to suspend his forward movement. By 30 September, he had gained about 8 miles and reached a line facing the enemy's third and strongest line of fortifications, the Kriemhilde Stellung. This obstacle was supposed to have been overwhelmed on the second day of the attack. On 29 September, Field Order No. 32 indicated that the attack would resume later. For the moment the three corps were to organize a defensive along the line Bois de la Cote Lemonte–Nantillois–Apremont-southwest across the Argonne. Veteran divisions relieved the most exhausted units at the front: the 1st Division replaced the 35th Division in I Corps, and the 2d and 3d Divisions replaced the 37th and 79th Divisions in V Corps. The 91st Division was withdrawn to the corps reserve, so that the VI Corps after that functioned with an entirely new group of organizations. These changes further complicated difficult problems of supply. Donald Smythe summarizes the circumstances graphically. "Whether because of incompetence or inexperience or both, the First Army was wallowing in an unbelievable logistical tangle. It was as if someone had taken the army's intestines out and dumped them all over the table."

German explanations for their successful defense emphasized American inexperience and flawed tactics. An officer from the 5th Reserve Corps who observed the action wrote: "American infantry is very unskillful [*sic*] in attack. It attacks with closed ranks in numerous and deep waves, at the head of which come the tanks. Such forms of attack form excellent targets for the activity of our artillery, infantry, and machine guns, if only the infantry does not get scared on account of the advancing masses and loses its nerve." Methods of coping with tanks had been identified. "The infantry allows them to approach closely and then fires upon them with machine guns, with rifles . . . and with artillery. Thereupon, the tanks generally turn back." Hand grenades also proved effective. If the tanks continued to advance, the infantry left them to the artillery.

The pause in the offensive was all the more galling to the Americans because the French on the left had made significant progress. Gouraud's Fourth Army was held up initially, but on 29 September, it overran the line of the Py River. Then on 1 October, it seized the strong point at Notre-Dame-des-Champs and on 3 October, another, Blanc Mont, this time with the valuable help of the American 2d Division. Pershing had released the experienced organization for this purpose. On 30 September–1 October, the French Fifth Army, operating farther west between the Vesle and the Aisne, pushed the Germans across the Aisne–Marne canal. By 7 October, the German defenders had retreated to positions behind the Suippe River and the line of the Arnes. However, the French seem to have paced their advance to match the progress of the American First Army on their right and the British Expeditionary Forces on their left.

Pershing put the best face on what was surely a severe disappointment. Writing to the Secretary of War Baker on 2 October, he claimed that "operations here have gone very well, but, due to rains and the condition of the roads have not gone forward as rapidly nor as far as I had hoped. . . . Our losses so far have been moderate." In his memoirs, he argued that the enemy had to weaken its order of battle elsewhere to hold the hinge of his defense on the western front, although he conceded that the enemy had fought well. "In this dire extremity the Germans defended every foot of ground with desperate tenacity and with the rare skill of experienced soldiers."

What had stopped the American attack, the first in the series that made up Marshal Foch's general counteroffensive? No one explanation is sufficient to explain the check administered to the First Army. Several complications combined to force suspension of the attack in front of the Kriemhilde Stellung.

Adhering to Foch's instructions, the First Army sought to gain surprise, but this effort did not succeed. Attempts to convince the enemy that the Americans would attack eastward toward Metz had some effect, but information about the Meuse–Argonne attack fell into enemy hands several days in advance. This misfortune allowed the German command to alert reinforcements who were able to move promptly into position soon after the beginning of the attack.

Of much greater significance was the inexperience of the American divisions. Pershing had to rely on undertrained troops during the initial phase of the Meuse–Argonne offensive, having used his battle-tested divisions at St. Mihiel. From a tactical point of view, the principal difficulties resulted from failure to coordinate infantry attacks and artillery fire. Methods developed elsewhere on the western front to deal with machine-gun nests were often ignored, leading to unnecessary casualties. Too often, green commanders and staffs ordered mass frontal attacks against well-sited weapons. Pershing had discounted warnings from the Allies that his divisional and corps commanders were not yet prepared for the challenge of the western front, but events of 26–30 September proved him wrong.

The most obvious of Pershing's difficulties was the extraordinary logistical tangle that soon developed behind the lines. Only two roads of any consequence led to the battlefield, and these traversed spongy soil that could not withstand heavy traffic. Congestion in the bottleneck between the First Army's depots and the huge force pinned down in front of the Kriemhilde Stellung prevented efficient supply of ammunition and food. It also inhibited forward displacement of artillery batteries. Hunter Liggett described conditions on the line. "The miserable roads began to have their effect on the second day. As the infantry advanced it lost the proper support of the artillery, which was unable to follow. The engineers and pioneers toiled furiously, but the task was an appalling one. Four years of shell fire had left the spongy soil of No Man's Land a troubled sea. . . . The rest of the region—a succession of half-obliterated trenches, water-filled shell holds and tangles of wire—defied transport; and when the artillery did slug its way through, it found itself at a disadvantage, at first, in the blind country."

Other critics have questioned Pershing's plan. Liddell Hart drew attention to the distance the attack must carry through difficult terrain before encountering the principal German fortifications. The German elastic defense based on clever use of machine guns and well-placed artillery, an expedient so beneficial to the French and British during their defensive battles from March to July, proved most effective, halting the Americans after their initial success. Braim stresses the ability of the defenders to concentrate fire on the Americans from three locations: the high ground in the Argonne forest, the hogback running north-south through the center of the narrow sector, and the heights east of the Meuse. He argues that Pershing should have included the entire Argonne forest in his sector or better still attacked east of the Meuse to neutralize the heights. Whatever one makes of these criticisms, it is certain that Pershing's plans did not give sufficient attention to the difficulties associated with advancing on a narrow front in difficult terrain against very strong positions that afforded excellent cover and concealment, many in flanking locations on high ground.

The check administered to the First Army after a promising beginning energized Allied criticism of General Pershing. Haig complained privately about the difficulties that the First Army had encountered, which struck him as like those of the Belgian army operating to his north. After noting reports that congestion had forced a halt in offensive operations for several days, he exploded: "What very valuable days are being lost! All this is the result of inexperience and ignorance on the part of the Belgian and American Staffs of the needs of a modern attacking force." Gen. Jean-Henri Mordacq, a member of Clemenceau's entourage who observed Pershing after the battle bogged down, recorded some striking impressions. "I could read clearly in his eyes that, at that moment, he realized his mistake. His soldiers were dying bravely, but they were not advancing, or very little, and their losses were heavy." Mordacq agreed with Haig's views on the causes of the American failure. "All that great body of men which the American Army represented was literally struck with paralysis because the 'brain' didn't exist, because the generals and their staffs lacked experience. With enemies like the Germans, this kind of war couldn't be improvised."

Foch shared these negative evaluations and attempted to retrieve matters by making significant changes in command. After informing Pétain that the Americans had been stopped more by the failure of their staff to manage logistical matters than by enemy action, he sent his principal staff officer, General Weygand, to Pershing with a devastating proposal. He wanted to send two or three American divisions to the French XXXVIII Corps operating on the right wing of the French Fourth Army just to the west of the American I Corps. A similar force would relocate east of the Meuse and join the French XVII Corps. A new French Army, the Second, would direct the troops located near the Argonne. Pershing would retain command of a reduced army on both sides of the Meuse. Weygand specified that the objectives assigned earlier would remain the same, but Pershing was to use his expanded force east of the Meuse to seize the heights between Damvillers and Dun-sur-Meuse. "The result would secure the flank of our general offensive toward the north and afford greater liberty of movement to our armies through the possession of the roads and of the railroad in the Valley of the Meuse."

Pershing immediately rejected the proposal. To accept it would have been tantamount to admitting failure, but to Foch he adduced other reasons for his opposition. Among them were his long-held objection to placing American troops under French generals; his intention to avoid "dismemberment of the American First Army at a moment when its elements are striving for success under the direction of American command"; and the logistical confusion that would result from the establishment of mixed commands. He assured the generalissimo that he would immediately launch attacks both west and east of the Meuse. Foch could only bow to Pershing's wishes, making the proviso that the American operations "start without delay and that, once begun, they be continued without any interruptions such as those which have just arisen."

Privately Pershing expressed great irritation at Foch's initiative, attributing it to Premier Clemenceau. He wrote at the time: "I will not stand for this letter which disparages myself and the American Army and the American effort. He [Foch] will have to retract it or I shall go further in the matter." Pershing presumably thought that Foch had overstepped his authority, which did not extend to local operational matters. In any event, Foch pulled back, and Pershing was left to galvanize his forces for a resumption of his offensive. A few days later, when Foch described this episode to Haig, the British commander opined that he could reach Valenciennes in forty-eight hours with three fresh American divisions. Foch responded that "it was impossible to get any troops from Pershing at the moment." After the war, Pershing admitted that serious shortages of transport had arisen, but he blamed the War Department for this circumstance. "After nearly eighteen months of war it would be reasonable to expect that the organization at home would have been more nearly able to provide adequate equipment and supplies, and to handle shipments more systematically." He admitted that "serious trouble, if not irreparable disaster" might have resulted, if the Allies had not met many of his needs.

Lack of progress on the Franco-American front disappointed Foch, but extraordinary events on the British front in Picardy, the other main element of the general counteroffensive, brought him the greatest satisfaction. On 27 September, the British First Army and Third Army attacked the Hindenburg line between the Sensee River and Villers-Guilain. The Canadian Corps burst across the Canal du Nord, the assault penetrating four miles into the German defenses on the first day. On the second and third days, the offensive broke completely through the Hindenburg line and reached the outskirts of Cambrai, a critical center of communications. Again, efficient combined operations, this time including armor, provided the margin of victory. The Hindenburg line was designed to resist bombardment but not tanks; it succumbed to attacks by infantry and armor closely coordinated with artillery fire.

On 29 September, another British Army, the Fourth, struck to the south between Vendhuile and Holnon on a 12-mile front against the German Second and Eighteenth Armies and moved swiftly across the St. Quentin Canal. General Debeney's French First Army, located to Rawlinson's right, also launched an attack, which made a less spectacular but measurable gain. Again, the Hindenburg line was breached completely, and the victorious Allied armies now conducted a pursuit of the enemy.

The American II Corps, which included the 27th and 30th Divisions, was attached to the Fourth Army during the attack across the St. Quentin Canal. It made a flawed but signal contribution to this success. Read's troops were located between the British III and IX Corps. They faced a difficult stretch of the Hindenburg line constructed over the Bellicourt tunnel that carried the St. Quentin Canal underground for almost

6 kilometers. Two days before the main attack, the Americans failed in an attempt to seize three German redoubts that protected the fortifications of the tunnel. Some attacking troops were cut off. Therefore, the assault of 29 September was made without artillery support. As in operations elsewhere, inexperience dogged the Americans, the 27th Division in particular becoming disorganized in a fog after losing many officers. German counterattacks either repulsed or pinned down the American infantry. Fortunately the 3d Division of the Australian Corps, ordered to pass through the 27th Division and to continue the assault to the Beaurevoir line of German fortifications (a reserve position behind the main line of resistance), eliminated German resistance.

The 30th Division fared somewhat better, crossing the ground above the Bellicourt tunnel and seizing the town of Bellicourt, although it was stopped short of its objectives. It also benefited from the support of the Australian Corps; the Australian 5th Division passed through and continued the attack successfully. Again, American divisions serving as part of a European command had encountered initial trouble but had acquitted themselves honorably. To the right of the 30th Division, the British 46th Territorial Division took advantage of the fog that had confused the Americans and crossed the St. Quentin Canal just below the southern exit of the tunnel. This success greatly compromised the German position. Further assaults extended the initial penetration. By 4 October, the Fourth Army had smashed through the Beaurevoir defenses.

Meanwhile, on 28 September, the Flanders Group of Armies struck still another of Foch's blows in Flanders between Dixmude and the Lys River on a 17-mile front against a depleted force of about five German divisions. Success came immediately. The German first line of defenses fell on the first day and the second line came under strong attack. On the second day, Dixmude was taken. So were Passchendaele Ridge, the scene of desperate fighting in 1917, and the Messines–Wytschaete line. The attack on the Lys then slowed, but just to the south, General Birdwood's British Fifth Army captured La Bassee, Lens, and Armentieres. These actions soon forced Ludendorff to give up the channel ports, and they threatened indispensable rail communications. No American units participated in this action, but two divisions were sent to the Flanders Group of Armies for future operations.

On 29 September, French and British troops attacked the center of the German line between La Fere and Peronne. The Allies now were engaged all along the western front from Dixmude to the Meuse, a distance of 250 miles. Everywhere the German Army had suffered defeat, although in one sector, the Meuse–Argonne, it had prevented a breach of its principal fortifications. Signs of exhaustion appeared everywhere. For example, the German Eighteenth Army, retreating to a line of defenses east of the Hindenburg line, felt that it must receive a reinforcement of five divisions. Otherwise it would assume "no responsibility . . . for holding the position" that it was supposed to defend. The American 30th Division reported that German prisoners of war were "quite fed up and glad to be out of the war. The opinion of the men was that Germany is on its last legs." Ludendorff was confronted with the greatest crisis of the war.

Thus Haig's forces accomplished what Pershing's First Army had failed to achieve: a rapid, complete breach of the enemy's principal fortifications guarding the

Lille–Strasbourg railroad lines. The British success was all the more remarkable be-cause it came against the strongest concentration of German forces on the western front. Ludendorff had thinned his defenses elsewhere to strengthen the positions in front of the British First, Third, and Fourth Armies. Liddell Hart noted that forty British divisions and two American divisions faced thirty-seven German divisions be-tween St. Quentin and Lens. Maurice counted only thirty-one British and two Ameri-can divisions against thirty-nine enemy divisions on the front of the three British Armies. The Allies enjoyed a much more pronounced margin in the south. Ludendorff had only twenty divisions to cope with thirty-one French divisions and thirteen double-strength American divisions, the latter equivalent to twenty-six of the enemy, a disadvantage to the defenders of about three to one. Haig had urged the American attack on Foch in the hope that it would force Ludendorff to move divi-sions from the front of the British, but the field marshal's forces crossed the Hinden-burg line before any German troops were transferred to the American front.

The combined impact of the Allied attacks between 26 and 29 September, but most especially the British smash through the Hindenburg line toward Maubeuge, elicited a rapid response from Ludendorff. Already convinced that Germany could not win the war, Ludendorff fell completely apart at the news of the British victories, which came as the Bulgarian army collapsed on the Salonika front. He professed to attribute his panicky actions of 28–29 September mainly to the Bulgarian defeat. This explanation was in all likelihood a means of shifting the onus of military failure from his army to that of a lesser ally. On 1 October a foreign office representative at Spa noted: "I get the impression that they [the high command] have all lost their nerve, here, and that, if things come to the worst, we can justify our action to the outside world by Bul-garia's behavior." On 28 September, Ludendorff informed Hindenburg that he deemed it necessary to make a peace offer immediately and to seek an early armistice. "The position could grow only worse, on account of the Balkan position, even if we held our ground in the West. Our one task now was to act clearly and firmly, without delay." Hindenburg then said that he had come to the same conclusion and concurred with Ludendorff's suggestion. They agreed that the armistice must permit a "con-trolled and orderly evacuation of the occupied territory and the possible resumption of hostilities on our own borders." They did not believe that Germany would have to abandon territory conquered in the east, "thinking that the Entente would be fully conscious of the dangers threatening them as well as ourselves from Bolshevism."

On the same day, Foreign Minister Paul von Hintze in Berlin skillfully executed what was later called a "revolution from above" by negotiating with Reichstag leaders. He recognized that significant changes must take place in the German government, if it wished to approach President Wilson in search of an armistice and peace negotia-tions. Certain leaders favored this course. Klaus Schwabe argues that von Hintze and his supporters believed Germany "had to entrust the role of peace mediator to Wilson alone because his conditions were more favorable than anything which Germany could expect from its European opponents and because the interests of Germany and the United States coincided on the issues of freedom of the seas and freedom of trade." Besides, the American peace terms were well known, and it would be difficult for Wilson to ignore an initiative from Berlin. Governmental changes would allow the

established regime to survive the difficult process of obtaining an armistice and negotiating a peace settlement. Above all, it was necessary to initiate parliamentary government.

On 29 September, a crown council held at Spa with Kaiser Wilhelm, Foreign Minister von Hintze, Ludendorff, and Hindenburg attending, made the necessary arrangements. It was decided to make an appeal to President Wilson, bypassing France and
Britain, because the American peace program was much less draconian than that of
the Entente Powers. On the same day, unbeknownst to the High Command, the kaiser
decided to propose establishment of parliamentary government. The chancellor,
Hertling, refused to concur in this measure, but von Hintze remained firm, and his
views prevailed. Hertling's resignation cleared the way for a new premier, the moderate Prince Max of Baden, who was acceptable to Wilson. One of Ludendorff's officers,
Maj. Baron Erich von dem Bussche, was sent to Berlin to explain matters to the Reichstag leadership. Hindenburg left the front, going with the kaiser to Berlin. Ludendorff
explained why he remained behind: "I was, unfortunately, indispensable at Spa, owing
to the position in the field." Ludendorff was anxious to hasten the peace process, but
he denied that extreme military exigency was the reason, citing instead his wish to
"avoid further loss of life" and his assumption that "the earlier we began [the process
required to arrange peace] the more favorable would our position be at the com-
mencement of negotiations." He was among those who believed that Wilson would
resist the more damaging Entente war aims. Meanwhile, if his troops gained a breathing space, they could regroup on the German border for a possible resumption of
hostilities.

On 2 October, the final step was taken to inaugurate peace negotiations: it was decided to send a message to President Wilson proposing an end to the war. Von dem
Bussche explained the High Command's views to the Reichstag leadership. He observed that although Germany had used up its reserves, the army could continue to
fight. It could for "an incalculable period, inflict heavy losses on our enemies and
leave a desert behind us, but we could not win that way." This consideration explained
why Hindenburg and Ludendorff had decided that "an effort should be made to bring
the fighting to an end so that the German nation and its allies might be spared further
sacrifices." Von dem Bussche was at pains to discuss the role of the American troops.
They had provided the necessary bulge in manpower, although they "were not in
themselves of any special value or in any way superior to ours. At those points where
they had obtained initial successes, thanks to their employment in mass, their attacks
had been beaten off in spite of their superior numbers." Their contribution was "to
take over large sections of the [inactive] front and thus make it possible for the English and French to relieve their own veteran divisions and create an almost inexhaustible reserve."

The acting chancellor, Friedrich von Payer, adopted Prince Max's view that Germany should avoid a request for an immediate armistice because it was a sign of
weakness. He asked Hindenburg to clarify the reasons for the shaken High Command's insistence on immediate action. Hindenburg gave oral answers to several
questions. How long could the army keep the Allies out of Germany? The field marshal was uncertain, but he hoped that the enemy could be held until the coming

spring. Should the government expect an early collapse? Hindenburg did not think so. Was the emergency so critical that immediate action was necessary to obtain an armistice? Hindenburg noted his letter of that day to the chancellor in which he had urged action without delay. Was the field marshal aware that territorial losses might result, especially Alsace-Lorraine and the purely Polish areas of the eastern provinces? Hindenburg recognized that Germany might lose French-speaking areas of Alsace-Lorraine, but he saw no need to surrender territory in the east. Payer also wanted Hindenburg to review a draft of the note to be sent to President Wilson. This document did not reach the field marshal, or so it was claimed.

On 3 October, Prince Max became chancellor, and he immediately signed the peace note to President Wilson, which proceeded through Swiss channels to its destination on 6 October. It proposed an armistice and peace negotiations based on the Fourteen Points and other presidential pronouncements, an act that led to further correspondence between Washington and Berlin. Wilson responded on 8 October, posing some questions. Did Germany accept the entire American program in principle? Did Prince Max speak for his people only or for those who had so far conducted German policy? The president specified that Germany would have to remove its army from all occupied territories. Schwabe summarizes the main purposes of the document. "It tried to commit Germany irrevocably to the Wilsonian peace program. It precluded the Central Powers from deriving a military advantage from a possible armistice. It expressed doubts about the authority of the new German government to conduct the proposed negotiations." Prince Max quickly responded on 12 October: Germany accepted the Fourteen Points in principle; the peace conference would deal only with details of their application. He spoke both for the German government and its people.

Meanwhile, the Entente leaders, purposefully excluded from the discussion, manifested anxiety and even irritation. Wilson's demands were much less stringent than those contained in the confidential understandings between the Allied Powers known as the "secret treaties." On 8 October, a joint meeting of the Allied Naval Council and the Permanent Military Representatives specified various terms of armistice. General Bliss, the American Military Representative, refused to sign the terms, pleading lack of instructions. Privately he was critical of them. "Judging from the spirit which seems more and more to actuate our European allies, I am beginning to despair that the war will accomplish more than the abolition of German militarism while leaving *European* militarism as rampant as ever."

On 14 October, President Wilson made a stern reply to the second German communication, but it eventually led to a German-American deal. In this note, Wilson stated that the Allies would decide upon procedures for evacuation of occupied territories, rejecting some proposals on this question from Prince Max, and would not agree to an armistice that might permit resumption of hostilities. He also included a broad hint that the kaiser should abdicate and that others responsible for German policy should resign. The president thus reflected the Allies' wish that he take a firm position, but he also kept open the door to peace negotiations.

Wilson's stiff note created great alarm in Berlin, but Prince Max decided that Germany's best hope remained the American leader. He was anxious to reach agreement; he wanted to place the president "in the position of *arbiter mundi* and further give him the opportunity of trying to moderate the fanatical aspirations of his 'Associates.'" On 20 October, Prince Max agreed to Wilson's conditions, outlining a program of electoral reform and enhanced powers for the Reichstag. This response satisfied Wilson, although it greatly annoyed the British. On 23 October, the president notified Prince Max that he would now submit the correspondence to the Allies. Germany accepted this note on 27 October.

The stage was now set for climactic negotiations in Paris. To represent the United States in these deliberations, President Wilson dispatched Colonel House to Paris.

NOTE

David Trask, *The AEF and Coalition Warmaking*, chapter 6: Foch's General Counteroffensive, Part I: 26 September to 23 October 1918 (Lawrence: University Press of Kansas, 1993), pp. 115–37. Reprinted with the permission of the University Press of Kansas.

Three

Armageddon

The Destruction of Louvain

Leon van der Essen

Apart from requisitions and constant vexations, the Germans had committed no excesses in Louvain after their entry on August 19th. They continued to take hostages, who took it in turn to live at the town-hall and were responsible for the behavior of their fellow-citizens. Every day, in all the churches of the place, an urgent warning was given at the instance of the German authorities, telling the inhabitants to remain calm and promising them, in that case, not to take any more hostages.

The troops which reached the town the following week, however, seemed to be animated by a violently anti-clerical spirit. They followed the priests who showed themselves in public with buffoonery, insults, and even threats. They were also very excitable. One day, when a municipal official was taken through the town, preceded by soldiers with drums, and forced to read a proclamation, the Germans hurried up at once from all sides in the hopes of seeing a civilian executed.

The attack by the Belgian 2nd and cavalry divisions on the German positions between Malines and Louvain on the day of August 25th produced considerable excitement in the town. The gun-firing was distinctly heard, and became more violent in the course of the afternoon. It drew closer.

On this day Louvain was crammed with troops. Some 10,000 men had just arrived from Liège and were beginning to take up quarters in the town. A few hundred hussars were coming along the Malines road, covered with dust and leading their horses by the bridles. It was plain that the struggle was not going well for the Germans and that re-enforcements were necessary. At the town-hall dispatch-bearers followed one another quickly, bringing messages which made the members of the *Kommandantur* anxious. At 5 p.m. firing was heard of particular violence, and seemed to be extremely close to the town. At this moment some horsemen galloped through the streets, giving the alarm. At once officers and soldiers ran together and formed up in a disordered column. Motor-cars were coming and going every way, and ranging themselves up confusedly on the borders of the boulevards. Artillery and commissariat wagons were mixed up with them. Along the roads the horses, lashed till they bled, stiffened themselves and rattled along in a mad dash the guns which were going to re-enforce the German troops on the Malines road. As if to raise the confusion to its height, carts were coming back full-tilt and in the greatest disorder from the field of battle, their drivers all excitement, with revolvers in their hands. After the departure of the hastily formed battalions a great silence fell upon the town. In view of the gravity of affairs, everybody had gone home, and soon nothing more was heard except the ever closer and more distinct sound of guns.

Suddenly, at 8 p.m., when twilight had already fallen and everyone, in obedience to the rules of the occupying army, had to be already at home, a shot rang out, followed rapidly by two more, and then by a terrible fusillade. This was heard simultaneously at several points of the town, in the Boulevard de Tirlemont, at the Tirlemont Gate, in the Rue de Tirlemont, at the Brussels Gate, in the Rue and Place de la Station, in the Rues Léopold, Marie-Thérèse, and des Joyeuses-Entrées. With the cracking of rifles was mingled the sinister "tac-tac" of machine guns. The windows of the houses splintered under a hail of bullets, the doors and walls were riddled by the machine guns. In their cellars and other places where they had taken shelter on the first shots the inhabitants heard, through the din, the quick and crowding steps of the soldiers, the noise of whistles followed at once by volleys, and at times the heavy sound of a body falling to the ground. Those who had ventured to go up to their upper stories or attics soon saw the heavens reddened with a dreadful light. The Germans had set fire to several quarters of the town—the Chaussée and Boulevard de Tirlemont, the Place and Rue de la Station, and the Place du Peuple. Soon, too, the Palais de Justice, the University with the celebrated Library, and the Church of St. Pierre were ablaze, systematically set on fire with fagots and chemicals. Through the streets the German soldiers were running like madmen, firing in every direction. Under the orders of their officers, they smashed in the doors of the house, dragged the inmates from their hiding-places, with cries of "*Man hat geschossen! Die Zivilisten haben geschossen!*" (There has been firing! Civilians have fired!), and hurled hand-grenades and incendiary pastilles into the rooms. Several of the inmates were hauled out and instantly shot. Those who tried to escape from their burning houses were thrust back into the flames or butchered like dogs by the soldiers, who were watching along the pavements, with their fingers on the triggers of their rifles. From several of the houses the officers had the objects of value taken out before giving the order to burn them. Every one who showed himself in the street was shot down. In the Rue de la Station an officer on horseback, bursting with rage, was directing the incendiaries.

In the morning certain of the inhabitants, who had passed the night in their cellars or their gardens, ventured to go out. They then learnt that the Germans pretended that a plot had been hatched amongst them, that there had been firing on the troops, and that the whole responsibility for what had happened was thrown on the civilians. From dawn squadrons of soldiers entered the houses, searched them from top to bottom, and turned out the inhabitants, forcing them towards the station. The poor wretches were compelled to run with their hands uplifted. They were given blows with the fists and with rifle-butts. Soon a large number of townspeople were collected in the Place de la Station, where dead bodies of civilians were lying on the ground. During the night a certain number of people had been shot, without serious inquiry. While they were being hustled along, the townspeople were searched by officers and soldiers, and their money was taken from them (some officers gave a receipt in return), as well as any objects of value. Those who did not understand an order, who did not raise their arms quickly enough, or who were found carrying knives larger than a penknife, were at once shot. While these horrible scenes were enacted, the guns were constantly booming in the Malines direction, but the noise gradually grew more distant. In the streets numerous civilian corpses lay, and in some places corpses of German soldiers, who had been killed by one another in the night. Victims of panic and obsessed by the thought of francs-tireurs (guerrilla warriors), they had fired on every group which they met in the darkness. Fights of this kind had taken place in the Rue de Bruxelles, near the station, in the Rue de Paris et Vieux-Marché, the Rue des Joyeuses-Entrées, near the canal, and in the Rue de Namur. On all sides lay dead horses. The Germans had unharnessed them from their wagons, driven them into the streets and killed them, to lend belief to an attack by civilians.

As the houses burned and the soldiers continued to loot and to drive the inhabitants down the streets, the townspeople who had been carried off to the station were brutally separated into two groups. The women and children were shut up in the station and the tram-shed, the men ranged up in the Place de la Station. The Germans selected by haphazard from among them the victims destined to be executed. Some of them had to lie on their stomachs, and were butchered by shots in the head, neck, or back. Others were collected in groups, surrounded by soldiers with fixed bayonets, and carried off to the outskirts of the town, to the accompaniment of curses, threats, and blows. They were forced to march and countermarch through Herent, Thildonck, Rotselaer, Campenhout, etc. Wherever they went the prisoners saw houses in flames and corpses of civilians stretched on the road or charred by fire. In the country district of Louvain the Germans had committed the same excesses as in the town itself. In order to terrorize them, these groups of prisoners were hunted along the roads, without any precise object except to drive them mad. Sometimes they were made to stop, and a mock shooting took place. They were forced to run, to lift up their arms, etc. Those who fell through fatigue or attempted to escape were slaughtered. When the mournful procession passed through a village they found their ranks swollen by numbers of inhabitants of these places, who had already spent the night in the church. At last, after having thus wandered over the country for hours, several of these groups were taken back to Louvain and put on board cattle-trucks. Piled on to these like cattle, old men, women, children, and able-bodied men were dispatched to Germany. We cannot stop to describe the tortures which the deported had to endure on the journey and the cruelties inflicted on them by the fanatical inhabitants of the towns through which they passed. Some were taken to Cologne and exhibited to the crowd; others were sent as far as Münster, where they were interned.

During these explosions of violence on the part of the troops there was no respect of persons. Dutch, Spaniards, South Americans pleaded their neutral status in vain; they were jeered at and subjected to the same outrages as the Belgians. The flags of foreign nations floating over certain houses were no protection to them. The Spanish *pédagogie* in the Rue de la Station was burnt, and in the house of Professor Noyons, of Dutch nationality, a pile of fagots was lighted.

Meanwhile those of the inhabitants who had not fled towards the station, or who had not been driven in that direction, were running madly about the streets. A large number took refuge in the Hospital of Saint-Thomas, in the neighborhood of the Institut Supérieur de Philosophie. About 9 a.m. on Wednesday, August 26th, the shooting ceased and quiet temporarily returned. A picket of soldiers traversed the streets, taking an unarmed policeman with them to announce that able-bodied men must come together in certain places to help to put out the flames. The civil guards were specially invited to repair, in civilian clothes, to the St.-Martin barracks. All who obeyed the summons were made prisoners and taken, some to the station, bound for Germany, others to the neighboring villages, where they swelled the troops of prisoners already there. Several groups were taken to Campenhout in particular. After spending the night there, insulted and threatened with death all the time, they were ordered the next day or the day after to Louvain and shut up in the Riding School. The atrocious scenes were witnessed. Women went mad and children died.

On this Wednesday the soldiers started again to fire at intervals, to plunder, and to burn. They could be seen strolling about the town, drunk, laden with bottles of wine, boxes of cigars, and objects of value. The officers let them do it, roared with laughter, or set the example themselves. The Vice-Rector of the University and the Prior of the Dominicans were led through the town, escorted by soldiers, and forced to stop at certain spots to read a German proclamation warning the people "not to fire again upon the soldiers." A gloomy comedy, indeed! In several places soldiers were seen entering the houses and the gardens, firing shots, so as to prolong the mystification and the looting. Some walked along firing phlegmatically into the air. If a house was of fairly good appearance, a group of soldiers would assail it with shouts of "There was firing from here," and at once began to loot.

On the third day, Thursday, August 27th, some soldiers went through the town in the morning, announcing to the terrified population that Louvain was to be bombarded at noon and that everyone must leave at once. Often they added special instructions to go to the station. Those who obeyed these orders were put on to cattle-trucks and sent to join their hapless fellow-citizens in Germany. Others, better advised, took refuge at Heverlé, the property of the Duke of Aremberg, a member of the Prussian House of Lords, who was serving in the German army, and there they were not molested.

Along the Tirlemont and Tervueren roads rolled the wretched flood of fugitives, old men, women, children, invalids, nuns, priests, in a rout which cannot be described. German soldiers followed, compelling the unfortunates to raise their arms, striking them and insulting them. The fury of the Germans raged particularly against the priests. On the Tirlemont road several of them were arrested, taken to a piggery, and stripped of everything. They were accused of having incited the people to revolt, and there was talk of shooting them. One officer, more humane than the rest, had them released. The scenes were the same on the Tervueren road. There the Rector of the University, several ecclesiastical professors, the President of the American Seminary, and a number of Jesuits were treated in a disgraceful fashion and penned in a field. A young Jesuit, Father Dupierreux, on whom was found a diary with notes on the war, some of them very unflattering to the invaders, was shot before the eyes of his colleagues. Certain of these priests were taken to Brussels, where they were at last released. The Rector of the University, some professors and monks were set free through the intervention of a Dutchman, M. Grondys, who was present at the sack of Louvain.

At 11 o'clock on this Thursday, August 27th, the town was dead. Nothing could be heard to break the profound silence except the sinister crackle of houses on fire. Then, the inhabitants having disappeared, the regular sack began. There was no more talk of bombardment. The sack was organized methodically like the burning, which also continued at the same time. The doors of wardrobes and drawers of desks were smashed with rifle-butts. Safes were broken open with burglars' tools. Every soldier took his pick amid the heap of furniture spread over the floor. Silver-plate, linen, works of art, children's toys, mechanical instruments, pictures—everything was taken. Whatever could not be carried off was broken. The cellars were emptied. Then the looters finished up by depositing their filth in all the corners.

This lasted eight days. Every time fresh troops reached Louvain, they rushed on their prey. Recalling his entry and his stay at Louvain on August 29th, a Landsturm soldier from Halle wrote in his diary: "the battalion . . . arrive dragging along with it all sorts of things, particularly bottles of wine, and many of the men were drunk. . . . the battalion set off in close order for the town, to break into the first houses they met, to plunder—I beg pardon, I mean to requisition—wine and other things too. Like a pack let loose, each one went where he pleased. The officers led the way and set a good example."

And Gaston Klein, the soldier in question, concludes: "This day has inspired me with a contempt I could not describe."

The burning continued, simultaneously with the sack, down to September 2nd. On that day the last houses were set on fire in the rue Marie-Thérèse. In the evening drunken German soldiers were still dragging to the station heavy bags full of things stolen in the Rue Léopold.

On the afternoon of Friday, August 28th, the Germans committed a particularly odious crime. From August 20th the little town of Aerschot had been abandoned to the mercy of all the troops passing through. The parish priest of Gelrode had been put to death there in barbarous circumstances, and the burning of houses and terrorization of the remaining inhabitants had gone on. On the morning of August 28th a large group of people from Aerschot was carried off in the direction of Louvain. When they reached the Place de la Station they were made to wait, being told that they were to be put on a train and deported to Germany. While the human herd stood there, suddenly, without motive, some enraged soldiers began to fire into the mass. Some were killed and wounded, including women and children. Certain German soldiers, who took two of the wounded to the Hospital of St. Thomas, could not themselves conceal the disgust inspired in them by this barbarous act.

Meanwhile some energetic citizens, among whom was M. Nerinckx, professor of the University, had somehow managed to form a new municipal council, with the help of some members of the old council who had escaped the massacre or had returned after the early days of terror. By their firm attitude they were at last able to obtain from the commandant of the town the cessation of all acts of disorder on the part of the troops.

Such is the story of the sack of Louvain. What was the motive of it? We shall not stop to consider the odious and lying accusation made against the inhabitants by the military authorities and adopted by the Emperor himself in his famous telegram to the President of the United States. It has been reduced to nothing by the evidence of disinterested neutrals and by the inquiries of an Austrian priest, made on the spot.

In Louvain itself the following explanation is given. On the night of August 25th, at the moment when soldiers and vehicles were coming back in disorder from Malines, some shots rang out. The German soldiers in the town imagined, some that the enemy was coming, others that the civilians were beginning an attack. The former fired on their own comrades, taking them for Belgian or French soldiers; the latter riddled the fronts of the houses with bullets. The supposition is that there was a mistake, and then a panic.

It must be the truth with regard to a great number of German soldiers. We have already said that the soldiers quartered in Louvain seemed very nervous, that the troops who flocked back into the town during the battle were very excited; and, on the other hand, it is established that during the night several groups of Germans fired on one another in the streets. In such a state of mind, constantly haunted by visions of francs-tireurs, the German soldiers were very liable to sudden panic. A single shot was sufficient to produce it. We have the histories of Aerschot, Liège, Namur, and above all Andenne, to guide us on the subject.

Now, the evidence of witnesses establishes that a few moments before the fusillade began a shot was heard, followed immediately by two others. By whom was this shot fired? That will probably never be known. Was it fired by an unnerved sentry, by a drunken soldier, by a civilian? Considering the numerous warnings given to the townspeople, the threats of the Germans themselves, the excited state of the troops returning to the town, and the numbers of the soldiers in the garrison, it is very unlikely that a civilian would have been guilty of this act of folly, knowing that thereby he was exposing the whole population to nameless horrors. The fate of Aerschot was in every one's memory. Those events were recent.

If the first shot was fired by a German soldier, did that soldier act with the intention of starting a catastrophe? Was he obeying superior orders, and was he giving the signal for the carrying out of a German military "plot"?

Some have replied to the German accusation with a charge of premeditation on the part of the invaders. Louvain must have been condemned in advance, they say, and the attack of the Belgian troops on August 25th can only have hastened the execution of the plan.

History, while rejecting the German accusation, will demand serious proofs before accepting the victims' counter-accusation of German premeditation. Doubtless the German methods of terrorization do not entirely exclude the possibility of systematic and premeditated destruction of a town. But did this premeditation exist positively in this one particular case of Louvain? That is the whole question.

After carefully examining the mass of documents within our reach, we believe we may say that, in the present state of the evidence, it is impossible to consider proved the charge of premeditation with regard to Louvain—premeditation signifying to us the plan conceived long beforehand of giving Louvain up to the flames.

No doubt there are singular facts which, at first sight, seem to justify the defenders in their hypothesis of German premeditation. The fusillade breaking out almost simultaneously at several points some distance apart, the several centers of incendiarism started at the same time, the presence of a company of incendiaries armed with up-to-date appliances, the luminous signals said to have been sent up a few moments before the fusillade began, certain remarks let drop by soldiers or officers, the removal of the German wounded on the eve of the disaster, the warnings given long in advance to the inhabitants living in places 20 to 30 kilometers away from Louvain by soldiers or officers—the whole setting of the drama, taken in its entirety, cannot fail to be suspicious.

Still, when one examines the weight of these facts, one by one, many of them lose their conclusive force. The data are not precise enough or are insufficiently established; the facts and the words themselves seem capable of different interpretations.

On the other side, certain facts seem to negate premeditation, in the sense which we attach to the word. It is established that many soldiers, and even officers, believed for a moment that "the French were there." On the hypothesis of a preconceived plan, would they not have understood that the first shots were the signal for the massacre? At the start, and in the night, the Germans fired upon one another; there can be no doubt of that. This can be easily understood on the hypothesis of a panic, less easily on that of a German plot.

We therefore exclude, provisionally, the supposition of a German plot, conceived long before its execution. It does not seem to us proved by the documents published so far.

What we do not exclude is the hypothesis of premeditation on the part of the soldiers. In the state of excitement in which they were, particularly those coming back in disorder from Malines, they may have fired a shot, knowing that "the rest" would follow. This story was repeated so often in other places that we have the right to apply it hypothetically in the case of Louvain.

There is more. On the night of the 25th and the following days, certain soldiers and non-commissioned officers fired shots, so as to have a pretext for continuing the pillage. Many of the soldiers and officers may have believed, at the beginning, for a few moments, that they were being attacked by the enemy entering the town or that a civilian attack was taking place. But this mistake cannot have lasted long. It remains established that, in cold blood and without any idea of a serious inquiry, the military authorities persisted in the error and subjected Louvain to eight days' martyrdom, without raising a finger to stop the orgy. Whether the responsibility fell upon Major von Manteuffel or must be referred back to the highest personalities in the Empire does not matter. It is the prolonged sack of the town, without previous inquiry, which makes what has been called "the crime of Louvain" so enormous.

Such an inquiry was possible. The example of Huy proves that. On August 25th Major von Bassewitz, commandant of that place, published the following order of the day:—

August 25, 1914.

Last night shooting took place. It has not been proved that the inhabitants of the town were still in possession of arms. Nor has it been proved that the civil population took part in the shooting; on the contrary, it would seem that the soldiers were under the influence of alcohol and opened fire under an incomprehensible fear of an enemy attack.

The conduct of the soldiers during the night produces a shameful impression, with a few exceptions.

When officers or non-commissioned officers set fire to houses, without permission or order from the commandant, or in the present case from the senior officer, and when they encourage the troops by their attitude to burn and loot, it is an act of the most regrettable kind.

I expect severe instructions to be given generally as to the attitude towards the life and property of the civil population. I forbid firing in the town without officers' orders.

The bad conduct of the troops has had as its result the serious wounding of a non-commissioned officer and a soldier by German shots.
Von Bassewitz, Major,
Commandant.
If this had been the state of mind of the military authorities in Louvain, it is certain that there would not have been the horrors which we have described above. We cannot help thinking that the military authorities, when once the machine was accidentally thrown out of gear, were not at all annoyed. They took care not to give the necessary sign to avert the consequences.

How many victims were there at Louvain? We do not know. The Capuchin Father Valère Claes himself discovered 108, of whom 96 had been shot, the others having perished in the ruins of the houses. In his Pastoral Letter, Cardinal Mercier speaks of 176 persons shot or burnt in the whole neighborhood of Louvain and the adjoining communes. With regard to material destruction, 1,120 houses were burnt in the area of the commune of Louvain, 461 in the adjacent commune of Kessel-Loo, and 95 in that of Héverlé, these three parts making up the urban district of Louvain. In Louvain itself, apart from private houses, fire destroyed the Church of St.-Pierre, the central University buildings, the Palais de Justice, the Académie des Beaux-Arts, the theater, and the School of Commercial and Consular Science belonging to the University.

The Church of St.-Pierre was methodically set on fire, as was the university Library. A Josephite Father called the attention of the officer in command of the incendiaries to the fact that the building which he was about to set on fire was the Library. The officer replied, "*Es ist Befehl*" (It is ordered). It was then about 11 p.m. on Tuesday, August 25th.

This was not the end, however, of the excesses committed by the Germans during the first sortie of the Belgian troops from Antwerp. The region round Louvain and the villages situated between this town and Malines were engulfed in the "punishment." Bueken, Gelrode, Herent, Wespelaer, Rymenam, Wygmael, Tremeloo, Werchter, Wesemael, Wackerzeel, Blauwput, Thildonck, Rillaer, Wilsele, Linden, Betecom, Haecht were partly burnt and plundered, a number of the inhabitants being shot. Others were dragged along for many hours, loaded with insults, used as shields against the enemy's troops during the battle, and finally chased in the direction of the Belgian lines. Some were thrown into wells after being horribly ill-treated. Here, too, the German soldiers were bitter against the priests. The Rev. Father Van Holm, a Capuchin, and Father Vincent, a Conventual; Lombaerts, parish priest of Boven-Loo; de Clerck, parish priest of Bueken, and Van Bladel, parish priest of Herent, were killed, as also were a Josephite Father and a Brother of Mercy. The parish priest of Wygmael and Wesemael were shamefully treated. Finally, in this neighborhood the Germans committed the same outrages against women and young girls as in the neighborhood of Hofstade, Sempst, etc. Crimes of a Sadic character were also found. Neither old men, women, nor children were respected.

NOTE

From Leon van der Essen in Charles Horne, ed., *Source Records of the Great War*, volume II (No place of publication: National Alumni, 1923), pp. 151–64.

The Historic First of July

Philip Gibbs

1

With the British Armies in the Field, July 1, 1916 The attack which was launched today against the German lines on a 20-mile front began well. It is not yet a victory, for victory comes at the end of a battle, and this is only a beginning. But our troops, fighting with very splendid valour, have swept across the enemy's front trenches along a great part of the line of attack, and have captured villages and strongholds which the Germans have long held against us. They are fighting their way forward not easily but doggedly. Many hundreds of the enemy are prisoners in our hands. His dead lie thick in the track of our regiments.

And so, after the first day of battle, we may say: It is, on balance, a good day for England and France. It is a day of promise in this war, in which the blood of brave men is poured out upon the sodden fields of Europe.

For nearly a week now we have been bombarding the enemy's lines from the Yser to the Somme. Those of us who have watched this bombardment knew the meaning of it. We knew that it was the preparation for this attack. All those raids of the week which I have recorded from day to day were but leading to a greater raid when not hundreds of men but hundreds of thousands would leave their trenches and go forward in a great assault.

We had to keep the secret, to close our lips tight, to write vague words lest the enemy should get a hint too soon, and the strain was great upon us and the suspense an ordeal to the nerves, because as the hours went by they drew nearer to the time when great masses of our men, those splendid young men who have gone marching along the roads of France, would be sent into the open, out of the ditches where they got cover from the German fire.

This secret was foreshadowed by many signs. Travelling along the roads we saw new guns arriving—heavy guns and field-guns, week after week. We were building up a great weight of metal.

Passing them, men raised their eyebrows and smiled grimly. . . . A tide of men flowed in from the ports of France—new men of new divisions. They passed to some part of the front, disappeared for a while, were met again in fields and billets, looking harder, having stories to tell of trench life and raids.

The army was growing. There was a mass of men here in France, and some day they would be ready, trained enough, hard enough, to strike a big blow.

A week or two ago the whisper passed, "We're going to attack." But no more than that, except behind closed doors of the mess-room. Somehow by the look on men's faces, by their silences and thoughtfulness, one could guess that something was to happen.

There was a thrill in the air, a thrill from the pulse of men who know the meaning of attack. Would it be in June or July? . . . The fields of France were very beautiful this June. There were roses in the gardens of old French chateaux. Poppies put a flame of colour in the fields, close up to the trenches, and there were long stretches of gold across the countryside. A pity that all this should be spoilt by the pest of war.

So some of us thought, but not many soldiers. After the misery of a wet winter and the expectations of the spring they were keen to get out of the trenches again. All their training led up to that. The spirit of the men was for an assault across the open, and they were confident in the new power of our guns. . . .

The guns spoke one morning last week with a louder voice than has yet been heard upon the front, and as they crashed out we knew that it was the signal for the new attack. Their fire increased in intensity, covering raids at many points of the line, until at last all things were ready for the biggest raid.

2

The scene of the battlefields at night was of terrible beauty. I motored out to it from a town behind the lines, where through their darkened windows French citizens watched the illumination of the sky, throbbing and flashing to distant shellfire. Behind the lines the villages were asleep, without the twinkle of a lamp in any window. The shadow forms of sentries paced up and down outside the stone archways of old French houses.

Here and there on the roads a lantern waved to and fro, and its rays gleamed upon the long bayonet and steel casque (helmet) of a French Territorial, and upon the bronzed face of an English soldier, who came forward to stare closely at a piece of paper which allowed a man to go into the fires of hell up there. It was an English voice that gave the first challenge, and then called out "Good-night" with a strange and unofficial friendliness as a greeting to men who were going towards the guns.

The fields on the edge of the battle of guns were very peaceful. A faint breeze stirred the tall wheat, above which there floated a milky light transfusing the darkness. The poppy fields still glowed redly, and there was a glint of gold from long stretches of mustard flower. Beyond, the woods stood black against the sky above little hollows where British soldiers were encamped.

There by the light of candles which gave a rose-colour to the painted canvas boys were writing letters home before lying down to sleep. Some horsemen were moving down a valley road. Further off a long column of black lorries passed. It was the food of the guns going forward.

A mile or two more, a challenge or two more, and then a halt by the roadside. It was a road which led straight into the central fires of one great battlefield in a battle line of 80 miles or more. A small corner of the front, yet in itself a broad and far-stretching panorama of our gunfire on this night of bombardment.

I stood with a few officers in the centre of a crescent sweeping round from Auchonvillers, Thiépval, La Boisselle, and Fricourt, to Bray, on the Somme, at the southern end of the curve. Here in this beetroot field on high ground, we stood watching one of the greatest artillery battles in which British gunners have been engaged. Up to that night the greatest.

The night sky, very calm and moist, with low-lying clouds not stirred by wind, was rent with incessant flashes of light as shells of every caliber burst and scattered. Out of the black ridges and woods in front of us came explosions of white fire, as though the earth had opened and let loose its inner heat. They came up with a burst of intense brilliance, which spread along a hundred yards of ground and then vanished abruptly behind the black curtain of the night. It was the work of high explosives and heavy trench mortars falling in the German lines. Over Thiépval and La Boisselle there were rapid flashes of bursting shrapnel shells, and these points of flame stabbed the sky along the whole battle front.

From the German lines rockets were rising, continually. They rose high and their star-shells remained suspended for half a minute with an intense brightness. While the light lasted it cut out the black outline of the trees and broken roofs, and revealed heavy white smoke-clouds rolling over the enemy's positions.

They were mostly white lights, but at one place red rockets went up. They were signals of distress, perhaps, from German infantry calling to their guns. It was in the zone of these red signals, over towards Ovillers, that our fire for a time was most fierce, so that sheets of flame waved to and fro as though fanned by a furious wind. All the time along the German line red lights ran up and down like little red dancing devils.

I cannot tell what they were unless they were some other kind of signaling, or the bursting of rifle-grenades. Sometimes for thirty second or so the firing ceased, and darkness, very black and velvety, blotted out everything and restored the world to peace. Then suddenly, at one point or another, the earth seemed to open to furnace fires. Down by Bray, southwards, there was one of these violent shocks of light, and then a moment later another, by Auchonvilliers to the north.

And once again the infernal fire began, flashing, flickering, running along a ridge with a swift tongue of flame, tossing burning feathers above rosy smoke-clouds, concentrating into one bonfire of bursting shells over Fricourt and Thiépval upon which our batteries always concentrated.

3

There was one curious phenomenon. It was the silence of all the artillery. By some atmospheric condition of moisture or wind (though the night was calm), or by the configuration of the ground, which made pockets into which the sound fell, there was no great uproar, such as I have heard scores of times in smaller bombardments than this.

It was all muffled. Even our own batteries did not crash out with any startling thunder, though I could hear the rush of big shells, like great birds in flight. Now and then there was a series of loud strokes, an urgent knocking at the doors of night. And now and again there was a dull, heavy thunder-clap, followed by a long rumble, which made me think that mines were being blown further up the line.

But for the most part it was curiously quiet and low-toned, and somehow this muffled artillery gave one a greater sense of awfulness and of deadly work.

Along all this stretch of the battle-front there was no sign of men. It was all inhuman, the work of impersonal powers, and man himself was in hiding from these great forces of destruction. So I thought, peering through the darkness, over the beetroots and the wheat.

But a little later I heard the steady tramp of many feet and the thud of horses' hoofs walking slowly, and the grinding of wheels in the ruts. Shadow forms came up out of the dark tunnel below the trees, the black figures of mounted officers, followed by a battalion marching with their transport. I could not see the faces of the men, but by the shape of their forms could see that they wore their steel helmets and their fighting kit. They were heavily laden with their packs, but they were marching at a smart, swinging pace, and as they came along were singing cheerily.

They were singing some music-hall tune, with a lilt in it, as they marched towards the lights of all the shells up there in the places of death. Some of them were blowing mouth-organs and others were whistling. I watched them pass—all these tall boys of a North Country regiment, and something of their spirit seemed to come out of the dark mass of their moving bodies and thrill the air. They were going up to those places without faltering, without a backward look and singing—dear, splendid men.

I saw other men on the march, and some of them were whistling the "Marseillaise," though they were English soldiers. Others were gossiping quietly as they walked and once the light of bursting shells played all down the line of their faces—hard, clean-shaven, bronzed English faces, with the eyes of youth there staring up at the battle-fires and unafraid.

A young officer walking at the head of his platoon called out a cheery good-night to me. It was a greeting in the darkness from one of those gallant boys who lead their men out of the trenches without much thought of self in that moment of sacrifice.

In the camps the lights were out and the tents were dark. The soldiers who had been writing letters home had sent their love and gone to sleep. But the shell fire never ceased all night.

4

A staff officer had whispered a secret to us at midnight in a little room, when the door was shut and the window closed. Even then they were words which could be only whispered, and to men of trust.

"The attack will be made this morning at 7.30."

So all had gone well, and there was to be no hitch. The preliminary bombardments had done their work with the enemy's wire and earthworks. All the organisation for attack had been done, and the men were ready in their assembly trenches waiting for the words which would hold all their fate.

There was a silence in the room where a dozen officers heard the words—men who were to be lookers-on and who would not have to leave a trench up there on the battlefields when the little hand of a wrist watch said "It is now."

The great and solemn meaning of next day's dawn made the air seem oppressive, and our hearts beat jumpily for just a moment. There would be no sleep for all those men crowded in the narrow trenches on the north of the Somme. God give them courage in the morning. . . .

The dawn came with a great beauty. There was a pale blue sky flecked with white wisps of cloud. But it was cold and over all the fields there was a floating mist which rose up from the moist earth and lay heavily upon the ridges, so that the horizon was obscured. As soon as light came there was activity in the place where I was behind the lines. A body of French engineers, all blue from casque to puttee, and laden with their field packs, marched along with a steady tramp, their grave, grim faces turned towards the front. British staff officers came motoring swiftly by and despatch riders mounted their motor cycles and scurried away through the market carts of French peasants to the open roads. French sentries and French soldiers in reserve raised their hands to the salute as our officers passed.

Each man among them guessed that it was England's day, and that the British Army was out for attack. It was the spirit of France saluting their comrades in arms when the oldest "poilu"[1] there raised a wrinkled hand to his helmet and said to an English soldier, "Bonne chance, mon camarade!"

Along the roads towards the battlefields there was no movement of troops. For a few miles there were quiet fields, where cattle grazed and where the wheat grew green and tall in the white mist. The larks were singing high in the first glinting sunshine of the day above the haze. And another kind of bird came soaring overhead.

It was one of our monoplanes, which flew steadily towards the lines, a herald of the battle. In distant hollows there were masses of limber, and artillery horses hobbled in lines.

The battle line came into view, the long sweep of country stretching southwards to the Somme. Above the lines beyond Bray, looking towards the German trenches, was a great cluster of kite balloons. They were poised very high, held steady by the air pockets on their ropes, and their baskets, where the artillery observers sat, caught the rays of the sun. I counted seventeen of them, the largest group that has ever been seen along our front; but I could see no enemy balloons opposite them. It seemed that we had more eyes than they, but to-day theirs have been staring out of the veil of the mist.

5

We went farther forward to the guns, and stood on the same high field where we had watched the night bombardment. The panorama of battle was spread around us, and the noise of battle swept about us in great tornadoes. I have said that in the night one was startled by the curious quietude of the guns, by that queer muffled effect of so great an artillery. But now on the morning of battle this phenomenon, which I do not understand, no longer existed. There was one continual roar of guns which beat the air with great waves and shocks of sound, prodigious and overwhelming.

The full power of our artillery was let loose at about 6 o'clock this morning. Nothing like it has ever been seen or heard upon our front before, and all the preliminary bombardment, great as it was, seemed insignificant to this. I do not know how many batteries we have along this battle line or upon the section of the line which I could see, but the guns seemed crowded in vast numbers of every caliber, and the concentration of their fire was terrific in its intensity.

For a time I could see nothing through the low-lying mist and heavy smoke-clouds which mingled with the mist, and stood like a blind man, only listening. It was a wonderful thing which came to my ears. Shells were rushing through the air as though all the trains in the world had leapt their rails and were driving at express speed through endless tunnels in which they met each other with frightful collisions.

Some of these shells firing from batteries not far from where I stood ripped the sky with a high, tearing note. Other shells whistled with that strange, gobbling, sibilant cry which makes one's bowels turn cold. Through the mist and the smoke there came sharp, loud, insistent knocks, as separate batteries fired salvoes, and great clangorous strokes, as of iron doors banged suddenly, and the tattoo of the light field guns playing the drums of death.

The mist was shifting and dissolving. The tall tower of Albert Cathedral appeared suddenly through the veil, and the sun shone full for a few seconds on the golden Virgin and the Babe, which she held head-downwards above all this tumult as a peace-offering to men.[2] The broken roofs of the town gleamed white, and the two tall chimneys to the left stood black and sharp against the pale blue of the sky, into which dirty smoke drifted above the whiter clouds.

I could see now as well as hear. I could see our shells falling upon the German lines by Thiépval and La Boiselle and further by Mametz, and southwards over Fricourt. High explosives were tossing up great vomits of black smoke and earth all along the ridges. Shrapnel was pouring upon these places, and leaving curly white clouds, which clung to the ground.

Below there was the flash of many batteries like Morse code signals by stabs of flame. The enemy was being blasted by a hurricane of fire. I found it in my heart to pity the poor devils who were there, and yet was filled by a strange and awful exultation because this was the work of our guns, and because it was England's day.

Over my head came a flight of six aeroplanes, led by a single monoplane, which steered steadily towards the enemy. The sky was deeply blue above them, and when the sun caught their wings they were as beautiful and delicate as butterflies. But they were carrying death with them, and were out to bomb the enemy's batteries and to drop their explosives into masses of men behind the German lines.

Farther away a German plane was up. Our anti-aircraft guns were searching for him with their shells, which dotted the sky with snowballs.

Every five minutes or so a single gun fired a round. It spoke with a voice I knew, the deep, gruff voice of old "Grandmother," one of our 15-inch guns, which carries a shell large enough to smash a cathedral with one enormous burst. I could follow the journey of the shell by listening to its rush through space. Seconds later there was the distant thud of its explosion.

Troops were moving forward to the attack from behind the lines. It was nearly 7.30. All the officers about me kept glancing at their wrist-watches. We did not speak much then, but stared silently at the smoke and mist which floated and banked along our lines. There, hidden, were our men. They, too, would be looking at their wrist-watches.

The minutes were passing very quickly—as quickly as men's lives pass when they look back upon the years. An officer near me turned away, and there was a look of sharp pain in his eyes. We were only lookers-on. The other men, our friends, the splendid youth that we have passed on the roads of France, were about to do this job. Good luck go with them! Men were muttering such wishes in their hearts.

6

It was 7.30. Our watches told us that, but nothing else. The guns had lifted and were firing behind the enemy's first lines, but there was no sudden hush for the moment of attack. The barrage by our guns seemed as great as the first bombardment. For ten minutes or so before this time a new sound had come into the general thunder of artillery. It was like the "rafale" of the French soixante-quinze,[3] very rapid, with distant and separate strokes, but louder than the noise of field-guns. They were our trench-mortars at work, along the whole length of the line before me.

It was 7.30. The moment for the attack had come. Clouds of smoke had been liberated to form a screen for the infantry, and hid the whole line. The only men I could see were those in reserve, winding along a road by some trees which led up to the attacking points. They had their backs turned, as they marched very slowly and steadily forward. I could not tell who they were, though I had passed some of them on the road a day or two before. But, whoever they were, English, Irish, or Welsh, I watched them until most had disappeared from sight behind a clump of trees. In a little while they would be fighting, and would need all their courage.

At a minute after 7.30 there came through the rolling smoke-clouds a rushing sound. It was the noise of rifle fire and machine-guns. The men were out of their trenches, and the attack had begun. The enemy was barraging our lines.

7

The country chosen for our main attack to-day stretches from the Somme for some 20 miles northwards. The French were to operate on our immediate right. It is very different country from Flanders, with its swamps and flats, and from the Loos battlefields, with their dreary plain pimpled by slack heaps.

It is a sweet and pleasant country, with wooded hills and little valleys along the river beds of the Ancre and the Somme, and fertile meadow-lands and stretches of woodland, where soldiers and guns may get good cover. "A clean country," said one of our Generals, when he first went to it from the northern war zone.

It seemed very queer to go there first, after a knowledge of war in the Ypres salient, where there is seldom a view of the enemy's lines from any rising ground—except Kemmel Hill and Observatory Ridge—and where certainly one cannot walk on the skyline in full view of German earthworks 2,000 yards away.

But at Hebuterne, which the French captured after desperate fighting, and at Auchonvilliers (opposite Beaumont), and on the high ground by the ruined city of Albert, looking over to Fricourt and Mametz, and further south on the Somme, looking towards the little German stronghold at Curlu, beyond the marshes, one could see very clearly and with a strange, unreal sense of safety.

I saw a German sentry pacing the village street of Curlu, and went within 20 paces of his outposts. Occasionally one could stare through one's glasses at German working parties just beyond sniping range round Beaumont and Fricourt and to left of Fricourt the Crucifix[4] between its seven trees seemed very near as one looked at it in the German lines.

Below this Calvary was the Tambour and the Bois Français, where not a week passed without a mine being blown on one side or the other, so that the ground was a great upheaval of mingling mine-craters and tumbled earth, which but half-covered the dead bodies of men.

It was difficult ground in front of us. The enemy was strong in his defences. In the clumps of woodland beside the ruined villages he hid many machine-guns and trench mortars, and each ruined house in each village was part of a fortified stronghold difficult to capture by direct assault. It was here, however, and with good hopes of success that our men attacked to-day, working eastwards across the Ancre and northwards up from the Somme.

8

At the end of this day's fighting it is still too soon to give a clear narrative of the battle. Behind the veil of smoke which hides our men there were many different actions taking place, and the messages that come back at the peril of men's lives and by the great gallantry of our signalers and runners give but glimpses of the progress of our men and of their hard fighting.

I have seen the wounded who have come out of the battle, and the prisoners brought down in batches, but even they can give only confused accounts of fighting in some single sector of the line which comes within their own experience.

At first, it is certain, there was not much difficulty in taking the enemy's first line trenches along the greater part of the country attacked. Our bombardment had done great damage, and had smashed down the enemy's wire and flattened his parapets. When our men left their assembly trenches and swept forward, cheering, they encountered no great resistance from German soldiers, who had been hiding in their dug-outs under our storm of shells.

Many of these dug-outs were blown in and filled with dead, but out of others which had not been flung to pieces by high explosives crept dazed and deafened men who held their hands up and bowed their heads. Some of them in one part of the line came out of their shelters as soon as our guns lifted, and met our soldiers half-way, with signs of surrender.

They were collected and sent back under guard, while the attacking columns passed on to the second and third lines in the network of trenches, and then if they could get through them to the fortified ruins behind.

But the fortunes of war vary in different places, as I know from the advance of troops, including the South Staffords, the Manchesters, and the Gordons. In crossing the first line of trench the South Staffordshire men had a comparatively easy time, with hardly any casualties, gathering up Germans who surrendered easily. The enemy's artillery fire did not touch them seriously, and both they and the Manchesters had very great luck.

But the Gordons fared differently. These keen fighting men rushed forward with great enthusiasm until they reached one end of the village of Mametz, and then quite suddenly they were faced by rapid machine-gun fire and a storm of bombs. The Germans held a trench called Danzig-avenue on the ridge where Mametz stands, and defended it with desperate courage. The Gordons flung themselves upon this position, and had some difficulty in clearing it of the enemy. At the end of the day Mametz remained in our hands.

It was these fortified villages which gave our men greatest trouble, for the German troops defended them with real courage, and worked their machine-guns from hidden emplacements with skill and determination.

Fricourt is, I believe, still holding out (its capture has since been officially reported), though our men have forced their way on both sides of it, so that it is partly surrounded. Montauban, to the north-east of Mametz, was captured early in the day, and we also gained the strong point at Serre, until the Germans made a somewhat heavy counter-attack, and succeeded in driving out our troops.

Beaumont-Hamel was not in our hands at the end of the day, but here again our men are fighting on both sides of it. The woods and village of Thiépval, which I had watched under terrific shell-fire in our preliminary bombardments, was one point of our first attack, and our troops swept from one end of the village to the other, and out beyond to a new objective.

They were too quick to get on, it seems, for a considerable number of Germans remained in the dug-outs, and when the British soldiers went past them they came out of their hiding-places and became a fighting force again. Farther north our infantry attacked both sides of the Gommecourt salient with the greatest possible valour.

That is my latest knowledge, writing at midnight on the first day of July, which leaves our men beyond the German front lines in many places, and penetrating to the country behind like arrow-heads between the enemy's strongholds.

9

In the afternoon I saw the first batches of prisoners brought in. In parties of 50 to 100 they came down, guarded by men of the Border Regiment, through the little French hamlets close behind the fighting-lines, where peasants stood in their doorways watching these first-fruits of victory.

They were damaged fruit, some of these poor wretches, wounded and nerve-shaken in the great bombardment. Most of them belonged to the 109th and 110th Regiments of the 14th Reserve Corps, and they seemed to be a mixed lot of Prussians and Bavarians. On the whole, they were tall, strong fellows, and there were striking faces among them, of men higher than the peasant type, and thoughtful. But they were very haggard and worn and dirty.

Over the barbed wire which had been stretched across a farmyard, in the shadow of an old French church, I spoke to some of them. To one man especially, who answered all my questions with a kind of patient sadness. He told me that most of his comrades and himself had been without food and water for several days, as our intense fire made it impossible to get supplies up the communication-trenches.

About the bombardment he raised his hands and eyes a moment—eyes full of a re-membered horror—and said, "Es war schrecklich" (It was horrible). Most of the offic-ers had remained in the second line, but the others had been killed, he thought. His own brother had been killed, and in Baden his mother and sisters would weep when they heard. But he was glad to be a prisoner, out of the war at last, which would last much longer.

A new column of prisoners was being brought down, and suddenly the man turned and uttered an exclamation with a look of surprise and awe.

"Ach, da ist ein Hauptmann!"⁵ He recognised an officer among these new prison-ers, and it seemed clearly a surprising thing to him that one of the great caste should be in this plight, should suffer as he had suffered.

Some of his fellow-prisoners lay on the ground all bloody and bandaged. One of them seemed about to die. But the English soldiers gave them water, and one of our officers emptied his cigarette-case and gave them all he had to smoke.

Other men were coming back from the fields of fire, glad also to be back behind the line. They were our wounded, who came in very quickly after the first attack to the casualty clearing stations close to the lines, but beyond the reach of shell-fire. Many of them were lightly wounded in the hands and feet, and sometimes 50 or more were on one lorry, which had taken up ammunition and was now bring back the casualties.

They were wonderful men. So wonderful in their gaiety and courage that one's heart melted at the sight of them. They were all grinning as though they had come from a "jolly" in which they had been bumped a little. There was a look of pride in their eyes as they came driving down like wounded knights from a tourney.

They had gone through the job with honour, and had come out with their lives, and the world was good and beautiful again, in this warm sun, in these snug French villages, where peasant men and women waved hands at them, and in these fields of scarlet and gold and green.

The men who were going up to the battle grinned back at those who were coming out. One could not see the faces of the lying-down cases, only the soles of their boots as they passed; but the laughing men on the lorries—some of them stripped to the waist and bandaged roughly—seemed to rob war of some of its horror, and the spirit of our British soldiers shows bright along the roads of France, so that the very sun seems to get some of its gold from these men's hearts.

To-night the guns are at work again, and the sky flushes as the shells burst over there where our men are fighting.

Notes

From Philip Gibbs, *The Battles of the Somme* (New York: George H. Doran, 1917), pp. 21–37.

1. Poilu, literally "hairy one" was a slang term used to refer to French soldiers.

2. Atop the cathedral in the French town of Albert sits a statue of the Virgin Mary holding the Baby Jesus up to the heavens. A German shell knocked the statue 90 degrees, making it appear that the Virgin was holding the Baby from falling to the ground below. The statue was visible to men on both sides during the Somme campaign, and men ascribed to it various meanings. It finally fell in 1918, but was rebuilt after the war.

3. The French 75mm artillery gun.

4. The Crucifix was a cross-shaped portion of the German trenches briefly captured by the British on July 1, but soon recaptured by the Germans.

5. "Oh, there is a captain!"

Between Mutiny and Obedience

Leonard V. Smith

The manpower of the 5e DI[1] remained essentially constant from the summer of 1916 through the mutinies. As noted earlier, the division suffered approximately 5,500 casualties in the Douaumont engagement, over 40 percent of its entire strength.[2] Although given the surviving documentation one can make only a reasonable approximation concerning the replacements, probably one-third of them were recovered wounded and about two-thirds new recruits (these a mixture of soldiers from the youngest classes and men previously classified as unfit for active duty).

In such documentation as survives, the age distribution in the division seemed a matter of the foremost concern, despite the image of the bearded, ageless *poilu*. The division had indeed aged since August 1914, even allowing for differences in perceptions of age between that time and the present. By March 1917, for the three regular-army regiments (the 74e RI, 36e RI, and the 129e RI), approximately 40 percent were between 19 and 24 years old, some 50 percent between 25 and 35, and about 10 percent between 36 and 42. For the one reserve regiment (the 274e RI), the respective figures are 17 percent, 45 percent, and 38 percent. Some 60–70 percent of the soldiers in the division came from the prewar recruitment areas of Normandy and Paris and its suburbs, the remainder from other parts of France.

The 5e DI sector at Les Eparges varied between about seven and ten kilometers during its time there. Considering that according to the 1916 infantry regulations, only about one-third to one-sixth of the troops were supposed to be in the front line of trenches at any given time, this meant a thin disposition of manpower throughout the sector. At least as the French told it, in no area of the sector did the terrain work in their favor. To be sure, they held much of the high ground. But given the abiding weakness of French artillery, this proved less of an advantage than might be expected. Indeed, high ground could actually work to their disadvantage, given the German skill at digging tunnels for high explosives under enemy positions, known simply as mining. In other areas of the sector, such as around the village of Les Eparges itself, both French and Germans held high ground, with the low ground as No Man's Land between them. This put frontline soldiers in an unusually exposed position. In the southern part of the sector, the Germans had a heavily wooded area to their rear, which made it difficult for the French to gauge the extent of their defenses.

Command interest in what transpired in trench warfare proved inversely proportional to hopes for decisive results during pitched battle. British commanders had a particularly keen interest in constantly harassing the enemy *before* they had a large field army on the continent; French commanders acquired this interest after they had spent much of theirs. Tony Ashworth's description of World War I high-command expectations—constant barrages, mining, or raids of enemy positions—is thus more accurate for the time the 5e DI spent in the Eparges sector than had been the case earlier.

The 1916 infantry regulations reflected this emphasis on aggression between pitched battles. A section requiring constant fire by snipers stated in bold letters: "Trench warfare is neither a truce nor guard service; it is a phase of the battle." The most minute enemy movements were to be watched closely, and every opportunity taken to inflict casualties. "The adversary must feel in front of him a vigilant hatred," the regulations continued, "and must know that we want no rest before his defeat."

Orders dated 26 July 1916 from Nivelle, at that time the IIe Armée commander in charge of the entire Verdun sector, further underscored these expectations. He sought to "render our front inviolable" through maintaining an aggressive defense, a sort of "offensive defense," in which the defender kept the initiative by continuously harassing the enemy. Three ways existed of doing this: artillery, digging mines under the enemy positions, and raids. Concentrated and precise artillery, Nivelle argued, could prevent the installation of new trench mortars (the feared *Minenwerfer*), and immobilize those already in place. Mining and raids could "take advantageous positions whose possession would reinforce our defensive organization and would menace other enemy positions."

The man in charge of carrying out Nivelle's orders was Mangin's successor, Gen. Henri de Roig-Bourdeville. Although he and Mangin were approximately the same age and shared some similarities in their career paths, in other respects the contrast was notable. General de Roig had risen from the ranks without the drama of Mangin's more erratic record. A volunteer in the colonial army, he graduated (without distinction) from Saint-Maixent, the school for promotable NCOs. He spent ten years in the North African colonies before the war, and was posted in metropolitan France thereafter. He commanded a reserve infantry regiment that served ably in August 1914, and by January 1915 had been given a brigade. General Lebrun, the 3e CA[3] commander, praised him in his evaluation of September 1916 as "extremely active, conscientious, and hard-working. Sure judgment." Apart from his personal dossier, information on the personality of de Roig does not abound. Henri Dutheil, the 5e DI staff secretary who had such an unwholesome fascination with Mangin, remarked simply: "He had the methodical, slow, calm manner of the director of a factory. But the flame, ah!, where was it, the claws of the lion, the talons of the eagle?"

Whatever his anatomical or spiritual defects, de Roig played a role in consistently endeavoring to scale down the expectations of his superiors of constant aggression in the Eparges sector. He clearly understood how little harm his artillery could inflict on the Germans. Considering the number of shells consumed at Verdun and along the Somme, and with another major offensive planned for the spring, a division not engaged in pitched battle inevitably found itself on short artillery rations. In a report of 22 December 1916, de Roig noted that "without having a very great density, the barrages are sufficient" for countering enemy barrages. But the division's ability to defend itself would be "very much too weak," however, if the enemy attacked along the whole 5e DI front. He called "dangerous" a proposal to remove some 240mm cannons, whose range and size made them "an element of the moral support of our troops." Brilliant aggressive results were plainly not to be anticipated from the 5e DI artillery.

Mining held no more promise. As noted, though the French held a considerable amount of high ground at Les Eparges, this meant that it was actually much easier for the Germans to mine than the French, which they did in the fall of 1916 with impunity, given the weakness of the French artillery. In a report stinging to the point of impertinence, the major in charge of construction in the front lines explained his decision to order all mining stopped on 18 December 1916. Given the insufficient supply of both men and materiel, he considered further effort simply pointless. Two acetylene lamps requested three weeks previously had still not arrived, and "the lack of mining tools has already rendered this type of work particularly difficult and has paralyzed all productivity." In his comment on the report, the brigade commander added that "we must not forget that the front in the Eparges sector represents 7km of front lines . . . and that I have only one incomplete company on average of every half kilometer to occupy, maintain, rebuild the multiple lines and communications trenches within that half kilometer."

This left raids. The basic problem of raids in the Eparges sector was outlined by 10e Brigade commander Colonel de Monthuisant in August 1916. As noted, the area south of the village of Les Eparges was mostly heavily wooded, concealing what were presumed to be thick and complicated defenses. An attack on either side of the salient around Les Eparges, Monthuisant noted, "would no longer be a question of a raid, but an offensive on a front of 1,000 to 1,200 meters by at least two regiments side by side, without counting the reserves needed." He concluded that "personally, I do not think that the military results . . . are worth the effort of an enterprise on the scale indicated above." He suggested raids involving one or two battalions at most, "no longer to gain an advantageous position, but simply to gain a foothold in the enemy lines, to create there a threat that would prevent the free disposition of the reserves."

By November 1916, senior officers resisted even this. Battalion commanders from the 10e Brigade cited the onset of winter and the basic military pointlessness of the enterprise. The commander of the 1e Bataillon of the 36e RI, for example, commented bluntly that "the terrain in which the raids would have to operate is truly a chaotic one in which, after the mortar fire, it is impossible at night to walk for twenty meters without the risk of sinking twenty times." Now that the forest had lost its leaves, it was possible to see from aerial reconnaissance that the enemy trenches were "well-organized," and that "a raid would only have a chance of success if it could be executed quickly, which is impossible." Moreover, he went so far as to say that the French themselves had an interest in maintaining the "live and let live" system for the time being.[4] "At the moment, our situation is so precarious that a violent reaction on the part of the enemy could be fatal." De Roig duly reported this conclusion to his own superiors.

Militarily speaking, then, the 5e DI in the Eparges sector proved at least as much and perhaps more the object than the perpetrator of aggression in trench warfare. During the eight months the division spent there, it suffered approximately 1,000 casualties, an average of some 125 per month (just under 1 percent of the total strength). Although these figures do not compare with losses during pitched battle, they are certainly "active sector" figures. They certainly sufficed to keep soldiers' minds focused on the ubiquitous possibility of death and serious injury. But as the next section will argue, and like the casualty figures at Verdun for the French army as a whole, the significant change is not so much in the absolute numbers of casualties, but how those casualties were perceived.

Soldiers' Dilemma: Entrapment versus Defeat

Simply put, the crisis in trench warfare involved an increasing sense on the part of the soldiers of the 5e DI that trench warfare at Les Eparges had no more military utility than pitched battle at Verdun. *Tenir*[5] held little for them but incarceration in the trenches and the constant and pointless danger. The problem, however, centered around finding an alternative given existing military technology and the fact that the Germans continued to hold northeastern France and Belgium hostage. Recognizing the military uselessness of their efforts meant recognizing that France had lost the war. This dilemma—entrapment versus defeat—became more and more clearly focused in the months before the 1917 mutinies.

Guy Hallé of the 74e RI provided a moving account of a new descent into foucauldian despair at Les Eparges. Immediately after Douaumont, Hallé sought almost desperately to find meaning in the division's efforts there. One day, the regiment was ordered to assemble for a distribution of decorations. Hallé sought a special link in the ceremony to those killed at Verdun. As the survivors assembled, they looked to him like "phantom companies, with so few men in them that once the regiment was brought together, our hearts were torn by sorrow." His own words best describe the ceremony itself:

> The colonel gave the command: "Au drapeau [To the flag]." The bayonets glistened motionless and the clarions sounded. One often laughs at military parades, me like the others, for all their artificiality, their showiness, and their staged poses. I assure you that no one wanted to smile at that moment.
>
> The thoughts of all were over there, on the slopes of Douaumont, in the grey smoke of the powder, with the dead.

But once Hallé's unit entered Les Eparges, the same sense that he felt leaving the trenches in front of Douaumont of helplessness in the face of ubiquitous death returned. In a vignette set in August 1916, his company was posted in the southern part of the Eparges sector. All of a sudden, a German shell came flying out of the woods on the other side of No Man's Land. At first the veterans of the unit thought nothing of it: "The Germans often fire by surprise like this, the only danger in a reasonably tranquil part of the sector." Shortly however, a soldier showed up in shock and so badly wounded in the legs that his shoes were soaked with blood: "Without him saying anything, we understand that there are dead over there."

This indeed proved the case, as the shell fell among a group of men playing cards. As with his comrade killed back at Verdun, Hallé was all too aware that he could just as easily have been the victim. A group of men new to the unit became quickly socialized to life at Les Eparges. "Around us the men are troubled and shaking," he wrote. He continued somewhat callously, showing the rapid deterioration of the special link with the dead back at Douaumont: "It's a good thing we have the rookies of the section, who arrived after Verdun and who haven't seen much yet. We disperse them, because this isn't a very nice place, and right away we busy ourselves carrying away the corpses, to remove as much as possible the traces of the horrible, stupid death of these three unhappy men."

By October, with poor weather setting in, Hallé linked trench warfare in the Eparges sector in October 1916 more closely than ever to incarceration on the battlefield. By that time a lieutenant commanding a company, Hallé described a closed-off world of semihumans. They were cut off not only from "real life" back home, but even from the war itself, in the sense of war as some comprehensible exercise of force toward some justifiable end: "What are we doing there, we poor numbed creatures, our hearts broken and crying with our very blood for peace, for love, for light, and the sweetness of seeing again everything that is so far away, so far away. We feel separated from all this by distance without limit and by infinite suffering." Per Hallé's title and insistent use of the term *là-bas* (down there), the world of the trenches has become simply "out there somewhere," identified principally by the suffering of the men incarcerated there *avec ceux qui souffrent* (with those who suffer).

When the "real world" of the civilian society and the closed world of the trenches collided, Hallé proved unable to cope with it. In November 1916, he received a letter from the wife of a man reported missing. Such letters always arrived, he complained, "on a fine day when we are resting, when the nerves loosen up a bit, and we feel ourselves coming alive again." The woman was aware that mine explosions had been reported in the sector of the 74e RI. Hallé knew the whole story. A mine explosion at the base of the ridge made a crater at least 180 meters long, and caused a landslide that buried one whole section (some 40–50 men). But since only two bodies were recovered and no physical evidence existed of the death of the others, regulations required them to be classified as "missing."

Although Hallé sincerely liked and admired the soldier whose wife wrote the letter, he decided not to respond, consciously numbing himself to the human tragedy of the situation. For the time being, he chose an almost unfeeling detachment, not only from the world behind the lines, but even from the dead man himself. He rationalized that officers were not formally obliged to answer private letters. He continued with remarkable candor: "One often responds even so out of sympathy. But me, I never had the courage. . . . When all's said and done, I think that sometimes it's better not to respond. This unhappy woman will understand that he is dead. It is useless to tell her in so many words what has happened. No, truly, it is better not to say."

By this time, absolute numbers of casualties in the 5e DI mattered little. Hallé scarcely cared that over the course of the whole time the 5e DI spent in the Eparges sector less than 1 percent of his men would become casualties each month, and that very few of these would suffer the fate of being buried in a mine explosion. What counted was that the possibility of horrible death without useful military purpose existed everywhere, just as it did at Verdun. Looking at his men one day, he wondered, "who will be the first to fall?" He was well aware that he was as likely a candidate as anyone else, since as he wrote: "We are all equal before death, and my hide is worth the same as yours, you poor fools who mutter and murmur as I pass." At one point, he dreamt of being able to release each of his men from the trenches. He provided an intriguing glimpse into what may have been passing through officers' minds in May 1917, when having left the special logic of the trenches, they were now expected to order their openly resisting men back there: "Go on, you're free, go home. If back there, you still suffer sometimes, at least you can try to forget, draw from the good life, all that will make your body happy, all that will set your heart at rest, in making you forget your sorrow."

Two other memoirs, by men new to the 74e RI, provide a striking contrast in ways soldiers could be socialized into life in Les Eparges and the dilemma facing soldiers there. Private Legentil, of the Class of 1916,[6] joined the 74e RI as a machine gunner just after Douaumont. He began learning the role of the *poilu* even before he entered the trenches for the first time in the Eparges sector. During an extended medical inspection while his unit was out of the front lines, he wrote: "We got to know the old-timers of the section, who were quite few, having left many comrades on the slopes of the fort of Douaumont. There was nothing to do [during the inspection], and these survivors of Verdun occupied themselves just getting drunk."

Also before he actually entered the front lines, he learned from his new comrades the difference between battlefield soldiers and others in uniform, and the art of cleverly defying authority when exercised by the wrong sort of person. During his company commander's leave, an ex-cavalier second lieutenant who had not been at Douaumont had been left in charge: "He did his work with zeal, and wanted to order the old-timers around as though they were back at the barracks. This didn't work at all." Somehow, the second lieutenant was able to get his mistress into the encampment, and as Legentil recalled, "for several nights, we had a veritable *charivari* underneath the windows of his bedroom. We avenged ourselves a bit." When the company commander returned, "we only had to do some parade marches and some practice fire."

Once in the lines after 23 June, Legentil was just as quickly socialized into disillusionment with the bleak prospects of trench warfare in Les Eparges. At first, he could still hear the battle raging at Verdun to his north. But in his sector "the days passed quite monotonously, marked only by some small artillery exchanges or an encounter with a night patrol that would provoke a short alert." When violence did come, it was often unpredictable and deadly. He described a mortar barrage on 23 June, just after he entered the sector:

These are curious projectiles, launched by small trench mortars. You can follow their capricious trajectory, and they fall to earth pirouetting in a great snort. You often have time to take cover, because they only come one at a time, and they don't always explode. On the other hand, wounds from these projectiles are often very grave, because they explode into a small number of very large pieces of twenty centimeters or even more!

He found a mine explosion even more frightening. On the evening of 27 September, a huge explosion went off like an earthquake in Legentil's subsector, followed by a violent artillery barrage. Some thirty men were killed outright or buried alive. The explosion created a huge crater; by the eerie light of flares, Legentil could see French and Germans scurrying to occupy its rim. He remarked: "an epic struggle, as cruel as it is murderous, for very meager results."

When the weather deteriorated by October, he had to endure another form of entrapment—the mud. Legentil described an unusually painful trip moving his machine gun to the front lines. The men had to crawl for three hours through a "thick and glutinous bed of mud" to get to the assigned position. Dragging bulky and heavy ammunition proved especially painful: "How will we get there? Good will, human resistance, has its limits. We stop every hundred meters, despite the comments of the liaison agent, who is in a hurry to get us into position so he can go take a nap." On days when the "live and let live" system did not prevail, their dehumanizing situation became complete: "In fact, once day broke, you had to sit down, and a big devil like Caron [a comrade] had to lie down so as not to be seen from the front. Painful hours, interminable days, without even being able to stand up to take a couple of steps, not even for bodily functions. Naturally, you relieve yourself the best you can, where you are."

Another newcomer to the division, Capt. Paul Rimbault, socialized himself very differently. Indeed, his is the only memoir from the 5e DI, in which the author identified more with the official language of "commander" than that of "soldiers," as those categories have been used here. Like Hallé, Rimbault commanded a company, and actually lived in trench conditions similar to those of his soldiers. But if Hallé and Legentil reacted to the dilemma of trench warfare in Les Eparges with a sense of helplessness bordering on despair, Rimbault struggled to maintain continuity with values he expressed before the war on military society and military authority. The result is an almost schizophrenic account, in which he juxtaposes sympathy with his men with considerable alienation from and disillusionment toward them.

According to his military resume, Rimbault had joined the army as a volunteer back in 1896. In 1904, he graduated from Saint-Maixent (the officer training school for NCOs) as a second lieutenant in 1904, and was promoted to lieutenant in 1906. He was still a lieutenant at age thirty-two in August 1914. The fact that he had remained at the same rank for eight years suggests that had the war not intervened, his professional status would not have changed.

In 1912, Lieutenant Rimbault had published a pamphlet for soldiers about to complete their two years of military service. The pamphlet outlined soldiers' continuing military duties and provided a guide to the preferred attitudes toward the army and toward war as conscripts prepared to reenter civilian life. Rimbault left no doubt that he considered the military hierarchy the sole source of legitimate authority on the battlefield: "To follow his leader everywhere, this is the first virtue of the soldier in combat." He appears also to have been a true believer in the doctrine of the offensive. Rimbault gave his readers the surprising assurance that "if you flee [on the battlefield], you will certainly get killed. If you go forward, you have 90 chances out of 100 to get out of it without a scratch."

Before joining the 74e RI, Rimbault had served several extended stretches in trench warfare, though his record does not indicate experience in major pitched battles. He arrived with the regiment in late October 1916, that is, after the onset of bad weather and in a period of heightened German activity. Hallé and Legentil by this point clearly suffered from the spiritual malady so closely identified with French soldiers in World War I, *le cafard*. Upon first inspecting the listening posts in advance of the front lines, he observed that "the existence of these poor devils who live over there is terrible. They are no longer men, they are piles of mud." But even his description of his first efforts to socialize with his men suggests that he was much more interested in maintaining emotional detachment from them than was Hallé (also a company commander); "Finally, one chats with them for a bit, gives them a cigarette, a bit of drink. It gives them pleasure; it also proves to them that one is thinking of their misery."

For his own part, he concluded stoically that his part of the Eparges sector "isn't of such a bad character; apart from the mortars, one can live his life here." Although his own living conditions could not have differed greatly from those of Hallé, Rimbault wrote much more of "their" suffering in the trenches than "our" suffering. He also differed from a number of more senior officers in the division cited previously in seeing some advantage to conducting raids as late as January 1917. Rimbault described the planning of one raid in some detail, though he said nothing about its execution. His concluding statement on the raid rather blithely asserted that it pleased his men as much as himself. But it also showed that he was not completely unaware of the concept of proportionality at Les Eparges: "The men like these little operations a lot, in which there is little risk and much profit. At the same time, one must not abuse them, lest a sector be wrecked uselessly and the time there be rendered, if not untenable, at least difficult."

Rimbault's memoir was divided into two parts, one a rudimentary diary that without explanation covered only the period from July 1915 to July 1917, the other a series of short commentaries on topics ranging from diplomacy to war profiteers. The most revealing expression of his complicated views on French soldiers after Verdun was an essay written in February 1917 called "The Simple *Bibi*." On the one hand, he praised the tenacity of the French soldier: "He is there, now and forever, armed and ready, looking the Boche in the eye without flinching." Indeed, this capacity for accepting *tenir* "has saved the country."

But on the other hand, Rimbault believed that the French soldier of February 1917 had passed his military prime. He maintained somewhat naively that back in 1914, the French soldier "had faith in his bayonet, that is to say in his valiance. He ignored the terror of the machinery of modern warfare." By 1917, however, "the simple *bibi* has lost fifty percent of his value." Rimbault believed that the French soldier had been worn down by disappointment, through fruitless offensives, wartime propaganda laden with untruths, and the impersonal nature of trench warfare itself. Most remarkably, this prewar professional officer maintained that they had become "more citizens than soldiers. . . . they are egalitarians, who bear a strong grudge toward their commanders and those behind the lines, who shun serried ranks, military fashion, everything that gives the appearance of an army." Like Mangin, he suggested that the hope for the renewal of the *furia francese* lay with black African and other colonial troops.

If Hallé and Legentil responded to the dilemma of stagnated warfare by early 1917 with an internalized sense of entrapment and despair, Rimbault responded with an externalized sense of disillusionment with the soldiers he commanded. He continued to have great faith in his own commanders' capacity to win the war, and with the exception of the essay just cited, he had far more to say about his military superiors than his military inferiors. Rimbault's identification with the military hierarchy became even closer in the spring of 1917.

Beginning in late 1916, a new documentary source emerged for examining opinions of the soldiers of the 5e DI, reports from the mail censors or *Contrôle Postal*. Soldiers' letters had been opened and read by their superiors at least since 1915. Mangin referred to them with some regularity in letters to his wife as evidence of his men's high morale. But over the course of 1916, surveillance of correspondence became centralized under a new office attached to the General Staff, the Service de Renseignement aux Armées (SRA). SRA records comprise primarily reports on samples of letters read, with summaries and many direct quotes.

These reports seem too linked to a prearranged bureaucratic agenda for them to be analyzed quantitatively, despite frequent attempts to do so both during the war and subsequently. Staff officers, I would suggest, wrote the reports more to please than to inform. They tended to find "morale" invariably holding up well, whatever external evidence might have existed to the contrary. Displeasing sentiments were frequently cited, but most often as exceptions that prove the rule of soldierly docility. In short, postal censorship records are neither more nor less "representative" than published memoirs, though for very different reasons. They serve most usefully as another form of literary evidence, in that they put words to phenomena suggested by broader circumstances. As Annick Cochet observed, "family correspondence of the common soldier in fact situates itself at the meeting point between the individual and the collective," that is, where individuals describe collective experiences. Letters constitute a unique form of literary evidence, since they were not intended for publication and were not written by literary figures. As letters were destined for a personal rather than a collective readership, they tended to be shorn of the public artistic ambitions that influence even the most self-consciously humble published accounts.

I propose here simply to illustrate echoes of views expressed by Hallé, Legentil, and Rimbault. Like the three authors of memoirs, soldiers in the ten months preceding the mutinies were thinking deeply about the dilemma of entrapment versus defeat. Two mutually contradictory sentiments appeared consistently in the reports: the sense expressed by Hallé and to a lesser degree Legentil that the principle of *tenir* in trench warfare had come to signify nothing more than control, misery, and death; and the abiding interest in winning the war so critical to understanding Rimbault. Most soldiers, I would suggest, held both the views simultaneously. In the spring of 1917, soldiers had to choose which of these sentiments was more important.

Of course, deep concern that the war might never end was hardly new, and surfaced in the first reports citing soldiers from the 5e DI. A report of 1 July 1916 quoted a soldier from the division (not further identified): "there is reason to despair, truly. . . . The newspapers lie to us and will lie to us again, because they are not better placed than the combattants to judge certain things greatly embellished by the journalists."

Expressions of misery figured more prominently in the reports beginning in October and November 1916, as the weather deteriorated and as German activity in the sector increased. "I am not blind," wrote a sergeant of the 274e RI to his mother, "and I see very well that this is not the last winter of the war. For a long time, the government and the civilians have sacrificed the *poilus*, as they say. As long as there are still *poilus*, the war will continue. We are caught in the machinery; sooner or later we will all pass through it in our turn."

Moreover, a strain of opinion existed that matters on the Western Front would get worse rather than better. A stretcher bearer from the 129e RI wrote to a friend: "You say that the hardest part is over. I don't share this opinion, because the longer the war lasts the worse it gets. After more than eighteen months of battles, Verdun passed all preceding battles; this summer the Somme—even more horrifying! In this way, the spring of 1917 will surpass Verdun and the Somme for the belligerents of the two camps." Even though they knew their letters were being read by the authority structure, some soldiers expressed clear premutinous opinions. A soldier from the 274e RI, whose letter was described in the report as "the most outrageous" of its genre, made unfavorable comparison between the lot of the frontline soldier and that of the convict. He wrote in January 1917:

> Considering the way we are led, convicts are happier than we are, and back there they don't risk their lives. It is disgusting to be French. . . . The real criminals aren't under fire. . . . The law protects them, while the fathers of families get their heads broken. We are only old men, and I assure you that our reflections are more bitter than enthusiastic.

But many soldiers never entirely rejected *tenir*, even if they accepted it simply as the worst alternative except for all the others. "As far as I'm concerned," wrote a corporal from the 74e RI in August 1916, "I have decided to carry it through to the end, understanding very well the sacrifice that France demands of me, making to her willingly the sacrifice of my life." Such sentiments appeared as regularly as sentiments of despair in SRA reports, and were construed by the staff officers writing them as confirmation of the identity between soldierly and command expectations.

Perhaps the most curious manifestation of soldiers' abiding interest in winning the war involved expressions of actual enthusiasm for the offensive planned for the spring of 1917. A sergeant from the 129e RI wrote in January 1917 that "we have confidence in the great spring offensive, which we *must hope* will be decisive, because, with Nivelle, we have an amazing man from the artillery who has proved himself at Verdun and in whom we have confidence." A soldier (not identified but probably an officer or an NCO) whose views were reported as indicative of the "dominant impression," went further in March 1917, when the 5e DI was behind the lines in the last stages of training for the offensive:

> The celebrated formula "On les aura! [We shall have them!]" begins to become "On les a! [We have them!]." The retreat of the Germans is noted by all the men as a certain sign of their weakness,[7] and has raised in their ranks the hope of striking revenge that they fore-

see on the horizon; all burn with desire to join their comrades attacking first for this offensive, so much yearned for. Their morale is excellent, completely up to the situation.

Soldiers could imagine a leap of faith in the early spring of 1917, not dissimilar to Rimbault's faith in the command structure, and Nivelle and Mangin's faith in the *barrage roulant*.[8] The key concept is the notion expressed by the sergeant from the 129e RI that soldiers had to hope that the next offensive would prove conclusive. Their most basic hope, perhaps, was to reconcile their despair with trench warfare with their abiding interest in winning the war.

In a different idiom, the courts-martial also underscored the impasse between soldiers and commanders at Les Eparges, which paralleled the impasse between the French and the Germans. Beginning in November 1916, by which time Hallé and Legentil noticed a serious decline in their spirits, convictions for desertion rose to their highest levels yet. The previous records had been set during the Battle of Verdun, 12 for April 1916 and 13 for May. After declining to 6–7 per month for the summer of 1916, convictions rose sharply—16 in November, 19 in December, 17 in January 1917, and 18 in February. Only in March 1917 did they decline, after the division had been withdrawn from Les Eparges. The argument of this chapter suggests that deserters came to regard the closed world of trench warfare at Les Eparges as providing many of the emotional and physical hardships of pitched battle. But many more opportunities to resist by deserting existed at Les Eparges than at Verdun—notably the physical dispersion of the division along a seven- to ten-kilometer front, and the granting of leaves.

In this context, the court-martial evolved into an instrument for the management (as opposed to the repression) of desertion. Although this meant that the *conseil de guerre* in many way functioned more coherently than had been the case previously, it also meant an institutional confession that the disciplinary dilemma of just what to do with errant soldiers had worsened considerably. The particular disciplinary approach at Les Eparges seems clearer than had been the case earlier. Recidivists and those considered likely in some way to "contaminate" otherwise obedient soldiers had their sentences carried out. Of the fifty sentences carried out between June 1916 and April 1917, thirty-five (or 70 percent) were for soldiers already convicted by a *conseil de guerre* in wartime. No soldiers were executed, or even given death sentences. It thus bears pointing out that carrying out sentence for desertion had the paradoxical effect of rendering the desertion successful. Although a special section *conseil de discipline* had set up in December 1916, its effect seems to have been minimal. The line dividing service in the trenches at Les Eparges from incarceration continued to become obscure.

One 5e DI officer recognized this situation even before the dramatic rise in desertion convictions. In a report dated 19 September 1916, Major Ménager, commanding the 1e Bataillon of the 36e RI, explored the causes of the "moral depression and lack of military spirit" in the front lines. The first factor he cited was the incorporation into each company of five or six men found guilty by courts-martial. He commented that "they are nearly all certain to profit from an amnesty at the end of the war, and they boast about it. . . . It is regrettable that the courts-martial are not more severe." Particularly galling for Ménager and his men was the practice of sending soldiers from the rear into the front lines for limited periods (about thirty days) in lieu of a prison sentence. Not surprisingly, this had "an absolutely deplorable effect" on the rest of the soldiers. Ménager noted one incident in which the men complained to their officer: "The rest of us, we foot soldiers, they consider us convicts! So will they send us to the rear to be punished?"

This being the case, the question to pose in concluding this chapter is not so much why so many soldiers were deserting from the 5e DI at Les Eparges, but given how low the potential risk was, why so few. Memoirs, letters, and military justice records indicate that soldiers plainly were developing serious reservations about what they were doing in the trenches. But for the vast majority, the ill-tempered compromise between soldiers and commanders of *tenir* had not been pushed to the breaking point—at least not yet. Ménager brought to bear the old Napoleonic axiom of "*ils grognent mais ils marchent encore* [they grumble but they still march]" to insist that his men still wanted to resolve the dilemma of entrapment versus defeat. Under conditions he probably could not have foreseen, the 1917 mutinies would prove him correct: "But one thing is certain. If they grumble, they still march and they will always march because their hearts are all in the right place, because above all they love their country, because they love their regiment, and they want to support its glorious reputation. I affirm that one will never call in vain on their fine sentiments."

Indeed, after the division had left Les Eparges in February 1917, General de Roig made the considerable leap of faith that all was well. Now that the division had left the sector and its various encumbrances, nothing remained to inhibit the exercise of command authority. "The long sojourn in the trenches," he admitted, had indeed raised the possibility of "a diminution in the combative value of the troops of the division." But after a period of rest and training in a camp in March 1917, he added hopefully, "the bad habits have disappeared." He concluded with a less than prophetic statement of the division's role in the "final" offensive planned for April:

> The maneuvers of the division have proven that everyone, commanders and soldiers [*chefs et soldats*], has not lost anything of their qualities of intelligence, endurance, and discipline. . . . The morale of all, enhanced by the present events, is excellent, and the 5e Division will certainly know how to show itself worthy of its past in the coming battles.

NOTES

From Leonard V. Smith, *Between Mutiny and Obedience: The Case of the French Fifth Infantry Division during World War I* (Princeton: Princeton University Press, 1994), pp. 156–68. © 1994 Princeton University Press. Reprinted by permission of Princeton University Press.

1. The Fifth French Infantry Division. "RI" refers to a regiment.
2. The recapture of Fort Douaumont was a bloody part of the massive Verdun campaign of 1916.

3. Third Army Corps

4. See reading number 3.4

5. Literally "to hold on," "*tenir*" came to mean holding on the defensive.

6. Men eligible to be drafted in 1916.

7. In fact the retreat was part of a larger German move back to stronger positions known collectively as the Hindenburg Line.

8. The rolling barrage was a technique whereby artillery preceded infantry by several hundred yards in an attempt to provide direct support for a ground advance.

The Live and Let Live System

Tony Ashworth

At the outset of this study, we must distinguish between problems of the origins of truces and problems of their persistence through time. Concerning origins, we want to know when and where tacit understandings first occurred, and also how they happened during battle, where each antagonist was ostensibly intent upon killing the other. Exactly when and where the first truce emerged can never be known; but the view that truces appeared for the first and last time during the Christmas of 1914 is incorrect. The Christmas truces were neither the first nor last instances of live and let live; for some truces occurred before the Christmas truce, and others for the duration of the war. A more correct view is that several forms of truce occurred throughout the trench war, and that truces briefly yet vividly emerged in the form of overt fraternisation on a widespread scale during the 1914 Christmas. The event can be likened to the sudden surfacing of the whole of an iceberg, visible to all including non-combatants, which for most of the war remained largely submerged, invisible to all save the participants. But how and when did truces first happen? Which activities were first involved?

Some evidence suggests that the first understandings were associated with meals, the times and conditions of which were common to each side. Both British and German rations were brought up to their respective trenches at about the same time each evening, and a British N.C.O. noticed this practice as well as its effect on truce formation as early as the first week of November 1914—which is around the beginning of trench war. The N.C.O. whose unit had been engaged in trench war for some days, observed that:

> The quartermaster used to bring the rations up . . . each night after dark; they were laid out and parties used to come from the front line to fetch them. I suppose the enemy were occupied in the same way; so things were quiet at that hour for a couple of nights, and the ration parties became careless because of it, and laughed and talked on their way back to their companies.

Probably the N.C.O.'s supposition that British and German ration parties were not only doing the same thing, but were aware of it, was correct. Concerning the growth of the process where each antagonist made assumptions about the other's behaviour, and then acted on these assumptions, it seems quite possible that men who are forced to take account of each other's behaviour in the battle in order to stay alive, will not stop when the pace of battle decelerates for whatever reason. The process of mutual empathy among antagonists was facilitated by their proximity in trench war and, further, was reinforced as the assumptions made by each of the other's likely actions were confirmed by subsequent events. Moreover, by getting to know the 'neighbour' in the trench opposite, each adversary realised that the other endured the same stress, reacted in the same way, and thus was not so very different from himself.

Again in respect of mealtimes, the early growth of this process is illustrated by a Private Hawkings of the 5th division who was looking over the parapet of his trench on the morning of 1 December 1914:

> I could observe the earthworks of a trench on the other side of the road. Soon after dawn a man looked out of this trench . . . and slid into ours. It was a sergeant . . . who had come to see how we were getting on. He warned us against peering lightheartedly over the parapet and opined that our earnest curiosity had not been greeted with a shower of bullets was probably due to the large breadth of no-man's-land, poor morning visibility and Fritz enjoying his breakfast.

No doubt Fritz was busy with his breakfast. No doubt, too, that such knowledge influenced not only Private Hawkings but other trench fighters up and down the line. Certainly, breakfast truces later in the war became a common mode of live and let live, and Liddell Hart, the trench fighter and military historian, described them thus, 'Unforgettable too, is the homely smell of breakfast bacon that gained its conquest over the war reek of chloride of lime, and in so doing not only brought a tacit truce to the battle front, but helped in preserving sanity.'

Similarly, ration party truces quickly became a custom of the quiet front, for instance, in April 1915, they were so well established on part of the 27th division's front that a private remarked, 'At night we went on ration parties across the open, which we came to regard as safe'; and, in the summer of 1915, Ian Hay of the 9th division was writing that:

> It would be child's play to shell the road behind the enemy's trenches, crowded as it must be with ration wagons and water carts, into a bloodstained wilderness . . . but on the whole there is silence. After all, if you prevent your enemy from drawing his rations, his remedy is simple: he will prevent you from drawing yours.

But on an active front, of course, each side considered the other's rations as a prime target.

Thus, early in the war and in spite of it, both sides were learning that each had similar priorities and needs, and it seems that this realisation first crystallised around basic needs such as food and warmth. For instance, in December 1914 but before Christmas, the same Private Hawkings was a sentry in an advanced post near a similar post manned by Germans. The weather was bitter. Hawkings was told to keep a sharp lookout, but he assumed that 'If the members of the Fritz post were as cold, wet and sleepy as I, they wouldn't be inclined to interfere with me.' The Germans, it seems, reasoned likewise, for the night passed in peace as neither side provoked the other.

At some point in this empathic process where each antagonist learned that the other shared his needs and priorities, overt fraternisation, rather than covert trucing, was always a possible outcome as, for example, where fraternisation might be necessary to satisfy a shared need. Concerning the common need for warmth, a German officer before the Christmas of 1914 commented upon 'The fraternisation that has been going on between our trenches and those of the enemy, when friend and foe alike go to fetch straw from the same rick to protect them from the cold and rain and to have some sort of bedding to lie on—and never a shot is fired.' Accordingly, the energy of each side was sometimes directed against their common enemy—winter—but such energy was not in all cases channeled back into warfare when conditions improved. One does not know whether this process had evolved among few or many units before the Christmas truces. Certainly, there is evidence that it had occurred in some battalions, but, equally, there is evidence that it had not occurred in others. Some battalions did not participate in the Christmas fraternisation, and whether there is a connection between the growth of empathy and the restriction of aggression before Christmas, and truce participation on Christmas Day, is an interesting question, but one which cannot be answered fully here.

Nevertheless, such a connection seems to make sense, and can be illustrated in the case of the 2/Scots Guards.[1] Towards the end of November 1914, some Scots Guards raided the German trenches at night, and according to one officer:

> The morning after the attack, there was almost a tacit understanding as to no firing, and about 6.15 a.m. I saw eight or nine German shoulders and heads appear, and then three of them crawled out a few feet in front of their parapet and began dragging in some of our fellows who were either dead or unconscious . . . I passed down the order that none of my men were to fire and this seems to have been done all down the line. I helped one of our men in myself, and was not fired on, at all.

The unintended consequence of such *ad hoc* truces was that antagonists were rendered more conscious of their similarities and less aware of their differences, and in so far as the mutual perception by enemies of their differences promotes war, the perception of similarities weakens it.

Thus it is probably no coincidence that, several days after the above truce, the same officer described in a letter plans for Christmas festivities which included gestures of goodwill for the Germans:

> We return to the trenches tomorrow, and shall be in them on Christmas Day. Germans or no Germans . . . we are going to have a 'ell of a bust, including plum puddings for the whole battalion. I have got a select little party together, who, led by my stentorian voice, are going to take up a position in our trenches where we are closest to the enemy, about 80 yards, and from 10 p.m. onwards we are going to give the enemy every conceivable form of song in harmony, from carols to Tipperary. . . . My fellows are most amused with the idea, and will make a rare noise when we get at it. Our object will be to drown the

now too familiar strains of 'Deutschland über Alles' and the 'Wacht am Rhein' we hear from their trenches every evening.

Not surprisingly, a Christmas truce occurred between the Scots Guards and the Germans. Moreover live and let live had existed in some form on the battalion's front before Christmas, and hence the fraternisation of Christmas was neither a wholly spontaneous, nor an isolated event, but the substitution of an overt for a covert form of peace. More generally, the whole of the Christmas truces might not have been a spontaneous event as is often supposed but a visible and vivid manifestation of the already existing undertone of trench war.

Now attention shifts from the origin of truces to the more complex problem of their persistence. The two problems are different: the fact that a truce emerged at breakfast, or when rations were brought up, or when rain flooded the trenches, does not explain why the *ad hoc* agreement persisted after breakfast, or when rations had been brought up, or when the sun appeared. Neither does the origin of truces in non-combat activities explain their diffusion throughout, and persistence within, combat activities. Now, communication among parties to a truce was necessary for a truce's origin as well as its persistence, and if we understand how trench fighters communicated with each other, we will also learn a lot about the persistence of truces throughout the war. Such communication posed unique problems with live and let live, since it had to happen not only *within* each army, that is, among compatriots, but also *between* each army, that is, among antagonists. In principle, the former does not seem difficult, but the latter is more puzzling, for instance, how was peace negotiated in the midst of battle? Moreover truces in war were fragile things, for if either side suspected the other of duplicity, a pre-emptive strike was at all times possible as well as prudent. Some truces were destroyed, no doubt, by pre-emptive aggression, but others persisted for months. How did each adversary not only reveal to the other the wish to restrict aggression, but also stop the spread of suspicion for as long as the truce lasted?

But first we will discuss the less complex question of communication among compatriots. Obviously, the unofficial rules of peace were not officially published and passed among trench fighters for their information; yet all veterans knew of the rules whether they concurred with them or not. How was this knowledge conveyed within each army? There are two situations here: one involved experienced trench fighters, and the other inexperienced troops fresh from the home front. In the first, a circulation of veterans into and out of the line was occurring at all times as battalions were rotated in and out of divisional sectors, while divisions moved in and out of corps and army sectors. Given this continuous movement of men, how could a truce remain stable on a sector for several months? The second case concerns the circulation of new troops. Freshly trained soldiers were frequently fed into the war either singly or in drafts to make a unit up to strength or as whole units, such as battalions and division, as in the build-up of the B.E.F. during 1915–16. As part of their training, soldiers acquired the official image of trench war, namely, of perpetual conflict where 'there was no cessation of gun, trench mortar and rifle fire, nor neglect of mining, raids and small actions for local purposes.' But where trench fighters first experienced war upon a quiet front the inconsistency of image and reality caused much surprised comment.

The reaction of a member of the 51st division was typical: 'there was . . . an uncanny stillness in the air, broken occasionally by some spasmodic firing. It was very difficult to imagine that this place had any connection with a world war—it seemed so quiet.' Likewise a medical officer of the 23rd division commented:

> It was my first visit to the trenches. . . . There was still none of that roar of cannon and rattle of machine guns which we in our innocence had imagined went on more or less continually in trench warfare.

The 'innocence' of some newcomers amused the old soldiers; for instance, one young soldier arrived in the front line calling out excitedly, "hi mate, where's the battle? I want to do my bit.' But clearly such enthusiasm might disturb the peace. In both the above situations the general problem should be clear enough: the persistence of truces was consistent neither with their constant renegotiation by seasoned antagonists entering into and exiting from the line, nor with their constant rediscovery by successive units of unseasoned men. How, then, did truces stay stable through time?

Let us take the last case first: exactly how and when were the rules of the game passed on to new troops? In the B.E.F. (British Expeditionary Forces) fresh divisions usually went for an official tour of instruction into trenches held by veterans, and where the line was quiet the newcomers were often instructed in the art of peace as well as war. Such a situation was described by a private of the greenhorn 47th division who with others of his section had been instructed and now were about to take over the trenches from their tutors and, for the first time, hold them alone. The private spoke with the outgoing soldiers:

> The man Mike gave some useful hints on trench work. 'It's the Saxons that's across the road' he said, pointing to the enemy lines which were very silent. I had not heard a bullet whistle over since I entered the trench. On the left was an interesting rifle and machine gun fire all the time. 'They're quiet fellows, the Saxons, they don't want to fight any more than we do, so there's a kind of understanding between us. Don't fire at us and we'll not fire at you.'

Likewise a unit of the 29th division took over trenches in France for the first time and was told by an N.C.O. of the garrison relieved that 'Mr. Bosche ain't a bad feller. You leave 'im alone: 'e'll leave you alone.'

In much the same way when a single newcomer joined a seasoned unit, he might be told by an old hand both of his official duties and of the unofficial rules guiding their performance. R. C. Sherriff, who served with the 24th division, described such an incident where one officer takes his new colleague around the trenches. Together they crawl along a sap into no-man's-land. A German trench is nearby:

> 'Yes' said Trotter . . . 'that's the Bosche front line. Bosche looking over this way now, maybe, just as we are—do you play cricket?' he added. . . . 'A bit' said Raleigh, 'could you chuck a cricket ball that distance?' 'I think so' 'Then you could do the same with a Mills Bomb (hand grenade). . . . But you won't though' said Trotter. . . . 'Come on, let sleeping

dogs lie. If we was to throw a bomb you can bet your boots the old Bosche would chuck
one back, and Mr Digby and Mr 'Arris (the soldiers occupying the sap) . . . are both married men. Wouldn't be cricket would it?'

One can agree with Trotter: not that it isn't cricket; but neither is it war. Yet Trotter's
brief homily on the undertone of war is neat.

We see then that the conventional image of trench war held by freshly trained
units and individuals was modified, as the new soldiers experienced both the reality
of a quiet sector and were initiated into the undertones of the war by their colleagues, and thus the stability of truces was assured. Neither was this stability
effected by the circulation of experienced men moving in and out of the line for the
official relief procedure allowed outgoing trench fighters to communicate the existence of tacit truces to incoming troops. Concerning trench relief, an official manual
laid down:

> The first essential is a careful preliminary reconnaissance. Whenever a unit is about to
> take over a new line of trenches, parties from it will visit the trenches previously, by day
> if possible. In the case of a battalion, the party should consist of the C.O., adjutant and
> machine gun officer, and at least one officer and one N.C.O. from each company.

Thus some incoming troops had direct knowledge of the line to be relieved and
doubtless told others both of their own impressions, and also of the tenants' description. An officer of the 37th division described the take over of a new sector from the
French:

> I made a preliminary tour of the whole line with Taudieres, a young French officer . . . of
> the French regiment we were relieving . . . it was the French practice to 'let sleeping dogs
> lie' when in a quiet sector . . . and of making this clear by retorting vigorously only when
> challenged. In one sector which we took over from them they explained to me that they
> had practically a code which the enemy well understood: they fired two shots for each
> one that came over, but never fired first.

A private soldier of the 56th division described the same situation, 'the necessary
arrangements were made for taking over our new section of front. These included a
visit by several officers to the firing line, and, as usual on these occasions, we waited
eagerly for their return in order to question . . . their mounted orderlies on the quiet-
ness or otherwise of our sector.'

The above refers to troops moving from one sector to another; but most reliefs
concerned different units moving in and out of trenches in the same sector, and in
such cases a reconnaissance was not always necessary. Such reliefs were described by
the adjutant of the 49th division:

> One relief is very much like another. . . . The trench seems endless, but, at last the front
> line is reached. Other men covered with mud and wearing equipment are waiting there.
> The relief goes smoothly. Sentries are changed, duties are handed over, the latest intelli-

gence about 'Fritz' or 'Jerry' is imparted. 'Quiet tour. Not a casualty in our company. He doesn't fire if you lie doggo.'

In this way a truce could persist for months, despite the continual circulation of soldiers in and out of the line, as the troops departing told those incoming of the existence of a truce, and thus constant renegotiation with the enemy was unnecessary.

The second problem is the more complex one of communication among antagonists, and here I shall distinguish direct and indirect truces, this distinction referring to different means of communication between antagonists. Direct communication involved the use of either verbal or written symbols, such as the spoken word with overt fraternisation. Indirect communication involved symbols unique to, and evolved in, the world of the trench fighter and it assumed one of two general forms: inertia or ritualisation. It is important to grasp that fraternisation, inertia and ritualisation were at one and the same time means of communication and forms of live and let live. The analysis starts with direct truces.

Insofar as opposing trenches were within speaking or shouting distance of each other, commonsense suggests that truces were negotiated verbally and reaffirmed by the same means for so long as they persisted. The most famous of such truces were those of Christmas 1914 when nine British divisions held a front line of approximately thirty miles throughout which verbally arranged truces of varying length of time occurred. The manner of the starting and ending of a typical Christmas truce was described by an officer of the 6th division. He met his German counterpart in no-man's-land where both agreed that neither wished to shoot on Christmas Day, although each had strict orders to allow no truces. A 24-hour truce was informally concluded and courteously ended at the agreed hour:

> At 8.30 I fired three shots in the air and put up a flag with 'Merry Christmas' on it, and I climbed on the parapet. He put up a sheet with 'Thank you' on it and the German Captain appeared on the parapet. We both bowed and saluted and got down into our respective trenches, and he fired two shots in the air, and the war was on again.

The reaction of high command to these truces was immediate and negative, but on the whole appears to have taken the form of admonishment and warning; for instance, one battalion recorded that the truces, 'drew down the wrath of general headquarters,' who further demanded the names of the officers responsible but eventually dropped the matter. But the truces caused an army routine order to be issued asserting that soldiers 'were in France to fight and not fraternise with the enemy.' For the Christmas of 1915 special measures were taken by high command to prevent a recurrence and these seem to have been successful, since only some units of the Scots Guards are recorded as having fraternised with the enemy. The reaction of high command was unequivocal. Two officers of the Scots Guards were court martialled; one was acquitted, and the other convicted and reprimanded. According to one officer, all leave in the battalion was stopped.

Despite the proscriptions of high command, verbally arranged truces were possibly widespread and probably the most common form of live and let live during the first few months of trench warfare. At about this time, an eyewitness wrote of British trench fighters that:

> They began to take something more than a professional interest in their neighbours opposite. The curiosity was reciprocated. Items of news . . . were exchanged when the trenches were near enough to permit of vocal intercourse. Curious conventions grew up, and at certain hours of the day . . . there was a kind of informal armistice. In one section the hour of 8 to 9 a.m. was regarded as consecrated to 'private business,' and certain places indicated by a flag were regarded as out of bounds by the snipers on both sides.

The custom which conferred immunity to an enemy on the loo is less curious, perhaps, than another where one side gave impromptu entertainments to the other. For example, we find in a battalion history that:

> On . . . the 4th April, the Germans made an organised effort to obtain a truce, which . . . lasted about two hours. While it was still dark, the Germans could be heard talking excitedly in their trenches which were not many yards away from our own. Later they began to sing and to shout remarks to the 1/2nd Londons and to the Leinsters . . . who returned the compliments with interest . . . it was amusing to see the heads of Germans popping up and down like marionettes, behind their trenches, to the accompaniment of loud laughter. A German, standing on his fire step, juggled with three bottles; and when his 'turn' was ended, another German—a very small man—walked out as far as his own wire, struck an attitude, and hurriedly scampered back. A third then stood up and boldly challenged our men to play a game of 'soccer' against them in no-man's-land, but was immediately howled down when he confessed that they cold not provide a football.

Overt truces involving direct communication were not confined to the early part of trench war; for instance, in 1918—the last year of the war—along the front of the 38th division, 'where the lines approached, there was an exchange of messages, cigarettes and visits. By May the whole division was fraternising until a peremptory order from the G.O.C. stopped the practice.' Whereas the latter truce involved large numbers of men along a divisional front, other direct truces occurred throughout the war on a much smaller scale, for example, a soldier of the 33rd division wrote, 'some of our sapheads were only fifteen yards from the German saphead. Each side could have easily thrown their bombs into one another's saps, but this was very rarely done and they generally lived in peace with one another; sometimes they held conversation.' While some trench fighters generally lived in peace, others as Junger pointed out were, 'forever puzzling out the best possible ways of slinging over bombs with hand made catapults.' The choice of aggression was always possible. Overt truces were arranged either in face-to-face situations by word of mouth as in the above illustrations, or, if the distance between trenches precluded face-to-face contact, trench fighters shouted across no-man's-land. Thus on parts of the 8th division's front during October 1915, the Germans frequently shouted over 'promising not to fire if we would not'; on moving to a quiet sector, a battalion of the 51st division heard the Germans shout, 'We Saxons, you Anglo Saxons, don't shoot,' and apparently all went well, for a few days later the Saxons, 'shouted . . . that Prussians were relieving them, and asked us to give them hell.' Written messages were sent to the enemy either upon a notice board raised above the trenches, or, more ingeniously but less effectively perhaps, inside defused missiles. For instance, opposite the 12th division, the Germans intimated a wish for the quiet life on a notice board which read, 'Don't fire East Surreys, you shoot too well'; on the front of the 18th division, bad weather prompted some light-hearted banter, 'a Teutonic voice was heard to call out "another dugout fallen in Tommie?" And . . . our neighbours across the way hoisted a board with the following inscription (in English) painted on it: "'On and after the 13th inst. you can have these bloody trenches.'" Using another means of communication, some sociable Saxons put a written message into a defused rifle-grenade, and dispatched the harmless missile into the trenches of a unit of the 12th division. The message read, 'To the opposition. We have sent by rifle grenades some newspapers. When you get it, stick up a white flag and we don't shoot. Wait a minute and newspapers come by non exploding grenades. Is peace in sight? Please answer.' A unit of the 46th division recorded that:

> the infantry opposite . . . were Saxons, and inclined to be friendly with the English. On one occasion the following message, tied to a stone, was thrown into our trench: 'We are going to send a 40 lb bomb. We have got to do this, but dont want to. It will come this evening, and we will whistle first to warn you.' All of this happened. A few days later they apparently mistrusted the German official news, for they sent a further message saying 'Send us an English newspaper that we may hear the verity.'

Similarly, Robert Graves, serving then with the 2nd division, remarked that his battalion—the 2/Royal Welch fusiliers—received a message in a defused grenade from the 'German Korporals' to the 'English Korporals' inviting the latter to a 'good German dinner.' In the 1st division, the Germans made 'coy advances' on the front of the 1/Gloucestershire Regiment and 'fired over a friendly message in a trench mortar bomb.' But it was most unlikely that either this regiment or the 2/Royal Welch responded in kind, since both were elite units with reputations for aggressive trench fighting.

Some truces occurred for a specific and limited purpose; for instance, heavy rainfall made mutual aggression very difficult; for the trenches were flooded and mud made rapid movement impossible, and in these conditions an *ad hoc* truce not infrequently emerged. An officer of the Guards division recorded that, 'the rain brought the trenches tumbling in, and the mud was so bad that they simply could not be used. The Germans and ourselves were walking about on the top in full view of each other, neither side wanting to shoot'; an officer of the 50th division described a similar bad weather truce:

> fortunately Fritz was in much the same plight and did not bother us. He was only about 200 yards away, and at almost any hour of the day we could see two or three of them standing about on the top. We did not snipe at them, and they left us alone. . . . Almost every day both British and Boche lose their way and get into the enemy lines.

It might be thought that bad weather gave trench fighters no choice but to stop the killing for a while. But that was neither the case nor the view of high command. For example, on the 8th division's front, some trenches were two feet deep in water, and others entirely flooded; yet under these seemingly impossible conditions, the 1/Worcester Regiment made the first raid of the trench war. In the same division another battalion with flooded trenches instantly fired upon Germans who quitted their flooded trenches in order to bail them out. The choice of aggression was possible even under extreme conditions.

Once started *ad hoc* weather truces were sometimes prolonged and progressed to further exchanges between antagonists. For instance, in the 24th division, a weather truce lasting for several days developed into good morning greetings, friendly conversations and night truces between working parties; during one of the latter a British officer, walking by mistake into the German working party, got stuck in the mud and was pulled out by his orderly. The logical outcome of such direct truces was, perhaps, the type of situation witnessed by Winston Churchill when visiting the French front line:

> The lines are in places only a few yards apart . . . the sentries looked at each other over the top of the parapet: and while we were in the trench the Germans passed the word to the French to take cover as their officer was going to order some shelling. This duly arrived.

Another British officer accompanied Churchill and described similar events:

> On the front we were on the Boche signals if the art. [artillery] is going to fire and shows the no. of rounds by holding fingers up. They inform the French of the arrival of an officer by pointing to their shoulders & yesterday shouted 'pauvres Français, explosion.' Measures were accordingly taken, & whilst we were there sure enough they exploded a comouflet.

No doubt the French in their turn similarly obliged the Germans.

Incidentally, it has been asked why Churchill wrote no war memoirs. He served with the Grenadier Guards for several weeks and as a battalion commander in the 9th division for several months. The 9th division held a front where live and let live was not infrequent, so that unless he described the latter, Churchill did not have a great deal to tell. Moreover most persons are familiar with a usual form of war memoir and would have expected the same from someone of Churchill's reputation. The state of the line was described by Ian Hay whom Churchill met and described as, 'the author of those brilliant articles *The First Hundred Thousand*.'

But to return to our theme: the British high command, perhaps aware of the outcome of uncurbed truces, were implacably opposed to all truces, whether these were brief events of no military consequence, or had some precedent and moral justification in the rules of war. The temper of high command can be gauged from the following events: after a minor attack, a battalion of the 16th division was invited by the Germans to collect its wounded in no-man's-land. Before the British and German commanders could stop it, a truce had been established and spread quickly along the front of the units concerned. The British battalion commander knew that despite its humane purpose the incident was 'highly irregular.' Further, and unfortunately for him, the truce occurred a short time after another for the same purpose had been conceded by the British to the Germans. The latter had caused the divisional headquarters to underline the order against fraternisation by a memo which stated:

> The Divisional Commander wishes it to be clearly understood by all ranks that any understanding with the enemy of . . . any . . . description is strictly forbidden. . . . No communication is to be held with him . . . and any attempt on his part to fraternise is to be instantly repressed. . . . In the event of any infringement . . . disciplinary action is to be taken.

High command convened a court of inquiry into the above truce and issued even more stringent orders. The truce involved several hundred men along a battalion front; yet small-scale truces involving a few men along a few yards elicited from high command an equally severe response, as the brief event below recorded by an officer of the 39th division showed:

> a German officer and perhaps twenty of his men . . . with friendly cries of 'Good morning, Tommy, have you any biscuits' . . . got out of their trench and invited our men to do the same . . . our men were told not to fire upon them, both by C. and the other company's officer on watch; . . . there was some exchange of shouted remarks and after a time both sides returned to the secrecy of their parapets.

When high command heard of this the two officers responsible were arrested, and shortly afterwards were marched off in open arrest to take part with their battalion in the battles of the Somme.

Although verbally arranged truces occurred intermittently for the duration of the war and were permanent in this sense, they were neither pervasive nor continuous. In the first case, overt truces could not exist without physical nearness and therefore could not diffuse into weapon groups which fought each other over long distances. For example, the opposing artillery and trench-mortar groups, unlike the opposing infantries, did not interact in face-to-face situations, and therefore could not arrange truces directly. Secondly, with rare exceptions, direct truces occurred neither in continuous succession, nor regularly at infrequent or frequent intervals; on the contrary, such truces were mostly irregular and ephemeral, since being highly visible they were easily repressed by high command, and therefore were never a serious and widespread problem.

However, live and let live involved indirect and covert forms as well as direct, overt forms, and the former were an adaptation to the legal sanctions of high command, which threatened the existence of overt forms of live and let live. Accordingly, antagonists conveyed the wish to restrict aggression not only directly and personally, but also indirectly, impersonally and over long distances. Such communication involved a language of trench warfare, that is, a set of non-verbal symbols understood by trench fighters, but not outsiders, whereby antagonists who neither saw, spoke nor wrote to each other, nevertheless managed to convey reciprocally the wish to exchange peace. The process of indirect communication among antagonists assumed two main forms: inertia and ritualisation. These, like overt fraternisation, were simultaneously forms of live and let live. Like direct truces, indirect truces occurred throughout the war; but unlike the former, the latter took a more subtle, less visible form and, as a consequence, were less vulnerable to the control of high command. As indirect communication was possible over long distances, such truces were pervasive involving artillery, trench-mortar and machine-gun weapon groups as well as the infantry. Moreover, as they could not easily be put down by high command, indirect truces continued without hindrance for many months on some sectors and were thus, from the point of view of high command, a serious and endemic problem of trench war. It seems that when referring to the undertone of trench war, Blunden had in mind these covert understandings which unlike overt truces were pervasive as well as continuous and subtle yet effective.

It was not the case that only one of the three forms of live and let live could exist on a sector at a given time, that is, a truce based upon either verbal contract, or inertia or ritualisation; on the contrary, all three forms could and sometimes did co-exist. For example, it could happen that infantry groups—hand-bombers—fraternised at sapheads, while machine-gunners remained inert, and the opposing artilleries ritualised aggression. The sectors where all three forms of live and let live existed, and where all weapon groups exchanged peace were described in the literature as 'very quiet' or 'absolutely peaceful' or 'like a convalescent home.' Such sectors were not frequent and were, perhaps, as rare as active sectors where no agreements existed, and all weapon groups exchanged aggression. On the other hand, many sectors were a mixture of war and peace, that is, of exchanges of peace as well as exchanges of aggression and these were more frequent than either very quiet or very active sectors.

All three forms of exchange existed for the whole of the war; at the same time, it will be argued below that, in the early phase of trench war, live and let live typically took the forms of overt truces and inertia, whereas, in the later phase inertia and ritualisation were more characteristic. But this is a matter of relative frequency only; for some fraternisation occurred in 1918, and some ritualisation occurred as early as 1914.

Having distinguished direct and indirect truces, and illustrated the former, we can now examine inertia both as a means of communication and as a form of live and let live. Not infrequently in trench warfare, a suspension of hostilities happened for no conscious decision or specific agreement, but merely because each side seemed disinclined to aggress the other. Antagonists sometimes shared a vague, general and passive attitude of mind. Although both sides would instantly retaliate against the other's aggression, generally neither would initiate aggression nor otherwise provoke the other, and, accordingly, both sides remained passive and inert. Such inertia should not be mistaken for the absence of either the ability or opportunity to aggress the enemy. Lack of capability was quite another thing. For instance, the British artillery was short of shells on the 4th and 46th divisional fronts in the spring of 1915, and, in consequence, the gunners were incapable of anything but inertia. Yet this shortage, which the press called 'the Shells Scandal' does not entirely explain the quiet which at that time prevailed on the front of the 46th division, and which an infantry officer of that unit described thus, 'Life in S.P. 4 was gloriously lazy. The weather was perfect, the enemy was most peaceful, and there was little to do but lie on one's back and smoke, or write long imaginative letters home. . . .' Unlike the gunners, the infantry had ammunition but chose not to use it. Thus the quiet of the front derived not only from the British gunners' shortage of shells, but also from the British infantry's inclination for inertia, which the German infantry shared—for it takes two to make peace. It is this latter voluntary type of inertia which concerns us here.

Inertia can be thought of as a negative situation void of meaning and communication, but, certainly, this was not true of inertia in trench warfare. In most sectors and at most times each side had the choice of either aggressing or not aggressing the enemy. In the situation where each antagonist had this choice, the non-aggression of one was neither negative nor meaningless to the other; on the contrary, it was as positive and meaningful as the alternative act of aggression. Mutual aggression was in a real and obvious sense mutual communication; for when trench fighters fired against each other, neither doubted that the other's intent was to kill or injure. Similarly, the choice of non-aggression instead of aggression was equally an act of communication, and this must be absolutely grasped by the reader, otherwise trench warfare will not be understood.

This crucial point must be spelt out: when the British (or German) trench fighter remained passive, the German (or British) thereby understood that either a special reason existed for the British (or German) non-aggression or the British had chosen not to aggress. The former possibility aside, the British choice of non-aggression where the contrary was possible meant to the German that the British desired peace. At the same time, the British passivity was not unconditional, and the Germans knew that if they responded to inertia with aggression, the British would retaliate in kind. On the other hand, the Germans knew also that to reciprocate the British inertia would establish a set of mutually contingent exchanges where neither side exercised its choice to aggress the other. As a means of communication, inertia was ambiguous, for it was sometimes difficult to decide whether inertia was a peace overture or not; notwithstanding this ambiguity, seasoned trench fighters generally understood the meaning of each other's passivity, and each remained inert in the expectation—and only in the expectation—that the gesture would be understood as well as reciprocated. Where this expectation was not realised, the exchange of aggression commenced, but where it was confirmed, the exchange of peace was either established or reinforced, or both. Moreover, the ambiguity of inertia as a means of communication diminished as peace exchanges continued and increased, and as each antagonist felt more confident of the other's response. Indeed inertia might be manipulated by an elite unit which would refrain from action to induce in the enemy a false sense of security that could be exploited by sudden aggression. Generally, however, inertia in trench war symbolised a willingness to give up the choice of aggression; it also served as a means of communication and was a form of live and let live. The meaning of inertia as exchange and communication among antagonists in trench was put in a nutshell by the poet Charles Sorley, an infantry officer of the 12th division, '—without at all "fraternizing"—we refrain from interfering with Brother Bosche seventy yards away, as long as he is kind to us'; and elsewhere Sorley wrote that trench fighters, 'have found out that to provide discomfort for the other is but a round about way of providing it for themselves.'

We have seen that high command took instant legal action against fraternisation, but how did high command react to inertia? What was the attitude of the generals to covert truces, and what action if any, was taken? Sorley perceived the problem facing high command, 'the staff know that a sense of humour won't allow of this sitting face to face in a cornfield for long, without both parties coming out and fraternising, as happened so constantly a few months ago,' and, further, he reckoned that inertia would continue till trench fighters, 'have their heads banged together by the red capped powers behind them, whom neither attempts to understand.' While they might not understand the generals, trench fighters could not ignore them; but exactly how did high command bang heads together?

Although tacit truces were less visible than fraternisation, high command was well enough aware of their existence; for the lack of fighting activity showed up on situation reports which the generals regularly received from front line units. Moreover members of high command sometimes visited the front where they witnessed events which might not be mentioned in an official report. For instance, a staff officer of the 51st division noted of a certain time in the war that: 'the diaries of senior officers contain frequent references in which they found the enemy working in daylight in full view, unmolested through want of initiative on the part of local commanders.' But even where trench fighters walked around openly, inertia, unlike fraternisation, was neither a violation of specific orders nor a court martial offence. Nevertheless inertia was opposed by high command from the start of trench war because it was contrary both to the spirit of the offensive, which pervaded the military theory of the time and to an official British directive of 1915 which made active trench war mandatory.

In respect of the former, while no belligerent had a definitive doctrine of attack and defence in trench war, all existing manuals firmly asserted the necessity of the offensive spirit. The British *Field Service Regulations 1914* stated, "Success in war depends more on moral than on physical qualities. Skill cannot compensate for want of courage, energy and determination. . . . The development of the necessary moral qualities is therefore the first of the objects to be attained.' Similarly, the German regulations instructed that, 'resolute action is . . . of the first importance in war. Every individual, from the highest commander to the youngest soldier, must always remember that supine inaction and neglect of opportunities will entail severer censure than an error in conception of the choice of means.' One might object that these were principles for a war of movement and thus either redundant or of little relevance to a static war within trenches. But this was not so. Firstly, the spirit of the offensive was conceived as a principle applicable to all wars and all situations. Secondly, trench war was in some respects similar to siege war, and manuals contained a tactic of the latter which stressed the need for offensiveness when an army was on the defensive. For example, the British F.S.R. ran:

> the general principle which governs the defence of fortresses is that the offensive is the
> soul of defence. . . . The most effectual means of defence is counter attack. It imposes

caution on the part of the besieger, and imparts an inspiriting influence to the defender's troops, besides rendering them more fit for field operation in the event of the siege being raised.

Clearly inertia was incompatible with the offensive spirit conceived to animate both attack and defence. On 5 February 1915, Sir John French reiterated these principles to army commanders in a G.H.Q. memorandum which laid down official guidelines for the conduct of trench war. The British commander-in-chief stressed the importance of constant activity and of offensive methods in general against the enemy even though the B.E.F. was on the defensive; he asserted that aggression must be encouraged since it would improve the morale of British troops and exhaust the enemy both morally and materially, and, further, that aggression was the most effective form of defence.

It might be misleading to say that Sir John's memo established what was later called the British *policy* of active trench war, as neither the tactic nor technology of trench war had by that time been evolved, but the memo did establish the *principle* of active trench war. However, the February memo had a limited effect for reasons we will later examine, and the advance of inertia continued; by September 1915, Sir John French was alluding to some veterans as 'sticky' on account of their 'trench habit'—indeed the lack of the 'trench habit' was a reason why he chose inexperienced rather than experienced troops as reserves for the battle of Loos.

In March 1916, a British training manual based largely on 1915 events identified inertia as both endemic and problematic, asserting in a section named 'The Offensive Spirit in Trench Warfare' that 'There is an insidious tendency to lapse into a passive and lethargic attitude against which officers of all ranks have to be on their guard, and the fostering of the offensive spirit . . . calls for incessant attention.' The attitude of the French and German high commands towards inertia was the same as the British. The official French manual for infantry officers (1917) affirms that 'The war of the trenches is neither a relaxation nor a guard duty; it is a phase of the battle. It is necessary that the adversary feel in front of him a vigilant hatred and know that we wish no rest before his defeat. It is necessary that each hostile company go back from the trenches with the loss of at least twenty men.' The German high command's concern for the fighting spirit goes back to April 1915 at least, when it was noted that 'the infantry had become enfeebled by trench warfare, and had lost its daring.' In 1917, Ludendorff appointed officers to divisional and army H.Q.s to lecture 'with a view to maintaining the fighting spirit of the army'; but Rudolf Binding, an officer of divisional cavalry who was selected for one of the latter posts, had been lecturing already to young officers on the spirit of field service regulations and had stressed the error of 'supine inaction.'

All this shows the several high commands' knowledge of, and concern for the problem, and inertia was clearly neither part of official policy nor something to which high command turned a blind eye. The next question is clear: what could high command do about inertia? And the short answer is—not a great deal in the early part of the war. During 1915 the British high command could do little against inertia except issue to combat units general directives to harass the enemy. General directives are less effective than specific orders as a means of control; for the great discretion of the former allows a subordinate to choose either evasion or compliance, whereas the latter give a subordinate no choice but to comply—or risk legal sanctions. In 1915, however, high command was unable to issue specific orders for aggression, since such orders meant spelling out, with more detail than was then possible, the methods of attack in trench warfare. Precise orders presupposed a specialised tactic and technology of trench warfare, and at this time the latter existed only in rudimentary and unstandardised form. For instance, from 1916 raids were frequently ordered by high command. But in 1915 this was not possible, for the raid was not distinguished from other minor operations, nor were raiding tactics and weaponry developed. Further, few battalions had had actual experience of raiding at this time. Thus high command had limited control over combat units in 1915 and could do little about inertia but issue general directives which affirmed the need for constant aggression, but which could neither set in motion a specific tactic of trench warfare nor otherwise spell out exactly how to aggress the enemy.

By no means all British units remained passive, however. Some were forced to counter the aggression of elite German units, while others made it a point of honour to harass the enemy or responded to the spirit of high command orders. But for whatever reason, to be active was to innovate, improvise and specialise, and 1915 was marked by the gradual growth of specialised tactics and technology of trench warfare, that is, a body of technical rules, expert skills and weapons for attack and defence in trench war. While its progression was somewhat uneven and *ad hoc* within and between opposing armies, this technology was basically the same on both sides; for should one side gain advantage by innovation, the other had to imitate or otherwise counter so as to survive. For example, German trench-mortars were more advanced than either British or French at the start of the war, but Allied trench-mortars improved and the German advantage was reduced by the end of 1915; similarly, the British pioneered the raid, a major form of attack in trench war, but the Germans countered by developing their own raiding expertise. In respect of the infantry, elite battalions assumed the innovating role and exploited the opportunities offered by trench warfare for combat at close quarters through simultaneously adapting old weapons and evolving new.

Typical of these elite units was the 2/Royal Welch Fusiliers which, according to its battalion history, began to innovate as early as December 1914: 'The germ of specialism began to sprout vigorously at this time as new means of offence and defence were brought out.' The energy with which the elite battalions went about the task of developing the new technology is illustrated in the history of the 1/Royal West Kents, which asserts of 1915 (and generally) that, 'When in the front line the time was spent in small aggressive actions calculated to make life uncertain for the enemy . . . either we or the enemy were constantly retaliating. . . . We always made ourselves as obnoxious to the Hun as orders and circumstances would allow.' Both the 2/Royal Welch and 1/Royal West Kents were regular battalions, but some new army battalions were also very active in 1915; for instance, in the 37th division, the 10/Royal Fusiliers took over from the French a quiet front which was quickly turned into a hornet's nest.

At this point it will be useful to summarise and underline some parts of our argument in this chapter. A distinction has been drawn between problems of the origin and the persistence of live and let live. In respect of origins, truces emerged before the Christmas of 1914 and first occurred in non-combat activities concerned with the fulfillment of basic needs. Probably these early truces were *ad hoc* and short-lived arrangements but once established they tended to persist and to evolve in accord with a circular process of cause and effect: live and let live entailed indirect or direct communication among enemies, and such communication implied mutual empathy, while empathy encouraged the evolution of live and let live in two way—firstly, be reinforcing existing truces, and, secondly, by spreading truces into combat activities.

Accordingly, it seems that both sides soon started to make assumptions about each other's behaviour in respect of areas unrelated to war. For example, each side speculated that if we allow the enemy to breakfast in peace, they will allow us the same in return, since like us they are hungry. Mutual empathy was implied in such reasoning and this increased as assumptions were affirmed by events. Moreover the meaning of inertia both as a means of communication and as a mode of live and let live grew less ambiguous as empathy advanced. As a result empathy extended simply and logically to the thought that if we leave the enemy absolutely in peace they will also leave us in peace. When this expectancy was realised, the diffusion of truces from non-combat to combat activities had occurred. The peace within the war now persisted. All this concerns indirect communication, but the latter also communicated directly, for instance, by word of mouth. No doubt this was made easier as some Germans spoke English, having worked in the U.K., often in the catering trade; there was a joke about this: one day in the line a British Tommy shouted 'Waiter,' and fifty Fritzes stuck their heads up above the trenches and said 'Coming Sir.'

High command was hostile both to overt and covert truces. Fraternisation was visible, and the authorities quickly and effectively moved against persons involved; in consequence, such truces were not endemic, although they occurred at intervals throughout the war. On the other hand, inertia was a subtle and tacit thing. High command could neither identify nor prove that certain persons at certain places and times had colluded with the enemy. The generals defined inertia as a problem of morale rather than law, but their directives were ineffectual as a counter to inertia which became widespread during the early part of the war. In conclusion, a picture should be emerging by now of soldiers who were not so dominated by events that they were entirely powerless. If they chose, trench fighters could exercise some control over the matter of life and death.

NOTES

From Tony Ashworth, *Trench Warfare, 1914–18: The Live and Let Live System* (New York: Holmes and Meier, 1980), pp. 24–47.

1. Second Battalion, Scots Guard Regiment. See reading 2.5.

Four

Home Fronts

Letters from a Lost Generation

Vera Brittain

Roland Leighton (Vera's Fiancé) to Vera

France, 20–21 April 1915

Your two last letters came one last night and one the night before, and I read them by candle-light sitting on the little wooden bench outside my dug-out. I am sitting there now writing this, while the sun shines on the paper and a bee is humming round and round the bed of primroses in front of me. War and primroses! At the moment it does not seem as if there could be such a thing as war. Our trenches are in the middle of a vast wood of tall straight trees—at least the support and reserve trenches are inside the wood, the fire trenches on the front edge. We have held the whole of this wood since the beginning of November and it is all a maze of small paths and isolated huts and breastworks. My own dug-out is in the second line, about 180 to 200 yards behind the fire trenches on the wood-edge. Hence the possibility of having primroses planted in front, behind the shelter of the breastwork. Half my platoon is in this support line and half in the fire trenches, so that I have to divide my time equally between them, except that of course I have my meals and sleep (when I have the time) down here, where there is cover from view, if not altogether from fire. As a matter of fact the wood is all exposed to shell-fire; and two of our men since yesterday morning have been hit by snipers as far back as in the third line. One bullet whistled past my head as I was shaving this morning just round the corner. Yesterday afternoon we were shelled for some time; and had our first man killed—shot through the head.

The portion of the line we are holding here is one of the best known, and much too strong now to be retaken by the Germans. It is probable that they will keep us here for some time—perhaps as long as two months. We are to be relieved by the 8th Worcesters every four days, have four days' rest in billets a few miles back, and then come in again for another four days. We are to go out to billets tomorrow Wednesday morning.

It is very nice sitting here now. At times I can quite forget danger and war and death, and think only of the beauty of life, and love—and you. Everything is in such grim contrast here. I went up yesterday morning to my fire trench, through the sunlit wood, and found the body of a dead British soldier hidden in the undergrowth a few yards from the path. He must have been shot there during the wood fighting in the early part of the war and lain forgotten all this time. The ground was slightly marshy and the body had sunk down into it so that only the toes of his boots stuck up above the soil. His cap and equipment were just by the side, half-buried and rotting away. I am having a mound of earth thrown over him, to add one more to the other little graves in the wood.

You do not mind my telling you these gruesome things, do you? You asked me to tell you everything. It is of such things that my new life is made.

Wednesday 21st

I had no opportunity to finish this yesterday.

We are going out of the trenches this afternoon at 4.0 o'clock. It is now 11.30 a.m. I shall be glad of the rest, as it has been a tiring four days here. I was up nearly all last night mending the barbed wire entanglements in front of our trenches, and this morning can hardly keep my eyes open. There is nothing glorious in trench warfare. It is all waiting and taking of petty advantages—and those who can wait longest win. And it is all for nothing—for an empty name, for an ideal perhaps—after all.

R.

Vera to Roland

Buxton, 23 April 1915

As we left the Hospital we stopped for a few moments to talk to one of the wounded soldiers— a little elderly man who had been at Neuve Chapelle. His appearance made a great impression on me; he did not look unnerved, or even painfully ill—but very, very sad.

Back to Oxford to-morrow

Vera to Roland

Micklem Hall, Brewer Street, St Aldate's,
Oxford, 25 April 1915

I received your letter dated April 20th this morning. Yes, tell me all the gruesome things you see—I know that even war will not blunt your sensibilities, & that you suffer because of these things as much as I should if seeing them,—as I do when hearing of them. I want your new life to be mine to as great an extent as is possible, & this is the only way it can—Women are no longer the sheltered & protected darlings of man's playtime, fit only for the nursery & the drawing-room—at least, no woman that you are interested in could ever be just that. Somehow I feel it makes me stronger to realise what horrors there are. I shudder & grow cold when I hear about them, & then feel that next time I shall bear it, not more callously, yet in some way better— . . .

I am wondering just how ever I am going to stand the next eight weeks—not because of the discomfort of my surroundings but because of their pleasantness. I remember once at the beginning of the war you described college as 'a secluded life of scholastic vegetation.' That is just what it is. It is, for me at least, too soft a job. . . . I want physical endurance; I should welcome the most wearying kind of bodily toil. To sit at my table & do a Latin prose feels not only a physical but a mental impossibility. Perhaps I am doing just what I ought—perhaps it is the best way to prepare for a future in which I am beginning to think it may be more eminently desirable & glorious to earn my own living than even I thought before. But just at present this sort of work is becoming impossible. Instead of doing it, I sit dreaming over it, thinking of you among barbed-wire entanglements at night, & of you suffering from the horrors of war & yet keeping your essential personality—as I see you are in your letters—untouched by them all. I think of the dead man in your regiment & how you might have been he. And all this is doing no one any good. Two people who finished their exam last term have gone down to nurse. If it hadn't been for pass Mods. I would have done the same; as it is I have to stop here & finish that, else the two last terms & my father's money & the college's are all thrown away, & if I came back here it would be beginning 3 years all over again.

But, as you know, I am going to nurse in the Long [Vacation], & if the war shows no signs of ending I am not sure that I shall come up again till it is over, but stay & nurse more. Suffering myself makes me want nothing so much as to do all I can to alleviate the sufferings of other people. The terrible things you mention & describe fill me, when the first horror is over, with a sort of infinite pity I have never felt before. I don't know whether it is you or sorrow that has aroused this softer feeling—perhaps both. Sorrow, & the higher joy that is not mere happiness, & you, all seem to be the same thing just now. Is it really all for nothing,—for an empty name—an ideal? Last time I saw you it was I who said that & you who denied it. Was I really right, & will the issue really not be worth one of the lives that have been sacrificed for it? Or did we need this gigantic catastrophe to wake up all that was dead within us? You can judge best of us two now. In the light of all that you have seen, tell me what you really think. Is it an ideal for which you personally are fighting, & is it one which justifies all the blood that has been & is to be shed?

I suppose you know that a most terrible battle is raging just about 10 miles north of you—& may possibly spread south. I saw in the paper to-day that as long as the Germans hold Menin, they can extend the battle by pouring in as many troops as they wish between Ypres & Armentières. Is there any chance of this? The paper calls this second battle of Ypres the most important conflict of the war & the Germans are getting the best of it. They say the victory of the British at Hill 60 was nothing to the immense advantage the Germans have gained the last few days. They are making a second desperate fight for Calais, are pouring in thousands of troops through Belgium, & are using asphyxiating bombs—another international law broken. All the Allies have fallen back. If this is to go on it seems the war must be interminable. Even the papers admit a decisive victory to the enemy so it must be a tremendous one. Surely, surely it is a worthy ideal—to fight that you may save your country's freedom from falling into the hands of this terrible & ruthless foe! It is awful to think that the very progress of civilization has made this war what it is—particularly intellectual progress, without a corresponding moral progress. Just to think that we have got to the stage of motors, aeroplanes, telephone & 17 inch shells, & yet have not passed the stage of killing one another.

At the end of your letter you seem to imply that you think I meant a kind of faint reproach when I spoke of a barrier between us. I meant nothing of the sort; no one could realise more clearly than I that for everything to be left off—I pray temporarily—in the middle was hard, but better so. Of course I know that reverence & reserve are incomplete without one another—before I met you I have let people know how they appeared to me because they seemed to imagine it was unnecessary to use more than a very slight amount of either one or the other. These qualities have a very strong influence in me, & for that very reason their presence in you is the last thing I could wish removed. But what you call sacrilege is only sacrilege when it comes too soon—at the right time it is the culminating point of the very reverence we both admire. My letter was a passionate regret aroused by the emotion in yours; not however a regret because anything we did ought to have been done differently, but because the progress of a very precious thing has to stop awhile with its culminating point still unreached. It is not unnatural surely to know a thing is right & yet regret that it has to be.

You speak of 'anticipation'—it is very sweet to think that such a thing may be again, & that you in spite of everything have hope enough to look forward. Now you are in the midst of it all, do you still feel you will come through to the end? I always am thinking how you said 'I am coming back,' & that one day our dreams will come true.

Roland to Edward Brittain (Vera's Brother)

Flanders, 27 April 1915

Am writing this in the trenches somewhere in Flanders, sitting on a plank outside a dug-out. There is nothing much doing at present, it being just after lunch when the snipers usually cease from sniping and our gunners have not yet begun to drop their afternoon shells into the German trenches. The latter are anything from 50 to 250 yards away at this part of the line. We are holding the front edge of a wood—a wood very famous in the history of the war—and our support and reserve trenches are hidden away inside. Half of my platoon is in the fire trench and half back in the second line. I have spent the morning in building a new traverse, and at present what with being very tired and sitting in a July sun I am feeling almost too sleepy to write. I didn't go to bed at all last night but went out instead with an R. E. [Royal Engineers] Captain to inspect wire entanglements etc. in front of our position (and incidentally nearly came to a bad end by being mistaken for Germans and fired at by one of our own men. Luckily the damned fool was in too much of a funk to fire straight!) Nearly everything in the way of work is done at night-time and we rest during the day. We have 4 days in and 4 days in billets a mile or so back. We came in on Sunday night and are due to go out again the day after tomorrow. Our position here is very strong, and in consequence life tends to become somewhat monotonous in time. The snipers are a chronic nuisance, but we do not get shelled very often, which is a distinct advantage. We have been here 10 days and have had only 1 killed and 6 wounded (none seriously). Armstrong got a bullet through his left wrist & has been sent home—lucky devil! They have stopped all leave other than sick leave now, so that I may be stuck out here for an indefinite period. As far as I can see, the war may last another two years if it goes on at the same rate as at present.

I seem to have kept you in disgraceful ignorance of my movements lately. Folkestone, Boulogne, Cassel, Steenwerek, Armentières, and —— are my meanderings to date, and we seem stuck where we are now until this part of the line advances. It is all very interesting here and I am enjoying it immensely. My only fear is that, being a rolling stone, I may find it monotonous in time if we stay here always on the same job.

When are you coming out to join me? In time for us to go down Unter den Linden arm in arm?

Let me know any news of Tar [Victor Richardson] if you can. He hasn't answered my last letter.

Roland to Vera

Flanders, 29 April 1915

I never remember having written a letter at this time of the morning before. It is just after dawn and everything is very still. From where I am sitting I can see the sun on the clover field just behind the trenches and a stretch of white road beyond. There are birds singing in the wood on our left, and small curls of blue wood-smoke from the men's fires climbing up through the trees. One of our Machine Guns has been firing single shots every few minutes with a cold and lazy regularity that seems singularly in harmony. Everyone else except the sentries is asleep.

I am the officer on duty from 3.30 a.m. till 8.0 a.m., when I shall go to sleep again until about half past ten. Meanwhile I have to keep awake, walk up and down the line every hour to visit all the sentries, and give any orders that may be necessary. As a matter of fact we are usually awake most of the night and go to sleep at odd times during the day. When you are never allowed to take your clothes off, it ceases to be any trouble to go to bed, or to get up.

We have left our trenches in the wood, and have been since 6 p.m. last night holding another piece of the line about a mile and a half further to the South. We came at a few hours' notice to relieve a Regular Brigade which is being sent on to Hill 60. These are more the conventional type of trenches here—one long ditch, as it were, with a high sandbag parapet and dug-outs in the front wall. There is much less room of course than when there was a large wood behind to walk about in. Also, there are no primroses or violets here, but only sandbags and boarding and yellow slag. Which is perhaps as it should be.

7.30 a.m.

Have just come back from my rounds. A French biplane went up a few minutes ago and is circling round and round over the German lines. They have got two anti-aircraft guns and a Maxim trying to hit him. It is a marvelous sight. Every minute there is a muffled report like the pop of a drawn cork magnified, and a fluffy ball of cotton wool appears suddenly in the air beside him. He is turning again now, the white balls floating all around him. You think how pretty it all is—white bird, white puffs of smoke, and the brilliant blue of the sky. It is hard to realise that there is danger up there, and daring, and the calculating courage that is true heroism.

. . . He is out of range now.

Midday

I have just read your letter, written on the 25th. I cannot answer it now—not as I should like. For one thing I have a lot of men's letters to censor before the post goes—prosaic and unimaginative most of them, but a few make me feel like a Father Confessor, and also two other officers are sitting by me chattering inanities. I will write again this evening, or tomorrow morning early, when I can do so alone.

I am taking care of myself as much as I can, and don't put my head over the parapet. Only yesterday a man in the regiment we relieved was shot through the head through doing that. He died while being carried out. An officer who saw it happen gave me some gruesome details which I will not repeat. All I myself saw were the splashes of blood all the way along the plank flooring of the trench down which they carried him. It was his own fault, though, poor devil.

Roland to Vera

Flanders, 1–3 May 1915

Yesterday we got rushed off suddenly to occupy a line of support trenches, and had to stay in them till 3.30 a.m. this morning. We are to hold them again this evening, I believe; which, with nothing more inspiring to do than sit still in the rain for the most part of the night, does not sound inviting. Still, at the worst it is good practice, and you can listen to the undulating roar of a distant artillery bombardment from the direction of Ypres not with equanimity but with a certain tremulous gratitude that it is no nearer. Someone is getting hell, but it isn't you—yet.

This morning I took a digging party of 50 men about 2 miles the other side of our wood (we are not actually in it any longer, but we keep in the neighbourhood). They had to deepen a support trench on the slope of a hill behind our line. We were out of range of rifle fire but all the buildings near had suffered badly from the shells. It was a glorious morning and from where we were on the hill we could see the country for miles around. It looked rather like the clear cut landscape in a child's painting book. The basis was deep green with an occasional flame-coloured patch in the valley where a red-roofed farm house had escaped the guns. Just below the horizon and again immediately at our feet was a brilliant yellow mustard field. I left the men digging and went to look at some of the houses near. All the windows were without glass and the rooms a mass of debris—bricks, tiles, plaster, rafters, a picture or two, and even clothing buried among the rest. There were shell holes through most of the walls and often no walls at all. One large château had been left with only the outside walls standing at all. I enclose a rather pathetic souvenir that I found among the rubbish in the ruins of one of the rooms— some pages from a child's exercise book. Soon after I came back to the trench a German howitzer battery that had caught sight of us sent over 38 3.5" shells, which fortuitously hit nearby, though they were all within thirty or forty yards of us. Luckily you can always hear this sort coming and we had time to crouch down in the bottom of the trench, which is the safest place in these circumstances. When the shell hits the ground it makes a circular depression like a pudding basin about a yard and a half across by 18 inches deep, burying itself deep down at the bottom. The explosion blows a cloud of earth and splinters of shell into the air, so that when they fire a salvo (all four guns together) the effect is rather terrifying and you wonder if the next one will come a yard or two nearer and burst right in the trench on top of you. I do not mind rifle fire so much, but to be under heavy shell fire is a most nerve-racking job.

Vera to Roland

Oxford, 1 May 1915

I was up at 3.45 this morning for the famous May Morning ceremony . . . as the clock struck four all the people turned towards the tower & became absolutely silent. Then immediately after, as the sun was rising, the choristers on the top of Magdalen tower sang the May Morning Latin hymn, turning towards the sun. . . . I could quite easily have wept at the beauty & pain of it. I couldn't help thinking how different everything is from what we pictured it would be, & how you had meant to be here, & how you would have loved it if you had been . . .

The battle in the Ypres district seems altogether rather a sad affair. We have stopped the German advance & the fury of it has died down for the present, but it seems to have cost us a great deal, to get back a few, not nearly all, of the trenches etc. they took from us. The casualty lists are long, especially among Territorial Regiments. They seem to be bearing all the strain that Kitchener's Army was meant for in the spring. The 'Times' is depressing & talks about the war lasting well into next year. It certainly doesn't look like ending soon when the enemy are still capable of such terrific onslaughts. It would be so much easier to work & hope if one hadn't to do it indefinitely. But I suppose it is weak to want things to be easy. When I read your letters & find how you never complain of anything by so much as a word, dear, although I know you shrink from horror & ugliness just as much as I do, I feel I am not being one little bit brave.

I hear Mother is sending you out some socks for your men. I am glad you are giving us some faint idea at last of things you want. I do feel such pleasure in sending them.

Goodbye for the present—very best of love—

V.

P.S. those green envelopes which don't have to be censored are a very pleasing idea. Not that your letters ever suffered much from over—'reserve'! But it makes it easier to write to people, doesn't it, when your letters are not going beneath the eyes of someone intermediate, though impersonal.

Vera to Roland

Oxford, 7 May 1915

It is horrible to think of you under shell fire, & in support trenches. I suppose you really are very near the vast chaos that was Ypres—if not actually in it. I wonder, if all this ever ends—sometimes I feel as if nothing but the end of the world could finish it—& you are still left to us, if you will be very different. I suppose you are bound to be—people, especially those who sensibilities are fine & keen, can't go through this sort of thing & remain the same. Your letters, certainly, don't seem to illustrate you as fundamentally altering, but they do show you to me as becoming very much more all I have known you to be. It seems so characteristic of you to be facing death one moment, & seeing so clearly the beauty of the world, & life, & love, in the next. I am glad my letters arrive so soon after I write them. I like to think of you receiving & reading them, & wonder what you feel when you see my writing on the envelope, and if it is anything like I feel when I see yours. Sometimes, in my nightmare moments, I think that perhaps one day he will not read the words meant only for him, into which I have put so much of all that is me . . .

My great object at present is to get this term over. . . . I don't think another term here while the war is in its present condition (and you in yours) would be tolerable. And—if I have to bear still more, it will be in action, not in scholastic seclusion, that I shall have to find the necessary strength—if indeed I could ever find it. . . . This at least I know—that if at any time I have to face the loss of you, dear, nothing I have done before will be possible for a very long time to come. Every letter makes me realise how near you are to that great Fact . . .

Roland to Vera

In the Trenches, Flanders, 9 May 1915
6.30 a.m.

One of my men has just been killed—the first. I have been taking the things out of his pockets and tying them round in his handkerchief to be sent back somewhere to someone who will see more than a torn letter, and a pencil, and a knife and a piece of shell. He was shot through the left temple while firing over the parapet. I did not actually see it—thank Heaven. I only found him lying very still at the bottom of the trench with a tiny stream of red trickling down his cheek onto his coat. He has just been carried away. I cannot help thinking how ridiculous it was that so small a thing should make such a change. He could have walked down the trench himself an hour ago. I was talking to him only a few minutes before . . .

I do not quite know how I felt at the moment. It was not anger (—even now I have no feeling of animosity against the man who shot him—) only a great pity, and a sudden feeling of impotence . . .

It is cruel of me to tell you this. Why should you have the horrors of war brought any nearer to you? And you have more time to think of them than I. At least, try not to remember: as I do.

11 a.m.

A glorious summer day, which helps one to forget many things. Today we have been instructed to 'give a demonstration of frightfulness,' i.e. to make ourselves as generally objectionable as possible. We began at 4.30 a.m. by exploding 1600 lbs. of guncotton under a German trench, and are progressing favourably with the help of machine guns, rifle grenades, and trench mortars. They have been shelling us a little. I hope they will not take to using any of their poisonous gas; although we have just been served out with respirators and goggles as a protection.

I should so like to write you a really long letter as an adequate recompense for letters that help me to live, in an atmosphere where the commonplace is perhaps more a thing to be feared than the terrible. But you will understand.

Vera to Roland

Oxford, 11 May 1915

Last Friday was the sort of day that made one begin to wonder if it was possible for the world to continue—horror piled on horror till by the time night came, I should think the whole of England was full of despair. First one opened the Times & read of Allies' reverses both in Flanders & Galicia, Germans poisoning wells & using gases, war-clouds rising between China & Japan, possible intervention of America on the wrong side, & a long casualty list of about 200 officers. Then at midday I saw on the placards of the ultimatum having been sent to China, & at tea time read that a man I know had been killed in action. As a finale to all this, last thing at night the sinking of the Lusitania was announced with its loss of 1500 lives. It was the sort of day that contained about as much as you would want to think about for a year under ordinary circumstances.

Mrs. Leighton seemed a little anxious because she had not heard from you for some time, but said she supposed we couldn't expect many letters now you were in the thick of the actual fighting, as she thinks you are.

Tell me honestly, are you? It won't make it any easier, dear, if you try not to let me know. Are you anywhere near the gas area? I suppose the Censor will allow you to tell me this. He has never objected to anything you have put so far. I suppose we are now in the midst of just what has been prophesied for the Spring all along. How much darker, I wonder, will it have to get before the dawn comes? At any rate it gives one practice in how to suffer & steel one's self against shocks,—if that is any comfort.

I hear that when Edward goes out it will almost certainly be to the Dardanelles. I hope it may not be soon. I wish he had not to go there, as it takes so long for news & letters to come. It must be terribly hot too, & I believe is much stricken with smallpox & cholera—though of course it has not as yet the accumulation of war horrors that there is in Flanders . . .

I approached the Principal here the other day on the subject of provisional notice for a year—in case of Red Cross work. She told me I needn't take any steps at all with regard to college until 3 months before the beginning of next term, which means about the middle of July. I hope by that time enough will have happened to clear up my indecision.

Edward to Vera

Maidstone, 13 May 1915

We came here on Sunday and go to Wrotham by train every morning—10 miles away—march up a hill for about 4 miles and dig trenches which are almost an improvement on those at the front. The country up there is more beautiful than any inland country I have met with in England and the trenches extend or will do when completely finished for 90 miles. . . . It is awfully boring for the officers having to watch the men dig and to measure as they go long; occasionally I dig myself but am not really allowed to, as we are supposed to superintend. We are only here for a fortnight, then I think back to Sandgate for a fortnight and then to a camp near Guildford. We are still very short of rifles and I don't know when we shall go out; it is quite likely that we shall go to the Dardanelles. I want to transfer to the Field Artillery but it is very difficult.

Roland to Edward

Flanders, 13 May 1915

Dear Edward,

I was so glad to get your letter—a very charming one, may I say, if tinged with ennui somewhat and more still with the 'lacrimae rerum' . . . I needn't tell you how much I should like you to be over here after all for many reasons. But I don't know about the Artillery. They say that it takes 5 years to make a gunner, but that's all balls. When you first mentioned it I thought that you'd probably get out quicker where you are, but I've been talking to one or two Artillery officers about it and they are more hopeful. The Regular R.F.A. [Royal Field Artillery] is the thing to get into, I gather. They are hard up for officers in the Regulars now and will allow Territorials (and Kitchener's Army too, I suppose) to transfer if recommended by a Brigadier or great nut and able to pass the Medical Exam. . . . Anyhow it's worth trying, and the Gunners have a topping time over here compared to a damned footslogger. Of course when they do get it they get it Hell—Germans rushing on towards the gun 100 yds away, and your horses half mad, and the trees broken, and two men and a boy left out of your battery to get away with. I was talking to a Canadian Artillery Officer yesterday who was in that recent show at St Julien near Ypres, and they seem to have had perfect Hades.

I don't quite know how you are to manage to work your transfer, though. You won't be able to do it by going straight at it—at least, I think not. As one who has had many experiences, and many disappointments, and ultimate success, in trying to get round Red Tape and Army Orders I can only advise you to get hold of somebody at Whitehall or elsewhere who actually knows of a job for you. It is absolutely useless writing to the War Office: practically useless writing to an individual unless he knows you already. . . . Of course I am in a way at the wrong end of the string here, inasmuch as you will need some training in England first. But I might come across an opening in the Infantry somewhere . . .

Personally I am going on much as usual—alternately about 4 or 5 days in the trenches & 4 days rest in billets. Nothing much doing where we are. On Sunday we had a Divisional order to be 'frightful' to distract the attention of our friends opposite from what the French were up to further to the South. We began at 4.0 a.m. by exploding 1600 lbs. of guncotton under part of their trench, & continued at intervals with rapid fire, Machine Guns, trench howitzers, rifle grenades, artillery shelling etc. until evening. There was a devil of a noise but nothing much else, and beyond knocking down a bit of parapet and barely missing my dug-out with a diminutive shell of sorts they seemed quite docile about it.

To me this war seems still to be a long job & in a sense only just beginning. The French have been doing remarkably well, though, these last two or three days. Someone will have to get a move on soon; I don't look forward to stopping where we are during the hot weather. The whole country is a muck-heap. (E.g. three days ago while digging a machine gun emplacement just to the front of my bit of trench we had to cut through 3 dead bodies to get there.)

Perhaps everything will end suddenly. Qui sait? As far as I can see there is still a large percentage of the English population that hasn't yet realised that there's a war on at all.

However—

I was very pleased to hear both from you & from the Old Block himself that he is getting on so well now. I suppose the Royal Sussex will not see him again, will they? I wish I could have seen him before I came away. So you think you may be amused—again? (Why again?) Tar the confirmed bachelor and a hospital nurse! Well, after all—yes, it is all very amusing. Et tu, Brute?

Vera to Roland

Oxford, 13 May 1915

Your letter written on the 9th arrived this morning. Do my letters really help you to live? I wish they could do more & ensure your life. Your description of that man's death made me feel a little as you say you did when you saw him lying dead . . .

Why was it cruel of you to tell me about it? It would be much more cruel if you didn't, when I asked you to. I should feel very hurt indeed if you were to try to shield me from things, instead of letting me share them, and I am ready to do. I wouldn't think of denying that horror & death & war are terrible things & made me suffer too, but there is something which even while it is impotent is yet stronger than they; & claims your frankness. It is easier to say 'forget' than to do so, but I would rather be unable to forget than be given nothing to remember. Perhaps when it is all over & the beautiful things in life come back, it may be possible to forget the sorrows they replace. But till then—I will be satisfied if I am called upon to remember.

Even if it is making us both very sad, that is all we can expect at present. I always think of the sorrow I saw in the face of the little private I met at the Hospital, who had been in Neuve Chapelle, & wonder, if ever I see you again, if you will wear that kind of look. Your expression was sad & serious enough before, too; as if you felt the griefs and responsibilities of the world more than most people. Perhaps you did—& do. I am glad you sent your private's few belongings home. It was like you to think of that. War seems either to make people quite callous, or more sensitive. I would rather you were one of the latter, though I suppose it makes it harder for you—now.

I see by the casualty list to-day that a Major Dore of your regiment has been wounded. Is that a result of your outburst of frightfulness? And do such instructions portend a taking of the offensive?

You never seem to go into billets now or to get any sleep. Do you have to stay in the trenches all the time, & aren't there enough people for you to exchange with? . . . I keep reading names in the paper where trenches have been lost or re-taken & wonder if that is where you are. I found an excellent map of Ypres & district (about 20 mile radius) in the Times. It is now on my wall & I look up all the names.

I notice in your last two or three letters you have seemed a little distressed because you think my letters are more frequent than yours. Please don't be. I wish I could make you realise how unspeakably precious your letters are, & then you would know that you don't need to apologise for their shortness. You don't want me, do you, to deprive myself of the joy of writing as much as I do, just because you can't answer as often, or to the same extent?

If I have more time to think, I also have more time to write—which just now is better than thinking. And when you tell me my letters help you to live, I mean to write more & more. . . . I know you think—so much—even when you can't write, & that you do write as often as you are able,—and there is nothing better I would ask. Sometimes I rather suspect you write to me when you are tired out with work & want to sleep, when a little rest would do you much more good than writing to me. I don't like to think you do that. It is for me a great deal you must take care of yourself.

Is the commonplace more to be feared than the terrible even in Flanders? It certainly is here. One rises to the occasion when a sudden call is made upon one's endurance; it is the long long hours of suspense & depression that lie on one's mind as a kind of dull heaviness & at times make one nearly mad. That is another reason why you mustn't shrink from telling me the dreadful things you yourself experience; I can bear them better than the burden of every day.

I have just had a letter from one of my great friends at school, whose brother, who is in the Buffs, was wounded near St Julien on the 3rd & is now in hospital in London. There are only 3 officers, including him, left of his battalion & only 159 men out of 5000. North of Ypres must indeed have been hell. This man hadn't slept or had his clothes off for 24 days before being wounded. They had to hold their trenches while under shell fire without a single gun to help them, and watched the Germans forming to attack them without being able to do anything. Their trenches were taken & as he was lying wounded he saw the Germans bayoneting his men & several of his friends, who were wounded. . . . He is a very nice boy; I wonder how he will be affected by this awful experience. He also got a whiff of the poisonous gas, & says it half blinded & made him sick for hours. I do hope, whatever else happens to you, you won't have to suffer from that. It is such an unsporting & diabolical method of warfare. I suppose we shall have to stoop to the same methods if nothing else will stop them. Is there any antidote at all to the poison? . . .

I do hate to think of you seeing that man dead, & feeling as you must have felt about it. I think I would rather it had been me that had seen it & felt it. You are after all so inappropriately placed in your present surroundings—& yet so splendid. I should love to see you in the trenches looking thoroughly dirty & untidy, since I have only been permitted so far a vision of absolute immaculateness. I wonder if I should even recognise you. It is an aggravation to me that though I can often visualise the faces of perfectly uninteresting people whom I don't care for at all, I can never quite see yours in my imagination. But one more look—if only . . .

Goodbye again, & ever so much love—

V.

Vera to Edward

1st London General Hospital, 15 June 1916
We have suddenly become very busy here, and are expecting still more large convoys. In consequence all leave has been stopped until further notice—a thing which has never happened while I have been here, busy as we have sometimes been. So it is very lucky you came when you did, as I certainly should have got no leave now. Our own ward is quite full—chiefly with Canadians. Even off-duty times are apt to get curtailed; one is even liable to miss them altogether. Some of our cases are very bad indeed and we are in for a busy morning to-morrow with six operations.

Edward to Vera

France, 26 June 1916

Dearest Vera,

The papers are getting rather more interesting, but I have only time to say adieu.

EHB

Vera to Edward

1st London General, 28 June 1916

I believe I heard the guns here a day or two ago. What a clamour must be going on! One anxiety is more than enough; & sometimes I feel quite glad that Roland is lying where the guns cannot disturb Him however loudly they are & He cannot any more hear the noise they make.

Vera to Edith Brittain (Her Mother)

1st London General, 1 July 1916

The news in the paper—which was got at 4.0 this afternoon—is quite self-evident, so I needn't say more about it. London was wildly excited & the papers welling madly. Of course you remember that Edward is at Albert & it is all around there that the papers say the fighting is fiercest—Montaubon—Fricourt—Mametz—I have been expecting this for days as when he was here he told me that the Great Offensive was to begin there & of the part his own regiment had to play in the attack . . . please be sure to wire to me at once anything you may hear about him—don't think you could tell me better in a letter whatever it is. Naturally I am very anxious indeed & I want to know anything you may hear as soon as you hear it. In great haste.

Editor's Note: Early on the morning of 1 July 1916, Edward led the first wave of the attack of his company in the great British offensive that was to go down in history as one of the most terrible days of slaughter in the annals of the British Army; the first day of the Battle of the Somme. While his company was waiting to go over, the wounded from an earlier part of the attack began to crowd into the trenches. Then part of the regiment in front began to retreat, throwing Edward's men into a panic. He had to return to the trenches twice to exhort them to follow him over the parapet. About ninety yards along No-Man's-Land, Edward was hit by a bullet through his thigh. He fell down and crawled into a shell hole. Soon afterwards a shell burst close to him and a splinter from it went through his left arm. The pain was so great that for the first time he lost his nerve and cried out. After about an hour and a half, he noticed that the machine-gun fire was slackening, and started a horrifying crawl back through the dead and wounded to the safety of the British trenches.

Edward to Vera

France, 1 July 1916

Dear Vera,

I was wounded in the action this morning in left arm and right thigh not seriously. Hope to come to England. Don't worry.

Edward

Victor to Vera

4th Batt. The Royal Sussex Regt., Purfleet, 2 July 1916

Thank you very much for your letter. It is very good of you to say that you enjoy our occasional evenings in Town. I am afraid I must have seemed rather unsympathetic on Monday. I did not mean to be, but it seems to me that I do not understand you as well as I ought. Perhaps some day I shall be less slow and get to know you better. I could tell from one or two things you said the other night that you have summed me up remarkably well . . .

So far the hardest fighting seems to have been North and South of Albert—round Hébuterne and Fricourt—rather than actually opposite Albert itself. You must be finding the suspense too terrible for words—there is nothing on earth so bad as waiting from day to day knowing that the dearest person in the world is in such awful peril. I had a farewell note from Edward on Thursday written on the leaf of a notebook.

'. . . I am so busy that I have only time for material things. And so I must bid you a long long adieu.' By the way this note was written on page 106 of the book: 106 is one of my lucky numbers—my only one as far as I know. Let's hope it is a good omen.

Geoffrey Thurlow to Vera

France, 4 July 1916

Dear Vera,

Please excuse my audacity in addressing you in this way instead of the stiff and formidable alternative 'Miss Brittain'—Mrs. Brittain once said that you had no objection to it—also for me writing, but I've been thinking about you all more than usual lately and know what a trying time you must be having. May Edward be as well looked after as I was out there—thus I can wish him nothing better.

Vera to Edith Brittain

1st London General, 5 July 1916

I hope they will send him to England soon; I expect they will but we hear hundreds, & probably thousands of them, are waiting to come across as there are so many the boats cannot take them quick enough. He might even come to-day as the large number of officers we were expecting yesterday did not arrive . . .

I think we are very lucky, his wounds in those places are not likely to be at all dangerous though they may be painful & long in healing. At any rate he is out of it for some time. . . . It would be funny if he turned up here. I only wish he would. . . . At last I can get a decent night's rest which I haven't had since the battle began although we get so tired.

Editor's Note: By coincidence Edward was sent to the 1st London General. On 5 July, a fellow VAD rushed into Vera's ward to tell her that Edward had been in the convoy of wounded officers who had arrived during the night. After receiving permission from her Matron to visit him, Vera hurried to Edward's bedside. He was struggling to eat breakfast with only one hand, his left arm was stiff and bandaged, but he appeared happy and relieved. Edward would remain in the hospital for three weeks before beginning a prolonged period of convalescent leave.

Vera to Edith Brittain

1st London General, 21 July 1916
[Edward] is leaving the Hospital on Monday as the further treatment he required cannot be obtained here . . . the doctor has promised to get Edward 3 months leave, which is very pleasant, & then of course there will probably be light duty after that. . . . We don't know what to do to get through the work & I often have to go without off-duty times. We have got the Hospital absolutely full to overflowing now, and yesterday we were actually told that somehow or other we have got to find 520 more beds! That will make us nearly 3000; I don't know how we are going to do it, but the orderlies' barrack room is being turned into a ward . . . & every available inch of ground is being covered with tents—tents in the middle of Camberwell . . . our meals get cut short, & we get so tired we don't know where to put ourselves.

Geoffrey to Vera

France, 13 August 1916
Thanks very much for your long letter which I got yesterday by the same post as one from Mrs. Brittain who rather amused me by saying that if she had had a chance of saying goodbye 'it might have included a kiss & in my mind's eye I can see your face!!' Well of all objectionable habits I think kissing is the worst . . .
No! Edward hasn't said anything about his arm, but he wouldn't no matter how bad. I'm awfully sorry to hear about it and only hope it will get well quicker than the usual neuritis which takes a long time doesn't it? Also that he won't have to come out here again.

Edward to Vera

14 Oxford Terrace, London, 24 August 1916
Father . . . brought up with him a letter from France addressed to me which mentions the following:—
    To/ 2Lt. E. H. Brittain
    (regiment etc)

The G.O.C. congratulates you on being awarded the Military Cross by the Commander in Chief.

Vera to Edith Brittain

1st London General, 25 August 1916

Isn't it unspeakably splendid about Edward's Military Cross! And how like him to send you a postcard, when anybody else would have wired; he takes it with the utmost placidity . . . he was wearing it to-day . . . other officers turn round & look at him, & he never appears to notice it. . . . He says he will undoubtedly get promotion now—though what does it matter if you are a 2nd Lieutenant all your days, when you are an M.C.!

Geoffrey to Vera

France, 28 August 1916

A hasty line to thank you for your letter which I got this morning. . . . (This dugout is full of weird insects which descend from the ceiling with a flop and settle on your hair, paper etc.—in fact anywhere) . . .

Well! For many things life is rather delightful here. When you see potatoes & cabbages growing well on the parados it seems singularly out of keeping with the rest. Machine guns are jolly active here at nights. Just outside our Coy HQs are two graves of French soldiers and further down one of a 'soldat allemande.'

. . . Expect Edward would prefer you to go to France wouldn't he? Please don't let him write until he is more or less all right. He said in his last card that in a few days he would write at 'Immense Length.' Well! Much as I'd like that he's not to do it.

(Another insect descends with a flop.)

Yesterday it rained on and off and we got slightly damp.

Just got the news that Roumania has come in on our side which is quite cheery. Please excuse this disjointed note but where I might be Interesting I am forbidden.

Geoffrey to Edward

France, 29 August 1916

I am sitting in a dark dugout, writing this with aid from a guttering candle. My fatigue men have gone away while it rains—Lander just came in to say that it has stopped so I shall have to carry on.

It has just started again so we can go on for a bit. Well! I had only time to send off a p.c. saying how damn glad I am that you've got the Military Cross—always thought you would do something great. If you are well enough I wish you would overcome your innate modesty & let me know all about it—please excuse my inquisitiveness but one likes to know how etc etc. That is one thing I've always longed for & shall long in vain, for I haven't much courage. Yesterday afternoon some whizzbangs arrived about 50 yds away which absolutely put the wind up me. At Ypres we used to watch them going to Hellfire Corner about same distance with almost joy. Still such is life. We shall be moving up shortly & I'm not looking forward to it much as am a bit off colour. Summer is over I think and rain has come. There is another strafe going on to the right a bit. [Enemy airplanes] seem to be getting quite offensive.

It is rather delightful to find cabbage & potatoes growing wild on some parts of parados in front line trenches don't you think?

(Day has arrived from Sappers so must stop once again!)

Much later 6.15.

After Day came our new Padre who stayed a long time so hence this interval. . . . (Really the amount of these little black beetles which flop down from the ceiling is unending.)

There has just arrived a magnificent storm: masses of black clouds, vivid lightning & great rolls of thunder. Nowadays one is reminded of 'So all day long the noise of battle rolled, Among the mountains to the northern sea. etc' When you were here didn't you yearn sometimes to see the sea again. It seems so clean when compared to land. . . . How is Victor Richardson? Please remember me to him when you see him again . . .

Him that thou knowest thine

G.R.Y.T.

P.S. I was asked to Toby's 21st dinner a few days ago & sat next to a perfect twit who insisted on [calling] me 'old darling.'

'Pass the salt will you please, old darling etc etc' in drawled out tones. Really such people shouldn't exist!

Vera to Edith Brittain

1st London General Hospital, 1 September 1916

The two people going on the hospital-ship are off to-morrow; I expect it will be my turn soon. . . . It is quite possible that I may be ordered abroad without being told definitely where I am going—the two who are going on the hospital-ship haven't the least idea where it is going. . . . It would be rather thrilling to arrive somewhere or other at night after a long voyage & say to one another 'Where (literally) in the world is this?'

NOTE

From Alan Bishop and Mark Bostridge, eds., *Letters from a Lost Generation: First World War Letters of Vera Brittain and Four Friends* (Boston: Northeastern University Press, 1999), pp. 86–104 and 263–72.

An English Wife in Berlin

Evelyn Blücher

BERLIN, February 1916.—One daily hears stories which show the weariness of killing on both sides. A youth, just home on leave for the first time, was telling his sister the other day his experience. He had been out since the beginning and had been on every front in turns, but he says his time in Belgium at the very beginning was the most fearful of all, and the franc-tireur's warfare the most ghastly part of it.

One night, when they were just settling down to sleep after a hard day's march, they were ordered out to take a village where the inhabitants were supposed to have been shooting on the troops. No very definite inquiries were made as to the truth of these statements, but for safety's sake it was thought best to burn the village. And so these young officers were given the order to march into it in the middle of the night, and to kill every one they met in a house with a light in the window. In the first house which he entered with his men they met a woman coming down the stairs. They had to carry out their orders, and killed this woman, and so on throughout. Next morning a hundred men were brought out, and the order was to stand them against the village walls and shoot every tenth man.

The wives, the mothers, all the women of the village were there imploring mercy, but no mercy was allowed to be shown. These men, who were not even permitted to be blindfolded, were shot before the eyes of their womenfolk.

And this boy returns to his family to "enjoy" his few days' leave, and his family are disappointed that he does not seem to enjoy it, that he seems preoccupied, that the things that used to amuse him now no longer seem to interest him.

BERLIN, March 5, 1916.—Here we are in March, and in ordinary times we should be rejoicing that winter is nearly over and spring coming, but now one feels nothing but dread, for it means that the armies will come out of their winter quarters and slaughter will begin once more.

March 2 has become a real nightmare with me, it being the date of the opening of the new submarine campaign. The description I have heard of the large German submarines makes me tremble. So confident are the Germans of their success that they say they can even bear the brunt of battle with America, for they are strong enough to cross the ocean and return in safety. Many are even hoping for war with America, so that they need exercise no consideration, but torpedo every single thing on the sea without discrimination or warning. Shocks are in store for us all, I fear. One cannot pretend indifference.

Verdun is the chief subject of interest at present, and in Germany it is now looked upon as likely to be one of the decisive victories of the war. They say it is only a matter of a few days before the whole fortress is taken, and that the terrific losses among the French fill even them with horror. Whereas on the other hand one reads in the English papers "that the Verdun attack has been a failure."

Ossip Schubin the novelist (she is a Bohemian, with all the Bohemian hatred of the Germans and Hungarians) told me a terrible story. Some Bohemian soldiers were ordered to enter a Serbian village and shoot all the inhabitants, including the women and children. They tried to refuse, but a second detachment was called up to urge them on at the point of the bayonet. The lieutenant who had to carry out this order went out of his mind at the horror of it. The soldiers then turned on the captain and shot him, saying, "Do your dirty work yourself."

That reminds me of another episode, equally horrible. There are a number of Austrian Serbians, that is to say, Serbs who have become Austrians by migrating into Croatian territory. Now, as Austrian subjects, they have been called upon to fight against their own race. One day, in a house where they were quartered, they assembled in a room—sixteen of them—to discuss the matter. An Austrian heard them say that it was a hard job for them, and the sixteen were shot to a man! . . . Is this not the reign of terror?

Mr. Dresel, an American friend of mine, has been to visit the Bavarian prison camps, and tells me that the prisoners are much better off now than at first. One commandant told him that he knew how well the German prisoners were being treated in England, and so they were trying to do the same here.

I feel very proud, because he told me that all the officers asked after me and sent me messages. There is quite an amount of freedom allowed them. They go into the town and to a gymnasium there, and the German and English officers have grown quite friendly towards one another and say it is about time both countries made concessions. I asked him if he had been allowed to see them alone, and he told me there were now new rules permitting them to go for a walk with any of them singly if they wish.

He had gone out with one or two, "but," he said, "you know what the English are; it is a long time before you can get an Englishman's confidence. If you do get it, you get it for ever, but they are reticent and dignified. You can't get an Englishman to complain!"

It is good to hear that, isn't it? It isn't that I don't know it, but I love people to tell it to me. Mr. Dresel told me he noticed a new class of men getting into the English army now—rankers that have risen.

We lunched at Count Moltke's yesterday. He is the Danish Minister. The Jacksons were there and several other Americans; we were about thirty in all. The tension between Germany and America is so great now that no one dared venture on the subject at all, even at a so-called neutral party like this.

BERLIN, March 10, 1916.—There is great political news this week. Admiral Tirpitz is going—he has sent in his resignation and it has been accepted. Out of all the obscu-

rity one thing appears to be certain, viz. that there are two parties, one headed by Tirpitz and his friends, the other apparently by Bethmann-Hollweg and the emperor. I
want the Emperor to get his due in this matter at least. He has long been against these
very drastic measures, and does all he can, it seems to me, to prevent any avoidable
cruelty. Now too it is distinctly difficult for him, and many say he is actually jeopar-
dizing his throne; for Tirpitz has Bülow with him, and they are both strong men with
many friends. Of course Tirpitz is being regretted by every one officially, as he is
looked on as the maker of the German fleet and the creator of the modern submarine,
which he has always regarded as the only effective weapon for modern naval warfare.

The military and naval authorities are furious with the Foreign Office, and call
them half-hearted; but their reply is that one must take into account the position of
Germany after the war. The Foreign Office also says that submarine warfare has not
been a success from the beginning, and that England was not in the least on the way
to being "starved out" after the first submarine blockade. To accomplish this they
would have needed at least 200 submarines, sufficient to form a chain round England;
and then if England had invented something to break the chain, as she has actually
done, the enormous expense and sacrifice would all have been in vain.

I think a good deal of the Foreign Office. They seem to me to be smoothing things
down, and will do much towards a better understanding between Germany and other
peoples. As for Tirpitz, they say his fury is indescribable. They gave out as the reason
for his retirement that he had broken down and needed rest; so he walked with his
wife up and down the Wilhelm Strasse for two hours to prove to the crowd that it was
not true, but that he was in the best of health. The next day he appeared in tall hat
and frock coat, to show that he had been "deprived of his uniform" (or rather to let
the people think he had), and talked to his wife in a loud voice so that the crowd
should be able to hear, and even addressed them. If this is true it points to trouble. It
is a little as though Tirpitz and Bülow were trying to threaten the Emperor.

I hear that the Emperor went to Verdun to see how things were going, and saw a
whole company of men blown up by a French mine. The sight was so terrible that he
had a nervous shock and has been ill since.

We met old Zeppelin at a party the other night. He looks a dear old man. They say
he flies over Munich and drops flowers on to the heads of the people below! A lady
said she would not relish bombs dropped instead of flowers. "Oh," said Zeppelin, "I
am sure I wish I could always drop flowers."

BERLIN, March 12, 1916,—There is great excitement here to-day about the *Möve*, and
the Commander, Count Dohna, whom we know well, has just arrived back and is
staying at this hotel.

He is much fêted, he has received the "pour le mérite," and looks splendid, just like
an English officer. It is interesting to watch how proud they all are of him, from the
lift boy upwards!

Both the steamers that conveyed Prince Salm home—the *Malojah* and the *Meck-
lenburg*—have been sunk by him. One took the Prince to Tilbury and the other to
Holland. No wonder Prince Salm noticed that all the men had life-belts slung over
their shoulders!

Some one came in to-day and told me that there is a so-called "cripple brigade" near Verdun. Men that have lost a finger, or who are disfigured but able-bodied, are used at the front again for odd jobs of one kind or another. This "cripple brigade" had the sad task of burying 4000 corpses outside Verdun! Some of them go out with the feeling that as they are not much more use, they may as well be shot dead out there. Poor fellows, it is so tragic!

BERLIN, March 14, 1916.—I have been in bed with what people say is influenza, but I feel inclined to call it "Ersatz" illness. Everyone is feeling ill from too many chemicals in the hotel food. I don't believe that Germany will ever be starved out, but she will be poisoned out first with these substitutes!

Just as I write this, some one comes in from household shopping, a thing I never have to do, being in a hotel. She looks quite unhappy, and says that really England is succeeding, as food is getting so dreadfully scarce. Her butcher told her that he is seriously thinking of closing down. She could get no potatoes, no sugar even. The shopkeepers told her that the soldiers don't get meat more than three times a week now, and even vegetables are scarce!

Then again one hears that so much is due to over-organization. The "Magistrat" forbids the selling of butter, sugar, etc., until all has been bought up and distributed equally and justly. In the meantime masses of butter and other stuffs get spoilt. So, they say, the Bolle dairy gave their butter to a big soap factory for the making of soap, as the butter had got bad through lying by so long, and in this way it was not entirely wasted. And potatoes and such-like lie by waiting to be bought up, and the poor clamour for food. It is all terrible, and what it is going to lead to no one knows.

My husband has just returned from a journey to Vienna. He stayed there a week and saw the "whole of Austria," so to say, in that short time. The chief topic there, he told me, is the hatred of Italy—the smart thing is to go to the Italian Front. The hatred of Russia is not great enough to call forth any enthusiasm on that side.

The other topic is criticism of their ally—Germany. There does not seem to be any love lost between those two allies, and they say that Turkey too is getting restive and tired of the whole thing. Erzerum was a very hard blow to the Turks, and they do not appreciate being left to their own resources. This I heard from the former Turkish Ambassadress, who lives here.

Prince Ernst Günther (Duke of Schleswig-Holstein and brother to the Empress) sat next to me at dinner the other night—we were dining with Count and Countess Colloredo. He told me of his experiences at the Western Front. It was he who picked up Captain Ivan Hay and drove him in his car to his destination, a prison camp. They could not help laughing at the fact that, had there been no war, they would have met that very month shooting in Silesia, as guests of Prince Pless.

He just missed seeing the Duchess of Sutherland when she was nursing in Brussels. He said they were very old friends, and he would have liked to see her in her capacity of nurse. He gave directions for her to receive special treatment and every possible attention, but did not know if these orders had been carried out.

Once, to, he nearly came face to face with his cousin and great friend, Count Gle-ichen, a relation through the Hohenlohes. They were in command on opposite sides and quite a few miles within sight of each other.

Poor Prince Ernst Günther spoke so sadly of all the friendships with his relations in England being cut off. He said: "One feels it, when those whom one has looked upon as intimate friends speak openly of their hatred of one's relations. How could Lord Charles Beresford say of my brother-in-law: 'The head of the assassin, William the Kaiser, should be hung from the highest tree in Potsdam as just retribution for all his cold-blooded murders'? Do you think in your heart that a man like Lord Charles really and truly believes that the Emperor is personally responsible? I can understand the people still thinking that kings are all-powerful, but surely no one else does."

I murmured some inane reply, for what could I say? But I should have loved to quote the words my husband used some days ago: "All governments nowadays are pacifists naturally, but frightened of their own peoples. Monarchs and governments are literally shaking in their shoes for fear of what the people will do, who have been called upon to make such superhuman sacrifices. The Emperor is the only monarch who did assert his authority, even until half-way through the war, though even he cannot do so any longer; but as he was the only one who ever could do so he is now blamed for all."

By the way, it was amusing to see Prince Ernst Günther take his "bread card" from his pocket and put it on the table beside him. It showed how deeply what the French call the "discipline de l'appétit" has sunk into the heart of the nation!

BERLIN, March 1916.—Here are some extracts from a private document, supposed to be a true account of the state of England and English feeling at the time (January 1916), compiled by a so-called neutral, but in reality a German, who obtained a pass-port and went over to England for the purpose.

His foremost impression was that it is the people who are now keeping on the war, in spite of the Government being fully ripe for peace overtures. The latter have lost control of the nation, and are simply tools in their hands.

Goethe's well-known verse:

Die Geister die du riefest, die wirst du nicht mehr los (You will never again be free from the spirits that you call), may be aptly applied here.

Lord Derby is the hero of the hour, his working of the conscription question hav-ing made a great impression for the time being. They say he was very sceptical himself at first as to the results.

Sir Edward Grey, like so many of the responsible men in the history of the war, is not strong enough to face the stern and immeasurable actualities which now confront him. Some say he is only a puppet moved by stronger and more unscrupulous wills. He is said to believe in the possibility of an eventual understanding with Germany, al-though here he is almost the most unpopular Englishman alive.

His position is growing more and more untenable, as the people are in such a state of inimical excitement that anything smacking of leniency towards Germany is looked upon as un-English and treacherous.

A parallel might be drawn between his case and that of Bethmann-Hollweg here in Germany, who is being almost as impatiently and thoughtlessly criticized as Grey in England.

The Cabinet of twenty-two seems to be the object of an increasing dislike and aversion on the part of the people, who are expressing their opinions more forcibly and less refinedly every day. "You have led us into the mess, now pull us out again!" I can imagine how gladly the "22" would pull them out if they only knew how. It certainly is easier to get stuck in the mire than to get out of it again.

Lord Kitchener, the "butcher of Omdurman," as he is usually called here, has lost prestige on both sides of the North Sea. Those small affairs which he was formerly engaged in must have been like playing at war compared to this world conflict.

The pacifists, it is said, meet with small regard on the part of the people, and tend more to excite the belligerent instincts of the "great unwashed" than to pacify them. I could imagine that open-air meetings of the pacifists, systematically arranged all over England, would be the best means possible for winning over the people, including "conscientious objectors," to accept compulsory service.

John Bull, reborn as St. George, radiant and beautiful in shining armour, goes out to destroy the venomous dragon of "German militarism" by force of arms, and one of the hugest jokes of history is exhibited to the astonished world!

The names of Sir Aldyn (sic), Morley, Bryce, as well as McIver, Middleton, Lorebourne (sic), Aberdeen, Gladstone, Beecham (sic), and Charles Mosterman (sic), are mentioned as leaders in the pacifist movement!

The most popular figure, says the report, is Lloyd George, the munition-man, who has donned the mask of a ferocious man of war, haranguing the masses, and assiduously providing food for the iron beasts of war, all for the sake of his own private ambitions.

Bonar Law is described as being a connecting link between the fanatical Unionists, who are clamouring for a general election, and the much harried Parliament, who, in their reverential awe of themselves as divine instruments for working out England's salvation, are still glad enough to cling to his strong personality, as a middleman in the dizzy whirl of events.

Will there be a general election or not? is said to be the burning question of the day. Should a new Government come in, we may expect the war to last another twenty years, which may the gods forbid.

I have heard the reason why such a huge number of unwounded prisoners were taken at Verdun. It was because they were rendered senseless by a new gas bomb invention. I was pleased at what seemed to me quite a humane use of this terrible gas, but I was soon disillusioned. I was told that the same thing had been done a little while before with 700 men, but a day later only 100 were still alive; the 600 had died from the after-effects of this gas—their lungs had shriveled up and prevented breathing, so suffocation had set in and killed them!

The people continue to be very restless; I hear that in other towns they have resorted to energetic measures for getting more food. In Cologne the mayor had to unlock the market twice in the middle of the night; once they hung a dead cat before his door, with the eyes gouged out, and an intimation that that would be his fate if he did not look after the people better. They also tried to mob the Town Council when sitting. The peasants now jeer at the town-breds, who have to spread their bread with *Kunsthonig* (artificial honey), while they, the peasants, have a thick layer of their own butter and a slab of ham on top!

My sister-in-law in Bonn gives a description of disturbances much in the style of those in Cologne. She says: "Yesterday there was a fearful mob and a fight in the Rathausstrasse for lard. It was the day for waiting outside the stores for this article; the town provides it for the people on certain days, and who arrives first is first served. A carriage with rich people in it drove up, and the inmates were served before the others, which caused a riot. The policemen had to use their swords, for the crowd nearly lynched them. The mob broke the windows of the police station."

BERLIN, April 1916.—Last night we dined at Baron von Jagow's and met the Dutch Minister and his wife, M. and Mme. Gevers.

As a change from the everlasting American crisis, which is becoming monotonous, a Dutch crisis had just sprung up; so it behoved us to avoid politics, and we crept delicately round the thin ice of the dangerous topics which were on the tip of our tongues.

It seems that England has just been proved to have sunk a Dutch merchantman, and is adopting a somewhat threatening attitude towards the neutrality of Holland; which is all very well in its way, but a Dutch neutrality in favour of England would be so very much better, seen through insular spectacles.

We were again struck by the difference between England's and Germany's diplomacy. If Germany happens to sink a ship, protected by American guardian-angels, the whole world knows of it at once, and the inevitable crisis springs up. If England, on the contrary, sinks a ship belonging to one of the long-suffering neutrals, by mistake, the matter is hushed up at once, and only some obscure notice of it appears in a list of shipping casualties, and the regrettable accident is lost to sight.

English diplomacy is certainly marvelous. The Germans call it by other names sometimes, not very nice ones, but would give a good deal if they themselves could catch the knack of it.

The practical, hard, matter-of-fact "uprightness" and "downrightness" of the Prussian character in general misses those finer lights and shades of what is generally known as tactfulness, and in its exaggerated from often leads to the virtue (or vice, as you take it) of a somewhat blundering form of diplomacy since the giant Bismarck resigned his post of steering the ship of Germany through the stormy seas of history.

A few days later we lunched with Dr. Solf, the Colonial Minister. Herr von Zimmermann, the Under Secretary of State, was there too. The policy of these two men is to refrain from taking any part in the war of abuse carried on by the Press against England, in wise forethought of the critical colonial question for Germany in the future.

Dr. Solf is one of those clear-seeing men who understand how complicated every phase of the struggle becomes through the vindictive vituperation of the Press. For this reason he is himself very much abused by certain members of the military party. For men like Kessler and Falkenhayn the sword is the only solution possible, and all methods of a milder nature are regarded as signs of effeminate weakness. A friend told me that the Kaiser is practically kept under supervision by men like Falkenhayn, who never allows any one to speak to him alone, he always being present at every audience. Prince Münster tried to do so in vain. They are afraid of the Kaiser's kind heart. At dinner one night the Kaiser said to Prince Münster: "Münster, I have had a letter from Lady O——, asking me to find out where her missing nephews are." A peal of scornful laughter arose from the other guests at table. A German Kaiser, they said, had other work to do than to search for missing English officers. The Kaiser remained silent, but on rising from the table asked Prince Münster to try and get some news for Lady O——.

The other day an article appeared in one of the daily Berlin papers, entitled "Englische Krankheit," and warning men in high positions not to allow themselves to be influenced by English women who are married to Germans, "as English women seem to have a dangerous knack of getting the men to look at things from their point of view."

Of course, every one here is wondering which of us is meant, and we are ourselves very much amused at this candid homage to the fascinating powers of English women, in spite of their being so often condemned as utterly under-educated from the German schoolmaster point of view. It is in any case not very complimentary to German women.

The fall of Tirpitz has been ascribed in some quarter to Princess Pless's influence over the Kaiser, on the ground that she had talked him over into using less drastic measures towards the English.

This is, of course, nonsense, as Princess Pless has never seen the Kaiser alone since the beginning of the war. And as for her being admitted to Headquarters because she is English, that is another ridiculous exaggeration. She was once at Headquarters, it is true, but as they happened to have settled them at her own house, they could not really turn her away. She had, however, to keep entirely to her own apartments, and had no intercourse with the Staff at all.

BERLIN, April 4, 1916.—I was suddenly rung up on the telephone by Sir Roger Casement, saying he must see me at once. I was somewhat surprised, as I thought he was ill in bed at Munich. He was, a few days ago, when we heard of him last.

However, although I was not keen on seeing him, I telephoned back to say that I would do so for a few minutes. Little did I think what a scene was before me.

The poor man came into the room like one demented, talked in a husky whisper, rushed round examining all the doors, and then said: "I have something to say to you, are you sure no one is listening?"

For one moment I was frightened. I felt I was in the presence of a madman, and worked my way round to sit near the telephone so as to be able to call for help. And then he began: "You were right a year ago when you told me that I had put my head into a noose in coming here. I have tried not to own you were right, and I did not like to tell you when you kept on urging me to get out of the country, that I realised from the moment I landed here what a terrific mistake I had made. And also I did not want to tell you that in reality I was a prisoner here. I could not get away. They will not let me out of the country.

"The German Foreign Office have had me shadowed, believing I was a spy in the pay of England, and England has had men spying on me all the time as well.

"Now the German Admiralty have asked me to go on an errand which all my being revolts against, and I am going mad at the thought of it, for it will make me appear a traitor to the Irish cause."

And at these words he sat down and sobbed like a child. I saw the man was beside himself with terror and grief, and so I tried to get a few more definite facts out of him, and told him there is a way out of every difficulty if he would only tell me more.

But he said, "If I told you more, it would endanger the lives of many, and as it is, it is only my life that has to be sacrificed." I made all sorts of suggestions, but all he would say was: "They are holding a pistol to my head here if I refuse, and they have a hangman's rope ready for me in England; and so the only thing for me to do is to go out and kill myself."

I argued him out of this, and at last he went away after giving me a bundle of farewell letters to be opened after his death. As he went out of the door, he said: "Tell them I was loyal to Ireland, although it will not appear so."

He asked to see me again, but as I am watched like every one else here, and as there was evidently some political intrigue on, I had to refuse.

NOTE

From Evelyn Blücher, *An English Wife in Berlin* (New York: E. P. Dutton, 1920), pp. 116–31.

Home Fires Burning

Belinda J. Davis

The collective power of Berliners of lesser means returned with a vengeance in the late winter and spring of 1917. They coalesced in calls for equal distribution of food among themselves and demanded the government address both official measures and private acts that compromised this equality. Poor urban consumers riveted their attention on the black-marketing that blossomed in this cold winter, largely displacing conflicts among themselves once more. The renewed street protest was closely tied to the shop-floor unrest of February and April. The well-studied strikes of April 1917, which began in Berlin metalworks and spread around the country, have often been perceived as the first sign of serious political unrest in Germany. Scholars have often interpreted the strikes, like the revolution of November 1918,[1] as a popular revolt against the attempted tyranny of a government that had imposed total war on German society. But popular fury through the war arose as heatedly from the inability of Prussian and imperial officials to impose their authority as firmly and as effectively on the food question as many would have liked.

In spite or perhaps because of the single-minded focus of the Supreme Army Command (OHL) on winning the war, civilian and military authorities reacted with redoubled responsiveness to street and shop-floor protests alike, committing the highest officials to the tasks of equalizing food distribution and prosecuting speculation. In turn, as late as the fall of 1917, Berliners and other Germans still maintained some faith in the Government's good intent, if not in its ability to execute it, and this, along with the promise of peace negotiations in the East, kept Germans from following the revolutionary path of their eastern neighbors. Indeed, poor urban Germans wanted to believe that officials represented their best chances at getting food. Nonetheless, government food scandals rocked Berlin in the fall and winter of 1917, pitching residents into numb despair. By the end of the year, hope even for officials' good intentions was wiped out by the image of cynical authorities who indulged in speculation themselves at the expense of just distribution among the larger population. Even as Foreign Office authorities announced renewed prospects for peace in the East, poorer Berliners concluded they should no longer place any faith in the Wilhelmine regime.

Peace, Freedom, and Bread?

The year 1917 opened to desperate calls for an equalization of food distribution, by working-class and lower-middle-class Berliners and especially by women, on and off the shop floor. Groups of normally rationed protesters in Berlin as well as in other cities continued to decry special rations for the ill or for children. But the focus now lay elsewhere. Women in the war factories demanded an equalization of rations among munitions workers, and the normally rationed called for the equalization of rations overall. One after another, the deputy commanders reported renewed unrest around the country, including concerning the continued "privileged treatment" of war-industry workers—and especially hardest laborers. Hardest laborers sought to retain their special supplements; still, they too joined the campaign for equalization by protesting differences in supply among the various factories.

By the early months of the year, however, these segments of the population began to turn their wrath away from one another and toward what they all perceived to be the far larger enemy under the controlled economy: profiteering in all its forms. Profiteering was, of course, the long-standing wartime enemy of poor Berlin consumers. It was first in the course of the fully controlled economy that, correspondingly, the black market burgeoned as a full-scale alternative to buying regulated foods. Police reports were full of incidents of "hoarder trips" taken by so-called hoarder men (likely including many women). Berliners observed dealings "roundabout" and "through the back door," as officials ordered police to vigilantly prosecute such activity.

For patrons of the black market, even this horrid period passed without more than discomfort and considerable expenditure of time, money, and energy, despite Michaelis's avowal that "everyone, even state ministers," was only barely surviving on turnips. (As sailors stationed in Kiel noted, they too would like to eat their turnips in the fashion of the officers: with lots of meat.) Evelyn Blücher, like those outside the capital, wrote of great dinner parties thrown by high society during the peak of the crisis over meat and fat.[2] Those with stores to spare claimed they would rather feed them to their friends than hand goods over to the authorities, despite the protest many had made publicly on behalf of the poor. Evidence of such polarized access to food supplies qualifies aggregate figures offering evidence that Germans ate more than rations allowed. Still even wealthier Berliners complained of regional disparity, calling for redistribution of goods from the agricultural areas of Greater Berlin, as well as other areas of the country, especially Bavaria. Concerns for such "underdistribution" brought in protests from around the city: from Steglitz, a district of functionaries, and wealthy Schmargendorf, Südende, and Zehldendorf as well as from Friedrichshain and Lichtenberg, offering an impressive, apparently united urban consumer front in deed now as well as in word. In part for this reason, poorer Berlin consumers continued to focus their animus primarily on the seller rather than the buyer of black-market goods and to deflect blame out of the city altogether.

The press continued to reflect and reinforce the anxieties of poorer Berliners, running daily pieces on the black market in the first months of the year. Newspapers de-

livered warnings to the hoarding farmer, the greedy middleman, and the retail trick-
ster, challenging their "patriotic disposition." They provoked readers with titles pro-
claiming farmers' views: "We'd Rather Feed the Pigs with It." They boldly proclaimed
the existence of massive hidden supplies, preserved, foddered, sold on the black market, or even allowed to rot, spurring poorer consumers to unrest by the relentless repetition of such accusations. At the same time, many newspapers provoked fury by
continuing to accept advertisements from black-market sellers. The damning articles
passed easily under the censors' eyes. Military authorities allowed such pieces to appear as long as they did not directly attack the state or fatherland. Yet the press indeed
excoriated the government and its various arms for their failure to suppress the speculation. The *Reichsbote* expressed deep vitriol against the "shameless hoarders and
profiteering merchants" who traitorously preyed on economically vulnerable women.
The paper judged most sharply, however, officials' "gentle treatment" of these traitors.
The *Berliner Tageblatt* offered wholehearted support for a Reichstag representative's
admonition to his colleagues and "the government" for the failure to fulfill their premier obligation, provisioning the people.

Police as well as the deputy commanders around the country helped maintain the
pressure on their superiors. Police observed popular appreciation for authorities' bid
for peace in the West and, failing that, their subsequent pursuit of unrestrained submarine warfare as a move to break the blockade (and an appropriate act of
vengeance). However, they noted, "an enormous portion of the population doesn't
care about the war at all any more" and exhibited a growing lack of faith in the military as well as the civilian administration. Poor prospects for food created a broad
"hotbed" for antiwar sentiment. In the wake of the split in the Social Democratic
Party (SPD) and the conference of left-wing SPD women, policemen expressed new
fear for the effect of "radical women" on the street protesters. It is indeed clear that
Spartacists and independent Social Democrats turned their attention increasingly to
the desperate women in the streets demanding food as a central potential mass revolutionary force. The annual March demonstration, populated by radical women and
youth, gained greater attention and interest than in previous years. Participants held
aloft a large, bright banner that vilified the Kaiser: "Curse the King, the King of the
Rich, who can't know our misery, who won't rest until he has exacted the last from us
and lets us be shot like dogs." Police observed the scene but declined to intervene.

Demonstrators still vehemently protested merchant trickery and treachery and the
offices that failed to control such activity. They deplored merchant policies that forced
them to buy one-third of their bread supplement in flour (if flour were to be had) or
one-third of their coal allotment in useless coke. In mid-March women, expressing
the deep "hatred" and "resentment," created unrest in the central market hall that required reinforcements to put down, as they protested against the expensive fish that
adorned the market stalls in place of the cheaper fish that was advertised. The scene
recalled the old Berlin legend of the "women's band" that was supposed to gather to
end a great famine by fishing together at night on the Spree River. But there was no
fish for these shoppers, and no end to the famine.

Street protest over government failures was matched by disruption on the shop
floor, in a series of one-day strikes in Berlin metalworks on 3 and 10 February.

Workers struck over wages, food supplies, and the general "food calamity," as well as perceived failures by the ZEG (Central Purchasing Authority) to stem profiteering. At the time of these first broad wartime strikes in Berlin factories (soon repeated around the country), women constituted the majority of war-industry workers. Munitions worker Martha Balzer noted with pleasure the widespread press response in February to "the demonstration of Britzer women," the more than 500 women, predominantly but not exclusively from the war factories, who stormed the communal offices of this working-class suburb adjoining Neukölln, claiming to be "speakers for the people." Balzer observed the extra ration cards protesters exacted from communal officials, more evidence that only continued protest brought desired ends.

In contrast to their relatively positive representation of the street protest and even of the shop-floor unrest generally, police responded dismissively to the participation of hardest laborers in the strikes, claiming that they were better than anyone else in Berlin. Police conflated protest on and off the shop floor in the battle for "equitable" distribution, making a case for the "generalized agitation" rather than for the interests that divided the populace. Groener responded in early March, recommending special supplements be targeted to the population of protesters, above all women, children, and adolescent youth. In turn, although the OHL's foremost commitment was to producing munitions, officials reacted more responsively to the demands of street protesters than of war-industry workers, better to the demands of general munitions workers than of hardest laborers, and better overall, by some measures, to women than to men.

Despite the OHL's "radical militaris[m]," Reich- and Prussian-level authorities continued to announce measures that sounded impressively earnest, vowing to revamp the system of special rations and to institute a general principle of equal food distribution that truly reckoned with both legal and illegal forms of special privilege. In the first months of the new year the KEA (War Food Office) and military officials adjusted special supplements to flatten distribution, despite concern especially among men in the war industry. Officials were just as responsive to popular condemnation of food speculation, despite their reliance on Junkers, speculators, and wealthy consumers for political and material support. In December 1916 the KEA had issued an edict in its most forceful language to date, banning "food profiteering, food displacement, and chain trade." Early in the new year, the Berlin police commissioner charged the War Profiteering Office (KWA) to execute the sense of the edict. Governor of Pomerania Wilhelm von Waldow launched a national initiative claiming a more dependable way for localities to purchase and distribute good for their residents, easing tensions between city and countryside. Prussian officials set up a revamped Potato Office with greater authority to oversee production as well as distribution. Feeling fresh power, Batocki publicly demanded the KEA be given enforceable control over policy on a national level. Prussian ministers overruled their colleague Schorlemer's objections to provide new powers to the Prussian Commissariat for the Provisioning of the People, giving it the control that the KEA had lacked over all Prussian civilian agencies concerning food. They put in charge of it former head of the Grain Authority Georg Michaelis on 21 March.

Berliners were hopeful despite a fresh snowfall. Perhaps at long last they had their food dictator and evidence that the government would respond properly and effectively. Working-class Berliners looked favorably toward Michaelis. They perceived him to be a forceful proponent of government control over food, as in the debate over public kitchens, and a successful adversary of agricultural particularism. Above all, poorer Berliners perceived the new powers and prestige of the commissariat as an important sign of the responsibility and obligation officials seemed to accept for the fate of the population. In this context the populace appreciated Michaelis's close ties to the military leadership. Unfortunately, his appointment in late March came simultaneously with an announcement of a prospective 25 percent cut in bread rations, following closely on the cut in January. Attempting to take hold of the situation, however, Michaelis spoke before the Berlin city assembly, spelling out a plan for controlled, equal distribution of bread. He announced that, this time, war-industry workers, including hardest laborers, would bear an equivalent reduction in their bread rations. In this way he cast a positive light on this dreaded measure for the broad population of poor consumers, even at the risk of renewed shop-floor unrest. Indeed, new measures throughout the remainder of the year removed virtually all privileging of war-industry workers, including hardest labors, as particularly strong or as offering unusual service to the nation.

Authorities now embraced equalized distribution generally. Michaelis described the system of differentiated distribution, in retrospect, as one that simply was not working. "One tried it," he noted, "with a system of supplements for heavy and heaviest laborers and the sick [, and with] special supplements for the elderly, women in childbed, children, etc. The administration became ever more complicated. Each worker claimed to be a heavy laborer." Correspondingly, members of the general, normally rationed population asserted that each person warranted "special supplements." At the same time, Michaelis acknowledged ruefully, "women's wallets were filled with food ration cards of every kind, but the rations were often so minimal that it wasn't even worth picking them up." Military officials concurred. Berge observed, "A simplification of the system of heavy, heaviest, munitions, and special laborer supplements is urgently desired, especially because . . . regulated differentiations and fair apportionment isn't possible. This is eliciting pitched discontent and jealousy among the workers without supplements." He finished with the popular recommendation that "all defense worker supplements . . . be abolished, and in its place the general rations of the 'non–self-provider' should be raised." Bundesrat officials agreed to a new meat card that would equalize distribution of this product among all Germans. The Städtetag put together a new system of benefits explicitly for the population of lesser means, acceptable because of the open way the category was defined. Through this new equalization, women lost the opportunity to be characterized as especially strong. But the broader urban populace read this change as acknowledgment of the needs and sacrifices of the greater population, as consumers and as producers alike.

Michaelis took a stance no less energetic toward profiteering and deception, promising reform of both the KEA and the ZEG and demanding "unified action" by military officials nationwide, through the deputy commanding generals. Batocki followed enthusiastically with demands that, following KWA efforts, officials redouble efforts to prosecute speculation and confiscate goods generally, on behalf of disadvantaged urban residents, "without regard for the implications for after the war." Berge's office banned "hoarder trips," proposing to install precious military forces at all train stations, conduct regular searches, and recommend heavy penalties against transgressors. Kessel promised a "search through the villages" to ferret out sources of food to bring into the city under official aegis. Officials moved concertedly to draw in the churches and private organizations in generating massive propaganda against blackmarketing and hoarding. The KWA announced the prosecution of over 24,000 cases of profiteering to date, claiming to root out another 4,000 cases each month. The KWA and Michaelis announced that Berlin police now pursued black market offenders as a primary task, protecting the populace rather than defending the government against the populace.

Bethmann weighed in with specific promises for domestic political reform, even as the OHL put a new request for war credits before the Reichstag. On 27 February Bethmann publicly committed to the pursuit of peace, democracy, and bread; the link between these concepts was tight and transparent, at least for every poor urban consumer. Bethmann elaborated plans for the new orientation of domestic politics he had so vaguely spoken of a year earlier. The Kaiser made his own direct pledge, acknowledging a new low in the regime's legitimacy. In his Easter edict on 7 April, the Kaiser promised revision of the Prussian three-class voting system. People in the streets responded generally with satisfaction, though they voiced their hope still for immediate, visible changes in their circumstances. The government's continued acknowledgment of its obligations toward its subjects may have prevented revolution at this point in the war in Germany, as it took place in March in Russia.

The press reported some policy successes as the winter waned, observing that in contrast to speculating "hoarder men," on the whole, residents returning to Berlin by train carried food only in their own bellies, having managed, "as the Berliners say, to have eaten themselves silly." Police claimed satisfaction that they had apprehended the shadowy (male) figures who lurked in the toilets of meal halls scalping bread and meat coupons. And yet, despite reforms, new offices, and prosecutions, black-marketing still flourished. This was in part a function of authorities' very success in "representing" urban consumers. High-level officials failed to call forth (if they ever had) the moral imperative that might spur farmers to turn over all their goods to authorities, and merchants to sell to poor consumers at fixed prices. Farmers, especially Junkers, were little pleased to be characterized as enemies of fellow Germans, above all by a regime they felt had deserted them and privileged urban dwellers, above all Berliners. One Pomeranian farmer claimed she would much rather sell her cows than "slave away" to produce butter for Berliners. By the spring of 1917 most farmers had relatively little investment in the war and even in the incumbent regime.

Authorities ran up against the practical problems of redistributing black market food once they did confiscate it, moreover. The press spread the rumor (often true) that when government agents did seize provisions off trains, they left foodstuffs on the station platform indefinitely, where they simply spoiled. This was certainly not the kind of equality of distribution for which Berliners had hoped. In early April tons of goods sat in the station of the Alexanderplatz city train just outside the central market, "leaking fluid," emitting rotten smells, and thoroughly enraging thousands of passersby as police stood around protecting the goods. Worse still for authorities, every Berlin paper announced the news; Dr. Carl Falck of the KWA found it a public relations nightmare.

In this context authorities themselves dreaded the response of Berliners and others to news of the revolution in Russia. Berliners paid close attention to the revolution, as much in light of renewed prospects of peace with that country as in terms of following Russia's example. Authorities noted that "news of the role played by industry workers in the movement in Russia has made an impact on German workers, for they believed they can spread their influence considerably further, in both their own factories, and on the political leadership." But hungry capital residents remained at least as attentive to the specifics of officials' latest food policy successes and blunders, despairing that Michaelis could not avoid the decrease in the bread ration (despite equalizing the burden) set to take effect in mid-April. Where was the bread in the "peace, freedom, and bread" Bethmann had promised? Officer Kurtz believed indeed that "interest for the events on the fronts, the revolution in Russia, and America's declaration of war [was] completely suppressed by the concern for food." This was not political apathy but, rather, continued investment in a different kind of politics. He repeated the familiar message: "The view remains firm that food would remain in sufficient supply, if a just system of distribution from the producer to the consumer were imposed. This belief has become all the stronger by the observation that food is consistently available on the black market, at usurious prices.

A sudden drop in the availability of potatoes on the eve of the cut in bread rations brought about "the worst imaginable mood all around." Poor consumers around the country joined Berliners in condemning what they feared to be efforts by authorities to patronize protesters with vacuous promises and "*false* pacification." Then delegates of Berlin metalworks and other works declared a demonstration strike for 16 April, the day after the cut in rations was to take effect. The result of Michaelis's promise to cut bread rations equitably was to provoke hard and hardest laborers to join their "light-working" counterparts in the factories and protesters on the streets, indeed taking on Bethmann's mantra as their own. Workers were little impressed by Batocki's new guarantees to the trade unions to provision workers; many resented the erosion of their special position. Many on and off the shop floor complained that the kaiser's edict did "only half the job," in part because it deferred the explicitly political rewards until after the war, but more centrally because it came without the bread that the kaiser had promised they deserved. Michaelis nervously demanded to hear immediately and directly all reports of unrest and strikes that arose specifically from food difficulties, while Spartacists disseminated their brochure titled *Hunger*, encouraging still more radical tactics. Hindenburg stepped in to recategorize political police once more, despite the movement toward equality, to ensure that they received at least as much as any of the workers who might protest—though this strategy had the potential to backfire.

Officials now moved to bring protesters more directly into the project of control and distribution. Worker's deputies met with the Berlin city council, along with Wermuth and high-level government officials, on Friday, 13 April. The authorities promised that all food, including previously unregulated luxury goods, would be under strict government control and that they would, moreover, establish new mass dining halls "without differentiation by status or type of work." On the eve of the planned worker walkout and broad demonstration, set for 16 April, Groener announced plans on behalf of the War Office and State Commissariat to appoint workers to run the business of the Distribution Office, including determining the method of distribution. In contrast to the military leadership's interest in personalizing delivery of food, the new plans explicitly allowed workers (here men) to take food home to their wives, whose own sacrifices required this. Though the scheme was a gambit to put the onus of food distribution on workers' shoulders as well as a last desperate attempt to ward off potentially catastrophic unrest, once more the highest-level officials seemed to be espousing democratization while promising greater control. In response, worker deputies promised to try to prevent unrest, though they claimed workers now lacked all faith in the government. But this claim is open to some question.

On Monday, 16 April, more than 200,000 metal-, munitions, and other workers failed to show up for work or walked off their shift, by wartime standards a formal act of unprecedented size. Demonstrators from many factories, including numerous war-industry works, spread throughout the city. Most struck specifically "against government measures on the food question," though the food question remained intimately connected to issues of relations between state and society. A large portion of the striking factory workers failed to join the formal demonstration that shop stewards had planned for 9:00 a.m. But there were plenty of impromptu gatherings in the streets, by factory workers and others. Oppen noted with regret that there were many attacks on bakeries, particularly in the sensitive area between police headquarters (the "red fortress") in Alexanderplatz and government buildings. Many groups succeeded in moving close to the inner sanctum of the municipal, Prussian, and imperial government, demonstrating in the thousands in Leipziger Street, just short of the Kaiser-Wilhelm bridge spanning the Spree River near the imperial palace, and in Alexanderplatz, site of the city's central market, where police could not deter people from gathering. Police prevented most demonstrators from reaching Wilhelm Street and Unter den Linden, though radical Social Democratic youth pushed their way through.

Workers felt pleased with the day's events. The walkout had been planned as a demonstration strike, and the great majority of workers intended to return to work by Tuesday or Wednesday. As a demonstration strike this action seemed to indicate for many the potential of successful response; it was a warning communicating a set of demands that strikers believed officials could and might meet. Particularly after the Friday night meeting before the strike, many workers felt that their message had been successfully expressed. At the same time many men in particular were nervous about remaining off the job, as military officials had quietly threatened to send strikers to the front lines. Most strikers showed little immediate enthusiasm for the suggestion of a fresh walkout on May Day, in protest against poor treatment of radical labor leader Richard Müller.

Although *Vorwärts*[3] was interested in denying the political aspect of the April strikes, for most of the protesters it appears that demands were political in the most specific and immediate sense: in having a voice beyond the franchise, in asserting the need for better representation, and in claiming their rights above commitment to a free market and demanding confiscation and redistribution of property to ensure basic needs. These demands were in certain respects more radical than those expressed by the shop stewards, which included a non-annexationist peace, extension of the franchise, and liberation of political prisoners. They were also demands that authorities had already afforded legitimacy. Strikers and demonstrators within and outside the war factories were heartened by "the willingness to oblige on the part of the government."

There are many reasons to see the April strikes as closely related to the ongoing protest in the streets. The latter was not epiphenomenal; the pattern established in making specific, material demands and retreating when those demands were met formed the model for the April strikes as well. The two sites of unrest did not feature distinct populations but, rather, populations that flowed from one location to the other. At least half of the strikers were women, who were also well-represented at meetings to plan for the strikes. In the days before the strike, working-class women in the streets who were not war-industry workers discussed the participation of their husbands as well as their sons and daughters in the prospective unrest. In Berlin, women appear to have formed the majority of protesters overall, though distinct populations were difficult to observe. The greater number of women makes sense in terms of women's majority in the local metal and munitions industry, their immunity from conscription, their ongoing presence in the streets as consumers, and finally their greater numbers generally on the homefront. Continued public (and police) support for poor women protesters in the streets may have prevented observers from publicly condemning the strikers, though some lashed out at strikers specifically while defending consumer protesters. Oppen noted that this large-scale unrest exposed a process of "political fermentation" throughout the city, spreading from street to factory and back, that would become increasingly visible in the coming months.

To protesters' relief and, for many, vindication, Michaelis still appeared to be listening, directly acknowledging opinions of protesters from both the shop floor and the streets. This was the kind of dictator poor urban protesters had hoped for: one who would use his enormous power to represent their interests. On the heels of the strike, Michaelis issued all-new, overriding principles of food distribution, which metropolitan officials attempted to follow, entirely reshuffling and simplifying the existing process. By early May, imperial officials erected a new food distribution office for Greater Berlin. The State Distribution Office (Staatliche Verteilungsstelle, SVS) quickly began its work in earnest, defining its task as the "equitable provisioning of the population of Greater Berlin with food and other items of daily need." Branch offices opened around the country, following nationwide unrest, offering workers representation on their boards. Broad segments of the populace perceived this step as legitimation once again of both greater control and a more participatory government. The *Reichsbote* reported that the revamped system of supplements was "especially well received and gratefully acknowledged by those—for example, the munitions workers—who no longer receive many special rations," while the normally rationed were thereby able to avoid public kitchens. Police, too, reported general cautious "content" by early May.

Yet once more the hopefulness faded in the following weeks, as basic foods still remained in short supply. The mayor of Charlottenburg reported in June that potato deliveries to both public kitchens and factory canteens were cut by half, but this cut was not followed by apparent greater general availability of the tuber at private vendors or at municipal sales outlets. General Heinrich von Scheüch, soon to assume the position of war minister, noted that German workers continued to express resentment for the unequal distribution of food within the factories. Scheüch warned of the compromise of popular "resistance" to both disease and unrest that might permit serious outbreaks at any moment. In turn SVS officials in Berlin voiced concern for the response of hard and hardest laborers to the changes in the supplements. At the same time, "the unequal treatment" between war-industry workers and their non–war-industry counterparts was still "creating great unrest . . . dissolving the advances that the introduction of the term 'munitions industry' brought with it." Exasperated authorities responded that it must be made clear to workers "that no more can be given them, and that their own wives and children will suffer at the raising of any special supplements," reconfirming that productive labor was not to be the only measure of national contribution. As shipments of raw supplies necessary to factory production (including the war industries) dwindled and arrived inconsistently, moreover, industrialists laid off many workers, beginning in the spring and summer of 1917. Layoffs included above all women workers, who now lost any remaining privileges and swelled the ranks of the normally rationed.

Substitute People

Poorer consumers became all the more convinced that black-marketing remained the real culprit, as the new equalized distribution of products under official control brought little relief. This suspicion was exacerbated in the summer of 1917 by the problem of substitution. Authorities had promised to compensate for the cut in bread rations by increasing rations in other foods such as potatoes, meat, fish, vegetables, and eggs. Consumers found none of these foods easily available or affordable in early April. This was not the first substitution problem. In the preceding months police and the press had reported consumers' frustration that even turnips were no longer available, though propaganda continued to urge their consumption to compensate for the lack of potatoes. One resident of Leipzig observed dryly that she did not mind eating rat; it was rat substitute she objected to. For poorer Berliners, the chicanery, cultural affronts, and actual health threats posed by the burgeoning market in ersatz or substitute foods, not to mention absence of the original items, brought them yet again to the point of protest in the summer of 1917.

The notion of "ersatz" was relatively positive at the outset of war. Military leaders expressed enthusiasm for the potential contributions of science to the war effort. In light of the embargo, they were thrilled that scientists could provide them with ersatz, or artificially produced, fixed nitrogen for gunpowder. Many officials hoped that the

new science of nutrition could ease the burden of the economic war by providing ersatz foods. As early as 1915 national commissions on ersatz coffee and tea had regulated the traffic of the various products sold under these names. This seemed harmless enough. As Germany had no imperial markets in bean coffee, most of the population had never drunk anything but domestic coffee, made from inexpensive chicory
and sugar beets (though naturally for them the latter was "real" coffee). Other substi-
tutions emerged with the first shortages: potatoes for bread, and vice versa; margarine
and jam for meat fat and butter. The population accepted the substitution of one food
for another when they recognized a limited gap between the nutritional and sociocul-
tural values of the two foods. Attitudes toward this gap relaxed of necessity as food
grew more scarce. In August 1916 women rioted violently in Kattowitz, shouting
"Bread! Bacon! Fat! Potatoes! Away with jam!" Now, one year later, consumers in
Berlin happily accepted jam as a bread spread.

Serious problems surrounding ersatz foods arose first in the turnip winter, in the
form of thousands of food substitutes, the most prominent of which was the loathed
swede turnip. In early 1917 the swede turnip constituted the primary food in the
households of most Berliners, a substitute for most other foods. There was no regular
means to prepare the indigestible fodder turnip, and nothing was available to improve
the root's much hated flavor. Officials and private organizations encouraged urban
consumers to think broadly about the turnip as mousse, cutlets, or pudding, offering
recipes composed of increasingly few ingredients. This propaganda made Berliners all
the more "bitter," as reports tellingly characterized the situation, when even the turnip
was not available for purchase by the spring and summer of 1917. If this was moreover
the most infamous example of an unwelcome substitution, it was not necessarily the
worst. Berliners traded jokes about ersatz foods, from the uses put to old battle horses
(which probably were eaten) to mattress stuffing to ration coupons themselves. A
woman worker from Lichtenberg described the substitute goods as dangerously
fraudulent and the government's propaganda as likewise so, from assertions about the
nutritional value of saccharine to the promotion of soap powder that exploded in her
kitchen. Women responded cynically to ongoing government campaigns to collect
genuine gold, iron, money, and even the hair off their heads, while everything they
took in was artificial and inferior. As officials concocted schemes to extract protein
from dragonfly wings, resourceful tradespeople cut often injurious "stretchers" into
good food and watered scarce milk for infants until it was a "transparent blue." Merchants thereby reinforced divisions between themselves and urban consumers, recalling the fears of food adulteration that had constituted one of the few common concerns among consumers across class lines before the war had broken out.

The case of coffee provides one example of how products sold as substitutes lost
their relation to the original item. Officials constituted coffee as a "most important
food," against the advice of the food experts, due to its cultural role in the German
diet. Just before the institution of the KEA in 1916, the Bundesrat established the War
Committee for Coffee, Tea, and Substitute Goods. Germans had to drink coffee with
their *Stulle*, or coffee break sandwich; it was as basic an accompaniment to bread as
the bread's spread. (For many workers, it might alternately be a pull of schnapps, although authorities did not find this a problem for the "German" diet. Beer produc-

tion, in Bavaria a most important food, was banned in northern Germany first in the summer of 1917 to encourage land use for more nutritional crops.) Conversely, one did not normally drink coffee without eating a roll or like product, reinforcing the connection between coffee and food; to desire a cup of coffee signified the expectation of bread. Germans of all classes drank coffee (bean or chicory) for breakfast, in the afternoon, and often before retiring. Virtually the national drink, Germans consumed it above all in the big cities. The product contained no nutritional value or, in working-class chicory coffee, even caffeine. Yet Germans did not celebrate the drink for its warmth alone. Most herbal infusions were "tea" and, therefore, not acceptable substitutes. When substitute teas were offered on the market, people often refused them, not just because they tasted disgusting "but, rather, because 'the German doesn't drink much tea, and is rather used to his coffee.'"

Based on the cultural importance of coffee, its scarcity by the second year of the war had caused no small uproar in Berlin. The KEA acknowledged "the meaningful influence that coffee and quasi-coffee drinks had on the general morale of the population," also noting that a warm drink helped make repetitive food, potatoes and dry bread, edible. In 1916 officials had planned to set aside roasted grains for use as substitute coffee. But the entry of Romania into the war closed off these supplies and set the production of coffee in competition with that of the bread with which coffee was drunk. The KEA attempted to take control of the situation, publishing lists of permitted substitutes for coffee (including ground walnut shells and corn powder) as well as for thousands of other food products—from 837 certified forms of substitute sausage to over 3,500 approved pseudo-soft drinks.

By the early spring of 1917, however, officials had lost control again. Berliners had entered the phase of "ersatz ersatz," or "surrogates" (*Surrogaten*). In the absence of common substitutes, substitutes for the substitutes were used, which were often illegal and of ever more dubious quality. Capital residents decried foul products merchants sold as ersatz coffee and as substitutes for all other foods. Skalweit notes, in perhaps an overly generous spirit, that "made up in nice packages, they offered the German housewife at least the pleasant deception that she was enriching the supply of her kitchen." But merchants offered replacements on the basis of some physical approximation, with increasingly little concern for taste, nutritional value, or safety. They packaged and sold yellow powder of indeterminate origin as dried egg; white powder, as dried milk. Washing soda mixed in starch constituted butter, sold under one of the new "fantasy names"—and at fantasy prices. The *Berliner Volkszeitung* lamented, "Coffee has disappeared, the finer substitutes have disappeared; only the price, the price, has remained." Surrogates contributed to the upheaval and disorientation of the war experience, as nothing was what it seemed to be, and the "good" and the "bad" were indistinguishable.

As of spring 1916, officials required producers of substitute products to list contents on their packaging. Consumers consequently expressed outrage when they discovered the contents of the products they purchased, inasmuch as they were actually listed. Ash constituted 85 percent of a product offered as ersatz pepper; many substitute foods contained the "indigestible remains of animals." Yet many desperate consumers continued to buy these products, inducing the onset of "substitute sickness," a syndrome representing the combined effects of insufficient nutrition and the consumption of many nonfood and even toxic items. In August 1917 Oppen himself deplored the sale of bread "in part so bad, that in many cases it has caused intestinal disorders." Consumers began angrily bringing their flour to authorities to be inspected for its content. Officials outside Berlin reported similar stories in understated fashion: "If one is to imagine that one is later to eat this grain as bread, it is little wonder that the aggravation in the populace grows ever greater."

In light of these circumstances, the term "ersatz" took on new meaning. While before the war it had signified simply a substitute, it had now come to mean "fake" or "artificial," "inferior substitute," and even "wretched." Berliners were by now extremely sensitive to artificial dealings on the market, activity that did not conform to government regulations. The press characterized officials themselves as "unconscious provocateurs" for allowing merchants to offer such artificial goods to "the German housewife" and rendering necessary the use of substitutes in the first place. The quality of the goods moreover seemed to constitute the identity of those who consumed them. If swede turnips rendered Berliners equivalent to animals, ash pepper suggested they were less than animals. Those who manufactured and sold surrogates had the ability to determine this identity.

Women working in munitions were disturbed by another association with the term "ersatz." In cooperation with the trade unions, who sought to codify women's place in the factory as temporary, the OHL designated these women "substitute workers" (*Ersatzarbeiterinnen*) for men at the front. Fellow workers and managers increasingly subjected women to this reminder on the shop floor. National Women's Service volunteers themselves adopted the notion of women workers as a "female substitute army." As "ersatz" came to mean "inferior" or "second-rate," this promoted tensions within the factories. In late 1916 and early 1917 working-class women felt strongly needed and wanted, at least by the OHL. Bourgeois women played an auxiliary role to their productive work. By mid-1917, as factory owners began laying off women for lack of raw materials to produce munitions, and as the trade union leadership gained greater negotiating power with the OHL, the role of working-class women as munitions workers lost some of its luster. Labor leaders were successful in halting some new efforts to refit factories to accommodate a growing female labor force, on the basis of women's "substitute" nature. By the late summer of 1917, as industrialists let even more substitute workers go, they advertised the need for *Facharbeiter*, skilled or "qualified" workers with a sense of "quality." Officials leaked the term "pile of second-raters" (*Ersatzhaufen*) to refer to the straggling reinforcements now called up to the front—those not "man" enough to have been sent earlier.

The notion of the ersatz food came to be used as a metaphor for the depreciating quality of life overall. The term "fake person" (*Ersatzmensch*) arose in this period, signifying someone in wretched condition. The term evoked both the poor state of the individual, waiting for "real" life to begin again, and to the way one felt as a result of eating ersatz foods. By the summer of 1917, as ersatz and surrogate goods were another rallying point for poor urban consumers, members of the "ersatz" labor force joined their counterparts outside the factory gate in ever greater numbers. Berliners and urban Germans still retained some desperate hope in the existing regime's intent and ability to transform their miserable lives. But this experience suggested yet again that even the highest-level officials were simply incapable of controlling the domestic crisis as the war continued to drag on. Poor women in the streets of the capital wondered aloud about the purpose of fighting the war for Germany when the lives of so many Germans, on the battlefront and on the homefront, were thus ruined. A girl from Schneidemühl reported in her diary that her mother and brother returned from a visit to Berlin in July "wretchedly thin and pale." Fortunately for her family, her grandmother was able to revive them with thick pea soup and bacon cracklings; most Berliners lacked such opportunities for relief.

In light of this deepening misery, it was at the height of the summer of 1917 that Berliners began to envision the agonies of a fourth war winter even while the sun's heat beat down on their heads during their daily queues. In July German troops battled Americans alongside Frenchmen and Britons, and Italy and even Russia showed no signs of immediate retreat; despite passage of the peace resolution in the Reichstag, poorer Berliners feared they had to plan for the worst. The experience of the preceding winter left such an indelible impression on Berliners that they spent much of the summer of 1917 in coal lines talking about it. The combination of deficient food and fuel along with the ignominies of surrogate foods was more than many people felt they would be able to bear again. Deputy commanders reported in July, "The matter is very serious. The population won't go along with another winter without sufficient coal. To starve and to freeze is just too much."

Berliners tried to store up coal, wondering if an end to the war would even change the circumstances. But even in these warm months they most often failed because of direct competition with the war industries, which burned the fuel voraciously year-round, as well as with the bakeries. The deficiency of coal continued to wreak havoc on municipal transport. In turn, coal dealers themselves, along with food merchants, claimed difficulty in transporting supplies from train stations, while consumers lacked access to public transportation to carry the goods long distances themselves. Adults wore out their cardboard shoes walking these distances, while children trudged barefoot beside them. Officials responded directly to popular complaints once more, issuing nontransferable ration cards for coal in July. Still, coal to fill the coupons remained unavailable except on the black market.

The summer of 1917 held other ominous prospects for the *Minderbemittelte* of Berlin. In June landlords began complaining of high taxes on their mortgages, as the city sought sources to help fund the swollen range of services it now attempted to provide. Landlords threatened to subvert the city's intentions by passing these costs on to their tenants, including the wives and mothers of soldiers, whom it was technically illegal to evict. Poorer families remained concerned about being forced out by high rents, to make way for single men and women who came from outside the city to work in war-industry factories. Berge refused the request of local mayors to ban rent increases, demonstrating little of the concern he had for rising food prices. On 1 July, as many landlords announced new rates to begin 1 October, poorer Berliners had a new burden of worry in anticipation of the coming fall and winter. Soldiers' wives and other war dependents in Neukölln banded together in early July, warning of a rent boycott for which they thought they might have better popular support than they had had in the fall of

1914. In response Bundesrat officials quickly reported efforts to better enforce existing controls. But in the end council members did nothing on the matter, at least for the current lease cycle. Their attention seemed focused almost exclusively on questions of food and demands of the broad population of poor consumers on those issues.

Poorer Berliners resorted once more to protest, with a new intensity, urgency, and "a certain heated frenzy" matching the warm summer days. Erupting first in mid-May, in the streets and on the shop floor, food demonstrations and unrest became more sustained during July, spreading across the country. Officer Schrott reported, "The market halls are daily stormed by hundreds of women. . . . It often comes to wild [wüste] rows, lootings, and even to blows. . . . There is great tension and hatefulness among the people." The Alexanderplatz market, near government offices and next to police headquarters, was the site of daily, violent "battles" over food. Police noted with bitterness that anyone with money or connections avoided the public market altogether, relying on new, illegal "delivery companies." By this point in the war, anyone on the streets or in marketplaces was likely a protester, lacking the resources to pursue other means to obtain food.

Demonstrations in the summer of 1917 were indeed considerably more violent than they had been at any time in the war to date. Officer Schneider observed a typical "stormy scene" in the weekly market in Lichtenberg, as 300 women gathered at the stand of greengrocer Haase of nearby rural Marzahn, "indignant over the high price ... and excited to the extreme." As women attacked the stand, Haase "saved himself only by fleeing quickly. However, the women pursued him, howling and screaming, till he sped up to a tremendous gallop, and the women gave up the pursuit." Would-be consumers demonstrated such fierceness that many farmers themselves stopped coming to market, particularly in Lichtenberg and in the northeast section of the city, where this violence was most concentrated. The summer unrest also regularly included trips by women to local offices of official agencies to express their demands directly and to exact a direct reply. As a recurrent practice, this represented a quantum escalation in confrontation. Lichtenberg police commissioner Lewald reported typically, "Several women left the [Viktoria] market for the city hall to demand bread and potatoes. . . . They asked where they could buy bread. . . . Then they went down the street to the baker and violently took thirty breads without paying for them." Such descriptions evoke the period before the French Revolution at a point when hungry women demanded that representatives of the king and state directly provide them with bread.

Spreading out from Berlin and its central suburbs, unrest encompassed the wider region, including small towns and villages. Officer Borchert reported acts of assault and battery by women in Niederschöneweide, southeast of the city and home to many AEG workers. In an area relatively quiet since the October 1915 butter riots, women now stormed the offices of local authorities demanding to know the whereabouts of potatoes and why other areas had gotten some. Borchert reported the women then hitting a shopkeeper with his own broom and insulting a policeman for his "fat belly" (no vacant affront in those days), which, Borchert added, was an accurate epithet. Observers reported regular "crass remarks" and "direct imprecations" against the government, civilian and military, for the failure to totally control supply and to end the war, which protesters asserted authorities had promised to do. Theodor Wolff observed that the government must now provide "real representation of the people" if it were to survive. This was the government's last best chance.

Police and others now characterized even this violence as "reasonable." Lewald described the protesters first storming the magistrate's office, then "violently" appropriating bread, as "nationally thinking women" whose "patience in bearing these cares [was] exhausted." He opined that it was "high time" for officials to absolutely ensure adequate supplies to the "broad masses of the population." Though he often found it necessary to edit his own very charged remarks in mood reports by this period, Oppen let stay his own assertion that officials were bringing Berliners to their last vestige of reason. From outside the capital, the *Bremer Bürger Zeitung* reported most sympathetically on the psychological toll that maldistribution, substitution, and the prospect of more of the same took, especially on the population of lesser means. The article warned that both the injustice and the actual physical deficiencies resulting from this maldistribution destroyed the "reason" of "otherwise rational people." Police contrasted such protesters with others—such as shell-shocked soldiers—acting through lack of reason though contributing nonetheless to the "frenzied" street scene. They declared to their superiors that "discussions with thoroughly reasonable women confirm[ed] that a portion of the population [was] truly starving."

Official and private observers in Berlin and the country expressed "little wonder" at this unrest and "surprise" that these "understandable" protests were not worse. *Der Deutsche Kurier* explained that "women and girls" crowded before the various market stalls had to constantly negotiate small confrontations, "because there is no other possibility." The paper urged KEA and Privy Council officials to observe these "images of the market" directly and to try to buy goods there themselves—and then to take action as appropriate. Recalling their earliest reports just after the Berlin butter riots, deputy commanders claimed that Germans exercised "astonishing patience"; police warned, however, that popular faith in both civilian and military officials, now nearly two years after the October 1915 unrest, was severely eroded.

Police expressed their own diminished faith ever more poignantly. Hertzberg, police commissioner of Charlottenburg, wrote to Oppen with concern regarding the truly "serious character" of the summer riots, imploring him to dispatch additional manpower. But political police observed in the riots of June and July 1917 that their uniformed counterparts were conspicuously absent. Officer Schneider called it "noteworthy" that only one uniformed policeman was visible at the market at the time of the scene at Haase's produce stall, and that this officer was "otherwise occupied at the cherry stand." Describing the same scene, Kurtz noted that "the women" explicitly "used the momentary absence of police at the marketplace to really give Haase a taste of their fury." The low profile of uniformed police in the marketplace may have been caused by more than simply insufficient forces (and even interest in pursuing their own sources of food); indeed, two plainclothes political policemen were stationed to watch the Lichtenberg market. Whether from sympathy, apathy, or fear, police were clearly reluctant to intervene as shopping women expressed their wrath, storming market stands and officials' offices in turn. Police reported ill response to their attempts to assert authority; demonstrators ignored, mocked, and even assaulted the gendarmes. Still they continued to describe their own role as defending poor women in the streets, a function simultaneously of direct orders and of their growing distance from their high superiors. Policemen prevented men, including veterans, from walking to the front of the line. They arrested merchants for acting "impolitely" and thereby further "straining the nerves" of poor shoppers, even as those shoppers exhibited violent behavior. Military officials considered replacing police with military personnel to better impose order by controlling the women themselves, but they feared that common soldiers would be little less sympathetic to protesters.

Earlier, police and other observers had defended marketplace protesters on the basis of their economic demands, though the effects had been political. Now officials and the broad public increasingly characterized protests and unrest on the streets and accompanying demands themselves as explicitly political. This view of women's strategies to get what they needed during the war sheds light on the standard political history of the era. It explains why working-class and lower middle-class women appeared indifferent to the question of voting rights, promoted by the League of German Women's Groups and, above all, by the Majority Social Democratic Party as the primary political question. The notion that the vote was not a very meaningful political tool under the prevailing circumstances may also have contributed to the mild response to the Kaiser's 1917 "Easter edict," though hungry women considered it an important symbolic gesture. A demonstration for franchise reform called by the socialists for early July also fizzled out for lack of popular interest. Social Democratic representatives forced the matter before the Prussian parliament in November 1917, demanding evidence of the state's intent to repay the country's workers for their contributions to the nation and to the war effort. However, as Officer Dittman noted, "the broader mass of workers view[ed] the whole affair without much interest" by the time the proposal was debated in the spring of 1918. Poorer women were more concerned about food for the moment than about a formal political right that could not even be exercised in the foreseeable future. It was also clear that they wielded considerable power and control without this formal and abstract right, and where that power failed them, the vote was of little use.

The highest German authorities found still more impressive measures to communicate to urban consumers especially the seriousness with which government viewed the plight of the people; these measures also reinforced official commitment to steward domestic as well as diplomatic matters. In August the OHL, with the help of the Reichstag, steered Bethmann out of office for his inability to control—and appear to control—the domestic situation. The civil cabinet and military leadership moved Prussian food commissar Georg Michaelis in as chancellor, in part on the basis of Michaelis's perceived expertise on the food question, his reputation as a strong proponent for tight controls on production and distribution, and his image as champion of the cities. Customarily viewed by historians as a puppet of the OHL without independent political standing or qualifications, Michaelis's role as chancellor may be better understood as a symbol to the populace of the urgency with which the highest civilian and military leaders viewed the crisis on the homefront.

Michaelis had his work cut out for him. Oppen questioned in a draft report of late July, "How much longer can this ever growing pressure to rebellion be held back!" Continuing in a statement he would excise from the final version, Oppen wrote, "The broad masses of the population are riveted to the food question. . . . The greater population is inclined to think the continued sacrifices for further battles are simply not worth it and any peace is better than a continuation of war." As chancellor, Michaelis took quick action. He began by replacing the weak-willed Batocki with Wilhelm von Waldow, who in turn set to work to combat black-marketing, the "greatest pestilence of the people of this world war."

In September and October 1917 Berliners and others watched, waited, and hoped once more. Most groaned as the OHL ordered new military forays, as Admiral Alfred von Tirpitz announced the foundation of the Fatherland Party, committed to peace only with annexations. They applauded as Reichstag representatives voted down a bill committing to such a peace, resolving instead to continue negotiations with Russia and Ukraine—negotiations for peace and for wheat. At the same time, new rent increases took effect on 1 October. Imperial officials announced another reduction in the butter rations and declared the cessation of fat allowances altogether. Rumor spread that KWA officials spent their time searching schoolchildren for smuggled food at the train station. Police announced still-deepening popular anger, especially within the civil service. Capital residents threatened that they could not hold out for one more war winter. Then Berliners read the news that military officials were pushing Michaelis out of office before he ever had the chance to make good on the expectations accreted to him as food dictator. Authorities attempted to sweeten the pill with methods they had used before. Waldow announced an October appeal to black marketers to cease their activity, followed by threats of stiffer penalties. He announced the sudden discovery of fruit that had been "lost" between rural Werder and Berlin. Berliners would soon see it, in the form of jam, as a substitute bread spread. Poorer Berliners grudgingly welcomed this news. This was a step in the right direction, at least, of actually getting food on the table, pathetic as it seemed.

Waldow's jam thus bore the weight of enormous expectations in the fall of 1917. Though not a central food, jam was at once a symbol of the government's new control over goods, an acceptable substitute for butter and meat fat, and a sign of the potential of new bread as peace negotiations continued with Russia and Ukraine. But the jam failed to appear after all. With the advent of cold weather, capital residents were beside themselves. Berliners discussed the missing jam as intensely as they did the new revolution in Russia. It was the missing jam that set Berliners moving "above all in a radical direction." Ludendorff himself linked food unrest in Germany directly with the Russian Revolution, claiming now that military interests demanded calming of the domestic unrest. To this degree Ludendorff, too, was hostage to popular pressures, despite his claim that he remained free of such concerns. Although Ludendorff may have thought in terms of swift and peremptory police and military action against unrest, it is important to note the limits of his ability to put such a plan in place.

The expectations officials themselves created had once again induced the deepest disappointment at their failures. Government propaganda "awoke in the Berlin population . . . belief that a regulated distribution of jam would take place." In mid-November a single distribution of jam occurred. Then nothing. "Again, one was left with nothing to spread on one's bread," Officer Faßhauer concluded. Residents of working-class Neukölln in particular were all the more enraged when it appeared that other districts of Greater Berlin had received more jam than they, despite promises that the bread spread would be equitably distributed. In response the Neukölln city council wrote to Waldow pressing for "measures that would ensure the equitable distribution of remaining food supplies, as well as the combating of profiteering." Berliners questioned their own wisdom in continuing to put stock in officials' promises and felt angry for having accorded authorities their vestigial faith.

The jam fiasco was only the most prominent of numerous scandals that made headlines in the fall and winter of 1917, in Berlin and around the country, accumulating evidence not only of the ineptitude of the new authorities but also of their cynical corruption. The *Bremer Bürger Zeitung* reported on the August "potato exposé," citing a Hanover newspaper on an event in Bochum. A member of the Bochum city council revealed that authorities allowed a farmer to turn over half his potatoes for later use in schnapps production. The *Berliner Morgenpost* ran an article titled "The Surplus Food Supply: Excess in the Munitions Industry," which presented new evidence of official maldistribution in the war factories. Berliners voiced their conviction now that the government simply could not fulfill its responsibilities to the populace, despite what really seemed to be officials' best efforts. Poorer consumers charged that officials themselves were creating new problems through their stupidity, lack of vision, and inability to co-ordinate and execute plans. Berliners read with horror of a scandal over butter in which several communal officials in Berlin-Friedrichsfelde were convicted of playing an illegal role themselves in the evident "displacement." With impeccable timing, a fresh cut in butter rations followed on the heels of this news, reducing official rations from 50 to 30 grams per person per week (about 2 tablespoons)—as available.

Before the implications of the butter scandal sank in, a new disgrace erupted, freighted with the rapidly accelerating lack of faith in the government and suspicions concerning officials' good intentions. At the end of November 1917, Neukölln city leaders presented a confidential position paper to the KEA, alleging that high-level officials had allowed some communal authorities to exceed legal price ceilings in their attempts to buy up food; this explained the unequal jam distribution. Indeed, the paper argued, Neukölln officials themselves had been regularly forced to transgress price ceilings to get any potatoes and other basic foods for their predominantly working-class population, because of the "greed of merchants," cultivated by the military regime. *Vorwärts* got hold of the piece and published it prominently in a special supplement under the title "Collapse of the Waldow System"; a follow-up article suggested "things were getting crazier and crazier." With the help of the press, the public interpreted the accusations as evidence of high officials' thoroughgoing betrayal of urban consumers, whose suppliers (private and public) were evidently forced to compete illegally for food supplies. Waldow himself soon emerged as more actively pernicious than his hated predecessor had ever been.

The populace had long suspected such abuses of the system, but concrete evidence of the corruption and mismanagement spurred the deepest dismay and despair. The defense of communal officials, that they felt they had to overstep the price ceilings in order to ensure supplies for their own residents, little impressed those in the streets. Lacking the means to engage actively in the black market, poorer consumers had staked their claims in the potential of the high officials to make the controlled economy work, to fulfill their needs, and to legitimate their relationship with the state. Officials hastened to ensure consumers that their confidence, such as it was, was still warranted. Authorities tried to spread the message "through the entire Berlin press" that they continued to fight hard and successfully against both the outer and inner enemies of the German people, though newspapers now showed little cooperation. As for direct propaganda, one deputy commander observed that by December, those responsible could not always commandeer the paper on which to print such communications.

The Neukölln exposé was pivotal to a transformation that took place in Berlin in December 1917, a culminating moment offering a final and dramatic bit of evidence of consumers' worst fears. The government had at best demonstrated "impotence" in performing its duties. Now—finally—a large population of working-class and lower middle-class Berliners lost faith in the existing regime's ability and even willingness to act on their behalf and in their interests. "The people held steadfastly to the idea that the government . . . acted itself as a profiteer, offering wares to the people at enormous prices," police observers noted of this time. New relations between state and society remained legitimate, but the reigning government lost authority to participate in that relationship. If poor urban Germans had retained some shred of faith in the government's willingness to represent them even as the new liberal government fell in Russia, they now began to think differently. Recognizing the gravity of the situation, the Kaiser hurried to voice his own condemnation of officials who were involved in the Neukölln scandal, in the form of a pamphlet that quickly reached wide distribution. The public demonstrated only greater outrage, taking the Kaiser's condemnation as a sign of admission of official corruption. By the first week in the new year, the magistrate in Berlin urged the Kaiser not to release further copies of the pamphlet—advice that Wilhelm followed. It was too late; the damage was done.

Now the law of the land was "everything through cheating," Helmut von Gerlach claimed, charging paradoxically that "the black market has become the normal form of traffic in goods," with the aid of the government itself. Gerlach averred that the new chancellor, Georg Graf von Hertling, was intimately involved in the system of corruption and flouted Bundesrat orders to permit his native Bavaria to withhold food from the rest of the country. This was the legacy of 1917 for the final year of the war. Just as women of little means had played a leading role in negotiating the domestic responsibilities of the German state, so were they essential in signaling the end of trust in the competence, good faith, and legitimacy of the Wilhelmine state.

Notes

From Belinda Davis, *Home Fires Burning: Food, Politics, and Everyday Life in Berlin* (Chapel Hill: University of North Carolina Press, 2000), pp. 190–218. (c) 2000 by the University of North Carolina Press. Used by permission of the publisher.

1. See reading 6.4, Richard Watt, "The Kings Depart," for more.
2. See reading 4.2, Evelyn Blücher, "An English Wife in Berlin," for more.
3. The Socialist Party newspaper.

The Politics of Race

Jennifer D. Keene

That World War I citizen-soldiers truly were civilians in uniform became apparent whenever racial tensions emerged: both white and black soldiers brought racial agendas into the army that made race relations unpredictable and volatile. From the army's perspective, citizen-soldiers' pursuit of their respective goals had little to do with the overall military mission of defeating Germany. Conflicts between white southern soldiers' desire to minimize the visibility of blacks and black soldiers' hopes to improve their societal status by serving as combatants had great potential to side-track soldiers into waging their own internal civil war. Soldiers never saw their racial clashes as detrimental to the nation's international crusade, but army officials did. They had little faith that whites would control themselves in racially motivated situations or that blacks would willingly subordinate their own campaign for equality to winning the war.

As might have been expected at such a dreadful period in American race relations, most army commanders (with a few notable exceptions) concurred with white soldiers on the need for segregation, but the demands of the war sometimes forced the army to place black soldiers in close proximity to whites and even in positions of minor authority. Whenever white soldiers protested these arrangements, army commanders accommodated their demands. This pacification bore consequences that transcended the parameters of this particular debate. For in acquiescing to these demands, the army compromised its own unilateral authority to set internal military policy and direct the behavior of all troops regardless of their preferences. What was at issue was how much power army commanders would have to forfeit in tackling the unprecedented challenge of turning millions of citizen-soldiers into a viable mass army. Citizen-soldiers' ability to dilute the principle of unquestioning obedience offers a compellingly vivid illustration of the powerful role these troops played in shaping the wartime army.

The Army's Dilemma

Early on, the General Staff decided both to use most black troops in noncombatant capacities and to maintain white majorities at all training camps. While for the most part quelling the apprehensions of white civilians that military service might create black terrorist bands, these decisions neither eliminated racial conflict in the army nor sealed the fate of black U.S. soldiers. These policies chiefly clarified where recruiters should send black draftees and how they should assign them, but absorbing black recruits in an uncontentious and expeditious manner became an uphill struggle. Consequently, General Staff officials and division commanders continued to discuss possible revisions to their initial mobilization decisions throughout the war.

These unending policy discussions strikingly portray how racial instability preyed on the minds of army officials, especially when they realized the consequences if they faltered in containing it. In the summer of 1917, newly overwhelmed with a large number of black recruits whom they could not absorb easily, General Staff policymakers considered assigning black drafted troops as cooks and assistant cooks in white combatant units. This scheme would help the army immediately absorb at least 35,000 of the 75,000 black troops anticipated from the first draft, advocates argued. As important, these assignments would relieve white combat troops of fatigue duties, thus increasing the number of hours they could spend training each day.

General Staff policymakers rejected this proposition several times, however, even though it complemented their decision to use drafted black troops primarily as laborers. Assigning black and white troops to the same units might, they believed, push racial tempers to the breaking point. Brigadier General C. H. Barth, commander of the 81st Division, training in Camp Jackson, South Carolina, tried to allay this concern, telling the General Staff that southern officers with whom he had spoken felt that "there would be no friction between races in consequence of such assignments . . . [because] no colored man would be in position to give orders to any white man." Members of the War Plans Division remained unswayed, however. Even if white soldiers accepted the proximity of black, they noted, such an arrangement had the potential to damage army discipline even more severely than outright racial rioting. Few soldiers enjoyed general fatigue duties, and reserving it for black troops would only confirm the lowly status of this work. White soldiers might subsequently refuse such assignments, thereby creating a mutinous situation. "There is a present wide-spread objection in the service to the performance of duties of a menial nature, but to admit their menial quality by assigning such duties exclusively to an inferior race would make it well nigh impossible to persuade white men to ever again resume these duties," Lieutenant Colonel J. W. Barker concluded in the General Staff's third review of the plan. If white soldiers refused to work in the kitchen, who would substitute when black kitchen workers became ill? Officers used kitchen police duty as a common company punishment for rule infractions, but army authorities knew they did not have the power to punish white soldiers by detailing them to work with black soldiers. To prevent these limitations in their power over white troops from becoming explicit, General Staff officers rejected this suggestion. The gain in training time did not outweigh the potential damage such assignments could inflict on army authority.

War Plans Division officials also remained leery of black advancement organizations, which they suspected would immediately protest these assignments unless they made black men eligible for all positions in white units. Among themselves, these officials frankly admitted the desire to avoid antagonizing black organizations by sponsoring such a blatant policy of inequality. Implicit in their concern not to "unnecessarily emphasize the inferiority of the colored race" lay an apprehension that such a policy would dishearten black soldiers as well as their civilian leaders. So while the assignment of black labor units to training camps exempted white troops from general maintenance duties, white troops remained responsible for fatigue duties within their units. This two-year exchange highlights an important goal of army racial policy—to maintain disciplinary control by segregating black and white troops as systematically as possible. It also underscores how the army tried to juggle the competing concerns both of white and black civilians and of white and black citizen-soldiers when formulating racial policy.

Army planners believed that they could formulate distinct personnel plans for white and black soldiers, but because racially motivated mobilization policies influenced the structure of the wartime army, they affected all members of the organization, white and black, in some way. White racial prejudices directly affected the military experience of black soldiers by limiting their combat opportunities. Decisions made about the treatment of black soldiers also, however, influenced the fate of white soldiers. Maintaining a white majority in each mobilization camp undermined the initial intention to form regional units in the national army. Army planners originally adopted a plan to preserve the local integrity of individual units after considering the prohibitive cost of transporting troops to training camps far from their homes. Men might be happier and easier to discipline, army planners reasoned, if they entered the army with men from the same region. Yet because some sections had higher concentrations of blacks than others, the army could not automatically send men to the camp closest to their home and still keep an acceptable racial balance. Instead, the army sent black men from Alabama, Florida, Mississippi, North Carolina, Oklahoma, and Tennessee to train and to work in the North. When the draft in southern states did not provide enough white men to fill up the divisions organizing in southern camps, the army had to ship white draftees from northern and western states to train in Camp Gordon, Georgia, and Camp Pike, Arkansas. Subsequent replacement and classification procedures further diluted the local integrity of most units, but racial policies provided the critical first push to abandon this principle.

Yet the army, like American society, remained an imperfectly segregated institution. Placing black and white soldiers in the same camp (the General Staff had rejected a plan to concentrate black soldiers in two mobilization camps), in the same ships, and the same French towns guaranteed contact, and conflict, between the two races. Black and white soldiers may not have served in the same units, but it proved impossible to isolate members of the same army working together toward a common war goal. Army officials believed that they had settled the most pertinent racial questions by assigning blacks to noncombatant positions, giving them little military training, and keeping a white majority in every camp. But camp commanders discovered that citizen-soldiers, white and black alike, did not hesitate to enlist the aid of their respective civilian supporters to bolster their stand against an official decision they deemed unacceptable.

The court-martial of Captain C. Rowan, who refused to allow his white troops to stand in a formation that included a black unit in Camp Pike, Arkansas, on March 25, 1918, revealed both the impossibility of complete segregation and the importance of outside political pressure. The first series of complaints from Rowan, which the governor of Mississippi telegrammed to President Wilson, included charges that the brigade commander, Colonel F. B. Shaw, was "forcing white privates to cook for negro soldiers." By the time of his court-martial, investigators dismissed most of his accusations except the one charging that white and black units had stood next to one another in formation. Rowan called this formation order illegal because racial "intermingling" violated the self-respect of white soldiers. "They are all Southerners and it would have been a direct violation of the customs they had abided by all during their lives," Rowan's counsel argued during his court-martial for willful disobedience of orders. On the surface, his conviction reaffirmed the principle of unquestioning obedience to orders, but concerned citizens and congressmen descended on Camp Pike to ensure that the camp commander was not giving orders that, in their view, white men could justifiably disobey. Rowan was dismissed from the army, but Major General Samuel D. Sturgis, the camp commander, thereafter forbade brigade commanders to place black and white units in the same formation. Secretary of War Baker also assured the president that the commanding general of the camp was offending "neither Southern nor Northern sensibilities" with his racial polices. In this camp, therefore, the commander carefully censored orders to avoid another confrontation with white troops and civilians.

Black soldiers also had advocates to whom they could appeal, although often with less satisfactory results. The black press publicized incidents of discrimination against black soldiers, and the War Department found itself investigating rumors that black soldiers were being "exposed in places of special danger in order to save the lives of white soldiers." Emmett J. Scott, Charles Williams, and Major William H. Loving were three black men who provided the bulk of official information, supplemented by the observations of white intelligence officers, to army officials and to black advancement organizations about black troops. Scott, secretary of the Tuskegee Institute and an associate of the late Booker T. Washington, began advising the secretary of war on racial matters in October 1917, but he had minimal power to remedy army racial problems. He received a steady stream of complaints from black soldiers throughout the war, which he could only pass on to the Intelligence Division to investigate. Although he occasionally visited the camps, Scott concentrated on persuading War Department officials to open more skilled and commissioned positions to educated blacks. He noted with pride after the war that whereas blacks had previously only served in cavalry and infantry units, during this war, blacks had served in every technical branch of the organization. Charles Williams began surveying camp conditions in March 1918 for the Federal Council of Churches, but filed all his reports and recommendations with the War Department. His background as a welfare worker made him especially curious about the harmful recreational habits of black soldiers. The Intelligence Division sent Major William Loving, a retired black army officer, to investigate the morale of black troops. His postwar report, which severely criticized army treatment of black soldiers, carried a good bit of weight with Brigadier General Marlborough Churchill, director of the Military Intelligence Division, because he had always regarded Loving as "a white man's negro." The situation must indeed be serious, Churchill concluded, if Loving criticized it. Although each investigator had a somewhat different agenda, each tried, at one point or another, to persuade policymakers to abandon strict segregation. The peaceful interracial relationships cropping up in some camps across the country, they argued, suggested that a strong commander could enforce an official effort to promote equality in the army.

Civilian allies helped white and black soldiers articulate their grievances to high-ranking army officials, but citizen-soldiers also manipulated the racial tempo of army life themselves. Because most white army officials shared the racial beliefs of white soldiers, the potential for conflict with white soldiers over racial matters appeared slim. Yet in the camps, commanders often unintentionally set up situations in which they could not express their sympathy or support for white soldiers' racial preferences without diluting their own (and the institution's) insistence on unquestioning obedience.

Simply walking through the camp gates brought black and white troops into contact with members of the other race whom the army had invested with some official authority. In an effort to minimize the hours white troops lost from training, black noncombatants were assigned to share the task of guard duty with white military police (MPs), although they did not serve in guard units together. Black sentries rarely carried guns, but they nonetheless checked passes and admitted visitors to the camp. Camp officials faced a dilemma when white soldiers refused to recognize black guards as legitimate representatives of army authority. Black skin in their eyes gave them license to disobey, and they could often find junior officers who supported their actions. A company officer's reaction when a white stevedore in his unit complained to him that a black sentry had stopped him from leaving Camp Hill, Virginia, without a pass aptly illustrated this dynamic. Rather than disciplining the soldier for his unauthorized attempt to leave camp, the lieutenant armed himself and twelve of his men and confronted the black guard. When the sentry explained that he only was obeying his orders to turn back every man who did not have a pass, the lieutenant, an investigator noted, said: "Damn the order! My men must not be stopped!" when the officer of the day arrived at the gate and asked the lieutenant to clarify exactly what he had meant by the words "Damn the order!" the lieutenant made it clear he would not allow a black guard to stop his men. Convinced that his guards could not enforce an order white troops deemed inappropriate, the officer of the day did nothing to punish the white troops for disobeying it.

White troops also invoked their own definition of appropriate military authority to justify their disobedience of black officers. At Camp Pike, Arkansas, the assignment of black officers to the Central Officers' Training School prompted a rash of disciplinary problems among the white troops stationed in the camp. "There is ever present a great danger of infraction of the rules of discipline as regards proper saluting and recognizing the authority of the colored officer by virtue of his commission over the white soldier," Colonel C. Miller complained to General Staff officials. An overwhelming number of men refused to salute black officers, and Miller claimed that he could not force them to do so. Unless the adjutant general removed the black officers from the camp, Miller feared, white troops would soon lose all respect for army authority. White officer candidates also disliked saluting black officers, but because their commissions depended upon their exemplary conduct as students, Miller expected less immediate trouble from them. Even when white soldiers agreed to recognize the superior rank of a black officer, they often found a way to make their true feelings clear. Mississippi troops, for example, saluted the black officers from Camp Zachary Taylor, Kentucky, they met in Camp Merritt, New Jersey, but added "Damn you!" under their breath. Black officers fared better in Camp Hancock, Georgia, because they did not "look for salutes" from white soldiers, a demeanor army officials encouraged all black officers to adopt.

Refusals to arrest white soldiers who physically assaulted black soldiers accompanied the tendency to rescind unpopular racial orders and to discourage black officers from demanding salutes from white soldiers. Sergeant David Myers returned to Camp Gordon, Georgia, with two black eyes and a bruised face after a group of white MPs, who were corporals, beat him for wearing sidearms through town. Ignoring his rank, one corporal demanded that he remove his sidearms. When Myers responded too slowly, the corporal warmed: "Hey dar nigger, why so mart bout taken off dem sidearms [sic], don't you know that you is down in Georgia?" before the group jumped on him. The camp authorities refused to prosecute the white corporals; instead, they concentrated on persuading Myers to drop his complaint against them.

Black troops proved no more willing than whites to obey authority figures of the other race, however, if they saw a means of preserving their racial dignity. Subjected to continuous abuse from whites, black soldiers counterattacked whenever possible. In August 1918, two white MPs arrived in the black troop housing area in Camp Funston, Kansas, to disperse a group whose loud yelling outside an open air theater was disrupting the show inside. When the MPs ordered the men to disperse, only a few complied. The others, MP Leman B. Johnson reported, jeered at them, "telling him that he couldn't do anything, and also telling him to 'About Face' and 'Squads Right' and laughing at him and telling him that he couldn't make any arrest." Determined to enforce their order, the MPs decided to arrest one particularly belligerent soldier. As the MPs approached him, he fled into a ditch, picked up a rock, and stood poised ready to hurl it at the two white men. "I then pulled my pistol," Corporal Leon Michaelis, the other MP, testified later, "and told him if he threw the rock I would shoot him. The other colored soldiers had been throwing rocks and near-beer bottles and other missiles during this time." When the man turned and ran toward the barracks, Johnson raised his pistol and shot him in the shoulder. Within minutes an angry crowd encircled the two white men. Two black noncommissioned officers hurriedly advised them to hide in the barracks across the street and wait for the guard. The guard, a group of unarmed black soldiers, successfully dispersed the crowd while the two white men waited under cover. Johnson was not arrested for shooting the black soldier.

For black soldiers, obeying white officers became synonymous with accepting the demeaning position that military authorities in general had imposed upon them: challenging white officers therefore became a viable way for them to reassert racial dignity. Lieutenant Corbett witnessed the gestation of this sort of race consciousness when a black troop train in France stopped near him and he ordered the black combat soldiers to come down off the boxcar roofs and find places inside the boxcars. One soldier refused to obey his order, and the sight of this lone black man defying a symbol of white authority prompted his comrades to support his actions vocally. "I was told by one man that he was no dog, I presume meaning the man I was ordering down, and this was followed by several outcries . . . one in particular I do recall was 'we'll take no orders from no white man.'" Soldiers began pouring off the train to join the group of agitated soldiers until a black corporal appeared and succeeded in coaxing the men inside the troop coaches. The black officers in charge, however, made no motion to protect the white officer, whom they no doubt knew was receiving the kind of treatment they endured so often from white troops. Racial violence was an undisputed fact of army life, Corporal Lloyd Blair, a member of the black 92nd Division, noted years later, because "we couldn't get along with the white to [sic] much."

To army officials the dissolution of the principle of unquestioning obedience to orders emerged as the most vexing aspect of citizen-soldiers' tendency to reject racially offensive directives or to ignore rank and justify disobedience in terms of the skin color of the man wearing the uniform. White soldiers usually won immediate concessions from army officials, who, when faced with their insubordination, revised offensive policies and abandoned the black soldiers charged with enforcing them. Occasionally, however, army officials stuck by their policy decisions if no potential disciplinary problem existed. Ill black and white soldiers, for instance, sometimes found themselves assigned beds in the same army hospital wards. When Private Roy Chesebro fell ill from his inoculations, he landed in the hospital for thirty days, "the only white soldier in the ward." Army officials ignored the objections white troops raised. "While the negro soldiers are segregated in the army, they are not separated from whites in hospital," Colonel D. W. Ketcham of the War Plans Division explained to the chief of staff. "[I]n hospitals, patients have to be classified by diseases rather than with reference to other considerations and, moreover, while men are sick in bed there is scarcely any opportunity for friction due to race troubles." The surgeon general, however, advised the Red Cross to segregate its convalescent houses for soldiers. Although ill white troops could not act on their racial prejudices, white doctors could and did. Black army observers noted that many white doctors refused to treat blacks. Loving, for example, reported from Camp Zachary Taylor that black soldiers suffering from venereal disease went untreated, because white doctors "must actually handle the privates of colored men in order to get results," and they refused to do so.

Racial relationships within the army proved extremely complex, and even more important, unpredictable. In some areas, full-blown racial riots broke out among soldiers. In others, white and black soldiers coexisted peacefully, even harmoniously. Black advancement officials argued that the constructive relationships found in some camps offered another viable alternative for the army besides always siding with white racists. Given the divided white opinion on appropriate racial practices, these black advancement advocates claimed that the army could have the deciding vote by forcing white soldiers to conform to mandated egalitarian policies. Given their own conservative views on race, few army officials agreed with the principle of integration or the idea that they possessed the power to force troops to comply with such a radical notion. They had no interest in making either the wartime or the professional army a place for social experimentation. Traditionally, the army stationed its four black regiments far away from white soldiers and civilians, in garrison posts along the Mexican border, in Hawaii, and in the Philippines. Race relations in the professional army had deteriorated significantly since the 1906 Brownsville riot shattered a forty-year lull in racial violence between black soldiers and white civilians, and the 1917 Houston riot seemingly gave the General Staff evidence that this dangerous new trend might continue. Their wartime experiences only reinforced professional officers' commitment to using segregation to maintain racial peace. But the suggestion that the army take an activist role in enforcing civil rights was not as far-fetched as it may have sounded at the time, although it required civilian, not military, leadership to succeed. Thirty years later, the military used its authoritarian power to force troop acceptance of President Harry Truman's 1948 decision to desegregate the armed forces, even though civilian society continued to embrace Jim Crow practices.

The Search for Predictability

Entering the army with distinct racial ambitions, white and black soldiers found many reasons to disagree during their service. But white and black soldiers also discovered grounds for cooperation. Two riots, one in Charleston, South Carolina, and one in Camp Merritt, New Jersey, illuminate how citizen-soldiers responded to these competing forces in the wartime army. Significantly, race relationships between soldiers did not simply mirror the prevalent racial tensions of civilian society but also evolved in response to pressures specific to the military environment.

The U.S. Army uniform, which most citizen-soldiers wore proudly during the national emergency, had perhaps the greatest potential to create a bond between black and white soldiers. It was a badge of honor that unified otherwise dissimilar men, not only symbolizing faithful service and their status as defenders of the nation, but distinguishing them both from civilians and from members of other armies. The General Staff recognized the symbolic importance of the uniform by advising commanders not to issue the uniform white soldiers wore to black noncombatant troops. But like many army policies, this one was haphazardly enforced, and in many camps black and white soldiers wore some similar version of the national uniform.

The civilian police in Charleston, South Carolina, dramatically under-estimated the strength of the uniform as a rallying point for American soldiers when they arrested a drunk black soldier they found wandering down a street one night. Their brutal treatment of the soldier corresponded with regional racial custom, and conceivably MPs arrested black soldiers in the same brutal way. But this harassment quickly lost its racial legitimacy when the arrest evolved into a confrontation between civilians and soldiers, rather than between white and black men.

On December 8, 1918, a crowd of about thirteen soldiers and sailors gathered on a street corner in Charleston to watch a white policeman arrest Private Colis Sylvester, a black soldier who had consumed a pint of whiskey. Private Fred Carrier, a white soldier and military guard, walked up to the policeman and told him that he knew Sylvester. Carrier offered to take him back to camp and turn him over to the military police. As he reached for Sylvester's arm, the policeman raised his club and struck his prisoner on the head. The crowd witnessing this assault stood by shocked, and "one of the sailors passed the remark '[R]emember, you are hitting a United States uniform,'"

Carrier testified. To which the policeman responded, "Fuck the uniform!" Clearly, the civilian policeman expected support from the white soldiers and sailors in the crowd. Instead, he turned their initial curiosity about the arrest into a defense of the uniform they all wore. "As he hit the stevedore someone yelled 'beat him up,'" Carrier recalled, and the military members of the crowd responded by pulling Sylvester away from the policeman and carrying him away from town toward camp.

A few blocks later, the crowd met an assembled block of police reserves, who, with drawn pistols, rearrested Sylvester and another black soldier. The police claimed they made this additional arrest after "they were cursed violently by the soldiers and sailors and attacked by them." The servicemen later denied assaulting the policemen, alleging that they only asked where the police were taking Sylvester. By this point the original crowd of thirteen men had swelled. "After the police had arrested the soldiers . . . a crowd of several hundred people, composed of both white and colored, soldiers, sailors and citizens, started to the police station," the investigating officer noted in his report. The soldiers and sailors in the crowd demanded that the police release the prisoners and arrest the policeman who had cursed the uniform. The police, fearing a riot, began dragging the soldiers they identified as the ringleaders, including Carrier, into the jail called the U.S. Guards to come and "quell the riot." When the Guards arrived, they discovered a large gathering standing patiently outside the jail waiting for a response to their demands, and no evidence that the crowd had tried to break into the jail. By midnight, the Guards had cleared the streets by ordering all soldiers back to their quarters.

Despite the participation of both black and white troops in the disturbance, civilian authorities continued to depict it as a race riot. They pursued their crusade against black soldiers by choosing to free the white soldier they had arrested while prosecuting all black prisoners. The town courts convicted every black soldier arrested that night and imposed fines or sentences of up to thirty days' hard labor, which they were powerless to enforce. Military authorities, however, rejected the racial overtones that the civilian authorities interjected into their interpretation of the incident. Major General Henry G. Sharpe, the commander of the Southeastern Department, refused to censure or to quarantine black troops near Charleston, negating racial friction as the reason for the clash. Instead, he told the mayor, the enlisted men were reacting to the unnecessary brutality used while arresting "a member of their command . . . and that a member of your Police Force had cast reflections on the uniform of the United States Army, and the men wearing it." To avoid future clashes, Sharpe urged civilian authorities to turn all men in uniform over to the army for prosecution in military courts.

This incident is striking in part because it occurred in the South, where civilian communities had been particularly successful in imposing their racial customs on both army officials and black soldiers. Clashes between white civilians and black soldiers commonly occurred, and clearly the Charleston police at first viewed their arrest of Sylvester as just another trophy they could claim in their campaign to keep black soldiers "in their place." Yet, the police did not appreciate that in the reordered worldview of white soldiers and even, it appears, among some white civilians, protecting the uniform came before punishing a disorderly black soldier. However, if white soldiers had agreed with the police interpretation of events, the camp commander would likely have punished black troops under his command. White soldiers always retained the power to sanction some racial behavior as legitimate and to judge other actions as contentious.

Ironically, however, peaceful coexistence between black and white soldiers and the decision of some civilian recreational officials to integrate their facilities often troubled army officials as much as outbursts of racial violence. In some camps, white and black soldiers negotiated racial truces that enabled them to share recreational facilities; in others, the camp commander required it. Black and white soldiers at one time or another contentedly shared facilities in Camp Devens, Camp Funston, Camp Lee, Camp Meade, Camp Merritt, Camp Travis, and Camp Upton. In these cooperative situations, white and black troops played games together, watched movies and shows, or wrote letters for each other. A white lieutenant in Camp Shelby, Mississippi, went as far as to organize a series of baseball games between his black labor outfit and a unit of white engineers. The YMCA provided general recreation to troops in the camps, and the willingness of YMCA secretaries and white troops to accept black soldiers in camp YMCA huts varied tremendously. In some camps, the Y established separate huts for black soldiers, while in others black soldiers frequented all existing facilities. Other organizations, including the Knights of Columbus and the Jewish Welfare Board, established integrated huts in the larger camps. "In all camps the K. of C. [Knights of Columbus] displayed the word 'WELCOME,' which meant all that the word implied," an investigator concluded in his survey of camp conditions. "There was absolutely no discrimination practiced by this organization."

Such racial reconciliation worried army officials, who feared that this tranquility could not last, and that violence was bound to explode at some point. The shared access policies pursued by some camp welfare secretaries and a few northern commanders created further problems by inspiring black advancement organizations to continue pressing army officials to guarantee equal treatment throughout the military.

The race riot at Camp Merritt, New Jersey, the port of embarkation, on August 18, 1918, sent a strong message throughout the army about the inevitable consequences of social integration. Black and white troops at Camp Merritt lived in close quarters and shared all recreational facilities for a short period of time while they waited to embark for France. The fragility of racial truces resembled the "live-and-let-live" pacts that emerged along the Western Front. Informal racial and enemy truces both could end suddenly when the range of behavior one group of men accepted proved intolerable to the next occupants of a camp or trench. Just as newly assigned troops often turned a quiet sector into an active one, the arrival of new troops in camp could terminate established racial agreements abruptly. Embarkation camp officials bore the burden of disciplining a completely transient population, whose officers had often already sailed for France. These circumstances magnified the problems associated with maintaining stable race relations. "There have been outbursts of friction before," William Lloyd Imes, a black YMCA secretary in Camp Merritt acknowledged. "Whenever Southerners are also in camp and near the hut used by the men [black and white] in common, there are many insults passed and threats." Nonetheless, YMCA secretaries had without incident ignored requests from embarking white troops that they bar black troops from recreational facilities.

When the 155th Infantry, a unit filled with recruits from Mississippi, arrived in Camp Merritt, they, like many groups of southern soldiers who had entered the camp before then, demanded that the YMCA segregate the facilities near their quarters. As he had done many times before, the white secretary in charge of Hut #2 refused. A note he discovered by the stamp counter the next afternoon indicated that this time a tenacious stance might not work. If the Y secretary did not meet their demands, these troops planned to rectify this offensive racial situation themselves. The note read:

> You Y.M.C.A. men are paying entirely too much attention to the niggers, and white men are neglected. Because of this, if it is not corrected by sundown, we are coming to clean this place out. (Signed), Southern Volunteers

Tension grew throughout the day as isolated scuffles broke out between white and black soldiers, but no encounter evolved into a mêlée. Finally, at 6:30, twenty-five "Southern Volunteers" marched into the YMCA and confronted the five black soldiers they found there writing letters. The white troops threw these black soldiers onto the street. The YMCA secretary followed the men out of the building, stood at the entrance, and closed the building to all soldiers until white soldiers agreed to accept the presence of black soldiers. As accounts of the incident spread back to the barracks from those who had witnessed it, alarm swept the camp. Black troops gathered outside their barracks to prepare for an anticipated attack, while the "Southern Volunteers" searched other public buildings. They soon discovered a black soldier playing the piano in the main auditorium and rushed up to him. The soldier immediately rose, pulled out his knife and successfully defended himself by cutting one of the white assailants on the neck. "By this time the military police had come, so that no further trouble occurred in this building," Imes recalled. "The barracks trouble [however] was now very much aflame, and two shots were heard. No one seemed able, up to this time, to state who fired these shots or where they were fired, but the alarm had been given." Confused soldiers milled about trying to locate the origin of the shots when thirteen guards from the 50th Infantry ran up and positioned themselves directly in front of the black soldiers' barracks. Within minutes the nervous white guard fired into the crowd, wounding three men inside the barracks and killing Private Edward Frye. The guard had fired without orders, misinterpreting the agitated black troops standing outside their barracks as instigators of the riot. "Greatest credit must be given the colored officers of a contingent of men from Camp Sherman, who were just across the road from the Camp Taylor men, into whom the guards had fired and who held their men in restraint from attacking the guard from the rear," Imes noted. The potential for further violence quickly dissipated when the authorities moved white troops to the opposite side of camp and quarantined all black troops until they left for France a few days later.

The General Staff Intelligence Division, fearful that a racial war might engulf the entire camp, immediately launched an investigation. The Camp Merritt riot underscored to the General Staff the value of strict segregation as the most effective way to control race relations. Camp YMCA officials and the investigating intelligence officer, Major L. B. Dunham, recommended a different course, however, in the days immediately following the riot. Dunham urged officials to support the secretaries' effort to integrate camp facilities. "If it is impossible for the white Southern troops to get along with negro troops, it is conceivable that the Government could make arrangements whereby the entire quota from any State could be raised from the white population," Dunham wrote angrily in his initial report. "It seems to me that, until the whites are willing to assume this burden, they should act in a decent manner toward the colored troops." Echoing this sentiment, camp YMCA officials urged the military authorities to endorse their endeavor to provide equal service for all soldiers.

The position of Camp Merritt's YMCA mirrored the order Major General J. Franklin Bell had given in Camp Upton, New York, when clashes between white and black troops began in April 1918. When a few white men from a newly arrived Texas regiment walked into a camp YMCA, they were stunned to see two black soldiers inside writing letters. "Being unaccustomed to such scenes, the group threw them out the window," Charles Williams reported. Bell assembled his officers the next morning and told them that all recreational facilities, including YMCA buildings and theaters, remained open to white and black troops. Bell warned them that hereafter "the officers in charge of both parties would be held strictly responsible for the acts of their men." Men who disobeyed these orders would never, he promised, get overseas.

The principles outlined in this verbal order appealed to those who felt that army officials had the power to improve societal race relations. General Staff officials let Bell's order stand, but they had no intention of seeing it as a precedent. Captain G. B. Perkins, chief of the Military Morale Division, agreed with Emmett Scott that Bell's speech "met the situation squarely" but based his conclusion on the erroneous assumption that Bell was censuring only northern troops. A similar order, he argued, was "likely to be interpreted somewhat differently when both the white and the colored soldiers are from the Southern section of the Country or when the white soldiers in the camp come from the southern states and the colored soldiers come mainly from the Northern states." Certainly, the northern location of Camp Upton explained the indifference of neighboring civilians to Bell's order, and in the South, civilian protest had already forced many changes in camp racial policies. Without explicitly noting their obvious unwillingness to see such a general policy in place, General Staff officials argued that the army did not have the power to enforce a mandate for integrated recreational facilities. Perkins concluded that if the YMCA secretaries had been more conciliatory toward white soldiers in Camp Merritt, the riot never would have occurred. In the future, Perkins recommended, when racial friction emerged "some wise person, preferably colored . . . should talk to the [black] soldiers, advising them regarding their conduct and urging them to use every reasonable means to avoid disturbances."

As might have been expected, given this interpretation of events, the Camp Merritt authorities made little effort to convict the guard of killing Private Frye. The one black NCO called to testify at the trial two months later could not identify which guard had shot and killed Frye, so the guards were acquitted. "It appears that there has been an unfortunate miscarriage of justice in connection with this affair," Loving noted dismally. Black troops passing through Camp Merritt after the riot continually questioned YMCA secretaries about the fate of the white assailants. The response they received demonstrated to them that once again army authorities had refused to punish white troops for an unjust attack on black soldiers.

The General Staff's conclusion championed the principles that Major General Charles C. Ballou, commander of 92nd division, had outlined for the black troops training in Camp Funston, Kansas. Ballou's infamous Bulletin #35 ordered black soldiers to stop pressing for equal treatment when they visited the town next to camp. Ballou issued the bulletin to defuse a heated dispute between black soldiers and white civilians after a theater owner refused to admit a member of the 92nd Division. Ballou instructed his troops in their responsibility to avoid antagonizing nearby civilians. Although the theater owner had broken the law by discriminating against the black sergeant, Ballou stated, "the sergeant is guilty of the GREATER wrong in doing ANYTHING, NO MATTER HOW LEGALLY CORRECT, that will provoke race animosity." Ballou told his troops to stay out of places where whites did not want them, or they would suffer severe consequences. "White men made the Division," he said, "and they can break it just as easily if it becomes a troublemaker." General Staff members concurred fully with this sentiment after the Camp Merritt riot. The "cases of unsatisfactory relations add weight to the opinion that the separation of the two races within the army organization is the policy of wisdom," intelligence officers concluded after the war.

Army officials' receptivity to strident segregationist demands revealed their concern about disciplinary control as much as it unveiled their own racist beliefs. The choices that army officials made during the war reflected how vulnerable they felt, or made themselves, to the weight of white soldiers' racial preferences, but the army paid a price for exacerbating the sense of isolation from the war's purpose that their status as noncombatants already had thrust upon black soldiers. The army's blatant discrimination in favor of whites precipitated enormous anger and hostility among the black rank and file, and disciplining this increasingly alienated segment of the army population further distracted army officials from the military goal of winning the war.

The Repercussions for Black Soldiers

The army's tendency to appease white opinion both within and without the military had serious long-term repercussions for black U.S. soldiers. In early policy discussions about how to assign black recruits, General Staff officials never doubted the army's ability to train these men for combat, especially since black units had compiled illustrious records in the Civil War and the Spanish-American War. Instead, they spoke of balancing political and manpower demands. By the spring of 1918, however, the General Staff began for the first time during the war to justify its decision to limit the number of black combat units in terms of defects inherent in the black race. "The poorer class of backwoods negro has not the mental stamina and moral sturdiness to put him in the line against opposing German troops," Colonel E. O. Anderson concluded in a memorandum on the black draft in May 1918. "The enemy is constantly looking for a weak place in the line and if he can find a part of the line held by troops composed of culls of the colored race, all he has to do is to concentrate on that." These same officials now argued that black soldiers found the adjustment to army life harder than whites. "The negro is frequently not accustomed to orderliness, moral or physical discipline, not even to ordinary cleanliness and sanitation. One colored private had complained bitterly because he had to comb his hair and take a bath every day," a typical intelligence bulletin read. Army authorities also claimed that they could not trust a racial group who seemed more committed to winning their own political battles than to victory on the battlefield. Officials speculated that German propagandists had infiltrated black communities and planted stories that black servicemen served as shields for white soldiers at the front. Such rumors circulated so widely by June 1918 that the War Department cabled Pershing to send them a publishable statement refuting these charges.

The army responded to this supposed subversive threat by launching a comprehensive investigation into black soldiers' activities. Intelligence officers compiled mountains of reports detailing the intentions of "troublemakers" to raise questions of equality and opportunity. Black troops concerned with these issues soon became dissatisfied with their army life, intelligence officers concluded, and were likely to instigate racial disturbances. Numerous operatives cited German propaganda as the cause of black soldiers' dissatisfaction, not the mistreatment black soldiers complained of to investigators. The stinging critique German propaganda pamphlets offered of racial segregation in American society had haunting accuracy. "Can you go to a restaurant where white people dine, can you get a seat in a theatre where white people sit, can you get a Pullman seat or berth in a railroad car? . . . there is nothing in the whole game for you but broken bones, horrible wounds, broken health or death," leaflets that German aviators dropped among the few American black troops near the front lines proclaimed.

After the war, this image of the black soldier as "the enemy within" stuck. Postwar studies noted that while African-Americans' subordinate position in civilian society taught them to depend on white men for leadership, the injustice blacks often encountered bred strong feelings of resentment against whites. "It would be futile for us to try to believe that the negro has no particular state of mind against us, he undoubtedly has," cautioned one postwar report. Rather than using this collection of evidence to create policies designed to remove the reasons for resentment and the appeal of enemy propaganda, the war induced a new, damaging period of institutional racism, in which officials viewed African-American soldiers as incompetent, untrustworthy, and dangerous.

Whenever racial friction emerged in any camp during the war, black troops were usually the ones who lost their pass privileges, received additional quarantines, or were court-martialed. When black troops directly questioned discriminatory quarantine rules, army officials simply responded that all soldiers had to endure quarantines to check the spread of infectious diseases through army training camps. Privately, however, army officials acknowledged these lengthy quarantines kept black troops under supervision in one section of the camp. In a few camps, troops took matters into their own hands and organized efforts to rush the gates and get into town for the night. Most of the men Ely Green led in a charge of the gates one night at Camp Stuart, Virginia, an auxiliary camp near Newport News, had not left camp since entering the army. Scheduled to depart for France the next day, "I began thinking to how I would love to hold a little brown baby in my arms once more. I hadnt [sic] been close to a woman in a month. The men were talking of breaking camp. They were restless, I knew. I was too," Green recalled. The men eluded the guards by throwing blankets over the perimeter fences and obstructing the guards' view of the escapees. Green cautioned the men to stick close together throughout the evening. "Dont [sic] any one get lost," he counseled them. "If you do you will be court-martialed. We must stick together." This strategy worked well, because only Green, the group's ringleader, got caught when the men returned to camp, and even he was released to sail with his unit the next day.

Many black soldiers who broke rules formulated to limit their interaction with white soldiers had less luck and got a quick and severe reminder of their second-class status. "The military police," at Camp Sevier, Charles Williams reported dismally "is composed of all southern soldiers, who are careful to see that the Negro soldiers stay in their place." MPs regularly threw black soldiers into the guardhouse, where their jailers indiscriminately beat them, put them to work, or let them go. Private Adams Glatfeller, training in Camp Gordon, Georgia, approvingly noted to his brother the trepidation he observed in the black prisoners who occasionally marched through camp. "You know they are afraid of a white person," Glatfeller wrote. Officials hoped the severity of the punishments given to black soldiers would deter other rebellious black soldiers from challenging army authority. When three black soldiers were convicted of raping a white woman outside Camp Dodge, Iowa, camp officials decided to hang them publicly so that everyone in the camp, white and black alike, would see the swift retribution aberrant black soldiers received.

Such tactics successfully subdued many black soldiers, but they also left them dispirited, sentiments clearly reflected in a heart-wrenching letter Private Stanley Moore wrote to his sister from Camp Travis, Texas:

> My dear Sister,
> Your letter received and always glad to hear from you. I can't say that I like the Army life, it is a hard life to live and they are so mean to the colored boys here. They curse and beat them just like they were dogs and a fellow can't even get sick. Oh! it is an awfully mean place. I will be so glad when they send me away from here.

Moore soon got his wish, and reported to his sister that things had improved for him in his new army home in Camp Funston, Kansas. His good luck did not last long, however, because medical examiners soon classified him as unfit to serve overseas and sent him back to Camp Travis.

Army officials made supervising black soldiers a high priority, but not supplying them. The equipment and housing requirements of white troops took precedence over the needs of black troops when the army allocated scarce resources. Inadequately housed and clothed black noncombatants consequently endured hardships more appropriate to the front line than in a stateside training camp. Some of the worst conditions existed in Camp Hill, which housed the black stevedores working at the Newport News embarkation port. "During the coldest weather Virginia has experienced in twenty-five years, the stevedores lived in tents without floors or stoves," forcing some to stand out around fires all night to avoid frostbite, Williams reported. Promised clothing within a month of their arrival in camp, these men worked in the sleet and snow loading and unloading ships "without overcoats, rain coats, or even good shoes." These men had nowhere to bathe, nor did they receive a change of clothing until January 1919. "Cases are known," Williams continued, "where men had only one suit of underwear for two or three months. As a result, many of them were covered with vermin."

Conditions like these seriously impaired the morale of black noncombatant soldiers. Added to reduced military training opportunities, these miserable living conditions further weakened their resolve. Most did not receive adequate housing or recreational facilities until after the war, when demobilizing white soldiers vacated their quarters. First Lieutenant Howard Jenkins, a morale officer in Camp Travis, reported encouragingly that moving black soldiers into barracks, improving rations, securing three afternoons off for the men, and opening a YMCA recreational room "have been important factors in decreasing A.W.O.L.s and other offenses to a very small percentage." This improved morale came too late to do the army much good.

Black troops gained significant social freedom while serving overseas, however. "A new race riot was staged in Winchester[,] England[,] between the southerners in the Camp Wheeler outfits and American negroes who were camped there," the debarkation intelligence officer reported to Washington. "It was reported, as has been reported many times before, that people in England always give American negroes a big reception and show them big times. . . . The negroes of the outfit, it was said, began boasting about it to the southerners at Winchester and a free for all fight followed." Nothing angered southern white troops more than friendships or sexual relationships between Frenchwomen and black soldiers. Sergeant Green, the same soldier who engineered the escape from Camp Stuart discussed above, was walking back to camp from St. Nazaire one afternoon with a group of white soldiers when they came upon a line of black troops waiting in line outside a whorehouse. "There was about fifteen Negro soldiers standing in line as if they were going to mess. These white souldiers [sic] began yelling at these Negro souldiers telling them that not to get too use to white womans. You won't have them when you get to America," he recalled. "The Negroes yelled back: 'Go to Hell.'" First Lieutenant William Powell reported from St. Sulpice that "almost daily there are reports coming into this office of the growing friction between the white and colored soldiers in this camp." The point of contention once again was competition for Frenchwomen. One Sunday, Powell saw a crowd of black soldiers gathering, and asked one of them what the problem was. "He replied, 'that a white guard had pulled a gun on a black boy who was talking to a white woman' and there 'would be trouble' if this continued."

French people, unfortunately, "do not look upon the Negro exactly in the same way that the white people of American do," Brigadier General W. S. Scott, the commanding general at St. Sulpice, concluded, although white American soldiers did their best to enlighten them. Black soldiers soon discovered that white U.S. troops were busy spreading rumors among the civilian population that blacks were rapists, thieves, and had tails. Anxious to develop a strong working relationship with their new allies, French military officials tried to eliminate these offensive interracial relationships.

Colonel Linard, a member of the French Mission attached to the U.S. Army, advised French Army headquarters to alert French officers that praising black soldiers and allowing unlimited interracial contact between friendly French civilians and black soldiers hurt white American troop morale. Sexual encounters between black soldiers and Frenchwomen even troubled those lobbying for equal treatment. Major Loving, a stalwart defender of black soldiers throughout the war, nonetheless advised the War Department to ship black soldiers back home quickly once the Armistice had been signed. Black soldiers, like all other soldiers, he warned, would seek sexual diversions after the war, and because no white man "wants to see colored men mingling with white women . . . I cannot see anything but an American race war in France."

Throughout the war, the army nearly always sided with white soldiers when they complained about unjust racial practices. These accommodations, coupled with the disciplinary revolution under way in nonracial matters, illustrate the powerful institutional position that white troops occupied. As the war wore on, winning the allegiance of these troops became more and more important to army officials. They increasingly viewed citizen-soldiers as comrades whom they could count on for future political support, rather than antagonists. It soon became apparent, however, that the army had little ability to direct citizen-soldiers' budding political consciousness. Encouraged to contemplate the nation's democratic war goals, both white and black citizen-soldiers developed ideas of their own about where American priorities should lie in the international crusade being pursued by the United States. The problem of discipline and loyalty came to encompass more than whether soldiers would obey unquestioningly or maintain peaceful race relations. American officials soon realized that the more faith U.S. soldiers invested in the democratic purpose of the war, the more determined they became to forge relations with the French and Germans that reflected their own definition of national war goals.

NOTE

From Jennifer D. Keene, *Doughboys, the Great War, and the Remaking of America*. (Baltimore: Johns Hopkins University Press, 2001), pp. 82–104. (c) 2001 Johns Hopkins University Press. Reprinted with permission of the Johns Hopkins University Press.

Five

The End of the War

The Fourteen Points

President Woodrow Wilson

January 8, 1918

Gentlemen of the Congress:

We entered this war because violations of right had occurred which touched us to the quick and made the life of our own people impossible unless they were corrected and the world secure once for all against their recurrence. What we demand in this war, therefore, is nothing peculiar to ourselves. It is that the world be made fit and safe to live in; and particularly that it be made safe for every peace-loving nation which, like our own, wishes to live its own life, determine its own institutions, be assured of justice and fair dealing by the other peoples of the world as against force and selfish aggression. All the peoples of the world are in effect partners in this interest, and for our own part we see very clearly that unless justice be done to others it will not be done to us. The program of the world's peace, therefore, is our program; and that program, the only possible program, as we see it, is this:

I. Open covenants of peace, openly arrived at, after which there shall be no private international understandings of any kind but diplomacy shall proceed always frankly and in the public view.

II. Absolute freedom of navigation upon the seas, outside territorial waters, alike in peace and in war, except as the seas may be closed in whole or in part by international action for the enforcement of international covenants.

III. The removal, so far as possible, of all economic barriers and the establishment of an equality of trade conditions among all the nations consenting to the peace and associating themselves for its maintenance.

IV. Adequate guarantees given and taken that national armaments will be reduced to the lowest point consistent with domestic safety.

V. A free, open-minded, and absolutely impartial adjustment of all colonial claims, based upon a strict observance of the principle that in determining all such questions of sovereignty the interests of the populations concerned must have equal weight with the equitable claims of the government whose title is to be determined.

VI. The evacuation of all Russian territory and such a settlement of all questions affecting Russia as will secure the best and freest cooperation of the other nations of the world in obtaining for her an unhampered and unembarrassed opportunity for the independent determination of her own political development and national policy and assure her of a sincere welcome into the society of free nations under institutions of her own choosing; and, more than a welcome, assistance also of every kind that she may need and may herself desire. The treatment accorded Russia by her sister nations in the months to come will be the acid test of their good will, of their comprehension of her needs as distinguished from their own interests, and of their intelligent and unselfish sympathy.

VII. Belgium, the whole world will agree, must be evacuated and restored, without any attempt to limit the sovereignty which she enjoys in common with all other free nations. No other single act will serve as this will serve to restore confidence among the nations in the laws which they have themselves set and determined for the government of their relations with one another. Without this healing act the whole structure and validity of international law is forever impaired.

VIII. All French territory should be freed and the invaded portions restored, and the wrong done to France by Prussia in 1871 in the matter of Alsace-Lorraine, which has unsettled the peace of the world for nearly fifty years, should be righted, in order that peace may once more be made secure in the interest of all.

IX. A readjustment of the frontiers of Italy should be effected along clearly recognizable lines of nationality.

X. The peoples of Austria-Hungary, whose place among the nations we wish to see safeguarded and assured, should be accorded the freest opportunity to autonomous development.

XI. Rumania, Serbia, and Montenegro should be evacuated; occupied territories restored; Serbia accorded free and secure access to the sea; and the relations of the several Balkan states to one another determined by friendly counsel along historically established lines of allegiance and nationality; and international guarantees of the political and economic independence and territorial integrity of the several Balkan states should be entered into.

XII. The Turkish portion of the present Ottoman Empire should be assured a secure sovereignty, but the other nationalities which are now under Turkish rule should be assured an undoubted security of life and an absolutely unmolested opportunity of autonomous development, and the Dardanelles should be permanently opened as a free passage to the ships and commerce of all nations under international guarantees.

XIII. An independent Polish state should be erected which should include the territories inhabited by indisputably Polish populations, which should be assured a free and secure access to the sea, and whose political and economic independence and territorial integrity should be guaranteed by international covenant.

XIV. A general association of nations must be formed under specific covenants for the purpose of affording mutual guarantees of political independence and territorial integrity to great and small states alike.

In regard to these essential rectifications of wrong and assertions of right we feel ourselves to be intimate partners of all the governments and peoples associated together against the Imperialists. We cannot be separated in interest or divided in purpose. We stand together until the end. For such arrangements and covenants we are willing to fight and to continue to fight until they are achieved; but only because we wish the right to prevail and desire a just and stable peace such as can be secured only by removing the chief provocations to war, which this program does remove. We have no jealousy of German greatness, and there is nothing in this program that impairs it. We grudge her no achievement or distinction of learning or of pacific enterprise such as have made her record very bright and very enviable. We do not wish to injure her or to block in any way her legitimate influence or power. We do not wish to fight her either with arms or with hostile arrangements of trade if she is willing to associate herself with us and the other peace-loving nations of the world in covenants of justice and law and fair dealing. We wish her only to accept a place of equality among the peoples of the world,—the new world in which we now live,—instead of a place of mastery.

NOTE

From Woodrow Wilson, The Fourteen Points Speech, 1918. www.yale.edu/lawweb/avalon /wilson14.htm.

Views on a Prospective Armistice

Ferdinand Foch and John Pershing

Marshal Ferdinand Foch, Commander in Chief of the Allied Armies to Prime Minister
Georges Clemenceau
Personal and Secret

18 October 1918

You saw Field Marshal Haig last Sunday; perhaps he spoke with you about conditions for an armistice, but in any case, today on this subject I understand the following:

Field Marshal Haig considers German military strength strong enough that we should count upon it for the near future. Further, he judges that the advancing of the season makes possible a delaying action on the part of the enemy that would permit him to regroup his forces on a shorter front, delay through destruction and bad weather the pursuit of allied forces, and assure the dictatorial German government of the possibility of the defense of German soil; in sum, to continue the war for an indeterminate period of time. We could undercut this tactic with an armistice that would put a quick end to the war, while imposing on the enemy the necessary conditions: evacuation of Belgium, Luxembourg, and Alsace-Lorraine.

These conditions seem sufficient to Field Marshal Haig to permit the allies to invade the Southern and Northern German states simultaneously in the case of a rupture of the armistice.

Field Marshal Haig has just left for London, where he must stay until the 20th and where he will be consulted on the state of the British Army and the military situation. These are undoubtedly the views he will develop.

I cannot agree with this timid manner of viewing the situation:

1. The military power of the Germans is in such a state of material and moral disorganization that it will not be able to offer serious resistance if we do not give it respite, whatever its form of government.

2. The simple evacuation of Belgium, Luxembourg, and Alsace-Lorraine does not give us a single guarantee for necessary reparations and, if the armistice is broken, does not furnish us with the means for breaking enemy resistance beyond the Rhine River where the Germans will resist all crossings.

In communicating Marshal Haig's views, which you may already know, to you without delay, I have the honor of letting you know that I hold to the propositions contained in my letter of the 8th of this month.[1]

Foch

Paris, October 30, 1918

To the Allied Supreme War Council,
Paris.

Gentlemen:

In considering the question of whether or not Germany's request for an armistice should be granted, the following expresses my opinion from the military point of view:

1. Judging by their excellent conduct during the past three moths, the British, French, Belgian and American armies appear capable of continuing the offensive indefinitely. Their morale is high and the prospects of certain victory should keep it so.

2. The American army is constantly increasing in strength and experience, and should be able to take an increasingly important part in the allied offensive. Its growth, both in personnel and materiel, with such reserves as the Allies may furnish, not counting the Italian army, should be more than equal to the combined losses of the allied armies.

3. German man-power is constantly diminishing and her armies have lost over 300,000 prisoners and over one-third of their artillery during the past three months in their effort to extricate themselves from a difficult situation and avoid disaster.

4. The estimated strength of the Allies on the Western front, not counting Italy, and of Germany, in rifles is—

Allies...............................1,563,000
Germany...........................1,134,000

An advantage in favor of the Allies of 37%

In guns—

Allies.................................22,413
Germany............................16,495

Advantage of 35% in favor of the Allies.

If Italy's forces should be added to the Western front we should have a still greater advantage.

5. Germany's morale is undoubtedly low, her allies have deserted her one by one and she can no longer hope to win. Therefore we should take full advantage of the situation and continue the offensive until we compel her unconditional surrender.

6. An armistice would revivify the low spirits of the German army and enable it to reorganize and resist later on, and would deprive the Allies of the full measure of victory by failing to press their present advantage to its complete military end.

7. As the apparent humility of German leaders in talking of peace may be feigned, the Allies should distrust their sincerity and their motives. The appeal for an armistice is undoubtedly to enable the withdrawal from a critical situation to one more advantageous.

8. On the other hand, the internal political conditions of Germany, if correctly reported, are such that she is practically forced to ask for an armistice to save the overthrow of her present government, a consummation which should be sought by the Allies as precedent to permanent peace.

9. A cessation of hostilities short of capitulation postpones if it does not render impossible the imposition of satisfactory peace terms, because it would allow Germany to withdraw

her army with its present strength, ready to resume hostilities if terms were not satisfactory to her.

10. An armistice would lead the Allied armies to believe this the end of fighting and it would be difficult if not impossible to resume hostilities with our present advantage in morale in the event of failure to secure at a peace conference what we have fought for.

11. By agreeing to an armistice under the present favorable military situation of the allies and accepting the principle of a negotiated peace rather than a dictated peace the allies would jeopardize the moral position they now hold and possibly lose the chance actually to secure world peace on terms that would insure its permanence.

12. It is the experience of history that victorious armies are prone to overestimate the enemy's strength and too eagerly seek an opportunity for peace. This mistake is likely to be made now on account of the reputation Germany has gained through her victories of the last four years.

13. Finally, I believe that complete victory can only be obtained by continuing the war until we force unconditional surrender from Germany, but if the Allied Governments decide to grant an armistice, the terms should be so rigid that under no circumstances could Germany again take up arms.

Respectfully submitted,

(signed) John J. Pershing

Commander-in-Chief, American Expeditionary Forces

NOTES

From Ferdinand Foch and John Pershing, Views on Prospective Armistice, Documents from the French Service Historique de l'Armée de Terre, Château de Vincennes, 6N70.

1. Foch's letter of October 8, 1918 insisted that conditions for an armistice must include German evacuation of Belgium, Luxembourg, and Alsace-Lorraine, as well as the creation of three allied bridgeheads across the Rhine River, and the imposition of reparations. The letter also called for Germany to surrender to the allies railroad stock, industrial resources, and military equipment in the areas they evacuated.

The Military Collapse of the German Empire

Wilhelm Deist

In the past two decades research in Germany into the history of the First World War has mainly concentrated on the beginning and end of the war. A large number of substantial investigations have been undertaken into the outbreak of war and its immediate antecedents, as well as into the end of the war and the revolutionary consequences of the events of October 1918. Political, especially party political, developments and economic problems under pressure of war have not been neglected, but they have not been nor are at the centre of academic interest, nor is the military course of the war.

The political component in the conduct of leading military men—Moltke, Falkenhayn, Hindenburg, Ludendorff and Groener—has been subjected to critical analysis in the relevant accounts, but the analysis of the military situation and the interpretation of military decisions have been noticeably left in the background. The same goes for the description and analysis of the conduct of war in 1918. The political implications of Ludendorff's decision to take the offensive in the spring and summer of 1918 have been emphasized. It is pointed out that the general overextension of resources led to the 'black day' of the German army, 8 August 1918,[1] and finally forced the First Quartermaster-General, after a much-discussed interval of indecision, to acknowledge defeat at the end of September by the request for an armistice. Such interpretations, based on decisions at the top, pay insufficient attention to the instrument the military leaders had to use, the army itself. Moreover, there is no consensus as to how far the overstretch of resources made itself felt among the troops on the Western Front. While Gerhard Ritter notes that from May 1918 a 'great role' was played by 'mutinies' during transport, 'desertion,' and 'surrender without resistance,' Karl Dietrich Erdmann remains of the opinion that, apart from the general decline in fighting spirit after 8 August 1918, the 'Germany Army in its entirety' had remained 'cohesive until its demobilization.' This can only mean that no general weight or significance should be attached to possible signs of disintegration. It is, however, beyond doubt that, besides the well-researched causes of the political collapse and revolutionary overthrow of the old system, the condition of the many million-strong army of the Western Front played a considerable, even decisive, role in the course of events during October and November 1918. This is, therefore, a matter of clarifying one of the essential preconditions for the German Revolution 1918–20, which has been rather lost sight of among the intensive research into the political actions of the workers' and soldiers' councils.

An investigation into the development of conditions in the army during 1918 comes up against the well-known difficulty that the records of the formations and of the commands in the field army were destroyed in the fire at the Army archive in Potsdam in 1945. There is, however, valuable and so far hardly used material in the voluminous publications of the Reichstag Committee of Inquiry into the Causes of the German Collapse. Together with evidence from memoirs and from other remaining fragments, this makes possible a more precise delineation and supplementation of the picture that has so far dominated our view of the changing inner structure of the army from the spring to the autumn of 1918. Further, we have at our disposal the concluding volume from the Reich Archive, completed at the end of the Second World War but not published till 1956, which on the basis of the records provides important relevant details.

This volume is, moreover, one more example of the almost unbearable, deliberate lack of realism in the older official history of the war. In these accounts the war is essentially reduced to a record of leadership decisions and their execution in the military staffs at various levels. Their language, for long stretches cool and detached, reinforces the illusion of rationality in the activities described. Many exponents of this type of military historiography find this organized atmosphere of disembodied rationality attractive even now. The result is that historical facts and the circumstances and consequences of historical developments are obscured rather than brought to our awareness.

The military defeat of the empire was made manifest in the request for an armistice by the Supreme Army Command (*Oberste Heeresleitung*, OHL) at the end of September 1918. Its first and essential cause was, however, the decision to conduct the war offensively against the Allies in the West. This decision was also brought about by OHL, and represents one of the few truly strategic choices which the German leadership was able to make in the course of the whole war. OHL, and above all Ludendorff, had succeeded in committing all those with a real say in the conduct of the war, even their Austro-Hungarian ally, to this decision. It is comparable with the decision to embark upon unrestricted submarine warfare in January 1917; indeed, it drew conclusions from the failure of this strategic aim in 1917, for now it was a matter of winning a decisive military victory over the Allied armies in France and Belgium before the deployment of the American army in western Europe.

In the situation in which the Reich and its allies found themselves at the turn of the year 1917/18, any strategic decision was fraught with high risks. The position of the Central Powers was marked by the devastating economic and social consequences of the Allied blockade and by the foreseeable exhaustion of human and material resources, but also by the uncertain and therefore inflated expectations based on the imminent peace treaty in the East and on the economic advantages arising from it. The risk lay above all in the likelihood that with this decision OHL would expend resources incapable of replacement.

Against this background one would have expected that a long-drawn out process of decision-making at the highest political and military level would have been embarked upon. Its purpose would have been to reach a conclusion about the fundamental problem of conducting the war in 1918: whether the available resources should be used for an offensive or defensive strategy. Such a process never took take place. As early as April 1917 Ludendorff toyed with the idea of a decisive western offensive. The general then clung to this fundamental concept of the offensive in the often adversarial discussions concerning the most suitable form of operations that took place from October onwards.

At this stage the question was still entirely open as to whether a political offensive, which would have had to focus on a declaration about the restoration of Belgium, should precede the military attack. Indeed, it could render such an attack, a very last resort, redundant. This question was put to OHL repeatedly, but replies were evasive and unsatisfactory, and such initiatives remained entirely without result. These circumstances are yet another indication of the almost unlimited position of power, compared with 1917, now occupied by OHL within the governing structures of the late Empire.

This still does not answer the question why the alternative to an offensive strategy was not more seriously debated within the military leadership itself. Ludendorff was well aware of the advantages of a defensive strategy and adopted it successfully in the first half of 1917 admittedly in the confident expectation that unrestricted submarine warfare would guarantee victory. Until August 1918 Ludendorff clung to the conviction that the war would need to end in outright victory. The ideas of OHL, particularly of Hindenburg and Ludendorff, about the aims to be attained by the war are well known; for both officers they included extensive annexations in East and West. It proved possible even before the start of the western offensive to take an essential step in that direction with the treaty of Brest-Litovsk.[2] This annexationist *diktat* was widely welcomed by the political representatives of the Reich, even by the Social Democratic Party in the Reichstag, though there were criticisms of detail. It highlights the strength of the so-called war aims movement of which OHL was the forceful exponent. As part of this constellation the military leadership left no stone unturned to propagate their notions concerning war aims. It was no accident that the immediate reaction to the resolution of the Reichstag of 19 July 1917, in which a majority supported a compromise peace, was an order to establish the comprehensive propaganda organization 'Patriotic Education.' This organization, with a profusion of effort, was intended, disclaimers and denials notwithstanding, to influence and mould opinion in the army and navy, and also among the civilian population, in accordance with the internal and external objectives of the war aims movement. Against this background it is not surprising that the idea of a strategic defensive was never seriously discussed in the officer corps and particularly not in the staffs. OHL could therefore count on the unreserved agreement of the officer corps with their decision to conduct the war offensively. There is thus no doubt that the military leadership was guided by political aims in the decision they imposed. 'Military calculations,' runs the judgment of a competent critic, 'were entirely overborne by the notion, not rationally founded, that a victorious conclusion was attainable.'

The risks inherent in the decision to conduct the war offensively were made obvious during the military preparations, undertaken with great energy and circumspection. The concentration of military resources on the Western Front meant denuding the secondary fronts in the East, South-East, and South. In the months from November 1917 to March 1918 alone thirty-three divisions were withdrawn from these areas, and further formations followed. This weakening enabled the Allies in the late summer to seize the initiative on these fronts as well, so that it was here that the descent into defeat of the Central Powers showed its first conclusive results.

With the concentration of forces in the West, it became possible to equal the enemy in numerical strength. At the beginning of the offensive in March 1918, about five million men (including labour battalions) faced each other. The limitation of German resources is apparent, however, when it comes to the reserves of manpower to be taken into calculation. At the end of 1917 there were still 612,000 men at the disposal of OHL in the home country. In addition, one could count on approximately 400,000 recruits born in 1900, who would become available only in the autumn. The material inferiority of the German West Army showed itself most clearly in guns of all calibers (14,000 against 18,500), aircraft (3,760 against 4,500), and especially in armoured fighting vehicles (10 against 800). OHL believed, however, that it could compensate for this general inferiority through concentration of men and material in the areas of attack. This left the problem of how to carry the attack beyond the enemy's positions to an operational breakthrough. For this OHL developed a special system of attack, which was entrusted from the beginning of the year to so-called 'mob.[ile] divisions.' These divisions were given preferential treatment in weapons and equipment, and in them was concentrated the offensive power of the western army. In contrast there were the so-called trench divisions, less well equipped in all respects. This divisional nomenclature revealed the greatest problem of the German offensive. The transition from trench to mobile warfare required in the first place the mobility of forces, but the means for this were extraordinarily limited. Thus only 23,000 mainly iron-wheeled lorries were available, while the Allies could muster 100,000 rubber-tyred lorries. In spite of all efforts, it proved impossible to equip the 'mob. divisions' with a sufficient number of horses, so that, for example, only a part of the heavy machine-guns and the light mine-throwers were horse-drawn. These factors highlight the military risk OHL was willing to incur with this offensive—for the sake of political goals.

A further essential element in the conduct of war received relatively little attention in the volume of the Reich Archive: the physical and psychological factors, even though important evidence from the records had already been given in testimony to the Committee of Inquiry of the Reichstag. Nor have the impressive observations dating from April and May 1918 of Colonel von Thaer, revealed in 1958, given rise to a more general investigation of this question. The picture remained of an army gravely weakened in its fighting force, yet left untouched by the signs of disintegration on the home front, which returned still 'firmly structured' to the revolutionized home country, conscious of having remained 'unbeaten in the field.'

A history of the changing inner structure of the army in the course of the war years remains, therefore, a research objective. The images that obtrude are full of sharp contrasts. The innumerable photographs from August 1914 reflect an optimism, a certainty of victory, and a self-confidence which even the first heavy engagements could not shake. It is not these images that are characteristic of the First World War, but those from the trenches, from the battles of attrition around Verdun and on the Somme: the individual or the small group lost in an almost apocalyptic environment.

The literary evidence, from Werner Beumelburg through Ernst Jünger to Arnold Zweig, signals a transformation of values and behaviour which ran counter to the hierarchical system of the military apparatus. They convey a vision and a feeling about life which has no longer much in common with the views prevailing before the war. A mass experience of this kind could not be without repercussions for the inner structure of the army. An early consequence of these slowly changing conditions were the efforts of military and civil authorities, beginning in the spring of 1916, to maintain 'morale' at home and in the army. The decline in morale was attributed not merely to the difficulties in food supplies on the home front but also to news and tales about 'abuses' in the army.

There was a fierce clash of opinion about these 'abuses' among the experts giving evidence to the Reichstag's Committee of Inquiry. In spite of the polemics exchanged by the two main experts, Martin Hobohm and Erich-Otto Volkmann, a common denominator can be detected. Both agree that the 'abuses' consisted of a broken relationship between officers and men. The experts differed widely, however, on the causes, extent, and evaluation of these findings. Even in retrospect it is hardly possible to paint an accurate picture of the indubitably disturbed relationship from the many often contradictory examples. One is more likely to find their true character if one looks for the causes of these symptoms.

In the first place, one has to stress the fundamental significance of the peculiar form of warfare prevailing on the Western Front since the end of 1914. Trench warfare and battles of attrition leveled social differences; the community of front-line soldiers knew no class barriers; the Imperial Army took on the character of a militia. The form of warfare emphasized the gulf between front and rear, and the border was not an organizational but a practical one: the reach of the enemy artillery. In the front area so defined there developed the community of the frontline soldiers later so exaggerated by propaganda, in which the role of the officer, especially as company commander, was unchallenged, particularly if he behaved responsibly as part of this community. Behind the front and in painful contrast to the conditions prevailing there, the gulf between officers and men in the sense of military hierarchy continued, and in fact became more acute.

A competent observer has described how sharp and profound the break was by looking at three crucial conditions of the soldier's life: 'security of life, accommodation, nourishment.' This man, a chief medical officer of the reserve, shows convincingly that the widely documented gross differences between the situation of staff and administrative officers on the one hand and troops on the other were inherent in the system. Excesses unavoidable in a gigantic organization like the wartime army and misuse of the hierarchically ordered privileges exaggerated these differences even further, to the disadvantage of the troops. The black market of the home front also operated in different guise in the field army. Although officers were by no means the only beneficiaries of this system, they were held responsible, since they exercised the power of command. There was the additional feeling of a loss of rights arising from an inadequate complaints procedure. When, on top of this, exhausted formations and units were employed on drill in their rest quarters, then bitterness could become 'hatred of officers.' The military leadership tried in vain to master these 'abuses' by issuing orders and commands, but of necessity they shied away from measures designed to change the system.

The consequence of the continuing 'abuses' was the increasing inability of the higher military command to take cognizance and account of the inner state of the fighting troops. In this connection it is significant that the only measure, beyond existing regulations, taken by OHL to strengthen the moral and 'mood' of the troops was the establishment of 'Patriotic Education.' Such 'Education'—in line with the offensive intention and strategic decision of OHL—was in accord with the domestic and foreign political programme of the war aims movement, but with the fighting troops it could, given the conditions outlined, only have the opposite of the effect intended.

With the setting up of 'Patriotic Education,' OHL had indirectly recognized that political arguments and aims were required to achieve the militarily essential mobilization of moral and personal resources. But since OHL's political message was more or less identical with the domestic and foreign ideas of the war aims movement, with particular emphasis on anti-parliamentarism, it came into conflict with the changed conditions of military leadership required by industrialized warfare. A remark of the Bavarian Colonel Mertz von Quirnheim in July 1917 shows, however, that a different way of thinking could also be found within OHL.

> What a tremendous impression it would make if General Ludendorff (through the voice of Hindenburg) were to declare: 'Yes, OHL is also in favour of universal suffrage for Prussia, because Prussian soldiers have fully deserved it.' I believe Ludendorff would be carried aloft in triumph, all danger of strikes etc. would be removed, the impression abroad would be tremendous. How beautifully one could dress up such a proclamation! But General Ludendorff lacks all understanding for such an exploitation of political ideas for the purpose of the war. He thinks he can keep up the spirit of the people in perpetuity with forceful phrases.

It was not incompetence or lack of imagination that prevented such a step, but the fact that, for Hindenburg, Ludendorff, and the military leadership as a whole, it would have revolutionized the position of the army in the power structure of the empire.

When all these elements, so important for the inner state and the motivation of the troops, are taken into account, then the extent and the profound impact of the transformation process undergone by the army since August 1914 become evident. The general physical and psychological exhaustion after nearly four years of war was anything but surprising. 'Callous, mutual mass murder' continuing for years was exacting its toll. The cohesive power of the army had been sharply diminished. A large group benefiting from the privileges conferred by the system contrasted with the grey mass of the troops. Bitterness about these conditions had become deeply embedded, and the yearning for peace, for an end to the war, was general and strong, undoubtedly also influenced by the political conflicts at home over war aims and the Prussian franchise.

In the autumn of 1917 there had already been incidents with reserve transports, and there were difficulties with the transfer of formations and units from East to West. In November 1917 up to 10 percent of the troops were using the transports to desert. The military leadership was unable to get on top of this problem, and the number of deserters increased. Nevertheless, all the available information indicates that the 'mood' in the preparatory phase and the early days of the March offensive was scarcely touched by these symptoms; on the contrary, and in view of the adverse conditions, it can only be described as extraordinarily good. The idea of ending the war, the cause of all the grief, through a last great effort had clearly overcome the mood of resignation prevailing up to then in the field army and on the home front. One testimony for these sentiments is a letter from a Silesian estate inspector of pronounced nationalist views, who was serving as a corporal on the Western Front. 'Let us hope the party gets going the sooner the better, so that these injustices that stink to heaven will come to an end, so that we can all eat out of one pot again, and there will be no more masters and slaves.'

The 'big battle in France' began on 21 March with the attack of three armies against the sector of the front held by the British, between Cambrai and St Quentin, in the area of the Somme battles of 1916–17. The aim was to inflict a decisive defeat upon the British forces, and to separate them from the French armies, because it was assumed 'that England would be more amenable to peace.'

The decision to attack in this sector had been preceded by a long debate about the operational execution of the strategic decision. There had above all to be an answer to the question whether one should seek the operational breakthrough in one great effort, with the risk that a failure of the operation would force a return to the defensive. Already in April 1917 Ludendorff had held the view that 'one would have to try out a number of different places in succession' in order to continue the attack, with emphasis on the weakest place on the enemy front. He stuck to this fundamental premise, strongly supported by the Chief of Staff of the Army Group Crown Prince Rupprecht, Lieutenant-General von Kuhl. This procedure was not without risk either. The intention to wear the enemy down in several successive attacks, as Ludendorff later put it, must lead to the attrition of the transport resources allocated to the mobile divisions. Therefore the tendency would be to diminish the chances of success of all further operations. Of even greater weight was the consideration that such an operational procedure would expose the fighting spirit of the divisions to continuous stress, when this spirit was mainly nourished by the hope of putting an end to the war in a last great effort.

The offensive, planned under the codename Michael, brought surprising successes—almost overwhelming successes, given the vain efforts of both sides over the years to escape from the war of position. The three armies (17th, 2nd and 18th), with a strength of nearly 1.4 million men, not only overcame the deeply-echeloned system of enemy positions but penetrated far into the hostile hinterland, the Second Army about 45 km, the 18th Army around 60 km. The decisive operational breakthrough was, however, not achieved. The attack had to be broken off on 5 April, since the fighting force of the armies was exhausted. The supply of the troops during the offensive and in the extended salient now established—the front line increased from 90 to 150 km—could not be satisfactorily guaranteed.

The offensive of the 4th and 6th Armies in Flanders and against the dominating heights of Kemmel lasted from 9 to 29 April and followed the logic of OHL's plans.

Again there were surprising successes and again logistical problems could not be overcome. This offensive again failed to bring OHL any nearer the goal of a politically effective success against the British army.

The impact of the failure of the Michael offensive on the troops was very accurately described by a General Staff officer, Colonel von Thaer, while the battle in Flanders was still going on.

> We now have for this attack between Kemmel and Bethune quite a few divisions that have just taken part in the March offensive, which there again lost their best officers and men and which have now been barely filled with personnel that is unfortunately of declining value. I must say that I do not much like the troops which have been deployed here. Officers and men express great disappointment that the March offensive has ground to a halt but that now regardless one attack is to follow upon another. Their hopes had been too high that this great blow would end the war in March. They had gathered up all their courage and energy for this. Now there is disappointment, and it goes very deep. That is the main reason why even attacks well prepared by artillery peter out as soon as our infantry moves beyond the heavily shelled zone.

These observations acquire their full significance when interpreted in the context of the fragile 'mood' preceding the start of the spring offensive.

The 'mood' could not but be affected by the heavy losses, which even in the reserved language of the medical reports for the three participating armies were described as 'extraordinarily high.' Of the initial strength of just 1.4 million men, more than a fifth (305,450) had been lost in the period 21 March–10 April. Certain divisions of the 17th Army were reduced by 'nearly a third' in the first ten days. It was of special significance that it was above all the 'mobile divisions' that were affected, for in them OHL had deliberately concentrated the offensive power of the field army. The reports repeatedly stress the severity of losses of officers, which proportionately were above those of the men and which were again concentrated in the mobile divisions. The company and platoon commanders were worst affected, namely that group in the officer corps to whom had passed, according to Thaer, 'the moral influence' among the men. These circumstances are even reflected in the volume from the Reich Archive, the language of which is entirely attuned to the thought processes of the staffs and veils the real conditions at the front.

During the succeeding offensive operations of two armies in Flanders, to which the observations of Colonel von Thaer refer, eleven of these already 'exhausted,' 'battle-fatigued' divisions were again deployed. With 55 divisions deployed altogether this was a very high percentage, indicating the limits of military resources. The 'mobile divisions' had become 'attack divisions,' of which the equipment and training were in decline compared with the former, and which were in particular less mobile because of their acute and damaging lack of horses. The losses of the 6th Army in Flanders from 1 to 30 April amounted to a total of 63,469 men against an average effective strength of 361,142, without taking into account the 15,605 lightly wounded and/or sick men who had returned to duty in the course of the month. The losses of the 4th Army in the same period were somewhat lower: against an average effective strength of 421,221 men they amounted to 59,209, excluding the 17,774 men returned to duty. The total 'wastage' of soldiers on the Western Front rose from 235,544 in March to 257,176 in April. From the account of the Reich Archive it appears that the attacking divisions operated much more cautiously, and that the lines reached hardly ever corresponded to the daily objectives laid down by the leadership. A few days after the start of the offensive the Chief of Staff of the 6th Army, Colonel von Lenz, reported on 14 April to his army group: 'The troops are not attacking, in spite of orders. The offensive has got stuck.' There could be no harsher expression of the change of mood, produced by the exhaustion, hopelessness, and heavy losses of the fighting troops.

Gerhard Ritter sees the decisive cause for the 'gradual decline of the fighting morale of the German Army in the final months of the war' in the spreading 'feeling' among the troops that they were 'being used up, in an ultimately futile and senseless way, in constantly renewed attacks, which had no prospect of success.' It is possible to give precision to this judgment by pointing to the inability of the German army, even in the final days of the March offensive, to solve the logistical problems—munitions and supply—decisive in any attack. Therefore the 'feeling' of the troops very early on affected their behaviour, which by April is reflected in the observations of Thaer and in the reports of Lenz. Ludwig Beck expressed the opinion, in an often-quoted letter of November 1918, that since the middle of July the troops simply 'did not hold any more,' 'because they did not want to.' Adopting this judgment, one could define the position in the first days of the April offensive by saying that the will to attack, still present in the first days of the March offensive, had vanished: that the obvious overextension of resources had produced paralysis.

This conclusion is not contradicted by the initially highly successful offensive against the Chemin des Dames and against Reims from the end of May to the beginning of June 1918. These great successes were the result of surprise and undoubtedly superior artillery, which it proved possible to maintain in the further course of the offensive. Nonetheless the force of the attack flagged as quickly as that of the Flanders offensive. This is not surprising, since the strength of 27 of the 36 attacking divisions had already been decimated in the March offensive. The losses of the 7th and 1st Armies in the period 21 May–20 June amounted to 125,000 men, and were thus appreciably lower (about an eighth of average effective strength) than in the two preceding offensives. The 'total wastage' of all armies on the Western Front, which had been 'only' 114,504 men in May, rose again in June to 209,435 and was therefore near the March figure.

Confronted with these losses, with the widely noted state of exhaustion of the troops, and with many a warning voice, Ludendorff and OHL were not prepared to make a fresh analysis of the military situation and to revise, if necessary, their strategic decision. On the contrary, OHL in mid-May still made clear their intention 'to beat the enemy, to hit him substantially, wherever the prospects were best.' At the beginning of June it was stated: 'We will continue our attacks and dictate the law of action to the enemy.' Quite apart from strategic considerations, operational aims were pushed increasingly into the background. When in April Ludendorff was asked about the operational aim of the Flanders offensive, he scorned the word 'operation' and declared, 'we will punch a hole in it. Then we will see further. We did the same in Russia.'

The only aim of the sheer activism thus expressed could be to wear down the enemy, but the German leaders had admitted that they lacked the human and material resources for this.

The two statements in the situation report of 5 June 1918, that 'the Entente had suffered one of its worst defeats' and that for the German side 'a basis had been created for further successes,' reflect the strange mixture of realism and blindness characteristic of the decisions of OHL. The Allies had certainly suffered heavy defeats, but the German side had thereby created the conditions for their own military defeat. Thus, to give a further example, at a time when their own troop levels were rapidly falling and those of the enemy just as rapidly rising, the length of the front between the Meuse at Verdun and the Flanders coast had increased between 20 March and 25 June by 120 km, from 390 to 510 km. The consequence was the successful counterattack by the Allies at Villiers-Cotterêts on 18 July and the defeat of the 2nd Army East of Amiens on 8 August.

How could there have been such a misjudgment of its own resources by OHL? Colonel von Thaer had put his observations about the state of the army quite early, at the beginning of May, to Hindenburg and Ludendorff with abundant clarity. Ludendorff reacted more directly, more impulsively than Hindenburg. He pitched into the Colonel: 'What does all your gloom-mongering amount to? What do you want me to do? Do you want me to make peace *à tout prix*?' (at any cost). It was a very revealing remark: again it was a matter of war aims; again it became obvious that for Ludendorff political aims prevailed over sober, military calculation. With an offensive planned for 1918 on such premises and degenerating into mere military activism, OHL smashed the still-available military potential and risked the provocation of a strike by the soldiers.

After the failure of the Michael offensive, the old complaints about 'abuses' in the relations between front and rear, between officers and men, surfaced again and became even more significant. Living conditions for the troops of the attacking army had worsened considerably in contrast to conditions in the rear. In the front line, where the thrust of the attack had exhausted itself, men were lying in improvised positions, which by order of the military leadership were not built up into a system of positions suitable for defence. In the long run—and as the hopes placed in the operational impact of the separate attacks progressively vanished—this situation was bound to reduce the fighting force of the units and formations. Some leading officers recognized this danger very quickly, but Ludendorff and OHL refused for too long to draw the obvious conclusions. For the men and the logistical problems caused by the attacks had serious repercussions, since the provision of munitions and especially food was not always sufficiently secure. The drastic result was that in all the attacks plundering of enemy stores occurred, which in some cases, particularly when alcohol was involved, led to ugly scenes. Colonel-General von Einem, the Commander of the 3rd Army, voiced the opinion already in early May that the army had degenerated into a 'gang of thieves' and added at the end of June: '*One* motive for the bravery of our infantry in this attack is the lust for plunder.' A guards division put forward the suggestion that every battalion should establish a booty platoon, to prevent arbitrary actions while securing the spoils for the battalion in question. This showed the extent to which discipline had become eroded. The 'abuses' which led to these symptoms were shaping the 'mood' of the troops. The chairman of the German Artisan Federation, basing himself on observations 'recently' made and passed to him, summarized them in a letter to Ludendorff on 11 August. 'Everything conspires to heighten even further the unbelievable bitterness of the men. We see in this a looming danger for the future development and the existence of the German Reich.'

The 'looming danger' had already assumed very concrete shape in the phenomenon of 'shirking.' It existed before the offensive started and was particularly evident in the East-West transports beginning in the autumn of 1917. Although there are naturally no reliable statistics about the extent of 'shirking,' one has to assume from all available reports and information that it was widespread.

In Army Group Crown Prince Rupprecht it was not unusual, according to the records of its commander, for the strength of a replacement transport to have diminished by 20 per cent when it arrived with its relevant formation. The term 'shirker' indicates that it was rarely a case of straightforward desertion. A variety of forms, not now capable of reconstruction, were sought and found to escape service in the front zone and to become submerged in the giant organization of the field army. The increasing movement of formations from one attacking front to another facilitated this behaviour. Deliberate absconding without permission from a unit was one method, for it earned the culprit a sentence under martial law of two to four months' prison. Another characteristic example of how to escape front-line service: those recovering in the military hospitals of the field army were not released to their reserve battalions, but directly to their front-line units. If they arrived there with defective equipment, they were sent back. The collecting-points then established to guarantee full equipment could not cope with their task, for the equipment was simply disposed of!

The first influenza epidemic, with more than half a million cases, hit the army in June/July, and materially aggravated the situation. The medical services had already been unable at the beginning of the offensive, when the number of wounded and sick 'exceeded all previous experience,' to cope with the demands in their accustomed manner. In particular the care of the walking wounded and slightly sick, whose numbers cannot be exactly determined but certainly ran into hundreds of thousands, posed insuperable difficulties. This mass streamed back from the front, took little notice of the procedures laid down for their maintenance, and had only one aim: to secure transport back home. It is well known that some trains for taking the lightly wounded home were simply stormed, and made the journey according to their own timetable. Such scenes occurred during all the offensives. The medical authorities were compelled as early as April to seek the help of the army. In the end the stream of wounded and sick had to be sent in the desired direction through chains of sentries. This behaviour of hundreds of thousands makes their rejection of the war abundantly clear.

The Chief of Staff of the Army Group Crown Prince Rupprecht, Lieutenant-General von Kuhl, repeatedly testified after the war that the commands had not succeeded in bringing 'shirking' under control or even in taking effective action at railway stations. That such events were not confined to this single army group is shown by the proposal put to Ludendorff on 21 July by General von Lossberg, in the wake of the successful Allied attack at Villiers-Cotterêts. He recommended, amongst other things, the construction by all undeployed units in East and West of deeply echeloned, operational defence zones in the rear. Their purpose would be to 'shut off the army's region from the home region,' to catch 'the large number of so-called shirkers' and bring them back to 'discipline and order.' Although there are no statistics about the extent of 'shirking'; Erich-Otto Volkmann's estimate of 750,000 to one million men in the last few months of the war seems in no way excessive, given the conditions reported in the reserve transports and in the care of the lightly wounded and sick. This estimate makes clear the dimensions of the problem, in the face of which the military command was helpless. The military instrument for the conduct of the war, the army, was in the process of disintegration.

Lossberg's proposal shows the full gravity of the situation brought about by developments at the front and the rear in mid-July 1918. In addition, the numerical weakness and exhaustion of the front-line troops made it imperative to take back and shorten the front. Ahead of the spring offensive, the regulation strength of a battalion was fixed at 850 men. In July the average battalion strength in more than a third of the 196 divisions of the army groups Crown Prince Rupprecht and German Crown Prince had sunk to 600 or less. Even this figure conceals the weakening of the fighting troops since 21 March 1918. According to the 'medical report,' the effective strength of the West Army only declined from 3,882,655 men in March to 3,582,203 men in July; but the total wastage in these five months amounted to nearly one million men, among them 125,000 dead and 1,000,000 missing; the American army in Europe grew by approximately the same number, just under one million men, in the months April to July. These figures give an idea of the continuous process of erosion of the front. In addition, according to a competent observer, the reserves which ultimately reached the front largely lacked the will and motivation to identify completely with their allotted military task. This was true of all ranks of the reserves, and was independent of the social stratum from which the reserves had been recruited. There is no stronger indication of this erosion than the need, before every engagement, to keep back a reserve of leaders from among the small number of tried officers and non-commissioned officers, in order to ensure that the troops still had leaders after the first wave of attack.

Ludendorff refused, because of his political aims, to acknowledge this clearly perceptible condition of the army after the failure of the Michael offensive. Only the defeat of the 2nd Army east of Amiens on 8 August 1918 forced him to return to military realities. He still refused, until the end of September, to draw the military and political conclusions from the total overextension of resources for which he was responsible. His behaviour in October indicates that his military judgment was even then clouded by wishful thinking.

In the mean-time the process of erosion on the Western Front had advanced further. According to reports by Lieutenant-General von Kuhl, the army, already reduced by nearly a million men in the attacks up to mid-July, lost another 420,000 in dead and wounded and 340,000 in prisoners and missing between 18 July and the armistice. The *fighting* strength of battalions declined dramatically. There is a report, from early October, about the condition of a corps in the 2nd Army, with a nominal strength of seven and one-third divisions: the infantry *battle* strength of this corps amounted to a total of 2,683 men, with 83 heavy and 79 light machine-guns. The corps had reserves of 2,050 men and covered a front line of 6.5 km. Even if this is an extreme example (a matter which is difficult to judge), it nevertheless shows up the deterioration of the army since March 1918. Information supplied by armies, corps, and divisions in the first few days of November about the fighting strength of formations shows that the leadership could count on scarcely a dozen divisions classified as 'fully combat-ready' or 'combat-capable' in the whole area from the Belgian coast to the Upper Rhine. The army was a shadow of its former self. Ludwig Beck, then a major on the staff of the Army Group German Crown Prince, described the situation in a memorable phrase when he wrote that the front was like 'a spider's web of fighters.'

It is reported that Ludendorff was particularly shaken when on the fateful 8 August an attack division was greeted by retreating guard troops with cries of 'strike-break-ers,' 'war-prolongers.' Such cries were merely the manifestations of a mass movement which had spread with explosive force since the failure of the offensive that had carried such high hopes and which had been met by a general refusal. This movement could express itself only very cautiously and covertly under the conditions of command and obedience. The characteristics which research has revealed about the mass movement of the workers in those years can be transferred to the symptoms reported in the army of the Western Front, appropriately modified by the different circumstances. Here also it began with the far-reaching loss of authority by the established powers as a result of glaring 'abuses.' The movement was furthered by the concentration of large masses in circumstances destructive of 'existing social, and political ties.' The rules of military discipline kept spontaneous action within narrow bounds. With the army this potential for protest, even more than with the mass movement of workers, showed its strength 'in immediate criticism, in negative action' and its weakness 'in the moment of success.' The hopelessness spreading since April and the horrendous losses provoked an ever more massive refusal, with the negative consequences evident in the 'spider's web of fighters' within an army still comprising millions. The only aim of the refusal, of the covert strike of soldiers, was an end to the war, and it was thus the political answer to the politically motivated actions of Ludendorff and the military leadership. The mass movement of soldiers on the Western Front was the essential cause of the admission of political and military failure wrung from Ludendorff on 29 September.

Bethmann Hollweg's assistant, Kurt Riezler, reports that the Chancellor expressed the view in July 1914 that a war, whatever its outcome, would produce a 'subversion of the whole existing order.' The guarantor of the existing order—in the meaning understood by Bethmann Hollweg—was the armed force of the empire, the army, and especially its officer corps. By 1914 it had become the integrative symbol of all the political forces of the Right and the Centre, and it kept the Left in check. The question was how this balance, in the long run undoubtedly fragile, could be made secure. Some circles held the opinion that 'A war would strengthen patriarchal order and sentiment,' but industrialized war, on the contrary, destroyed the laboriously maintained balance. The Supreme Command, compelled to adapt the military arm to the conditions of modern war, contributed substantially to this shift of balance. The war also undermined the structural basis of the military instrument, of the guarantor of 'the existing order.' The unity of the officer corps disintegrated in the battles of attrition, under the constant pressure and demand for higher performance. Above all, the officer corps and the military leadership were confronted with the paradox that they could only conduct the war with the help of the political and social forces against which they believed themselves compelled to defend the 'existing order.' OHL tried to overcome this dilemma by siding from a political point of view decisively and openly with the dominant forces of the prewar order. The result was that Ludendorff was forced to admit on 29 September that 'OHL and the German army have reached the end. . . . The troops can no longer be relied on.' The military command had therefore lost control of its irreplaceable instrument. Just as Groener had stated in November 1916 that the war could not be won against the worker, so Ludendorff was now faced by the fact that the war could not be waged, let alone won, without the soldiers. The fate of the empire and the army was thus sealed.

The revolution was finally unleashed by the revolt of the sailors of the High Seas Fleet, appropriately described as 'rebellion against the military authorities and the monarchical establishment legitimating them, but with strictly limited aims.' The refusal of obedience in the fleet was, however, only the tip of the iceberg. Essential preconditions for revolution were created by the mass movements at home and in the war zone. With the covert strike movement among the soldiers the aims, while undoubtedly remaining limited, became somewhat extended: on the one hand it was a question of ending the existing predominance of the military hierarchy in state and society; on the other the demand for a change in the social order was massively reinforced. The initially more or less non-violent nature of the revolution arose essentially from the mass movement of the soldiers. In comparison the 'paralysis of decision' in the leading military echelons in the face of the first signs of revolution played a minor role. Without taking into account the preconditions created for the practical political conduct of the soldiers' councils by the covert strike of soldiers, it is impossible to arrive at an adequate evaluation of the role of the councils in the first phase of the revolution.

The covert strike of the soldiers also had effects of a quite different kind. It was a necessary element in the genesis of this mass movement that it developed in isolation from the German public. This circumstance, and the strongly pronounced propaganda and information policy of OHL, ensured that the German people were totally misinformed about the development of the military position from April 1918. This was particularly the case with the so-called educated classes and almost without exception with the political representatives of the Reich, including the leaders of the Majority Social Democrats. The reactions of the party leaders to the lecture by Major von dem Bussche-Ippenburg about the military situation on 2 October cannot otherwise be explained, especially as the exposition of the major was a long way from matching reality. The suddenness of the event, the breathtaking speed of the cataclysmic domestic and foreign developments in October, the remaining lack of clarity, deliberately promoted by Ludendorff, about the real military situation on the Western Front—all this prevented a reassessment of previous positions and their modification in the new circumstances. The difficulty of forming fresh perspectives was inherent in the situation, but should not be neglected in judging political actions, particularly those of the Social Democratic leaders.

The sudden and chaotic collapse of a system hitherto opposed in principle only by a small political minority deprived the broad middle strata of their general political orientation. It thus prepared fertile ground for wild hypotheses and attempts at explanation, all of which served the purpose of suppressing or making tolerable the bitter and repugnant reality. The stab-in-the-back myth perfectly met this requirement. It used accustomed categories and was, even in its exaggerated form, not new. Major General von Seeckt had already expressed it in the crisis of July 1917: 'What are we really fighting for? The home front has attacked us from behind, and therefore the war is lost.' This distorting statement was now consciously used as a political weapon. In this area OHL also pointed the way when Ludendorff told officers of the General Staff on 29 September 'now those circles must be brought into the government . . . whom we have above all to thank for having brought us to this point. . . . Let them now eat the broth they have cooked for us.' The shifting of responsibility for the disaster, long in preparation, now assumed concrete form. At the very moment of defeat the formula was discovered which helped to obscure among large sections of the population the recognition of the causes of collapse, and to give a propaganda ploy the appearance of reality. While recognizing with surprising clarity the real issues, the chairman of the Pan-German League stated to its executive committee on 19 October that 'the situation should be used for a fanfare against Jewry and the Jews as lightning conductors for all injustices.' The stab-in-the-back myth was thus endowed with its devastating anti-Semitic force.

The covert strike of the soldiers was the political answer to the overextension of all resources of the nation in the service of a military policy with illusory domestic and foreign aims. The mass movement among the soldiers aimed in the first place for an end to the war, but was also a decisive precondition for the revolution and determined its form and content. At the same time, the suddenness of its success provoked a counter-movement which was to have, by means of grotesque self-deception, simple suppression, or even deliberate propagandistic falsification of events, more permanent political consequences than the mass movement of the soldiers.

Notes

From Wilhelm Deist, "The Military Collapse of the German Empire," *War in History* 3 (2): 186–207. (c) 2001 Edward Arnold (Publishers) Ltd. (www.hodderarnoldjournals.com). Reprinted with permission of the publisher.

1. On August 8, 1918 at the Battle of Amiens the Germans suffered a stinging defeat. Of greatest concern to the German high command was the high number of men who surrendered rather than fight, indicating a serious decline in German morale.

2. The treaty that ended Russian participation in the war. Germany seized vast Russian stores of grain, oil, and weapons as well as a million square miles of territory containing sixty-two million people.

Diggers and Doughboys
Australian and American Troop Interaction
on the Western Front, 1918

Dale Blair

Last century Australia fought in four major wars: the First World War, the Second World War, Korea and Vietnam. A constant ally in those conflicts was the United States. For both nations, sizeable portions of their adult male populations participated in military operations. As a consequence, the perceptions of different generations of Australians and Americans toward one another have been shaped and transmitted within the extraordinary parameters of war.

The First World War saw a largely positive interaction between Australian and American soldiers. Although thrown together for only a short time, the two forces left an indelible mark on each other. The fleeting nature of this marriage, and the fact that the union occurred on neutral political and geographical ground, undoubtedly contributed to the goodwill exhibited by the respective armies. There were, however, other determinants at work that allowed for the bonding of the "diggers" and "doughboys." Both nations celebrated a "frontier" tradition that advanced distinct and robust masculine traditions. Both had been British colonies, though the road to nationhood had followed quite different routes. Nevertheless, of vital importance to the relationship was a shared antipathy toward the British, one heightened by a respect forged in the fire of the front line during the latter part of 1918. It is the nature of those factors that this article strives to identify.

The American declaration of war on 6 April 1917 arguably shifted the Great War's status from a European war to a World War. Nevertheless it would be twelve months before American mobilisation allowed sufficient numbers of U.S. soldiers to arrive in Europe and significantly bolster the Allied armies. Most Australians were thankful of the American decision to enter the war, as they saw it as an obvious source of relief for themselves. An Australian Imperial Force gunner stated the case plainly: "Of course as more Yanks come in then more Aussies should be able to get away." Above all, American manpower offered real hope for bringing the war to a decisive conclusion.

The first significant contacts between diggers and doughboys occurred in June of 1918. This came after the British commander-in-chief Douglas Haig made a request to his American counterpart, General John Pershing, for U.S. troops to be used in a defensive role in the event of an emergency. The American 27th and 33rd Divisions, and later the 30th, 78th and 80th Divisions, were moved closer to the front near Amiens to fulfil that need if required.

It was among the soldiers of the 27th, 30th and 33rd Divisions that the most enduring memories of Australian soldiers were felt. The fact that these represented only three of forty-three U.S. divisions also meant that knowledge of the Australians was limited in the American experience. Conversely, the Australian view of Americans was more widespread. Five A.I.F. divisions represented the totality of the Australian presence on the Western Front, and thus the entire Australian force had some contact with the Americans.

The training of American troops under British command was to follow a three-step process. This entailed the attachment of American platoons to larger formations, then companies, eventuating in the placement of whole larger American formations in the front line with independent command authority. Because U.S. divisions were large, being nearly double the size of standard equivalent British formations, the attachment of American platoons to Australian battalions reflected a pragmatic breakdown of the larger-size American units to enable the men to "mix" more readily.

The first significant action involving diggers and doughboys was the Australian attack on Hamel in July 1918. In that operation Lieutenant-General Sir John Monash was planning to eradicate a German salient to improve his line for future moves near Amiens. The Fourth Army commander, General Sir Henry Rawlinson, offered Monash the use of the recently-arrived 65th Brigade of the 33rd U.S. Division. The incorporation in the Australian battle plan of ten companies of infantry, from the 131st and 132nd Regiments, was to prove a controversial one.

The use of the doughboys hardly constituted the "emergency" to which Pershing had previously acquiesced. On learning of the projected deployment of American troops during a visit to the front, Pershing ordered their withdrawal on the basis that they were inadequately trained and that their use was contrary to the earlier agreement. Major General G. W. Read, commander of the American II Corps to which the allocated companies belonged, was advised to withdraw the doughboys. A day before the attack, six companies were withdrawn and the Australian plan adjusted to cover their loss. When it appeared that the remaining four companies would also be withdrawn, Monash objected strenuously and threatened to cancel the attack. He was unmoved by Rawlinson's concern that he (Rawlinson) might be despatched to England if he proceeded in violation of Pershing's wishes. The preservation of the confidence in Australian and American troop relations, Monash argued, outweighed the fate of an Army commander. Ultimately, Haig accepted responsibility for the use of the four companies of doughboys, deeming the improvement of the position to be of more critical and immediate importance to future operations than Pershing's objection.

At Hamel the Americans were considered to have performed well. One Australian who observed a doughboy company in action noted: "If they showed a fault it was as always with first class fighting men until they get experience—the fault of excessive keenness, so that they suffered some casualties by pressing on into our barrage, but the 'Australians' are lavish in admiration of their 'dash.'" This *élan*, though born largely of ignorance and excessive enthusiasm, was fundamental to the maintenance of respect on the part of the Australians. The first signs of a friendly rivalry were evident, too, and Sapper William M. Telford remarked that its existence did "Fritz no good."

During the battle, American runners and stretcher-bearers were paired with Australians to assist in their training. The value of this pairing of experience with inexperience soon came to the fore as the commander of the 131st Infantry attested: "Considerable opposition was met near the western edge of Hamel where there were some dug-outs. A reserve platoon of Americans led by Lieutenant Symons worked around to the flank overlying the position. The lieutenant was wounded but his runner, the only Australian with the platoon, took charge and cleared up the situation."

Despite the close association of the diggers and doughboys in this phase, American ignorance of the Australians' distinct view of themselves was evident. Captain Will Lewis Judy noted that he thought this combined operation represented "the first time American troops fought side by side with their enemy of our own revolutionary days, the British." Australians would have recoiled (and do) at such association. The lack of distinction between Australian and British had become a vexatious issue for the diggers late in the war. They had become intensely sensitive to the failure of British authorities to distinguish between Australian and British operations. The main reason for this was that Australians had come to believe the British, generally, were not up to the Australian standard. They perceived Australian successes to be unheralded by such generic reportage.

Antipathy toward the British, however, was something that both diggers and doughboys shared. As such it provided a powerful bonding agent. The Australian contempt for the British command and of the fighting qualities of the English was little concealed. A report by the Commanding General, 27th U.S. Division, distinguished between the attitudes of Australian officers and enlisted men toward their comrades-in-arms. The "diggers" were reported as manifesting an open and "intense criticism" that bordered on "bitterness" while the Australian officers were considered to have been more circumspect in registering their dissatisfaction, expressing it informally.

American relations with the British do not appear to have been as cordial as with the dominion forces. Robert E. Smith of the 120th Infantry thought "The British islanders were never very friendly or willing to try to get along." Although he excluded the Scots from his assessment, he believed the "British outlook on Americans was in conflict." Private Leslie Charles White of the 129th Infantry recalled having "trouble with the British" and thought them neither friendly nor good soldiers. It is possible that American perceptions of English soldierly qualities—which they had not had adequate opportunity of witnessing first hand—were influenced by contact with the Australians' contemptuous denigration of the Tommies.

Pershing's lower echelon commanders and men also shared the contentious issue of American command independence that coloured his relations with the British. Private L. Wolf of the 129th Infantry wrote: "The English wanted to boss our command off the earth and so did the French—we got along with the other foreign countries." This view was confirmed by Sergeant Merritt C. Pratt, 131st Infantry, who remembered English NCOs trying to laud it over his men by insisting they salute British Sergeant-Majors which was not liked at all (mirroring the legendary disinclination of Australians toward such military protocol). Pratt was happier serving with the Australians whom he classed as the best fighters he had ever seen and who also "disliked the British soldier."

For the diggers, the tension with the British was due in part to them being part of a fledgling nation trying to prove itself worthy within the family of the British Empire. The Americans, on the other hand, had already enjoyed nearly a century and a half of independence, won bloodily from the "mother country." The doughboys' antipathy was partly historic. Sergeant Fred P. Jones, 108th Engineers, stated that the British "still remembered the Revolutionary War and if they didn't we reminded [them] of it." If this undertaking was widespread among American soldiers, one could well understand a certain coolness of attitude from the British.

Relations between Americans and British were the subject of an extended treatment by Lieutenant Colonel Calvin H. Goddard of the U.S. Army War College. Many of the comments made by soldiers in the U.S. Army's World War One survey were borne out in Goddard's study. Goddard identified the relationship between the Americans and English as being relatively poor and lacking in generosity. Americans considered the English inferior in physique, initiative and morale—factors axiomatic to Australian perceptions. Regarding the comparative fighting qualities of the two forces, he conceded that the sub-standard drafts reinforcing the British armies and the exhaustion from years of combat had diminished the fighting capacity of the British Expeditionary Force (BEF). That aside, the BEF was still seen as possessing courage and tenacity.

Goddard believed the Americans rated the Australians highly and saw themselves as equals. A feature of the Australian method was identified as being the combination of caution and aggression that restricted casualties while at the same time gaining objectives "handsomely." Some aspects of Australian behaviour, however, were repugnant to the Americans. The "systematic looting" of the American dead by the "diggers" was a case in point. Australian officers were said to have dismissed such incidents in a "light-hearted manner."

That such looting occurred seems beyond doubt given the pragmatic admission of one Australian soldier:

> Most of our men souvenired the Americans before they were buried and some got great hauls of money (in French notes of course) as most Americans were wealthy and had plenty of money on them. This was quite alright as we may as well have had the money and made use of it (which we did) instead of burying it with them.

Yet, for the Americans, the lengths to which some Australians were prepared to go was nothing short of disgraceful. The commander of the 27th Division, Major General John F. O'Ryan, while full of approbation for the Australians, could not hide his revulsion at the knowledge that an Australian soldier had allegedly cut off a dead American officer's finger to acquire a ring. O'Ryan clearly did not doubt the veracity of the claim noting that the Australians were well known for moving "over the fields with gunny sacks seeking whatever was of value." It was suggested that ill feeling from such incidents was offset by the lavish praise the Australians directed at the Americans.

The Australians' capacity for self-sufficiency was a trait that was also observed to have crossed the lines of acceptable military efficacy. An example was offered by the commanding general of 60th U.S. Brigade. He noted that Australian artillery communications were "astonishingly efficient" in that they were still open when neighbouring lines had been cut. The reason, he ventured, lay in the fact that the Australians "would themselves cut anybody else's wire if necessary to keep up communications." Irrespective of whether such an unlikely act was true or whether the story was apocryphal, the American general's perceptions of Australians as ruthlessly opportunistic comrades in arms was manifest.

The treatment of prisoners was also a contentious area. One criticism of some interest was that of Sergeant James V. Armfield, 105th Engineers, who voiced disapproval at the "treatment of prisoners by British non-coms [non-commissioned officers]." He did not elaborate on the nature of that treatment but presumably it referred to acts that fell outside the guidelines of the Hague Convention and common decency. It was obvious though, that the Australians were passing on their own hard-nosed attitudes in regard to military expediency to the inexperienced doughboys who had not yet adapted their civilian sensibilities to the fighting mores of the front line. According to Private Willard M. Newton of the 105th Engineer Train, he was able to glean from the Australians "lots of things that are important to a soldier who has not been in battle." It was clear, too, that the impressionable doughboys were uncritically accepting of Australian claims of German "torture" and "extreme cruelty" toward their prisoners. On such issues the Australians' veteran status gave added credibility as Newton noted, "We believe them, for they have been in this war long enough to know." The Australian advice was not to allow oneself to be captured or as, Newton implied, take prisoners: "They have no use for the Huns."

It was in battle that Australian-American relations would be tested in the most extreme way. When it came to combat performance, the Australians had reached a high level of competence by the time the Americans arrived. The Americans on the other hand were an unproven quantity. The manner in which they proved themselves on the battlefield was critical to Australian assessments. It was during the attack on the Hindenburg line, in which the American II Corps comprising the 27th and 33rd U.S. Divisions was attached to Monash's Australian Corps, that sizeable numbers of both forces came in contact with the other.

After the crucial assault against the St. Quentin Canal on 29 September 1918 and the breaking of the Hindenburg Line, Australians following up the initial attack remarked on the numerous American dead. Gunner A. G. MacKay, camped in a trench where a heap of thirty Yanks lay in front, thought the Americans had erred in sending unguarded prisoners to the rear. This was a common practice though it was believed, in this instance, that the prisoners simply reinforced German machine-gun and artillery positions that had been by-passed. Another Australian artilleryman put the "lanes of American dead" down to their lack of strategy or initiative and to "bad fire discipline." The Americans had gamely "rushed headlong at entrenched machine-guns" rather than employing tactics of fire and movement to outflank the enemy. They had thus fallen prey to the German tactic of leaving gaps in the wire to entice inexperienced troops into the fields of fire concentrated there. The perceived failure of the Americans to "mop up" was central to Australian criticisms of the American attack and permeates personal Australian accounts of the battle. Allegedly, supporting Australians subsequently informed the Americans that it was pointless them sending back any more prisoners, as they would not be allowed to pass.

Australia's official war historian, C. E. W. Bean, resisted such notions in his account. He concluded that the Americans had not rushed forward impetuously and that the chief resistance had not come from by-passed Germans or those sent rearward but from "supports and reserves attacking normally from the front." He believed that the Americans had been set too difficult a task for inexperienced troops.

To circumvent some of that inexperience, a special "Australian Mission" was organised to facilitate liaison between the American divisions attached to the Australian Corps during the Battle for the Hindenburg Line. Major General E. G. Sinclair-Maclagan headed the mission of two groups drawn from the 1st and 4th Australian divisions. Eighty-three officers and 127 NCO's participated in the Mission. One group under Brigadier General C. H. Brand was attached to the 27th Division; the other, under Brigadier General I. G. Mackay, went to the 30th Division. At the outset it was stipulated that the duties of the Mission were to be entirely advisory and not executive.

The prime purpose of the Mission was to assist in the preparation for the attack of 29 September. Australian officers and NCOs supervised the taping of start lines and positioning of troops. The commander of the 54th U.S. Infantry Brigade, Brigadier General Palmer E. Pierce, was particularly thankful for the invaluable services and lessons the Australians provided in regard matters of supply, including the provision of hot meals to the men at the front. The NCOs were recalled on the 28 September but the officers were to remain until after the attack.

One task undertaken by the Australian intelligence officers was to supervise the production of contour maps to familiarise the officers and men with the ground over which the regiments had to attack. In the case of the 107th, these maps were never completed as the regiment was ordered forward and few of its personnel saw even the incomplete version.

Pre-battle advice and planning given by Lieutenant Hill, the Australian intelligence officer attached to the 107th Regiment, and his accompanying sergeants, seems to have been valued. However, his recommendation that a battalion command post ought to be positioned a 1000 yards behind the company lines rather than between the first and second waves, as was thought appropriate by the enquiring Captain Egan, appears to have been quietly dismissed as unacceptable to American "machismo." Hill cut something of a dramatic figure as he hurried the Americans toward their jump-off line, the pegging of which he had supervised a few hours earlier. He had lost his tin-hat and had tied a handkerchief around his head—perhaps to give a theatrical brush to events as the handkerchief's protective qualities were certainly dubious.

When the American attack began to go awry, the Australian officers assumed a central role in assessing and endeavouring to restore the situation. From the field messages of the II Corps, it is evident that the Australian officers were being relied on for advice. During the afternoon of 29 September, Lieutenant Colonel A. G. Salisbury was on hand to advise Colonel Boswell of likely outcomes during the absence of reports from 54th Brigade patrols sent out in the morning. Lieutenant Bowman of the 1st Battalion, AIF, was cited as having provided "valuable assistance" to the 115th U.S. Machine Gun Battalion, while an Australian surgical team under Major A. W. Holmes à Court gave assistance at the Americans' main dressing station at Villers-Faucon.

Brigadier-General Iven Mackay, on learning of the failure of the 27th Division and of the disorganisation of the 30th Division (though it was largely successful in gaining its objectives), immediately went forward to assist. To Major General Edward M. Lewis, GOC 30th Division, he wrote down a series of instructions in regard to the reorganising and controlling of units and employment of staffs. He arranged for these instructions to be set in train in the rear echelons, and at divisional headquarters, and then personally went forward to the headquarters of the attacking 59th and 60th Brigades to instruct the commanders of those units. Later in the afternoon, Mackay accompanied General Lewis to Headquarters 5th Australian Division, to arrange details for the withdrawal of the Americans.

The extent of the 30th Division's disorganisation was borne out in Major W. F. L. Hartigan's report to G-3. Assembly points for stragglers were unknown, and stragglers in large numbers clogged the division's rear. Hartigan personally assembled and directed five hundred strays back to the front. Men bringing in prisoners singly rather than in groups, men escorting wounded comrades, and others seeking attention for superficial injuries such as backs hurt from falling in shell-holes, all contributed to the congestion. Inhibiting the efficient management of the problem was a lack of training and initiative on the part of the American NCOs. Many did not have compasses—a reflection of the supply problems and shortages that afflicted the American Expeditionary Force (AEF) generally—and this caused the mist and smoke that limited visibility in the early phase of the battle to be doubly blinding. They exhibited a marked disinclination to join other units, or form new temporary squads to move the battle forward. This attitude also precluded any willingness to assume higher command responsibilities in the face of missing or disabled officers. The American advance was further compromised by a lack of understanding on the part of company officers and NCOs about their unit's objectives and mission. Many of the problems were the same as had afflicted the untested Australians at Gallipoli, and were symptomatic of green troops and staffs in battle. That the 30th Division achieved its objectives in the face of such inexperience is perhaps testament to the men's exuberance and desire to succeed, as well as the exactness of the preparatory planning of Monash. Unlike the 27th Division, the 30th had not been compromised by having to commence its attack from behind the initial start line.

At the 27th U.S. Division, Brigadier-General Brand recorded in detail the ramifications of that formation's operational rawness. After the battle, Brand provided some corrective notes to Major General O'Ryan about how the Americans could improve future performance. Among the twenty-six points outlined, the more salient criticisms were that the staff officers were too headquarters-bound, thus often allowing unreliable information to find its way to Brigade and Divisional headquarters; too much optimism clouded or blinded judgement; too many officers went forward in the first waves and became unnecessary casualties, thus contributing to a shortage of officers and loss of unit cohesion; and written communications from the field were poor, with too great a reliance on telephone communication and not enough runners. All these things, according to Brand, militated against providing a clear picture of the attack's progress. Combined with poor rear echelon organisation, they further impeded the ability of the Americans to react promptly.

The alleged exuberance of the doughboys might well have been due to their greenness and desire to perform well. Another possibility that has been suggested is that they were victims of an ambiguous doctrine from Pershing, who oscillated between planning for trench warfare and subscribing to the virtues of, and preference for, open warfare. As a consequence, fighting commanders entered the line with no clear conceptual understanding of their commander-in-chief's expectations. U.S. Army successes were subsequently won by the costly tactic of smothering German machine-guns with American flesh.

Nevertheless, the desire to engage with the Germans in open warfare was evident in the demeanour of the doughboys, according to a British officer who observed the training of the 27th Division. He thought the prospect of the fight rather than the immediate, even if seemingly menial, tasks of preparation was a source of distraction to the Americans:

> The men are anxious for active operations rather than the work of trench warfare and have not realised the necessity for acquiring proficiency with the spade.

Deficiencies were undoubtedly carried into battle. An American officer stated, in relation to the training of the 30th Division, that it was "very apparent that our men expose themselves unnecessarily and do not hug the folds of the ground or crawl as they should."

Along the St. Quentin Canal, while doctrinal factors might have contributed to the American losses, the 27th Division's assault was initially compromised by the earlier failure of the British III Corps to secure the German strong-points located at the Knoll, Gillemont Farm and Quennemont Farm. This was, as Bean termed it, "a serious complication." In Monash's pre-battle planning it was expected that these positions would have been secured prior to the doughboys' arrival. When the Americans took over the line, an attempt was made by the 106th U.S. Regiment to clear the German outposts but this proved a singularly disastrous operation. The 108th pushed forward in the afternoon of 27 September to relieve the disorganised remnants of the 106th, a process that was not completed, owing to inexact knowledge of the 106th's position, until the early hours of 28 September.

With the ground still not taken by 29 September, the main attack was to proceed with the 27th Division left to clear the contested ground and make up the lost yardage as best it could. Unfortunately, confusion over whether unsupported and wounded Americans still lay out in front prior to the main attack resulted in the supporting barrage remaining on its originally planned line rather than being brought back. As compensation, additional tanks were allocated to the 27th Division to help them fight their way forward. Without adequate artillery support to suppress the unconquered outposts confronting the doughboys, the task set O'Ryan's men was an onerous one.

It was little wonder that the leading regiments of the 27th Division, the 107th and 108th, struggled on 29 September to make up the ground and suffered excessive casualties as a result. Nevertheless, the displeasure of the Australians at the confusion ahead of their advance and the disorientation within the American command was being clearly communicated through II U.S. Army Corps headquarters. The vicinity of Guoy, Le Catelet and Bony was, contrary to plan, swarming with Germans. A battalion of Americans supposed to be occupying the ground had not been heard from and was feared lost, seemingly confirming the statement of a captured German colonel that 700 American prisoners had been taken.

An Australian artillery officer accompanied a battalion of the 107th toward Guoy and returned at 5 p.m. to confirm the rough fighting and occupation of Le Catelet by the Germans. The officer was Lieutenant W. O. Pasefield and he reported seeing the Americans undertake repeated bayonet charges and stated, "I saw more fighting on this day than I have seen during my experiences." It was probably this same officer who was reported as saying the 107th's fighting to have been the hardest he had seen during the war.

A consequence of the stiff fighting in front of the 27th Division's line of advance and on its right around Bellicourt, before the 30th Division, was the severe artillery barrages brought down by the Germans in support of their frontline troops. The Australian artillery and ambulance columns moving forward in accordance with the planned timetable were caught unawares by the hold up toward their front. As they descended into the valley before the German line they came under the view of artillery observers and the roads were deluged with shells. The result was mayhem with "horses and men . . . running in all directions." Stretcher-bearers were sent forward in the mid-afternoon and relay posts were established on the outskirts of Bellicourt, but due to the incessant shell-fire it was dusk before loading posts could be established to clear the mounting stretcher cases from the front.

Sergeant Merritt D. Cutler, of the 107th Regiment, thought the battle resembled a scene from *Dante's Inferno*. The sight of so many of his wounded comrades compelled him to seek assistance to remove the wounded and dying from the maelstrom. He came across a couple of Australians who were moving toward the front and he was, despite the reticence of one, able to gain help and a stretcher from the other who replied: "Sure, Yank, I'll go; we're in this bloody thing together."

Although the failure of the 27th Division and, to a lesser extent, the confusion in the 30th Division were observed by the diggers first-hand, condemnation found little place in the personal letters and diaries of Australian soldiers who recorded the fighting along the St. Quentin Canal. While English failures were belittled and enshrined in ANZAC mythology, in this instance it was the unswerving gallantry of the Americans—as ill-advised as it might have been—that left the greatest impression on the Australians.

If Australian attitudes were shaped by perceptions of American bravery and potential, American attitudes were similarly shaped by Australian efficiency and aggression. Colonel Spence of the 117th Infantry believed the division had been fortunate to have served with and received the co-operation of the British and Australians. He thought the Australians were "wonderfully aggressive fighters."

Post-war views of the Americans, especially those of the ageing veterans who participated in the U.S. Army's WWI Research project, were overwhelmingly positive in regard to the Australians. While many also spoke generically of good relations with the British, those of the 27th, 30th and 33rd Divisions often singled out the Australians and other Dominion troops as being outstanding. George Leonhardt, 105th Engineers, considered the Australians to be "real men." Richard H. Brooks, a corporal in the 120th Infantry Regiment, wrote: "I thought more of the Australians and Canadians than I did the British. They would say 'Don't shoot, don't shoot' (fear of retaliation), but those Australians were OK." Second Lt. Roby G. Yarborough, 120th Infantry, rated the Australians as "excellent" but believed the British to be "too cautious." Henry Bacon McKay was another clearly not enamoured by His Majesty's forces: "We disliked and laughed at the British"; the Australians, in contrast, were "liked and admired."

There was, too, in the relationship between diggers and doughboys a degree of narcissism. Each saw something of themselves in the other. Lieutenant Kenneth Gow of the 107th Regiment was fond of the Aussies and described them as "more like ourselves than any of the other allies." It was this recognition that possibly produced some of the empathy the Australians held for the Americans. Observing the doughboys' greenness, an Australian sergeant noted, "Their enthusiasm is just great, but of course they are just as we were in early 1915." Australians were keenly aware of the bloody lessons that lay before the Americans.

Overall, a spontaneity characterised Australian and American relations that was absent in American and British relations. That is not to say that Americans and the British were incapable of shared views. Indeed, Australian discipline (or perceived lack of) was one point on which Americans and the British sometimes concurred. Private Charles D. Ebersole, 129th Infantry, thought the Australians "very good" and "very democratic," though "somewhat undisciplined." In this regard the British professional view of what army discipline ought to be was akin to Pershing's preferred "West Point"–styled U.S. Army. American bureaucracy did not pass unnoticed as one Australian declared: "Their administration was top-heavy, and they ran a paper war at least three times ours." Both American and British discipline and protocol jarred against the Australian soldiers' more casual outlook.

To conclude, if a prevailing Australian view of the Americans is required, it is best encapsulated in the assessment of Lieutenant W. A. Carne:

At the very outset, the newcomers made no secret of their admiration of the Australians. Indeed, their outspoken regard . . . was almost embarrassing. On the other hand, the 'diggers' were well disposed towards such a friendly lot of men, and the two parties got on splendidly together. But when it came to the business in hand, Company members were appalled at their ignorance and want of perception. . . . In spite of their extreme rawness, Company officers agreed that they would prove very staunch in action if well led. . . . The wide difference between the two parties made thoughtful Company members realise how very far they themselves had travelled since Gallipoli days, and what a vast amount of experience they took for granted, and looked for in troops in France.

It was this reflection of themselves, along with the shared antipathy toward the British, and mutual recognition of bravery and performance on the battlefield, that allowed Australians to generously accept the Americans on the Western Front in 1918.

Note

From Dale Blair, "Diggers and Doughboys: Australian and American Troop Interaction on the Western Front, 1918," *Journal of the Australian War Memorial* 35 (Dec. 2001). http://www.awm.gov.au/journal/j35/blair.htm. Reprinted with permission.

Six

Peace

Peacemaking, 1919

Harold Nicolson

1

In this, the second volume of my trilogy, I have tried to deal with the transitional phase between pre-war and post-war diplomacy and to give some picture of the Paris Peace Conference. I had intended at first to cast this study also in the form of a biography and to centre my story around the personality of Mr. Woodrow Wilson or Mr. Lloyd George. I found, however, that such a concentration of theme would convey no impression of the appalling dispersal of energy which was the actual key-note of the Paris Conference. The sharp perspective, the personal continuity, given by the biographical method would have proved inimical to my purpose. I am well aware that in abandoning my original intention I have lost immeasurably in construction, interest, and financial profit. Yet in adopting such a method I should have been simplifying the issues, rather than furnishing a picture of the confusions and complications which actually occurred. I decided, therefore, that I should merely describe the Peace Conference as I experienced it myself.

Here again I was faced with a difficulty. I realised the impossibility at this stage of furnishing any connected narrative of the Conference in terms either of subject, or of time-sequence. On the one hand many vital documents are still unavailable, and on the other hand the consecutive method would create no accurate impression. The important point to realise about the Paris Conference is its amazing inconsequence, the complete absence of any consecutive method of negotiation or even imposition. The actual history of the Conference will one day be written in authoritative and readable form. What may remain unrecorded, is the atmosphere of those unhappy months, the mists by which we were enshrouded. My study, therefore, is a study in fog. The reader should not look for any continuous lucidity. It wasn't there.

I have, I think, read most of the many books which since 1919 have been published about the Peace Conference, some of which are admirable and some the reverse. Yet from all these books I have derived the impression that something essential was absent, and I am convinced that this vital omission was the omission of the element of confusion. It is that element, and that only, which I have endeavoured in this volume to record.

The memory of those congested days is very vivid to me. It has been fortified by reading the diary which I kept at the time. I have decided to print, as the second half of this volume, the major portions of that diary, feeling convinced that in its chirpy triviality it reflects better than any comments of a disillusioned middle age the very atmosphere which it is my desire to convey. My criticisms of my own diary are however implicit rather than explicit. I was, at the time, young and pardonably excited. No special self-excuse is needed for such faults.

Yet my main thesis, I trust, will be apparent. It is this. Given the atmosphere of the time, given the passions aroused in all democracies by four years of war, it would have been impossible even for supermen to devise a peace of moderation and righteousness. The task of the Paris negotiators was, however, complicated by special circumstances of confusion. The ideals to which they had been pledged by President Wilson were not only impracticable in themselves but necessitated for their execution the intimate and unceasing collaboration of the United States. We felt that this collaboration might possibly be intimate but could not possibly be unceasing. It was thus the endeavour of men like Clemenceau and Lloyd George to find a middle way between the desires of their democracies and the more moderate dictates of their own experience, as well as a middle way between the theology of President Wilson and the practical needs of a distracted Europe. These twin gulfs had to be bridged by compromise, and to a later generation these compromises seem hypocritical and deceptive. Yet were they not inevitable? And is it to be expected that human nature, having but recently indulged in the folly of the Great War, could suddenly manifest the calm serenity of almost superhuman wisdom?

I do not answer these questions. I leave them as interrogatives to be answered by some future generation. All that I hope to suggest is that human error is a permanent and not a periodic factor in history, and that future negotiators will be exposed, however noble their intentions, to futilities of intention and omission as grave as any which characterised the Council of Five. They were convinced that they would never commit the blunders and iniquities of the Congress of Vienna. Future generations will be equally convinced that they will be immune from the defects which assailed the negotiators of Paris. Yet they in their turn will be exposed to similar microbes of infection, to the eternal inadequacy of human intelligence.

It is with saddened regret that I look back to-day to that November morning when Mr. Lloyd George announced the Armistice from the steps of Downing Street. The scene, to this moment, is impressed indelibly upon my mind. I was working in the basement of the Foreign Office, in a green and violet dug-out which but a few weeks before had provided shelter against the air-raids of the Germans. I was preparing for the eventual Peace Conference. More particularly, on that morning of November 11, I was studying the problem of the Strumnitza enclave.

Having worked for an hour, I found that I required a further map. I went upstairs towards the tower where our map-room was installed. On my way there I called in at the office of the Chief Clerk to order some further tin boxes for my needs at the Conference. I strolled to the window and looked down upon No. 10 Downing Street. A group of people stood in the roadway and there were some half a dozen policemen. It was 10:55 a.m. Suddenly the front door opened. Mr. Lloyd George, his white hair fluttering in the wind, appeared upon the door-step. He waved his arms outwards. I opened the window hurriedly. He was shouting the same sentence over and over again. I caught his words. 'At eleven o'clock this morning the war will be over.'

The crowd surged towards him. Plump and smiling he made dismissive gestures and then retreated behind the great front door. People were running along Downing Street and in a few minutes the whole street was blocked. There was no cheering. The crowd overflowed dumbly into the Horse Guards Parade. They surged around the wall of the Downing Street garden. From my post of vantage I observed Lloyd George emerge into that garden, nervous and enthusiastic. He went towards the garden door and then withdrew. Two secretaries who were with him urged him on. He opened the door. He stepped out into the Parade. He waved his hands for a moment of gesticulation and then again retreated. The crowd rushed towards him and patted feverishly at his back. My most vivid impression of Mr. Lloyd George derives from that moment. A man retreating from too urgent admirers who endeavour hysterically to pat him on the back. Ought he to have gone? Having gone, ought he to have retreated so boyishly? That scene was a symbol of much that was to follow thereafter. Having regained the garden enclosure, Mr. Lloyd George laughed heartily with the two secretaries who had accompanied him. It was a moving scene.

So the Germans had signed after all. I returned to my basement and the Strumnitza enclave. When I again emerged the whole of London had gone mad.

It was in this manner that I heard of the coming of peace.

2

Many years have elapsed since those November days when I, in my green and violet basement, pored over the problem of the Strumnitza enclave. I am to-day aware that during the same period the rulers of the world were preoccupied by problems of even graver significance.

It is necessary, when examining the legal basis of the Peace Treaties, to concentrate at the very outset upon the question whether the triangular correspondence which took place in October between Washington, Berlin and the capitals of the Associated Powers constituted a contract in the legal sense of the term. Before we proceed a page further it is essential to state the following problem; 'Did the Germans lay down their arms in reliance upon a pledge given them by their enemies that the ensuing peace terms would conform absolutely to the twenty-three principles enunciated by President Wilson? If so, did the Allied and Associated Powers observe, or violate that pledge once Germany was at their mercy?'

The problem is so material to any record of the Peace Conference that I feel obliged to repeat the practice of my predecessors upon this thorny path and to recapitulate in my first chapter the main features of the pre-Armistice agreement (the 'pactum de contrahendo') between Germany and the victorious Powers. The essential documents can be summarised as follows. On October 5 Prince Max of Baden, after many anxious telephone messages to German Headquarters, addressed an official Note to President Wilson in which he begged him to negotiate a peace on the basis of his own Fourteen Points and his nine subsequent principles and to facilitate the immediate conclusion of the Armistice. On October 8 President Wilson replied in the form of three questions: (a) Did the German Government themselves accept the Fourteen Points as the basis of the desired Treaty? (b) Would they at once withdraw their troops from all foreign soil? (c) Could they give assurance that the present and future government of Germany would be placed on a truly democratic basis? On October 12 the Chancellor replied in the affirmative to each of these three questions. He added that his 'object in entering into discussions would be only to agree upon practical details of the application' of the 'terms' contained in President Wilson's Fourteen Points and his subsequent pronouncements. On October 14 President Wilson again addressed the German Government. He told them that no armistice could be negotiated which did not 'provide absolutely satisfactory safeguard for the maintenance of the present military supremacy' of the Allied and Associated armies. He added that submarine warfare must at once be discontinued, and that a democratic and representative government must be installed in Berlin. On October 20 the German Chancellor replied accepting these conditions. On October 23 President Wilson informed the German Government that, having now received their assurance that they unreservedly accepted the 'terms of peace' embodied in his own pronouncements, he was prepared to discuss with his associates the grant of an armistice on this basis. He repeated that its terms must exclude all possibility of the resumption of hostilities. He hinted that the path of peace would be smoothed by the prior disappearance of 'monarchical autocrats.' He added that he had communicated to the Associated Governments the correspondence which had passed between himself and the German Government and had asked them whether they for their part would be 'disposed to effect peace upon the terms and principles indicated.' On November 5 the President transmitted to the German Government the replies he had received from his associates. The Allied Governments had declared their willingness to conclude a Treaty with the Government of Germany on the basis of the 'terms of peace' enunciated by the President subject to two qualifications. The first of these bore upon the question of the Freedom of the Seas. The second extended the principle of 'restoration' so as to cover 'all damage done to the civilian population of the Allies and to their property by the aggression of Germany by land, by sea, and from the air.' The German government, on the receipt of this assurance at once dispatched their emissaries to receive the armistice terms. The terms of this Armistice had been drafted in Conference by the Supreme Council at Versailles: they were such as to place Germany at the complete mercy of the Allied Powers by land and sea: they were signed in the Forest of Compiègne at 5 a.m. on Monday, November 11.

In my next chapter I shall describe my own veneration for the Fourteen Points; I shall summarise those points and their attendant principles; and I shall show how nineteen out of President Wilson's twenty-three 'Terms of Peace' were flagrantly violated in the Treaty of Versailles as finally drafted.

For the moment I am concerned only with the pre-Armistice agreement under which Germany consented to surrender on the explicit understanding that the peace terms thereafter to be imposed upon her would conform absolutely to Wilsonian principles, and would in fact be merely 'the practical detail of application' of those twenty-three conditions on which alone she had consented to lay down her arms. I have summarised above the exchange of correspondence in which this agreement was embodied. Yet this is not the whole story. Sufficient import has not, except by Mr. Winston Churchill, been given to Colonel House's "Interpretation' of the Fourteen Points which preceded their acceptance by the Associated Powers. Colonel House, at the time, was the Representative of America upon the Supreme War Council at Versailles. It was that body which approved the Armistice Terms as drafted, and through which the Allied Powers accepted President Wilson's 'Terms of Peace.' Colonel House's 'Interpretation' or 'commentary' of or on the Fourteen Points is thus a document of very vital importance.

This 'commentary' was, on October 29, 1918, cabled to President Wilson for his approval. It contained the following glosses upon the Fourteen Points and the New Principles. The expression 'open covenants' was not to be interpreted as precluding confidential diplomatic negotiation. By the Freedom of the Seas the President had not intended to abolish the weapon of blockade, but merely to inculcate some respect for private right and property. The President himself advanced the engaging theory that in future wars, because of the League of Nations, there 'would be no neutrals.' Under this double gloss, paragraph 2 of the Fourteen Points became the vaguest expression of opinion. The demand for free trade among the nations of the earth was not to be interpreted as precluding all protection of home industries. Far from it. All that it entailed was the 'open door' for raw material, and the prohibition of discriminatory tariffs between members of the League of Nations. The point regarding 'disarmament' implied only that the Powers should accept the theory in principle, and should agree to the appointment of a Commission to examine the details. The German Colonies might, when the time came, be in principle regarded as the property of the League of Nations, and thus be farmed out among desirable mandatories. Belgium was to be indemnified for all war-costs since every expense to which that unfortunate country had been exposed since August of 1914 was an 'illegitimate' expense. France on the other hand, was not to receive full war costs, only a full indemnity for the actual damage done. Her claim to the territory of the Saar was 'a clear violation of the President's proposal.' Italy, for reasons of security, might claim the Brenner frontier, but the German populations which would thus be incorporated within the Italian frontier should be assured 'complete autonomy.' The subject races of Austria-Hungary should have complete independence conditional upon a guarantee for the protection of racial and linguistic minorities. The mere offer of autonomy 'no longer held.' Bulgaria, on the other hand (a country with whom the United States were not at war, and on whom they had in the past conferred great educational and philanthropic benefits) was to be compensated for having entered the war against us. She was to be given not only the Dobrudja and Western Thrace, but Eastern Thrace as well, as far even as the Midia-Rodosto line. Constantinople and the straits were to be placed under international control. Central Asia Minor was to remain Turkish. Great Britain was to obtain Palestine, Arabia and Iraq. The Greeks might possibly be accorded a mandate over Smyrna and the adjacent districts. Armenia was to be created as an independent state under the tutelage of some great Power. Poland must have access to the sea, although such access implied a difficulty. That difficulty was the severance of East Prussia from the rest of Germany. Colonel House was careful to warn the President that this solution would not be an easy solution. And finally the League of Nations was to be the 'foundation of the diplomatic structure of a permanent peace.'

I do not wish to imply that Colonel House, in presenting this, his interpretation to the Associated Powers, was guilty of any desire to modify the fourteen commandments. I have the most profound respect for Colonel House—considering him to be the best diplomatic brain that America has yet produced, yet I confess that a most undesirable obscurity hangs over his 'interpretation.' Was it on the basis of that interpretation that the Allies accepted the Fourteen Points, the Four Principles and the Five Particulars, as the basis of the eventual Treaty of Peace? If so, then the Enemy Powers should assuredly have been informed at the time. I write subject to correction, since the exact documents, the exact exchange of suggestion and agreement, are not to-day available. Yet it is difficult to resist the impression that the Enemy Powers accepted the Fourteen Points as they stood; whereas the Allied Powers accepted them only as interpreted by Colonel House at the meetings which culminated in his cable of October 29. Somewhere, amid the hurried and anxious imprecisions of those October days, lurks the explanation of the fundamental misunderstanding which has since arisen.

In any case we, the technical staff, the civil servants, had no knowledge of Colonel House's 'Interpretation.' We also looked upon the Fourteen Points and their attendant pronouncements as the charter for our future activity. As I shall show, a great gap widened between our terms of reference, and the eventual conclusions. Had we known of Colonel House's glossary, we might, in April, have seized upon it as a justification for our backsliding. Yet it was not until many years later that I even heard of this glossary. And I cannot, for one moment, pretend that it influenced my attitude to the slightest degree. I betrayed my own allegiance to the Fourteen Points. The purpose of this book is to give some indication, some slight clue, as to the reasons for, or rather the atmosphere of, that betrayal.

My intention in writing this record is, however, not to comment upon documents; my sole endeavour is to recapture states of mind. I am aware that I can make no claim to recapture any state of mind other than my own—a most insignificant capture. Yet I contend that what I felt at the time was also felt by ninety-five per cent. of those who, although not politicians, were actively concerned with public affairs. When I use the term 'We,' I use it as defining the many people who in Paris felt and thought as I did myself. And, as such, we were representative of wide, and not wholly unintelligent, sections of opinion. I think that my own state of mind regarding the contractual basis of the Armistice and the ensuing Treaty did in fact represent an average point of view, which was widely and not wholly unreasonably, held; and I have no recollection that *at the time* the divergence between our own conception of the 'pactum de contrahendo' and the interpretation given to it in Germany presented itself in terms anything like so extreme as those in which it has since been stated.

On the one hand we were convinced that with the crumbling of the western defences—with the collapse of Austria, Turkey and Bulgaria—Germany in any case was beaten to her knees. We were relieved when the Armistice was accepted, since it meant a shortening of the war: but we were convinced that had Germany refused to surrender it would have been a matter of months only, perhaps only of weeks, before her complete capitulation could have been enforced on German soil. On the other hand, in that autumn of 1918, we honestly believed that only upon the principles of President Wilson could a durable peace be founded. In other words, it never entered our heads that we had purchased the surrender of Germany by an offer of the Fourteen Points. The former seemed to us inevitable in any case: the latter, at the time, we took for granted. To argue otherwise is to attribute to November of 1918 ideas and ambitions which did not emerge into the open until the following March.

Excerpt from Nicolson's Diary

June 28, Saturday

La journée de Versailles. Lunch early and leave the Majestic in a car with Headlam Motley. He is a historian, yet he dislikes historical occasions. Apart from that he is a sensitive person and does not rejoice in seeing great nations humbled. I, having none of such acquirements or decencies, am just excited.

There is no crowd at all until we reach Ville d'Avray. But there are poilus at every crossroad waving red flags and stopping all other traffic. When we reach Versailles the crowd thickens. The avenue up to the Château is lined with cavalry in steel-blue helmets. The pennants of their lances flutter red and white in the sun. In the Cour d'Honneur, from which the captured German cannon have tactfully been removed, are further troops. There are Generals, Pétain, Gouraud, Mangin. There are St. Cyriens. Very military and orderly. Headlam Morley and I creep out of our car hurriedly. Feeling civilian and grubby. And wholly unimportant. We hurry through the door.

Magnificent upon the staircase stand the Gardes Républicains—two caryatides on every step—their sabers at the salute. This is a great ordeal, but there are other people climbing the stairs with us. Headlam and I have an eye-meet. His thin cigaretted fingers make a gesture of dismissal. He is not a militarist.

We enter the two anterooms, our feet softening on to the thickest of savonnerie carpets. They have ransacked the Garde Meubles for their finest pieces. Never, since the Grand Siècle, has Versailles been more ostentatious or more embossed. 'I hate Versailles,' I whisper to Headlam. 'You hate what?' he answers, being only a trifle deaf. 'Versailles,' I answer. 'Oh,' he says, 'you mean the Treaty.' 'What Treaty?' I say—thinking of 1871. I do not know why I record this conversation, but I am doing this section of the diary very carefully. It will amuse Ben and Nigel. 'This Treaty,' he answers. 'Oh,' I say, "I see what you mean—the German Treaty.' And of course it will be called not the Treaty of Paris, but the Treaty of Versailles. 'A toutes les gloires de la France' (To all the glories of France).

We enter the Galerie des Glaces. It is divided into three sections. At the far end are the Press already thickly installed. In the middle there is a horse-shoe table for the plenipotentiaries. In front of that, like a guillotine, is the table for the signatures. It is supposed to be raised on a dais but, if so, the dais can be but a few inches high. In the nearer distance are rows and rows of tabourets for the distinguished guests, the deputies, the senators and the members of the delegations. There must be seats for over a thousand persons. This robs the ceremony of all privilege and therefore of all dignity. It is like the Aeolian Hall.

Clemenceau is already seated under the heavy ceiling as we arrive. 'Le roi,' runs the scroll above him, 'gouverne par lui-même' (The king governs by himself). He looks small and yellow. A crunched homunculus.

Conversation clatters out among the mixed groups around us. It is, as always on such occasions, like water running into a tin bath. I have never been able to get other people to recognize that similarity. There was a tin bath in my house at Wellington: one turned it on when one had finished and ran upstairs shouting 'Bath ready' to one's successor: 'Right ho!' he would answer: and then would come the sound of water pouring into the tin bath below, while he hurried into his dressing-gown. It is exactly the sound of people talking in undertones in a closed room. But it is not an analogy which I can get others to accept.

People step over the Aubusson benches and escabeaux to talk to friends. Meanwhile the delegates arrive in little bunches and push up the central aisle slowly. Wilson and Lloyd George are among the last. They take their seats at the central table. The table is at last full. Clemenceau glances to right and left. People sit down upon their escabeaux but continue chattering. Clemenceau makes a sign to the ushers. They say 'Ssh! Ssh! Ssh!' People cease chattering and there is only the sound of occasional coughing and the dry rustle of programmes. The officials of the Protocol of the Foreign Office move up the aisle and say, 'Ssh! Ssh!' again. There is then an absolute hush, followed by a sharp military order. The Gardes Républicains at the doorway flash their swords into their scabbards with a loud click. 'Faites entrer les Allemands' (Bring in the Germans), says Clemenceau in the ensuing silence. His voice is distant but harshly penetrating. A hush follows.

Through the door at the end appear two huissiers with silver chains. They march in single file. After them come four officers of France, Great Britain, America and Italy. And then, isolated and pitiable, come the two German delegates. Dr. Müller, Dr. Bell. The silence is terrifying. Their feet upon a strip of parquet between the savonnerie carpets echo hollow and duplicate. They keep their eyes fixed away from those two thousand staring eyes, fixed upon the ceiling. They are deathly pale. They do not appear as representatives of a brutal militarism. The one is thin and pink-eyelidded: the second fiddle in a Brunswick orchestra. The other is moon-faced and suffering: a privat-dozent. It is all most painful.

They are conducted to their chairs. Clemenceau at once breaks the silence. 'Messieurs,' he rasps, 'la séance est ouverte' (the session is begun). He adds a few ill-chosen words. 'We are here to sign a Treaty of Peace.' The Germans leap up anxiously when he has finished, since they know that they are the first to sign. William Martin, as if a theatre manager, motions them petulantly to sit down again. Mantoux translates Clemenceau's words into English. Then St. Quentin advances towards the Germans and with the utmost dignity leads them to the little table on which the Treaty is expanded. There is general tension. They sign. There is a general relaxation. Conversation hums again in an undertone. The delegates stand up one by one and pass onwards to the queue which waits by the signature table. Meanwhile people buzz round the main table getting autographs. The single file of plenipotentiaries waiting to approach the table gets thicker. It goes quickly. The officials of the Quai d'Orsay stand round, indicating places to sign, indicating procedure, blotting with neat little pads.

Suddenly from outside comes the crash of guns thundering a salute. It announces to Paris that the second Treaty of Versailles has been signed by Dr. Müller and Dr. Bell. Through the few open windows comes the sound of distant crowds cheering hoarsely. And still the signature goes on.

We had been warned it might last three hours. Yet almost at once it seemed that the queue was getting thin. Only three, then two, and then one delegate remained to sign. His name had hardly been blotted before the huissiers began again their 'Ssh! Ssh!' cutting suddenly short the wide murmur which had again begun. There was a final hush. 'La séance est levée' (The session is over) rasped Clemenceau. Not a word more or less.

We kept our seats while the Germans were conducted like prisoners from the dock, their eyes still fixed upon some distant point of the horizon.

We still kept our seats to allow the Big Five to pass down the aisle. Wilson, Lloyd George, the Dominions, others. Finally, Clemenceau, with his rolling satirical gait. Painlevé, who was sitting one off me, rose to greet him. He stretched out both his hands and grasped Clemenceau's right glove. He congratulated him. 'Oui' says Clemenceau, 'c'est une belle journée' (Yes, it is a good day). There were tears in his bleary eyes.

Marie Murat was near me and had overheard. 'En êtes-vous sure?' (Are you sure?) I ask her. 'Pas du tout' (Not at all) she answers, being a woman of intelligence.

Slowly the crowd in the room clears, the Press through the Rotonde, and the rest through the Salle d'Honneur. I walk across the room, pushing past empty tabourets, to a wide-open window which gives out upon the terrace and the famous Versailles view. The fountains spurt vociferously. I look out over the tapis vert towards a tranquil sweep of open country. The clouds, white on blue, race across the sky and a squadron of aeroplanes races after them. Clemenceau emerges through the door below me. He is joined by Wilson and Lloyd George. The crowds upon the terrace burst through the cordon of troops. The top hats of the Big Four and the uniforms of the accompanying Generals are lost in a sea of gesticulation. Fortunately it was only a privileged crowd. A platoon arrives at the double and rescues the Big Four. I find Headlam Morley standing miserably in the littered immensity of the Galerie des Glaces. We say nothing to each other. It has all been horrible.

And so through crowds cheering 'Vive l'Angleterre' (for our car carries the Union Jack) and back to the comparative refinement of the Majestic.

In the car I told Headlam Morley of a day, years ago, when Tom Spring Rice had dined with the Prime Minister. He was young at the time, myopic and shy. The other guests were very prosperous politicians. When the women had gone upstairs they all took their glasses of port and bunched around the Prime Minister. Tom was left out. Opposite him was Eddie Marsh, also at a tail-end. Eddie took his glass round to Tom's side of the table and sat beside him. 'Success,' he said, 'is beastly, isn't it?'

Headlam Morley agreed that success, when emphasised, was very beastly indeed.

Celebrations in the hotel afterwards. We are given free champagne at the expense of the tax-payer. It is very bad champagne. Go out on to the boulevards afterwards.

To bed, sick of life.

NOTE

Nicolson, Sir Harold, *Peacemaking, 1919* (London: Constable & Co., 1933), pp. 3–17. Reprinted with the permission of the Estate of Sir Harold Nicolson.

British Diplomacy
The Hussein-McMahon Letters

Sir Henry McMahon, British High Commissioner in Cairo, to Hussein Ibn Ali, the Sherif of Mecca

I have received your letter of the 29th Shawal, 1333, with much pleasure and your expression of friendliness and sincerity have given me the greatest satisfaction.

I regret that you should have received from my last letter the impression that I regarded the question of limits and boundaries with coldness and hesitation; such was not the case, but it appeared to me that the time had not yet come when that question could be discussed in a conclusive manner.

I have realised, however, from your last letter that you regard this question as one of vital and urgent importance. I have, therefore, lost no time in informing the Government of Great Britain of the contents of your letter, and it is with great pleasure that I communicate to you on their behalf the following statement, which I am confident you will receive with satisfaction.— The two districts of Mersina and Alexandretta and portions of Syria lying to the west of the districts of Damascus, Homs, Hama, and Aleppo cannot be said to be purely Arab, and should be excluded from the limits demanded.

With the above modification, and without prejudice to our existing treaties with Arab chiefs, we accept those limits.

As for those regions lying within those frontiers wherein Great Britain is free to act without detriment to the interests of her ally, France, I am empowered in the name of the Government of Great Britain to give the following reply to your letter:

(1) Subject to the above modifications, Great Britain is prepared to recognise and support the independence of the Arabs in all the regions within the limits demanded by the Sherif of Mecca.

(2) Great Britain will guarantee the Holy Places against all external aggression and will recognise their inviolability.

(3) When the situation admits, Great Britain will give to the Arabs her advice and will assist them to establish what may appear to be the most suitable forms of government in those various territories.

(4) On the other hand, it is understood that the Arabs have decided to seek the advice and guidance of Great Britain only, and that such European advisers and officials as may be required for the formation of a sound form of administration will be British.

(5) With regard to the vilayets of Bagdad and Basra, the Arabs will recognise that the established position and interests of Great Britain necessitate special administrative

arrangements in order to secure these territories from foreign aggression, to promote the welfare of the local populations, and to safeguard our mutual economic interests.

I am convinced that this declaration will assure you beyond all possible doubt of the sympathy of Great Britain towards the aspirations of her friends the Arabs and will result in a firm and lasting alliance, the immediate results of which will be the expulsion of the Turks from the Arab countries and the freeing of the Arab peoples from the Turkish yoke, which for so many years has pressed heavily upon them.

I have confined myself in this letter to the more vital and important questions, and if there are any other matters dealt with in your letters which I have omitted to mention, we may discuss them at some convenient date in the future.

It was with very great relief and satisfaction that I heard of the safe arrival of the Holy Carpet and the accompanying offerings which, thanks to the clearness of your directions and the excellence of your arrangements, were landed without trouble or mishap in spite of the dangers and difficulties occasioned by the present sad war. May God soon bring a lasting peace and freedom of all peoples.

I am sending this letter by the hand of your trusted and excellent messenger, Sheikh Mohammed ibn Arif ibn Uraifan, and he will inform you of the various matters of interest, but of less vital importance, which I have not mentioned in this letter.

(Compliments).

(Signed): A. HENRY MCMAHON.

The Sykes-Picot Agreement

Sir Edward Grey, British Foreign Minister to Paul Cambon, French Ambassador to Great Britain

15 May 1916

I shall have the honour to reply fully in a further note to your Excellency's note of the 9th instant, relative to the creation of an Arab State, but I should meanwhile be grateful if your Excellency could assure me that in those regions which, under the conditions recorded in that communication, become entirely French, or in which French interests are recognised as predominant, any existing British concessions, rights of navigation or development, and the rights and privileges of any British religious, scholastic, or medical institutions will be maintained.

His Majesty's Government are, of course, ready to give a reciprocal assurance in regard to the British area.

Sir Edward Grey to Paul Cambon,

16 May 1916

I have the honour to acknowledge the receipt of your Excellency's note of the 9th instant, stating that the French Government accept the limits of a future Arab State, or Confederation of States, and of those parts of Syria where French interests predominate, together with certain conditions attached thereto, such as they result from recent discussions in London and Petrograd on the subject.

I have the honour to inform your Excellency in reply that the acceptance of the whole project, as it now stands, will involve the abdication of considerable British interests, but, since His Majesty's Government recognise the advantage to the general cause of the Allies entailed in producing a more favourable internal political situation in Turkey, they are ready to accept the arrangement now arrived at, provided that the co-operation of the Arabs is secured, and that the Arabs fulfil the conditions and obtain the towns of Homs, Hama, Damascus, and Aleppo.

It is accordingly understood between the French and British Governments—

1. That France and Great Britain are prepared to recognize and protect an independent Arab State or a Confederation of Arab States in the areas (A) and (B) marked on the annexed map, under the suzerainty of an Arab chief. That in area (A) France, and in area (B) Great Britain, shall have priority of right of enterprise and local loans. That in area (A) France, and in area (B) Great Britain, shall alone supply advisers or foreign functionaries at the request of the Arab State or Confederation of Arab States.

2. That in the blue area France, and in the red area Great Britain, shall be allowed to establish such direct or indirect administration or control as they desire and as they may think fit to arrange with the Arab State or Confederation of Arab States.

3. That in the brown area there shall be established an international administration, the form of which is to be decided upon after consultation with Russia, and subsequently in consultation with the other Allies, and the representatives of the Shereef of Mecca.

4. That Great Britain be accorded (1) the ports of Haifa and Acre, (2) guarantee of a given supply of water from the Tigris and Euphrates in area (A) for area (B). His Majesty's Government, on their part, undertake that they will at no time enter into negotiations for the cession of Cyprus to any third Power without the previous consent of the French Government.

5. That Alexandretta shall be a free port as regards the trade of the British Empire, and that there shall be no discrimination in port charges or facilities as regards British shipping and British goods; that there shall be freedom of transit for British goods through Alexandretta and by railway through the blue area, whether those goods are intended for or originate in the red area, or (B) area, or area (A); and there shall be no discrimination, direct or indirect against British goods on any railway or against British goods or ships at any port serving the areas mentioned.

That Haifa shall be a free port as regards the trade of France, her dominions and protectorates, and there shall be no discrimination in port charges or facilities as regards French shipping and French goods. There shall be freedom of transit for French goods through Haifa and by the British railway through the brown area, whether those goods are intended for or originate in the blue area, area (A), or area (B), and there shall be no discrimination, direct or indirect, against French goods on any railway, or against French goods or ships at any port serving the areas mentioned.

6. That in area (A) the Baghdad Railway shall not be extended southwards beyond Mosul, and in area (B) northwards beyond Samarra, until a railway connecting Baghdad with Aleppo via the Euphrates Valley has been completed, and then only with the concurrence of the two Governments.

7. That Great Britain has the right to build, administer, and be sole owner of a railway connecting Haifa with area (B), and shall have a perpetual right to transport troops along such a line at all times.

It is to be understood by both Governments that this railway is to facilitate the connexion of Baghdad with Haifa by rail, and it is further understood that, if the engineering difficulties and expense entailed by keeping this connecting line in the brown area only make the project unfeasible, that the French Government shall be prepared to consider that the line in question may also traverse the polygon Banias–Keis Marib–Salkhab Tell Otsda–Mesmie before reaching area (B).

8. For a period of twenty years the existing Turkish customs tariff shall remain in force throughout the whole of the blue and red areas, as well as in areas (A) and (B), and no increase in the rates of duty or conversion from ad valorem to specific rates shall be made except by agreement between the two Powers.

There shall be no interior customs barriers between any of the above-mentioned areas. The customs duties leviable on goods destined for the interior shall be collected at the port of entry and handed over to the administration of the area of destination.

9. It shall be agreed that the French Government will at no time enter into any negotiations for the cession of their rights and will not cede such rights in the blue area to any third Power, except the Arab State or Confederation of Arab States without the previous agreement of His Majesty's Government, who, on their part, will give a similar undertaking to the French Government regarding the red area.

10. The British and French Governments, as the protectors of the Arab State, shall agree that they will not themselves acquire and will not consent to a third Power acquiring territorial possessions in the Arabian peninsula, nor consent to a third Power installing a naval base either on the east coast, or on the islands, of the Red Sea. This, however, shall not prevent such adjustment of the Aden frontier as may be necessary in consequence of recent Turkish aggression.

11. The negotiations with the Arabs as to the boundaries of the Arab State or Confederation of Arab States shall be continued through the same channel as heretofore on behalf of the two Powers.

12. It is agreed that measures to control the importation of arms into the Arab territories will be considered by the two Governments.

I have further the honour to state that, in order to make the agreement complete, His Majesty's Government are proposing to the Russian Government to exchange notes analogous to those exchanged by the latter and your Excellency's Government on the 26th April last. Copies of these notes will be communicated to your Excellency as soon as exchanged.

I would also venture to remind your Excellency that the conclusion of the present agreement raises, for practical consideration, the question of the claims of Italy to a share in any partition or rearrangement of Turkey in Asia, as formulated in article 9 of the agreement of the 26th April, 1915, between Italy and the Allies.

His Majesty's Government further consider that the Japanese Government should be informed of the arrangement now concluded.

The Balfour Declaration

Foreign Office

November 2nd, 1917

Dear Lord Rothschild,

I have much pleasure in conveying to you, on behalf of His Majesty's Government, the following declaration of sympathy with Jewish Zionist aspirations which has been submitted to, and approved by, the Cabinet.

"His Majesty's Government view with favour the establishment in Palestine of a national home for the Jewish people, and will use their best endeavours to facilitate the achievement of this object, it being clearly understood that nothing shall be done which may prejudice the civil and religious rights of existing non-Jewish communities in Palestine, or the rights and political status enjoyed by Jews in any other country."

I should be grateful if you would bring this declaration to the knowledge of the Zionist Federation.

Yours sincerely,

Arthur James Balfour

NOTE

From British Diplomacy. The Hussein-McMahon Letters. Sir Henry McMahon, British High Commissioner in Cairo, to Hussein Ibn Ali, the Sherif of Mecca, October 24, 1915. http://www.lib.byu.edu/~rdh/wwi/1916/mcmahon.html; http://www.yale.edu/lawweb/avalon /mideast/sykes.htm; http://www.yale.edu/lawweb/avalon/mideast/balfour.htm.

A Peace to End All Peace

David Fromkin

I

"Diplomacy by Conference" was a phrase, attributed to Maurice Hankey, that described Lloyd George's proceedings in the postwar years. It became the standard description of the unreal world in which the Prime Minister lived. Divorcing himself as best he could from the other responsibilities of his office, he spent more than three years in attending international meetings aimed at shaping the postwar world. The meetings among the Allies began almost as soon as the armistices were signed, and developed into a way of life. Lloyd George, between 1919 and 1922, attended no fewer than thirty-three international conferences; and, even before they began, had engaged in informal meetings, such as those with Clemenceau and with Wilson in London at the end of 1918. The formal preliminaries to the Peace Conference began in Paris in January 1919, and shifted to other locations from time to time. At issue were the terms to be imposed upon the German, Austro-Hungarian, and Ottoman empires, and their ally, Bulgaria. The decisions about the Ottoman Empire were agreed upon for the most part at the First Conference of London (beginning in February 1920), were confirmed in the Italian Riviera resort town of San Remo (April 1920), and were embodied in a treaty signed at Sèvres, a residential suburb of Paris, on 10 August 1920.

With respect to the negotiation of the peace settlement in the Middle East, the decisive fact was that it took so much time. Of all the peace treaties, that with the Ottoman Empire was the last to be concluded. Beginning with the informal discussions between Lloyd George and Clemenceau after the armistice, it took sixteen months to reach agreement on substantive matters, and another four months to dispose of remaining issues and sign a treaty. In all, it took nearly two years to conclude the peace treaty with the Ottoman Empire; at the outset Lloyd George had predicted that it would take about a week.

Because of the long delay, situations were allowed to develop, and decisions were required to be made, that in the end proved more important than the terms of the treaty itself. The Allied statesmen thought that they had determined the future of Arabic-speaking Asia by what they did at San Remo, and of the Turkish-speaking Ottoman Empire by what they did at Sèvres; but what they did not do in 1918 and 1919 proved to have more influence on the future of both.

At the outset Lloyd George had stated that it would be impossible for his country to support indefinitely its 1,084,000-man army of occupation in the Ottoman Empire. Churchill and the General Staff, it will be recalled, had impressed upon him the need to reach a settlement while he still had the troops to enforce it. By the summer of 1919, some six months later, the British Cabinet was told that the army of occupation was down by more than two-thirds to 320,000 men. As the army melted away, its commanders adhered to a timetable of withdrawal that imposed a series of deadlines upon the Prime Minister at the Peace Conference, as did the continuing drain of British financial resources.

In the north, along the Caucasus frontier with Russia, British troops had remained in place in the hope that the United States, Italy, or France could be persuaded to replace them and defend newly independent Armenia, Georgia, and Azerbaijan if Russia or Turkey should revive sufficiently to attack them. But Britain lacked the men and money to undertake the job, and was eventually forced to abandon her charges to their fate.

In ordering British forces to leave these formerly Russian territories, the Prime Minister disregarded the strong objections of Winston Churchill. For all his recent enthusiasm for retrenchment, Churchill was a firebrand on the communist issue and was prepared to send men and money into Russia to overthrow the Soviet regime. Even Maurice Hankey, who believed that "in the coming years Bolshevism was the greatest danger to Europe," described Churchill as "quite barmy in his enthusiasm for the anti-Bolsheviks"; Churchill was obsessively determined to keep British troops north of the Turkish frontier to help the Whites fight the Reds in the Russian Civil War. Lloyd George's political fears were of a different sort. The Prime Minister told Hankey that he was anxious to get all British troops out of all formerly Russian territories to keep them from becoming "restless"; by which he presumably meant that he wanted to keep them from being infected with the revolutionary virus. Pursuant to his orders, British forces north of the Russian-Turkish frontier were evacuated in the summer of 1919.

To the south of the old Russian frontier, in mountain valleys where the present Turkish borders run with those of Syria, Iraq, and Iran, lay the area imprecisely known as Kurdistan, where British officials thought of sponsoring another of their protectorates. The area fell within the sphere promised to France in the Sykes-Picot Agreement, so the British envisaged a series of autonomous Kurdish states, to be advised by British political officers, which the French were to be asked to concede in the Wilsonian spirit of self-determination for the Kurdish people. The Kurds are an ancient mountain people who have never known unity, and whose energies have been channeled into violent quarrels with neighbors, especially Arabs and Armenians. A British attempt to organize them in 1919 resulted in three uprisings, as the Kurds turned against the British newcomers; soon afterward, British troops pulled back from Kurdistan, too.

II

Within Turkey, the British position continued to disintegrate. The British authorities still relied on the Armistice of Mudros. The brief armistice document dealt almost entirely with naval and military matters, requiring the Turkish authorities to demobilize all their armed forces except those required to maintain internal order. Ottoman troops piled up their weapons and munitions in dumps. British officers supervised the surrender, riding through the countryside in twos and threes. The armistice terms permitted the Ottoman authorities to remain in control of the Turkish-speaking remnant of their empire, subject to the Allies' right to occupy strategic points should a situation arise that threatened their security. In practice, British naval control of the seacoast, coupled with control of the communications and transportation systems, took the place of military occupation of Turkey.

The capital city, Constantinople, remained in theory unoccupied, although Allied forces were much in evidence. The British fleet was anchored there, and, in a triumphal ceremony, the French General Louis Franchet d'Esperey, the Allied commander in Ottoman Europe, rode into the city on a white charger.

The Ottoman government formed to negotiate the armistice was dismissed soon afterward by Mehmed VI, who had become Sultan in June 1918 and was chiefly concerned with retaining his throne. To this end, his policy was to seek favor with the Allies, and when Turkish politicians began to oppose Allied claims and proposals, the Sultan dissolved Parliament and ruled by decree. Soon afterward Mehmed appointed his brother-in-law to head the government as Grand Vizier, thus completing the change back from constitutional to personal rule.

The Sultan's government was not, however, unchallenged. Civilian and military networks of the Young Turkey Party operated throughout Anatolia, and the War Office—Enver's fiefdom—remained largely under their control. They plotted against the new Sultan and his ministers, and hoped to force the Allies to offer milder peace terms.

Outside the capital city, all authority was on the wane. In the interior there was an upsurge of brigandage and communal strife. This breakdown of order throughout Asia Minor was a cause of concern to the Allies, especially when it resulted in threats to the safety of Christians. When Greek villages behind the Black Sea port of Samsun were attacked by Turkish Moslems, the Allies demanded that the Grand Vizier take action. Alarmed, the Grand Vizier consulted the Acting Minister of the Interior, who advised that there was no way to bring the situation under control from Constantinople—an officer would have to be sent into the field to deal with matters on the spot. The Acting Minister suggested the name of his friend, General Mustapha Kemal, the hero of Gallipoli, whose opposition to Enver had kept him from receiving the major command appointments during the war that were his due. The suggestion was adopted and Kemal succeeded in obtaining exceptionally broad civil and military powers as Inspector-General of the Ninth Army, covering most of Anatolia.

On the evening of 6 May 1919 he embarked for Samsun. It was the beginning of one of the great political voyages of the twentieth century. At midnight Wyndham Deedes—the British Intelligence expert on Ottoman affairs—sped to the Sublime Porte to warn the Grand Vizier not to let Kemal go, only to learn that he was too late.

Kemal had already set off for Samsun, and his purpose—as Wyndham Deedes seems to have divined—was to rally forces throughout Turkey to resist Allied peace terms if they proved too harsh. Those forces consisted in large part of Ottoman troops in the unoccupied center and east of Turkey, and—armed with the Sultan's commission and his own formidable skills—Kemal planned to put himself at their head.

III

In 1918–19 Turkey was dark—and cold. Fuel was scarce, and the lights of Constantinople were kept dim. Elsewhere, too, the lands that at the outset of the war had formed the Ottoman domains entered into a sort of twilight existence, defined in terms of international law by the Regulations annexed to the 1907 Hague Convention Respecting the Laws and Customs of War on Land. As the occupying power in most of these domains, Britain's obligation was essentially to keep things as they were under Ottoman law until some final determination as to their fate should be made.

Such a determination would take the form of a treaty of peace between the Ottoman Empire and its conquerors. On the Ottoman side, no difficulty suggested itself; the Sultan lived in the shadow of British warships and in fear of losing his throne, and presumably would sign almost any document the British naval commander placed in front of him. All that the Allies had to do was decide among themselves what terms they wanted to impose.

That situation changed fundamentally in May 1919 when President Wilson and Prime Minister Lloyd George decided to play the Greeks off against the Italians in Anatolia. The unintended effect of the decision was to arouse Greek hopes and Turkish fears that Greece had come back to Asia Minor to stay. Moslem Turkish hatred of the two large Christian populations in their midst—Greeks and Armenians—had always exerted a powerful force, and did so again even in Turkey's exhausted state. While the Allied statesmen were looking the other way, Ottoman soldiers in the interior of Anatolia regrouped and returned to seize their weapons from the dumps where they were deposited.

Within days after the news of the Greek landing at Smyrna became known, Inspector-General Mustapha Kemal was ordered to return to Constantinople—and disobeyed. Instead he met with three colleagues, at the ancient provincial capital city of Amasya, to draft a declaration of independence. Disregarding the Sultan's government as a captive of the Allies, Kemal attended a regional nationalist congress at Erzerum, in the east of Turkey, and then assembled a national congress at Sivas, in the interior of Anatolia, midway between Erzerum and Ankara. He won the allegiance of a number of army officers his own age and younger, many of whom, like himself, had been associated with the military wing of the C.U.P.;[1] for the most part he carried with him the majors and colonels rather than the generals. He also seems to have taken over leadership of the military and civilian resistance networks organized by the Young Turks, although he prudently disclaimed any connection with the officially disbanded C.U.P. Despite Kemal's strong secular bias, Moslem holy men proved to be his strongest adherents.

The Allied leaders knew little about Mustapha Kemal, the lean, tough-minded, hard-living officer in his late thirties who inspired and led the rebellion against them.

Neither the British Foreign Office nor British Intelligence was even able to tell the Prime Minister whether Kemal was acting for or against the Sultan.

Unaware of what was happening in Turkey, the Allied leaders in Europe continued to meet in conferences that were intended to decide Turkey's fate. At a conference in London on 28 February 1920, the Allied leaders were amazed by the news that an army of 30,000 Turkish troops under Kemal's command had defeated a small French contingent at Marash in southern Anatolia. What surprised them—Lloyd George later claimed—was not so much the outcome of the battle (for the French were greatly outnumbered) but the revelation that Kemal's army of regulars existed. According to Lloyd George, this was the first that he and his colleagues had heard of such an army. "Our military intelligence had never been more thoroughly unintelligent," he later wrote in his memoirs, typically putting the blame on others.

IV

As Kemal's revolt spread through Anatolia, a parallel movement developed in the Arabic-speaking south of the Ottoman Empire, where the token French presence along the seacoast at Beirut, Tripoli, Sidon, and Tyre presented a tempting target to Moslem militants in Damascus. The French intruders on the coast of Syria and Lebanon threatened to overthrow the delicate balance of Christian and Moslem religious communities, evoking a reaction not unlike that against the Greeks in Turkey.

Britain allowed inland Syria, like inland Anatolia, self-rule. In theory the Syrian administration was headed by Feisal, who was away at the Peace Conference. In practice it was administered by people over whom he had little control, and who feuded bitterly with one another. For more than a year after the Ottoman retreat, inland Syria—with its capital at Damascus—was administered, if somewhat chaotically, by Arabs, and the novel habit of independence, once contracted, was not one that they wished to surrender.

A British Intelligence chief warned the Foreign Secretary in London in 1919 that the Arab government in Damascus and Kemal's movement in Turkey were preparing to enter into an alliance. But the Arab and Turkish movements were not as alike as he supposed: Kemal was a nationalist in the western sense of the word, while in Arab Damascus, though everybody now spoke the fashionable language of nationalism, it was not a native tongue. Of the Arabic-speaking leaders who governed from Damascus in 1919, most—perhaps four out of five—had not been adherents of an Arab national identity or of Arab independence as late as 1918. The Syrians among them were mostly from landowning families, with a stake in maintaining the established order. An analysis of the occupational groups from which they were drawn shows the leadership made up in large part of Ottoman soldiers and officials, many of them from Iraq and Palestine, who were out of a job. Most of them had remained loyal to Turkey during the war with Britain.

In the year since the Ottoman army had left Damascus, and under the noses of the distracted British, who were thinking about France, the Ottoman Arabs who had opposed them during the war had taken back control of the liberated province. The Ottoman Arabs, however, were fragmented along geographical lines in their current political concerns. Those from communities like Jerusalem denounced Zionism in Palestine; those from Baghdad complained of the British in Mesopotamia; and the Syrians wanted to expel the French from their seacoast and from Lebanon. Meanwhile, leaders of the traditional pro-Ottoman anti-Feisal ruling families were pitted against ambitious young militants seeking their political fortunes. Behind the rhetoric of the political parties and the renascent secret societies lay obscure family and local conflicts. It was a confused and confusing political situation, in which Feisal's position was secured essentially by the support of Britain, visibly represented by General Allenby's armies, and by the common Arab supposition that because of Feisal, Britain would oppose the colonialist designs of France.

In retrospect it can be seen that Britain entered 1919 with a period of grace of less than nine months in which to bluff France into backing down; by the summer of 1919 financial pressures and social unrest forced Lloyd George and the War Office to recognize that a timetable for British withdrawal from Syria could no longer be postponed. On 4 September 1919 the Prime Minister convened a conference of his advisers at the vacation house of his friend Lord Riddell, near Troubille on France's Normandy coast, to consider what should be done about the Middle East. Only a few days before Riddell had recorded in his diary that Lloyd George was "angry with the French for their attitude concerning Syria. He said that the Syrians would not have the French, and asked how the Allies could compel them to accept mandatories who were distasteful. . . . His attitude to the French has changed greatly. . . . He continually refers to their greed." Yet he and his advisers saw no alternative but to abandon the field to the French.

On 13 September 1919 the British government announced that withdrawal would take place in November, leaving the French and Feisal to settle matters between themselves. According to the British leaders, they thereby honored their commitments both to France and to the Arabs. It was a disingenuous claim. The British had pretended that Feisal headed a great Arab army in Syria, but government officials were aware that this was a pretense without substance. For the British army to leave was to leave Feisal to the mercy of the French. To Kitchener's followers in Britain and the Middle East, this meant a betrayal of all they had worked for; while to the French, the nine-month attempt to face them down, even though it was abandoned, was unforgivable.

For Feisal, the nervous prince with the worry-bead fingers, the British announcement of withdrawal was another sudden turning in the labyrinth of deception through which he tried to wend his way. There was, however, a teasing, tantalizing possibility that briefly opened up before him. Clemenceau, willing as always to accommodate British preferences in the Middle East—if politically possible—was prepared to let Feisal be king of Syria (since that is what Britain wanted) if Feisal would meet him halfway. The French Premier agreed to enter once again into negotiations with the Arab leader, aimed at securing recognition of France's minimum terms: that France would rule a Greater Lebanon, and that Syria, though independent, would become a French client state. But these French terms placed Feisal in the middle, between colliding forces. The militant Arabs of Damascus who claimed to be his followers, but who had no particular attachment to him, were prepared to allow him to call himself their ruler only so long as he could keep the French out; while the French were prepared to let him rule only if he could succeed in bringing them in. Feisal, a stranger in the land of Syria, was in no position to do anything but mediate. All he could do was obtain concessions from Clemenceau and then try to obtain concessions from the Arab militants in Damascus.

Early in January 1920, Feisal and Clemenceau arrived at a secret accord—secret, because Clemenceau, seeking to become President of France, did not want his opponents to be able to claim he had been weak on Syria—permitting Feisal's Arab state its independence, but with exclusively French advisers. The accord was designed to lead to a French Mandate, but only of the loosest sort. Feisal then left for Damascus to see if he could persuade the Arab leadership there to accept its relatively mild terms; but his mission proved to be another blind turn in the political labyrinth for on 17 January Clemenceau, rejected in his bid for the presidency, gave up his political career. Alexandre Millerand, Clemenceau's successor as Premier, lacked his inclination to save Britain's face in the Middle East, and therefore saw no need either to allow Syria her independence or to let Feisal mount her throne.

V

At the beginning of 1920, with Britain no longer blocking French ambitions in Syria, the way was clear for the two Allies finally to formulate the terms they would impose upon the defeated Ottoman Empire. The terms upon which they then agreed were that the Arabic-speaking portions of the empire were to be detached and divided between the two European powers, with Palestine and Mesopotamia to be kept by Britain; Arabia was to remain independent under British-influenced monarchs, Egypt and the Gulf Coast already having been take by Britain; and Syria, including Lebanon, was to go to France. Palestine, including Transjordan; Syria, including Lebanon; and Iraq were all destined for eventual independence, if one believed the language of the League of Nations Mandates, pursuant to which the Allies awarded these territories to themselves. But France, in particular, regarded the pledge of independence as window-dressing, and approached Syria and Lebanon in an annexationist spirit.

Apart from the Dodecanese islands, most of the Aegean islands and European Turkey (eastern Thrace) were ceded to Greece. Smyrna, and the district of western Anatolia of which it was the leading city, were to be administered by Greece for five years, after which a plebiscite would be taken, presumably leading to incorporation of the area within the Kingdom of Greece. The Dardanelles, where the Royal Navy could make itself felt, were placed under international control, and along with Constantinople became hostages guaranteeing Turkey's good behavior in such matters as the treatment of Christian minorities. In eastern Anatolia, Armenia was granted independence, and Kurdistan was given autonomy. Turkish finances were placed under British, French, and Italian supervision. Within these limits, and subject to these restrictions, what little remained of Turkish-speaking Anatolia was to remain nominally independent under the Ottoman Sultan.

Such were the terms, agreed upon in London and San Remo in the first half of 1920, that were dictated to the Sultan's government—which reluctantly signed the treaty imposed upon it in August 1920, in the French suburban city of Sèvres. As only France's Poincaré seems to have noticed, it was an inauspicious choice for the site of a treaty upon which Europe intended to rely; Sèvres was known for its china, which was fragile and easily broken.

Lloyd George was the only one of the original Big Four who remained in his position when the final peace treaty was signed. He was also the only British Cabinet minister at the beginning of the First World War who remained in the Cabinet throughout the war until its conclusion. The only British politician to survive the war, he was the only Allied leader to survive the peace; but the Ottoman settlement, of which he was so proud, was to prove his undoing.

NOTES

From David Fromkin, *A Peace to End All Peace: The Fall of the Ottoman Empire and the Creation of the Modern Middle East* (New York: Holt, 1989), pp. 403–11. Reprinted with permission from the author.

1. The Committee for Union and Progress, otherwise known as the Young Turk movement.

The Kings Depart

Richard Watt

Because the *Freikorps* were to play such an important role in the period of German history which followed these early-January days, it is worthwhile to study their background.

In their formation, the *Freikorps* owed much to two concepts which were legacies from the old Imperial Army. One of these was the status of the Army officer in Germany; the other was the techniques of the *Sturmtruppen*—storm troops—which the Army had developed during the war.

The officer of the Imperial Army had occupied a unique place in the German social scheme. In a nation where it seemed that almost everyone wore some type of uniform, where many persons, whether of noble birth or not, bore some sort of official title or had been awarded some type of medal or decoration, the Army officer was supreme. He was frequently a member of the nobility; failing this, he was certainly from the upper reaches of the bourgeoisie. He was usually the product of one of the famous cadet schools. Although he was given his commission by his King, not even the Kaiser would have dared to award it until the candidate's acceptance had been approved by every single officer in his prospective regiment. The Imperial Army officer was outside the jurisdiction of civil law and responsible only to the military code, which, incidentally, obliged him to punish on the spot any display of insolence or disrespect by a civilian. Everyone deferred to the military officer. Prior to 1914 it was said that "the young lieutenant went through life as a god, the lieutenant of reserves as a demigod."

Much had changed during the few wartime years. The tremendous growth of the Imperial Army and the casualties which the relatively small (fifty thousand men) officer corps sustained had resulted in an explosive increase in its size. By the end of the war there were some 270,000 German officers. It had not been possible to maintain the same exalted social standards as before in selecting the new officers. But they thought themselves fully the equals of the prewar officers, whom they regarded with awe and whose manners they aped.

Given these circumstances, it is not surprising that when peace came the officer corps of the German Army comprised a caste apart, a large percentage of which was unprepared for a return to civilian life. Sullen and bitter, these suddenly declassed men found themselves stripped of everything they cared about: they had lost a war, lost an Emperor, lost their prestige, and lost their profession. The breakup of the Imperial Army left the bulk of the officer corps wandering purposelessly about the cities and the old garrison towns. "I find," was the typical reflection of one of the officers, "that I no longer belong to this nation. All I can remember is that I once belonged to the German Army."

Another influence on the character of the *Freikorps* was the development of a special type of attack-troop formation within the Imperial German Army. By 1916 it had been discovered that there was a need for a number of small units, generally of battalion size, consisting of specially trained, equipped and conditioned shock troops. These elite formations, the *Sturmbataillone*, were carefully husbanded far behind the front line until it was time for a major raid or an assault. Then the *Sturmbataillone* were raced to the front by truck to lead the attack. They did not look like ordinary infantry. The German Army regarded them as "the perfected form of the front-line fighter."

> He did not march with shouldered rifle, but with unslung carbine. His knees and elbows are protected with leather patches. He no longer wears a cartridge belt, but stick his cartridges in his pockets. Crossed over his shoulder are two sacks for his hand grenades. . . . Thus he moves from shellhole to shellhole through searing fire, shot and attack, creeping, crawling like a robber, hugging the ground like an animal, never daunted, never surprised . . . always shifting, cunning, always full of confidence in himself and his ability to handle any situation . . ."

An array of special equipment had been created for those *Sturmtruppen*: carbines, lightweight machine guns, small flamethrowers, all designed to be brought forward with breakneck speed during an action. To supplement their special training and superb equipment, the storm troops were given extra privileges. The enlisted men were issued pistols, worn only by officers in the rest of the Army. Their food was the best the German Army had to offer. They got more leave than the rest of the Army. They were allowed to choose their own special unit insignia, for which they generally picked the silver death's head reserved in the past for the cavalry. Nothing was spared to reward these superb troops for the bravery, the blood lust and the merciless efficiency which were demanded of them.

The elite among this elite were the officers of the storm-troops battalions—the *Stosstruppführer*. They were a meticulously selected group—unmarried, never older than twenty-five, and perfect physical specimens. A special intimacy grew up between the enlisted men and their officers. They spoke to one another using the familiar *du*, a manner of address which was utterly unthinkable in the rest of the Army. The storm battalion itself was called by the name of its commander. When the storm battalion attacked, the officers went forward ahead of their men. They were ever braver, together and more merciless than their men. "The turmoil of our feelings," wrote a young *Stosstruppführer*, "was called forth by rage, alcohol and the thirst for blood. As we advanced heavily but irresistibly toward the enemy lines, I was boiling over with a fury which tripped me . . . the overpowering desire to kill gave me wings. Rage squeezed bitter tears from my eyes. . . . Only the spell of primeval instinct remained."

In response to their successes, a whole body of legend grew up about the famous storm troops and their officers. They were called "the New Man, the storm soldier, the elite of Mittel Europa," a "completely new race, cunning, strong and packed with purpose."

But when the war ended it was the storm trooper and the stormtroop officers who were the most lost and bewildered members of the disintegrating German Army. They were later described by Herman Goering as "fighters who could not come debrutalized." They had no particular ideological convictions and no special political outlook. All they knew was fighting and the tradition of the "front-line soldier."

These were the elements which, mixed together, made up the various little armies that were soon to be called the "*Freikorps*": the officer who could not conceive of returning to civilian life; the restless young soldier yearning for some sort of new German life; and the storm trooper tradition of ruthless efficiency.

The first *Freikorps* had its origin on December 12, 1918, when, in the horror of the general dissolution of the field army, Maercker had appealed to his corps commander, General von Morgen, for permission to form a "Corps of Volunteer Rifles." Morgen instructed Maercker to draft and submit to him a scheme of organization for the volunteer group. This was immediately done. It bore the title "Organizational Directive for the Volunteer Rifle Corps." The directive and the subsequent "Conditions for Admission to the Corps of Volunteer Rifles" were instantly approved by Morgen and the Supreme Command.

These documents make interesting reading. It is a common supposition that the *Freikorps* were ultrareactionary gangs formed of White-Guardist types under the iron control of the most monarchial elements of the General Staff. This was not the case. The events of the German Revolution had convinced the more perceptive members of the officer corps, particularly the levelheaded Groener, that if the Army was to survive it must make certain concessions to the rank and file. Nor did the office corps think that this was necessarily bad. Maercker intended to recruit only the very best fighting elements of the old field army and to organize them on the lines of the storm troops. Each infantry company would be practically self-sufficient, like a miniature division in the old field army; it would have its own trench-mortar section, its own transport and its own heavy mortars. Obviously a high degree of initiative, flexibility and imagination would be required of the enlisted men who made up these rifle companies. The *Kadaverdisziplin* of the old Imperial Army had no place here. A different sort of relationship between officers and privates must be developed, somewhat similar to that which had grown up in the *Sturmbataillone*.

In any event, Maercker's organizational directive, while insisting that "iron discipline was absolutely necessary," also conceded that "discipline should be founded upon ready and consenting obedience." The order dwelt at length on the newly created post of *Vertrauensleute*—"trusted men." These men, who were to be elected by the privates in each company, were given unprecedented privileges. The officers were required to consult with them on such matters as food and leave. The "trusted men" had the right to bring complaints against any officer or noncommissioned officer, and these charges had to be investigated by a senior officer.

On December 22, Maercker's directive having been approved, he published the "Conditions for Admission to the Corps of Volunteer Rifles," which spelled out the terms under which men would be enlisted. Only soldiers who had completed their military training in the old Imperial Army were acceptable to Maercker. Each man enlisted for a period of thirty days, which was renewable every month. He could leave by giving fifteen days' notice. A generous scale of pay and allowances was published, and service in the Volunteer Rifle Corps counted for retirement and pensions just as did service in the Imperial Army. As to the matter of an oath of loyalty, both the Supreme Command and Maercker gave considerable thought to the form this should take. Obviously some form of pledge of allegiance had to be given. To swear loyalty to the old monarchy was out of the question. To pledge fealty to the "Ebert-Haase government" was also impossible. Haase was an Independent Socialist and could be counted upon to condemn the formation of this corps once he heard about it. As Maercker said, "No one could ask me to swear loyalty to the person of Herr Haase, who in 1914 had declared he wanted to undermine the Army in order to set the world revolution in motion." In the end each volunteer was required to sign a statement pledging only, "I will loyally serve the provisional government of Chancellor Ebert until the National Assembly has created the new constitution."

The Majority Socialists could have asked for nothing more. But it is significant of the confusion of the times that they knew little or perhaps nothing about the Volunteer Rifle Corps. No doubt distance had something to do with this. Maercker's Volunteer Rifles had set up their headquarters in a secluded Franciscan convent at Salzkotten in the province of Westphalia; shrewdly, Maercker was not calling attention to his corps in its early days. Despite this seclusion, he had no difficulty in obtaining volunteers. His old infantry division, the 214th, like every other division in the Imperial Army, had broken up, but in it there had been a nucleus of hardy souls willing to remain with Maercker as volunteers. It is difficult to assess their motives with any exactitude. Doubtless this first *Freikorps* had its share of professional soldiers who knew no trade, had no family and could not conceive of life outside the barracks. Other volunteers were motivated by patriotism and sincerely believed that they were Germany's salvation against a wave of Bolshevism. Still others were motivated by a brutal hatred for the *Etappe*, the rear, which they had begun to see as the source of their wartime defeat and suffering.

Whatever their motives, it is significant that out of a single infantry division a sufficient number of tough veteran soldiers could be found to form, within a few days after the publication of the organizational directive, a "section" consisting of three infantry companies and a battery of artillery. Getting enough volunteers, however, was not the end of Maercker's organizational problems. The men had to be fed, paid, armed and clothed. The Supreme Command could supply only the money; the rest was Maercker's responsibility, and it proved to be a tremendous burden. He and his staff officers visited depot after depot in frantic succession, hearing the same story in practically every case: the troops guarding the supply dumps had disappeared, and whatever was stored had been looted. It was ominous that Maercker had great difficulty in finding small arms and ammunition for his men. In the few supply depots where any sort of order still existed, the local soldiers' councils had taken over, and they refused to give him any of the stores. Neither the Supreme Command nor the staff of Maercker's own army corps could provide him with transport. They referred him to the Seventeenth Corps motor park, but there he again found himself too late. As Maercker described it, everything was in "Russian conditions." A sad spectacle met my eyes—lorries, guns, munitions wagons, artillery, lay scattered about. . . . Everything was rusted, broken, beyond use; the axle trees were twisted, the copper plates wrenched off and sold." Maercker could not even find enough winter coats for his men. He appealed to the Supreme Command and then to the War Ministry in Berlin. No one could help him. Bitterly he reflected that the situation was truly desperate when neither the German government nor the Supreme Command of the German Army could find enough overcoats for a few companies of infantry.

Eventually some unpillaged supply dumps were found, and enough equipment was scraped together to outfit Maerckers' troops. The Supreme Command had sent three popular generals to help with recruiting, and by late December the Volunteer Rifles had nearly four thousand men. A staff of the officers began work devising a doctrine for clearing streets, defending public buildings and controlling mobs. As fast as these tactics were worked out, the troops were trained in them. On December 28, following the fiasco before the Marstall, Maercker's corps was ordered to move east to Zossen, where, on January 4, they appeared—almost miraculously, it seemed—before Noske and Ebert, stepping smartly across the snow-covered paradeground.

By January 4 Maercker's Volunteer Rifles were not the only *Freikorps* in Germany. In Kiel the Navy had put together several brigades composed of officers, petty officers and naval cadets. Each of the young company commanders was a former U-boat captain who had been decorated with the Pour le Mérite, the most coveted of Germany's military awards. The various naval brigades took the names of their commanders—the Ehrhardt Free Corps, the Löwenfeld Corps. In Berlin in mid-December a *Freikorps* had even been formed by a sergeant named Suppe, who had called together a group of his men from the Second Guards Regiment and appealed to their sense of honor; thus the Suppe Free Corps was born. Another *Freikorps*, known as the "Guard Cavalry Rifle Division" (Garde-Kavellerie-Schützen Division), was being put together out of the wreckage of several divisions of the old Imperial Guards.

As yet, in early January of 1919, there were not many of these volunteer corps—probably no more than a dozen—and each was still quite small. But they were proliferating, and some common threads ran through them. Most of them, for example, were copying Maercker's organizational directive. And most of them, even though they were "free" corps, were quite willing to accept orders from the Supreme Command or from the Ebert government, which, after all, was paying them. They were neither monarchist nor Socialist. They were merely tough, determined and anti-Bolshevik.

The "Spartacist Revolution" began in Berlin on January 6, 1919. It came as no surprise to the citizens of Berlin, who had seen huge strikes and riots become daily occurrences during the first week of the new year. In fact, the only people who were really caught unawares was the leadership of the new Communist Party.

During the first week in January the Ebert government, aware that its power was rapidly deteriorating, had finally abandoned all restraint in attacking the opposition to the left. The Majority Socialists had, after some fighting, managed to recapture the (Socialist Party newspaper) *Vorwärts* printing office which the Spartacists had seized on Christmas Day. Now they used their presses to publish a series of violent newspaper and pamphlet attacks on the left wing of the Independents, the Revolutionary Shop Stewards and the Communists—all of whom they lumped together as "Spartacists."

> The despicable actions of Liebknecht and Rosa Luxemburg soil the revolution and endanger all its achievements [*Vorwärts* charged]. The masses must not sit by quietly for one minute longer while these brutal beasts and their followers paralyze the activities of the republican governmental offices, incite the people more and more to civil war and strangle with their dirty fists the right of free expression . . .

The Majority Socialists ridiculed the Communists' announced intention of taking over the government only when they had obtained the support of the majority of the proletariat. They did not believe Rosa Luxemburg's claim that the left would never stage a *Putsch*. As it turned out, they knew the Communists' intentions better than the Communists did themselves.

The tension came to a head over the left-wing Independent Emil Eichhorn, who had held on to the Berlin police presidency ever since November 9. It was common knowledge that Eichhorn was filling up the police ranks with Spartacist sympathizers who, with their chief's approval, took only the most perfunctory notice of rioters against the Ebert government. He had declared his police to be "neutral" at the time of the Christmas Eve fighting in front of the Marstall, and he was outspoken in his opposition to the forthcoming elections for the National Assembly. All of this Ebert had felt constrained to accept as long as the Independents had remained in the government. When the Independents quit, the Majority Socialist newspapers let loose a volley of attacks on Eichhorn until, on Saturday, January 4, he was given notice of dismissal by the Prussian state government.

Eichhorn refused to be fired. Upon receiving the news, he reported directly to the headquarters of the Independent Socialists. The Independent leaders quickly met in turn with the Revolutionary Shop Stewards and the Communists, and a joint manifesto demanding Eichhorn's retention and appealing to the proletariat for a mass demonstration in his support was drafted and rushed onto the Berlin streets. At a meeting of the three left-wing parties it was agreed also to demand that the government give arms to the Berlin proletariat and disarm the *Freikorps*, about which the left had begun to hear rumors.

The mass demonstration took place on Sunday, January 5, in front of the police headquarters on the Alexanderplatz. The crowd filled the big square and extended for blocks east and west along the Königstrasse. Its size and vehemence astounded even the organizers of the protest, who had never seen a crowd like this before. Many of the demonstrators were armed. When the workers were addressed from the police-headquarters balcony by various prominent revolutionary figures, such as Ledebour of the Independent Socialists, Däumig of the Revolutionary Shop Stewards and, of course, Liebknecht, they responded with a deafening clamor.

In the midst of this demonstration Eugen Ernst, the new police president designated by the government, had the ill fortune to appear. He was roughly handled by the crowd, which would not even allow him to get near the headquarters building. Prudently he drove back to the Reich Chancellery. Then, in a scene of great enthusiasm, Eichhorn appeared on the Balcony and proclaimed his determination to remain in office no matter what the government might do. The crowd cheered wildly and, even as night fell, remained in the *Platz* to listen to speeches.

Meanwhile the officials of the left wing of the Independents, the Revolutionary Shop Stewards and the Communists all gathered within the building. There were seventy-one persons present, of whom only two, Liebknecht and Wilhelm Pieck, were Communists. This coalition made a momentous decision: to call a general strike, to support an armed attack upon the government and "to place Germany in the vanguard of the international proletarian revolution."

The decision was by no means unanimous. The leaders of the three parties had not originally come there with the intention of declaring the revolution. They had been aware that their respective organizations were far from perfected and that a good deal of agitation remained to be done. They must have realized that a declaration of revolution would be tantamount to civil war, and that this would be a blood affair which would have to be repeated in almost every major German city. It would not be enough to capture Berlin. If the other great cities were not won over, the Berlin proletariat could be cut off and starved out.

Nevertheless, the majority of the left-wing leaders at the meeting in police headquarters suddenly became absolutely certain that the revolution's hour had struck. They were overwhelmed by the enthusiasm of the unbelievably huge mass demonstration which was cheering outside on the Alexanderplatz. As they met, messengers came dashing in from all over Berlin to report that revolutionary workers had begun to occupy the newspaper offices in the Bell-Alliance-Platz, that the proletariat was attacking the railway stations, that an entire issue of *Vorwärts* had been seized at revolver point and dumped into a canal; and Dorrenbach rushed over to announce that his People's Naval Division was ready to go into action in support of the uprising. To those who gathered at the meeting it must have seemed that the revolution was actually taking place while they talked. Surely the mere fact that they were discussing it while sitting in the Berlin police headquarters, of all places, was proof that the Ebert government had collapsed. Obviously the workers were ready. They wanted only to be led. Glorious comparisons with the Smolny Institute in Petrograd came to every mind.

Practically everyone present was later to claim that, although it was the Revolutionary Shop Stewards who proposed the revolution, it was Liebknecht who carried the decision. Probably an element of competition entered into his motivation; it would have been intolerable to Liebknecht if the Revolutionary Shop Stewards had been permitted to lead this "second revolution." And he is said to have feared that if there was no revolution soon, the sailors of the People's Naval Division would feel he was betraying them. Be that as it may, his eyes shone, his face glowed and he radiated absolute certainty of revolutionary victory. Away from the moderating counsels of his party associates, Liebknecht was free to commit the Communist Party to the ultimate move. No one was there to remind him that the official Communist policy was still relentless agitation among the workers until, without the need for a *Putsch*, the party was summoned to power by the masses.

It is easy to see how under Liebknecht's exhortations, delivered to the accompaniment of the intoxicating clamor of the armed masses outside, the group at police headquarters was stampeded into a decision. The leaders of the masses could scarcely afford to be found timidly trailing in the wake of the masses. By a vote of sixty-five to six, the leaders of the left decided to summon the Berlin proletariat to revolution.

The next step of the combined group of Independents, Revolutionary Shop Stewards and Communists was to draft and send out into the nighttime streets a manifesto calling for that final revolutionary combination, the arming of the workers and the launching of a general strike. On the following day, Monday, January 6, the Ebert government would have to fall: there would be no electricity, no streetcars, no factories operating, no shops open; nothing would move on the streets of Berlin except an armed mass of workers. As the police-headquarters meeting continued into the night, the seventy-one men present approved the formation of a fifty-three–member "Revolutionary Committee." This committee immediately prepared another manifesto, to be published as soon as the general strike had taken effect, declaring that the "Ebert-Scheidemann government" was "deposed" and that the Revolutionary Committee had temporarily taken over governmental affairs. The second manifesto was set in type at once and held in readiness for the takeover.

That night and the next morning the Revolutionary Committee distributed arms to the workers. The general strike of January 6 began on schedule. A mammoth demonstration of some 200,000 workers paraded through the Berlin streets. Groups of workers succeeded in capturing the bourgeois newspaper offices and the Wolff Telegraph Agency. By the morning of January 7 the revolutionaries had seized the Brandenburg Gate and placed riflemen among the statuary at its top. From there they could now fire east down Unter den Linden, west across the Charlottenburger Chausee, and north and south along the Königstrasse. The Government Printing Office had been seized, as had the most important of the railroad stations. The revolutionaries took over and fortified the huge Bötzow Brewery. The Reichstag building was under attack and defended only by a scratch force of government bureaucrats hastily armed for the occasion.

News spread through the city that several of the remaining army regiments were about to march on Berlin in support of the revolution. The garrison in Frankfurt was said to have gone over to the revolutionaries also and to have entrained for the capital. In other cities of Germany—Brunswick, Düsseldorf, Dortmund, Nuremberg and Hamburg—revolutionary workers seized the bourgeois newspapers. In Bremen a Soviet republic was declared. Lenin, overjoyed at the news from Germany, was preparing an "Open Letter to the Workers of Europe and America" which lauded "the German Spartakusbund with its world-famous leaders" for its attack on the "imperialist robber bourgeoisie of Germany."

By Wednesday the Majority Socialist government controlled only a few of the major public buildings in Berlin; it had managed to hold on to the Reich Chancellery only by crowding the Wilhelmstrasse in front of the building with a couple thousand

Majority Socialist supporters. It could not issue appeals to the workers—the revolutionaries had taken over the *Vorwärts* office. Walled up behind their barricade of human flesh, Ebert and his government sat, depressed and practically helpless, wondering if they should flee Berlin. They did not dare go home, for fear they would be arrested. The general strike even made it impossible for them to go to a restaurant for dinner; finally a friend of one of the Majority Socialists, after being appealed to by telephone, made his way to the Chancellery with a hamper of food for the government.

Gustav Noske, the newly appointed Minister of Defense, had been forced to flee from inner Berlin on January 6. He had found it impossible to work in the Chancellery and had made his way on foot to the Army General Staff building, the famous old red house on the Königplatz. When he arrived, he found a huge revolutionary crowd preparing to storm the building. Clearly this was no place to stay. Telling Ebert that he was leaving the city to rally support—"Perhaps we'll have luck"—Noske summoned an automobile and fled the heart of Berlin along the road which led to Dahlem, a quiet section in the southwest suburbs of the city. Someone knew of a girls' boarding school there which was empty because of the holidays. At 3 p.m. on January 6 Noske arrived at the school and established his headquarters there, with an empty classroom as an office, a couple of tables shoved together as a desk, and a telephone screwed onto a plank.

The city of Berlin was, and still remains, one of the newest of the major cities of Europe. Before the Hohenzollern kings of Prussia erupted into prominence, it was little more than a glorified fishing and trading village on one bank of the River Spree. Then, as Prussia grew and prospered, the home city of its kings grew simultaneously. Between 1820 and 1918 Berlin expanded its population by more than ten times, and after 1871, when it became the capital of Germany, the growth had been particularly rapid. Government buildings, mostly constructed in the massive stone style ironically known as "Berlin renaissance," were built everywhere. The city was laid out along a series of broad avenues which converged, spoke fashion, in a number of central squares. Inner Berlin, the city's center, was dominated by the main thoroughfares, the massive government buildings, large parks such as the Tiergarten and the fashionable residential districts. The industrial districts, consisting principally of huge metalworking and electrical-equipment factories, dominated the northern, eastern and southern outskirts of the city. In the suburbs to the west lay the arsenals and munitions factories of Spandau. The eastern quarter of Berlin consisted of a sea of low brick working-class residences.

More than two million persons lived in Berlin, and most of them were industrial workers and their families. There were few ties to the soil among the city's proletariat; when they came from the farms to Berlin the workers quickly shook off their rural docility. Before the war most of the Berlin workers had been Social Democrats, a fact which the old Imperial Army had noted and because of which the army had preferred to take its conscripts from the farming regions. Although the Berlin worker was disciplined, efficient and hard-working, he was also very class-conscious and was convinced that he and his children were the victims of glaring social injustice. His experiences during the war had deepened this conviction. True, not every Berliner felt this way. But a very great many, perhaps the majority of the industrial workers, did, and these were the supporters of the three revolutionary parties—the left wing of the Independents, the Revolutionary Shop Stewards and the Communists, all of whom were now lumped together by the Ebert government under the collective term "Spartacist."

This was the city which the Ebert government had to defend and the populace against which it had to defend itself.

January 7 was the low point of the Majority Socialist government's fortunes. The first two days of this "Spartacist Week" had proved to Ebert and his colleagues that there was no hope of reaching any sort of compromise with the revolutionary parties. At a meeting in the Chancellery Commissioner Landsberg had reported, "the Spartacists have taken over the Railroad Administration Building, the Ministry of War is next in line in a few hours and then it will be our turn." Ebert had come to the conclusion that the first duty of any government is to survive, and this realization made decision easier. The Majority Socialists now gathered unto themselves every party or faction which could possibly support them in this crisis. Ebert and his fellow government members kept their heads. There was no more talk of abandoning the Reich Chancellery or of fleeing Berlin. Noske was in Dahlem organizing an army to reinvade the city. The Cabinet had decided to give him carte blanche—"We must not interfere with his decision."

Within the capital the government sought the support of the bourgeoisie, the monarchists, the conservatives, even the frankly counterrevolutionary elements which it had gone to great pains to hold at arm's length only a few weeks before. It issued a proclamation, addressed this time to "Fellow Citizens" (*Mitbürger*), not to the customary "Comrades" (*Genossen*), appealing for the support of every class. A constant vigil of Majority Socialists was maintained outside the Reich Chancellery. (They crowded the streets and paths around the building, but carefully refrained from standing on the grass, for there were signs which forbade this.) A corps of five thousand men was recruited from among the civil servants, armed and given the task of defending the major public buildings still left in government hands. These volunteers managed to drive the revolutionaries off the Brandenburg Gate and to set up machine guns atop it.

From the outset the government managed to rupture the revolutionaries' main potential source of armed power, the People's Naval Division. A Majority Socialist official, Anton Fischer, visited the Marstall and harangued the sailors, making promises of payment for their neutrality. For a little while the issue was in doubt. Dorrenbach, the sailors' leader, who on the wild night of January 5 had promised the support of the division against the government, ordered Fischer arrested. But the sailors, apprehensive over the future consequences of a government victory, arrested Dorrenbach himself, freed Fischer and declared their neutrality. Liebknecht, who had made the Marstall a sort of operational headquarters, was evicted from the building.

Prominent Majority Socialists were dispatched to the garrisons at Spandau and Frankfurt and came back with assurances of the soldiers' neutrality. But other soldiers were not neutral. The government, caring nothing at this point for the political implications of its action, summoned Colonel Wilhelm Reinhard, who was in the process of forming a *Freikorps* in Berlin, and ordered him to recapture the various newspaper offices located in the Belle-Alliance-Platz. Reinhard's corps had only nine hundred men, and with this pitiful force he had been lucky to hang on to the Moabit barracks in northern Berlin. But he quickly gathered a strong force made up of other embryo *Freikorps*—General von Röder's Volunteer Scouts, General von Hoffmann's Horse Guards Division and other little groups then forming under Generals Held, von Wissel and von Hülsen. Another *Freikorps* called the "Potsdam Regiment" was scraped together from the First Infantry Guards Regiment and various noncommissioned officers' schools at the Potsdam barracks. These were for the moment tiny organizations, but many of their "privates" still wore their old Army tunics, on which officers' shoulder tabs were plainly visible. Some companies consisted entirely of noncommissioned officers, and a large number of all ranks had been members of the wartime storm troops. All of them, with the exception of a couple of hastily put together bourgeois companies composed of very young students and older professional men, were veteran frontline soldiers.

On the night of January 9–10, the twelve hundred troops of the Potsdam Regiment, under the immediate command of Major von Stephani, occupied the Belle-Alliance-Platz in front of the *Vorwärts* building. Stephani had not forgotten the lesson of Christmas Eve at the Marstall. All the streets leading into the *Platz* were blocked off. No one was allowed to approach the troops which were being assembled. Anyone who did was greeted with an extended bayonet and the old Prussian sentry's warning cry, "*Zehn Schritte vom Leib!*" (Ten steps from my body!). Anyone who came closer was automatically considered an enemy and fired upon.

Stephani had a good idea of what he was up against. On the previous night he had dressed himself in worker's clothing and presented himself at the *Vorwärts* building as a revolutionary who had come to offer his services. This had given him a opportunity to inspect the building's defenses and prepare his plans for assaulting it. He gave the Spartacists defending the *Vorwärts* building only one opportunity to surrender. Then his trench mortars opened up. A large hole was immediately blasted in the front of the four-story masonry structure. Machine guns were carried across the rooftops, and they began to fire into the *Vorwärts* offices. Two howitzers were towed into the *Platz* directly in front of the building, and the gun crews shot point-blank at the building. A tank rumbled across the square and smashed in the front doors. It was followed by armored cars which drove up onto the front sidewalks and fired into the windows.

The defenders of the *Vorwärts*, who numbered only about 350, had barricaded themselves behind upturned rolls of newsprint. Their only weapons were small arms, and against the explosions of the artillery they could do nothing more than take cover behind these barricades. A few of the more intrepid revolutionaries sniped at the gunners in the square below, but when the building's entrance was blasted in the defenders knew the battle was lost. From the upstairs windows they began to wave white flags and handkerchiefs. The *Freikorps* soldiers paid no attention. Two huge mortar shells practically blew in the roof of the building, and then, covered by the smoke and the debris, squads of riflemen sprinted across the cobblestone *Platz*, hugged the walls of the building for a moment, tossed hand grenades through the windows and then dashed through the blown-in doors and up the stairs. Simultaneously, a company of *Freikorps* soldiers with a flamethrower burned down a high board fence at the back of the building and broke through the rear doors. They took about three hundred prisoners, marched them to a nearby barracks and shot a number of them down.

By eight-fifteen on the morning of January 10 the *Freikorps* had cleared out all the newspaper offices adjoining the *Vorwärts* on the Bell-Alliance-Platz. Some of the defenders had scrambled across the roofs to safety. The rest were prisoners. Reinhard's troops now turned to the reduction of other Spartacist strongpoints.

Noske had not been wasting his time at the girls' school in Dahlem. A scant five days had passed since he had fled the center of Berlin, but he and his staff had made every moment count. They had alerted Maercker's Volunteer Rifles at Zossen to prepare to march on the capital, and a *Freikorps* company had been brought to Dahlem to fortify the school against any possible attack. This was hardly necessary. The mere news that Noske was putting together a force to crush the revolution brought thousands of officers and soldiers to Dahlem, where his large and skillful staff quickly organized and armed them. Dahlem was a wealthy residential suburb consisting mostly of villas with large landscaped grounds. The area surrounding Noske's headquarters provided plenty of room. Troops were encamped and motor pools set up. A signal detachment was put together and telephone switchboards were installed; a radio station was erected and went on the air. Troop commanders and their staffs were appointed, and a map room was established. At the center of it all was Noske, working for days without sleeping. It is difficult to avoid the impression that he enjoyed all this. He was in his element, and he made no apology for the conservative character of his military staff.

> It was our great misfortune that no incomparable leader appeared in the ranks of the privates or the noncommissioned officers. . . . I was obliged, therefore, to fall back on the officers. It is quite true that many of them are monarchists, but when you want to reconstruct you must fall back on the men whose profession it is. An undisciplined army is a hollow mockery. . . . I sought out, one by one, the former officers and former officials, beaten and spat upon as they were, and it is with their help that I averted the worst.

The worst was indeed being averted. The revolutionary groups were showing themselves to be far weaker than had been suspected on January 5. On that fateful Sunday evening when the Revolutionary Committee had met at police headquarters, its supporters had seemed to be in control of the streets of Berlin. But after the initial successes of Monday and Tuesday the revolution had begun to falter. The Revolutionary Committee of fifty-three persons from three parties had proved grotesquely inefficient. The committee even had three coequal presidents, one from each of the sponsoring parties. The objectives of the groups varied just enough to make rapid decisions impossible. It was a far cry from the tightly knit Military Revolutionary Committee over which Lenin and Trotsky had presided at Petrograd in 1917. there was no small, cohesive revolutionary group in Berlin which could give instant orders to trained cadres leading the Red Guards in the streets. It was not that there was any shortage of armed workers. *Die Rote Fahne* later wrote:

> What was seen on Monday in Berlin was probably the greatest proletarian manifestation in history. . . . From the statue of Roland [in front of the City Hall] to the statue of Vic-

tory [at that time in the Königplatz] proletarians were standing shoulder to shoulder . . . they had brought along their weapons, they waved their red flags. They were ready to do anything, to give everything, even their lives. There was an army of 200,000 such as Ludendorff had never seen.

Then the inconceivable happened. The masses were standing from nine in the morning in the cold and fog. Somewhere their leaders were sitting and conferring. The fog lifted and the masses were still standing. Their leaders conferred. Noon came and, in addition to the cold, hunger came. And the leaders conferred. The masses were feverish with excitement. They wanted one deed, even one word to calm their excitement. But nobody knew what to say, because the leaders were conferring. The fog came again and with it the dusk. The masses went home sad. They wanted great things, but they had done nothing. Because their leaders conferred. They conferred in the Marstall, then they went to the police headquarters and continued to confer . . . they sat the entire evening and the entire night and conferred; they sat during the next morning. When dawn came, they either were still conferring or were conferring again.

There was no direction or coordination from the Revolutionary Committee. Where the armed workers had taken over a railroad station, a government office or a newspaper plant there was nothing left for them to do but entrench themselves and await a government counterattack. No one sent them instructions, no one gave them reinforcements, no one encouraged them to seize other buildings. After January 10 the Revolutionary Committee even ceased to meet.

As the days passed, even the general strike began to lose its effectiveness. It was a complete success in the metalworking factories and the other major industries where the Revolutionary Shop Stewards or the Communists were strong. But the movement had failed to achieve the principal objective of a general strike, the abrupt and total cessation of normal life. The workers in the electrical generating plants remained at their jobs as did the Berlin fire department, whose engines now toured the city picking up the dead and wounded. The telephones still worked. A young American Army lieutenant, part of a small prisoner-of-war repatriation contingent in Berlin, noted in his diary the bizarre situation on January 7: "Firing can be heard all over the city . . . [but] theaters are wide open and crowded. The city is mad, and without the slightest hesitation men wipe their bloodstained hands and come in from the street battles to the cabarets to dance and drink and dine with women."

Almost visibly the uprising was losing its momentum. Some of the right-wing members of the Independent Socialists, horrified at the bloodshed, returned to the Majority Socialists. Even the most revolutionary of the Independents were privately attempting to negotiate some sort of compromise agreement with the government. They had not bargained on Ebert's actually resisting their revolution, and they had no stomach for fighting in the streets. They did not seem to understand that they could not attack the Reichstag building while simultaneously negotiating for a return to their old seats on the council of People's Commissioners. The Independents could not bring themselves to the realization that revolutionaries must burn every bridge behind them.

Nor did the revolution proceed with the kind of ruthless energy that marked the October Revolution in Petrograd. When, on January 7, the Ebert government announced that no demonstrations or parades would be permitted on the Wilhelmstrasse in the vicinity of the Chancellery, the revolutionaries made only a tentative probe down this avenue which led to the citadel of German power, had a few shots fired over their heads by the handful of troops which were then guarding the Chancellery, and turned away.

On January 6, before the People's Naval Division declared its neutrality, a section of sailors was sent by Liebknecht to occupy the Ministry of War. There was practically no one to defend the ministry, since most of its staff had gone to Dahlem with Noske. To the officer left in charge the sailors displayed a written warrant authorizing their seizure of the building. Thinking quickly, the officer examined the paper and pointed out that it was not properly signed. The sailors took the document back, looked at it and saw that in fact there was no signature. Back they trooped to the Marstall, where they hunted up Liebknecht and got him to sign the paper. On their return to the ministry it seems to have dawned on the sailors that this was not the way to conduct a revolution. Musing on this, their leader threw away the warrant and drifted back to the Marstall.

The most confused spectacle of all was provided by the Communist Party itself. Rosa Luxemburg, Leo Jogiches and Karl Radek had been appalled when they learned that the January 5 conference of the parties of the left had decided to proclaim the revolution. They were not alone. The majority of the party's Zentrale was similarly horrified. They saw quite clearly that the proletarian movement was not yet ready for a real revolution, and they cursed the luck which had permitted Liebknecht to go almost alone to the meeting at police headquarters. The masses were not yet properly educated. The thing which Rosa Luxemburg had most feared, a premature uprising of the proletariat, had occurred. When Liebknecht came back to the *Rote Fahne* offices with the news of the revolution, Luxemburg cried out, "But Karl, how could you? What about our program?" Only the week before she had written: "It would be a criminal error to seize power now. The German working class is not ready for such an act.... It is useless, it is childish to overthrow it [the Ebert government] and replace it by another if the masses are not ready and able to organize Germany." Agitation and propaganda were both well short of their goals. Even if this uprising succeeded—and Luxemburg was sure it would not—it could be sustained only by Leninist policies of terror.

Radek was equally opposed to the uprising, but for somewhat different reasons. He certainly had no compunction about using terror, but as a highly experienced revolutionary, he was convinced that the German Communist Party was not ready for the revolution. The Bolsheviks in Petrograd had possessed much greater force in terms of revolutionary cadres and Red Guards, and still their revolution had been a close-run thing. He urged the party's leaders to withdraw from the Revolutionary Committee at once. If necessary, they should disarm the workers. It was what Lenin would do. Mistakes must be liquidated at once, however brutal that might seem.

Luxemburg and the other German Communist leaders could not bring themselves to do this. They realized that they themselves had aroused the workers. The party could not now abandon them. As doomed as this revolutionary attempt might be, they must share the workers' fate. It was "a matter of revolutionary honor." For this reason, *Die Rote Fahne* was forced to give the revolution its support. Luxemburg wrote:

> The masses followed the call of their leaders with impetuosity. . . . they are waiting for further directing and actions from their leaders. . . . No time must be wasted. Thorough measures must be taken immediately. Clear and urgent directives must be given to the masses and to the soldiers who remained faithful to the cause of the revolution. . . . Act! Act! Courageously, decisively and constantly. . . . Disarm the counterrevolution, arm the masses, occupy all positions of power. Act quickly!

Radek refused to go even this far. It was all madness. "A government of workers," he wrote to the Communist Zentrale on January 9,

> is unthinkable without an existing proletarian mass organization. At present the only mass organizations to be considered, the workers' and soldiers' councils, are of only nominal strength. . . . If the government should fall into your hands as the result of a coup d'état, within a few days it would be cut off from the rest of the country and would be strangled.

He went on to attack those who in their enthusiasm "transformed the protest demonstration [of January 5] into a struggle for political power. This," he said, "enables Ebert and Scheidemann to strike a blow against the Berlin movement which can weaken the entire movement for months." He pleaded with the Zentrale to abandon the fight. "The only force which can prevent this disaster is you, the Communist Party. You have sufficient insight to know that the fight is hopeless. . . . Nothing can prevent a weaker power from retreating before a superior force."

Radek was right. On the rainy evening of January 11, the various *Freikorps* of Gustav Noske began to march on inner Berlin.

A careful plan for the reconquest of Berlin had been worked out by Noske's staff. The first step involved a march of infantry, artillery, cavalry and armored cars into the heart of Berlin. This was completed by nightfall of January 11. Noske himself led these troops, perhaps only three thousand men in all, in a march which crossed Berlin from south to north. With Noske marching on foot at the head of a column made up of sections of Maercker's Volunteer Rifles and his own Iron Brigade from Kiel, the troops proceeded in ranks up to Potsdamer Strasse and turned east onto the Leipziger Strasse, then north again up the Wilhelmstrasse. They had now reached the center of Berlin and had not been fired upon. The city was wrapped in a dead silence except for occasional shots from the direction of the Belle-Alliance-Platz, several blocks east of the line of march, where Stephani's Potsdam Regiment was cleaning out the last of the revolutionaries hidden in the newspaper offices. A few civilians came to cheer the marching columns, and in response the soldiers began to sing some of the old army marching song—"Die Wacht am Rhein" and "O Deutschland hoch in Ehren." After the troops had crossed Berlin, they dispersed into the Moabit barracks, which were still held by Reinhard's *Freikorps*.

That night a detachment of Reinhard's command was dispatched to the Alexanderplatz to recapture the police headquarters, where Emil Eichhorn and his supporters were still barricaded. It attacked viciously. The artillery practically blew in the front of the building; then the assault section, under the command of a sergeant major named Schulze, charged the building and rapidly cleared it. Little quarter was give to its defenders, who were shot down where they were found. Only a few of them escaped over the roofs.

The next day Noske's plan developed according to schedule. Coming from the south, a blunt wedge of *Freikorps* pierced the center of Berlin and spread out to the east and west. They held a pie-shaped piece of the city comprising about a third of its area. From left to right the various contingents consisted of Hülsen's *Freikorps*, with headquarters at the Charlottenburg Palace; the Horse Guards Division under General von Hoffmann, with headquarters in the Eden Hotel; in the center of Berlin, Maercker's Volunteer Rifles, with headquarters in the palace of the Crown Prince, directly across from the imperial palace itself and commanding a full view of the Marstall, still held by the People's Naval Division; on Maercker's right, Röder's Volunteer Scouts, with headquarters in the Victoria School on the Neanderstrasse; then Wissel's *Freikorps* from the Thirty-first Infantry Division, with headquarters in the barracks of the old Telephone Corps near Treptower Park; and General von Held's Seventeenth Division Volunteers, who took over the town hall of Neukölln, on the extreme right. They were all under the command of General von Lüttwitz, who accepted his orders from Noske and the officers of Noske's staff. A network of communications between the various headquarters was insured by the immediate occupation of all the most important telephone exchanges.

By January 13 the *Freikorps* began operations. Working out from their wedge, they successively expanded the areas under their control. The troops deployed into skirmish formation and, working a few blocks at a time, searched the buildings, flushed out any Spartacist defenders and stationed machine guns and armored cars in the central squares. There were not enough men to throw a continuous cordon around the cleared areas, but there were enough to maintain general control over the sections of the city which the *Freikorps* occupied. It proved impossible for the revolutionaries to recapture a building which the soldiers had taken over. Demonstrations were equally impossible. Whenever even a small group of civilians gathered in a street an armored car appeared almost instantly, and under the threat of its machine guns the crowd would disperse. Anyone attempting to cross one of the bridges over the Spree was searched and interrogated. At night searchlight beams from the patrolling armored cars were flung down various streets to detect any demonstrations being organized. On January 13 the Revolutionary Shop Stewards called off the general strike, and by midnight of January 15 the city of Berlin was securely in the hands of the *Freikorps*. The "Spartacist Week" was over.

The leaders of the revolution were now hunted men. The conquest of the police headquarters had enabled the government to install at last its own police president, who instantly dissolved Eichhorn's "security force" and summoned back to duty the old pre-revolutionary police. These men now began to scour Berlin for the various members of the Revolutionary Committee. They quickly caught Georg Ledebour and

Ernst Meyer of the Independent Socialists. Leo Jogiches and Hugo Eberlein were captured in a raid on the Communist Party headquarters. Some of the party's leadership escaped arrest by fleeing to the relative safety of Frankfurt-am-Main, where a strong Communist organization existed. A reward of ten thousand marks was offered by the "Association for Combating Bolshevism" for the arrest of Karl Radek. But Radek, accompanied by Eichhorn, had fled the city.

The real prizes, Luxemburg and Liebknecht, remained uncaught. The *Freikorps*, knowing little of the Revolutionary Shop Stewards, were under the impression that the uprising had been inspired by the Communists. The Majority Socialists did not to correct this opinion. In the pages of *Vorwärts* they published a poem:

> *Many hundred dead are lying in a row,*
> Proletarians!
> Karl, Rosa, Radek and company don't care.
> None of them lies there, none of them lies there,
> Proletarians!

Toward the end of the uprising, *Die Rote Fahne* (which was suppressed on January 16) ran a bitter editorial by Luxemburg entitled "Order Rules in Berlin." In it she admitted the failure of the current revolution, but was optimistic about the eventual victory of the revolutionary movement. Addressing herself to the Ebert government, she wrote, "Your 'order' is built on sand. Tomorrow the revolution will 'rise again with clattering noise' and, to your horror, will proclaim to the sound of trumpets: I was, I am, I shall be."

As the *Freikorps* tightened their hold on the city, the search for Liebknecht became more and more intense. But he was not easily found. He had spent the last days of the uprising visiting each of the Spartacist strong points, attempting to encourage his followers. In company with the other Communist leaders, Liebknecht even went out for dinner at various small restaurants. Then the mortal danger which they were in finally dawned on them. Liebknecht made his way in disguise through the *Freikorps* lines and took refuge in the home of a working-class family in the Neukölln district.

Now, for once in his life, Liebknecht seems to have found a certain tranquility. There was nothing that he could do to stem the overwhelming *Freikorps* victory. There were no demonstrations to lead, no frantic speeches to make, no plans to lay, no articles to write. He passed hours reading fairy tales to the small daughter of the family who sheltered him. Liebknecht, who in Rosa Luxemburg's words had always lived "in a gallop, in eternal haste, hurrying to appointments with all the world, to meetings, committees, writing pads and slips of paper, jumping from auto into the electric and from the electric into the steam tram, his body and soul covered with street dust," had nothing to do. He knew that he was being searched for everywhere in Berlin and that the search was getting hotter every day, but he took comfort in the thought of the ultimate Communist victory: "The Calvary of the German working class is not yet over, but the day of salvation nears." Even the news that his wife and son had been captured did not upset his calm. They would all suffer, but the proletarian victory would come, of that he was certain.

On the night of January 14 Liebknecht left Neukölln, where the search was getting intense, for another hiding place, the apartment of a relative, a Frau Markussohn, at 53 Mannheimer Strasse in the Wilmersdorf district. Rosa Luxemburg and Wilhelm Pieck joined him there. The Red Rose was in a pitiable condition. She suffered from constant headaches. Her biographer says that she had become "taciturn and reserved." In the past "she had risen above her physical infirmities. But now it seemed . . . even her will could no longer triumph." At first thought it would seem that Wilmersdorf was a poor place for the Communist leaders to hide. It was an upper-middle-class area only a few blocks from the headquarters of the Horse Guards Division at the Eden Hotel. But doubtless Liebknecht hoped that this very proximity would save him from discovery.

He was wrong. At 9 p.m. on January 15 a patrol from the Horse Guards Division broke into the apartment and seized the three Communist leaders, who apparently had been betrayed by a neighbor of Frau Markussohn's. They were taken to headquarters in the Eden Hotel for questioning, in the course of which they were beaten. Later in the night automobiles were brought around to the back entrance of the hotel, and Liebknecht and Luxemburg were brought out separately. As Liebknecht emerged through the doorway, a *Freikorps* soldier, an enormously built private named Runge, raised his rifle and smashed it down on Liebknecht's head. More dead than alive, "Spartakus" was flung into a car. Six *Freikorps* officers climbed in, and the automobile drove off toward Moabit Prison.

A few moments later Rosa Luxemburg hobbled out through the same hotel doorway. She too was clubbed with Runge's rifle. She too, almost lifeless, was thrown into an automobile, which drove off under the command of a Lieutenant Vogel.

Meanwhile, the car bearing Liebknecht had stopped in the wooded Tiergarten a few blocks north of the hotel. Liebknecht was taken out of the car by the six officers, who later claimed that the vehicle had broken down. He was asked if he could walk and replied that he could. According to the *Freikorps* officers, he broke loose and was shot twice and killed while "attempting to escape."

No one knows whether Rosa Luxemburg was still alive when Lieutenant Vogel blew her brains out with a single shot. Her automobile was stopped and the body was thrown off the Liechtenstein Bridge into the ice-covered Landwehr Canal, from which it was not recovered until May 31. Leo Jogiches, who had once been Rosa Luxemburg's lover, dispatched a one-sentence telegram to tell Lenin of the murders: "Rosa Luxemburg and Karl Liebknecht have carried out their ultimate revolutionary duty."

When Friedrich Ebert learned of these murders he was, by every account, sincerely horrified and angrier than he had ever been seen before. He had not even been informed of the arrest of Liebknecht and Luxemburg. Only that day in a Cabinet meeting he had issued instructions that Liebknecht's wife was to be released. He told his government, "We have kept warning the troops to proceed with caution." Many of his followers were upset, too—but not necessarily on moral or humanitarian grounds. They felt that Liebknecht and Luxemburg were only two of the many victims of a *Putsch* which they more than anyone else had been responsible for starting; Scheidemann, for example, observed that "they had now become the victims of their own bloody terroristic tactics." It was generally agreed that the murder of the Communist leaders would inevitably result in their martyrdom and quite possibly in future Communist uprisings.

Ebert ordered an investigation of the affair, which the *Freikorps* commanders were able to frustrate. Lieutenant Vogel was convicted of failing to report a death and of illegally disposing of a corpse. He had no difficulty in obtaining a false passport and crossing the Dutch border. After waiting in Holland for a few months, he returned to Germany. He was never imprisoned. Private Runge served a sentence of several months for "attempted manslaughter."

It was now time for the election of delegates to the National Assembly. On the face of it, it would appear that the Majority Socialists had been successful. They had managed to defend their government against Bolshevism, and the elections for which they had struggled would take place on schedule. Germany would probably have a democratically elected government to draft a constitution and make peace with the victors. Ebert realized, of course, that there were other grave matters still to be dealt with: the Bavarian situation; Poland, where border warfare was already breaking out; and the Baltic States, where German troops were stemming the Russian Army's advance into Europe. Nor was the "Spartacist" menace yet dead, as the government would find out when it sent troops to the little town of Weimar. There was still a significant danger on the left.

What the government did not fully realize was that there was an equally great danger on the right. The moderate German labor movement was not irrevocably factionalized, and its largest element, the Majority Socialist, had allowed itself to become thoroughly compromised by the armed and resurgent right. Recruiting advertisements for scores upon scores of new *Freikorps* were beginning to appear in the Berlin papers. Within a few weeks the frustrated and vengeful Ludendorff would return from Sweden saying to his wife, "It would be the greatest stupidity for the revolutionaries to allow us all to remain alive. Why, if ever I come to power again, there will be no pardon. Then, with an easy conscience, I would have Ebert, Scheidemann and company hanged and watch them dangle."

The German kings had departed. The captains had not.

NOTE

From Richard Watt, *The Kings Depart: The Tragedy of Germany: Versailles and the German Revolution* (New York: Simon and Schuster, 1968), pp. 247–73. Reprinted with permission from the author.

Further Reading

Introduction

Becker, Jean-Jacques. *The Great War and the French People*. Oxford: Berg, 1993.

Bourne, J. M. *Britain and the Great War*. London: Routledge, 1989.

Chickering, Roger. *Imperial Germany and the Great War, 1914–1918*. Cambridge: Cambridge University Press, 2004.

Doughty, Robert. *Pyrrhic Victory: French Strategy and Operations in the Great War*. Cambridge, Mass.: Belknap Press of Harvard University, 2005.

Ferguson, Niall. *The Pity of War*. New York: Basic Books, 1999.

Hamilton, Richard, and Holger Herwig, eds. *The Origins of World War I*. Cambridge: Cambridge University Press, 2003.

Herwig, Holger. *The First World War: Germany and Austria*. London: Edward Arnold, 1997.

Jeffrey, Keith. *Ireland and the Great War*. Cambridge: Cambridge University Press, 2000.

Neiberg, Michael S. *Fighting the Great War: A Global History*. Cambridge, Mass.: Harvard University Press, 2005.

Sheffield, Gary. *Forgotten Victory: The First World War, Myths and Realities*. London: Headline, 2001.

Smith, Leonard, et. al. *France and the Great War*. Cambridge: Cambridge University Press, 2003.

Stone, Norman. *The Eastern Front, 1914–1917*. London: Penguin, 1975.

Strachan, Hew. *The First World War: To Arms*. Oxford: Oxford University Press, 2001.

Xu, Guoqi. *China and the Great War: China's Pursuit of a New National Identity and Internationalization*. Cambridge: Cambridge University Press, 2005.

Part One

Fischer, Fritz. *Germany's Aims in the First World War*. New York: Norton, 1967.

Foley, Robert T. *German Strategy and the Path to Verdun: Erich von Falkenhayn and the Development of Attrition, 1870–1916*. Cambridge: Cambridge University Press, 2005.

Fromkin, David. *Europe's Last Summer: Who Started the Great War in 1914?* New York: Knopf, 2004.

Joll, James. *The Origins of the First World War*. Second Edition. Harlow: Longman, 1992.

Keiger, J. F. V. *France and the Origins of the First World War*. New York: St. Martin's, 1993.

Lafore, Lawrence. *The Long Fuse: An Interpretation of the Origins of World War I*. Prospect Heights, Ill.: Waveland Press, 1971.

Mombauer, Annika. *Helmuth von Moltke and the Origins of the First World War*. Cambridge: Cambridge University Press, 2001.

Porch, Douglas. *March to the Marne: The French Army, 1871–1914*. Cambridge: Cambridge University Press, 1981.

Showalter, Dennis. *Tannenberg: Clash of Empires.* Dulles, Va.: Potomac Books, 2004.

Tuchman, Barbara. *The Guns of August.* New York: Ballantine, 1962.

Tunstall, Graydon. *Planning for War against Russia and Serbia: Austro-Hungarian and German Military Strategies.* New York: Columbia University Press, 1993.

Verhey, Jeffrey. *The Spirit of 1914: Militarism, Myth, and Mobilization in Germany.* Cambridge: Cambridge University Press, 2000.

Williamson, Samuel. *The Politics of Grand Strategy: Britain and France Prepare for War.* Cambridge, Mass.: Harvard University Press, 1969.

Zuber, Terence. *Inventing the Schlieffen Plan: German War Planning, 1871–1914.* Oxford: Oxford University Press, 2002.

Part Two

Bowman, Timothy. *The Irish Regiments in the Great War: Discipline and Morale.* Manchester: Manchester University Press, 2003.

Clayton, Anthony. *Paths of Glory: The French Army, 1914–1918.* London: Cassell, 2003.

Cru, Jean-Norton. *War Books.* San Diego: San Diego State University Press, 1931, 1976.

Gardner, Nikolas. *Trial by Fire: Command and the British Expeditionary Force in 1914.* Westport, Conn.: Praeger, 2003.

Griffith, Paddy. *Battle Tactics of the Western Front: The British Army's Art of Attack, 1916–1918.* New Haven: Yale University Press, 1994.

Schweitzer, Richard. *The Cross and the Trench: Religious Faith and Doubt among British and American Great War Soldiers.* Westport, Conn.: Praeger, 2003.

Sheffield, Gary. *Leadership in the Trenches: Officer-Man Relations, Morale, and Discipline in the British Army in the Era of the First World War.* New York: St. Martin's, 2000.

Simkins, Peter. *Kitchener's Army: The Raising of the New Armies, 1914–1916.* Manchester: Manchester University Press, 1988.

Spears, Edward. *Liaison, 1914: A Narrative of the Great Retreat.* London: Cassell, 1999.

Winter, Denis. *Death's Men: Soldiers of the Great War.* London: Allen Lane, 1978.

Part Three

Ashworth, Tony. *Trench Warfare 1914–1918: The Live and Let Live System.* New York: Holmes and Meier, 1980.

Braim, Paul. *The Test of Battle: The AEF in the Meuse–Argonne Campaign.* Shippensburg, Pa.: White Mane Books, 1998.

Ellis, John. *Eye Deep in Hell: Trench Warfare in World War I.* Baltimore: Johns Hopkins University Press, 1976.

Erickson, Edward. *Ordered to Die: A History of the Ottoman Army in the First World War.* Westport, Conn.: Praeger, 2001.

Gudmundsson, Bruce. *Stormtroop Tactics: Innovation in the German Army, 1914–1918.* Westport, Conn.: Praeger, 1989.

Horne, John, and Alan Kramer. *German Atrocities, 1914: A History of Denial.* New Haven: Yale University Press, 2001.

Lincoln, W. Bruce. *Passage through Armageddon: The Russian People in War and Revolution, 1914–1918.* New York: Simon and Schuster, 1986.

Morselli, Mario. *Caporetto, 1917: Victory or Defeat?* London: Cass, 2001.

Ousby, Ian. *The Road to Verdun: World War I's Most Momentous Battle and the Folly of Nationalism.* New York: Doubleday, 2002.

Philpott, William. *Anglo-French Relations and Strategy on the Western Front*. New York: St. Martin's, 1996.

Schindler, John. *Isonzo: The Forgotten Sacrifice of the Great War*. Westport, Conn.: Praeger, 2001.

Smith, Leonard. *Between Mutiny and Obedience: The Case of the French Fifth Infantry Division during World War I*. Princeton: Princeton University Press, 1994.

Travers, Tim. *The Killing Ground: The British Army, the Western Front, and the Emergence of Modern Warfare*. London: Allen and Unwin, 1987.

Watt, Richard. *Dare Call It Treason*. New York: Simon and Schuster, 1963.

Part Four

Audoin-Rouzeau, Stéphane, and Annette Becker. *14–18: Understanding the Great War*. New York: Hill and Wang, 2002.

Brittain, Vera. *Testament of Youth*. Reprint Edition. New York: Penguin, 2005.

Chambers, John Whiteclay. *To Raise an Army: The Draft Comes to Modern America*. New York: Free Press, 1987.

Chickering, Roger, and Stig Förster, eds. *Great War, Total War: Combat and Mobilization on the Western Front*. Cambridge: Cambridge University Press, 2000.

De Groot, Gerard. *Blighty: British Society in the Era of the Great War*. London: Longman, 1996.

Ekstein, Modris. *Rites of Spring: The Great War and the Birth of the Modern Age*. Boston: Houghton Mifflin, 1989.

Healy, Maureen. *Vienna and the Fall of the Habsburg Empire: Total War and Everyday Life in World War I*. Cambridge: Cambridge University Press, 2004.

Hynes, Samuel. *A War Imagined: The First World War and English Culture*. New York: Atheneum, 1990.

Keene, Jennifer D. *Doughboys, the Great War, and the Remaking of America*. Baltimore: Johns Hopkins University Press, 2001.

Kennedy, David. *Over Here: The First World War and American Society*. Oxford: Oxford University Press, 1980.

Kocka, Jurgen. *Facing Total War: German Society, 1914–1918*. Oxford: Berg, 1984.

Miller, Ian H. M. *Our Glory and Our Grief: Torontonians and the Great War*. Toronto: University of Toronto Press, 2002.

Offer, Avner. *The First World War: An Agrarian Interpretation*. Oxford: Clarendon, 1989.

Roshwald, Aviel, and Richard Stites, eds. *European Culture in the Great War: The Arts, Entertainment, and Propaganda, 1914–1918*. Cambridge: Cambridge University Press, 1999.

Part Five

Bruce, Robert. *A Fraternity of Arms: America and France in the Great War*. Lawrence: University Press of Kansas, 2003.

Coffman, Edward M. *The War to End All Wars: The American Military Experience in World War I*. Oxford: Oxford University Press, 1968.

French, David. *The Strategy of the Lloyd George Coalition, 1916–1918*. Oxford: Oxford University Press, 1995.

Schreiber, Shane. *Shock Army of the British Empire: The Canadian Corps in the Last 100 Days of World War I*. Westport, Conn.: Praeger, 1997.

Terraine, John. *To Win a War: 1918, the Year of Victory*. London: Cassell, 1978.

Trask, David. *The AEF and Coalition Warmaking, 1917–1918*. Lawrence: University Press of Kansas, 1993.

Travers, Tim. *How the War Was Won: Command and Technology in the British Army on the Western Front, 1917–1918*. London: Routledge, 1992.

Part Six

Boemke, Manfred, Gerald Feldman, and Elisabeth Glaser-Schmidt, eds. *The Treaty of Versailles: A Reassessment After 75 Years*. Cambridge: Cambridge University Press, 1998.

Cooper, John Milton, Jr. *Breaking the Heart of the World: Woodrow Wilson and the Fight for the League of Nations*. Cambridge: Cambridge University Press, 2001.

Fromkin, David. *A Peace to End all Peace: the Fall of the Ottoman Empire and the Making of the Modern Middle East*. New York: Henry Holt, 2001.

Fussell, Paul. *The Great War and Modern Memory*. Oxford: Oxford University Press, 1975.

Macmillan, Margaret. *Peacemakers*. London: John Murray, 2001.

Mayer, Arno. *Politics and Diplomacy of Peacemaking: Containment and Counterrevolution at Versailles, 1918–1919*. New York: Knopf, 1967.

Winter, Jay. *Sites of Memory, Sites of Mourning*. Cambridge: Cambridge University Press, 1995.

Index

About the Editor

Michael S. Neiberg is Professor of History and Codirector of the Center for the Study of War and Society at the University of Southern Mississippi. His publications include *Fighting the Great War: A Global History*; *Warfare and Society in Europe: 1898 to the Present*; *Foch: Supreme Allied Commander in the Great War*; and *Making Citizen-Soldiers: ROTC and the Ideology of American Military Service*.

Made in the USA
Las Vegas, NV
20 July 2021

26722231R00229